THE ARDEN SHAKESPEARE

THIRD SERIES

General Editors: Richard Proudfoot, Ann Thompson,
David Scott Kastan and H. R. Woudhuysen
Associate General Editor for this volume:
George Walton Williams

KING
HENRY VIII
(ALL IS TRUE)

THE ARDEN SHAKESPEARE

ALL'S WELL THAT ENDS WELL	edited by G.K. Hunter*
ANTONY AND CLEOPATRA	edited by John Wilders
AS YOU LIKE IT	edited by Juliet Dusinberre
THE COMEDY OF ERRORS	edited by R.A. Foakes*
CORIOLANUS	edited by Philip Brockbank*
CYMBELINE	edited by J.M. Nosworthy*
DOUBLE FALSEHOOD	edited by Brean Hammond
HAMLET	edited by Ann Thompson and Neil Taylor
JULIUS CAESAR	edited by David Daniell
KING HENRY IV Part 1	edited by David Scott Kastan
KING HENRY IV Part 2	edited by A.R. Humphreys*
KING HENRY V	edited by T.W. Craik
KING HENRY VI Part 1	edited by Edward Burns
KING HENRY VI Part 2	edited by Ronald Knowles
KING HENRY VI Part 3	edited by John D. Cox and Eric Rasmussen
KING HENRY VIII	edited by Gordon McMullan
KING JOHN	edited by E.A.J. Honigmann*
KING LEAR	edited by R.A. Foakes
KING RICHARD II	edited by Charles Forker
KING RICHARD III	edited by James R. Siemon
LOVE'S LABOUR'S LOST	edited by H.R. Woudhuysen
MACBETH	edited by Kenneth Muir*
MEASURE FOR MEASURE	edited by J.W. Lever*
THE MERCHANT OF VENICE	edited by John Drakakis
THE MERRY WIVES OF WINDSOR	edited by Giorgio Melchiori
A MIDSUMMER NIGHT'S DREAM	edited by Harold F. Brooks*
MUCH ADO ABOUT NOTHING	edited by Claire McEachern
OTHELLO	edited by E.A.J. Honigmann
PERICLES	edited by Suzanne Gossett
SHAKESPEARE'S POEMS	edited by Katherine Duncan-Jones and H.R. Woudhuysen
ROMEO AND JULIET	edited by Brian Gibbons*
SHAKESPEARE'S SONNETS	edited by Katherine Duncan-Jones
THE TAMING OF THE SHREW	edited by Barbara Hodgdon
THE TEMPEST	edited by Virginia Mason Vaughan and Alden T. Vaughan
TIMON OF ATHENS	edited by Anthony B. Dawson and Gretchen E. Minton
TITUS ANDRONICUS	edited by Jonathan Bate
TROILUS AND CRESSIDA	edited by David Bevington
TWELFTH NIGHT	edited by Keir Elam
THE TWO GENTLEMEN OF VERONA	edited by William C. Carroll
THE TWO NOBLE KINSMEN	edited by Lois Potter
THE WINTER'S TALE	edited by John Pitcher

* Second series

THE ARDEN SHAKESPEARE

KING HENRY VIII (ALL IS TRUE)

William Shakespeare and John Fletcher

Edited by
GORDON McMULLAN

THE ARDEN SHAKESPEARE
LONDON • NEW YORK • OXFORD • NEW DELHI • SYDNEY

THE ARDEN SHAKESPEARE
Bloomsbury Publishing Plc
50 Bedford Square, London, WC1B 3DP, UK
1385 Broadway, New York, NY 10018, USA

BLOOMSBURY, THE ARDEN SHAKESPEARE and the Arden Shakespeare logo
are trademarks of Bloomsbury Publishing Plc

This edition of King Henry VIII, by Gordon McMullan,
published 2000 by The Arden Shakespeare
Reprinted by Bloomsbury Arden Shakespeare 2009, 2011, 2013,
2015, 2016, 2017, 2018, 2019

Editorial material © Gordon McMullan 2000

The general editors of the Arden Shakespeare have been
W. J. Craig and R. H. Case (first series 1899–1944)
Una Ellis-Fermor, Harold F. Brooks, Harold Jenkins and
Brian Morris (second series 1946–82)
Present general editors (third series)
Richard Proudfoot, Ann Thompson, David Scott Kastan
and H. R. Woudhuysen

Bloomsbury Publishing Plc does not have any control over, or responsibility for,
any third-party websites referred to or in this book. All internet addresses given
in this book were correct at the time of going to press. The author and publisher
regret any inconvenience caused if addresses have changed or sites have
ceased to exist, but can accept no responsibility for any such changes.

A catalogue record for this book is available from the British Library.

A catalog record for this book is available from the Library of Congress.

ISBN: HB: 978-1-9034-3624-0
PB: 978-1-9034-3625-7

Series: The Arden Shakespeare Third Series

Typeset by Ehrhardt by Multiplex Techniques Ltd
Printed and bound in Great Britain

To find out more about our authors and books visit
www.bloomsbury.com and sign up for our newsletters.

The Editor

Gordon McMullan is a Lecturer in the Department of English, King's College London. His previous publications include *The Politics of Tragicomedy: Shakespeare and After* (co-edited with Jonathan Hope, 1992); *The Politics of Unease in the Plays of John Fletcher* (1994); and *Renaissance Configurations: Voices/Bodies/Spaces, 1580–1690* (edited, 1998).

For
Muriel McMullan,
Hilda Brooks
and
Suzanne Connell

CONTENTS

vii

LIST OF
ILLUSTRATIONS

GENERAL EDITORS' PREFACE

The Arden Shakespeare is now over one hundred years old. The earliest volume in the first series, Edward Dowden's *Hamlet*, was published in 1899. Since then the Arden Shakespeare has become internationally recognized and respected. It is now widely acknowledged as the pre-eminent Shakespeare series, valued by scholars, students, actors and 'the great variety of readers' alike for its readable and reliable texts, its full annotation and its richly informative introductions.

We have aimed in the third Arden edition to maintain the quality and general character of its predecessors, preserving the commitment to presenting the play as it has been shaped in history. While each individual volume will necessarily have its own emphasis in the light of the unique possibilities and problems posed by the play, the series as a whole, like the earlier Ardens, insists upon the highest standards of scholarship and upon attractive and accessible presentation.

Newly edited from the original quarto and folio editions, the texts are presented in fully modernized form, with a textual apparatus that records all substantial divergences from those early printings. The notes and introductions focus on the conditions and possibilities of meaning that editors, critics and performers (on stage and screen) have discovered in the play. While building upon the rich history of scholarly and theatrical activity that has long shaped our understanding of the texts of Shakespeare's plays, this third series of the Arden Shakespeare is made necessary and possible by a new generation's encounter with Shakespeare, engaging with the plays and their complex relation to the culture in which they were – and continue to be – produced.

THE TEXT

On each page of the play itself, readers will find a passage of text followed by commentary and, finally, textual notes. Act and scene divisions (seldom present in the early editions and often the product of eighteenth-century or later scholarship) have been retained for ease of reference, but have been given less prominence than in the previous series. Editorial indications of location of the action have been removed to the textual notes or commentary.

In the text itself, unfamiliar typographic conventions have been avoided in order to minimize obstacles to the reader. Elided forms in the early texts are spelt out in full in verse lines wherever they indicate a usual late twentieth-century pronunciation that requires no special indication and wherever they occur in prose (except when they indicate non-standard pronunciation). In verse speeches, marks of elision are retained where they are necessary guides to the scansion and pronunciation of the line. Final -ed in past tense and participial forms of verbs is always printed as -ed without accent, never as -'d, but wherever the required pronunciation diverges from modern usage a note in the commentary draws attention to the fact. Where the final -ed should be given syllabic value contrary to modern usage, e.g.

> Doth Silvia know that I am banished?
> (*TGV* 3.1.221)

the note will take the form

> 221 **banished** banishèd

Conventional lineation of divided verse lines shared by two or more speakers has been reconsidered and sometimes rearranged. Except for the familiar *Exit* and *Exeunt*, Latin forms in stage directions and speech prefixes have been translated into English and the original Latin forms recorded in the textual notes.

COMMENTARY AND TEXTUAL NOTES

Notes in the commentary, for which a major source will be the *Oxford English Dictionary*, offer glossarial and other explication of verbal difficulties; they may also include discussion of points of theatrical interpretation and, in relevant cases, substantial extracts from Shakespeare's source material. Editors will not usually offer glossarial notes for words adequately defined in the latest edition of *The Concise Oxford Dictionary* or *Merriam-Webster's Collegiate Dictionary*, but in cases of doubt they will include notes. Attention, however, will be drawn to places where more than one likely interpretation can be proposed and to significant verbal and syntactic complexity. Notes preceded by * discuss editorial amendations or variant readings from the early edition(s) on which the text is based.

Headnotes to acts or scenes discuss, where appropriate, questions of scene location, Shakespeare's handling of his source materials, and major difficulties of staging. The list of roles (so headed to emphasize the play's status as a text for performance) is also considered in commentary notes. These may include comment on plausible patterns of casting with the resources of an Elizabethan or Jacobean acting company, and also on any variation in the description of roles in their speech prefixes in the early editions.

The textual notes are designed to let readers know when the edited text diverges from the early edition(s) on which it is based. Wherever this happens the note will record the rejected reading of the early edition(s), in original spelling, and the source of the reading adopted in this edition. Other forms from the early edition(s) recorded in these notes will include some spellings of particular interest or significance and original forms of translated stage directions. Where two early editions are involved, for instance with *Othello*, the notes will also record all important differences between them. The textual notes take a form that has been in use since the nineteenth century. This comprises, first: line reference, reading adopted in the text and closing square bracket; then: abbreviated reference, in italic, to the earliest edition to adopt the accepted reading, italic semicolon and noteworthy alternative reading(s), each with abbreviated italic reference to its source.

Conventions used in these textual notes include the following. The solidus / is used, in notes quoting verse or discussing verse lining, to indicate line endings. Distinctive spellings of the basic text (Q or F) follow the square bracket without indication of source and are enclosed in italic brackets. Names enclosed in italic brackets indicate originators of conjectural emendations when these did not originate in an edition of the text, or when this edition records a conjecture not accepted into its text. Stage directions (SDs) are referred to by the number of the line within or immediately after which they are placed. Line numbers with a decimal point relate to entry SDs and to SDs more than one line long, with the number after the point indicating the line within the SD: e.g. 78.4 refers to the fourth line of the SD following line 78. Lines of SDs at the start of a scene are numbered 0.1, 0.2, etc. Where only a line number and SD precede the square bracket, e.g. 128 SD], the note relates to the whole of a SD within or immediately following the line. Speech prefixes (SPs) follow similar conventions, 203 SP] referring to the speaker's name for line 203. Where a SP reference takes the form e.g. 38 + SP, it relates to all subsequent speeches assigned to that speaker in the scene in question.

Where, as with *King Henry V*, one of the early editions is a so-called 'bad quarto' (that is, a text either heavily adapted, or reconstructed from memory, or both), the divergences from the present edition are too great to be recorded in full in the notes. In these cases the editions will include a reduced photographic facsimile of the 'bad quarto' in an appendix.

INTRODUCTION

Both the introduction and the commentary are designed to present the plays as texts for performance, and make appropriate reference to stage, film and television versions, as well as introducing the reader to the range of critical approaches to the plays. They discuss the history of the reception of the texts within the theatre and scholarship and beyond, investigating the interdependency of the literary text and the surrounding 'cultural text' both at the time of the original production of Shakespeare's works and during their long and rich afterlife.

PREFACE

Henry the Eighth – 'that Bluebeard', as Elsa Lanchester, playing Anne of Cleves in the film, *The Private Life of Henry VIII*, describes her future husband – is the most immediately recognizable of England's monarchs, a fame (or rather, notoriety) that can be attributed in roughly equal measure to the artistic abilities of Holbein and the ongoing cultural fascination with the King's murderous sex life. The play which is named after him and which appears last in the sequence of 'Histories' in the Shakespeare First Folio is rather less well known, though its success on the stage in the eighteenth and nineteenth centuries was a significant factor in the sustained visual familiarity of the King himself. In fact, if people know anything at all about *Henry VIII* at the beginning of the twenty-first century, they are more likely to know that it caused the destruction of the Globe theatre or that it has been the source of arguments over Shakespearean authorship than they are to have a close acquaintance with the actual text. But this would not have been the case a century ago, at the height of *Henry VIII*'s popularity on the stage, and it strikes me as a great pity that the play should be so under-appreciated now, because (and I may as well state this right away) I think it a splendid play and one that richly rewards close attention.

It is also a play which has been consistently misrepresented, both in performance and in criticism, both in its heyday and afterwards, and one for which the absorption of a certain amount of information about the immediate cultural and historical contexts out of which it emerged makes a great deal of difference to modern readers. I hope my Introduction provides those readers with what they need to understand both how the play may have been seen by its first audiences and what kinds of reaction it may have provoked – not because I believe that the task of the contemporary critic (or the contemporary director) is to 're-create' the 'original' conditions of production (a task which is patently impossible) but because it seems to me that adequate understanding of any early modern play can come about only through a productive negotiation between the historical and the current. I should perhaps add, too, that I have set out – in the Arden third series tradition initiated by Jonathan Bate in his edition of *Titus Andronicus* – not to follow the pattern of the 'conventionally ordered introduction to a Shakespearian text', defined by A.R.Braunmuller in his exemplary edition of *King John* as one which 'separates fact from opinion and places the former before the latter' (1), principally because I cannot see how I or any other editor can possibly fulfil such a daunting proposition. There may be some facts out there, but they can only be approached by way of opinion.

A few forewarnings. As with the earlier plays on historical subjects in the Shakespeare canon, *Henry VIII* depends heavily (sometimes word for word) on its sources, particularly Holinshed's *Chronicles*. It was the custom in the previous Arden series (Arden 2) to provide substantial extracts from the sources in an appendix, which had the obvious virtue of providing a coherent narrative of the historical events covered and of allowing that narrative to be read in the order in which it appeared in the source rather than in the play. In practice, though, relatively few students of the play ever bothered to turn to the back of the book to compare a particular section of Holinshed with the passage in question. So in order to facilitate the process of setting the play against its sources I have located quotations from those sources in the commentary notes at the bottom of the page. This makes some of the notes a little longer and more obtrusive than I would have preferred, but it seems to me very important that readers of this edition should be able to make the comparisons easily and immediately, particularly since, in this collaborative play, they need always to remain aware of the operations of multiple agency and attitude in the production of a dramatic text. The appropriate sections of the narratives of Holinshed and Foxe (as well as lengthy extracts from Samuel Rowley's Henry VIII play, *When You See Me, You Know Me*) can be found in Geoffrey Bullough's *Narrative and Dramatic Sources of Shakespeare* and in earlier editions: they can, of course, also be found in the originals of and later editions of the chronicles in question.

For this edition, I have been fortunate to be able to consult Jonathan Hope, linguistics adviser to Arden 3, on a number of questions of language, and his suggestions are identified in the commentary notes. At this stage, I want to note one or two general points about the discussion of language in this edition. Arden 3 editors have been encouraged to make fuller use of the *OED* than their predecessors, but it is worth bearing in mind that the date of an *OED* first citation for a word or meaning may well not represent the earliest usage. This is because such citations were restricted to printed sources which survived into the nineteenth century and these sources were inevitably not, because of the sheer enormity of the task, searched exhaustively (see Schäfer). Nonetheless, the *OED* is an enormous help to an editor, and all references are given in detailed form. The standard 'Shakespearean grammar' consulted by editors is Abbott (generally, the third edition of 1870), but this is now pretty comprehensively outdated, based as it is on prescriptive, rather than descriptive, ways of thinking about the English language. Readers with a specific interest in Shakespeare's use of language are advised to look at Jonathan Hope's essay 'Shakespeare's "Natiue English"' in David Kastan's *A Companion to Shakespeare* for a concise, engaging overview and at Charles Barber's *Early Modern English* for a detailed analysis. For questions of Shakespearean verse form, George Wright's *Shakespeare's Metrical Art* is very helpful. For Fletcher, no such books exist.

One other warning. As my own interest in practical theatre has grown over the last few years, so I have tried to make this a more 'theatrical' edition than I would ever have expected when I started work on it. But anyone who has ever seen a particular professional production in rehearsal, at dress rehearsal, in preview, on the press night and at the beginning, middle and end of a run, and has noted the changes of pace determined by alterations in personnel, venue or weather, or even by the closing time of the pub next to the theatre, will realize the depressing inadequacy of stage histories based on reviews in the press or single eyewitness accounts. As John Cox and David Kastan note in *A New History of Early English Drama*, '[d]rama is . . . a temporal art, ineluctably tied . . . to the event of its performance, for performance changes from one afternoon (or night) to the next in a particular run, and even more from one run to another, which might occur decades or even centuries apart, in what are, in effect, different cultures' (4). It is impossible, even with such resources as the fixed-camera videos the Royal Shakespeare Company have made of their productions since 1982, to regain a sense of what it was like to be in the audience for productions you never yourself saw. I hope I have developed a reasonable sense of the impact of the productions I discuss, but I have no doubt that much more could be said, if I could only get that time machine in the garage to work properly.

In the course of writing this edition, I have published four articles which have been to a greater or lesser extent reworked in producing the Introduction. These are 'Shakespeare and the end of history', *Essays and Studies*, 48 (1995), 16–37; ' "Our whole life is like a play": collaboration and the problem of editing', *Textus*, 9 (1996), 437–60; 'Swimming on bladders: the dialogics of Reformation in Shakespeare & Fletcher's *Henry VIII* ', in Ronald Knowles (ed.), *Shakespeare and Carnival: After Bakhtin* (1998), 211–27; and ' "Thou hast made me now a man": reforming man(ner)liness in *Henry VIII* ', in Jennifer Richards and James Knowles (eds), *Shakespeare's Late Plays: New Readings* (Edinburgh, 1999), 40–56. Readers of this edition who would like more detailed presentations of some of the arguments offered here are advised to have a look at the articles.

Jay Halio's Oxford edition unfortunately came out at too late a stage of the publication process of the present volume for me to be able to refer to it.

This edition has been a fair while in the making, and a lot of people have been helpful along the way. I wish therefore to offer rather more acknowledgements than is usually the case. My first acknowledgements must be to Richard Proudfoot, David Kastan and Ann Thompson, who have been exemplary general editors, patient, encouraging, informative and ironic, as and when appropriate. My greatest debt is to Richard, the true editors' editor, whose generosity with his knowledge, time and energy is hugely appreciated by those of us who have been fortunate enough to have our work supervised by him. David and Ann have been supportive editors and good friends: it is just a pity that David has such poor taste in soccer teams. I am grateful, too, to George Walton Williams, Associate General Editor, for detailed, helpful and characteristically entertaining suggestions.

I want also to acknowledge the dedication, hard work and friendship of a number of publishers' editors: I am especially grateful to Jane Armstrong, without whom the whole thing would never have happened in the first place; to Talia Rodgers and Sophie Powell at Routledge; to Nick Kind at Thomas Nelson; and in particular to Jessica Hodge at Nelson and then at Thomson Learning. The latter stages of the editorial process have been made (almost) pleasurable by Jessica's humour, efficiency and endless energy. I am grateful, too, to Hannah Hyam and Nicola Bennett for saving me from a range of errors.

I began work on this edition as a lecturer in the Department of English Literature at the University of Newcastle upon Tyne. I am grateful for support from Linda Anderson, Bruce Babington, Tom Cain, Judith Hawley, Mike Rossington, Ianthi Tsimpli and Karen Corrigan; and Claire Lamont was the best imaginable head of department. Mike Pincombe was a good friend and an essential resource, dropping me notes in his inimitable hand with commentary suggestions; and I am grateful to Celia Shephard, who read and asked perceptive questions about the play to help me ascertain the needs of a key group of readers.

I moved to King's College London in 1995, with the result that for a year or so Richard Proudfoot was, for his sins, not only my general editor but also my head of department. Peter Stallybrass and Ann Rosalind Jones were in London that year, and I am happy to acknowledge their many contributions, witting and unwitting, to this edition. Peter did a particularly good job of harassing my preconceptions about authorship until light finally began to dawn. I am grateful to my colleagues at King's for coping with conversations that always seemed to end up with some reference to *Henry VIII*. I am grateful too to my students ('the hope o'th' Strand'), especially to Lucy Munro for suggesting illustrations and offering research on genres, dates and companies, and to Eva Griffith for promoting *If You Know Not Me* and for resisting my Protestant perspective.

I want also to say thank you to Greg Doran for inviting me to participate in the rehearsal process of his 1996 RSC production, and to the cast (especially Jane Lapotaire, Paul Jesson and Iain Hogg) for putting up with my questions and impertinent suggestions. This would have been a lesser edition if I had not had the experience of watching theatre professionals of their calibre turning complex text into dynamic performance. I am grateful, too, to Patrick Spottiswoode and Andrew Gurr for encouraging me to become involved at the rebuilt Globe. I was fortunate to be able to run a workshop on the staging of certain scenes from *Henry VIII* on the Globe stage in March 1999 as part of the 'Winter Playing' season, and I would like to record my gratitude to Kate Raper, who directed the workshop (and who was also assistant director on the RSC production), and to Sarah Finch, Julia Office, Mary McNulty and the team for their enthusiasm and professionalism.

Friends have offered patience and abuse in roughly equal measure – notably Karl Horton, to whom I am grateful for his (largely) uncomplaining role as chauffeur in quest of the Field of the Cloth of Gold and for the clear demonstration of linguistic 'accommodation theory' that the journey afforded. Jonathan Hope has been consistently supportive and offensive for over a decade, ever since we ran a conference in Oxford as optimistic, job-seeking graduate students. In London, research days would not have been the same, either for me or for the profit margins of the cafés in Museum Street, without the company of Sue Wiseman. And I would like to thank Tom and Margaret Healy and other members of the London Renaissance Seminar – notably Helen Hackett, Sasha Roberts and Alan Stewart – for making me feel at home in the capital. I am also grateful to Judith Anderson, Clara Calvo, Michael Dobson, Ernst Honigmann, James Knowles, Mark Lawhorn, David Lindley, Annabel Patterson, Kristen Poole, Lois Potter, Maureen Quilligan, Anna Round, Nicholas Round, Conrad Russell, Peter Shaw, Emma Smith, Ruth Vanita and Stanley Wells for providing suggestions or references, or for letting me see work in progress. Those of us who knew Gareth Roberts, an Arden editor until his untimely death in February 1999, miss him very much.

I have received much-appreciated assistance from the staff of the British Library (at Bloomsbury, St Pancras and Colindale), the University of London Library, King's College Library, the Theatre Museum, the Bodleian Library, Cambridge University Library, the Shakespeare Centre and Shakespeare Institute libraries in Stratford-upon-Avon, the New York Public Library for the Performing Arts at the Lincoln Center, and the Huntington Library. I was fortunate to be able to spend four months at the Huntington in 1995, courtesy of a Mayer Fund Fellowship, and thus to experience the considerable hospitality of the library's Research Director, Robert C. Ritchie, as well as the helpfulness of his staff. I benefited from time spent with many people there, notably Marilyn Corrie, Larry and Susan Green,

David Kastan, J.M. Massi, Reid Mitchell, Jane Moody, Mark Valeri, Blair Worden and, most especially, Belinda Peters; also, at Santa Barbara, Lee Bliss; and at UCLA, Michael Allen, Lowell Gallagher, Arthur Little, Deborah Shuger and, especially, Claire McEachern. A.R. Braunmuller has been tremendously supportive, both in Los Angeles and in London: without his advice, this edition would have been a lesser piece of work and (more to the point) I would never have learned to order a quad decaf grande latte non-fat before such words had ever been uttered in Britain. I am grateful, too, to Reg and Mary Foakes for their hospitality, and I am just sorry that Mary is not around now to read this thank-you. Reg's edition of *Henry VIII* set the standard for subsequent editors; Reg himself has been more than generous with his time and knowledge. I hope I remember to do the same for the upstart who eventually presumes to replace *this* edition, which is (it goes without saying) definitive.

I am very grateful that my time in Pasadena coincided with Lorna Hutson's Huntington fellowship. For one thing, without her, I'd never have been able to keep up with the second series of *NYPD Blue*. More importantly, though, it was a privilege to be able to spend sustained time with a person whose breadth of knowledge and intellectual excitement is so infectious.

Both at the Huntington and later, I learned a great deal from, and shared wonderful times with, Allison Sneider, in spite of her preference for reading Shakespeare in the sauna.

I would like to dedicate this edition to three people: to my mother, Muriel McMullan, and to my aunt, Hilda Brooks; and to Suzanne Connell, who, on my very first day in the Robson Valley (and just in case I ever decide to work on *The Winter's Tale*), provided me with a unique and marvellous insight into Shakespeare's best-known stage direction.

Gordon McMullan
London, Los Angeles, and Newcastle upon Tyne

INTRODUCTION

An account of a conversation in 1910 between the actress Sarah Bernhardt and the actor–producer Sir Herbert Beerbohm Tree includes an impassioned plea by Bernhardt for truth in the representation of historical drama. 'A theatre', she is reported as saying:

> is a place where art seeks to present to the mind a real and living drama, something that once took place, something that was once as actual as our life to-day, a thing that happened. To do this three things are necessary – the genius of the actor, the genius of the painter, the genius of the costumier. The illusion is not complete without the truth of the impersonation, the truth of the place, the truth of the dress. The whole thing must be true.
>
> (*Era*, 17).

This account appeared during the enormously successful run of Tree's production of *Henry VIII*, and Bernhardt's words exemplify the premise of the spectacular Shakespearean stagings – based on meticulous research into every detail, from the food on the table to the colour of a doublet's silk lining – that were loved by Victorian and Edwardian audiences. The quest for artistic truth, at least as far as 'history plays' were concerned, depended for Bernhardt (and for Tree) upon a full sensory re-creation of an imagined original, and *Henry VIII* – its action drawn closely from chronicle history and its text peppered with detailed directions for staged state ritual – seemed the ideal vehicle for this vision of historical drama. Yet later in the twentieth century Donald Sinden, commenting on his preparations for playing Henry in Trevor Nunn's Royal Shakespeare Company production, observed (with obvious distaste) that 'if you study history you will find that

1

practically everything shown or talked about in the play is only a veneer of the truth' (Sinden, 265). For Sinden, this historical duplicity was a destructive flaw; yet by the time of the Nunn production both academics and directors (including Nunn himself) had already begun to acknowledge that the representation offered by *Henry VIII* of the 'something that once took place', of the 'thing that actually happened', of (in other words) the 'truth' of this play about truth, is both complex and elusive.

The disjunction between Bernhardt's ideal and Sinden's experience is, I will argue, symptomatic of *Henry VIII*. On the one hand, it is a play which undoubtedly does depend for its success upon the visible truth of its historical representation (no other 'history' play can boast anything like the extent and detail of those stage directions); at the same time, it appears wilfully to undercut that truth. Sinden's discovery of its historical duplicity clearly came as a surprise to him, yet even the briefest of glances at a history of the reign of Henry VIII ought to make it apparent that the play's engagement with 'what actually happened' in that reign is limited at best. Only a portion of Henry's life – and certainly little of what people generally know about that life (we see only two of the six wives, for instance) – is dealt with. Chronology is disrupted as historical events are shunted around for dramatic effect. The break with Rome – surely the most significant political event of the English century – is treated only obliquely. Moreover, on closer inspection, the play seems to be at least as much engaged with the politics and culture of the reign in which it was produced – that of James I (or VI, if you are a Scot) – as it is with the reign it ostensibly represents.

Henry VIII, I would argue, demands a much more radical understanding of the nature of truth than editors and critics (with one or two honourable exceptions) have tended to allow, even though questions of truth and authenticity have always been central to its history. The play itself, as the alternative title under which it was first performed – *All Is True* – suggests, is obsessed with truth. The word 'truth' itself turns up no fewer than

2

twenty-five times, and there are six occurrences of 'truly', one of 'true-hearted' and eighteen of 'true'. The Prologue alone offers two occurrences of 'truth' and one of 'true', first of all locating the concept within a nexus of faith, hope and expenditure – 'Such as give / Their money out of hope they may believe / May here find truth' (7–9) – then connecting it with a sense of deliberate selectivity or, perhaps, election – 'our chosen truth' (18) – and finally addressing the relationship between artistic intention and representation – 'the opinion that we bring / To make that only true we now intend' (20–1). This direct engagement with 'truth' right at the start – which is sustained throughout – is echoed in the history of the play's reception. Yet despite its consistent centrality to developments in the staging of early modern drama – as directors and actors made use of the play to establish competing versions of 'authentic' production – a clear understanding of the theatrical truth of *Henry VIII* remains remarkably elusive, at least in part because of the truncated versions of the play that were performed in the eighteenth and nineteenth centuries. Moreover, the very 'authenticity' of the play itself has been the source of extensive, and at times suffocating, debate as authorship analysts have struggled to determine whether or not the play can actually be called 'Shakespearean' – and therefore, within the framework of bardolatry, whether it is worthy of close critical attention at all.

Partly, but not solely, as a result of this, critical attitudes to *Henry VIII* have been largely negative. Well before the play's authorship was ever doubted, in fact, Pepys was unimpressed: 'though I went with resolution to like it,' he claims, the play 'is so simple a thing, made up of a great many patches, that, besides the shows and processions in it, there is nothing in the world good or well done' (Pepys, 5.2 (1 January 1664)). And despite the play's immense popularity on the stage in the eighteenth and nineteenth centuries (it was performed in every decade, and in every year of some decades, from the mid-seventeenth century well into the nineteenth century, and later nineteenth-century productions became showpieces of contemporary theatrical fashion), critics remained largely lukewarm about *Henry VIII*, treating it at best as 'minor Shakespeare', and often ignoring it altogether. Certain key roles – Katherine and Wolsey, in particular – were considered powerful, but the play from which they were drawn was felt to be deeply flawed.

Throughout this period, and certainly for the bulk of the twentieth century, the watchword of criticism was 'unity', and unity is something critics have felt to be particularly (even embarrassingly) lacking in *Henry VIII*, with its episodic structure and its lack of a single, obvious central character. Moreover, the kind of topical engagement that critics began to discover in the play was thought also to lead to inferior art – 'great' writing being located somehow outside and beyond the contingent – and collaborative plays, as *Henry VIII* was increasingly acknowledged to be, were anyway considered, by definition, inferior 'hackwork'. Only special circumstances, it was felt, could possibly have caused Shakespeare to work in such a time-bound and/or collaborative manner, and while it was acknowledged to be helpful to understand those special circumstances, there was no need to believe that a play produced in such a way could possibly match the detached, internally inspired product of a single imagination, particularly the unsurpassed imagination of England's national poet.

The play was thus considered by those who didn't like it to be disjoint and/or dissonant, and if they acknowledged the possibility of collaborative production, it was simply to blame Shakespeare's collaborator for ruining what might have been the last great Shakespearean history play: there is an exact correlation between dislike for the play and a determination to prove it to be mostly the work of someone other than Shakespeare. Those who did like and appreciate the play (including my predecessor as Arden editor, R.A.Foakes) fought just as hard to prove the play a singly-authored, coherent, Shakespearean whole. The most conspicuous (and most eccentric) of the handful of early-to-mid-twentieth-century critics who believed in the play's unity and made a strong case for its centrality to the Shakespeare canon was G. Wilson Knight, a scholar and amateur director whose critical work on Shakespeare – exceptional for its day in its insistence on looking beyond character and moral argument – had considerable influence in post-war Britain. For Knight, *Henry VIII*, viewed as 'authoritatively Shakespearean' (code for 'not the product of collaboration'), was no less than the culmination of the Great Author's grand, unifying vision of English nationalism and royalism. Rather than treating *Henry VIII* as a 'patchwork' of 'mere' pomp and ceremony, Knight viewed it whole, examining 'the great architecture of sequent pageants and their deeper meanings' to see in the play the grand finale of Shakespeare's history plays, which together represented 'the unfurling of a nation's history towards the destiny outlined in Cranmer's prophecy, . . . England's almost Messianic destiny' (Knight, *Crown*, 330).[1] The play was, in other words, the coherent embodiment of the dream Knight attributed to Shakespeare of an ideological unification of royalism and Christianity, a near-sacred text demanding reverence from morally engaged Englishmen.

For decades, Knight's view of *Henry VIII* – near-fascistic, inaccurate and ahistorical – was effectively the only one which

---

1 See also Knight, *Principles*, 221, 231, and Knight, 'Propaganda', 3, 54. The latter, an unpublished typescript with manuscript additions and alterations, is held in the British Library, and presents itself as a survey of Knight's efforts across the years to express the centrality of royalty to Shakespeare's 'vision'. Knight emphasizes his writings and his performances during the Second World War, when he devised and performed (with Henry Ainley, who had played Buckingham in Tree's 1910 *Henry VIII* and who, though ill, was persuaded out of retirement by Knight) a 'Dramatisation of Shakespeare's Call to Great Britain in Time of War' entitled *This Sceptred Isle*. It included Gaunt's speech in *Richard II* from which Knight drew his title, and which culminated in a section called 'The Royal Phoenix', featuring Cranmer's prophecy from *Henry VIII*. His focus on Shakespearean royalty is intensely nationalistic, yet he also insists that his 'mind was never wholly given to a one-way propaganda', recalling that in the summer of 1940 he was completing his book *Christ and Nietzsche*, 'with what some have regarded as its dangerously dramatic interest at one point . . . in the Nazi movement' – explaining that it was 'perhaps my many years of dramatic experience which prompts my attempts to understand both parties in *any* conflict' ('Propaganda', 8). Re-reading Knight for the purposes of this edition, I found it quite disturbing to recall (for all his undoubted critical abilities) that I was recommended his books by my schoolteachers as perfectly rational mainstream Shakespeare criticism.

treated the play as a coherent, purposeful dramatic text, and certainly the only one to give it a place of importance in the Shakespeare canon. This, happily, is no longer the case. Critical developments since the late 1960s have enabled a certain liberation both from the tyranny of unity and from the romantic philosophy that underlies the critical insistence upon solitary inspiration – not so as to replace order with chaos or to privilege artistic incompetence over genuine creative achievement, but instead to seek appropriate ways to read a range of literary texts, particularly early modern dramatic texts, whose mode of production means that they can only begin to be comprehensible outside the straitjacket of the 'unified whole'. By the end of the twentieth century, there had been enough exploratory productions of *Henry VIII* – notably those of Terence Gray, Tyrone Guthrie, Trevor Nunn, Howard Davies and Greg Doran – as well as imaginative critical readings – beginning with Lee Bliss's groundbreaking 1975 essay in *English Literary History* – for the dismissive view of the play to be largely banished. To be in a position to move beyond the constraints of the unified 'work' is to begin to appreciate this complex, ironic, multi-layered, collaborative text for what it is – or, perhaps better, for what it can become through a productive negotiation between the processes of its origin and construction and our own critical understanding of its possibilities.

Henry VIII is neither simply a 'thing made up of a great many patches', as Pepys thought, nor is it an uncritical and deeply conservative celebration of royal power and English national will, as Knight believed, nor is it a theatrical 'biopic' dependent for its success on the stage solely on the grandeur of its sets and the casting of famous actors in at least one of its three principal roles, as directors still sometimes seem to think. It is, on the contrary, a sophisticated play, at once celebratory and cynical about display, which meditates on the progress of Reformation in England, reading English life since Henry VIII's day as a series of bewildering changes in national and personal allegiance, and presenting history as the product of testimony that is by its very nature varied, contradictory and irresolvable. It is a play which is dependent upon the authenticity of the representations of history that it provides – exemplified in the precision with which the chronicle accounts of state ritual are reproduced – yet it is at the same time a play which questions both the possibility of precise reproduction and the validity of state ritual as an authentic representation of political will. The play was, moreover, written at a highly charged moment in national consciousness, a moment which brought to a head certain key issues of the relationship of past, present and future upon which its source texts had reflected and which provided an immediate context for its first audience's engagement with current events even as they watched an apparent representation of the past. It thus deliberately encouraged critical self-positioning on the part of the audience in 1613, inviting its members to imagine the texture of English history, and it deploys a range of dramatic strategies to reach the different constituent parts of that audience. And I would argue that the kind of productive anxiety about the nature of historical and political truth that it sought to produce in that audience can still have a powerful and unsettling effect on audiences and readers today.

This description of the play may well come as a surprise to some of the readers of this edition, accustomed as they probably are to the idea that *Henry VIII* is one of the least subtle and complex plays in the Shakespeare canon. But as Iska Alter argues in a provocative essay, 'many of the difficulties that we have come to regard as inherent' in *Henry VIII* are in fact 'theatrical constructs, created by the requirements of an older, culturally determined idea about what constituted effective and appropriate dramatic action' (Alter, 184). I hope here to suggest the inadequacy both of the constructs and of the idea. In this context, the best way to begin an assessment of the play is with a survey of its stage history, from its first recorded performances to the end of the twentieth century, because although the play lost in the latter half of that century the prominence on the stage it had when Sarah Bernhardt formulated her vision of 'truthful' drama in 1910, it has in the course of its afterlife been substantially more important to theatre practitioners than it has to literary critics. It has, in fact, had one of the longest and most stable theatrical histories of any play in the Shakespeare canon, something which has been both an immense advantage and also, for a range of reasons, an unfortunate burden.

AUTHENTICITIES: PERFORMANCE HISTORY

Discussions of *Henry VIII* tend inevitably to resolve into the question of truth, and the truth of the play, performatively speaking, has been seen to be embodied in the uniquely detailed stage directions provided in the earliest text we have of the play, that in the First Folio of 1623. Producers from the Restoration onwards have seen in these stage directions an invitation to demote the text in favour of theatrical effect. Richard Schoch, for instance, has described the controversy over the 'actor–historian' Charles Kean's Shakespeare revivals at the Princess's Theatre in the 1850s, as scholars and theatre professionals argued over the validity of the staging of historical spectacle, but he records that 'even those poetic purists who sickened at the sight of theatrical upholstery conceded that the lines of demarcation between "accuracy" and "show" in *Henry VIII* were imperceptible' (Schoch, 86). Kean, he notes, 'did not need to justify the scenic voluptuousness of *Henry VIII* with any . . . extrinsic argument' as he had been obliged to do for his production of *Macbeth* two years earlier, 'because spectacle and pageantry were already written into the text' (Schoch, 86). The attitude exemplified here has dominated the play's performance history (as public taste for historical spectacle declined, so did the frequency of productions of *Henry VIII*) and has rarely been questioned since, despite the fact that the (sometimes very real) dangers of the play's materiality in the theatre had been apparent from the very earliest performances.

Date and early performances

In the course of the first recorded performance of *Henry VIII* on the afternoon of 29 June 1613, the first Globe Theatre caught fire and burned down.[1] Several contemporary reports have survived of this event which I will discuss in due course; for now, I simply want to note that the fact of the fire enables us to be quite precise about the date of the earliest performances and, to a certain extent, about the way in which the play was received by its very first audiences. It is described in one of the reports as a 'new' play (it may possibly already have been performed at court as early as February, though this is unlikely).[2] It was probably also staged (very possibly prior to the Globe performances) at the Blackfriars Theatre, the indoor, so-called 'private' playhouse occupied by the King's Men in 1608, though, because of outbreaks of the plague, not brought into full use until 1610. The First Folio text – noteworthy, as I have observed, for the extent and detail of its stage directions – is assumed to represent the play as it was performed at the Globe, both because of the reports of the Globe fire and because the Blackfriars stage was smaller and less able to accommodate the sheer numbers of actors and extras demanded by the stage directions.[3] But there is in fact nothing to say that the play could not originally have been conceived on a more modest scale and then extended for performance at the larger venue. The company is known to have played other plays at both venues, so that reports of Globe performance do not necessarily mean that *Henry VIII* was

1 There is a curious irony in the fact that the play which was responsible for the destruction of the first Globe Theatre should open with a discussion of the Field of the Cloth of Gold, where the familiar round theatre design was first introduced to the English in the form of an immense polygonal tent (see Orrell, *Human*, 31–8).

2 See pp. 57–62, esp. Wotton letter discussed at pp. 59–62. Foakes (Ard²) believed that the play was first performed for the wedding of Princess Elizabeth and the Elector Palatine in February 1613 (see pp. 64–5), though he admits there is no actual documentary evidence for this (Ard², xxxiv).

3 According to the available evidence for casting the plays in the Shakespeare canon, King argues that, for *Henry VIII*, '[t]hirteen men can play twenty-two principal male roles, and three boys play three principal female roles; these sixteen actors speak 96% of the lines. Seventeen men can play eighteen small speaking parts and forty-nine mutes; seven boys can play two small speaking parts and nineteen mutes' (King, *Casting*, 93). See Appendix 7.

exclusively a Globe play.[1] More to the point, there would have been considerable historical resonance in performance at the Blackfriars, since the theatre was located in the very same hall in which the divorce hearing of Henry VIII and Katherine of Aragon, on which the play in many ways pivots, had taken place eighty-four years earlier. Henry seems too deliberately to draw the audience's attention to the location – 'The most convenient place that I can think of / For such receipt of learning', he announces at the end of 2.2, 'is Blackfriars' (2.2.136–7) – for the play not to have been written with performance at the newly-acquired theatre in mind. And though no documentary evidence exists for this, it does offer the interesting possibility that a proportion of the spectacle for which the play is known may well have been incorporated only after an initial run of performances at a theatre better suited to intimacy and irony than to pomp and sincerity.[2]

What can we infer about the staging of these early performances? Whichever theatre the play was first performed in, there seems to have been a 'state' centre stage (e.g. 1.2.8.4: 'KING *riseth from his state*'), a raised seat or throne covered with a canopy of some sort (e.g. 2.4.0.11: '*The* KING *takes place under the cloth of state*'), which may have remained on stage throughout (*TxC*, 619). Recent work on the first Globe, culminating in the construction of a replica theatre on the Bankside, has given us a fair idea of its probable shape and therefore of the staging of scenes which are dependent upon the particular space available (Orrell, *Quest*; Gurr & Orrell). If we knew more about the physical construction of the Blackfriars theatre too, we might have a better idea of possible alternative stagings for key scenes, notably that of Katherine's vision. The nineteenth century certainly made the most of the opportunity provided by the detailed stage direction for this

---

1 Seventeen editions of ten plays, including 1622 and 1630 Quartos of *Othello* and the 1631 Quarto of *The Taming of the Shrew*, list both the Globe and the Blackfriars on their title-pages. I am grateful to David Kastan for the precise figures.

2 Its location near the Inns of Court provided the Blackfriars with an audience of young law students keen to sustain their reputation for sophisticated appreciation of satire and iconoclasm.

moment, providing in Kean's 1855 production, for example, a cascade of angels, carefully lit to hide the ladder on which they were perched. In the twentieth century, productions have varied in emphasis between full stagings in this tradition and bare minimalism. Howard Davies (Royal Shakespeare Company, 1983), for example, paired the moment visually with an atmospheric dance sequence at Wolsey's masque in order to present the dream-vision as a redemptive version of the earlier scene (see Fig. 1), while Greg Doran, for the subsequent RSC production (1996), eschewed angels altogether in favour of simple spotlighting and a focus on the individual redemption of the Queen. We have no clear idea of how it might have been staged in 1613. Lighting effects – using candles and mirrors – would presumably have worked better in the darkness at the Blackfriars (if the theatre was in fact dark) than in daylight at the Globe, and it is possible that two rather different styles may have been adopted for the same scene even in the very first year of production.[1]

Costume would have been eclectic. The usual basis for this assumption is the Peacham drawing, traditionally thought to be the only extant contemporary depiction of a Shakespeare play in performance and ostensibly illustrating the lines from *Titus Andronicus* inscribed beneath it, which seems to show Elizabethan and Jacobean theatrical costume for plays with historical settings as a mixture of old and new: 'As the play addresses issues in contemporary history via a Roman setting,' Jonathan Bate observes, 'so the costumes mingle ages' (*Tit*, Ard³, 43). Recent work by June Schlueter, however, questions the connection between the illustration and *Titus Andronicus*, arguing that the Peacham drawing in fact depicts a related but distinct play (Schlueter, 172–83). Nonetheless, the assumption about costume, at least in relation to *Henry VIII*, appears to stand. The title-page of *When You See Me, You Know Me*, a slightly earlier play about Henry VIII, features an etching of the King in Tudor dress and the classic

---

1 Recent research seems to suggest that the Blackfriars was probably lit as much as possible by light from the windows rather than by costly candles.

1 Katherine's vision, with Gemma Jones as the Queen, from Howard Davies's production for the Royal Shakespeare Company, 1983

Holbein pose, legs straddled and arms akimbo, embodying the logic of the play's title (see Fig. 2); at the same time, there are several references in *Henry VIII* to the latest in Jacobean fashion (e.g. 5.3.46), and there is a general sense throughout the play of a significant blurring of lines between the Henrician and the Jacobean. There is also the suggestion of J.W.Saunders that the 'rail' mentioned at 5.3.86 ran around the edge of the thrust stage, thus implying that the imagined 'crowd' is in fact the audience, which might in turn imply the actors' invocation, if not use, of the yard as well as the stage for playing this scene and underline the juxtaposition the play effects of Henrician history and contemporary Jacobean life (Saunders, 70–1).

The scene which suggests the most imaginative use of theatrical facilities is 5.2, in which the action utilizes the different levels of the stage. Cranmer, to whom the King has given a signet ring with which to appeal over others' heads if need be, enters at one door in order to attend a Privy Council meeting to which he has been summoned, but finds his way barred. The King's physician, Butts, enters, possibly at the other door to give him time to 'pass along' (5.2.10), and, seeing Cranmer waiting in the company of 'boys, grooms and lackeys' (5.2.17), swiftly exits. He then reappears with the King *'at a window above'* (5.2.18.1), i.e., presumably, in the musicians' gallery above the tiring house at the rear of the stage. The King decides to eavesdrop, telling Butts to 'draw the curtain close' (5.2.33), a gesture which Bowers suggests 'removes what would have been a distraction for the audience if it had observed the King's reactions above to the events and dialogue below' (Bowers, 128); it would also allow the King to make his way quietly down the stairs as the scene progresses and put him sufficiently to the back of the audience's mind for his stage-level entry at 147.1 to create a powerful effect. Editions often start a new scene here, but this misses the point of the continuity created by Henry's listening above. The Councillors enter, presumably through the door on the other side of the stage at

WHEN YOV SEE ME,
You know me.
Or the famous Chronicle Hiftorie of king
Henrie the Eight, with the birth and vertuous life
of EDVVARD *Prince of Wales.*

As it was playd by the high and mightie Prince of Wales
his feruants.

By SAMVELL ROVVLY, feruant
to the Prince.

AT LONDON,
Printed for *Nathaniell Butter,* and are to be fold at his fhop in Paules
Church-yard neare S. *Auftines* gate. 1613.

2 Title-page of Samuel Rowley's *When You See Me, You Know Me*, London,
1613

which Cranmer has been waiting, and call him in. He has not of course exited, so he doesn't have to re-enter; the audience are apparently expected, from the moment of the Council's entry, to treat one side of the stage as the antechamber and the other as the Council chamber. The Councillors then debate with Cranmer and announce that he is to be sent to the Tower; he produces the King's ring; and Henry himself then enters at stage level to express his displeasure. No exit is marked for Butts, who is anyway hidden from sight once the curtain is drawn. The scene, imagined in this way, makes the most of the space available in the Globe (and presumably in the Blackfriars, which seems to have shared stage/gallery architecture with the larger theatre), of the absence of a restrictive set, and thus of the audience's willing imaginative participation in the action on the stage.[1]

It is not clear how soon the King's Men chose to revive *Henry VIII* at the rebuilt Globe, though evidence of the next recorded performance (which appears to be the first for which the title is no longer given as *All Is True*) suggests that the audience knew the play reasonably well. This took place in 1628 at the second Globe and offers a political perspective on the play which theatrical tradition has worked hard to erase. The performance was sponsored by the unpopular Duke of Buckingham as part of a deliberate dramatic campaign to improve his image in face of charges of political and military incompetence:

> On teusday his Grace was present at ye acting of K. Hen. 8 at ye Globe, a play bespoken of purpose by himself; whereat he stayd till ye Duke of Buckingham was beheaded, & then departed. Some say, he should rather

---

1 I am particularly grateful to the Globe 'Winter Playing' actors for the possibilities they opened up for me in relation to the action of 5.2: they tried out various combinations of side doors, discovery-space doors and musicians' gallery, and strongly endorsed a sense of shared engagement with the audience's imagination. For discussion of staging possibilities offered by the Blackfriars, see Lois Potter's Ard^3 *TNK*, 59–64.

have seen ye fall of Cardinall Woolsey, who was a more
lively type of himself, having governed this kingdom 18
yeares, as he hath done 14.

(Gell)[1]

This account has puzzled commentators, who see it as 'an extreme
illustration of the extent to which the king and his courtiers failed
to make (or at least affected to ignore)' topical associations
(Wiggins, 40). Yet if Buckingham was thinking about the play in
relation to his current circumstances, he would know three things:
that his namesake in the play died as a result of being framed, that
the Duke is effectively forgotten from the moment of his death,
and that the fall of Wolsey, later in the play, would provide an
opportunity for rather less flattering comparisons. Walking out of
the theatre at the moment of the Duke's assertion of his innocence would thus serve both to imply that the charges against him
were false and to ensure that the audience ignored the rest of the
play, including the possible comparisons with Wolsey – though
Gell's letter shows that in fact they knew the play well enough to
make this connection anyway.

Buckingham therefore need not have been 'insensitive to the
possibility of topical application' (Wiggins, 40): on the contrary,
he seems to have requested the play in order to make a political
point. But it is only if you attend to the play's implication that
the dramatic Buckingham was framed by Wolsey and not really
guilty that you see why he ordered it. Buckingham's sponsorship
of *Henry VIII* thus suggests that it was clear both to him and
to the audience that the play's Duke is innocent and therefore
that the play's King is perceived as being subject to Wolsey's

1   Buckingham sponsored a series of masques which were designed to put an improved
    gloss on his failed naval projects within the broad context of his sponsorship
    throughout his 'reign' of self-aggrandizing entertainments (he even had a masquing-
    room built at his London home). I am grateful to James Knowles for discussion of
    Buckingham and his masques. Janet Clare echoes Griffin's suggestion that the cur-
    tailment of the dialogue between the King and Buckingham in F *R3* (s3^v, after TLN
    2697) is the result of sensitivity about the later Duke (Clare, 199–100; Griffin,
    331–2).

machinations from the outset – which is not something that directors and critics of the play have always been keen to suggest. Moreover, Buckingham was not the only member of a pre-modern audience to see the potential for political irony in *Henry VIII*. When the play was performed for George I at Hampton Court in 1717:

> Wolsey's filching from his royal master the honour of extending pardon to those who resisted payment of the 'exactions' appeared so gross and impudent a contrivance that the courtiers laughed loudly at such an example of ministerial craft. His majesty, who was imperfectly acquainted with the English language asked the Lord Chamberlain the meaning of this mirth, and upon being informed of it joined in a hearty laugh of approbation.
>
> (Clark, 204)

Hugh Richmond takes this to be an example of a failure of seriousness in performance on a par with the eighteenth-century theatrical tendency to portray Gardiner as a clown (Richmond, 35; see pp. 22–3 below): I would argue instead that both Buckingham's sponsorship of, and later the Georgian court's reaction to, performances of *Henry VIII* represent characteristic responses by attuned politicians to a politically engaged play.

Performances 1660–1916

Acknowledgement of political engagement, however, goes against the grain of the play's production history after the Restoration. On his return to London in 1660, Charles II placed the theatre under his own patronage, granting a monopoly over theatrical activity to two courtier–managers, Sir Thomas Killigrew (King's Company) and Sir William Davenant (Duke of York's Company), thereby ensuring ideological control over what was performed. Part of the theatres' task was 'to return to the artistic forms popular "Before our Exile" as though nothing had happened', and Davenant keenly obliged (Dobson, *National*, 20; Davenant, 3).[1] He revived his own play *Love and Honour*, featuring the actor Betterton wearing the King's actual coronation robes, a verisimilar gesture which suggests why *Henry VIII*, with its extensive stage directions for royal ceremony, was keenly appropriated for the Restoration theatre. Surprisingly few Shakespeare plays were revived at this time, at least in recognizable form: the stage was dominated by plays from the Fletcher canon and, to a lesser extent, from Jonson's *Works*. *Henry VIII*, though, was one of the handful of plays from the Shakespeare canon which were successful without extensive adaptation (Dobson, *National*, 25–6).[2] Davenant's revivals of the play in fact served two purposes, participating both in the general royalist reworking of history, theatrical and political, and in Davenant's own self-aggrandizing construction of an 'apostolic succession', as reported by John Downes:

> The part of the King was so right and justly done by Mr. *Betterton*, he being Instructed in it by Sir *William* [Davenant], who had it from old Mr. *Lowen*, that had his Instructions from Mr. *Shakespear* himself, that I dare and will aver, none can, or will come near him in this Age, in the performance of that part.
>
> (Downes, C4[v]; Milhous & Hume, 55–6)[3]

Commentators seem to have accepted Downes's statement at face value and have used it as evidence that 'the realistic production style of the Restoration might plausibly reflect the author's

1 Davenant's *Prologue* was the very first court performance of the new reign and shared in the general project of misrepresentation of parliamentarians' attitude to theatre: 'They that would have no KING, would have no *Play*' (Davenant, 6). For assessment of this project, see, for example, Butler, 8–10; Wiseman, 10–16.
2 There is no sign, I should add, that *Henry VIII*'s revivers were aware of Fletcher's involvement in the play: they would simply have taken it as Shakespeare's from its inclusion in the 1623 Folio.
3 This account suggests that it had not been, as might be expected, Burbage who had played the King back in 1613, but the younger John Lowin, setting an early precedent for productions, including Tyrone Guthrie's in 1949, which have featured a Henry in the prime of his years.

18

own acting specifications' without registering the compromising influence of Davenant's attempts (including his claim that he was the Bard's illegitimate son) to present himself as Shakespeare's natural successor (Richmond, 30).[1]

When Davenant first revived *Henry VIII*, he did so in a manner which echoed his revival of *Love and Honour*, with a great deal of spectacle and royal pageantry (*London Stage*, 1.72–5). This production paid more attention to historical costume than did most other Restoration productions, and is therefore generally considered to have initiated the tradition of 'historical realism' that has informed most productions of the play since (see pp. 28, 30, 32–7). Pepys describes the actor playing Henry as being dressed 'as we see him painted', which Odell assumes implies that his costume created 'something approaching a resemblance to Holbein's portrait' (Odell, 1.205, 208). Certainly, the two extant portraits of Henry Harris as Wolsey in Davenant's production (which are 'the first known representations of an English actor in a Shakespearean role'(Edmond, 139)) depict Harris in distinctly sixteenth-century cardinal's clothing (see Fig. 3), though the etching which accompanies the text of the play in Rowe's 1709 edition shows that, while Henry was represented in the usual Holbeinesque manner, the nobles, whispering in the background, were in contemporary dress, with conspicuous turn-of-the-eighteenth-century coats and wigs (see Fig. 4).

Costume was not the only material practice made available for royalist appropriation. Davenant revisited Inigo Jones's pre-Revolutionary theatrical aesthetic by introducing elaborate scenery and a range of technological innovations. *Henry VIII* presented itself as prime material for scenic elaboration, and contemporary descriptions show that Davenant made the most of it: Pepys, who had mellowed to the play over a period of five

1 A.C.Sprague notes Lowin's influence as a reason for the likelihood of the preservation of 'Elizabethan stage business' in productions down the years: see Sprague, *Actors*, 76.

3 Henry Harris as Wolsey in Davenant's production.

years, saw it in December 1668 and admitted he 'was mightily
pleased, better than [he] ever expected, with the history and
shows of it' (Pepys, 9. 403–4 (30 December 1668)). Davenant's
production ran for a long time, though the production's focus on

4 Frontispiece to Rowe's 1709 edition, showing Betterton as Henry, dressed in Tudor costume, handing the intercepted letters to Verbruggen as Wolsey, with the nobles in the background, all in contemporary dress

spectacle and on sheer numbers on stage made it susceptible to mockery.[1] A character in an Aphra Behn play describes 'a broken six-penny Looking-Glas, that show'd as many Faces, as the Scene in *Henry* the Eighth' (*Lucky Chance*, C1ᵛ). In Villiers's *The Rehearsal* (1672), the protagonist Bayes, exasperated with the inability of the actors in a performance he is directing to keep time with the music, tells them that they 'dance worse than the Angels in *Harry* the Eight', and when he is boasting about the planned performance, he makes further telling comparisons:

> Now, Gentlemen, I will be bold to say, I'l shew you the greatest Scene that ever *England* saw: I mean not for words, for those I do not value; but for state, shew, and magnificence. In fine, I'l justifie it to be as grand to the eye every whit, I gad, as that great Scene in *Harry* the Eight.
> (*Rehearsal*, D2ʳ, G1ᵛ)[2]

Bayes's exaggerations make it clear that the actual play had long since been replaced by spectacle as the principal focus of attention.

Davenant's productions obviously were not taken quite as seriously as he might have preferred, and he seems almost to have encouraged this by casting Cave Underhill (well known for playing comic parts) as Gardiner, thereby initiating a tradition of presenting the bishop and sometimes Cranmer too as 'comic, ineffectual figures' and thus downplaying the complexities of the play's representation of Reformation (Richmond, 3, 35).[3] Narcissus Luttrell reports a performance in 1700 in which 'the actors ridiculed a christening, and Underhill represented the archbishop, which has given offence', and which arguably foreshadows, right at the outset of the eighteenth century, certain productions in the twentieth century –

---

1 Langbaine, writing twenty-five years later, notes that '[t]his Play frequently appears on the present Stage, the part of *Henry* being extreamly well acted by Mr. *Betterton*' (Langbaine, 457), and Betterton's last recorded appearance in the role comes as late as 1709.

2 As Villiers was the son of the Duke of Buckingham who had sponsored the 1628 performance, his distaste for *Henry VIII* is perhaps understandable.

3 Traces of this tradition were still apparent in Tyrone Guthrie's 1949 production and even arguably in Greg Doran's RSC version in 1996.

notably that of Terence Gray – which sought to debunk the conservative politics they attributed to the play (Luttrell, 4.712).

But ridicule was not the only response. In 1682 – the year of the ascendancy of the Catholic Duke of York, shortly to become James II – the Dorset Garden Theatre presented the first performances of John Banks's *Virtue Betrayed, or Anna Bullen*, a melodramatic and vehemently Protestant tragedy which was performed for fifty years as a complement (and sometimes as a rival) to performances of *Henry VIII*, with certain actors taking the same role in both plays (notably Barton Booth, who played the King in both during the 1720s).[1] The action picks up where *Henry VIII* left off, though history is wrenched even more out of joint to ensure that Wolsey becomes central to the plots against Anne, serving as a gauge both of the political climate and of the Cardinal's popularity in Restoration productions of *Henry VIII*. His objections to Anna Bullen – 'A *Lutheran* Queen upon the Throne of *England*', he rages, 'She to lie in the Bosom of our Prince!' (*Virtue Bertayed*, A6ᵛ) – echo the Wolsey of *Henry VIII* – 'I know her for / A spleeny Lutheran, . . . / . . . that she should lie i'th' bosom of / Our hard-ruled King' (3.2.98–101) – while Anna (whose personality seems more like the Katherine of the earlier play than the Anne) comes on in the first act as Queen, rejecting pomp and ceremony and clashing immediately with an unrepentantly scheming Cardinal.

Virtue Betrayed simplifies the emotions of each of the characters it shares with *Henry VIII*. The King is charmless and unsubtle, and he roars at Rochford for disturbing his meditations, as he does at Norfolk and Suffolk in the earlier play. Anna is both histrionic and genuinely guileless in comparison with the earlier Anne. She was, we learn, chastely in love with Northumberland's son Harry Piercy long before the King came along, has been forced to marry Henry, and is therefore free from blame for Henry's divorce from Katherine:

1 The play was revived occasionally after 1733, but not with any regularity. The last performance appears to have been in 1766; see *London Stage*, parts 1–4.

> Just Heav'n, whose is the Sin?
> Punish not me, I sought not to be Queen;
> But *Henry*'s Guilt amidst my Pomp is weigh'd,
> And makes my Crown sit heavy on my Head,
> To banish from his Bed the chastest Bride,
> That twenty Years lay loving by his side!

(B5ᵛ)

And though the toddler Elizabeth, in the course of a painfully sentimental dialogue, makes a reference to her 'Godfather *Cranmer*' (G2ʳ), it is in fact Anna herself who speaks a prophecy over the child, in language that echoes Cranmer's speech in *Henry VIII*: '[L]et me hold her but a Moment longer', she begs, 'And with this Kiss, that now must be my last, / Unlock a secret, which Heav'n dictates to me' (G5ᵛ). *Virtue Betrayed* replaces the knowing Anne Bullen of the earlier play with a figure of uncomplicated innocence and thus realigns and simplifies the play's engagement with Protestantism.

Eighteenth-century productions of *Henry VIII* itself – with Barton Booth succeeding Betterton and the famously unsubtle James ('Bellower') Quin also playing the King at Lincoln's Inn Fields – remained within the shadow of Davenant's spectacular aesthetic. Colley Cibber, who had played Wolsey earlier in the decade, revived *Henry VIII* in 1727 at the Theatre Royal, Drury Lane, in a production designed to celebrate the coronation of George II, with an interpolated scene – a pageant of 'The Military Ceremony in Westminster Hall' – which was appended as an afterpiece to a variety of other plays (*London Stage*, II.2, 946).[1] The play's popularity and its equation with royalism were underlined the following year when members of the audience (in an echo of the uncontrollable crowd of 5.3), hearing that the royal family were to attend a performance at Drury Lane, broke into the theatre to secure their seats. *Henry VIII* was performed five or six

1   See Genest, 3.302. It was also mocked at the rival Lincoln's Inn Fields Theatre in a satirical 'Burlesque upon the Ceremonial Coronation of Anna Bullen'.

times a year throughout the mid-eighteenth century, with Hannah Pritchard playing Katherine at Covent Garden in 1744 and Margaret ('Peg') Woffington in 1749 in productions which continued to incorporate the additional ceremonies.[1]

Frances Brooke, writer of the periodical *The Old Maid* (under the pseudonym 'Mary Singleton, Spinster'), satirically describes one Drury Lane production which was attended by the Moroccan ambassador. She comments on the ambassador's tendency to pay rather more attention to the audience than the stage, but notes that:

> at the entrance of *King Henry*, his attention was a little recovered to the performance; but his majesty had not proceeded half way through the scene, before he burst into a most immoderate fit of apparently contemptuous laughter, which he repeated very often thro' the whole playing of the part.
>
> (*Old Maid*, 221)

Brooke capitalizes on this to express her dislike both of Edward Berry's performance as the King –

> The manner in which this stranger was affected by it, amongst other considerations, fully convinces me that this character is most ridiculously burlesqued in the representation, and that both *Shakespeare* and the monarch are very inhumanly sacrificed to the polite taste and elegant distinction of the upper gallery
>
> (221)

– and of the interpolated action: 'upon the *Champion*'s entry [on] horse-back, he burst into such an immoderate fit of laughter as to fall quite back in his seat' (223). She also notes 'the absurdity of *Winchester*'s brandishing his cane at *Canterbury*, upon the close of

---

1 Woffington also played Anna in *Virtue Betrayed* in 1750, alongside Quin and Ryan, the Henry and Wolsey of the Covent Garden *Henry VIII*.

the council scene' (222), thereby confirming the continuation of comic versions of the play's clergy.

Drury Lane's dominance of *Henry VIII* culminated in 1761 in a production which put more emphasis than ever on costume and display, and which, as in 1727, incorporated a 'Coronation' scene (this time to mark the coronation of George III) which completely overshadowed the play itself. Both Covent Garden and Drury Lane put on special shows for the coronation, and Thomas Davies provides a harrowing report of the effects of competition between the managers of the two playhouses, claiming that Drury Lane's David Garrick – accepting that his rival John Rich 'had a taste in the ordering, dressing, and setting out these pompous processions, superior to his own' – simply revived the 'Coronation' scene 'with the old dresses which have occasionally been used from 1727 to 1761, a show which he repeated for near forty nights successively':

> The exhibition was the meanest, and most unworthy of a theatre, I ever saw. The stage indeed was opened into Drury-lane; and a new and unexpected sight surprised the audience, of a real bonefire, and the populace huzzaing, and drinking porter to the health of queen Anne Bullen. The stage in the mean time, amidst the parading of dukes, dutchesses, archbishops, peeresses, heralds, &c. was covered with a thick fog from the smoke of the fire, which served to hide the tawdry dresses of the processionalists.
>
> (Davies, 1.328–30)

Rich, by contrast, 'fully satisfied' his audience's 'warmest imaginations' with 'a profusion of fine cloaths, of velvet, silk, sattin, lace, feathers, jewels, pearls, &c.' (Davies, 1.330). The play, lost somewhere in the midst of all this tawdriness, was not performed again for over ten years.

The next notable production was that of John Philip Kemble at Drury Lane in November 1788, in which his sister Sarah Siddons played Katherine.[1] Kemble reduced the pomp – he completely omitted the coronation scene (possibly for financial reasons) – and gave new prominence to the roles of Wolsey and, in particular, Katherine, which became dominant throughout the nineteenth century. Though she is best known for her violent Lady Macbeth, Siddons was, by all accounts, a revelation as Katherine, able to move the audience profoundly both early in the play, when she swept proudly through the divorce hearing, and later, as she embodied the gradual erosion of the Queen's strength of mind and body. She must have been a formidable figure with whom to act. One theatrical legend claimed that:

> by simply saying, 'You were the Duke's Surveyor, and lost your office on the complaints o' the tenants', she put the actor to whom the words were addressed into such perspiring agony that as he came off, crushed by her earnestness, he declared that he would not for the world meet her black eyes on the stage again.
>
> (Clark, 214–5)

According to Michael Booth, the climactic moment of the divorce hearing came as she addressed Wolsey. In what was, he suggests, 'obviously [Siddons's] own piece of business', the other cardinal, Campeius, stepped forward when she spoke the words 'Lord Cardinal' (Booth, Stokes, Bassnett, 57). A contemporary describes her reaction:

> we feel it impossible to describe the majestic self-correction of the petulance and vexation, which, in her perturbed state of mind, she feels at the misapprehension of Campeius, and the intelligent expression of countenance, and gracious dignity of gesture with which she intimates to him his mistake, and dismisses him again to his seat – and no language can possibly convey a picture

---

1 This was Siddons's first performance in the role in London, though she had already performed the part in the provinces between 1778 and 1780 (Young, xlii).

of her immediate re-assumption of the fulness of majesty
glowing with scorn, contempt, anger and the terrific
pride of innocence, when she turns round to Wolsey, and
exclaims, 'to YOU I speak!'

(Genest, 8.303–4)

Kemble revived the play regularly after his move to Covent Garden
– performances which are presumably the source of Henry
Crawford's claim in Jane Austen's *Mansfield Park* (1814) that he
'once saw Henry the 8th acted' or 'heard of it from somebody who
did' (Austen, 279) – and his work on *Henry VIII* there marked two
directions for later stagings: his 1803 production was based on a
savagely cut text, and his more lavish 1811 production is notable as
the first to attempt the 'archaeological realism' that was to become
the dominant mode by the end of the century.[1] The chief legacy of
Kemble's productions, however (despite his curious decision in
1811 to omit 3.1, the scene in which Katherine clashes with, and
then succumbs to, the Cardinals), was the location of Siddons's
proud Katherine at the emotional centre of the play (see Fig. 5).

The extent to which the text was cut and rearranged in nineteenth-century productions varied. Kemble's were followed at
Covent Garden by those of William Charles Macready and at
Sadler's Wells by those of Samuel Phelps (which fluctuated from
a bare three acts, ending with the fall of Wolsey, to a fairly full
text). In 1848, Macready and Phelps joined forces at Drury Lane
to stage before Queen Victoria and Prince Albert a three-act version featuring the American actress Charlotte Cushman. The die
had been cast, and later productions demonstrated a willingness to
sacrifice large sections of the text to the exigencies of spectacle

1 The production seems also to have held a certain amount of topical significance.
   Jonathan Bate notes that it 'contained recognisable allusions to the "delicate investigation" into the conduct of the Princess Caroline (an attempt by the heir to the
   throne to get rid of his wife). 1811 was the year in which the king's insanity was
   finally acknowledged to be permanent and incurable, with the effect that the Regency
   was established' (Bate, 93). On the relationship between *Mansfield Park* and *Henry
   VIII*, see Armstrong, 58–89. As Armstrong notes, Elizabeth Inchbald, who wrote
   Lovers' Vows (1798), the play which is the cause of scandal in *Mansfield Park*, had
   played Anne Bullen in *Henry VIII* at Covent Garden in November 1783.

5 Mrs Siddons as Queen Katherine, artist unknown, undated

and the requirements of star actors. In the United States, Cushman appeared in a production at the Walnut Street Theatre in Philadelphia in April 1852 which ended at Katherine's death. In London, Charles Kean's production at the Princess's Theatre in 1855, which had a run of a hundred nights, was extensively cut to make time for elaborate staging, though it did at least feature all the scenes in the right order. Kean's production was both 'state-of-the-art' (it marked the first use of the focused limelight, for instance) and 'archaeological' (it depended on information gleaned from chronicle histories, museums and art galleries). It was also spectacular: one highlight of the production was a 'Grand Moving Panorama' which stretched from Bridewell to Greenwich, 'Representing London in the Time of Henry the Eighth', which then gave way to 'a spectacular scene of pageantry in the church of the Grey Friars, restoring as far as it is possible to conceive, the interior appearance of the edifice at the time' (Clark, 218).[1] Kean and his wife Ellen Tree toured Australia, Canada and the US in 1863–5 with a repertoire that included *Henry VIII*, and grandiose stagings of the play followed on both sides of the Atlantic.[2]

In the wake of Siddons's remarkable playing of Katherine, *Henry VIII* had become established as a vehicle for grandstanding performances by major actors and actresses. In the United States,

1 Clark adds that 'considerable trouble was taken that the scenery might be historically correct. The scene of the Old Palace Yard, Westminster, was copied from a drawing made by Antony van der Wyngaerde, in 1543, and preserved in the Bodleian Library at Oxford. That of the Council Chamber was a Restoration of the painted chamber at Westminster, from Capon's drawing in *Vetusta Monumenta*. In the room in the Queen's apartment at Bridewell Palace a chimney-piece designed by Holbein for that palace was introduced, built up from a drawing of it in the British Museum. The Queen's chamber in Kimbolton Castle was hung with tapestry, in accordance with authentic fact' (217–18).

2 The first US performance of the play had taken place in New York in May 1799. In the later nineteenth century, there was a production by Marcus Moriarty at the McVickers Theatre in Chicago in 1874 and Edwin Booth played Wolsey in 1871, 1874 and 1878 at his own theatre in New York, and in 1876 at the Arch Street Theatre, Philadelphia, opposite a variety of Katherines, beginning with Cushman. A later New York production, at the Garden Theater in 1892, starred the Polish actress Helena Modjeska, who played Katherine so touchingly (despite her apparently less-than-perfect command of English) that she was compared with Ellen Terry.

Cushman held sway over the play, as over many others: she played Katherine for decades, performing Wolsey, too, in 1859 (thereby neatly reversing the gendered stage practices of early modern London as she had done for her highly acclaimed Romeo), and in the spaces between her repeated retirements she performed solo shows which included speeches by both characters. Descriptions of her performances make her sound fairly blunt and static by modern standards, but she appears to have been deeply moving as Katherine.[1]

Monopoly of any role by a single actor or style, however, inevitably leads to stagnation, and as Kim Noling notes:

> nineteenth-century abridgements of the play 'for Katherine' sought to make her voice dominant to the end by drawing the final curtain at her death, thereby under-mining the dramaturgy that celebrates Henry and his heirs at the end of the uncut play.
>
> (Noling, 298n.)

It could thus easily be argued that the tradition which Cushman exemplifies of leading actresses performing Katherine's scenes quite independently of the entire play has had a detrimental effect on the play's stage history. The role in fact tends to be undertaken by highly capable, experienced actresses performing their own (in general, deeply sympathetic) Katherine in the midst of a director's produc-tion. The individuality of this connection between actress and role can produce considerable tensions, as Michael Billington makes clear when he writes of Peggy Ashcroft's approach to rehearsing the part:

> [H]er total immersion in the role made her almost pro-prietorial in her attitude towards it. 'Peggy herself', [Trevor] Nunn recalls, 'had become obsessed with

---

1 According to the theatre critic Henry Clapp, Cushman's Katherine was 'her crown-ing achievement, and, therefore, the highest histrionic work of any American actress' (Clapp, 86). He seems to have been especially impressed with her performance in 4.2: '[a]s the shadows deepened about the sick woman, Miss Cushman's power took on an unearthly beauty and sweetness which keenly touched the listener's heart' (89–90).

> Katharine of Aragon to the point where she brought into
> rehearsals every day a kind of defence of the character.
> She was on Katharine's side to the extent that she was
> against Shakespeare's. She would turn up with extra lines
> from the historical trial or from Katharine's letters and
> try to put them into the text. . . . I don't think I ever
> argued Peggy out of the conviction that she was not play-
> ing Katharine, but that she *was* Katharine.'
>
> (Billington, *Ashcroft*, 224)

The search for a performance which is 'truthful' to the historical
Katherine (as opposed, that is, to the character of Katherine in the
play) – and which reproduces on an individual level the problematic tradition of 'authentic' production – can thus create a
Katherine noticeably out of kilter with the rest of a given production. As it happens, though, a Katherine visibly detached from the
patriarchal world of the play can in fact work rather well, as the
Queen is excluded from the royal family, from politics, and then
finally from the world itself, offering a good (if fortunate) example of the contingency of interpretation.

The function of *Henry VIII* as a star vehicle was certainly one
factor which led to the erosion of the text during the eighteenth
and nineteenth centuries. But the principal cause, especially as the
nineteenth century progressed, remained the play's obvious availability for the kind of spectacular, tableau-dominated production
that Victorian audiences in particular adored. As we have seen, the
tendency to produce *Henry VIII* in as grand a manner as theatrical
facilities and funding would allow had been dominant since
Davenant's first revival, but late nineteenth- and early twentieth-
century producers took the mode to its logical extreme. The two
most spectacular productions of all were those of Henry Irving in
1892 and Herbert Beerbohm Tree in 1910. After a twenty-year
period of modest Shakespearean productions in London, Irving
revived Kean's penchant for historical spectacle. His Lyceum production set out:

with the aid of modern effects, by a lavish expenditure of money, a careful study of every possible archaeological authority . . . to make this the most perfect reproduction of court life in the days of Henry VIII, that this stage, or indeed the stage of any country, has ever seen.

(Scott)

For each of its fourteen scenes (much of Acts 4 and 5 were cut), Irving created an elaborate set – an 'authentic' reproduction, for instance, of a street in Tudor Westminster, with enthusiastic citizens leaning out of every window of carefully modelled, three-storied, wood-beamed houses. Ellen Terry's Katherine, William Terriss's Henry and Forbes Robertson's Buckingham (a role whose star-vehicle potential has effectively disappeared since) all received strong praise, as did Edward German's *entr'acte* music; it was, nonetheless, the visual grandeur of the production that received most comment.

Tree's 1910 production made even Irving's seem restrained. As far as Tree was concerned, and in the context of an age which, he believed, 'was characterized by great sumptuousness', *Henry VIII* was above all 'a pageant play': 'As such it was conceived and written,' he proclaimed, 'as such we shall endeavour to present it' (Tree, *Henry*, 89). In his quest to do justice to the play, Tree extended Irving's pictorial tableaux, his attempts to ensure archaeological precision and the sheer scale of his spectacle. He deployed a massive cast – 172 participants, consisting of 24 speaking parts (5 of them doubling), 20 Extra Ladies, 12 Extra Gentlemen, 4 Chorus Ladies, 8 Special Chorus Gentlemen, 19 Boys, 8 Girls, 2 Trumpeters and 75 Supers – and he commissioned vast sets for the key scenes. For the masque at York Place, for instance, he created a scene of immense opulence, deploying all the available technology:

The hall had a fan-vaulted ceiling and its stone walls were hung with tapestries of velvet and gold. Over the length of the carpet . . . hung four chandeliers of electric lights imitating candles. Twenty-five limes behind

> the proscenium, . . . two limes in the dome, a full array
> of amber and white floats and blue and white battens
> must have bathed the scene in the intense light often
> complained of by those sensitive to excessive brightness
> and glare in the theatre.
>
> (Booth, 141)[1]

Costume, too, was as striking as possible: in the banquet scene, 'the colour scheme [was] dominated by the host's rare crimson, and his royal guest's marvellous green, the single streak of blue flashed by the morris-dancers – they all help in a harmony of effect not destroyed even when the picture is broken up by the kaleidoscopic movements of mask and dance' (*Daily Mail*). And in a manner recognizable to anyone familiar with the criticism of A.C.Bradley (which he probably knew), Tree evoked the Bard himself in support of this extravagant approach: 'Surely no one reading the vision of Katharine of Aragon', he argued, 'can come to any conclusion than that Shakespeare intended to leave as little to the imagination as possible, and to put upon the stage as gorgeous and complete a picture as the resources of the theatre could supply' (Tree, *Thoughts*, 60–1) (see Fig. 6).

Tree, the Francis Ford Coppola of his day, oversaw a gruelling rehearsal process, typically extending into the early hours of the morning, and was apparently (unlike his cast and crew) without need of sleep:

> the men at their posts on the limelights would drop off to
> sleep, and the actors would lie about in the circle or in the
> boxes. Tree would disappear for hours to have supper or
> talk over some problem of the play, and return at three or
> four in the morning. The limelight men would spring to
> attention, the actors rush down on the stage, full of
> apologies for daring even to feel sleepy in his presence.
> And he would be as bright and energetic as ever.
>
> (Collier, *Harlequinade*, 95–6)

1 On the scale of Tree's production, see also Foulkes.

6 The trial scene from Herbert Beerbohm Tree's production, 1910

Despite the trauma induced by, and the apparent chaos of, this rehearsal method, Tree's productions ended up being organized and impressive on the stage, though the inefficiencies of the process often led to major last-minute changes, notably in this case the removal, at the final rehearsal, of what was left of Act 5 in Tree's reordering as a direct result of the extended running time required by the spectacle. Tree's *Henry VIII* thus finished with Anne's coronation (with the Kimbolton scene reordered as penultimate), the demands of staging outweighing any residual desire to respect the script. Tree was in fact happy to dismiss large sections of the text: 'It has been thought desirable', he noted:

> to omit almost in their entirety those portions of the play which deal with the Reformation, being as they are practically devoid of dramatic interest and calculated, as they are, to weary an audience.

> (Tree, *Henry*, 90)

Within the surviving scenes, too, Tree removed vast swathes of key lines, cutting, for instance, Henry's 'conscience speech' in 2.4 from 178 all the way to 227, subordinating complex motivation to visual effect.[1] The text thus became, to all intents and purposes, superfluous: one hapless reviewer, breathless with admiration at the range of colours on view in the first scene, observed that it all 'merges and blends into a glorious harmony, which needs no words to make it intelligible' (*East Anglian Daily Times*).

Clearly, little of this is to early twenty-first-century taste, but equally clearly (and despite journalistic criticism of Tree) a substantial portion of the Edwardian theatre-going public adored Tree's *Henry VIII*. His was the biggest, most lavish and most successful of all the spectacular Shakespearean productions of the period. Playing for eight months and 254 performances, it

---

1 Tree in the end cut 1,323 of the play's 2,810 lines, or 47 per cent (Richmond, 61).

had the longest uninterrupted single run of any Shakespeare play in England.[1] But it was also the high-water mark of productions of the play which emphasized large-scale archaeological 'authenticity'. The First World War brought with it irreversible social and aesthetic changes, and as theatrical tastes altered and resources shrank, the mode was no longer sustainable. Tree's production toured to the United States in 1916 (the tercentenary of Shakespeare's death) and played to packed houses, but American reviewers were less impressed than their British counterparts by what they saw as a frankly old-fashioned production. By this time, too, in an echo of Garrick's coronation *débâcle*:

> the scenery was showing signs of wear, which did not escape the eyes of the sharper critics. One, indeed, condemned the production as 'the frumperies of a puppet stage', hitting Tree just where English critics thought him strongest with the sub-heading 'Pictorially His Production of "Henry VIII" Is a Worn Echo of Another Day.'
>
> (Booth, 155, quoting *New York Evening Mail*)

What had once seemed a radical contemporary attempt to create an authentic reproduction of an earlier age now struck reviewers as a tired re-creation of a Victorian affectation whose time was up.

Performances 1916–2000

As a direct result of the fading of the spectacular style in the theatre (and because the play had become so closely identified with that style), *Henry VIII* became markedly less popular after 1916. Twentieth-century productions of *Henry VIII* can, broadly, be

---

1   It shared with other productions of *Henry VIII* the status that comes with 'command performance', revived on 5 July 1915 'in aid of King George's Actors' Pension Fund in the presence of Their Majesties, the same principals being aided by many other stage celebrities in minor parts' (Young, xlvii). *Henry VIII* may have been the last spectacular Shakespearean play on the Victorian–Edwardian stage, but the 'apogee' of the spectacular mode came with Max Reinhardt's 'immense recreation of a Gothic cathedral in the vastness of Olympia' for his mime-play *The Miracle* (1911), which had a cast of 2,000 (Booth, 159).

divided into two groups. On the one hand, there has been a fair number of 'conservative' productions which either persist with versions of the spectacular style as if it had never gone out of fashion, or else reject it firmly in favour of the quest for 'authentic' acting conditions and relatively restrained, fast-moving performance. On the other, there have been a few 'radical' productions which either treat the text as a piece of glorified propaganda and set out to debunk it, or else (in more recent cases) focus on certain ironies and political awkwardnesses they find in a text previously considered undilutedly conservative. What radical productions there have been, though (and there have been very few), have generally been ignored by their successors. Terence Gray's grotesque, Carrollesque production in Cambridge in 1931 and Margaret Webster's old-school ceremonial for the 1946 New York production offer contrasting examples of twentieth-century repertory-company stagings: there was no sign in Webster's production that Gray or anyone else had ever questioned the Victorian tradition she was blithely extending into the mid-century (see Fig. 7).[1]

Hugh Richmond has argued that all productions of *Henry VIII* to date, even consciously 'inauthentic' productions such as those of Gray and Howard Davies, have been dependent upon a Tudor aesthetic which has survived, perhaps against the odds, down the years. The cardboard cutout characters that featured in Gray's production, for instance, echoed the amplification of large-scale scenes with the use of dummy figures that had been a characteristic of Irving's or Tree's sets, and his playing-card costumes drew strongly on Tudor prototypes; while Davies's drably coloured costumes were still dependent on Holbein, simply shifting their source from his paintings to the monochrome of his drawings. This conservatism, even in 'radical' productions, stems

---

1 Webster had already directed an epic amateur production of *Henry VIII* ten years earlier in England: 'The Women's Institutes throughout the county of Kent joined together to do Shakespeare's *Henry VIII* as a pageant production in an outdoor setting. . . . The Baptism scene at the end was to bring together the entire cast of more than eight hundred people' (Webster, 368).

7 Margaret Webster's production of *Henry VIII* at the American Repertory Theater, 1946

directly from the sustained success of the play over the centuries. As Richmond points out:

> unlike almost all other Shakespearian plays, *Henry VIII* has an unbroken theatrical history from the time of Shakespeare himself, in which successive directors have drawn on received opinion about the author's own intentions and practical knowledge of how best these can be realised. In this play at least, no modern productions can avoid indebtedness to this inherited expertise.
>
> (Richmond, 9)

Richmond makes this observation approvingly, but as with the editorial tendency to use the 'received text' rather than return to the earliest reliable text as copy-text, there is a clear danger that each production of a play with an 'unbroken theatrical history' may inherit and compound the errors of the previous one. Precisely because of the longevity and continuity of the play's theatrical history, an absolutely fresh start has been impossible to achieve.

Certainly there has been no attempt at a full modernization of the play along the lines of the Eyre/McKellen *Richard III*. The only modern-dress (though definitely not 'fully modernized') performance of the play in the twentieth century (as far as I am aware) was Wilson Knight's propagandistic 'Call to Great Britain in Time of War', *This Sceptred Isle*, in which 'the concluding movement was given to *Henry VIII* [and] done in modern dress' (Knight, 'Propaganda', 28).[1] Knight's patriotic appropriation serves as a reminder of the continuing role *Henry VIII* has played at times of national crisis and triumph, a role which has helped sustain the conservatism exemplified in productions such as

---

1   See p.5n. Paul Jesson writes of an idea ('admittedly rather daft') he had for a *Henry VIII* set in the 'early twentieth-century, Henry as Edward VII . . . Katherine as Queen Alexandra, Anne Bullen as Lillie Langtry', adding that, though his idea was for a production that never happened, '[s]omeone will do it one day. It would at least point up the fact that Shakespeare was writing about history very recent to his own time' (Jesson, 115).

Webster's, which itself served as a celebration of the end of the Pacific War.[1] In Britain, Tyrone Guthrie's imaginative 1949 production, which was attended by George VI, was revived (shorn of some of its riskier, more imaginative elements) for the accession of Elizabeth II in 1953, with the new Queen and the Duke of Edinburgh in attendance for the first night. This propaganda function, which the play shares with the (these days) much better known *Henry V*, has consistently stifled attempts to explore new directions in production.

In the years following the fading of spectacular staging, 'truth' and 'authenticity' remained the principal subject of directorial attention, but focused now on the idea of the re-creation of Jacobean staging conditions rather than on the imaginative reconstruction of Tudor England. Tree himself, even in the midst of his massive verisimilitude, had cottoned on to the possibility of other versions of authenticity, drawing on the experiments of William Poel with 'Elizabethan' set design. Tree's large-scale tableaux would seem to be proscenium-arch material *par excellence*, yet he in fact deployed for *Henry VIII* the nine-foot apron stage that Poel had constructed for his earlier production of *The Two Gentlemen of Verona* at the same theatre. Poel's limited attempt to reproduce the Elizabethan/Jacobean thrust stage anticipated the later twentieth-century movement to re-create 'original acting conditions' – heralded by Tanya Moiseiwitsch's stage set for Guthrie's 1949 production, which in turn became the basis of the theatre at Stratford, Ontario, and later theatres at Minneapolis, Chichester and Stratford-upon-Avon – which culminated in the building of the reconstructed Globe in London. The principal result of these developments was to encourage a sparser, less cluttered style which facilitated much more rapidly paced productions and a consequent

---

1 Brooks Atkinson, writing in the *New York Times*, caught the triumphalist mood in his comments about the set designer: 'David Ffolkes, who hardly more than a year ago was dreaming of the theatre in a Jap [*sic*] prison labor camp, has designed one of the real magnificences of the modern stage. . . . It is as though he had poured into this pageant and show all the color and beauty pent up inside him during the years he was a war prisoner in the Orient' (Atkinson).

recovery of a full (or near-full) text, notably in Ben Greet's 1916 production, which played to critical approval at the Old Vic while Tree's American tour was in full swing, and in Robert Atkins' restrained 1924 production at the same theatre. This emphasis on fluency and pace has persisted since, even in productions still bearing the marks of the spectacular tradition.[1]

You might expect that an alternative source of new ideas for the play might have been found at this time in the new medium of cinema, but although *Henry VIII* was indeed one of the very first Shakespeare plays to be filmed, the motivation for the filming effectively pre-empted the possibility of a radical break with performative tradition, since the director was none other than Beerbohm Tree himself. He took the cast of his stage production to Ealing for a single day and made a twenty-five-minute, five-scene film for the Barker Motion Photography Company. Frustratingly, the film was made under an exclusivity deal which required the burning of all prints six weeks later, and no-one has found evidence of any surviving film (Ball, 82). Tree's film serves as a cinematic precedent, if not for films of *Henry VIII* itself (there has been no wide-screen movie of *Henry VIII* since), then for later epic cinematic renditions of Henry VIII's reign, which have, ironically, produced in turn a theatrical response in the continued deployment of a predictable Holbeinism familiar to audiences principally from film and television costume drama, notably Charles Laughton's and Keith Michell's versions of the reign.[2] Asked why he had chosen to direct *Henry VIII* at the Chichester Festival in 1991, Ian Judge replied candidly that he

---

1 Michael Coveney, reviewing the Doran production, enthused about the set – 'it opens like a golden casket, two huge doors fretted with gleaming metalwork, . . . characters cascading forth in . . . glorious costumes like waxworks on parade' – yet was also complimentary about the production's 'fluent staging' (Coveney).

2 Later filmed versions of Henry VIII's reign include Alexander Korda's *The Private Life of Henry VIII* (1933), starring Charles Laughton; Fred Zinneman's film version of Robert Bolt's play *A Man for All Seasons* (1966); and Charles Jarrott's *Anne of the Thousand Days* (1969). Keith Michell appeared as Henry in the 1970s BBC series *The Six Wives of Henry VIII*. There have also been any number of spectacular, 'authentically' detailed films of Elizabeth's reign, which develop the same visual tradition.

hadn't chosen it at all: he had accepted an invitation to direct something quite different but was asked by the organizers, once they had unexpectedly acquired the services of Keith Michell, to put on the Shakespearean play to allow the actor to reprise his King Henry.[1] Thus although the play itself has yet to receive full cinematic treatment, the production values traditionally associated with it remain apparent on the big screen. Shekhar Kapur's *Elizabeth* (1998), for instance, offers both spectacle (at its clearest in the film's coronation sequence) and Holbeinism (at a crucial point in the Queen's development, we see, stacked in a cellar and covered in cobwebs, Holbein's painting of her father in the classic stance) alive and well at the turn of the twenty-first century.

In this context and in the context of the BBC's success in televising coronations and other large-scale state events (itself productive of an escalation in the pomp of such events as the establishment seeks to reinvent royalty), it is pleasingly ironic that the notoriously low budget for the BBC Shakespeare series in the late 1970s resulted in a *Henry VIII* which, though meticulously archaeological in costume and architecture, denied the director the temptation to turn the tradition of pomp and ceremony into televisual spectacle (only glimpses are caught of processions) and obliged him to concentrate upon the possibilities offered by the TV close-up.[2] The production was by no means radical: there was little irony, and despite the absence of pomp, 'authenticity' of a kind was nonetheless sought by filming entirely on location – at Leeds Castle, Penshurst Place and Hever Castle, all stately homes with Tudor connections, in weather so cold that the actors'

---

1   Ian Judge, conversation with editor, 1996. Shaun Usher, reviewing the Doran production in the *Daily Mail*, obviously thought it high praise indeed to suggest that in Paul Jesson '[w]e have a new King!', going on to explain that '[t]hanks to the *Six Wives* TV series, and his return appearance in the 1990 staging of *Henry VIII* at Chichester, Keith Michell seemed to own the role, but now Paul Jesson takes it by force of personality and talent' (Usher).

2   The production (directed by Kevin Billington, 1979) was voted by members of the Shakespeare Association of America the most successful of the BBC films (though the number of duds in the series arguably makes this less of an accolade than it sounds).

breaths are visible pretty much throughout. Nonetheless, the BBC *Henry VIII* demonstrates that the TV camera can serve to narrow rather than enlarge the visual focus of the play in a manner which would perhaps have pleased Poel or Greet more than Tree. The centrality in the BBC production of the figure of Katherine – itself potentially a throwback to earlier productions – underlined this inwardness by emphasizing the clash between personal moral commitment and the flexible morality of political life, an emphasis which might have seemed glib had it not been for the dignified performance of Claire Bloom as the Queen. The film's small scale would have surprised both Tree and Barker, who clearly saw the medium of film as a means of sustaining visual opulence, but it perhaps suggests a workable, ongoing alternative to the epic style that has been so persistent in the play's performance history.

But it was repertory theatre rather than cinema that produced by far the most remarkable production of *Henry VIII* in the twentieth century, that of the Irish director Terence Gray for the Festival Theatre, Cambridge, in February 1931. Gray has by and large been dismissed as a director of Shakespeare: A.C.Sprague objected to the 'silliness and even travesty' apparent in his *Henry VIII*, and even Richard Cave, who sees Gray as 'one of the great shapers of our awareness of theatre today', suggests that, in this particular production, '[m]ere method won the day and meaning degenerated into nonsense' (Cave, 15, 53). But at least one early report suggests that beside Gray's production 'any other version' of the play would seem 'as inanimate as an old painting' (a throwaway dismissal of the entire Holbein tradition), and, as Cave's description implies, Gray has begun to be appreciated as a genuine experimental artist whose mission was 'a general onslaught against the formal and cultural conservatism of the English theatre' (Sprague, *Histories*, 11, n. 1; Rigby, *Eastern Daily Press*; Shaughnessy, 93, 95).

For Gray, historical drama offered the director a clear choice:

> [H]istory may be taken seriously, that is to say a dramatist
> may set out to create a pageant that brings before the eyes

of a modern audience a near representation of the outward semblance of a past epoch of the human race; or he
may take it satirically, that is to say as a means of poking
fun at, or otherwise bringing into light relief aspects of
the modern world by contrast with a caricature of an age
that is past.

(Gray, 6)

He made a clear decision to follow the second route, picking
Henry VIII as a representative culturally authoritative text in
order specifically to reject theatrical tradition, a choice echoed in
the programme notes: 'Shakespeare's histories . . . are theatrical
material and nothing more. Consequently, we need hardly apolo-
gise for not being solemn over their history' (*Review*, 5). Yet Gray
seems also to have been intent on finding a more appropriate mode
for a play which had been overlaid with ponderous theatrical
accretions – in other words, on locating a kind of authenticity. A
preview article claimed that 'Mr. Terence Gray expresses a hope
that his "modernist" production of "Henry VIII" at the Cambridge
Festival Theatre will, by its lack of elaborate "effects", enable
audiences to catch something of the same thrill as those who saw
it in Shakespeare's day' (*Liverpool Post*), and the programme notes
argued that the Festival Theatre offered an opportunity to 'bring
Shakespeare back into the theatre', with methods 'more distinctly
akin to the methods for which the plays were composed than to
the methods . . . which are known as the "Shakespeare tradition"'
(*Review*, 3) (see Fig. 8). Even this most radical production of
Henry VIII, then, still leant heavily on issues of 'authenticity'.

Visually speaking, though, the production was both striking
and deliberately alienating, appearing anything but 'authentic', at
least in the Irving/Tree sense of the word: the *Birmingham Post*
reviewer described it as resembling 'the garden party in "Alice in
Wonderland", as conceived by Lewis Carroll and illustrated by
John Tenniel' (*Birmingham Post*). The set consisted of a stark alu-
minium ramp which curved across the stage to disappear into
heavy blue curtains. A fair amount of the action took place in the

8 The trial scene, from Terence Gray's production for the Festival Theatre, Cambridge, 1931

auditorium. And the actors – on the premise that the original 'method of production was formalised rather than realistic' (*Review*, 2) – worked within a non-naturalistic 'dance-drama' mode, striking odd, exaggerated postures, miming 'concerted reactions to events as if they were puppets and some force had suddenly pulled their strings' (Cave, 52), and wearing Carrollesque playing-card costumes, which were viewed alternately as sinister and as 'vaguely Tudor' (*Birmingham Post*). The dancing and the costumes had an overtly deterministic effect, reducing the characters, as Robert Shaughnessy notes, 'to flat, manufactured and depersonalised playthings', and characterizing court politics as a 'ruthless and arbitrary game' (Shaughnessy, 104). Buckingham, for example, appeared as the 'Knave of Spades' in apparent disregard for the text's ambivalence about his guilt, while Wolsey 'wore stilt-like *cothurnoi* beneath his robes which made him tower above the other characters' but which he removed at his fall from power so that he 'literally seemed to wither in stature' (Marshall, *Theatre*, 66). The one exception to the rule of decharacterization appears to have been Mary MacDonald's Katherine, whose passion marked a deliberate and uncomfortable contrast with 'the prevailing artificiality' (Cave, 53), particularly since the courtiers all 'seemed ever more foolhardy in giving up their individuality to dance to the tune of Wolsey or Henry' (Cave, 52).

What remains unclear from the various reviews (many of which take their cue from the Cambridge context and refer to Gray's approach as 'ragging Shakespeare') is the way the production treated the text itself – whether the aim was to debunk a conservative, royalist play or to recover a submerged political irony within it. Gray's treatment of the last act provides a curious focus for this question: he rejected the tradition of finishing after Katherine's or Wolsey's final lines (a rejection in keeping with the conscious impersonality of the production) and kept going to the final scene, but reworked the scene savagely, Cranmer revealing that the baby in his arms was in fact a cardboard doll with a face 'of Elizabeth at the age of 60' (Rigby, *Maddermarket*, 107) and then joining the whole company to toss the baby into the audience, 'Punch-and-Judy fashion' (Cave, 53) and sprint out of the auditorium. This outrageous final moment – which echoes the production at Lincoln's Inn Fields in 1700 during which 'the actors ridiculed a christening' (Luttrell, 4.712; and see above, p. 22) – seems to suggest that, in the end, Gray perceived the play as fundamentally conservative, assuming that in order to achieve a radical break with previous productions he needed to work against the grain of the text rather than tap into any potential for subversion that might be found within it.

Gray's production (despite nods to tradition in, for instance, costume and the characterization of Katherine) thus effectively broke the mould, and three directors since Gray, all working at Stratford, have to a greater or lesser extent sustained the alienating approach to the play pioneered at the Cambridge Festival Theatre. Tyrone Guthrie – who in his autobiography 'seems loath to admit how deep an influence' the Cambridge Festival Theatre had on him, despite his period as director there (Cave, 71; Guthrie, 53–63) – was involved in two different productions of *Henry VIII*: a sumptuous and comic one in 1933, with Charles Laughton as Henry, and a much more energetic and indecorous one in 1949 at Stratford which was revived in 1950 and 1953 and which – by way of its use of a full text, its innovative staging, and the detailed attention paid to minor parts – made a substantial impact (see Fig. 9). Playing the full text allowed the production to dwell on particular ironies in order to offer the post-war audience an alienating glimpse of the fascist potential in royal ceremony.[1] Initially at least, the stage was kept disconcertingly busy:

> There is always something happening to titillate the eye or the ear. . . . Whilst Cranmer delivers his grandiose address in honour of the infant Princess Elizabeth, the

---

1 Despite this, elements of the opulent mode persisted in the production, particularly when it was revived for the coronation. It even featured a squad of soldiers from the local regiment, the Royal Warwickshires.

Duchess of Norfolk explodes in a mighty sneeze. In the scene where the scriveners take down Queen Katherine's plea for leniency, priests, scribbling away on their parchment, are rolled about the floor like bowls by careless courtiers.

(Hobson 1949)

Reviewers suggested that the director was having too much fun (Harold Hobson suggested that 'the main spirit of the production is comedic, any resemblances to Shakespeare being purely accidental'), and Guthrie seems to have been persuaded by critics' hostility and by the exigencies of the revival for Elizabeth II's coronation to tone down the ironies he had excavated. Muriel St Clare Byrne, in a substantial review for *Shakespeare Survey*, notes that 'the interruption of the Duchess's sneeze . . . was removed after the first night', but this was not the only piece of business at which critics baulked (Byrne, 129). Some, in their haste to object, seem to have mixed up actual textual elements with imposed directorial decisions: J.C.Trewin, for instance, objecting to the sneeze, adds that:

Mr. Guthrie – with his incorrigible sense of humour – can be naughty at times. Certainly he should not permit two comic gentlemen to gossip before the farewell of Buckingham.

(Trewin, *Lady*)

No matter how hard directors try, reviewers' fixed ideas about the play tend to colour their understanding of particular productions. R.A.Foakes's recollections arguably offer a clearer sense than do reviews such as Trewin's of the excitement of Guthrie's *Henry VIII*:

It would be worth emphasising the revolutionary nature of the production. Audiences at Stratford were used to a proscenium-arch stage. . . . Guthrie changed that: he made something of a thrust stage, used the depth of the resulting

9 The christening scene from Tyrone Guthrie's Stratford production, 1950

space, allowed actors to turn their backs on the audience, speeded up the pace by giving us a more or less continuous action, with swirling movements and varied groupings. The effect was startling: instead of actors delivering their lines to the audience, we had characters interacting in ways which brought the action to life with a new realism, and made the whole very exciting. In retrospect, it was not a significant political reading of the play, . . . but what the production did was to make the intrigues, the trials, the spectacles of the play vivid and full of energy.

> (Richmond, 90–1, quoting Foakes, private correspondence)

Guthrie thus found genuinely innovative ways to revitalize the play, even if he was prepared in reviving his production to reduce their impact.

Twenty years after Guthrie, Trevor Nunn directed *Henry VIII* for the RSC with Donald Sinden and Peggy Ashcroft as Henry and Katherine, providing clear contrast with his predecessor by offering a sombre version of the play which bore echoes both of Atkins's austerity and of Gray's alienations. As with the 1949 production, there were elements of Nunn's staging which irritated the reviewers and which were later toned down. Between the scenes, Nunn projected captions bearing 'contemporary' news reports of the events of the play, a device which was designed to encourage the audience to treat the characters on the stage (in the words of the Prologue (27)) 'As they were living', but which was omitted when the production transferred to London. Yet in apparent contradiction to this Brechtianism, Nunn's was possibly the most psychologically committed production of the play since Siddons, the absence of distractions focusing attention on the main roles and drawing out intense Method acting from the principals. One of its notable features was a close focus on Henry, resisting a uniformly bluff King and emphasizing his development across the play from initial irresponsibility to confident autocratic power. According to one reviewer, he:

threads his path through the play as if haunted by the murders he has not yet committed, his spirit wasted by the consciousness of years of lechery he as yet knows nothing of, the magnificent and aggressive Holbein body contradicted by the dead soul within. . . . [W]hen everyone else for the last time has left the stage, Mr Sinden's Henry also departs, but as he leaves he half turns, and momentarily gazes at the audience. His face . . . seems in some inexplicable way to be questioning the future, questioning it in fatigue and apprehension. . . . Mr Sinden's Henry is capable of both crime and poetry, as the bluff King Hal of tradition could never be.

(Hobson 1969)

(See Fig. 10.) The effect, as we have seen in Sinden's comments on his experience of acting Henry, appears to have been to uncover a productive duplicity in the play's politics which spectacular productions had hidden from view but which could begin to be

10 Donald Sinden as Henry and Brewster Mason as Wolsey in the masque scene from Trevor Nunn's production for the Royal Shakespeare Company, 1969

appreciated once again in the wary yet intoxicating political climate of the 1960s.

The play was next performed at Stratford in 1983 in a controversial production by Howard Davies which extended Nunn's political focus, treating *Henry VIII*, in the director's words, as 'a modern play, dealing with taxes, unemployment and social divisions' (Trewin, *Birmingham Post*). The results were mixed. On the one hand, the production was more comprehensively alienating than Nunn's (distinctly reminiscent, in fact, of Gray's), a 'cynical Brechtian anatomy of power politics' (Billington, *Guardian*). On the other, it struck some in the audience as slow and drab, if well meaning. James Fenton, writing in the *Sunday Times*, underlined the Gray connection, arguing that 'it is time we stopped imagining that the anti-realistic tradition in Britain is purely Brechtian' and suggesting that Davies's production 'offers the same kind of production [as Gray's] but without the pandemonium' (Fenton). The costumes and set, in deliberately low-key greys and ochres, as well as the extremely limited ceremonial, provided a wilfully bleak and sparse environment for political intrigue, with Weillian music underscoring the visual alienation. There were moments of overt modernizing, notably the enthusiastic chanting of football songs by the crowd in the Porter scene. Perhaps the most notably anti-realistic scene of all was 4.1, in which the audience watched a rehearsal for the coronation prior to the event itself, with the Gentlemen deploying dummies for the aristocrats and self-consciously reading out the stage directions, thereby deflating the actual coronation.[1] The application of such techniques to a Shakespeare production in the early 1980s could hardly be said to place it at the cutting edge of theatrical radicalism, but in the context of the play's staunchly conservative stage history (and despite Fenton's claim that '[t]he alienatory style of . . . Howard Davies has nobody left to argue with'), Davies's production served as a valuable extension of Gray's experiment with alternative production values.

---

1   The dummies arguably still extend aspects of traditional performance (they were used in spectacular productions to swell the crowd scenes) as well as echoing Gray (seep p. 38).

Since Davies, there has been just one RSC production of the play. Greg Doran's acclaimed 1996 staging at the Swan Theatre (which ran on into 1998 in various locations from New York to Tokyo) was more complex than most in its response to the play and its stage history. Doran was clearly well aware of his predecessors and consciously sought to work within the tradition of spectacle – 'discreet spectacle', though, in response to the size and shape of Stratford's second house – while at the same time engaging with some of the ironies that Nunn and Davies, in particular, had unearthed.[1] His aim was to:

> move beyond the Brechtian rejections of ceremonial by reclaiming the fullness of spectacle at the same time as demonstrating (and in order to demonstrate) its emptiness – to which end the ceremonial must be impressive, not pre-debunked.
>
> (Doran)

Thus the production began with a grand, glittering, slightly comic tableau of the Field of the Cloth of Gold, with the bulk of the cast gliding on stage in stiff, formal poses, only to reverse rapidly and awkwardly as lightning flashed and the rain of the 'hideous storm' (1.1.90) began (see Fig. 11). The masque at York Place, in one of the few echoes of Davies, became a 'bacchanalian orgy' with Paul Jesson as a big, blustering Henry whose majesty was sufficiently in question for Wolsey to pick him out only on the third or fourth attempt (Coveney; see also Jesson, 122). The figure of Anne was developed uneasily in relation to the audience's knowledge of her

1 'Discreet spectacle' are Doran's own words, and a useful, if paradoxical, description of the combination of semi-'authentic' space, closely placed seating and technological possibilities offered by the Swan Theatre. The choice of the Swan, with its small stage area, offered certain parallels with possible early performances at the Blackfriars (see pp. 9–10). Doran's production, as it happens, provided a continuation of the 'command performance' tradition. Prince Charles attended one night, and afterwards offered this insight: 'It makes you realize how little things have changed. When one is born into a certain position you have people advising you all the time, whispering in your ear. It's only when you get to my age that you begin to work out who's telling you the truth' (Jesson, 130–1).

11 The opening tableau in Greg Doran's 1996 production for the Royal
   Shakespeare Company

fate, and she reappeared at the end of the christening scene, hand
nervously held at her throat, to cast a final shadow over the celebrations. Throughout the production, close attention to the
details of speech aimed to bring out ironies of conversation, and
the play's background noise of whisper and rumour was quietly
evident at key moments.[1]

Reviewers of the production demonstrated their customary
persistence in assuming the basic weakness of the play and praised
both the director and the actors – reserving particular appreciation
for Jesson's Henry and for Jane Lapotaire's impassioned Katherine
(both of whom have written sensitively about their experience of
the roles) – for coping well with substandard material. Ann

---

1 There is still a tendency for audiences to expect, even to require, an unironic, ceremonial play. Audiences for the Doran production, in my experience at least, tended
  not to notice much of the irony and unease that had been discussed at length in
  rehearsal, wondering vaguely why the actors looked a bit shifty in the grand scenes
  and objecting to the actors in the gallery above talking to each other during the
  divorce hearing.

FitzGerald, for instance, noted the 'clear weaknesses in this collaboration', but suggested that Doran 'succeeds in surmounting' the play's problems (FitzGerald). Michael Coveney argued that in Doran's hands, *Henry VIII* seemed 'a much more sinuous and engaging piece than [he] had thought from the bland pageant of a Chichester revival [in 1990] or . . . the grimly Brechtian antispectacular that the RSC itself served up in 1983' (Coveney). And Michael Billington appreciated the 'good use' made of 'the space's opportunities for intimate spectacle', noting the 'visual unity' achieved by showing the King 'periodically emerging . . . in golden triumph while brutal realpolitik takes place on the forestage' (Billington, *Guardian*), thereby underlining Doran's genuine attempt to forge a path between the theatrical legacy of spectacle and the rejection of that spectacle effected by Gray, Nunn and Davies.[1]

The twentieth century thus offered a range of alternative perspectives on the play in performance, underpinned by contradictory visions of what constitutes 'authenticity'. Greet and Atkins's fast-paced, uncluttered productions of *Henry VIII* may have been conservative in the sense that they depended upon a belief in the 'recreation' of 'original staging conditions', yet they successfully broke with the prevailing ponderousness of Victorian/Edwardian productions. Gray's anti-realistic take may have been based on an assumption of the essential conservatism of the play which meant that ironies had to be imposed upon, rather than drawn out of, the text, yet there is no doubt of the startling, and instructive, impact his production had on its audience and on his successors (even if they tended not to admit it). Guthrie may have toned down the ironies he had originally introduced and succumbed to the habitual appropriation of *Henry VIII* for royalism, yet he found moments in the text which questioned the conservative assumptions that underlay even 'radical' productions such as that of Gray. Davies may still have depended visually upon a

---

1 On 'intimate spectacle', see p. 54n.

version of the traditional Holbeinesque mode, yet the Brechtian style he adopted for the play echoes Gray in questioning the assumption that versions of naturalism are the only possible direction for the play. Partly in response to Davies, Doran's production demonstrated the possibility of a synthesis of the spectacular, intimate and ironic styles which had come to seem mutually exclusive in the quest for contradictory authenticities. What is, in a sense, curious is the tentative, exploratory quality of each of these productions, a quality which suggests that, despite the longevity of tradition in performance of the play, at the beginning of the twenty-first century the afterlife of *Henry VIII* has, for all sorts of reasons, only just begun.

ALL IS TRUE: CULTURAL HISTORY

FALSTAFF   Is not the truth the truth?

(1H4 2.4.233–4)

The most persistent strand in attempts across the years to create a 'truthful' production of *Henry VIII* has been the idea that it might be possible to re-create for a contemporary audience the same effect that performances had on the play's very first audiences. Clearly, this has meant different things at different times – with Tree, Gray and Nunn, for instance, developing mutually incompatible ideas of what that 'authentic' effect might be – and the notion that it might be possible or desirable to remove the accretions of a play's performance history seems to me to deny the inescapable contingency of all theatrical work. But *Henry VIII* was undoubtedly a play of its moment, and for the purposes of this edition it is important to ask what the first audiences would have seen and understood when they made their way across the Thames one afternoon in the early summer of 1613.

There are several reports of the catastrophic events of 29 June 1613 – it was a major topic of gossip for letter-writing Londoners – and I will begin with that provided by a young merchant called Henry Bluett:

On Tuesday last there was acted at the Globe a new play called *All is Triewe*, which had been acted not passing 2 or 3 times before. There came many people to see it insomuch that the house was very full, and as the play was almost ended the house was fired with shooting off a chamber which was stopped with towe which was blown up into the thatch of the house and so burned down to the ground. But the people escaped all without hurt except one man who was scalded with the fire by adventuring in to save a child which otherwise had been burnt.

(Cole, 352)[1]

Bluett's account is confirmed in a letter of Thomas Lorkins:

London this last of June 1613
No longer since then yesterday, while Bourbege his companie were acting at ye Globe the play of Hen: 8, and there shooting of certayne chambers in way of triumph; the fire catch'd & fastened upon the thatch of ye house and there burned so furiously as it consumed the whole house & all in lesse then two houres (the people having enough to doe to save themselves).

(Lorkins)[2]

---

1   The Globe fire found an uncanny, tragicomic echo in a theatrical (non-)event a hundred or so years later which is curiously reminiscent of the crowd scene at Anne's coronation, in which '[g]reat-bellied women' are said to 'shake the press' (4.1.76, 78). During a production of *Henry VIII* on 26 October 1727 at Drury Lane, 'a Gentlewoman fancying she saw Smoke issue from under the Stage, as she sat in the Pit, during the Play Time, . . . and at the same time believing she smelt Fire, declared her Opinion so loud, and by her precipitate Endeavours to get out, gave such an Alarm all over the House, as was attended with the fatal Consequence of one Woman big with Child being press'd to Death, and several other Persons were very much bruised' (*London Stage*, 2.940, quoting *Daily Journal*, 28 October 1727).

2   See also Howes's 1615 augmentation of Stow's *Annals*: 'Also vpon *S. Peters* day last, the play-house or Theater called the *Globe*, vpon the Banck-side neere London, by negligent discharging of a peale of ordinance, close to the south side thereof, the Thatch tooke fier, & the wind sodainly disperst ye flame round about, & in a very short space ye whole building was quite consumed, & no man hurt: the house being filled with people, to behold the play, viz. of *Henry* the 8. And the next spring it was new builded in far fairer manner then before' (Stow 1615, 4ll^r; 926).

Both accounts agree, then, that the fire was started by 'chambers' (small cannons used to create sound effects), that it took hold very rapidly, and that it completely destroyed the theatre.[1] According to Lorkins, and in the context of the Prologue's claim (13) that a performance lasted 'two short hours', it seems to have taken about as much time to burn down the Globe as it would have done, in normal circumstances, to finish the play.

The fullest and most interesting account we have of the burning of the Globe comes from the diplomat Sir Henry Wotton. Writing to a friend about current political issues, he moves on to the week's sensation:

> Now, to let matters of state sleep, I will entertain you at the present with what hath happened this week at the Bank's side. The King's players had a new play, called *All is true*, representing some principal pieces of the reign of Henry VIII, which was set forth with many extraordinary circumstances of Pomp and Majesty, even to the matting of the stage; the Knights of the Order, with their Georges and garters, the Guards with their embroidered coats, and the like: sufficient in truth within a while to make greatness very familiar, if not ridiculous. Now, King Henry making a masque at the Cardinal Wolsey's house, and certain chambers being shot off at his entry, some of the paper, or other stuff, wherewith one of them was stopped, did light on the thatch, where being thought at first but an idle smoke, and their eyes more attentive to the show, it kindled inwardly, and ran round like a train, consuming within less than an hour the whole house to the very grounds.
>
> This was the fatal period of that virtuous fabric; wherein yet nothing did perish but wood and straw, and a few forsaken cloaks; only one man had his breeches set on

1   Ben Jonson specifies 'two poor chambers' as the culprits in his poem 'An Execration upon Vulcan' (Jonson, *Poems*, 368).

fire, that would perhaps have broiled him, if he had not
by the benefit of a provident wit put it out with bottle ale.
(Wotton, 2.32–3)

Comparison of this letter with Bluett's and Lorkins's produces
one or two discrepancies (Wotton's fire, for instance, is an hour
more ferocious than that of Lorkins) but also reveals Wotton's
account to be more than just a report: it is, in fact, an acute and
subtle critical reading of the play.

There is nothing to say that Wotton was actually present in
person at the Globe on the day in question, but he does nonetheless offer a detailed description of the play and of the catastrophe,
and he is quite clear about the order of events, the construction of
the theatre, and the relationship of the material facts of production to the outbreak of the fire. He confirms the title – *All Is True*
– that we must assume was the original one for the play when first
performed, though it was later changed to *The Famous History of
the Life of King Henry VIII* when it was placed last in the
sequence of plays on the reigns of English kings in the First Folio
(see also Woudhuysen). He notes, too, the episodic nature of the
play as 'representing some principal pieces' of Henry VIII's reign.
And he expands on certain details (he notes that the 'chambers'
which caused the trouble were set off to mark the arrival of the
King at Wolsey's party), emphasizing the 'many extraordinary circumstances of Pomp and Majesty' that characterized the play,
'even', as he says, 'to the matting of the stage'. But where Bluett
and Lorkins set out simply to describe the main news story of the
week, Wotton provides a moral narrative in which he notes both
the hubris of the dramatic representation and the destruction of
the theatre that follows directly from that representation, and
then, curiously, concludes with a carnivalesque *dénouement* which
alleges that 'nothing did perish' after all. In other words, he
describes not simply the accidental and more-or-less regrettable
burning-down of a public building but a *comœdia apocalyptica* –
an historical drama in which an all-consuming disaster has an

unexpectedly happy ending, mapping out the Christian pattern of crucifixion and resurrection – thereby adapting a Reformation genre to act as commentary both on the play and on the nature of theatre itself.

Wotton's attitude to the event of the play – both the production and the fire – is at once gleeful and unsettled. He claims he will 'let matters of state sleep' in order to report events on the Bankside, yet the scene he describes is itself quite clearly a representation of 'matters of state', and the representation, he assures us indignantly, was both accurate and demeaning – 'sufficient in truth within a while to make greatness very familiar, if not ridiculous'. This may suggest a specific satirical or allegorical intent for the play; it may also imply that all political plays, by their nature as public entertainments dealing with affairs of state, are inevitably trivializing. Either way, he offers an apocalyptic account of the event which has both political and theological overtones: a fire begins which is ignored by the people as an 'idle smoke' but which turns out rapidly to burn 'the whole house to the very grounds'. He also presents an impossible paradox – a 'fatal period' in which 'nothing did perish' (the burning of a 'wooden O' is, at least in one Jacobean signification, the destruction of a kind of 'nothing') – which is only resolved through slapstick: 'one man had his breeches set on fire, that would perhaps have broiled him, if he had not by the benefit of a provident wit put it out with bottle ale'. Suddenly, after the discomfort he has expressed over the ridiculousness of the play's representation of politics, Wotton invokes the spirit of carnival. Thus even as he condemns the essentially subversive nature of theatre (the nearer the players come to the 'truth', the more dangerous their representation) and embraces an event which marks a reflexive act of judgement upon them (judgement which is precisely a result of the dangerous accuracy of their representation), he celebrates their evasion of that judgement by way of the return of the subversive principle that has led to that judgement in the first place. The apocalyptic conclusion thus appears to have been reached only to find itself undermined by the return of the very impulse that provoked it in the first place.

Wotton's testimony on the subject of the Globe fire is thus more complex than it might at first appear. Its ambivalence about the nature of truth and about its own function as testimony is central to what is effectively the first critical reading of *Henry VIII*, and I will argue that this ambivalence finds its focus in the play's representation of the state of the Reformation in Jacobean England. As a metaphor for this – and before moving into detailed discussion of the cultural and political context in which the play intervenes – I want briefly to mention another fire: not this time the fire that destroyed the Globe, but one that took place in the same year which was both equally destructive and equally revealing. On the afternoon of 6 August 1613, a substantial section of the town of Dorchester, in the county of Dorset, was devastated by an uncontrollable blaze. The physical effect of this fire was considerable, but the psychological effect on the townspeople of Dorchester was (to modern eyes) out of all proportion, producing, in David Underdown's words, 'a sort of mass spiritual conversion', a 'recognition' on the part of many of the inhabitants 'that what was needed was a total reformation of the town' (Underdown, 4). Despite the fact that England had been a reformed nation, a Protestant nation, for the best part of a century (or at the very least since the beginning of the reign of Elizabeth I in 1558), English Protestants in James I's reign remained acutely aware of the limitations of reformation, of the possibilities of counter-reformation, and consequently of the need for continuous revival of the impetus to reform.[1] Underdown's engaging history of Dorchester in the years following the fire underlines this awareness, making it abundantly clear that the English Reformation was not a single, unique event, but an ongoing and

---

1 On the ongoing need for reformation, see Underdown, 59: 'The "yoke of Antichrist", White later declared, had been removed at Queen Elizabeth's accession, but the "perfecting of the work", the full reformation of the church, had been neglected or deferred for the current generation to complete.' On the varieties of reformation, see Haigh, especially 12–21.

uncertain process. I would suggest that without this sense of the uncertain state of the Reformation in the minds of many of James I's subjects, we will have an impoverished understanding both of the events of 1613 and of the play *Henry VIII*. And I will argue that, by way of its simultaneous engagement with the reigns of Henry VIII and of James I, the play occupies a space between the celebration of James's Reformation inheritance and the suggestion that that Reformation had never truly taken place.

Truth and topicality

One nineteenth-century editor found it hard to imagine how 'a play celebrating the elevation of Anne Boleyn, and the birth of her daughter Elizabeth' could possibly have been written and produced 'in the 10th year of James's reign', and preferred to believe that it dated from the last year or two of Elizabeth's life and that the 'allusive compliments to James' apparent in the text should be 'regarded as additions foisted into the piece at its representation during the new reign' (Campbell, 1.lii). But the letters of Wotton and the others provide the firmest dating evidence of any play in the Shakespeare canon, and it is therefore important to try to understand the play in the context of the particular time in which it was written.

The year 1613 was an extraordinary one for English politics and in particular for the politics of English Protestantism. James I's eldest son, Henry, Prince of Wales, heir to the thrones of England and Scotland, had died, suddenly and unexpectedly, in November 1612, producing overwhelming public grief.[1] The only comparable event in recent memory – in Britain, at least (the assassination of John F. Kennedy had a similarly profound effect in the United States) – was the death of Diana, Princess of Wales, though the sustained public mourning for Henry is, for several

---

1 'Never before had so many elegies been written on a single occasion, by such a wide range of practitioners' (Kay, 124). Kay lists some of the better-known poets who wrote elegies for Henry: Browne, Campion, Chapman, Donne, Drummond, Herbert, Heywood, King, Ralegh, Sylvester, Tourneur, Webster and Wither.

reasons, far more comprehensible than it was for Diana. He, too, was a charismatic figure with a keen eye for developing his own personal mythology, but he was also heir to the throne and, with his passion for military display and his allegiance to the dream of a wholly Reformed Europe, he appeared to offer the possibility of a new era for an England fully engaged with Continental Protestantism, a situation which was highly unlikely as long as James was on the throne. Henry's death shattered the millenarian hopes invested in him by militant Protestants and left a vacuum which was filled by popular endorsement of his personal enthusiasm for his sister Elizabeth's impending marriage to Frederick, the Elector Palatine (the most prominent Continental Protestant ruler), as ardour for English intervention in the struggle with Catholic Europe focused on their union. As a result, the wedding of Elizabeth and Frederick – postponed until February 1613 so as not to be wholly overshadowed by Henry's funeral – was taken up with a fervour verging on desperation.

Henry VIII shares in the mixed negative and positive emotions induced by this rapid succession of funeral and wedding.[1] The Prologue predicts a melancholy play – 'if you can be merry then, I'll say / A man may weep upon his wedding day' (Prologue 31–2) – and the two commentating Gentlemen note the pace of political and emotional change:

2 GENTLEMAN

                           At our last encounter,
The Duke of Buckingham came from his trial.

1 GENTLEMAN

'Tis very true. But that time offered sorrow,
This, general joy.

                                  (4.1.4–7)

1   As does *The Two Noble Kinsmen*, which arguably echoes the prevailing emotions of 1613 in its unique tragicomic conclusion (a wedding and a funeral, simultaneously), voiced most succinctly by Palamon: 'That we should things desire, which do cost us / The loss of our desire! That naught could buy / Dear love, but loss of dear love!' (5.4.110–12).

As R.A.Foakes points out, a play that incorporates the birth of Queen Elizabeth and engages with the English Reformation would clearly have been appropriate at a time of celebration for the marriage of a Protestant Princess Elizabeth, and he suggests – noting a series of verbal parallels between contemporary descriptions of the occasion and the Folio stage directions, and emphasizing the deliberate comparisons drawn between Queen Elizabeth and her young royal namesake in sermons and pamphlets at the time – that *Henry VIII* may well have been performed for the wedding itself (Ard², xxxi).[1] Whether or not this was so, there is no doubt at all that there is a firm relationship between *Henry VIII* and the political culture of 1612–13.[2]

This engagement with Jacobean politics has encouraged some critics to see *Henry VIII* as a Protestant propaganda play.[3] For

1   I have nothing to add to Foakes's account (and have benefited considerably from his work, as I hope the Commentary shows) except to note, as he does, that there is no actual primary evidence (in the form, for example, of a record of payment) of such a court performance, and to suggest that both the ambivalent politics I outline for the play and the thematic emphasis it places on divorce together make it less than obvious material for the celebration of a dynastic marriage.

2   The later example of Middleton's *A Game at Chess*, apparently 'written in haste' as a highly topical play but actually performed (with unprecedented success) several months after the events that motivated it, suggests that there is no reason why *Henry VIII* should have been performed for the wedding itself: by June 1613, Princess Elizabeth had left England (she departed for the Continent on 10 April) and the topic may have been a safer one. Julia Gasper, however, points out (with justification) that to perform a play 'largely concerned with divorce . . . at a royal wedding would surely have been an offence against taste and decorum' (Gasper, 'Reform', 207).

3   This is a perhaps surprising argument in view of repeated claims that Shakespeare was brought up as a recusant Catholic (see Honigmann, *Lost*). It is less surprising, however, in view of the allegiances of Shakespeare's collaborator John Fletcher. Fletcher wrote no apocalyptic allegories, no political pamphlets, and his many plays demonstrate an uneasy and rather unpredictable engagement with political and theological issues; but he did state his support for war with Spain when writing to his patron, the Countess of Huntingdon, and it is also relevant that one (wholly erroneous) report of sectarian volatility following the death of Henry specifies her husband, Henry Hastings, fifth Earl of Huntingdon, as the imagined target of rampaging recusants: '[O]rder is gon into most shires to disarme the papists; what secret cause there may be I know not, but the world here growes suspicious and apprehends great daunger from them, and many rumours are raised, as namely the last weeke that the earl of Huntington was slaine by them in his owne house; whereupon at Coventrie and Warwicke they shut theyre gates and mustered theyre souldiers, and at Banburie and those parts the people made barricados and all other manner of provision, as yf they looked presently to be assaulted' (Chamberlain, 1.410).

Frances Yates, *Henry VIII* was an unequivocally Protestant play which 'reflects the Foxian apocalyptic view of English history' (Yates, 70).[1] More recently, William Baillie, analysing a series of topical motifs in the play with distinct resonances for militant Protestants, sees the representation of 'the expansion of the monarch's personal authority in relation to the law, the sudden fall of a court favorite, and a divorce' as indications that the play was deliberately addressing Protestant attitudes to current events (Baillie, 248).[2] Donna Hamilton has extended these claims – particularly in respect of the currency of divorce as a sectarian issue – by arguing that *Henry VIII* is designed to discredit the 'Howard faction at court (a faction dominated by Catholics) by associating their values and projects . . . with Wolsey and the values he represents' (Hamilton, 164). These arguments are largely convincing, yet I would argue that the play has complexities that they do not fully address.

Twentieth-century 'topical' critics (working against the nineteenth-century theatrical tendency to cut Act 5) tended to place a great deal of weight on the final scene – and in particular on Cranmer's prophecy – to support the argument that *Henry VIII* projects a future for English Protestantism under James. Certainly, Cranmer's christening speech encourages the association of Elizabeth with the concept of truth that the play has emphasized. 'Let me speak, sir,' Cranmer urges the King, 'For heaven now bids me; and the words I utter / Let none think flattery, for they'll find 'em truth' (5.4.14–16). The child Elizabeth, he claims, 'promises / Upon this land a thousand thousand blessings, / Which time shall bring to ripeness' (18–20). In this time of revelation, he assures us:

1   Glynne Wickham, however, finds a very different aim, arguing that the play was designed to rehabilitate Katherine of Aragon, presumably to pave the way for Catholic matches in the future.
2   Baillie suggests that the play addresses both James's absolutist tendencies and the high-profile divorce of the Earl of Essex and Frances Howard; on the latter, see Lindley, *Howard*.

> Truth shall nurse her;
> Holy and heavenly thoughts still counsel her.
> She shall be loved and feared. Her own shall bless her;
> Her foes shake like a field of beaten corn,
> And hang their heads with sorrow. . . .
> God shall be truly known, and those about her
> From her shall read the perfect ways of honour. . . .
> (5.4.28–32, 36–7)

And he goes on to foretell James's accession as a time of peace and hope, treating 'truth' as a key attribute bequeathed to her successor by Elizabeth:

> Peace, plenty, love, truth, terror,
> That were the servants to this chosen infant,
> Shall then be his, and like a vine grow to him.
> Wherever the bright sun of heaven shall shine,
> His honour and the greatness of his name
> Shall be, and make new nations.
> (5.4.47–52)

'Truth', then, personified as a key attribute of the elect ruler, is emphasized in the prophecy as the foundation of the future reign and (particularly in the context of a prophecy spoken by a future Protestant martyr) invokes the resurgence at this time of an iconography of Truth that originated early in the Reformation.

'Truth' was the subject of intense ideological struggle in the course of the sixteenth century, and Elizabeth associated herself personally with the concept in order to imply that her accession was Time's gift to Europe's chosen nation after the tribulations of her sister's reign (see King, *Tudor*, 191–5, 228). This Protestant appropriation involved the annexing of visual, as well as verbal, icons (Chew, 69–70). We tend to think of early modern reformers as iconoclasts *par excellence*, yet the protagonists of reform knew an effective ideological weapon when they saw one, and despite their reputation as enemies of the visual image, they often preferred to reform, rather than to eradicate, Catholic iconography. Visual representations of 'Truth' are a good case in point. In England, medieval images of the harrowing of hell were reworked to depict 'the liberation of Christian Truth (as seen by Protestant reformers) from her captivity under the monster of Roman hypocrisy' (Saxl, 203). In these images, Truth is portrayed as a young woman trapped in a cave but saved from her fate by Time, depicted as an old man drawing her up into the open air. This tableau forcefully connects Time and Truth in an apocalyptic conjunction which implies that truth, though at present obscured, will be revealed to all at the day of judgement. It thus appropriates the Latin tag *veritas filia temporis* ('Truth the daughter of Time') to provide an iconography which offered an instant visual mnemonic for the Protestant insistence upon apocalypse (see Fig. 12).[1]

The *veritas filia temporis* iconography had acquired a new lease of life at the time of the first production of *Henry VIII* in response to James I's perceived indifference to the fate of continental Protestants. Thomas Dekker had forcefully dramatized the associations of the Time/Truth image early in the reign in his allegorical play *The Whore of Babylon*, and Thomas Middleton's 1613 pageant *The Triumphs of Truth* takes for granted the audience's knowledge of the typology of truth, presenting a 'lengthy struggle . . . between a female figure representing Truth . . . and idolatrous Error' (Norbrook, 'Reformation', 94), and concluding with fiery special effects to mark Truth's victory. But the death of Prince Henry marked the turning of the tide for this ideological weapon. An overtly apocalyptic masque with Truth as its central

---

1   The most memorable appropriation of *veritas filia temporis* came during the festivities for Elizabeth's coronation. As she moved along the traditional route from the Tower of London to Westminster Abbey, a series of symbolic pageants was enacted; seeing the fourth pageant from the distance, she asked what it was. 'She was told that it showed Truth the daughter of Time: "Tyme? qu*oth* she, and Tyme hath brought me hether", implicitly identifying herself with Truth. When she heard that Truth would present her with an English Bible, "she thanked the citie for that gift, and sayd that she would oftentimes reade ouer that booke"' (Hackett, 43, quoting *Queen's*, C2ᵛ).

12 *Veritas filia temporis* (Truth the daughter of Time), woodcut from William Marshall, *Goodly Primer in English*, 1535

figure (which David Norbrook has christened *The Masque of Truth*) had been planned by Henry himself for his sister's wedding, but it was cancelled immediately after his death.[1] This offered a very different view of Elizabeth's marriage from that held by her father, presenting the union not as the first of a planned series of cross-sectarian marriages designed to enforce European peace and harmony, but as a 'confessional alliance', in which James, as guardian of English Calvinist Protestantism, would ensure that the other European nations eventually turned to Protestantism. Without Prince Henry's continued patronage, the masque was never performed, and its cancellation underlines both the extent of Henry's loss to English militant Protestants and his father's lack of interest in an apocalyptic vision of the future of Europe (see Fig. 13).

'Truth', then, had very specific connotations in 1613 which suggest that a play produced at that time called *All Is True*, which emphasizes the concept of truth throughout, will be closely engaged with the politics of Protestantism. After all the tribulations we have witnessed in the course of the play, the prophecy with which the play closes appears to promise a decisive break from the nightmare of cyclical history. Cranmer presents the baby Elizabeth as the incarnation of Truth within an apocalyptic framework – 'Which time shall bring to ripeness' (5.4.20) – and the audience, uplifted by the grandeur of the scene and by the Archbishop's prophetic words, sees in the tableau of Cranmer and the child a reworking of the *veritas filia temporis* vignette, with Time standing protectively over Truth, rapturously predicting the final victory for English Protestantism.[2]

---

1 It was replaced by a conservative masque commissioned from Thomas Campion, a client of the Howard family, who (as Donna Hamilton has shown) had very different sectarian allegiances from Henry's circle (see *Lords' Masque*, 66; Hamilton, 173–80).

2 Even the arch-Catholic Gardiner, with vast irony, is given lines that unwittingly acknowledge the revelatory conjunction of Time and Truth embodied in the royal baby: 'The fruit she goes with', he says, 'I pray for heartily, that it may find / Good time, and live. But, for the stock,' he adds, savagely, 'I wish it grubbed up now' (5.1.20–3). Truth finding Time would hardly be Gardiner's ideal event, if he thought about it.

13 *Henry, Prince of Wales on Horseback*, painting by Robert Peake, c. 1611,
showing the Prince leading Time by the forelock

The Jacobean audience would, as R.A.Foakes noted, have been
attuned to two Elizabeths and two royal ceremonies: the prophecy
is thus directed at a series of futures, some already completed by
1613, others still projected, depending heavily for its success upon
the audience's hindsight, since the predictions which are known
already to have 'come true' (i.e. which are predictions for the
Henrician characters but not for the Jacobean audience) serve to
validate those as yet unfulfilled (Ard², xxxiii–xxxiv). This offers a
clear dynamic, celebrating (in John Margeson's words) 'not only

71

... the peace and security of Queen Elizabeth's reign, but also ... the idealised hopes, still felt by some in 1613, for the reign of James I' (Cam², 4). Cranmer thus deploys the myth of the phoenix (seen as a type of Christ's resurrection) to provide a 'natural' Christian framework within which to read James's succession:

> ... as when
> The bird of wonder dies, the maiden phoenix,
> Her ashes new create another heir
> As great in admiration as herself,
> So shall she leave her blessedness to one,
> When heaven shall call her from this cloud of darkness,
> Who from the sacred ashes of her honour
> Shall star-like rise as great in fame as she was
> And so stand fixed.
>
> (5.4.39–47)

James, as Elizabeth's heir (in mythic terms, if not in familial), is thus presented as the monarch for whom Protestant England has been waiting, in a direct line of inheritance from Henry VIII.

Yet for anyone with knowledge either of James or of the general attitude to Henry VIII in his reign, this does not really add up, since Cranmer ascribes to Elizabeth's successor aspirations which are at odds with those of James, who preferred peace and harmony to apocalyptic struggle. The plantation of America, for instance, promoted by militant Protestants and listed among James's 'predicted' achievements in Cranmer's speech – 'Wherever the bright sun of heaven shall shine,' Cranmer announces, 'His honour and the greatness of his name / Shall be, and make new nations' (5.4.50–52) – was viewed with suspicion by the King, who had an antagonistic relationship with the Virginia Company. Moreover, in context, the phoenix metaphor itself looks less convincing than it might. A parallel prediction in Dekker's *Whore of Babylon* by a figure representative of Rome ('Babilon') suggests the tensions that underlie Cranmer's words:

> [O]ut of her ashes may
> A second Phoenix rise, of larger wing,
> Of stronger talent, of more dreadfull beake,
> Who swooping through the ayre, may with his beating
> So well commaund the winds, that all those trees
> Where sit birds of our hatching (now fled thither)
> Will tremble, . . . yea and perhaps his talent
> May be so bonie and so large of gripe,
> That it may shake all Babilon.
>
> (Dekker, *Whore*, F2^v)

Juxtaposed with this, Cranmer's vision seems bloodless: the phoenix's 'talents' are blunt, and (as Julia Gasper has noted) although Cranmer makes several biblical allusions in the course of his prophecy, he refers each time to Old Testament prophets and resolutely avoids the Book of Revelation, the principal source text for Protestant apocalyptic visions of a final showdown with Rome (Gasper, *Dragon*, 97). In fact, Dekker's ferocity was directed at, not shared with, his sovereign, who showed no desire whatsoever to 'shake all Babilon': on the contrary, his principal interest lay in the establishment of peace across Europe through dynastic marriage. In this context, the direct connection that the prophecy appears to make between Henry VIII and James I as protagonists of a truly Reformed England is at best exhortatory, at worst unconvincing.

Royal reputations

Perhaps a stronger connection could have been drawn instead between Henry VIII and his young namesake, Henry, Prince of Wales, prior to his death. After all, the name of Henry VIII brings with it images of a powerful, militaristic, reforming king keen on a vigorous European foreign policy. And the young Prince Henry was, in Patrick Collinson's words:

> an ardent figure whose very name (as an echo of Henry VIII), together with a reputation for soundness in religion,

promised to bring about that convergence of military glory, macho monarchy and protestant zeal which was the natural potential of the English Reformation.

(Collinson, 130)

Official representations of Prince Henry, however, steered clear of making a direct connection between the two Henries, and on the odd occasion that a parallel was suggested, it was with a degree of circumspection.[1] The status of Henry VIII in the eyes of English Protestants in the reign of James I was, in fact, by no means secure. True, there was little doubt in the public's mind of the importance of the Henrician schism, and there were many images of Henry as a hero of the struggle against Catholicism: a good example is an engraving in John Foxe's *Acts and Monuments* (1583) in which Henry uses Pope Clement as a footstool while receiving the Bible from Cranmer and Cromwell (see Fig. 14). True, too, a popular cultural tradition – that of 'Bluff-King-Harry' – had been established under Elizabeth which showed Henry VIII in a positive light of sorts. He appears – as a kind of Prince Hal in a body more like that of Falstaff, and often in the company of his Fool, Will Summers – in a variety of Elizabethan prose works, most notably Thomas Nashe's *Unfortunate Traveller* and Thomas Deloney's *Jack of Newbury*, in which he is represented as a temperamental, boisterous character, partial to duelling and practical jokes, who evokes loyalty and patriotism wherever he goes. But this tradition would have had limited appeal for militant Protestants, since its ideological function is to divert attention both from the serious business of Reformation and from the actual violence and absolutism of Henry VIII's reign. It would, in

1   When the painter Robert Peake was commissioned to produce a portrait of the young Prince in 1603, he did indeed turn to an image (the best-known image) of Henry VIII as the basis for his work, but only as channelled through a depiction of a more unequivocally Reforming royal. The Prince's pose was based, predictably enough, on Holbein's famous painting of Henry VIII (as reproduced on the title-page of the appropriately named *When You See Me, You Know Me*), but specifically in the form in which it had been reinterpreted by an earlier court painter, William Scrots, for his portrait of Henry VIII's son, the boy King Edward VI (Strong, 114).

14 Engraving from Foxe, *Acts and Monuments* (1583), showing Henry using the Pope as a footstool

any case, seem an entirely inappropriate image for the young, earnest Prince Henry.

Jacobeans, like modern historians, did not make an automatic equation between the English Reformation and the Henrician schism, preferring in many cases to regard Henry VIII's children Edward and Elizabeth as the genuine reformers. This is apparent in a 1613 sermon which lists the royal Protestant inheritance:

> It was in the *defence* of Religion, that made *Dauid, Salomon, Iosias, Constantine, Edward* the 6. Queene

> *Elizabeth*, and our late blessed Prince *Henry* so honoured,
> that their names amongst all true hearted *Protestants*, are
> like a precious oyntment, their remembrance is sweet as
> hony, and as Musicke at a banquet of wine.
>
> (Price, *London's*, H2ʳ)

Henry VIII is conspicuous by his absence from this list (as, too, is
James I). Again, for William Warner, in his *Albion's England*
(reprinted in 1612), although Henry VIII was unquestionably the
king who had 'abolished the long time usurped Supremacie of the
Bishops of *Rome*', he was neither the first to think up the idea of
schism nor himself a truly successful reformer:

> [w]hatsoever by this death-prevented King the Father in
> Religion and Church-rites remained unreformed, was by
> his blessed Sonne King *Edward* the sixth happily per-
> fected[, b]ut more absolutely by his world-admired
> Daughter *Elizabeth*.
>
> (Warner, 398)[1]

This equivocation is typical: Protestants acknowledged the importance of the Henrician schism but could not forget Henry's prior
behaviour as Defender of the (Roman Catholic) Faith and thus as
a vigorous persecutor of Protestants (see King, *Tudor*, 138).[2]

Foxe, too, picks his words with great care when writing of
Henry VIII, noting that 'as touching the king, . . . here is nothing
spoken but to his laud and praise' (Foxe 1563, 682), yet offering
a series of equivocal metaphors for Henry VIII's actions:

---

1 Cf. Sir Thomas Browne's later assertion that '[i]t is an unjust scandall of our adver-
saries, and a grosse error in our selves, to compute the Nativity of our Religion from
Henry the eight, who though he rejected the Pope, refus'd not the faith of *Rome*, and
effected no more then what his owne Predecessors desired and assayed in ages past,
and was conceived the State of *Venice* would have attempted in our dayes' (Browne,
64–5).

2 King ('Henry') notes that Foxe deployed Stephen Gardiner, Bishop of Winchester,
as a scapegoat for Henry, deflecting much of the responsibility for persecution of
Protestants under Henry onto the Bishop; this attitude to Gardiner persists, as King
observes, in *Henry VIII*.

> Although it cannot be denied, but kinge Henry . . .
> deserued also prayse & renown for his valiant and vertu-
> ous beginninge: Yet if he had proceded so hardeli,
> according as happely he begonne: and like as he crakt the
> Popes crowne, and raysed his name, so if he had clene
> dispossessed him of al: or as he hadde once got the vicory
> [*sic*] ouer him, so if he had pursued his victory got: And
> . . . like as he had once unhorsed the Pope and put him
> out of the sadle, so if he had also taken awaye his trapers
> [i.e. trappings] and sturruppes wherby the prelates went
> aboute to set him on his horse againe. Then had his actes
> ioyning a perfect ende to his godly beginning, deserued a
> firme memory of much commendation.

(Foxe 1563, 675)

For Foxe, Henry was to be trusted only when he had godly advisers about him (he lists 'Quene Anne, L. Cromewel. B. Cranmer.
M. Denney, D. Buts' under this heading), but not 'when sinestre
and wicked counsaile vnder subtile and craftye pretences had got-
ten once the fote in' (682); and he concludes his assessment by
noting that '[t]he death of this kinge, as it tooke away a valiant, and
Martiall prince out of this life so it brought no little tranquility
and libertye to the church of England' (682). For Foxe's readers,
then, comparisons between Henry VIII and either James I or his
son would be neither comfortable nor appropriate.

There was one play, though, about the reign of Henry VIII,
written at an earlier date but revived in 1613, which seems to have
offered a positive connection of sorts between the reigns. Samuel
Rowley's *When You See Me, You Know Me* is a comical history
which draws heavily on the 'Bluff-King-Harry' tradition but
which offers the young Edward VI, not the festive, peremptory
Henry VIII, as the moral figurehead in the overt struggle between
Protestant and Catholic that the play depicts. According to Judith
Doolin Spikes, in a controversial essay on the notion of the 'Elect
Nation' in Jacobean history plays, the 'glorification of Prince

Edward' in *When You See Me* 'appears to mirror a hopeful expectation that the waverings of James and the uncertainties of his government might be peacefully resolved under his successor' (Spikes, 130). Although the play was written in 1604, when Henry was only ten years old and had yet to develop the militant identity and separate court that came to signal his differences from his would-be peacemaker father, it is noticeable that Edward is referred to in the course of the play as 'Prince of Wales' (even though historically plans for his investiture with that title had been curtailed by the death of his father), and certainly by 1613, when the play was reissued, it would be difficult not to think of the premature death of the young, vehemently Protestant Edward as a foreshadowing of the loss of Prince Henry.[1]

When You See Me looks to Edward, not to his father, to develop England into a truly Protestant nation. Edward is educated by Cranmer in Protestant ways of thinking, ensuring that he rejects the ideas he hears from his 'Sister *Marie* and her Tutors' (G3ᵛ), and develops a sense of his future leadership role in a country which 'stands wauering in her Faith, / Betwixt the Papists and the Protestants' (G3ᵛ). In the midst of the debate between Queen Catherine Parr and the Catholic Bishops Gardiner and Bonner, in which the King is seen to waver from one side to the other, Edward receives letters from his sisters. Mary encourages him to pray to the saints, Elizabeth 'to shun Idolatrie' (I2ᵛ), and he rejects his elder sister's advice, aligning himself with Elizabeth: 'in thy vertues will I meditate,' he announces, 'To Christ Ile onely pray for me and thee: / This I imbrace, away Idolatrie' (I2ᵛ). Edward is thus confirmed as a true believer, sharing Elizabeth's status as divinely appointed Protestant ruler. This makes the absence from *Henry VIII* of any mention of Edward (or of his mother, Jane Seymour) quite striking, though circumstances provide one obvious

1 The title-pages of *When You See Me* in 1605 and 1613 both state that the play was acted by the 'Prince of Wales his servants', who in January 1613 became the Elector Palatine's Men, suggesting a natural transfer of patronage to Princess Elizabeth's new Protestant husband as well as the company's presumed allegiance to the cause.

reason for the omission. It would hardly have been tactful for the King's Company to offer an image of Prince Henry in a play first performed so soon after his death. Moreover, since we cannot know exactly when *Henry VIII* was written, there is nothing to say either that the text was anywhere near its final form when the Prince's death was announced or indeed that, if it had been changed in the process of or prior to performance, the original version had been written with Henry in mind. In fact, while the Prince was alive, an Edward VI play would have been appropriate enough; but by late November 1612 it would be better to concentrate on a Princess Elizabeth with glorious prospects than on a Prince of Wales whose promise was abruptly curtailed.[1] Certainly, the Prologue to *Henry VIII* denies any relationship with *When You See Me*, warning that members of the audience who have come to see 'a merry, bawdy play, / A noise of targets, or to see a fellow / In a long motley coat guarded with yellow, / Will be deceived' (Prologue 14–17).[2] The carnivalesque degradation of the 'Bluff-King-Harry' tradition is thus rejected, and only the attributes required to make the King appear 'true' to the

---

1 It could be argued, too, that Shakespeare would have had a good personal, or at least professional, reason to avoid any reference to the young Prince of Wales. In probably the first of his plays performed at the Blackfriars theatre – *The Winter's Tale* – Shakespeare had provided an unwitting prophecy of the death of Henry – unwitting because Henry's death a couple of years later was sudden and unexpected, but prophetic because, as Simon Palfrey has argued, it seems already to have been clear to Shakespeare that the 'unspeakable comfort' that Henry's revived chivalric world seemed to promise was out of kilter with the way of things in James's reign: 'To silence Mamillius', argues Palfrey, 'is to kill not only the exclusive, aristocratic romance which the play from its inception appears both to invoke and undermine, but also any hope that the transformatory optimism of the genre might be brushed up into something new, something less beholden to courtly violence' (Palfrey, 112). On the other hand, since *The Winter's Tale* appears to have been performed as part of the celebrations for the wedding of Princess Elizabeth and the Elector Palatine, it is possible that the play's movement from the grimness of Mamillius's death to the optimism of the resurrection of Hermione may have taken on new and positive allegorical significance after Henry's death.

2 Joseph Candido has suggested, in an essay rejecting 'Providential' readings of the play, that Shakespeare's portrait of an erratic king 'is a distinctly "Rowleyan" one': Shakespeare and Fletcher's Henry VIII, 'like Rowley's, is neither "high-priest" nor villain; he is merely a robust and impulsive man [who] sways violently with the passion of the moment' (Candido, 54). This seems to me, though helpful, to underestimate both Henry's culpability and the relative complexity with which he is drawn in *Henry VIII*.

audience – i.e. the principal attributes that had come to be associated in popular culture with Henry VIII: the sheer size and energy of the man, his lechery and caprice, his peremptory 'Ha!' – are retained. The play rejects the crassness of the 'Bluff-King-Harry' model not in order to shield the King from the audience's critical gaze but to produce a Henry who is both much more complex and much more culpable than might otherwise be the case.

The conscience of the King

The King and his conscience are, after all, highly culpable. We first hear Henry discussing his restless conscience in Act 2, when he is momentarily regretting his decision to divorce Katherine.[1] 'O my lord,' he asks Wolsey, 'Would it not grieve an able man to leave / So sweet a bedfellow?' and before the Cardinal has had time to work out a reply, Henry provides his own answer: 'But conscience, conscience', he sighs, 'O, 'tis a tender place, and I must leave her' (2.2.139–2). It is clear that Henry is thinking in sexual terms, boasting of his 'ability' in bed and acknowledging his reluctance to give up an attractive partner. But to what, exactly, is he referring in the phrase 'tender place'? One possible answer is given in the next scene, and is underlined, as Paul Jesson notes (Jesson, 123), by the way in which Anne Bullen's opening line, 'Not for that neither' (2.3.1), can be played as an instant rejection of Henry's rhetorical (and hypocritical) question if, in performance, the two scenes are run together without a break (as would almost certainly have been the case at the Globe or Blackfriars). In 2.3, Anne's ostensible innocence is put under considerable pressure by her dialogue with a knowing Old Lady who seems to have been drawn from Rojas's *Celestina* (Round, 100–9), and it is the Old Lady's heavy innuendo when speaking of 'the capacity' of Anne's 'soft cheverel conscience' to receive the King's gifts, if she 'might please to stretch it'

---

1 As Judith Anderson observes, 'our crediting the King's words and our sympathizing with his troubles are seriously impaired by what we have heard about conscience already in this play, for example, from Buckingham, who has been legally condemned for treason: "And if I have a conscience, let it sink me, / . . . if I be not faithful" (2.1.60–1)' (Anderson, 128).

(2.3.31–3), that glosses his phrasing. In Henry's momentary expression of regret at what he is about to do, conscience – that 'faculty or principle which', as the *OED* puts it, 'pronounces upon the moral quality of one's actions or motives' and which was so central to the struggles of the Reformation – is placed in a frank and unsettling relation to sexuality, and has in effect become inseparable in the King's imagination from his lover's vagina.[1]

As this might suggest, Henry's masculinity is in crisis in this play. In the final scene he shouts out with happiness after Cranmer has spoken his prophecy over Elizabeth. 'Thou hast made me now a man', he cries, adding that 'Never before / This happy child did I get anything' (5.4.63–4) – a curious claim, since although none of Katherine of Aragon's male children survived beyond infancy, their daughter Mary was very much alive and the suggestion that Henry's masculinity has only now finally been established by his fathering of another baby girl is implausible. But his comments underline the anxiety in evidence throughout the play about the King's manliness, an anxiety which is at its most apparent in the narrative he offers in explanation of his 'conscientious', if rather belated, decision to part from Katherine on the grounds that, since she was his brother's widow, he should never have married her in the first place.

The narrative focuses on the debilitating effect that his failure to produce a male heir has had on his internal well being. He begins nervously – 'Now, what moved me to't' (to the divorce, that is), 'I will be bold with time and your attention: / Then mark th'inducement. Thus it came: give heed to't' (2.4.164–6) – and then he tries to explain:

> My conscience first received a tenderness,
> Scruple and prick, on certain speeches uttered
> By th' Bishop of Bayonne, then French ambassador,
> Who had been hither sent on the debating
> A marriage 'twixt the Duke of Orléans and

---

1   Anderson effectively makes this point, if rather obliquely: 'The least the "tender place" can mean here is a bed' (Anderson, 129).

> Our daughter Mary. I'th' progress of this business,
> Ere a determinate resolution, he –
> I mean the Bishop – did require a respite,
> Wherein he might the King his lord advertise
> Whether our daughter were legitimate
> Respecting this our marriage with the dowager,
> Sometimes our brother's wife. This respite shook
> The bosom of my conscience, entered me,
> Yea, with a spitting power, and made to tremble
> The region of my breast; which forced such way
> That many mazed considerings did throng
> And pressed in with this caution. First, methought
> I stood not in the smile of heaven, who had
> Commanded nature that my lady's womb,
> If it conceived a male child by me, should
> Do no more offices of life to't than
> The grave does to the dead: for her male issue
> Or died where they were made, or shortly after
> This world had aired them. Hence I took a thought
> This was a judgement on me, that my kingdom –
> Well worthy the best heir o'th' world – should not
> Be gladded in't by me. Then follows that
> I weighed the danger which my realms stood in
> By this my issue's fail, and that gave to me
> Many a groaning throe. Thus hulling in
> The wild sea of my conscience, I did steer
> Toward this remedy whereupon we are
> Now present here together[.]

$$(2.4.167–199)$$

Henry's masculinity is under direct threat here. We have already seen the implications of 'tenderness' (167), and 'prick' (168) is a basic enough pun. As the King tells the story, it is clear that doubt about Mary's legitimacy has had a penetrating effect on his selfhood: it impales him, 'enter[s]' him 'with a spitting power' (179–80). He even adopts a curiously maternal stance as his need for an heir resolves itself into a kind of phantom pregnancy, the 'danger' (194) that gives him '[m]any a groaning throe' (196).[1] The speech thoroughly compromises Henry's manliness, and despite his acknowledgement of the symptoms, there is no suggestion that he is aware that what lies behind his failure to father an heir might not be his wife's supposed inability to produce a healthy son but rather his own immoderation.

Early modern man inherited from classical tradition certain anxieties about sexual expenditure. Careful pacing of sexual activity was considered important, both because excess might lead to illness and 'because in sexual activity in general man's mastery, strength, and life were at stake' (Foucault, *Sexuality*, 125). The act of sex was thought to diminish a man, and he therefore had a responsibility to avoid indulging in excessive periods of sexual heat that might threaten his control of the sexual act and thus his manliness (*Seed*, 317).[2] It is heat that is at issue the first time we directly witness Henry's own brand of immoderation. When the King appears in disguise at Wolsey's party and dances with, and then kisses, Anne Bullen, the Cardinal attempts to divert his master. 'Your grace, / I fear, with dancing is a little heated', he says to Henry, who appears wryly to acknowledge the dangers implicit in his behaviour: 'I fear too much', he agrees (1.4.99–101). Wolsey then points out that '[t]here's fresher air . . . / In the next chamber' (1.4.101–2), and when Henry orders the dancers to lead their partners into the adjoining room, it seems that the Cardinal has succeeded in reminding his master of his responsibilities. But Henry immediately follows his order by ensuring that Anne remains his 'partner' (1.4.103) and announcing further drinking and dancing, and we find ourselves witnessing Wolsey's first failure to exercise control over his immoderate sovereign (a failure which implies that Anne's rise will in due course lead to Wolsey's fall).

---

1   In conjunction with the sailing metaphor, this echoes Prospero's oddly maternal experience adrift at sea with Miranda: 'Thou didst smile, / Infused with a fortitude from heaven, / When I have decked the sea with drops full salt, / Under my burden groaned, which raised in me / An undergoing stomach to bear up / Against what should ensue' (*Tem* 1.2.153–8).
2   See Laqueur for discussion of this and other (Aristotelian and Galenic) traditions.

Henry, the 'great voluptuary', is thus seen to be incapable of the moderation required of a 'proper' man. His inability to control his lust for Anne Bullen undermines the very manliness of the urges that drive him to flirt with her, both because he ought, as an 'able man', to be capable not only of expressing but also of controlling his passions and because his very enthusiasm for unlimited sexual activity threatens the future of the realm by sapping his procreative potential.

Moderation thus becomes a key issue in the contrast between good and bad that the play sets up, between Wolsey and Buckingham, between Wolsey and Cranmer, between Henry and virtually everyone else, a contrast which is dependent upon a basic humanist antithesis between:

> the intemperate prodigal whose concern with immediate gratification is expressed as the consumption of wealth . . . and the prudent or temperate man concerned with a longer-term calculation of profit.
>
> (Hutson, 'Chivalry', 45)[1]

Appropriately, it is not, as the nobles assume, Wolsey's letter to the Pope informing him of the progress of the divorce that at last provokes Henry's wrath, but the inventory of the secretly hoarded possessions that Wolsey has unwittingly included in the packet of letters he sent to the King. Wolsey is the very personification of excess, of immoderation: 'No man's pie', Buckingham tells us, 'is freed / From his ambitious finger' (1.1.52–3); he is a 'butcher's cur' (120), a 'keech' who 'can with his very bulk / Take up the rays o'th' beneficial sun / And keep it from the earth' (55–7). Cranmer, on the other hand, as the exemplary Protestant, is characterized by his sense of the eventual sorting of the wheat and the chaff at the day of judgement. This is, in fact, what makes Gardiner, Bishop of Winchester, so much more implacable as Cranmer's foe than Wolsey ever was. The play's Gardiner has a strong belief in the need for moderation and restraint (a characterization which would probably have amused the audience,

---

1   See also Hutson, *Usurer's*, 115–51, 173–4.

since the Southwark brothels had flourished on the manors of the Bishop of Winchester and the Globe stood within yards of the Bishop's palace), a belief which is most evident when he lectures a passing pageboy on the obligation to take rest in the hours of darkness even as the King plays cards by candlelight: 'These should be hours for necessities, / Not for delights; times to repair our nature / With comforting repose, and not for us / To waste these times' (5.1.2–5).[1] This Lenten rejection of pleasures, though, marks the opposite boundary of the temperate from that occupied by his master; in his failure to recognize that leading the temperate life does not entail the outright renunciation of pleasures but rather their proper distribution across the course of a life, he becomes the play's Malvolio.[2] It is, in fact, the paradoxical excess of Gardiner's zeal for and expression of his sense of the moderate and the appropriate that enables the unshakeably temperate Cranmer to escape his plot in Act 5. In view of the iconography of Truth and Time that, as we have seen, underpins the play, the resonances of 'temperance' accrue considerable significance.

Truth and temperance

In early modern England, 'temperance' seems to have signified both moderation and timeliness, both self-restraint and the ability to capitalize on the moment.[3] Certainly, in *Henry VIII*, the King's

---

1   On Gardiner and the stews, see Archer, 252.
2   See Foucault, *Sexuality*, 57–8; and cf. p. 22.
3   Hutson notes that the idea of temperance as a combination of moderation and timeliness is evident in Machiavelli's work and that in England a translation of Dominicus Mancinus's *De Quattuor Virtutibus* by George Turberville 'disseminated a similar if simplified version of the Ciceronian version of temperance for the unlearned reader' (Hutson, 'Chivalry', 47). Interestingly, she also notes that in 1544 Anthony Cope, who was chamberlain to Queen Katherine Parr, dedicated a translation of Livy to Henry VIII with a prefatory discussion of the brevity of opportunity afforded a man by Time and a consequent injunction that Henry 'tempre dispose and conueigh all his procedynges' to 'brynge theim to effecte, with prosperous successe', on the grounds that 'as [Occasion] cometh towarde a man, he may take sure holde of her, by hir longe heares[; b]ut in case he mysse to take than his holde, suffrying hir to passe by him: than is there no holde to be taken of hir behynde, but that she runneth awaie without recouerie' (Cope, A2ᵛ; Hutson, 'Chivalry', 48). It appears that the idea of temperance as signifying both moderation and timeliness was firmly established by Henry VIII's reign and even perhaps that it was possible to suggest politely that the King still had room for improvement in this regard.

15 *Henry VIII dining in the Privy Chamber*, drawing by an unknown artist of the
   North German School, probably dating from the early seventeenth century

failure of manhood is presented as a failure of temperance in both
senses, a failure to adopt an appropriately moderate lifestyle and a
failure to keep appropriate hours (see Fig. 15). This understanding
of the relationship of timeliness and manliness provides us with a
key perspective on the way in which the King is marginalized, personally and dynastically, at the culmination of the play. As we have
observed, the final scene depends in part for its success on the
iconography of Truth and on its particular association with Queen
Elizabeth, offering a vignette familiar from the image of *veritas filia
temporis* in which the baby Elizabeth, at the moment of her christening – her entry into membership of the Church of England – is
identified with the Protestant appropriation of Truth within an
apocalyptic framework. The visual image of Time deployed in the

debates over temperance was usually that of Time as Occasion, often represented iconographically as a young woman (or sometimes old man) being led by the forelock by a suitably temperate man (see Fig. 13), but here, as we have seen, it is clearly the other, apocalyptic image of Time and Truth that is invoked.

In order to function successfully in relation to the iconography, however, the *veritas filia temporis* vignette requires the presence of the figure of Time as Truth's father, a figure who would logically be represented by Henry, the baby Elizabeth's natural father. But it is clear that the role of Time cannot morally be taken by the play's Henry. His immoderation – his woeful lack of temperance – means that an identification with Time is out of the question. Thus, as we have observed, what the audience sees at this crucial moment of the play in the position of Truth's father is not Henry but Cranmer. It is Cranmer who extends the christening process by speaking the play's culminating prophecy of Elizabeth and of James, rhetorically generating the male heir whom Henry is incapable of fathering biologically. It is Cranmer who insists on the truth of his words and whose stance – that of an authoritative man in a protective, redemptive relationship with a young girl – becomes that of the iconographic representation of Time delivering Truth from the grip of hell.[1] Far, then, from providing a justification of Henry's assertion that his political and personal strength has grown by the end of the play (5.2.215) – Geoffrey Bullough, for example, believed that, though the play's Henry is 'a man of sensual lust and self-will', he does grow 'in wisdom and benevolence as the drama proceeds' (Bullough, 450) – the final tableau shows us a king whose intemperance is a failure of manliness and therefore of political efficacy and who must be replaced by a Protestant martyr as a symbolic

---

1   Placing Henry in the role would be particularly inappropriate (and Cranmer, as a martyr, notably more appropriate) since, if the origins of the image in medieval depictions of the harrowing of hell are taken into account, the stooping, redeeming figure in the tableau is that of Christ. Thomas Brightman (1609) specifically identifies 'Thomas Cromwell . . . as the avenging angel with the scythe in his hand, and Thomas Cranmer as the soul from out of the altar' (Firth, 170); he does not mention King Henry.

father-figure for a reformed England. The iconography thus decentres the King, removing him from full paternity and leaving the circumstances of Elizabeth's birth (and consequently her legitimacy) as shrouded as is her death in Cranmer's prophecy. Henry may claim to have been 'made a man' by this girl, by the 'getting' of Elizabeth, but Cranmer's unexpected centrality in this reworked iconographic tableau sets up Elizabeth and her reign as the offspring not of an intemperate, and therefore finally unmanly, monarch but of an alternative, spiritual figure who is far better placed, as a representative of the tribulations and therefore of the triumphs (not yet achieved but fully imagined) of the English Reformation, to provide an ideological bridge from Henrician to Jacobean England (see Fig. 16).

Moreover, a further, covert layer of iconographic potential in the christening scene exacerbates the discomfort of this moment for the audience. The reference to 'Saba' (the Queen of Sheba) in Cranmer's prophecy (5.4.23) obliquely associates the young Elizabeth with Solomon, implying her vicarious adoption of his attributes (notably that of wisdom) and echoing the equation that was made between Solomon and Frederick, the Elector Palatine, as his marriage to Princess Elizabeth approached in 1613.[1] It also extends the connections that had at various times been drawn both between Henry VIII and King David as restorers of true religion (most notably in relation to David as psalmist: see King, 'Henry') and between James I and David as kings who brought union to their respective nations (see Fig. 17).[2] David, though, was no saint,

1   The Queen of Sheba's visit to Solomon is recounted in 1 Kings, 10. James, in his *Basilikon Doron*, addressed to Prince Henry, advises his son to keep a virtuous court, so 'that when strangers shall visite your Court, they may with the Queene of Sheba, admire your wisedome in the glorie of your house, and comely order among your servants' (McIlwain, 33), presumably implying that his relationship to his son is like that of David to Solomon; Frederick therefore inherits Solomon's wisdom from Henry. As William Tate has pointed out, James himself was also at times associated with Solomon as well as David, though mostly after 1613.

2   The minister Andrew Willet, for example, made both connections: in his *A Treatise of Salomon's Marriage* (1612), he makes a direct correlation between Frederick and Solomon and, by implication, between Elizabeth and Sheba. Willet's *Certain Fruitful Meditations* compares the uniting of England and Scotland under James with that of Judah and Israel under David: 'I trust that God hath raised vp another Dauid to his Israel of England' (D4ʳ).

16 *Thomas Cranmer*, painting by Gerlach Flicke, 1546.

and the story of his relationship with Bathsheba, particularly
when read in the context of the marginalizing of Henry VIII at
this key moment of the play, offers an additional, politically unsettling possibility. The account in 2 Samuel, 11–12, of David's

17 *Henry VIII with a Harp, as David*, with Will Summers, his fool, from *Henry VIII's Psalter*, c. 1530–40

desire for and adultery with the beautiful Bathsheba, his arrangement for the death in battle of her husband Uriah, and his subsequent repentance for these sins following his denunciation by the prophet Nathan was one of the best-known of all Old Testament stories, and a tradition had developed which associated David's 'Penitential Psalms' with the Bathsheba story.[1]

---

1   The Penitential Psalms are a traditional grouping of Psalms 6, 32, 38, 51, 102, 130 and 143. On the iconography, see Ewbank, 'David', 3–40; Zim, 70–74; Parkes, 175, plate 88; Fisher, aa2ʳ; the tradition focused particularly on the image of David watching Bathsheba bathing. I am grateful to Richard Proudfoot for suggesting the relevance of the David and Bathsheba story. There is also a later, extra-biblical, visual tradition in which an old woman acts as go-between for David and Bathsheba, occupying a role similar to that of the eponymous panderess in Rojas's *Celestina*, who in turn may have influenced the characterization of the Old Lady in 2.3 (see Commentary, 2.3n.).

Reformation readings tended to treat the story baldly as an instance of the shame and inevitability of sin and the necessity of repentance, but it was a narrative which took on uncomfortable significance in respect of Henry's extra-marital activities.[1] Sir Thomas Wyatt, for instance – who was rumoured to have had an affair with Anne Bullen before the King met her, and who wrote verse translations of the Penitential Psalms – seems to have seen Henry and David as analogous, not as restorers of right religion but as royal lovers prepared to go to murderous lengths to consummate illicit desire (Zim, 73–4; Greenblatt, 115, 146–7).[2]

It would be hard to deny the implications this story held for Henry, particularly in view of the repeated deaths either at birth or in infancy of his male children, since David's penitence in the biblical story is such that God lets him live, but punishes him with the death of his first child by Bathsheba. It is the conception and birth of Solomon in the wake of this grim event that marks the return of God's favour. *Henry VIII* draws on this, implicitly equating Cranmer with Nathan and Henry with David – God's anointed, but not always entirely reliable, king. The birth of Elizabeth thus heralds the return of God's favour to His chosen nation in the wake of irreligious behaviour on the part of her father. This has its echo in the direct connection made in 1612–13 between Solomon and Frederick in treatises such as Willet's *Salomon's Marriage*: rechristening Princess Elizabeth's fiancé in this way makes the wedding a marker of the return of divine favour to England, and provides a fitting and optimistic conclusion to the play

---

1 Unadorned emphasis on shame and repentance partly embodied a reaction to a Roman Catholic tradition of fairly breathtaking licence in which David's desire for Bathsheba was interpreted as Christ's desire for his Church, Uriah became the 'Prince of this World', and David's adultery was conveniently reworked as his rescue of the Church from the Devil (Réau, 273–7; Zim, 70; Tyndale, 135^v–136^r).

2 Arabella Stuart, writing to James I on the touchy subject of divorce, mentions (presumably in reference to Henry VIII) certain English 'Princes' who 'have left [a precedent] as little imitable for so good and gratious a Kinge as your Ma^{ty} as Davids dealing wth Uriah' (Stuart).

which foreshadows the ultimate happy ending of the Protestant *comœdia apocalyptica*.[1]

Yet the Jacobean audience could make a further, dangerous, topical interpretation in the context both of the play's insistent juxtaposition of Henrician and Jacobean England and of some of the published responses to the death of Henry, Prince of Wales.[2] Peacham's *Period of Mourning*, for example, offers six overtly Spenserian 'visions', presenting different emblems of Henry as warrior for, and patron of, Truth (Peacham, B3ʳ).[3] The conspicuous omission of James from these apocalyptic visions implies that, with Henry gone, Truth lacks a warrior; it is only a short step from omission to implication and the suggestion that James was himself responsible, through negligence of the godly cause, for his son's death. It was even rumoured at the time of the funeral that James, jealous of his son's popularity, had had him murdered.[4] The David and Bathsheba story could thus be read as criticism not just of Henry VIII, but also of James I.[5] These uncomfortable images both foreground the play's underlying coherence as a *comœdia apocalyptica*, a play whose basic pattern is that of the story of Christian redemption, and at the same time underline the ways in which the play resists this linear

1   It would certainly make more sense to Protestants than the Solomon/James I correlation that was being established at this time. The first recorded occasion on which this particular typology was tried out became a fine example of royal immoderation: 'after dinner, the representation of Solomon his Temple and the coming of the Queen of Sheba was made. . . . The entertainment and show went forward, and most of the presenters went backward, or fell down; wine did so occupy their upper chambers. Now did appear, in rich dress, Hope, Faith, and Charity. . . . Charity . . . made obeysance and brought giftes, but said she would return home again. . . . She then returned to Hope and Faith, who were both sick and spewing in the lower hall' (McClure, 119–20).

2   On Prince Henry's death as divine retribution, see Kay, 134.

3   See the useful discussion of Peacham in Kay, 157–60.

4   On rumours of James's responsibility for his son's death, see Gardiner, 2.72.

5   Spedding unwittingly acknowledged this when deprecating the 'defects' of the play, suggesting that '[i]t is as if Nathan's rebuke to David had ended, not with the doom of death to the child, but with a prophetic promise of the felicities of Solomon' (Spedding, 116).

structure.[1] It is thus possible to read the last scene of *Henry VIII* in two ways, each of which is appropriate both to the Henrician subject matter and to the Jacobean context – as a propagandistic celebration of a direct line of Protestant monarchy from Henry to Elizabeth to James, and as an awkward, unsettling depiction of an England whose King has not fully understood the nature of his responsibilities towards the continuing Reformation. The play thus invites the members of its audience to interpret their own history, giving them the choice of seeing the play as either a celebration of Stuart power or a questioning of the state of the Reformation ten years into James I's reign.

Truth and textuality

To write a play about Henry VIII in 1612–13, then, is to tap into a history of equivocal representations that obliges the audience to seek its own interpretation of Reformation history, one only possible with the benefit of hindsight. I have no doubt that only a small portion, at best, of the audience would immediately have thought of the iconography of *veritas filia temporis* or the story of David and Bathsheba as they watched the last scene of *Henry VIII*, but I am equally sure that the bulk of the audience would have felt the political resonances of these visual and verbal originals and would therefore not have experienced the play as the unquestioning royalist propaganda that critics have traditionally

---

1   They also underline a certain continuity between Cranmer's speech and Henrician popular tradition. Alistair Fox notes that apocalyptic political prophecies were 'widespread' in the Tudor period, and that they 'had a far greater social and political importance than is often supposed[, providing] a means for Englishmen to objectify their fears and hopes concerning developments in Henry VIII's reign. . . . Politically, they were important because both supporters and opponents of Henry's reform policy used them as propaganda' (Fox, 78). He adds that these prophecies 'were an instrument whereby ordinary Englishmen could objectify their feelings about the course history was taking' (89–90): 'To see past and future political disturbances as part of an apocalyptic pattern with a happy outcome was to make them bearable. Moreover, the foreseen deliverance allowed people to invest their trust in the Tudor dynasty, and then when that dynasty seemed, to some, to be failing them after the break with Rome, to endure the dynasty in a hope that the real deliverance was yet to come' (91). On the importance of the political prophecy as a Tudor genre, see Taylor, *Prophecy*, and Firth.

assumed it to be. Both the self-consciousness of the deployment of textual undercurrents in the play and the lack of a linear dynamic make this quite impossible.

For one thing, Cranmer's prophecy may come as a final revelation and may offer Elizabeth's birth as the fulfilment of a *comœdia apocalyptica*, yet the play as a whole seems anything but apocalyptic in its treatment of time and narrative. For Paul Dean, *Henry VIII* offers no 'organic and cumulative movement toward a single concluding point' (Dean, 178), and Frank Cespedes argues that the play, despite its status as a 'history play', annuls teleology, emphasizing the uncertainties of narrative over the optimistic principle of providential history in order to question the availability of an 'omniscient' perspective on historical events (Cespedes, 416–17). As the action unfolds, we see a series of events offered sequentially rather than causally: Buckingham's fall at the hands of an ex-employee manipulated by Wolsey; Henry's political innocence in contrast with Wolsey's efficient control of events; Anne Bullen's rise and Katherine of Aragon's gradual decline; the eventual divorce of Henry and Katherine; the sudden decline and death of Wolsey; the death of Katherine; the birth of Elizabeth; and the attempt by the Privy Council to remove Cranmer. By the end of the council scene, Henry claims to be at the heart of a sustained, mutual process of political development – 'So I grow stronger, you more honour gain' (5.2.215) – and Cranmer's prophecy appears to confirm the progress that has been made (Ard^2, lxi). Yet, as we have seen, the final scene of the play offers at best highly circumscribed, provisional confirmation. For Ivo Kamps, 'despite the christening scene's power and pathos, Cranmer's effort to produce dramatic and historical closure . . . is undercut by other historical "voices" of the play' (Kamps, 105). Bill Readings takes this argument a stage further. For him:

> the play's purely sequential plotting mirrors the procession scenes: political power is to be understood less as a matter of actions in causal patterns giving rise to effects

than as a question of momentary precedence within an order that is given to the eye.

(Readings, 288)

The sequence of events, from this perspective, is arbitrary, and we are left with a strong sense that, for all the pomp and acclaim of the christening – and particularly since we are aware both of Henry's disappointment at the birth of a daughter and of the fractures within the hasty construction of a dynastic logic for the transition from Elizabeth to James – no great revelation or conviction of future revelation has been achieved.

Most critics have in fact argued that history is represented in the play not as pure sequence but as cycle. As Clifford Leech noted forty years ago, of all the 'late' plays, *Henry VIII* appears the most heavily invested in cyclical, rather than linear, time: 'Nothing is finally decided here, the pattern of future events being foreshadowed as essentially a repetition of what is here presented' (Leech, 29). *Henry VIII*, like *Troilus and Cressida*, '[l]eaps o'er the vaunt and firstlings of those broils, / Beginning in the middle' (*TC* Prologue 27–8), and we see each subsequent event in its past and future relations with others. We hear of earlier events which presage what takes place on stage in the theatrical present (the betrayal of Buckingham's father by his servant, for instance), and we witness events which will then be played back upon their perpetrators. All successes (for example, Wolsey's finding 'evidence' against Buckingham) will return to haunt the successful (thus, Henry's finding 'evidence' against Wolsey), and our knowledge of the history of Henry's life means that we know the way the King behaves towards Katherine and Anne will be replayed several more times with subsequent wives. This apparently irresistible repetition of events produces a grim irony which is more marked than in any other history play and is matched in the Shakespeare canon only by *Troilus and Cressida*, *Timon of Athens* and *The Two Noble Kinsmen*. For John Margeson:

95

[a]lthough *Henry VIII* is not continuously ironic in the way that *Troilus and Cressida* is, nevertheless the action, the characters and much of the dialogue are given an ironic colouring which creates a degree of scepticism in the audience about protestations of innocence or conscience and a sense that more than one interpretation of words and deeds is possible.

(Cam^2, 43)

Henry's crass, contingent reworkings of the concept of conscience, in other words, are only one example of a thoroughgoing scepticism about the possibility of access to the truth of motivation and of historical event that permeates the play.

To consider the nature of the play's scepticism, I want to turn back for a moment to Wotton's letter about the burning of the Globe and juxtapose it with another report of a spectacular event, Norfolk's description of the Field of the Cloth of Gold at the beginning of Act 1 (1.1.13–38). Critics agree that this opening scene is representative of the play as a whole 'in its insistence on the second-hand nature of our acquaintance with historical events' (Dean, 182), and Norfolk's testimony chimes with Wotton's in several ways. It is, as Gasper notes, 'an artful piece of time-release poetry . . . which appears to be a panegyric of the court, but which reveals more and more scepticism, disgust and ridicule the more often we read it' (Gasper, 'Reform,' 208). Initially, we are happy to take Norfolk's glorious description at face value as he describes himself to Buckingham as 'ever since a fresh admirer' (1.1.3) of the spectacle put on by the Kings of England and France during their meeting at the Field of the Cloth of Gold. 'Today the French, / All clinquant, all in gold like heathen gods, / Shone down the English', he reports (1.1.18–20), yet:

> . . . tomorrow they
> Made Britain India. Every man that stood
> Showed like a mine. . . .

> Now this masque
> Was cried incomparable; and th'ensuing night
> Made it a fool and beggar. The two kings,
> Equal in lustre, were now best, now worst,
> As presence did present them: him in eye,
> Still him in praise, and being present both,
> 'Twas said they saw but one, and no discerner
> Durst wag his tongue in censure.
>
> $$(1.1.20-22, 26-33)$$

The spectacle seems an exact correlative for the power of the kings and the significance of the occasion as the establishment of peace between two great nations. Yet within a few dozen lines we learn that the whole thing was a waste of time, producing only a temporary peace which 'not values / The cost that did conclude it' (88–9), and that the French have already broken the pact. As a result, looking back at the speech, we realize that it expressed a kind of relativism. The English and French are each viewed in light of the other, with no firm ground for judgement: 'The two kings, / Equal in lustre, were now best, now worst, / As presence did present them' (28–30). And we are forced to acknowledge the emptiness of the grand gesture that only a moment before had seemed both convincing and appropriate. Just as Wotton's letter narrates an apocalypse that is in fact nothing of the sort, so Norfolk's speech describes a significant occasion that turns out to be glitteringly meaningless.

As Lee Bliss observes, '[i]n the beginning all had seemed true to Norfolk and, in his report, to us; only in retrospect can we see how false, how truly unstable . . . that appearance was' (Bliss, 3). When we hear that the arrangement of events was such that even the exaggeratedly fictional story of Bevis of Hampton seems, in this context, credible (1.1.36–8), we realize that official ideology and actual truth are irreconcilable. We realize, too, that Norfolk's assertion that he is still an 'admirer' (3) of what he saw in France is itself a loaded comment. As Bliss points out:

> 'admire' did not signify wonder in the sense of approbation, but rather an ironic sense of amazement at the disparity between a dream of transcendent and transforming harmony and the disconcertingly mutable political realities of an impoverished nobility and a broken treaty.
>
> (Bliss, 3)

Norfolk turns out to be much less impressed than he had sounded initially. In his testimony, judgement and the truth on which judgement must be based are both entirely contingent, as is Buckingham's reaction. He appears to reserve judgement until he learns that it was Wolsey who 'set the body and the limbs / Of this great sport together' (1.1.46–7), after which he instantly dismisses the celebrations as 'fierce vanities' (54). And Norfolk himself, having made the occasion sound so spectacular and so convincing, happily takes up Buckingham's theme, treating the ceremony as the kind of thing you would expect from someone who lacks noble blood: 'There's in him stuff that puts him to these ends', he sneers, 'being not propped by ancestry' (58–9). Accolades are thus subject to attitudes, and we are put on our guard as we watch this play of ceremony and spectacle. Everything we see which at first appears impressive or convincing may well turn out to be a major disappointment.

It is clear that those observing royal spectacle, those interpellated by official ceremony, are just as frankly aware of the contingency of events as those further up the hierarchy. As the two Gentlemen provide their commentary on Anne's coronation procession, we hear the Second Gentleman respond knowingly to the new Queen's undoubted sexual charisma. He appears at first to be wholly caught up in the ceremony, but his rhapsody concludes with a suggestive, and politically dangerous, bathos. 'Heaven bless thee!' he cries out as he sees Anne –

> Thou hast the sweetest face I ever looked on.
> Sir, as I have a soul, she is an angel.
> Our King has all the Indies in his arms,
> And more, and richer, when he strains that lady,

– and then he adds, slyly: 'I cannot blame his conscience' (4.1.42–7). His friend ignores this knowing remark, but then himself returns to the transparent and unrestrained sexuality of the aristocracy just a few lines later. 'These are stars indeed –', says the Second Gentleman, in admiration of the courtly women as they process by, to which the First Gentleman adds, 'And sometimes falling ones', a remark risqué enough (laying bare, as it does, Anne's perceived route to power through sex) to produce the hasty retort 'No more of that' from his friend (54–5). Greatness is thus made both familiar and ridiculous.

The fact that we need to hear the Gentlemen's commentaries in order to establish a clear perspective on the events of the play underlines the opacity of individual motivation. As Anne Barton notes:

> [n]o soliloquies resolve the question of Buckingham's innocence or guilt, divulge Henry's genuine reason for divorcing Katherine, the extent of Wolsey's fidelity to the crown, or make it plain in what spirit Anne makes her way to Henry's bed. Judgement, as a result, or even understanding of these events which (in one sense) are being so accurately presented, becomes almost impossible.
>
> (Barton, 185)

We are denied access to the motivations of all those who experience power in the play, even once they have fallen from power and would appear to have nothing to lose by admitting what drove them on in the first place. Buckingham's last speech before execution seems to offer a formal occasion for us to learn the truth – traditionally, convicted criminals would confess their crimes and ask the King's forgiveness, and Buckingham claims that he is 'richer' than his 'base accusers, / That never knew what truth meant' (2.1.104–5) – yet his public testimony remains ambivalent.[1] He claims to forgive his enemies, yet looks forward to haunting them:

1 See Ives, 392, on the conventional pattern for a convict's last words.

> Be what they will, I heartily forgive 'em.
> Yet let 'em look they glory not in mischief
> Nor build their evils on the graves of great men,
> For then my guiltless blood must cry against 'em.
>   (2.1.65–8)

He claims he will 'cry for blessings' (90) on the King, yet he is careful to describe himself not just as Edward Bohun, Duke of Buckingham, but also as Lord High Constable, a title which would remind the audience of the Bohun family's proximity to the blood royal, quietly hinting that the real reason for his execution is the threat he could pose to the King simply by claiming his hereditary rights.[1] His language evokes Old Testament righteous indignation rather than the forgiveness for enemies enjoined in the Gospels, and his speech is expanded considerably from its source in Holinshed, obliging the audience to confront the contradictions of the verdict.[2]

We are denied access, too, to the motivations of those who are instrumental in bringing down the powerful. Once he hears the names of Court, Park and Hopkins, Buckingham immediately knows that it is his erstwhile surveyor who has betrayed him – or rather, he knows when he hears the names that his surveyor has been 'false' (1.1.222) and that Wolsey must have bribed him to provide the necessary information for the arrests that have been made. Sure enough, it is the Surveyor whom we see giving testimony against Buckingham before the King, encouraged by Wolsey, who tells him to '[s]tand forth, and with bold spirit relate' what he has 'like a careful subject . . . collected / Out of the Duke of Buckingham' (1.2.129–31). At the first climactic moment in his account, as he relates the Duke's report of the monk Hopkins's prediction that '[t]he Duke / Shall govern England' (1.2.170–1), Queen Katherine intervenes: 'If I know you well,' she says (and we can only assume that she does, because the man does not deny

1   See 2.1.102n.
2   See 2.1.64–6n.

the charge), '[y]ou were the Duke's surveyor, and lost your office / On the complaint o'th' tenants' (171–3). And she admonishes him: 'Take good heed / You charge not in your spleen a noble person / And spoil your nobler soul' (173–5). He protests that he will 'speak but truth' (177), but we have our warning, and we are already unsure of the signification of 'truth' in this play. The rest of the testimony, fragmentary and lurid though it is, is clearly enough to convince Henry of the Duke's guilt – 'He's traitor to th' height!' (214) – but the audience is surely left much less convinced. On closer inspection, this uncertainty stems not only from the fact that Wolsey is involved, nor from Katherine's observations about the possible (though unconfirmed) motivation of revenge, but from the multiple levels of the testimony: what we hear are second-hand narratives – the Surveyor's reports of the Duke's speech – and the crucial moment at which we first learn of Buckingham's ambition for the Crown comes during the Surveyor's report of the Duke's account of the monk's words.

The issue of testimony thus foregrounds the uncertainties of the play and its (for those uninclined to like the play) surprisingly subtle textuality. As Pierre Sahel notes:

> [m]ost of the events of *Henry VIII* are echoed – more or less unfaithfully – within the play itself. They are not dramatized but reported after having passed through distorting filters. Characters present incidents and occurrences – or, often, their own versions of incidents and occurrences.

> (Sahel, 145)

The effect of this filtering of events is to sustain a sense of radical uncertainty throughout the play. For Sahel, it is rumour which sets the tone: rumour sometimes as a political tool, sometimes simply as the 'buzzing' (2.1.147) which seems constantly to be going on in the background. There may be no actual figure of '*Rumour . . . painted full of tongues*' in *Henry VIII* as there is in *2 Henry IV* (Induction 0.1), but despite fears of suppression ('no discerner /

Durst wag his tongue in censure' (1.1.32–3), we are told of the Field of the Cloth of Gold), rumour is never silenced in this play. Indeed, a mutual relationship between rumour and truth is set up at the beginning of Act 2 in another of the Gentlemen's conversations. 'Did you not', asks the Second Gentleman, 'of late days hear / A buzzing of a separation / Between the King and Katherine?' (2.1.146–8). 'Yes,' replies his friend:

>   . . . but it held not
> For when the King once heard it, out of anger
> He sent command to the Lord Mayor straight
> To stop the rumour and allay those tongues
> That durst disperse it.
>
>   (148–152)

To which the Second Gentleman immediately retorts:

>   But that slander, sir,
> Is found a truth now, for it grows again
> Fresher than e'er it was, and held for certain
> The King will venture at it.
>
>   (152–5)

The clause 'held for certain' neatly captures the tone here: certainty and opinion have become indistinguishable from each other.

Truth, in this context, occupies the same space as slander: the two seem interchangeable, dependent simply upon the succession of events and the way things are viewed from moment to moment. Communication becomes a process which simultaneously transmits and degrades truth, an organic and inescapable infection: 'it grows again / Fresher than e'er it was'. The build-up to this exchange of rumour is both revealing and complex. The Second Gentleman drops a broad hint of occult knowledge: '[y]et I can give you inkling / Of an ensuing evil, if it fall, / Greater than this' (2.1.139–41). His friend's eager, staccato reply is a masterpiece of contradiction, desiring while denying the desire to know the truth (or, rather, the rumour). It also emphasizes faith, not just as trustworthiness but as belief: 'Good angels keep it from us. / What may it be? You do not doubt my faith, sir?' (141–2). To which the Second Gentleman responds, teasingly, 'This secret is so weighty 'twill require / A strong faith to conceal it' (143–4). 'Let me have it', cries the First Gentleman, 'I do not talk much' (144–5), a comment which provokes laughter in performance, since the only capacity in which we have seen the speaker is as a gossip and rumour-monger. The Gentlemen, then, fail to fulfil their ostensible role as choric figures. They do not cut through the confusion of events, as a chorus ought to do, offering an anchor of objectivity; on the contrary, their dialogue, as Bliss notes, 'pointedly fails to resolve the kinds of questions – truth or deception, guilt or innocence – which the play repeatedly raises' (Bliss, 5).

What becomes apparent is the isolated nature of testimony, defined not simply as one person's perspective on a coherent truth of which the witness sees only one facet, but rather as a unique report of an event seen by one person which can be performed by that person alone and which may share little or nothing with the event as reported by other witnesses (Felman & Laub, 206). This seems palpably true of the world of *Henry VIII*, in which multiple testimonies are never fully reconcilable. The play, in fact, seems to dwell on the radical and unbridgeable difference between the perspectives different witnesses have on the same event or character to the point at which the event itself cannot clearly be said to have happened or the character to have existed, at least in any fixed, stable form. Take, for instance, the contradictory descriptions of Wolsey given by Katherine and Griffith in 4.2. Katherine has learnt of Wolsey's death, and she speaks a frank epitaph:

> He was a man
> Of an unbounded stomach, ever ranking
> Himself with princes; one that by suggestion
> Tied all the kingdom. Simony was fair play.
> His own opinion was his law. I'th' presence
> He would say untruths, and be ever double

Both in his words and meaning. He was never,
But where he meant to ruin, pitiful.
His promises were as he then was, mighty;
But his performance, as he is now, nothing.
Of his own body he was ill, and gave
The clergy ill example.

(4.2.33–44)

Griffith, Katherine's gentleman usher, responds with an alternative epitaph, one which the Cardinal would presumably have preferred:

From his cradle
He was a scholar, and a ripe and good one,
Exceeding wise, fair-spoken and persuading;
Lofty and sour to them that loved him not,
But to those men that sought him, sweet as summer.
And though he were unsatisfied in getting –
Which was a sin – yet in bestowing, madam,
He was most princely: ever witness for him
Those twins of learning that he raised in you,
Ipswich and Oxford – one of which fell with him,
Unwilling to outlive the good that did it;
The other, though unfinished, yet so famous,
So excellent in art, and still so rising,
That Christendom shall ever speak his virtue.
His overthrow heaped happiness upon him,
For then, and not till then, he felt himself,
And found the blessedness of being little.
And, to add greater honours to his age
Than man could give him, he died fearing God.

(50–68)

Griffith thus counters Katherine's diatribe by offering an encomium. The effect is to present us with two quite distinct pictures of Wolsey which hardly overlap at all (except, perhaps, when

104

Griffith notes that the Cardinal was 'unsatisfied in getting – / Which was a sin'), and we see a fine example of testimony as the performance of isolated positions. Rhetorically, the two speeches are roughly proportionate; yet as far as motivations are concerned, there is presumably a wealth of difference, since Katherine's venom has been prompted by the savagery of Wolsey's behaviour toward her. What we hear from Griffith is rhetoric: we have no reason to think that he believes Wolsey to have been the exemplary figure he describes, but he feels the need to fulfil what would have been childhood habit for educated Jacobeans – to offer both sides of any debate with equal fluency and conviction. In other words, in Katherine's furious description and Griffith's bland counter-description, we see testimony as a form of rhetoric which is both deeply personal and thoroughly impersonal.[1] What we are not given is a sense of testimony as the recounting of the truth: as with the numerous pamphlets entitled 'A True Report' or 'A True Account' that were printed in the period, there is no need to assume that all is true.

Far from sustaining a sense of 'Truth' as a Protestant absolute, then, the play makes truth indeterminate. Since everyone, from Buckingham and his surveyor to Wolsey and Cranmer, claims an exclusive hold, a monopoly, over truth, the concept is under more strain than it can bear. And as, at the level of dialogue, we hear characters offering radically different assessments of other characters or of events which cannot be read as different perspectives on that character or event but rather as distinct performances, so, at the level of the play, we see radically different interpretations of the great events – and principally of the Reformation – that the play represents, requiring the audience to establish their own individual or communal assessment of those events. The play's emphasis on the concept of truth, then, signals not only its engagement with

1   As Tom Healy notes, Griffith's ambiguous response to Katherine's description of her vision – 'I am most joyful, madam, such good dreams / Possess your fancy' (4.2.93–4) – leaves us unclear whether we have witnessed 'a true vision or a staging of a fanciful dream' (Healy, 170), thereby sustaining his function as the provider of alternative viewpoints.

Jacobean politics – which is itself a much more complex and subtle engagement than has generally been acknowledged – but also its immersion in the question of the nature of testimony. The play's fascination with truth is a fascination not only with the immediate political and ecclesiological resonances of the term for its first audiences but also with the much broader issue of the ways in which truth is debated and established within a culture and particularly within that culture's conception of history.[1]

Truth and tragicomedy

Generic categorization is a way to distinguish between texts in terms of their relationship with, and treatment of, truth. Different genres offer very different kinds of truth, often apparently incompatible truths, as they provide their particular responses to, their 'unique angles of vision' on, the crisis which impels the plot (Kastan, *Shapes*, 33). Early modern writers seem, by and large, to have been far less concerned about precise categorization than we are (despite Sir Philip Sidney's well-known resistance to the mixing of dramatic genres in his *Apology for Poetry*), and the Shakespeare First Folio, although it at first sight appears to divide along crisp generic lines, presents a range of problems for anyone determined to establish firm boundaries. Why, for instance (to take three examples of plays usually thought of as having shared generic characteristics), do *The Tempest* and *The Winter's Tale* open and close the 'Comedies' section, while *Cymbeline* concludes the 'Tragedies'?

Henry VIII provides one of many generic puzzles, its apparently unplanned proximity to *Troilus and Cressida* in the Folio serving only to underline the difficulty of determining its genre. Critical interest has focused on three categories in the quest to establish the play's generic affinities: 'history', 'late play' or

---

1 See Kamps, 91–139, for a perceptive account of the challenges offered by *Henry VIII* to Elizabethan and Jacobean historiographies. For Kamps, the play is best seen 'not [as] a disunified play about history but a play about disunified history' (105). On questions of history, see also Patterson, 'All Is True', and Healy.

'romance', and masque. The play's title, subject matter, and location in the Folio at the end of the 'Histories' section – bringing the sequence of English kings' reigns (and of the legitimizing of the Tudor dynasty) as near to the Jacobean present as was permissible – appears to make it a 'history play'. Its chronological position within the Shakespeare canon, along with certain central formal and thematic concerns, however, suggest that its closest relatives are the 'late plays' or 'romances', the quartet of plays from *Pericles* to *The Tempest* that has traditionally been seen as the last flowering of Shakespeare's genius. On the other hand, the play's visual specificity, the grandeur of its ritual, and its presumed function as a royalist mythologization of the transition from Tudor to Stuart rule have led to comparisons with the court masque. Critics have in fact never been sure what kind of play *Henry VIII* is: as a result, it is frequently omitted from books both on the 'late plays' (Kiernan Ryan's collection, *Shakespeare: The Last Plays*, to take one recent example) and on the 'Histories' (Jean Howard and Phyllis Rackin's *Engendering a Nation*, to take another).

This latter omission seems particularly odd. Simply on the basis of the title under which it appears in the Folio, *Henry VIII* appears inescapably a 'history play'. Moreover, its echoes of, for instance, the episodic structure of the *Henry VI* plays or the representation of the origins of Reformation in *King John*, indicate close ties to earlier plays with historical subjects, and it makes enough allusions to the characters and events of *Richard III* for it to be thought of as a continuation of the story begun at the end of that play, when Richmond graduates to the crown as Henry VII. Certainly, the references Buckingham makes to his father seem almost clumsy reminders to the audience of what happened in *Richard III*, and the names of the aristocrats are, of course, the same from generation to generation. As Hugh Richmond notes, in Shakespeare's tetralogies we have already seen characters with the names Lovell, Norfolk and Surrey, as well as a series of royal Elizabeths, from Elizabeth Woodville, wife of Edward IV, to Elizabeth of York, wife of Henry VII, who lead us finally to the double Elizabeth of *Henry VIII*, Elizabeth I and Elizabeth Stuart (Richmond, 14). Yet *Henry VIII* is still perceived as fundamentally different from Shakespeare's other history plays. Blair Worden, for instance, notes that, where the earlier plays portrayed the struggles of medieval kingship, *Henry VIII* takes us 'into a Renaissance court: the court of the monarchy that has broken the medieval nobility and imposed new values and new rules of conduct', a distinction summed up neatly in his observation that:

> [w]hen in *Henry IV Part 1* Hal calls Hotspur a 'child of honour' (3.2.139) he is commending his manliness and courage: when in *Henry VIII* Katharine of Aragon calls Wolsey 'the great child of honour' (4.2.6) she is alluding to his receipt of royal favour.
>
> (Worden, 14)

Unlike the earlier plays, in which the nobility is 'warlike, . . . its power resting as much on its estates and its ability to arm its tenantry as on royal favour', in *Henry VIII* the nobles 'cower in the royal antechambers, dreading the royal anger', and the 'institutions and conventions of [the] court are designed to keep truth at bay' (Worden, 12).

The historical 'truth' of *Henry VIII* is thus arguably quite different from that of Shakespeare's other 'history plays', and some critics have insisted instead on the play's affinity with a genre associated more with Ben Jonson than with Shakespeare or Fletcher. Its emphasis on the visual and on ritual, together with the context of entertainments for the marriage of Elizabeth and Frederick, has led several critics to examine the relationship between *Henry VIII* and the court masque. This is an association made, especially in the early days of New Historicism, with the late plays as a group, but there seems to be a particularly close connection with *Henry VIII*: for John Cox, in fact, the play's 'singular dramaturgy can be seen as an experiment in adapting the principles of the court masque to the dramatic tradition of the public theaters' (Cox, 391). Certainly, the pattern of the final two scenes (the Porter scene and the christening) bears obvious comparison with the structure of the masque – presenting an antimasque of lower-class characters who are swept aside by the arrival of the main masque, which culminates in celebration of the monarch – and it is, of course, possible to stage the play as an elaborate courtly entertainment (which, as we have seen, productions in the nineteenth century did almost as a matter of course). But Cox's argument has a broader reach, suggesting that in *Henry VIII* 'Shakespeare [*sic*] goes beyond flirtation' with masque-form 'and actually weds the familiar conventions of popular drama with the spirit and principles of the refined court masque', so that the play becomes 'a celebration of Jacobean kingship' which 'delineate[s] the principles of James's rule, thus holding up the mirror to the King's greatness, just as the court masques do' (Cox, 391, 395, 394).

Yet Wotton's letter reminds us that there is more to this uncomfortable play than masques, and Cox usefully qualifies his thesis, arguing that:

> [w]hile fully meeting the masque's demand for royal compliment, *Henry VIII* explores the ambiguities of divine right and reveals an image whose truth encompasses more things on earth than are dreamt of in the heavenly philosophy of the masque.
>
> (Cox, 407)

We have seen the masque as a site of ideological struggle in the entertainments planned for the Palatine wedding: any assumption that because the play engages with the form of the masque the ending of the play – Cranmer's speech and Henry's reception of that speech – must be harmonious, must be 'a celebration of Jacobean kingship', ignores the fracturing of royal ideology, the undercurrents of sexual and procreative failure, and all the other ways in which that prophecy is undermined for the Jacobean audience. The masque is an idealistic, monolithic form which aims to harness the networks of allusion that might spoil the simplicity of its illusion; *Henry VIII*, on the other hand, as we have seen, wilfully deploys precisely the multiple referentiality that the masque denies. It seems clear, then, that the truth of *Henry VIII* is engaged with, but different from, that of the masque: there is a strong and conscious dependence upon the form, but this dependence is fundamentally ironic, providing ostensible ideological limitation to a situation of productive multiplicity.

The play's focus on the visual, however, taken in tandem with its concluding emphasis on the emotion of wonder and on the relationship of a father and a daughter, suggests an affinity with Shakespeare's 'late plays' or 'romances' which is difficult to deny, and some critics have attempted to make sense of the generic inconvenience of *Henry VIII* and its belatedness as a 'history play' by emphasizing its similarities not to Shakespearean history, but to the plays in the canon which immediately precede it chronologically – *Pericles*, *The Winter's Tale*, *Cymbeline* and *The Tempest*. Certainly, *Henry VIII* has several features traditionally associated with Shakespeare's 'late plays': it may not be expansive geographically or dependent on a poetic or prose romance as its source, but it does have a multiple character focus, at least one supernatural moment (Katherine's vision), and a conclusion that features a redemptive father-and-daughter tableau. Moreover, its juxtaposing of linear and cyclical concepts of time is strongly reminiscent of a basic pattern of the 'late plays'. Yet the scepticism of *Henry VIII*'s attitude to truth and to testimony, along with its insistent undermining of the emotion of wonder, makes its association with these plays less comfortable than this might suggest. Norfolk's cynical stance as a critical 'admirer' of the scene at the Field of the Cloth of Gold is a far cry from Miranda's innocent amazement at the 'brave new world' of men in *The Tempest* or the 'faith' and 'marvel' called for by Paulina when she conjures Hermione back to life in *The Winter's Tale*. And the way the play deals with the materials it ostensibly shares with the 'late plays' suggests that it has moved beyond their concerns into a bleaker and more uncertain space.

The 'late plays' themselves have been a consistent puzzle for critics, unsure how to locate them in an era in which, as I have suggested, exclusive categorization has been important in a way it simply was not for the Jacobeans. Edward Dowden, in 1877, was the first to deal with the problem by creating a new category, that of 'romance', and using that term to foreground the shared characteristics of the 'last plays'.[1] But as Stephen Orgel notes, while 'Dowden's generic ploy . . . enabled criticism to see the interrelations of these four plays more clearly, and probably served to disarm the most obvious rationalistic objections to their action', his new generic category 'has proved as obfuscatory as it has been enlightening' (Orgel, 2–3). Certainly, the co-option of these plays for late romanticism has produced a range of unhelpfully ahistorical attitudes. Shakespeare's late plays have, as Simon Palfrey observes:

> a reputation as courtly works, composed and performed within the ambit of state power, and complimentary to ruling decorums. Vast myths have been discovered at their core: they are redemptive journeys of nature and grace, the basic ethics those of aristocratic fortitude beneath a careless but ultimately beneficent destiny.
>
> (Palfrey, 1)

Palfrey notes literary tradition's insistence on a clear contrast between 'history plays' and 'romances', arguing that, for Shakespeare criticism, 'whereas history is a tale of irony – of hopes misconceived, gaps between intent and end, of massive hyperbole and *sotto voce* subversion – romance is history's impossible, itinerant, escapist corrective' (Palfrey, 1). If this is true, then *Henry VIII* is impossibly divided within itself, constructed of fundamentally incompatible materials. But tradition also acknowledges not only the dependence of Shakespearean 'romance' on the

---

1   Stephen Orgel has noted that 'Dowden's claims for his new Shakespearian genre in fact did little more than systematize an observation already made by Coleridge in his *Notes on "The Tempest"*, in which the play is referred to as a romance' (Orgel, 2).

comic forms out of which the early plays in the canon emerged but also the tendency of the 'late plays' to reassess those forms. In this sense, *Henry VIII*, in its insistent revaluation of the forms on which it depends, belongs firmly among the 'late plays'.

Perhaps *Henry VIII* is best viewed as a 'late play' not in the specific sense of the features it shares with the four plays in question but rather in the general sense of the concept of 'late writing' – the idea that authors, towards the end of their careers, tend to return to patterns associated with their early writings in order to rework them from the perspective of the experience of the intervening years.[1] Certainly, this could provide a transhistorical explanation for the retrospective quality of both *Henry VIII* and *The Two Noble Kinsmen* as they revisit the patterns and motifs of certain of Shakespeare's early plays in a new context. Ironically, though, one of the problems with which *Henry VIII* has traditionally had to contend is precisely its 'lateness' – in particular, its appearing to postdate the play most critics preferred to think of as the Bard's last, reading Prospero's surrender of his magical art in *The Tempest* as Shakespeare's retirement speech. Even the most recent criticism of Shakespeare's late plays sustains a belief in the moral, if not factual, finality of *The Tempest*: Palfrey, for instance, in a brief section explaining his exclusion of *Henry VIII* and *The Two Noble Kinsmen* from his 1997 study of the 'late plays', writes of 'the four romances as a discrete group, culminating in *The Tempest*'s valedictory perfection' (Palfrey, 31). And it is easy enough to construct a biography for Shakespeare in the period 1611–13 in which, snapping his quill after finishing *The Tempest*, the great playwright retires, rich and satisfied, to Stratford, only to discover that life there isn't too thrilling and that Heminges and Condell, his fellow shareholders and veterans of the company, are

---

1   One of the clearest examples of this tendency in more recent literature is Henry James's 'New York' edition, published late in his career, in which he reissued his earlier novels in either partially or wholly rewritten form (see Millgate). For a view of the nature of Shakespearean late writing which is very much a product of its time, see Muir.

keen to have him back to help ease his successor, Fletcher, into place. So he returns to London to show the younger man how it is done, and finally leaves for good once *The Two Noble Kinsmen* is finished. This tale allows for *The Tempest* to be the conscious conclusion of a career (followed by the inevitable comeback tour), and it compartmentalizes the later 'late plays' as a collaborative afterthought with which Shakespeare is at best only (literally) half engaged. But (as this last premise for disparagement suggests) the tale also requires a denial of the actual processes of production of drama in Jacobean England, since the idea of 'late writing', dependent as it is upon assumptions about the linear structure of a career and a certain biographical determinism, has to contend with one simple problem: that of collaborative production.

Shakespeare's is, after all, not the only 'career' into which this play fits; it inhabits also that of John Fletcher, his successor as company playwright. And while *Henry VIII* dates from the last year of Shakespeare's writing career, it has to be considered, in Fletcherian terms, as a (relatively) 'early' play. To view it as 'late work' can thus be only half appropriate, at best, and therefore fully compromised. I have incorporated a comparative chronology for Shakespeare and Fletcher as Appendix 2 in order to indicate the nature of the overlap between the two 'careers' in question. Put simply, Shakespeare was, by 1607, firmly established as the principal playwright for the King's Company, for whom he had recently produced a truly remarkable series of tragedies. Around the time the Company occupied the Blackfriars theatre, he began to write plays of a quite different type, expansive plays with elements obviously drawn from romance, grim comedies, tragicomedies, or plays which have all the elements of tragedy but conclude with a familial miracle. He stopped writing after he had written four such plays and apparently left London in 1610 or thereabouts, but he then wrote three more plays with Fletcher in 1612–13 and died three years later.

Fletcher, on the other hand, was only just becoming established in 1607. Within a couple of years, he had a series of successes with emotionally excessive, ironic tragicomedies written collaboratively with Francis Beaumont; and though his first solo play, *The Faithful Shepherdess*, failed on the stage, his next, *The Woman's Prize* – drawing overtly on Shakespeare's *The Taming of the Shrew* to provide a humorous, radical mock-sequel to that play – seems to have been more successful. After Beaumont's retirement, Fletcher continued to collaborate with other dramatists, writing three plays with Shakespeare in 1612–13 and establishing himself as his successor at the Globe, and then trying out several different creative partnerships before settling into a routine of working with Philip Massinger, with whom he went on to create at least fifteen plays, all for the King's Company. He caught the plague and died in the summer of 1625.

The overlap of these 'careers', though brief, appears to have been significant for both. Whichever way the immediate influence flowed, each wrote plays which were in the vanguard of the new fashionable genre – which we call 'romantic tragicomedy', for want of a better term – which dominated the stage up to and beyond the English Revolution. Though he had collaborated before (it was standard practice among early modern playwrights), Shakespeare had not written a series of three plays with any other writer: in Fletcher, he seems to have found a playwright with whom he could work, at least for twelve months. *Henry VIII* echoes Fletcher's pre-1613 work as well as that of Shakespeare, but it is less dependent on Fletcherian material for the obvious reason that, in 1613, there were far fewer Fletcher plays to work with: Shakespeare had been writing successful drama since the late 1580s, Fletcher only since 1606 or so. Fletcher's plays – mostly written, to this point, with Beaumont – did, though, establish a clear, if elliptical, relationship with the plays of Shakespeare right from the start. *The Woman Hater* of 1606 opens with a scene which satirizes the obscure motivations of Duke Vincentio in *Measure for Measure* (1604) (McMullan, *Unease*, 89–90). *Philaster* (1608–9) draws on *Hamlet* (1600); *Bonduca* (written somewhere in the period 1609–14) on *Cymbeline* (1610–11); and *The Woman's*

Prize (1611) assumes the audience's familiarity with *The Taming of the Shrew* (1589–90). *The Tempest* (1611), on the other hand, marks the influence going the other way, echoing the basic structure of Fletcher's *Faithful Shepherdess* (1608–9), in which a woman with magical powers, living in an isolated place and attended by a satyr, orchestrates events in order to heal spiritual and civil wounds and enable the various protagonists to return to the world of normality. The collaborative plays in fact suggest influence going both ways: *The Two Noble Kinsmen*, returning to Chaucer's *Knight's Tale* for its principal source, is a darker reworking of the materials of *A Midsummer Night's Dream* (1594–5), and *Henry VIII*, in addition to its obvious relationship with Shakespeare's earlier history plays, draws the basic form of its penultimate scene from Beaumont and Fletcher's *The Maid's Tragedy* (1610) (see Appendix 4).

As a result of all this interdependence, a few critics since Ashley Thorndike's groundbreaking (if overstated) *Influence of Beaumont and Fletcher on Shakspere* have attempted to suggest that Shakespeare's late plays emerged as a direct consequence of Fletcher's creation (in tandem with Beaumont) of the genre of romantic tragicomedy. This is a fraught subject on at least three fronts: one, whether or not the notion of crisp generic categorization is workable in the first place; two, whether the prefatory material to *The Faithful Shepherdess* can be accepted as a statement of the genre as it would develop (particularly in view of the failure of the play on the stage), and therefore whether an appropriate definition of Jacobean 'tragicomedy' can be achieved on the basis of that material; and three, whether the current dating for plays in the two canons can be accepted as more than educated guesswork.[1] I created a working chronology for Fletcher when I wrote on his plays, but I am aware of its highly provisional nature; equally, dates for the writing of *The Winter's Tale* and *Cymbeline*, in particular, appear impossible to pin down (it is even

---

1 On the relationship between Fletcher's preface to *The Faithful Shepherdess* and Jacobean tragicomedy in general, see McMullan & Hope, 1–7.

unclear which came first; indeed, there is no firm evidence that *The Tempest* post-dates either) (McMullan, *Unease*, 267–9). In this context, determining exact precedence for Shakespeare's 'late plays' and Fletcher's early work is largely futile: the point is that both playwrights were aware of, and in a sense collaborating with, each other's work for several years before they finally began to write plays together. Collaborative authorship is, anyway, only one of the intersections of influence that map the play's place within its sphere of production in a time before copyright. As Roslyn Lander Knutson has shown, the role of the playwright in the creation of new generic patterns was subject to the needs of the acting companies: it was typically the exigencies of competition, not free-floating individual creativity, that determined the nature and genre of a new play, as companies vied to establish and capitalize upon theatrical trends (Knutson, *Company*, 15–55; Knutson, 'Repertory', 461–80). To consider *Henry VIII* as one of the 'late plays', then, is not necessarily to treat it as a 'late work' in the restrictive, single-author-centred way outlined earlier, for at least two reasons: because Shakespeare's late plays and Fletcher's early plays are closely interwoven, and because both playwrights were writing for acting companies who paid very close attention to the output of their rivals and required their playwrights to ride the wave of new modes when and if they appeared to be successful.

The circumstances of the collaboration, while underlining the differences between *Henry VIII* and the four plays known as Shakespeare's 'late plays', also make it no surprise that *Henry VIII*, in the scenes attributed to Fletcher as well as in the 'Shakespeare' scenes, draws on and echoes those plays. Of the four – despite strong claims for *Cymbeline* as a play which, like *Henry VIII*, 'illustrate[s] . . . the problems that arise when history is conflated with romance' (Felperin, 178 and ff.) – the closest turns out to be *The Winter's Tale*. Both plays focus on a king whose immoderation has led to his lack of an heir and who turns belatedly to a daughter for the possibility of a future. And if you take as a point of comparison the emotion of 'wonder' – which has been a key concern in recent 'late play' criticism (see, for instance, Bishop, and Platt) – and consider the relationship between the opening scene of *Henry VIII*, in which Norfolk and Buckingham discuss the 'great sport' (1.1.47) of the meeting at the Field of the Cloth of Gold, and the penultimate scene of *The Winter's Tale*, in which three Gentlemen rehearse the events of the play and discuss the effect of the rediscovery of Perdita on court and kingdom, the relationship between the two plays becomes clearer. *The Winter's Tale*'s Gentlemen (who have their obvious counterparts in the 'walking gentlemen' of *Henry VIII*) debate the truth of Leontes' reunion with Perdita in a wonderfully productive dialogue which is easily mistaken for mere plot summary:

> SECOND GENTLEMAN   The King's daughter is found. Such a deal of wonder is broken out within this hour, that ballad-makers cannot be able to express it. . . . This news, which is called true, is so like an old tale that the verity of it is in strong suspicion. Has the King found his heir?
>
> THIRD GENTLEMAN   Most true, if ever truth were pregnant by circumstance. That which you hear you'll swear you see, there is such unity in the proofs. . . . Did you see the meeting of the two kings?
>
> SECOND GENTLEMAN   No.
>
> THIRD GENTLEMAN   Then have you lost a sight which was to be seen, cannot be spoken of. There might you have beheld one joy crown another, so and in such manner that it seemed sorrow wept to take leave of them, for their joy waded in tears.
>
> *(WT* 5.2.23–5, 27–32, 39–46)

The resonances for *Henry VIII* of this dialogue on 'truth' and its relations with 'pregnancy' and 'circumstance' are considerable; and it is no surprise that we revisit this conversation in a more sceptical way in the later play, as the encounter of the kings returns in a competitive frame at the Field of the Cloth of Gold and the effect of genuine wonder at a marvellous spectacle turns out to be temporary and disappointing. We have thus already moved beyond the naïve kind of wonder that *The Winter's Tale* itself, by way both of the lack of conviction displayed by the Gentlemen and the sheer weight of years and suffering that have gone by since the original crisis, registers as problematic. *Henry VIII* begins, in a sense, where the earlier play leaves off, drama- tizing the political and social ramifications of the unease signalled even within its reconciliations.

This engagement with the nature of truth is matched by the thematic dominance of time in *The Winter's Tale*, and the two issues combine in the play's exploration of the *veritas filia temporis* iconography. Shakespeare had already deployed this iconography in *Pericles*, the first of the 'late plays', and he returned to it in a rather more complex way in *The Winter's Tale*, turning to Robert Greene's *Pandosto* – subtitled *The Triumph of Time* – as his prin- cipal source.[1] For Inga-Stina Ewbank:

> [t]he *Pandosto* story itself fails to work out its motto . . . for it puts all the emphasis on Fortune, with her wheel, as the ruling agent of human affairs. Shakespeare, on the other hand, makes the Triumph of Time into a control- ling theme of his tale; and doing so he transforms what the conventional motto suggests – a simple victory of Time, the father of Truth – into a dramatic exploration of the manifold meanings of Time.
>
> (Ewbank, 'Triumph', 140)

Leontes' initial failure to trust in Time as revelation – since 'time, when not allowed to ripen, can only *make*, not *unfold* error' – leads directly to the loss of his virtuous wife and the catastrophic death of his son, turning (in other words) from Time the Revealer to Time the Destroyer (Ewbank, 'Triumph', 142). The second half

---

1   On *Pericles*, truth and time, see Barrett.

of the play, heralded by the choric figure of Time himself, demonstrates the process of Time's triumph, as human agency is subordinated to progress towards revelation and the play concludes in a celebration which is also a tense negotiation between the two temporal modes, destructive and redemptive. This offers a direct connection both with Fletcher's 1614 collaboration, *Four Plays in One*, which includes a masque entitled 'The Triumph of Time', and with the iconographic resonances of *Henry VIII*, ironic and sectarian though they are. Simply put, where *The Winter's Tale* focuses on the forms of Time, *Henry VIII*, as we have seen, explores the varieties of Truth.

Generically and iconographically, then, *The Winter's Tale* and *Henry VIII* have a great deal in common, and certainly more than 'late play' critics have generally cared to acknowledge. But the principal connection made between the two plays is the apparent similarity of the plays' spurned and rejected queens, Hermione and Katherine, as they react to their parallel situations as victims of cruel, self-obsessed husbands. Each, in the profound lack of agency that disables her resistance to the savagery of her husband, reflects both the other and the fundamentally patriarchal worlds they both inhabit. Each is the daughter of foreign royalty; each defends herself passionately yet unsuccessfully in a public courtroom; each rejects the ritual that sustains a patriarchal political realm; each believes in a version of the truth that her husband cannot understand; each appeals to a conscience that her husband appears to lack; and each loses the struggle, at least in the material world. Although, unlike Katherine, she is reborn, Hermione shares Katherine's failure of agency in the course of her self-defence; the nearest Katherine gets to the possibility of rebirth is the vision she is given of her heavenly prospects. At least, in Hermione's case, it is her own daughter who is recovered at the end: *Henry VIII* ends, to all intents and purposes, with Katherine dead and forgotten and her arch-rival Anne Bullen's child the centre of attention, and the hope she expresses for her daughter Mary at 4.2.136 is, of course, deeply ironic for a Protestant audience brought up on tales of Mary's sectarian ferocity. Yet the comparisons and contrasts typically drawn between Katherine and Anne are, unexpectedly, both problematic and, to a certain extent, illusory, and the function of Katherine in the play is far more complex and circumscribed than is generally acknowledged.

The character of the Queen

The crisis of the 'late plays' is always, in one way or another, a family crisis, and the breaking of deadlock in each of the plays is effected by or through women: Marina, Imogen, Perdita and Miranda unwittingly, Paulina consciously. As Wotton's emphasis on the problems of the 'familiar' might unintentionally suggest, much of the trouble in *Henry VIII* takes place within or in relation to the institution of the family, yet one crucial difference between *Henry VIII* and the 'late plays' is that the collaboration contains no itinerant, independent heroine. Katherine is perhaps the nearest in quality to a 'late play' heroine as she attempts to maintain an independent relationship with the King, yet she is consistently outmanoeuvred and finally effectively incarcerated. Anne appeals to Henry at least in part because of her apparent independence (which we judge, when we first see her, from her ability to evade Lord Sandys's charmless advances (1.4.45–8)), but from the moment of their meeting she is subject to his desires, and her behaviour and morals are quite different from those of a Marina or a Perdita. The child Elizabeth, on the other hand, is the only female figure permitted the promise of agency, but that agency is deferred, remaining unfulfilled within the confines of the play (and arguably within the audience's memory, too). Perhaps, then, the young heroine of the late plays is here divided into three – into Katherine the spiritual exile, Anne the beautiful and productive, and Elizabeth the hope of the future – even as she herself figures an ideal version of the Elizabeth of the Jacobean imagination. But none of the three has the independence of movement and the plot-driving quality of a Marina or an Imogen, or even the circumscribed agency of a Perdita or a Miranda.

Katherine pushes hard, though, both to sustain the original structure of her marriage and to keep things as they are and should be, and her rage for stability is one it is impossible for the audience not to share. Henry's brief reflection after Katherine has stormed out of the courtroom seems to sum her up: 'Go thy ways, Kate', he says, admiringly:

> That man i'th' world who shall report he has
> A better wife, let him in naught be trusted
> For speaking false in that. Thou art alone –
> If thy rare qualities, sweet gentleness,
> Thy meekness saint-like, wife-like government,
> Obeying in commanding, and thy parts
> Sovereign and pious else, could speak thee out –
> The queen of earthly queens. She's noble born,
> And like her true nobility she has
> Carried her self towards me.
>
> (2.4.130–140)

The audience has little choice, hearing this encomium, but to accept that Katherine is an exemplary woman in the mould of popular 'lives' of female saints or model matrons, and her behaviour throughout the play supports this description. Strangely, then, just as the play sets out to represent the process of Reformation and celebrate the birth of the Protestant Elizabeth, it seems to set up her hated sister's mother as a paragon of virtue. The early nineteenth-century critic Anna Jameson describes Katherine in terms that will by now be familiar:

> The character [of Katherine] when analysed, is, in the first place, distinguished by *truth*. I do not only mean its truth to nature, or its relative truth arising from its historic fidelity and dramatic consistency, but *truth* as a quality of the soul: this is the basis of the character.
>
> (Jameson, 2.274)

Jameson appeals to a romantic understanding of the concept of truth which, though current, indeed culturally dominant, in her own period, would have meant little to the Jacobeans, yet she shares this assessment of Katherine's character – certainly compared with all the other characters in the play – with generations of critics and theatre practitioners. Yet to what, exactly, is Katherine true? On the one hand, as an exemplary wife prepared to stand up to her unreasonable husband in order to sustain their marriage, she is true to a central principle of the reformation of manners; on the other, as a devout Catholic staunchly opposed to Reformation, she is true to Rome and the old order.

This presents a surprisingly complex problem because of the apparent disjunction between the responses to be expected from the audience in 1613 to these two principal aspects of her character. She is, after all, inescapably Roman Catholic: she appeals directly 'unto the Pope' (2.4.117) when she runs out of patience with the divorce hearing, and she insistently resists the onset of Reformation as personified in the Lutheran Anne. Yet she is no Gardiner – there was no popular vilification of Katherine after her death as there was of the bishop and of her daughter Mary – and she is set up from the second scene onwards in direct opposition to Wolsey, who embodies all that is corrupt in both court and Church. Perhaps disturbingly, bearing in mind her allegiance to Rome, she has in fact no apparent need for reformation, since her life on earth has been exemplary. She is, in many ways, an ideal embodiment of the reformation of manners as it was applied to the relations between the sexes and specifically to women, sustaining as she does, to the bitter end, the basic social structure, marriage, upon which political stability was held to depend. Her Catholicism, in other words, has more in common with reformed social and personal attitudes (as well, perhaps, as with James I's foreign policy) than it does with the Church of which Wolsey is a prominent member. Moreover, the heavenly vision she is given seems to establish her as a true Christian, welcomed by angels into the body of the elect. Though, as I have suggested, post-Renaissance productions have varied between what might be thought of as a 'Protestant' and a 'Catholic' version of the vision, the former sparse and internalized, the latter spectacular and externalized, there seems little doubt – at least to judge from the lengthy Folio stage direction – that the original audiences would have seen a spectacular version and therefore have no doubt about Katherine's state of grace.

Yet for some Protestant members of the audience, this vision – grace or no grace – would have been decidedly uncomfortable (just as Leontes' apparent admiration for a graven image in the last act of *The Winter's Tale* would have worried them), since visions of angels are associated with Catholic tradition in a way they are not with Protestantism. Moreover, as Judith Anderson has suggested, Katherine's vision is not as reassuring as we might initially assume. Though it seems to provide 'poetic recompense' for her sufferings, 'there is also an ironic recollection of her earlier declaration, "nothing but death / Shall e'er divorce my dignities"', and, by '[c]ombining poetic recompense and actual divorce' in this way, the play 'gives us cause to wonder whether Catherine's vision is just another anodyne or is true inspiration'. In other words, as far as the audience is concerned, the vision, while 'appealing', is also 'at the very least ambivalent' (Anderson, 134). Moreover, for all her ostensible detachment from worldly matters, Katherine's final speech (like those of Buckingham and Wolsey) clearly indicates both that she is still aware of material and ideological reality and that (understandably) she has yet to forgive Henry for his actions (4.2.163–4). In a specifically legal context, Katherine's deathbed requests constitute a deliberate, continued rejection both of the divorce and of Henry's legal moves to enforce his control of her property. As Ann Rosalind Jones and Peter Stallybrass note, she is here asserting 'her right to give away the money . . . that she is simultaneously asking Henry to give to her' (Jones & Stallybrass, 'Griselda', 19). And the bitter echo of the destruction of Jezebel in her last words (4.2.171–2 and n.) indicates her continued resentment of the King's callousness.

The position Henry's divorce-hearing encomium puts her in – as the ideal conduct-book wife nonetheless abandoned – is a reminder that Katherine is, like all dramatic characters, no matter how 'proud' or 'dignified', a construct, pieced together from prior textual material, and it is not just conduct books that create the Katherine of the play. Her status, for instance, as a foreign Queen of England – called, diminutively, 'Kate' (2.4.130) at a moment of intimacy which is really a political moment – reminds us of Hal's French Kate in the last act of *Henry V*. But, kneeling before her husband at her first entrance, she also reminds us of another, quite different Kate, as Sarah Siddons clearly realized when, in January 1790, she arranged and starred in a back-to-back performance of *Henry VIII* and Garrick's *Katharine and Petruchio*, an adaptation of Shakespeare's *The Taming of the Shrew*. As Hugh Richmond notes:

> Siddons surely perceived the irony of the late play seen as a wry corollary of the early one, since a wife as loyal as Queen Katherine earns only misfortune by meeting the specifications which a reformed Katherina Minola finally offers Petruchio.
>
> (Richmond, 44)

Henry's failure to acknowledge Katherine's status as an exemplar of the reformation of manners would, I am sure, have been just as apparent to the Jacobean audience in view of the continuing interest in *The Taming of the Shrew* implied by Fletcher's *Woman's Prize*, first performed just a year or so earlier, and it is a failure which is foregrounded throughout what has become known as the 'trial scene'. This is also the scene in which the intertextuality of Katherine's characterization is most apparent. We have noted the particular physical significance the divorce hearing would have had for an audience in the Blackfriars theatre, the very hall in which, eighty-four years previously, the papal inquiry into the status of Henry's and Katherine's marriage had taken place (a parallel which might also have led the audience to wonder about the truth of the dramatic proceedings they were witnessing). Other trials would also have sprung to mind, too, some fictional, some actual and recent. The 'actual' trials would include those of Arabella Stuart and, as the play was first performed, of Frances Howard, principal players in the two most notorious divorce cases of James's reign; the fictional would certainly include Vittoria Corombona's trial in John Webster's dark and violent tragedy *The White Devil*, first performed in 1612 at the rival Red Bull theatre in Clerkenwell. The most obvious parallel, however – and one which provides a fine example of the way in which the repertory of a given company developed in relation to those of other companies, since it was itself an influence on Webster's play – is with Hermione's trial in *The Winter's Tale*.

Katherine's defence of her marriage in the Blackfriars courtroom has strong resemblances to Hermione's resistance to Leontes' irrational jealousy. As Michael Dobson neatly phrases it, 'the King of Spain was Katharine's father, the Emperor of Russia was Hermione's, but they seem to have attended the same school of rhetoric' (Dobson, 'Costume drama', 22). 'Good my lords,' says Hermione, when her husband first accuses her of adultery, 'I am not prone to weeping, as our sex / Commonly are; . . .. But I have / That honourable grief lodged here which burns / Worse than tears drown' (*WT* 2.1.109–11, 112–14), and at her trial she relies upon her royal nature and the integrity of her past behaviour as her twin defences against false accusation:

> You, my lord, best know –
> Who least will seem to do so my past life
> Hath been as continent, as chaste, as true
> As I am now unhappy; which is more
> Than history can pattern, though devised
> And played to take spectators. For behold me,
> A fellow of the royal bed, which owe
> A moiety of the throne; a great king's daughter,
> The mother to a hopeful prince, here standing

18 *Portrait of a Woman, possibly Katherine of Aragon*, painting by Miguel de Sittow, 1503/4

> To prate and talk for life and honour, fore
> Who please to come and hear. For life, I prize it
> As I weigh grief, which I would spare. For honour,
> 'Tis a derivative from me to mine,
> And only that I stand for. I appeal
> To your own conscience, sir, before Polixenes
> Came to your court how I was in your grace,
> How merited to be so; since he came,
> With what encounter so uncurrent I
> Have strained t'appear thus. If one jot beyond
> The bound of honour, or in act or will
> That way inclining, hardened be the hearts
> Of all that hear me, and my near'st of kin
> Cry 'Fie' upon my grave.
>
> (*WT* 3.2.31–53)

Katherine, too, resists tears and stands upon her royal blood. 'Sir,' she says to Wolsey:

> I am about to weep; but, thinking that
> We are a queen, or long have dreamed so, certain
> The daughter of a king, my drops of tears
> I'll turn to sparks of fire.
>
> (2.4.68–71)

And, appealing like Hermione to her husband's degraded conscience, she too calls in her defence her exemplary past:

> Sir, I desire you do me right and justice,
> And to bestow your pity on me, for
> I am a most poor woman, and a stranger,
> Born out of your dominions, having here
> No judge indifferent, nor no more assurance
> Of equal friendship and proceeding. . . .
>   Heaven witness
> I have been to you a true and humble wife,
> At all times to your will conformable,

Ever in fear to kindle your dislike,
Yea, subject to your countenance, glad or sorry
As I saw it inclined. . . .
              Sir, call to mind
That I have been your wife in this obedience
Upward of twenty years, and have been blessed
With many children by you. If, in the course
And process of this time, you can report,
And prove it too, against mine honour aught,
My bond to wedlock, or my love and duty
Against your sacred person, in God's name
Turn me away and let the foulest contempt
Shut door upon me, and so give me up
To the sharpest kind of justice.
            (2.4.11–16, 20–25, 32–42)

The queens, in other words, emerging from the same mould and
sharing the same emotions, surely evoke equal sympathy in the
audience for each play.

Yet there are problematic resonances, too, in the conjunction of
these two plays. Incest is the darkest of shadows in the earlier 'late
plays', overtly in *Pericles* when the protagonist decodes the riddle
that tells the truth about Antiochus and his daughter, covertly in
The Winter's Tale when (in a sublimated version of the incest plot
in *Pandosto*) Paulina and Leontes clash uncomfortably over his
apparent sexual interest in the as-yet-unidentified Perdita (*WT*
5.1.220–7). And incest reappears in *Henry VIII* as the 'tenderness, / Scruple and prick' in Henry's conscience (2.4.167–8), the
belated bar to his marriage with Katherine. As Michael Dobson
observes, this 'play about a succession crisis, involving a man who
has married his brother's widow' would have had a familiar ring
for a Shakespearean audience, retracing as it does the relationship
of Gertrude and Claudius in *Hamlet* (Dobson, 'Costume drama',
21; see also Rosenblatt). In this return to the earlier play, Henry
becomes Claudius – the Satyr to the dead Arthur's Hyperion –

and Katherine, Gertrude. Fascinatingly, as Dobson notes, in recalling Gertrude, Katherine, 'post-menopausal and presented as a dead-end for the future of the Tudor dynasty, . . . simultaneously recalls the old Queen Elizabeth whom Gertrude partly figured' (22). Moreover, in pitching together *Hamlet* and *The Winter's Tale* in the construction of Katherine, the playwrights effect not the outright contrast you would expect, but a curious, sublimated correlation of Katherine and Anne Bullen. As Dobson observes:

> [t]he difference between the two cases is that whereas Hermione is on trial for adultery, Katharine is accused of incest, but the way in which the latter trial seems deliberately to recall the former invites us to parallel or conflate them, and thereby forcibly calls to mind a third famous legal process, the very one which causes *Henry VIII* to end where it does so that we won't have to see it: the judicial murder of Anne Boleyn on charges of adultery with, among others, her own brother.
>
> (Dobson, 'Costume drama', 22–3)[1]

Stephen Orgel has argued that Hermione's trial in *The Winter's Tale* inescapably brings to mind Anne Bullen's trial (so melodramatically staged in the later *Virtue Betrayed*); in replaying Hermione's experience in Katherine, the playwrights seem quite deliberately – and remarkably – to conflate Katherine with her arch-rival.

It might be expected that the crispest possible distinctions would be drawn between the two queens, and not just in terms of age. Katherine's Catholicism and Anne's Lutheranism provide the principal difference. Furthermore, where Katherine is

---

1 There is further irony in the fact that, when he first began to plan for the marriage to Anne, Henry sought a dispensation from the Pope to marry a woman with whose older sister he had already slept, since his earlier affair with Mary Bullen technically made his union with Anne incestuous. The irony, of course, is that Henry moved from a marriage which he repudiated as incestuous to another which, by sixteenth-century rules, was also incestuous. I am grateful to Maureen Quilligan for discussion of incest, authorship and the significance of Marguerite of Angoulême (see p. 133).

portrayed as the ideal chaste matron, Anne is presented to us in overtly sexual terms. Her character is determined for us dialogically in the first instance through the debate she has with her experienced, courtly and unscrupulous companion, the Old Lady, a dialogue in which Anne is enabled ostensibly to remain virtuous whilst in fact happily succumbing to the economic and social imperative of the King's offer. The terms of her relationship with the King and the state are clearly economic as well as frankly sexual: Anne is a precious 'gem / To lighten all this isle' (2.3.78–9), a 'fresh fish', who, unlike her friend, who has 'been begging sixteen years in court' and is 'yet a courtier beggarly', has her 'mouth filled up' before she has opened it (2.3.86, 82–3, 87–8) and whose 'thousand pounds a year' is clearly not given 'for pure respect' with '[n]o other obligation' (2.3.95–6). The Third Gentleman's description of Anne at the coronation sustains the pornographic tone of these remarks, implying the new Queen's general availability as she 'oppos[es] freely / The beauty of her person to the people' (4.1.67–8) and describing her as 'the goodliest woman / That ever lay by man' (4.1.69–70) (see Fig. 19).

Yet Anne is so overtly instrumental within the patriarchal frame that it becomes difficult to treat her as a 'character' in the traditional sense. She is a 'creature', rather, a vehicle for the birth of Elizabeth, barely adequately characterized as a foil for Katherine's virtues and strength of personality, and her negative qualities are repeatedly erased by the unsubtle reminders that, whatever we think of her liaison with Henry, the outcome will be Elizabeth. All that matters is the production of an heir, as Anne herself acknowledges in her words to the Lord Chamberlain – 'More than my all is nothing' (2.3.67) – if 'nothing' connotes 'vagina' and therefore sexuality / procreativity. We have seen the dispensability of mothers in Katherine's dismissal for failing to produce a son, and Gardiner callously dismisses Anne, too, assuming that she is about to bear a boy: '[t]he fruit she goes with', he says to Lovell, 'I pray for heartily, that it may find / Good time, and live. But for the stock, . . . / I wish it grubbed up now'

19 *Unknown Lady*, drawing by Hans Holbein the Younger, inscribed '*Anna Bullen decollata fuit Londini 19 May 1536*'

(5.1.20–3). This context of the instrumentality of women in a patriarchal culture makes it less curious than it might be that, at a subtextual level, at least, it seems so difficult to make black-and-white distinctions between Katherine and Anne.

The play seems, in fact, perversely to confuse the differences between the two queens, and thus to make the transition from Roman Catholicism to Protestantism, as both symbolized in and provoked by Henry's divorce and remarriage, a much more problematic and unresolved process than might at first appear. On the one hand, we see Katherine as the embodiment of the old, Roman Catholic England and Anne as the embodiment of the new, Reformation England. On the other, we see Katherine as the embodiment of a stability which is in many ways far more comfortable, comprehensible and credible than any new order, and we see Anne as the embodiment of divorce and schism, uncertainty and unpredictability. Moreover, where Anne is portrayed as a Bathsheba figure (though one for whom a wife rather than a husband must be destroyed), Katherine is depicted as a woman of strength and faith. And source study suggests, remarkably, that the climactic deathbed vision which effectively apotheosizes Katherine acts not to outline her transcendent separation from Anne and from the Reformation, but to engage her both with her rival and with the cultural transformation she resists.

While there is nothing in Holinshed to suggest that Katherine was the recipient of divine revelation before she died, two alternative sources have been suggested for her angelic vision. E.E.Duncan-Jones points out that another notable woman of the period, Marguerite of Angoulême, Duchess of Alençon and Queen of Navarre, is reported to have had such a dream just before her death (Duncan-Jones, 142). Marguerite is mentioned at 2.2.40 and 3.2.85–6 as Wolsey's preferred bride for Henry after the divorce from Katherine. The dream she is reported to have had is described in her funeral oration, published in 1550, and clearly draws on Catholic saints' legends: in her vision, she sees 'une très-belle femme tenante en sa main une couronne qu'elle luy monstroit et luy disoit que bien tost elle en seroit couronnée' ('a very beautiful woman holding in her hand a coronet which she showed her and told her that soon she would be crowned'), a scene very close indeed to Katherine's angelic vision in the play (*Sainte Marthe*, 105).[1] According to Duncan-Jones, Marguerite's 'piety . . . was well known in England during her lifetime' (143), and it would seem perfectly appropriate to transfer this association to Katherine, particularly as Marguerite was strongly opposed to the divorce (Jourda, 1.172). Interestingly, however, Marguerite was a reforming Catholic, a staunch defender of early French reformers – the young Queen Elizabeth had translated one of her early works as a gift for her Protestant stepmother, Queen Katherine Parr – and, although never herself a Protestant, she was celebrated by French Protestants as a friend of Calvin and Marot. The transfer of her dream to Katherine thus figures Katherine as a reforming Catholic, a far cry from Wolsey or Gardiner; at the same time, the incorporation of the idea of 'holy incest' in Marguerite's poem *Miroir de l'âme pécheresse* as a means for expressing intimacy with God has further, controversial resonances for Katherine's situation. It acts also as implicit criticism of Henry, since John Bale, in his edition of Marguerite's treatise *A Godly Meditation of the Christian Soul* (1548), 'eulogized the youthful translator, Princess Elizabeth, as an intellectual descendant of Anne Askew', a celebrated Protestant martyr under Henry VIII (King, *Tudor*, 209). And since Anne Bullen herself was believed (in error) to have been a lady-in-waiting to Marguerite and even to have been encouraged in her Protestantism by her, the deployment of Marguerite's dream for

1 Duncan-Jones adds in a footnote that 'Pepys heard from a Presbyterian minister, Mr. Case, "a pretty story of a religious lady, Queen of Navarre" on 20 Jan. 1668. He does not reveal what it was but since he goes on to say that another member of the company "told a good story of Mr. Newman, the minister in New England . . . foretelling his death and preaching his funeral sermon, and at last bid the angels do their office, and dies" it seems possible that the "pretty story of the Queen of Navarre" was that of her vision of the angel with the garland' (143).

Katherine's vision produces a quite remarkable sectarian conjunction.[1]

This conjunction, in itself unexpected, is outweighed by John Margeson's suggestion (Cam[2]) that the description of the vision may have been influenced by Holinshed's report of a dream experienced by Anne Bullen herself shortly before her death:

> this good queene was forwarned of hir death in a dreame, wherein *Morpheus* the god of sleepe (in the likenesse of hir grandfather) appeered vnto hir, and after a long narration of the vanities of this world (how enuie reigneth in the courts of princes, maligning the fortunate estate of the vertuous, how king Henrie the eight and his issue should be the vtter ouerthrow and expulsion of poperie out of England, and that the gouernment of queene Elizabeth should be established in tranquillitie & peace. . .
>
> (Holinshed, 940)

Looking forward to Elizabeth's reign after the death of her daughter Mary, this dream might appear anathema to Katherine, yet there is no doubt that it is a possible source – a dream-vision of impending death which offers a bright future and which offers, too, a connection between Katherine's vision and Cranmer's prophecy (as well, tenuously, as the song which opens 3.1, with 'Morpheus' slipping to 'Orpheus', whose music induces sleep). If so, it creates a remarkable, and wholly unlikely, conflation of personalities and reputations.

Yet, remarkable though this is, there is a further possible source for Katherine's dream which produces the most unlikely conjunction of all. In Heywood's *If You Know Not Me, You Know Nobody* (first published 1605), subtitled *The Troubles of Queen Elizabeth*, the young Princess Elizabeth is suffering at the hands of her

---

1   As it happens, Anne was never a member of Marguerite's household, though she seems to have known her fairly well. According to Ives, 'Marguerite became a noted – if somewhat eclectic – supporter of religious reform, and it was easy for men like Sander [a recusant exile and polemicist under Elizabeth] to conclude that Anne, the embodiment of heresy, had been first subverted by the duchess' (Ives, 40).

sister Mary, and she has a dream-vision which shares several features with Katherine's vision in *Henry VIII*. She dreams of friars 'offering to kill her' and of angels defending her, one of whom then 'opens the Bible, and puts it in her hands'. Waking, she asks her maid Clarentia if she has seen or heard anything and discovers that she has been dreaming. She is comforted by the dream, believing that it was the 'inspiration' of 'heaven' (D4^v). The parallels between this vision of angels and Katherine's are marked, and the conjunction it creates between Anne Bullen's daughter and the mother of 'Bloody Mary' is astonishing. To give Katherine a dream which is composed of visions dreamed by Anne Bullen, Marguerite of Angoulême and the young Elizabeth is to effect through Katherine a conjunction of Catholic saints' lives and a reforming tradition of prophetic dreams, as well as to create a quiet (but quite startling) religious, if not personal, *rapprochement* between the King's first two wives – implying that Katherine (whether or not she would admit it), in her staunch resistance to the corruption represented by Wolsey and Campeius, is in fact a kind of reformer. Certainly, the dream is more dependent upon the language of Revelation – especially 7.9 and 19.9 (see 4.2.82.3–5n. and 4.2.87–90n.) – than is Cranmer's prophecy.

As the play proceeds, then, the two queens seem to lose their distinct symbolic significance, and we begin to see the essential futility of the Henrician Reformation. The sequence of Henry's wives foreshadows the sequence of post- and counter-Reformation reigns, the apparently cyclical movement from Henry to Edward to Mary to Elizabeth, and underlines fears for the future after James's death (despite, or perhaps because of, James's plan to defuse the situation by marrying a daughter to a Continental Protestant and a son to a Catholic). The restless displacement of queens in Henry's life and reign, each change both conclusive and inconclusive, embodies the long-term process of Reformation: England moves from reign to reign in the hope of a religious resolution just as Henry moves from queen to queen in the hope of a son and heir. And this process comes under its severest metaphoric pressure in a passage early in Act 4 which is apparently without direct source, inserted into a scene otherwise very closely dependent upon the wording in Holinshed:

> Hats, cloaks –
> Doublets, I think – flew up, and had their faces
> Been loose, this day they had been lost. Such joy
> I never saw before. Great-bellied women
> That had not half a week to go, like rams
> In the old time of war, would shake the press
> And make 'em reel before 'em. No man living
> Could say 'This is my wife' there, all were woven
> So strangely in one piece.
>
> (4.1.73–81)

The procreative festivity of the scene, with its curious blend of violence and fecundity, embodies the hopes of Henry and his people for a male heir through Anne, but it is the Gentleman's last observation which arguably offers the most radical reading of English Reformation history in the course of the play, a reading which is both the logical corollary of the degradation of 'conscience' and a crushing repudiation of the assumption that the individual subject was the product of Reformation. In the moment of Anne's coronation – the first of the series of remarriages, opening the floodgates to a futile quest for a healthy heir – wives become indistinguishable, 'all . . . woven / So strangely in one piece', and this is seen to be especially true of royal wives. The play's characterization of the queens – embodying its uncomfortable attitude both to the reformation of manners and to the Reformation proper – is thus designed to ensure that no-one in the audience, least of all the 'godly', is permitted the luxury of a simplistic, black-and-white understanding of the Reformation.

Hidden reformations

One field in which the Reformation was perceived by the godly to remain unfulfilled was the law, specifically in respect of the absence of a legal basis in England for thoroughgoing ecclesiastical discipline. The legal system was gradually developing a broader reach in relation to matters of conscience: the founding of the court at Bridewell Hospital – in the former Palace premises next door to Blackfriars which were given by Edward VI to the City of London in the 1550s – marked the extension of legal involvement in the policing of sexual behaviour from an exclusive focus on prostitution (that is, on professional sexual activity) to fornication in non-commercial contexts (that is, to private illicit sexual activity), and the materialization of the erratic workings of conscience into a stable and practical process of equity is apparent, for instance, in the writings of Christopher St German (Archer, 251–6). But there was no overarching official remedy for what the godly saw as the failure of the English conscience to respond to divine precepts, particularly in relation to sexuality. A principal focus for anxiety in this regard, as Lorna Hutson has noted, was the issue of clandestine marriage, which typically took place across class boundaries and which appears to have been culturally associated with stage plays from early on. Hutson cites the 1574 Act of Common Council as an example of this: the Act specifies the 'inveglynge and alleurynge of maides, speciallye orphanes and good Cityzens Children vnder Age, to previe and unmete Contractes' as a prime example of the 'sondrye greate disorders and inconvenyences [that] have benne found to ensewe to this Cittie by the inordynate hauntynge of greate multitudes of people, speciallye youthe, to playes, enterludes, and shewes' (Chambers, *ES*, 4.273; Hutson, *Usurer's*, 184).

It is not surprising that there was a cultural association of clandestine marriage and theatre in early modern London. The clandestine contract furnished a principal trope of the Terentian comedy that was both a mainstay of grammar-school education in the period and a major influence on Elizabethan and Jacobean comedy and tragicomedy, and Hutson has eloquently demonstrated the way in which Elizabethan comedy in the Terentian tradition capitalizes on error and misdeed to facilitate an outcome more productive than any 'legitimate' plot could have done. A key Terentian plot involved the clandestine marriage of the male protagonist to a lower-class woman or courtesan/prostitute who turns out in the end to be a perfectly appropriate person – the daughter of an upper-class neighbour, say – for him to marry, a catastrophe (in the technical and positive sense of a reordering conclusion) which is typically announced by a character who turns up relatively late in the play and has knowledge hidden from the others. This, allied with folk traditions of the 'lost child', is a key pattern also in Shakespeare's 'late plays' (Marina is the clearest example, emerging chaste from the brothel at Mytilene), as Shakespeare returns to Roman 'New Comedy' for his plots after a lengthy gap in which classical tragedy was the principal underpinning of his work. *Henry VIII* – despite its proximity to, and association with, the 'late plays' – tends not to be thought of in this context. I wish to argue that it should be.

The play, after all, pivots on a clandestine marriage, that of Henry and Anne, a marriage which, for obvious political reasons, is awkwardly fudged and deflected. We are simply told, along with the amazed Surrey in 3.2, that '[t]he King already / Hath married the fair lady' (3.2.41–2), and the play evades mention of the awkward sequence of events by which Henry married Anne in secret in January 1533 yet Cranmer did not formally invalidate the King's marriage to Katherine until May of that year, a mere four days before Anne's coronation. The event is, nonetheless, tacitly present in Suffolk's awkward speech in response to Surrey's delight at the news. 'There's order given for her coronation', he says, but adds a warning – 'Marry, this is yet but young, and may be left / To some ears unrecounted' (3.2.46–8) – before offering a slightly nervous (because rhetorically superfluous) proleptic justification of the match:

> But, my lords,
> She is a gallant creature, and complete
> In mind and feature. I persuade me from her
> Will fall some blessing to this land which shall
> In it be memorized.
>
> (3.2.48–52)

We have already heard the Chamberlain on this subject when he visited Anne and the Old Lady (2.3.78–9), and we are aware that retrospective rejection of charges of illegitimacy is being laid on with a trowel. Moreover, if there is any suggestion in the text that Anne is to be seen as visibly pregnant at the coronation, it is well submerged – surfacing only obliquely, if at all, in the Third Gentleman's reference to '[g]reat-bellied women / That had not half a week to go' (4.1.76–7). Yet whatever evasions the text offers, the fact remains that the most public figure in the land, the head both of the state and of the Church of England, marries in secret in what can only be described as unfortunate circumstances and against the displaced paternal objections voiced by Wolsey:

> Anne Bullen? No, I'll no Anne Bullens for him:
> There's more in't than fair visage. Bullen?
> No, we'll no Bullens. . . .
> The late Queen's gentlewoman? A knight's daughter
> To be her mistress' mistress? The Queen's Queen?
>
> (3.2.87–9, 94–5)

The solution to the play's central problem – the lack of an heir to the throne – is thus the King's clandestine marriage to a woman of lower status in the face of 'paternal' disapproval, and I would argue that this can best be explicated as the simultaneous deployment and displacement of Terentian plot-structure – making *Henry VIII* the most unlikely of comedies.

By way of support, I want to outline a couple of representative Terentian plots: one from Terence himself, the other from Plautus (whose plays, though distinct, were generally discussed alongside those of Terence in grammar-school education). The first is Terence's *Andria* ('The Woman from Andros'), a play which was regularly cited and explicated by Renaissance theorists, including the tragicomic theorist Giambattista Guarini (whose work is in turn cited by Fletcher in his preface to *The Faithful Shepherdess*), and has been a principal focus too for modern scholars of Terentian influence on Shakespeare (see Baldwin, Herrick). *Andria* relates the story of Pamphilus, a young man who is in love with a slave girl called Glycerium but whose father plans to marry him to Philumena, his old friend Chremes' daughter, who is in fact loved by another young man, Charinus. Pamphilus is helped by a wily slave to resist his father's plan, and after a variety of errors, misunderstandings and discoveries – including the revelation that Glycerium is pregnant by Pamphilus – a stranger arrives in town and breaks the news that Glycerium is not a slave at all, but Chremes' long-lost daughter and therefore Philumena's sister. The play ends happily with marriage for the pairs of lovers, a conclusion which retrospectively validates the illicit sexual encounter of Pamphilus and Glycerium and legitimates the child of their union.

The second representative plot is that of Plautus's *Amphitryo*, one of two Plautus plays which serve as sources for *The Comedy of Errors* (and which has strong similarities to the events narrated in Natalie Zemon Davis's fascinating account of *The Return of Martin Guerre*).[1] Mercury, who appears as a version of the slave trickster, helping fool mortals on Jupiter's behalf, tells the story of his master's desire for a mortal woman, Alcmena, who is married to Amphitryo, and his miraculous appearance at her door in the shape of her husband soon after Amphitryo has gone off to battle. They have sex, Alcmena becomes pregnant, and her husband, on his actual return, wants to know who is responsible. Eventually, after much confusion, Alcmena gives birth to the prodigy Hercules, whose astonishing physical development and heroic

1 These similarities were noted in the narrative of the trial of Arnaud du Tilh written by one of the judges, Jean de Coras; see Coras, A4^{r-v}; Davis, 111n.; Hutson, *Usurer's*, 191–6.

behaviour confirms his miraculous nature and legitimates her encounter with Jupiter in everyone's eyes, including those of her husband. The encounter of god and woman takes place in disguise (the ultimate bed trick) and the product of that encounter is miraculous, so that Alcmena's responsibility for the act is erased in two ways: sleeping (as she thinks) with her husband, surprised as she is by his apparent change of character in a short space of time, can only be an indication of true wifely, obedient behaviour, and the child produced as a result of the encounter is prodigious, a further indication of divine sanction (indeed, divine responsibility in a material sense) for what she has done. Alcmena thus manages both to have illicit sex and to behave in a godly manner.

The surprising dependence of the structure of *Henry VIII* on the Terentian plot that these two plays, in their different ways, exemplify will by now be apparent. As Ruth Nevo notes, the aim of Shakespeare's comic plots is 'recovery: the finding of what was missing or lacking at the start', and the same is true, as we have seen, for *Henry VIII* (Nevo, 6). What is missing is an heir: by the end of the play, that heir has been produced and the dual problem of her origin and her sex has been effectively erased. The Terentian pattern thus operates in displaced form. The King is the protagonist of this unexpected comedy, while Wolsey is both the disapproving father and the slave trickster intent on helping both his master and himself. Henry meets Anne in disguise, so that she does not initially know who she is dealing with; he gets her pregnant and marries her clandestinely; Cranmer then acts as the *persona ad catastrophen machinata* (the character with hidden knowledge who confirms the actual legitimacy of the apparently illicit action) to enable Anne's effective translation from whore to Queen. Thus, what looks initially like an inappropriate match between a king and a whore is validated in due time by the birth of the prodigious issue, Elizabeth. As a result, the already crowded field of generic attributions of *Henry VIII* is thrown into further disarray, suggesting a comic direction for the last days of the 'history play', and offering a further take on the play's engagement with Protestantism.

In this context, what is of particular interest is the use made of the clandestine marriage plot by reforming writers as a trope of apocalypse. A good example of a Protestant play which depends upon the Terentian plot – or at least on a modified version of that plot – is John Foxe's *Titus et Gesippus*. Foxe is not exactly the first name to spring to mind in a catalogue of Renaissance playwrights, yet the martyrologist did, when young, write two plays which offer a sense of the way in which English Protestant thinking appropriated classical texts and patterns which might otherwise seem decidedly un-Christian. *Titus et Gesippus* is a tragicomedy in which the protagonist, Gesippus, gives up his bride out of true faithfulness to his friend Titus. Later he goes to visit his friend, is not recognized in Rome, and is about to be hanged as a robber when Titus, recognizing him at last, charges himself with the crime instead in order to save his friend. The two are finally saved by the confession of the true robber, and Titus helps Gesippus find an even better wife than the one he gave up in the first place. Though this is ostensibly a play of male friendship and not a comedy of the sexes, there are Terentian elements in the pattern of the plot; in the presence of a trickster figure, Phormio; in the double marriage; and in certain specific names drawn directly from *Andria*, including Chremes (Gesippus's father) and Pamphila (the woman Gesippus marries at the end of the play, a former sweetheart of Titus).

Foxe effectively rewrote *Titus et Gesippus* as a *comœdia apocalyptica* in his later play *Christus Triumphans*, which follows the fate of a representative soul under threat from Satan and the Antichrist (the Catholic Church, that is) until Christ finally saves him, and which concludes with a prophecy of revelation to come at an indeterminate but deeply longed-for time. The two plays, though ostensibly different in nature, in fact provide the same basic tragicomic plot, as they move through failures of recognition and other confusions towards a happy ending. Their similarities demonstrate the acquisition of the Terentian plot for Protestantism (freed from the 'immoral' elements of classical exemplars), as the confusions and eventual reordering conclusion of Roman comedy are reworked as apocalyptic history.[1] In *Christus Triumphans*, according to the play's late-seventeenth-century editor, '*[i]ctu uno actuque sales ediscere Plauti, / Et Christi hisce datur*' ('In a single stroke and act, you may learn the wit of Plautus and with it that of Christ') (Foxe, *Christus*, B1^{r-v}).

Thus although *Henry VIII* has been written off for centuries as a play of loosely connected episodes with no overall unifying structure, it would in fact have had a perfectly understandable framework for its first audiences, since what the Protestant playgoer saw was a 'reformed' play drawing on classical sources for its plot structure. As a result, the apparently disparate episodes we are offered from Henry VIII's reign form a comprehensible sequence which is then available for subversion. What Protestants marked out from the Terentian plot was the manner in which a providential outcome emerged from apparently unpromising circumstances: the initial sexual congress may be shady and improper, but the issue is heaven-sent; at the same time, the improper behaviour remains improper, despite its recuperation by way of the progenitive outcome. In the context of increased policing of sexual impropriety, notably the act of clandestine marriage, the celebration of a providential outcome of a royal clandestine marriage is necessarily uncomfortable. The nature of the Henrician Reformation is thus irredeemably double: it is an event which precipitates godly change, yet it is at the same time an event precipitated by ungodly behaviour.

1   For Marvin Herrick, *Christus Triumphans* is a good example of the tradition known as 'Christian Terence', 'a large body of academic plays written for the most part by schoolmasters for the instruction of students' (Herrick, 61–2). Herrick also notes the place of the Christian Terence plays in the development of tragicomedy, the principal mode of Shakespeare's and of Fletcher's work after 1607: 'The plays of the Christian Terence anticipated almost every characteristic . . . of the secular tragicomedy that flourished in western Europe at the close of the sixteenth and the beginning of the seventeenth centuries' (62). John Hazel Smith notes that the *dénouement* of *Christus Triumphans*, 'a preparation for a wedding, is a clear use of a long theological tradition inherited from the apocalyptic source and from some Roman comic practice' (Smith, 39).

One scene of *Henry VIII*, more than any other, has either been omitted altogether or else heavily cut, and that is 5.3, the scene featuring the Porter and his Man. Formally, the scene has the function of an antimasque, a brief period of anarchy erased by the return of the christening procession and redeemed by Cranmer's prophecy of peace and stability; it is also, in its way, tragicomic – threatening violence, yet concluding in celebration. Clearly, it serves a very practical theatrical function at this point in the play: as the BBC script editor puts it (noting that it is the only scene cut in the television version), '[i]t's a classic example of needing a scene with only about two people in front of the tabs while every-body else is getting ready for the big walk down at the end' (BBC, 19). But the scene has, I would argue, a significant symbolic, as well as practical, function: it is, in fact, in many ways paradigmatic of the play as a whole in its resistance to the formalities of Reformation. The blurring of distinctions, the difficulty of con-trolling popular energy, the contradictory effects of celebration, and the mockery of the transience of fashion all act to tie the scene closely to the rest of the play, and its dismissal at the hands of crit-ics and directors is evidence of the way in which *Henry VIII* has been persistently misread across the centuries. Its significance stems from its engagement with the extra-temporal realm of fes-tival, as it plays games with time in order to establish a framework for truth which is contemporary as well as historical, and it serves both to contradict the ostensible calm and control of the final, prophetic scene and to foreground the actual confusion and uncertainty behind the ritual with which the play concludes.

The ostensible logic of the chaos is celebration of a royal event, but from the beginning the topography of order is confused – 'Do you take the court for Parish Garden?' (5.3.1–2) demands the Porter of the crowd – and the absence of motivational clarity is apparent in his double question: 'You must be seeing christenings? Do you look for ale and cakes here?' (8–9). As the latter question indicates, the crowd that besieges the court bears the hallmarks of carnival: the phallic humour in the reference to the 'strange Indian with the great tool' (32) and in the sad few remaining inches of the Porter's Man's once-proud four-foot cudgel; the personification of consumption as an anonymous voice in the crowd claims to 'belong to th' larder' (4); the grotesque figures of the red-faced man and the haberdasher's wife in the Porter's Man's narrative. The intransigence of this crowd and the violence required to contain them demonstrate the ease with which carnival can turn to violence: the Porter's Man points out that the only way to move the crowd would be to 'sweep 'em from the door with cannons', adding that they 'may as well push against Paul's as stir 'em' (11, 14). Celebration has thus become siege, and the Porter's Man provides a graphic account of the manoeuvrings of the opposing forces in a carnivalesque battlefield:

> That fire-drake did I hit three times on the head, and three times was his nose discharged against me. He stands there like a mortar-piece, to blow us. There was a haberdasher's wife of small wit near him, that railed upon me till her pinked porringer fell off her head, for kindling such a combustion in the state. I missed the meteor once and hit that woman, who cried out 'Clubs!', when I might see from far some forty truncheoners draw to her succour, which were the hope o'th' Strand, where she was quartered. They fell on; I made good my place; at length they came to th' broomstaff to me; I defied 'em still, when suddenly a file of boys behind 'em, loose shot, delivered such a shower of pebbles that I was fain to draw mine honour in and let 'em win the work.
>
> (41–55)

This comically violent scene is credible as Henrician festivity; at the same time, in its resistance both to the peace that is celebrated in the final scene and to the war that would be the only alternative, and in its sheer detail, it expresses the audience's London, the London of 1613.

For one thing, the Porter and his Man are anachronistically aware of the place of the Jacobean stage on the boundary between civic order and chaos, apparent in the Porter's identification of the 'file of boys' (53) with the riotous 'youths that thunder at a play-house and fight for bitten apples' (57–8) as well as in the confusion of court and Parish Garden. Certain details of dress – linked to the earlier equation of Reformation and the cycle of changing fashion – locate the scene firmly (and humorously) in 1613, most notably the 'pinked porringer' lost by the haberdasher's wife (a particularly self-conscious example of the latest in Jacobean fashion, worn appropriately enough by the wife of a hatmaker) and the person 'i'th' chamblet' addressed by the Porter at the end of the scene (chamblet was a material freshly in fashion in 1613, and, as a particularly costly cloth, a hint either that the crowd is made up of people from a broad social spectrum or else that the siege has come unexpectedly out of a gathering of people in their Sunday best) (Linthicum, 218–9).

In the crowd's response, the official equation of James's daughter Elizabeth with Henry's daughter Elizabeth receives popular validation; at the same time, the very fact that the events of the Reformation are being played out in what is recognizably a Jacobean, not a Henrician, scene, suggests both the pace and at the same time the incompletion of the events depicted. The penultimate scene thus foregrounds the play's juxtaposition of two different historical periods, treating Henry VIII's reign as if it were contemporary for the Globe or Blackfriars audiences ('Think ye see / The very persons of our noble story / As they were living', as the Prologue (25–7) suggests) and reading Jacobean England in direct continuity with Henrician England. At the same time, things had changed so much in a few decades that the Jacobean audience would no doubt have felt a certain sympathy with the Third Gentlemen in his confusion over the name of the newly christened Whitehall: 'I know it,' he says, 'But 'tis so lately altered that the old name / Is fresh about me' (4.1.97–9). By underlining the speed and vigour with which political change can take place as well as the fundamental continuities between Henrician and Jacobean experience, this scene – like the play as a whole – creates a dramatic space within which the outcome of the English Reformation is still very much at stake.

ORIGINALS: TEXTUAL HISTORY

In the prologue to his account of the mutiny on the *Bounty*, the historian Greg Dening admits that, as a spin-off from his textual endeavours, he set himself 'the summer relaxation of completing [a] wooden model of the *Bounty*' (Dening, 5). But, he asks himself, which *Bounty*? 'Will this model', he wonders:

> be the *Bounty* of the Deptford Naval Yard plans or the adaptations made of them? . . . Will I set the mainmast a little lower following Bligh's plan to lower the power of her sails, or shall I raise it following his second thoughts at the Cape of Good Hope?
>
> (5)

In other words, he wants to know, 'When was the *Bounty* the *Bounty*?' and he is by no means sure that there is an answer.

These are the kinds of question that an editor must also ask of the process of 'establishing the text' – because, as Dening observes, 'what model' (or, for our purposes, what fixed text of a performed event) 'will ever catch process?' (6). A text – perhaps especially a dramatic text, and certainly a text belonging to a canon which has been the subject of minute, obsessive attention for centuries – is never still, never stable, is always reflective of change (in attitudes to interpretation, to dramatic production, to textuality); as a result, the 'establishment' of a play-text is both a necessary and a time-bound action, an action which is both (to use Dening's words) a 'freezing' and a 'falsifying' (5). And while the textual history of *Henry VIII* is simplicity itself in comparison with *King Lear*, say, or *Othello* – each of which exists in more than one authoritative form – the play is in several ways, as I have

147

suggested, a play about change, about the negotiation of change and the denial of change, and its textual condition is part and parcel of that concern.

In editing a play-text, there are three factors that an editor must take into account: the event of performance, the process of production of the performance script as a text for readers, and the composition of the target readership of the edition. Each of these factors will determine the text that appears in the edition, and each of them militates against stability. The fact that the plays in the Shakespeare canon were written for performance and only after they had had their time on the stage were presented in the form of a book means that any single text can represent only a frozen moment in the life of the performed play. Any performance is, in its way, unique: it can only offer one take on the possibilities offered by a script; and a professional playwright does well to keep this in mind. Playwrights who do try to maintain a hold over what happens to the script once it has left their hands are generally fighting a losing battle. Ben Jonson's attempt to present the reading public with an authorized version of his plays was virtually unique in the period: to do so he was obliged to make substantial alterations (for instance, rewriting sections of originally collaborative plays which had been written by his coadjutor, not himself). English Renaissance playwrights in fact sold their plays to an acting company (Shakespeare to the company in which he was a shareholder, the King's Men): once acquired, the play was the company's to do with as it pleased and no longer the property of its writer. In this context alone, it is impossible to say of an early modern play-text that its meaning can be determined solely in relation to its author's intentions.

There are, nonetheless, certain crucial questions which any intelligent reader of an early modern play will eventually ask precisely because (rightly or wrongly) the traditions of literary criticism (and of legal, theological, and other forms of textual interpretation) place such central importance on authority and authorship. Whose words are we reading at any given moment? In the case of *Henry VIII*, are they those of Shakespeare? Of Fletcher? Of some anonymous scribe making a fair copy of the playwright('s/s') rough drafts (or 'foul papers', as they were known)? Of the compositors at the printing house, who set the text into type? Of the proofreader at the printing house, who checked the typesetters' work and corrected it? At each stage of this process, change can enter in: collaborators may rework, cross out or reinstate each other's material; scribes may misread foul papers or correct omissions or errors in the manuscript before them; compositors in turn may misread the handwriting of scribe or playwright, may decide to even out stylistic differences apparent in a collaborative text, may (will, almost certainly) make simple mechanical errors; proofreaders may, in attempting to correct what appears to be a compositor's error, introduce further change.

In other words, the one thing we do know is that at no point when we are reading a play in the Shakespeare canon or any other early modern canon can we be absolutely sure that we are reading the words that were written (never mind 'intended') by the writer whose work we believe (hope) we are reading. In the case of *Henry VIII*, the text we have seems to have reached us as the product of two compositors working from copy put together by two playwrights who were in turn working from multiple narrative sources, the chief of which, Holinshed's *Chronicles*, was itself the product of collaborative writing. This copy was written not as a text for mechanical reproduction but as a score for a stage play which came to life only in production by a highly successful acting company, and was performed in (and thus written for) at least two theatres as well as, in all likelihood, the court before it was committed to print in the First Folio. The questions asked of the origins of this play are therefore necessarily complicated, and much of the (relatively limited) critical and editorial attention that *Henry VIII* has received over the years has dwelt on or pronounced upon the play's origins and in particular on the question of authorship. I chose not to begin my introduction with a lengthy and possibly off-putting discussion of these topics because editions of *Henry VIII* have too often begun in this way, with the effect that critical comment is interminably delayed and frustratingly abbreviated. But in order to do this, I have had to leave certain obvious questions in the air, and it is now time to attempt some answers. In this concluding section, therefore, I shall comment, in order, on my copy-text (i.e. the text chosen as the basis for this edition, the First Folio text of *Henry VIII*), on the process of modernization of that text for this edition, on the origins of that text in earlier texts (i.e. 'sources'), and on the evidence for and ramifications of collaborative production.

Text and modernization

If Shakespeare's old colleagues Heminges and Condell had organized the First Folio chronologically and had included every play in which Shakespeare had had a hand, then *Henry VIII* would in all likelihood have been the penultimate play (after *Cardenio* and before *The Two Noble Kinsmen*), and might well have been titled *All Is True*. If they had ordered chronologically just the plays they did include in the Folio, then *Henry VIII* would have come last. But they chose a different running order, organizing the book on the basis of broad generic categories, and *Henry VIII* appears on folios t3^r–x4^v – i.e. pp. 205–32 (p. 216 is mispaged '218', as can be seen by comparing the page numbers of folios v2^v and v3^v, reproduced on pp. 151–2 (Figs. 20, 21) – as the twenty-fourth play in the volume, in the second section, entitled 'Histories', within which plays are arranged not in the order in which they were written but in the historical order of kings' reigns. *Henry VIII*, or to give it the full title under which it is listed, *The Famous History of the Life of King Henry the Eight* (which was most probably substituted for the performance title *All Is True* for purposes of continuity with the titles of the other history plays), addressing as it does history more recent than the others and even incorporating the birth of Elizabeth – the Queen who had ruled until a decade before the play was performed – is thus the tenth and last, coming

218 · *The Life of King Henry the Eight.*

Car. Whil'ft our Commiffion from Rome is read,
Let filence be commanded.
King. What's the need?
It hath already publiquely bene read,
And on all fides th'Authority allow'd,
You may then fpare that time.
Car. Bee't fo, proceed.
Scri. Say, *Henry* K. of England, come into the Court.
Crier. *Henry* King of England, &c.
King. Heere.
Scribe. Say, *Katherine* Queene of England,
Come into the Court.
Crier. *Katherine* Queene of England, &c.
    The Queene makes no anfwer, rifes out of her Chaire,
    goes about the Court, comes to the King, and kneeles at
    his Feete. Then fpeakes.
Sir, I defire you do me Right and Iuftice,
And to beftow your pitty on me; for
I am a moft poore Woman, and a Stranger,
Borne out of your Dominions : hauing heere
No Iudge indifferent, nor no more affurance
Of equall Friendfhip and Proceeding. Alas Sir :
In what haue I offended you? What caufe
Hath my behauiour giuen to your difpleafure,
That thus you fhould proceede to put me off,
And take your good Grace from me? Heauen witneffe,
I haue bene to you, a true and humble Wife,
At all times to your will conformable :
Euer in feare to kindle your Difike,
Yea, fubiect to your Countenance: Glad, or forry,
As I faw it inclin'd? When was the houre
I euer contradicted your Defire?
Or made it not mine too? Or which of your Friends
Haue I not ftroue to loue, although I knew
He were mine Enemy? What Friend of mine,
That had to him deriu'd your Anger, did I
Continue in my Liking? Nay, gaue notice
He was from thence difcharg'd? Sir, call to minde,
That I haue beene your Wife, in this Obedience,
Vpward of twenty yeares, and haue bene bleft
With many Children by you, If in the courfe
And procefle of this time, you can report,
And proue it fo, against mine Honor, aught
My bond to Wedlocke, or my Loue and Dutie
Against your Sacred Perfon; in Gods name
Turne me away : and let the fowl'ft Contempt
Shut doore vpon me, and fo giue me vp
To the fharp'ft kinde of Iuftice. Pleafe you, Sir,
The King your Father, was reputed for
A Prince moft Prudent; of an excellent
And vnmatch'd Wit, and Iudgement. *Ferdinand*
My Father, King of Spaine, was reckon'd one
The wifeft Prince, that there had reign'd, by many
A yeare before. It is not to be queftion'd,
That they had gather'd a wife Councell to them
Of euery Realme, that did debate this Bufineffe,
Who deem'd our Marriage lawful. Wherefore I humbly
Befeech you Sir, to fpare me, till I may
Be by my Friends in Spaine, aduis'd; whofe Counfaile
I will implore. If not, i'th'name of God
Your pleafure be fulfill'd.
Wol. You haue heere Lady,
(And of your choice) thefe Reuerend Fathers, men
Of fingular Integrity, and Learning;
Yea, the elect o'th'Land, who are affembled
To pleade your Caufe. It fhall be therefore bootleffe,

That longer you defire the Court, as well
For your owne quiet, as to rectifie
What is vnfetled in the King.
    Camp. His Grace
Hath fpoken well, and iuftly: Therefore Madam,
It's fit this Royall Seffion do proceed,
And that (without delay) their Arguments
Be now produc'd, and heard.
    Qu. Lord Cardinall, to you I fpeake.
Wol. Your pleafure, Madam.
    Qu. Sir, I am about to weepe; but thinking that
We are a Queene (or long haue dream'd fo) certaine
The daughter of a King, my drops of teares,
Ile turne to fparkes of fire.
Wol. Be patient yet.
    Qu. I will, when you are humble; Nay before,
Or God will punifh me. I do beleeue
(Induc'd by potent Circumftances) that
You are mine Enemy, and make my Challenge,
You fhall not be my Iudge. For it is you
Haue blowne this Coale, betwixt my Lord, and me;
(Which Gods dew quench) therefore, I fay againe,
I vtterly abhorre; yea, from my Soule
Refufe you for my Iudge, whom yet once more
I hold my moft malicious Foe, and thinke not
At all a Friend to truth.
Wol. I do profeffe
You fpeake not like your felfe: who euer yet
Haue ftood to Charity, and difplayd th'effects
Of difpofition gentle, and of wifedome,
Ore-topping womans powre. Madam, you do me wrong
I haue no Spleene against you, nor iniuftice
For you, or any : how farre I haue proceeded,
Or how farre further (Shall) is warranted
By a Commiffion from the Confiftorie.
Yea, the whole Confiftorie of Rome. You charge me,
That I haue blowne this Coale: I do deny it,
The King is prefent: If it be knowne to him,
That I gainfay my Deed; how may he wound,
And worthily my Falfehood, yea, as much
As you haue done my Truth, If he know
That I am free of your Report, he knowes
I am not of your wrong. Therefore in him
It lies to cure me, and the Cure is to
Remoue thefe Thoughts from you. The which before
His Highneffe fhall fpeake in, I do befeech
You (gracious Madam) to vnthinke your fpeaking,
And to fay fo no more.
    Queen. My Lord, my Lord,
I am a fimple woman, much too weake
T'oppofe your cunning. Y'are meek, & humble-mouth'd
You figne your Place, and Calling, in full feeming,
With Meekeneffe and Humilitie; but your Heart
Is cramm'd with Arrogancie, Spleene, and Pride.
You haue by Fortune, and his Highneffe fauors,
Gone flightly o're lowe fteppes, and now are mounted
Where Powres are your Retainers, and your words
(Domeftickes to you) ferue your will, as't pleafe
Your felfe pronounce their Office. I muft tell you,
You tender more your perfons Honor, then
Your high profeffion Spirituall. That agen
I do refufe you for my Iudge, and heere
Before you all, Appeale vnto the Pope,
To bring my whole Caufe 'fore his Holineffe,
And to be iudg'd by him.
    She Curtfies to the King, and offers to depart.
                          Cont.

20 Folio v2^v from the First Folio, 1623, containing Katherine's 'coals' speech; it was set by Compositor B and includes the variant *Queen.* and *Qu.* SPs

Actus Tertius.   *Scena Prima.*

Enter Queene and her Women as at worke.

Queen. Take thy Lute wench,
My Soule growes sad with trouble,
Sing, and disperse 'em if thou canst: leaue working:

SONG.

ORpheus with his Lute made Trees,
  And the Mountaine tops that freeze,
Bow themselues when he did sing.
To his Musicke, Plants and Flowers
Euer sprung; as Sunne and Showers,
There had made a lasting Spring.
Euery thing that heard him play,
Euen the Billowes of the Sea,
Hung their heads, & then lay by.
In sweet Musicke is such Art,
Killing care, & griefe of heart,
Fall asleepe, or hearing dye.

Enter a Gentleman.

Queen. How now?
Gent. And't please your Grace, the two great Cardinals
Wait in the presence.
Queen. Would they speake with me?
Gent. They wil'd me say so Madam.
Queen. Pray their Graces
To come neere: what can be their busines
With me, a poore weake woman, falne from fauour?
I doe not like their comming; now I thinke on't,
They should bee good men, their affaires as righteous:
But all Hoods, make not Monkes.

Enter the two Cardinalls, Wolsey & Campian.

Wols. Peace to your Highnesse.
Queen. Your Graces find me heere part of a Houswife,
(I would be all) against the worst may happen:
What are your pleasures with me, reuerent Lords?
Wol. May it please you Noble Madam, to withdraw
Into your priuate Chamber; we shall giue you
The full cause of our comming.
Queen. Speake it heere.
There's nothing I haue done yet o'my Conscience
Deserues a Corner: would all other Women
Could speake this with as free a Soule as I doe.
My Lords, I care not (so much I am happy
Aboue a number) if my actions
Were tri'de by eu'ry tongue, eu'ry eye saw 'em,
Enuy and base opinion set against 'em,
I know my life so euen. If your busines
Seeke me out, and that way I am Wife in;
Out with it boldly: Truth loues open dealing.
Card. Tanta est erga te mentis integritas Regina serenissima.
Queen. O good my Lord, no Latin;
I am not such a Truant since my comming,
As not to know the Language I haue liu'd in: (ous:
A strange Tongue makes my cause more strange, suspiti-
Pray speake in English; heere are some will thanke you,
If you speake truth for their poore Mistris sake;
Beleeue me she ha's had much wrong. Lord Cardinall,
The willing'st sinne I euer yet committed,
May be absolu'd in English.
Card. Noble Lady,

I am sorry my integrity shoul breed,
(And seruice to his Maiesty and you)
So deepe suspition, where all faith was meant;
We come not by the way of Accusation,
To taint that honour euery good Tongue blesses;
Nor to betray you any way to sorrow;
You haue too much good Lady: But to know
How you stand minded in the waighty difference
Betweene the King and you, and to deliuer
(Like free and honest men) our iust opinions,
And comforts to our cause.
Camp. Most honour'd Madam,
My Lord of Yorke, out of his Noble nature,
Zeale and obedience he still bore your Grace,
Forgetting (like a good man) your late Censure
Both of his truth and him (which was too farre)
Offers, as I doe, in a signe of peace,
His Seruice, and his Counsell.
Queen. To betray me.
My Lords, I thanke you both for your good wills,
Ye speake like honest men, (pray God ye proue so)
But how to make ye sodainly an Answere
In such a poynt of weight, so neere mine Honour,
(More neere my Life I feare) with my weake wit;
And to such men of grauity and learning;
In truth I know not. I was set at worke,
Among my Maids, full little (God knowes) looking
Either for such men, or such businesse;
For her sake that I haue beene, for I feele
The last fit of my Greatnesse; good your Graces
Let me haue time and Councell for my Cause:
Alas, I am a Woman frendlesse, hopelesse.
Wol. Madam,
You wrong the Kings loue with these feares,
Your hopes and friends are infinite.
Queen. In England,
But little for my profit can you thinke Lords,
That any English man dare giue me Councell?
Or be a knowne friend 'gainst his Highnes pleasure,
(Though he be growne so desperate to be honest)
And liue a Subiect? Nay forsooth, my Friends,
They that must weigh out my afflictions,
They that my trust must grow to, liue not heere,
They are (as all my other comforts) far hence
In mine owne Countrey Lords.
Camp. I would your Grace
Would leaue your greefes, and take my Counsell.
Queen. How Sir?
Camp. Put your maine cause into the Kings protection,
Hee's louing and most gracious. 'Twill be much,
Both for your Honour better, and your Cause:
For if the tryall of the Law o'retake ye,
You'l part away disgrac'd.
Wol. He tels you rightly.
Queen. Ye tell me what ye wish for both, my ruine:
Is this your Christian Councell? Out vpon ye.
Heauen is aboue all yet; there sits a Iudge,
That no King can corrupt.
Camp. Your rage mistakes vs.
Queen. The more shame for ye; holy men I thought ye,
Vpon my Soule two reuerend Cardinall Vertues:
But Cardinall Sins, and hollow hearts I feare ye:
Mend 'em for shame my Lords: Is this your comfort?
The Cordiall that ye bring a wretched Lady?
A woman lost among ye, laugh't at, scornd?
I will not wish ye halfe my miseries,

21   Folio v3ᵛ from the First Folio, 1623, showing the beginning of Katherine's 'cardinal sins' speech; it was set by Compositor I

...more Charity. But say I warn'd ye;
Take heed, for heauens fake take heed, leaft at once
The burthen of my forrowes, fall vpon ye.
  Car. Madam, this is a meere diftraction.
You turne the good we offer, into enuy.
  ...ture. Ye turne me into nothing. Woe vpon ye,
And all fuch falfe Profeffors. Would you haue me
(if you haue any Iuftice, any Pitty,)
(If ye be any thing but Churchmens habits)
Put my ficke caufe into his hands, that hates me?
Alas, he's banifh'd me his Bed already,
His Loue, too long ago. I am old my Lords,
And all the Fellowfhip I hold now with him
Is onely my Obedience. What can happen
To me, aboue this wretchedneffe? All your Studies
Make me a Curfe, like this.
  Camp. Your feares are worfe.
  Qu. Haue I liu'd thus long (let me fpeake my felfe,
Since Vertue findes no friends) a Wife a true one?
A Woman (I dare fay without Vainglory)
Neuer yet branded with Sufpition?
Haue I, with all my full Affections
Still met the King? Lou'd him next Heau'n? Obey'd him?
Bin (out of fondneffe) fuperftitious to him?
Almoft forgot my Prayres to content him?
And am I thus rewarded? Tis not well Lords.
Bring me a conftant woman to her Husband,
One that ne're dream'd a Ioy, beyond his pleafure;
And to that Woman (when fhe has done moft)
Yet will I adde an Honor; a great Patience.
  Car. Madam, you wander from the good
We ayme at.
  Qu. My Lord,
I dare not make my felfe fo guiltie,
To giue vp willingly that Noble Title
Your Mafter wed me to: nothing but death
Shall e're diuorce my Dignities.
  Car. Pray heare me.
  Qu. Would I had neuer trod this Englifh Earth,
Or felt the Flatteries that grow vpon it:
Ye haue Angels Faces; but Heauen knowes your hearts.
What will become of me now, wretched Lady?
I am the moft vnhappy Woman liuing.
Alas (poore Wenches) where are now your Fortunes?
Shipwrack'd vpon a Kingdome, where no Pitty,
No Friends, no Hope, no Kindred weepes for me?
Almoft no Graue allow'd me? Like the Lilly
That once was Miftris of the Field, and flourifh'd,
Ile hang my head, and perifh.
  Car. If your Grace
Could but be brought to know, our Ends are honeft,
You'd feele more comfort. Why fhold we (good Lady)
Vpon what caufe wrong you? Alas, our Places,
The way of our Profeffion is againft it;
We are to Cure fuch forrowes, not to fowe 'em.
For Goodneffe fake, confider what you do,
How you may hurt your felfe: I, vtterly
Grow from the Kings Acquaintance, by this Carriage.
The hearts of Princes kiffe Obedience,
So much they loue it. But to ftubborne Spirits,
They fwell and grow, as terrible as ftormes.
I know you haue a Gentle, Noble temper,
A Soule as euen as a Calme; Pray thinke vs,
Thofe we profeffe Peace-makers, Friends, and Seruants.
  Camp. Madam, you'l finde it fo:
You wrong your Vertues

With thefe weake Womens feares. A Noble Spirit
As yours was, put into you, euer cafts
Such doubts as falfe Coine from it. The King loues you,
Beware you loofe it not: For vs (if you pleafe
To truft vs in your bufineffe) we are ready
To vfe our vtmoft Studies, in your feruice.
  Qu. Do what ye will, my Lords:
And pray forgiue me;
If I haue vs'd my felfe vnmannerly,
You know I am a Woman, lacking wit
To make a feemely anfwer to fuch perfons,
Pray do my feruice to his Maieftie,
He ha's my heart yet, and fhall haue my Prayers
While I fhall haue my life. Come reuerend Fathers,
Beftow your Councels on me. She now begges
That little thought when fhe fet footing heere,
She fhould haue bought her Dignities fo deere. *Exeunt.*

Scena Secunda.

Enter the Duke of Norfolke, Duke of Suffolke, Lord Surrey, and Lord Chamberlaine.

  Norf. If you will now vnite in your Complaints,
And force them with a Conftancy, the Cardinall
Cannot ftand vnder them. If you omit
The offer of this time, I cannot promife,
But that you fhall fuftaine moe new difgraces,
With thefe you beare alreadie.
  Sur. I am ioyfull
To meete the leaft occafion, that may giue me
Remembrance of my Father-in-Law, the Duke,
To be reueng'd on him.
  Suf. Which of the Peeres
Haue vncontemn'd gone by him, or at leaft
Strangely neglected? When did he regard
The ftampe of Nobleneffe in any perfon
Out of himfelfe?
  Cham. My Lords, you fpeake your pleafures:
What he deferues of you and me, I know:
What we can do to him (though now the time
Giues way to vs) I much feare. If you cannot
Barre his acceffe to'th'King, neuer attempt
Any thing on him: for he hath a Witchcraft
Ouer the King in's Tongue.
  Nor. O feare him not,
His fpell in that is out: the King hath found
Matter againft him, that for euer marres
The Hony of his Language. No, he's fetled
(Not to come off) in his difpleafure.
  Sur. Sir,
I fhould be glad to heare fuch Newes as this
Once euery houre.
  Nor. Beleeue it, this is true.
In the Diuorce, his contrarie proceedings
Are all vnfolded: wherein he appeares,
As I would wifh mine Enemy.
  Sur. How come
His practifes to light?
  Suf. Moft ftrangely.
  Sur. O how? how?
  Suf. The Cardinals Letters to the Pope mifcarried,
And

22 Folio v4^r from the First Folio, 1623, showing the end of Katherine's 'cardinal sins' speech; it was set by Compositor B and contains the variant *Quee.* and *Qu.* SPs

after *The Life & Death of Richard the Third*, the play in which the audience had seen the establishment of the Tudor dynasty (*TxC*, 28). After it, at the beginning of the section called 'Tragedies' in the table of contents, comes *Troilus and Cressida*, not, as listed, *Coriolanus*, which follows immediately afterwards as the volume resumes the stated order.[1]

The textual history of *Henry VIII*, which exists in early form only in the First Folio, is fairly straightforward. As I have noted, in tackling *Henry VIII*, I have not had to deal with the kinds of problem that face the editor of, say, *King Lear*, for which there are two quite distinct versions, Quarto and Folio (in modern terms, cheap paperback and serious collected edition), the differences between which have to be assessed, accounted for and negotiated.[2] This doesn't, unfortunately, mean that the text of *Henry VIII* is free from problems which require the editor to make certain decisions – there are several densely phrased passages which make interpretation difficult (Norfolk's 'spider-like' speech at 1.1.57–66, for instance), and the question of the play's authorship has been a constant problem since the middle of the nineteenth century – but as a text it raises few of the complex issues of priority and authority that affect a play such as *King Lear*. It is generally assumed that the text of *Henry VIII* was set from a carefully prepared manuscript in a single hand, though there is disagreement over whose that single hand might be. Montgomery argues that two features of the text suggest that it was produced from a scribal, rather than authorial, transcript: the spelling of the word 'has' as 'ha's', which is associated with neither Shakespeare nor Fletcher and which runs across sections of the text which for various reasons are associated with both compositors (see pp. 155–8), and the unusually high

1   Work on *Henry VIII* was in fact held up because of problems experienced by the Jaggards (the printers of the First Folio) over *Troilus and Cressida*, which had originally been due to appear after *Romeo and Juliet*, but which was eventually set as the very last task of the Folio and inserted between *Henry VIII* and *Coriolanus* (Hinman, 2.231–64 ; *TC*, Ard[3], 401ff.).

2   Attentive readers of both Arden 2 and Arden 3 will realize that editing *Henry VIII* is merely the beginning of a forty-year apprenticeship before the tyro is ready to edit *Lear*.

number of round brackets (mostly removed from the current edition in the process of modernization, but conspicuous in F), again a feature associated with neither playwright and which runs across the stints of the two compositors.[1]

One feature that immediately strikes the reader of the First Folio text of *Henry VIII* – and it is a feature which, as we have seen, has had a significant impact on the play's reception over the centuries – is the inclusion of substantial stage directions, most notably 'The Order of the Coronation' at v6^v, but also at t3^v, t4^r, t5^v, t6^r, t6^v, x3^r, and particularly at v2^r, x1^v and x4^r. As a result, it has sometimes been stated that the text was set from a prompt-book, yet the stage directions provided are, as often as not, detailed descriptions of state ritual drawn direct and at some length from Holinshed, and not the kind of terse, practical directions usually found in play-texts which can be seen to have stemmed from prompt copy. Montgomery suggests that what he believes to be a duplicated music direction at 2.4.0.1 may stem from theatrical annotation 'which either the scribe or the compositor incorporated into the main direction' (*TxC*, 620), but I am not convinced by his argument (see 2.4.0.1n.). There is no other evidence of this sort: as Greg put it, the copy for *Henry VIII* 'could have been used as a prompt copy, but there is no indication that it was' (Greg, 425).

One of the editor's tasks – and this is particularly important for a play for which there is evidence, or suspicion, of collaborative authorship – is to determine who set the type at the printing house. This is because a compositor will have characteristic ways of dealing with certain practical matters: he (there were, as far as I know, no women compositors in Jacobean England, though women did

---

1   For Montgomery's argument and statistics, see *TxC*, 618–9. One candidate for scribe is Ralph Crane, who 'may have been a more senior figure in the Folio's editorial team' than has been assumed, and is known for (amongst other features) his enthusiasm for brackets (Honigmann, *Texts*, 73). Recent work by E.A.J.Honigmann, however, suggests that Crane was not responsible for the Folio *Henry VIII*. While there is a fair number of phrases, sentences and paragraphs enclosed by brackets, there is only a small number of 'swibs' ('single words in brackets'), a feature emphasized by Honigmann as Crane's most distinctive characteristic (Honigmann, *Texts*, 59–76).

occasionally own or run printing houses) may spell certain words in a particular way, may opt for a particular form of letters for a speech prefix, may adjust in a particular way to deal with inaccuracies in the casting-off process (whereby preliminary estimates are made of the quantity of manuscript copy which is likely to fit onto a given printed page).[1] Studies of compositors' habits have led to the conclusion that *Henry VIII* was set by two compositors (neither of whom can be assigned a personal name) – Compositor B (who set more type for the First Folio than all the other compositors, now thought to be as many as ten in total, put together) and another, currently known as Compositor I, who according to Gary Taylor was a 'journeyman' (i.e. not a master craftsman) and who made a noticeably higher number of errors than his colleague.

In 1958, in connection with his Arden 2 edition of the play, R.A.Foakes made an analysis of the typesetting of *Henry VIII*, marking differences in spelling habits between the sections and assigning them to Compositors B and A respectively (Foakes, 'Folio'). On the basis of consistent differences in the spellings of words such as 'go/goe', 'do/doe', and 'here/heere', as well as of speech prefixes such as 'Buc/Buck' and 'Qu/Quee', he assigned fifteen pages to Compositor A (t4^r–v2^r; v3^r, v3^v; x3^r–x4^v) and thirteen to Compositor B (t3^r, t3^v; v2^v; v4^r–x2^v). Charlton Hinman, in his exhaustive study of the printing of the Folio, confirmed Foakes's assignment of sections, but replaced his assumption that the second compositor was A with the assertion – based, as it happens, on characteristic spellings (i.e. characteristics ascertained in other texts) of 'go', 'do' and 'here' – that it was a third man, whom he called C. Since that time, the characteristics of a raft of other compositors have been identified in the Folio, and B's partner in *Henry VIII*, newly associated (on the basis this time of particular, consistent spellings of suffixes) with whoever set certain pages of the Folio *Hamlet*, has been redesignated by Taylor as Compositor I (Taylor, 'Shrinking'). Hinman's machine collation of the First

---

1   For a brief but precise account of casting-off, see Moore, 11.

Folio disclosed no significant press-variants in *Henry VIII*, noting that 'the proof-reading that was done for the Histories . . . was even at its best sporadic' (Hinman 1.281).[1] The following table, modified from Hinman to incorporate line numbers from the current edition, demonstrates the order in which the text was set by pages and serves as a useful reminder that compositors did not set plays in the order in which we read them and that their response to textual anomalies therefore depended on how accustomed they had grown to the text they were dealing with at the time.

ORDER OF COMPOSITION OF FOLIO TEXT

Compositor B	Compositor I
t3^v (1.1.36–137)	t4^r (1.1.138–1.2.11)
t3^r (Prologue 0.1–1.1.35)	t4^v (1.2.12–128)
t2^v (*R3*)	t5^r (1.2.129–1.3.18a)
t2^r (*R3*)	t5^v (1.3.18b–1.4.40)
t1^v (*R3*)	t6^r (1.4.41–2.1.16)
t1^r (*R3*)	t6^v (2.1.17–127)
v4^r (3.1.109–3.2.30)	v3^v (3.1.0.1–108)
v4^v (3.2.31–130)	v3^r (2.4.119b–238)
v5^r (3.2.131–240)	v2^r (2.3.20–2.4.0.16)
v2^v (2.4.1–119 SD)	v1^v (2.2.60b–2.3.19)
v5^v (3.2.241–356)	v1^r (2.1.128–2.2.60a)
v6^r (3.2.357–4.1.3)	x3^r (5.2.20–125)
v6^v (4.1.4–90)	x3^v (5.2.126–5.3.15)
x2^v (5.1.98–5.2.19)	x4^r (5.3.16–5.4.28)
x2^r (5.1.0–97)	x4^v (5.4.29–Epilogue 14)
x1^v (4.2.80–173)	
x1^r (4.1.91–4.2.79)	

1   Charlton Hinman created a machine known as the 'Hinman Collator', which allowed him to compare a considerable number of copies of the First Folio with the one he had chosen as his copy-text and to enhance beyond all recognition our understanding of the process of its printing (Hinman, 1.8, 243–4).

A glance at the three folio pages reproduced on pp. 151–3 (Figs 20–22) will make one compositorial characteristic immediately clear. When setting speech prefixes for Queen Katherine, Compositor I prefers to set the full word *Queen*; Compositor B, on the other hand, prefers a shorter form (*Qu* or, at most, *Quee*), only setting the full word *Queen* when it prefixes a half-line and is therefore needed to fill what would otherwise be white space. A comparison between folios v3^v and v4^r, which contain 3.1, show that Katherine's speeches are uniformly prefixed *Queen* on v3^v, whereas they are prefixed either *Quee* or *Qu* on v4^r. This is one indication that the setting of this scene was shared between B and I. Such information about compositors might seem to be, literally, of no more than academic interest, but for anyone interested in knowing who may actually have written the play (particularly in view of the dominance of issues of authorship and authority in nineteenth- and twentieth-century interpretation), it is significant, since editors wish to differentiate as clearly as possible between the characteristics of the different agents engaged in the creation of the text, particularly if there is reason to believe that more than one playwright was involved. I will return to this in due course in the section on collaboration.

Figs 20–22 are designed partly to demonstrate the features of the text which have led editors and critics to fret over the identities of playwrights and compositors, and partly to serve the more general function of reminding anyone not used to dealing directly with early modern printed texts of the substantial differences of spelling and punctuation between those texts and modern practice. In the foreign country of the past, they did things differently, and any attempt on our part to erase those differences is bound to be, whether we realize it or not, an act of vandalism. Editors tend not to like modernized texts, partly because by the time they get to edit an early modern text they have become accustomed to, and fond of, the peculiarities and idiosyncrasies of such texts, but also because they regret the obligation to protect the reader from the curious and possibly off-putting experience of tackling an alien text belonging to an alien culture. It is undoubtedly true that a modernized text denies the modern reader that alienation and therefore a substantial part of the experience of engaging with the past; but it is also true that editions are created for readers and that old-spelling editions have a limited readership, a readership determined by experience with old texts. Editors modernize in order to make such texts as accessible as possible for a modern reader or actor, and they therefore do so as thoroughly as possible.

Modernizing involves both spelling and punctuation. Neither was fixed in the early modern period, and inconsistencies and opacities are frequent and endemic.[1] The textual notes not only provide chronological evidence of suggested emendations, but also draw attention to the more marked differences between Jacobean and modern spelling and punctuation in particular instances. I have completely modernized the punctuation of the play, most notably removing the numerous round brackets that appear in F and replacing them with whatever marks seem appropriate in a modernized text (principally, though by no means always, with dashes), but I began with, and have borne in mind throughout, the practice of the First Folio text. This is, of course, a basic rule, but it cannot by any means answer every possible question about the implication of a particular example of punctuation; so often, 'accidentals' (as punctuation and other non-substantive marks are known) turn out to be 'semi-substantives' (as accidentals are known when they clearly determine meaning). Decisions about spelling can have further implications, too, including for example the political. I have, after much internal struggle, chosen to capitalize aristocratic titles and titles of office (e.g. 'Duke of Buckingham', not 'duke of Buckingham'; 'Cardinal Wolsey', not 'cardinal Wolsey'). In view of the standard practice of historians, this makes a typical page of text in this edition look rather old-fashioned, and for someone who is not a royalist (the present editor, for instance) it grates slightly; but

---

1 For anyone interested in a brief overview of this subject, I recommend Vivian Salmon's very helpful essay in *Oxf (Orig)*.

experimenting with lower-case letters for these titles seemed to me to indicate that, in a play in which rank and title are of central importance, the reader might be caused unnecessary confusion by my deploying current practice in this regard.

The issue of modernized spelling is equally fraught. Early modern spelling is nothing if not inconsistent (it is well-enough known that Shakespeare seems not to have spelled his own name the same way twice). As Vivian Salmon observes, 'Shakespeare's plays appeared . . . at a time when printers, although apparently aiming at a standard form of spelling, had not yet finally succeeded in establishing one' (Salmon, xliii); spelling, in both manuscripts and printed books, is often determined not by any individual's preferences, but simply by material factors such as the space available on the page. For this edition, I have thoroughly modernized spellings throughout, on the Arden 3 principle that retaining for whatever reason a few 'typically Shakespearean' and perhaps familiar (to Shakespeare scholars) spellings serves only to create a form of the text which represents no known stage in the development of English orthography. I have also modernized such features as pronoun elisions (e.g. 'th'have', 'y'are', which become 'they've' and 'you're') which might be thought of as distinctively 'Fletcherian' (at least, they appear only in the scenes attributed to Fletcher), although since the modernized elisions do not appear in the 'Shakespeare' scenes, this arguably does not matter. The effect might nonetheless be to produce a more uniform text than that provided in the First Folio, a text which arguably participates in the general theatrical project to erase 'the perception of any differences that might have existed, for whatever reason, between collaborated parts', sustaining the theoretical primacy of individual creativity over collective production (Masten, *Intercourse*, 17). But these become questions of authorial attribution rather than of modernization, and I will return to them in due course.

Decisions to modernize or retain are never quite as simple as they might seem. At 3.1.16, for instance (and elsewhere in the play), the word 'an', meaning 'if', is retained, though obviously archaic, for the simple reason that the only alternative, 'and', would not convey the appropriate meaning to a modern reader. A more complex instance is the word 'comptroller' at 1.3.67. The modern equivalent in British English is 'controller', but I have left the F spelling alone in this case for several reasons. In the play it is used in a bureaucratic context, and in Britain for certain official occasions the office of comptroller still exists. This alone might not be enough to justify retention, since it is not entirely clear that occasional official or ceremonial usage means an otherwise archaic spelling counts as 'modern', but there is a further justification which also offers a further complication, since (as I am informed by my American general editor) in American English 'comptroller' is still the preferred form. To British ears, then, the word is an archaism; to American, it is not. My own assumption that it was an archaic form which might need modernizing was thus culturally determined, and the decision I made to retain 'comptroller' on grounds of occasional bureaucratic usage was confirmed for very different reasons once I learnt that a substantial portion of the projected readership for this edition would not necessarily perceive the word as an archaic form anyway.

Resources

Sources

In editions of early modern plays, sources are usually considered entirely separately from questions of authorship. Yet I find it hard to see the qualitative difference between two imagined scenes of writing – between, say, the scene of Shakespeare sitting at a table with the King's Company's copy of Holinshed beside him, creating one of his sections of the play with close reference to the *Chronicles*, and the scene of Shakespeare sitting at the same table with a draft of an earlier scene in Fletcher's handwriting, creating the same section with close reference to what his colleague has already written. In each case, Shakespeare would simply be doing what writers always do, consciously or unconsciously, that is, drawing upon available texts to provide them with material to which they respond and which they reshape and extend in relation to the specific and general contexts within which they are operating. This makes an adequate understanding of the books that Shakespeare and Fletcher were using (or the books that were, so to speak, providing Shakespeare and Fletcher with the words) crucial to understanding the play. I have chosen, therefore, to place discussion of the sources for *Henry VIII* here, immediately prior to my analysis of the play's authorship.

The cardinal rule in contemporary source study is that any text derived from a source is a *reading* of that source. Shakespeare and Fletcher do not just *use* their historical sources – the chronicle histories of Holinshed and Foxe, plus moments drawn from Speed and Stow – even when quoting effectively verbatim from them. On the contrary, there are, in the process of creating new drama from other dramatic or non-dramatic texts, principles of selection and omission which inevitably constitute an interpretation of those texts. Just as Stow, for instance, reads Wolsey's biographer Cavendish and, in omitting the latter's negative references to Anne Bullen, interprets and alters what he reads, so Fletcher and Shakespeare, dramatizing Stow's version of Cavendish, interpret and therefore re-create both Cavendish and Stow for their own particular theatrical purposes. At the same time, dependence upon certain sources is likely to determine how a writer approaches his or her subject: as a result, analysis of source material that concentrates only on what a writer *alters* in that source is likely to result in a partial view.

As Annabel Patterson has shown, Holinshed's *Chronicles* – published in 1577 and expanded ten years later into the version that provided the material for Shakespeare's history plays – is a carefully shaped and mediated account of English history (Patterson, *Holinshed*). Holinshed's prefatory note to the third volume (1587) makes it clear that he is offering a kind of history which aims to encourage independent critical thinking on the part of the reader:

> [C]oncerning the historie of England, as I haue collected the same out of manie and sundrie authors, in whom

what contrarietie, negligence, and rashnesse sometime is
found in their reports; I leaue to the discretion of those
that haue perused their works: for my part, I haue in
things doubtfull rather chosen to shew the diuersitie of
their writings, than by ouer-ruling them, and vsing a
peremptorie censure, to frame them to agree to my liking:
leauing it neuerthelesse to each mans iudgement, to con-
troll them as he seeth cause.

(Holinshed, A3^r–A3^v)

Patterson thus sees Holinshed's *Chronicles*:

not as the successor to Hall's *Union* (which was written at
the specific request of a monarch in order to sustain the
legitimacy of a dynasty), but rather as a counterstate-
ment: the evidence of diversity that historical inquiry
discovers must not, at whatever cost to the historian, give
way to the principles of unity and order.

(15)

She foregrounds those features which make the *Chronicles* seem
peculiarly appropriate as the principal source for the kind of play
that we have seen *Henry VIII* to be. For one thing, Raphael
Holinshed was in fact only one of a number of historians involved
in the construction of the *Chronicles*: collaborative history thus
underpins collaborative drama. Again, it is not surprising that a
play based closely on Holinshed – and especially on sections of the
Chronicles devoted to the surveillance and betrayal of individuals
by organized groups within the state – should be preoccupied by
issues of censorship, since the 1587 edition of the *Chronicles* was
itself subject to heavy castration at the command of the Privy
Council. Like the Jacobean dramatists, the Elizabethan chroniclers
had a tendency to test out the bounds of censorship, to 'teeter constantly on the edge of the illegal', in portraying the workings of the
arcana imperii (the secrets of state) (Patterson, *Holinshed*, 7).[1]

1 On dramatic censorship, see Clare; Dutton; Patterson, *Censorship*.

Yet for all the multivocality of the *Chronicles*, they do not lack forceful, leading attitudes to a whole range of issues, upon which *Henry VIII* clearly draws throughout. The play's ambivalence about Buckingham's execution, for instance, would appear to originate in the attitude towards that event and towards Wolsey apparent in Holinshed, which he in turn drew from Edward Hall and from Polydor Vergil (who, as Peter Gwyn notes in attempting to redress the balance (Gwyn, xix–xx), was highly critical of the Cardinal). Holinshed relishes outlining Wolsey's scheming against the Duke, couching all the accusations as reported speech and adding an aside:

> These were the speciall articles & points comprised in the indictment, and laid to his charge: but how trulie, or in what sort prooved, I haue not further to say, either in accusing or excusing him, other than as I find in *Hall* and *Polydor*, whose words in effect, I haue thought to impart to the reader, and without anie parciall wresting of the same either to or fro.
>
> Sauing that (I trust) I maie without offense saie, that (as the rumour then went) the cardinall chieflie procured the death of this noble man, no lesse fauoured and beloued of the people of this realme in that season, than the cardinall himselfe was hated and enuied. Which thing caused the dukes fall the more to be pitied and lamented, sith he was the man of all other, that chieflie went about to crosse the cardinall in his lordlie demeanor, & headie proceedings.
>
> (Holinshed, 864–5)

For all Holinshed's enthusiasm for a multivocal account of the past, then, he is no liberal historian *avant la lettre*.

Curiously, there is a tradition that Fletcher had no time for Holinshed. This is because of a line in *The Elder Brother*, in which a character called Miramont, in denouncing his brother Brisac, disparages the chronicler: 'Thou art an Asse then', he says, 'A dull old tedious Asse, th'art ten times worse / And of lesse credit than Dunce *Hollingshead* / The Englishman, that writes of snowes and Sheriffes' (*EB* 2.1.117–20). This would certainly seem an odd attitude, coming from a playwright who (if the attribution is accepted) worked so assiduously with Holinshed for *Henry VIII*, but it is dangerous to associate the attitudes of a dramatic character with those of the dramatist. The snobbish Miramont associates scholarly learning with gentility, and though he does not understand the classics, he vehemently wishes to defend classical learning in face of vernacular history:

> *Miramont.* . . . I beleeve, I have a learned faith Sir,
>   And that's it makes a Gentleman of my sort,
>   Though I can speake no Greeke I love the sound on't,
>   It goes so thundering as it conjur'd Devils;
>   *Charles* speakes it loftily. . . .
>
>   O he has read such things
>   To me!
> *Brisac.*   And you doe understand'm brother.
> *Miramont.* I tell thee no, that's not materiall; the sound's
>   Sufficient to confirme an honest man.
>   (*EB* 2.1.52–6, 60–3)

Brisac insists he will disinherit his scholarly heir in favour of his courtly younger son, and Miramont finishes up his counter-argument with the comment about Holinshed. The audience would hear this doubly, aware that Holinshed's *Chronicles*, as vernacular history, occupies a quite different place from classical history in the historiographical hierarchy, but aware, too, that Miramont is dismissing what he perceives to be 'vulgar' history because, in his undereducated but class-aspirational state, he wishes to associate himself only with categorically high culture.[1]

1 Public perception was such that an audience could be expected to understand why Miramont is given these lines. '*Hollingshead* the Englishman' (as opposed to, say, Tacitus the Roman) is associated with a certain kind of popular history ('snowes and Sheriffes'), and this leads a number of contemporary writers to dismiss the *Chronicles*. The nearest parallel (and probable source) for Miramont's attitude comes

Miramont's remark, in context, simply acknowledges Holinshed's role as a 'popular' historian, eliciting an independent, knowing response from the audience: it is not the style of the *Chronicles* but the ignorance of those who would dismiss it as inferior history that comes under fire.

Henry VIII clearly shares a great deal with the *Chronicles*. The play is, as we have seen, a 'meditation on the effects of the Reformation in England' (Patterson, *Holinshed*, 20), representing post-Reformation experience as an unsettling series of changes in the definition of 'truth'; it presents history as the product of diverse testimony, expressing this diversity as 'multivocality' (7); it addresses a broad-based audience in a way which interpellates (calls into being in an apparently natural but in fact constrained way) the individual member of that audience as 'a thoughtful, critical, and wary individual' concerned to negotiate 'the complex texture' of British national history (8). In other words, any adequate analysis of the sources of *Henry VIII* needs to treat not just the playwrights but also the audience as readers of history, responsive to the possibility of a range of political nuance in the ways in which chronicle history could be represented. Thus, for all that *Henry VIII* does follow Holinshed closely pretty much throughout, it would be far too simplistic to treat the play as little more than a versified chronicle. As the chronological chart in Appendix 1 suggests, *Henry VIII* plays fast and loose with the chronology it draws from the *Chronicles*. Time and motive are

from Nashe's Pierce Penniless, who warns against 'lay Chronigraphers, that write of nothing but of Mayors and Sheriefs, and the deare yeere, and the great Frost' (Nashe, 1.194). Gabriel Harvey, whose comment on the matter is also very close to Miramont's (though, being a marginal note in Latin in his copy of Livy's *Romanae Historia Principis,* inaccessible to Fletcher), writes of the 'many asses who dare to compile histories, chronicles, annals, commentaries . . . Grafton, Stow, Holinshed, and a few others like them who are not cognizant of law or politics, nor of the art of depicting character, nor are they in any way learned'. And he goes on to ask, tellingly: 'How long shall we yearn for a British Livy? Or when will there emerge a British Tacitus or Frontinus?' (Stern, 152). Spenser, though, had acknowledged a debt to Holinshed, and the Jacobean Spenserians echoed this: Samuel Daniel, in a preface to his *Collection of the History of England* (1626), noted his own debt to 'such Collections as by *Polydore Virgile, Fabian, Grafton, Hall, Holingshead, Stow* and *Speed*, diligent and Famous Trauailors in the search of our History' (Daniel, 4.82).

reordered to create dramatic structure. Buckingham's and Wolsey's falls are both intertwined and paralleled, and Katherine's fall is both connected and contrasted with theirs in a way it is not in Holinshed. Moreover, even when a speech is drawn directly from Holinshed, there are invariably subtle changes or developments which have a substantial dramatic effect.

In 2.4, for example, Katherine's major speech is almost entirely versified Holinshed, but with some important changes and additions, notably in the vehemence of the dramatic Katherine (see 2.4.39–42, 66–82, 103–119), and her departure from the courtroom has rather more impact in the play than it does in Holinshed's account (see 2.4.131–40). Again, the King's speeches in this scene also follow Holinshed closely, but with a number of crucial differences, including the peremptory nervousness with which Henry draws attention to the beginning of his narrative (see 2.4.164–6). The reputation of Henry as the king who initiated the Reformation, an image which lies behind the emphasis on Wolsey's duplicity and on Gardiner's machinations as causes of unease in the kingdom, is, as we have seen, questioned in complex ways in the play. This is presumably due in part to the influence of Foxe, who is quite clear that the schism came about despite rather than because of Henry VIII (though he is pragmatically happy to accept the 'conscience' issue and the lawfulness of the divorce because the remarriage produced Elizabeth).[1] From these and other such instances, it is quite clear that the play draws upon a much broader range of possibilities in its representation of Henry VIII's reign than that available from Holinshed alone.

It is thus essential to remember that, even in those parts of the play for which Holinshed is the principal source, it is by no means

1 Fletcher would arguably have been even more familiar than Shakespeare with Foxe's martyrology because of his family's involvement in the book. His grandfather had given Foxe an account of the martyrdom of Christopher Wade for the 1583 edition of the *Acts and Monuments* which notes the presence too, as a young boy, of the playwright's father Richard, who eventually became Bishop of London. The account is notable for making sure that Wade's last words include an endorsement not of Protestant nonconformism but of 'the doctrin of the gospel preached in king Edward his daies' (Foxe 1583, 2: 1679–80; McMullan, *Unease*, 1).

the *only* one. Particular scenes which have been attributed to one or other collaborator demonstrate a more complex blending of source materials than seems generally to have been assumed by editors and critics. For example, 3.2, already a complex scene attributionally (generally held to have been divided roughly in two by the playwrights), demonstrates a conscious variety of sources drawn on for strictly dramatic purposes. The first section is indeed dependent upon Holinshed, yet the opening conversation between the nobles is clearly dramatic extrapolation (see 3.2.1–3n.); the description of Campeius's departure – reported simply in Holinshed as 'cardinall *Campeius* tooke his leaue of the king' – appears to stem from either Hall or Foxe (see 3.2.56–60n.); and the remarks about Lutherans a little further on are reminiscent of certain passages in Rowley's *When You See Me, You Know Me* (see 3.2.99n., 99–104n.). Again, the manner of dependence on Holinshed is not always linear: Wolsey's fatal error is taken from Holinshed's account of the reign of Henry VII – a passage quite out of sequence with all the material about Henry VIII – where it is told of Thomas Ruthall, Bishop of Durham – and transferred to Wolsey, apparently under the influence of Holinshed's (and, possibly, Foxe's) description of the King's discovering certain incriminating letters sent by Wolsey to the Pope (see 3.2.124n.).

The second section of the scene, which (against the convention of attribution by whole scenic unit) authorship analysts have assigned to Fletcher, also echoes Holinshed on Henry VII, with further echoes of the phraseology of the story of Ruthall's error (see 3.2.213n.), but now other chronicles are drawn in, too. Part of Wolsey's soliloquy acknowledging his fall stems from Speed's recently published *Theatre of the Empire of Great Britain* (2.769): this is one of two apparent echoes of Speed, both in the second section of the scene (see 3.2.224n., 359n.), which then returns to Holinshed, extrapolating from the chronicle account of the confrontation of Wolsey and the nobles, and incorporating from slightly later in Holinshed the list of charges brought against the Cardinal (see 3.2.228–32n.). The entire ensuing argument is built up from one line in Holinshed (see 3.2.232–5n.), which goes on to list nine of the articles used to indict Wolsey in 1529, of which six are quoted in the play. *When You See Me* echoes (in a rather garbled way) two of the articles listed by Holinshed, though it is hard to say if this is a direct influence (see 3.2.304n.). Wolsey's language from here to the end of the scene, both in soliloquy and in dialogue with Cromwell, is crammed with biblical allusion (see, for example, 3.2.371n.), presumably implying his renewal as a Christian in the immediate wake of his downfall (though the powerful image of Lucifer falling '[n]ever to hope again' significantly darkens and questions this personal reformation); his swansong is modelled on Isaiah, 40.6–8 (see 3.2.352–8n.).

Finally, for the conversation between Wolsey and Cromwell with which the scene closes, the source appears to be not Holinshed, but Stow's appropriation in his 1592 *Annals* of the *Life and Death of Cardinal Wolsey* by Wolsey's gentleman usher, George Cavendish. Judith Anderson has helpfully analysed the relationship of the *Life of Wolsey* to *Henry VIII*, but editions to date have not recognized the extent of Cavendish's influence on the play. This relationship is not direct: there was no Tudor printing of Cavendish and there is 'no evidence that Shakespeare [or, presumably Fletcher] knew Cavendish's *Wolsey* directly'.[1] Nonetheless, Anderson argues, 'Cavendish's *Life of Wolsey* is at the heart of the treatment of Wolsey in *Henry VIII*, and to a greater extent than is usually recognised, [this treatment] is a conceptual paradigm of the play's . . . fundamental ambivalence' (Anderson, 136). If any influence from Cavendish has been acknowledged in the past, it has

---

1 See Anderson: 'It is usually assumed that whatever Shakespeare [*sic*] had of Cavendish's work he found in Holinshed's second edition, 1587, which in turn depends closely on Stow's *Chronicles* of 1580 for what it includes of Cavendish. . . . Stow's rendition of Cavendish in the 1592 edition[, however,] differs significantly from the second edition of Holinshed' (136). She argues that the dramatists' apparent knowledge of it – in the play's emphasis on 'the singular importance of Cromwell to Wolsey, the close nature of their relationship, and the rather tearful circumstances of their farewell' (142) – indicates its involvement in the fundamental ambivalence of *Henry VIII* (136). Anderson also effectively rejects Frederick Kiefer's claim that the play's presentation of Wolsey was influenced by the *Mirror for Magistrates* (Kiefer; Anderson, 227n.).

been assumed that that influence came via Holinshed or Stow's earlier *Chronicles* (1580), but the 1592 *Annals* more fully and faithfully renders Cavendish's work than does any of Stow 1580, Holinshed 1587 (which is dependent anyway on Stow 1580 for its rendition of Cavendish) or Speed's first edition of 1611. For Anderson, '[t]he most important difference between Stow 1592 and Holinshed 1587 is that the former preserves more faithfully the essential ambiguity of Wolsey's awareness that we find so forcefully present in Cavendish' (Anderson, 136), and while several of the passages in the play could have been drawn from Holinshed's version of Stow's earlier version of Cavendish, she argues that the play's treatment of the Wolsey/Cromwell relationship in the immediate aftermath of Wolsey's fall confirms Stow 1592 as a source.

Holinshed mentions Cromwell simply as one of Wolsey's 'chiefe counsell, and chiefe dooer for him in the suppression of abbeies', who, along with a number of Wolsey's servants, 'departed from him to the kings seruice' (913). Stow 1592, however, incorporated more from Cavendish, including the assertion that Cromwell's 'honest estimation' and 'earnest behauour in his masters cause, grew so in euerie mans opinion, how that he was the most faithfull seruant to his master of all other, wherein hee was greatly of all men commended' (Stow 1592, 927; cf. Cavendish, EETS, 113), and it is from this that the play draws its sympathetic depiction of the Wolsey/Cromwell relationship. The tearful nature of the farewell – 'Nay, an you weep / I am fallen indeed' (3.2.375–6); 'I did not think to shed a tear' (3.2.428) – has its origin in Stow 1592: 'beholding the goodly number of his seruants, [he] could not speak vnto them vntill the teares ran downe his cheekes' (Stow 1592, 924). And, again, the scene of Wolsey and Cromwell alone together, comforting each other, has its roots in Stow's account: 'My lord returned into his chamber lamenting the departure from his servants, making his mone to master *Cromwell*, who comforted him as best he could' (Stow 1592, 925). At the same time, though, the play is not entirely dependent on this source: while both Cavendish and Stow

make fairly explicit the future Lord Chancellor's ability to improvise success from Wolsey's downfall, the play plays down
Cromwell's pragmatism so as (it would seem) the better to present
him as an exemplary Protestant.[1]

In order both to summarize and to focus my analysis of the
play's deployment of source material, I want to return briefly to a
moment in 3.2 – to one turn of phrase, in fact, in Wolsey's swansong – which demonstrates the complex communicative
interaction taking place between stage and audience at the level of
a single metaphor. In keeping with his representation in chronicles from Cavendish to Holinshed, the character of Wolsey is
ambivalently drawn in *Henry VIII*. In many ways, he is the
embodiment of the grotesque: he invokes the physical language of
carnival; he is overweight and plebeian; and he embodies social
inversion. His origins mean that he is no Falstaff: neither gentleman nor buffoon, he is in many ways the personification of
intolerant authority. At the same time, as Buckingham's contemptuous 'beggar's book' remark makes clear (1.1.122–3), he can also
claim the status of underdog, enraging the aristocrats simply by
being of what they would call 'low' or 'no' birth. For them, 'being
not propped by ancestry', Wolsey is 'spider-like' (1.1.59, 62), less
than human because lacking either rank or respect. As a result, our
knowledge of the Cardinal's violence, cruelty and arbitrariness,
his orchestration of Buckingham's betrayal and his effective
acknowledgement of Campeius's allegation that he was responsible for the death of Gardiner's predecessor as King's secretary,
may still be tempered with a degree of sympathy.

By the time of Wolsey's downfall, in other words, we have seen
him in a variety of guises, and it is not clear how we are expected
to respond to his farewell speech. Do we empathize? Or mock?
Are we, like the earls, pleased to see him destroyed? Or are we
happy that he at least appears to claim the grace of repentance?
This ambivalence is exemplified in three lines: 'I have ventured,'

1 For a more detailed account of the relationship of Cavendish and Stow 1592 to
Henry VIII, see Anderson, 136–53.

says Wolsey, 'Like little wanton boys that swim on bladders, / This many summers in a sea of glory, / But far beyond my depth' (3.2.358–61). On the face of it, this is an acknowledgement that he was not suited, or born, to the power he achieved; and there is something touching about the analogy, a kind of childhood summer innocence destined for tragedy. Yet a glance at Speed's account of his death offers a telling resonance in the word 'bladder'. Far from being a touching analogy, these lines of Wolsey's can be seen as a tasteless joke on his corpulence and on the manner of his death. 'Formerly', recounts Speed:

> wee haue spoken of the rising of this man, who now being swolne so bigge by the blasts of promotion, as the bladder not able to conteine more greatnesse, suddenly burst, and vented foorthe the winde of all former fauours . . . whose death himselfe had hastened by taking an ouermuch quantity of a confection to breake winde from off his stomacke.
>
> (Speed, 2.769)

We may well recall Holinshed's introduction of the Cardinal as 'a proud popeling; as led with the like spirit of swelling ambition, wherwith the rable of popes haue beene bladder like puffed and blowne vp' (Holinshed, 837); and we realize that, for any member of the audience acquainted with these sources, and particularly with Speed, a fashionable history published only eighteen months earlier, the word 'bladder' would simultaneously evoke not only a kind of childlike naïvety and absence of agency but also a grotesque – both funny and cruel – image of the dying Wolsey.

Few members of the audience would have known Speed or Holinshed well enough to recognize at a conscious level the resonances of the apparently innocuous word 'bladder' at this moment. But I would suggest that this scene – establishing, as it does, a sustained irony by way of its imaginative deployment of source material – is typical of what is going on throughout the play at different levels, and that the cumulative effect takes *Henry VIII* a very long way away from the straightforward celebration of

Tudor history it has been thought to be. It is clear that 3.2, at least – and, certainly, a number of other scenes – cannot be thought of as 'mere' versified chronicle. On the contrary, while beginning time and again with Holinshed, substantial sections of the play are constructed from a broad and carefully meshed range of apposite sources, and this mesh of sources works to provide underpinnings which quietly work against the apparent grain of the text.

On the basis of the most recent authorship study, that of Jonathan Hope, it might be possible to make certain observations about the deployment of sources. The scenes attributed to Shakespeare, where they have any tangible source at all, are (with the exception of 5.1, which is based closely on Foxe) heavily dependent upon Holinshed, often following the *Chronicles* very closely indeed, developing chronicle prose into poetic dialogue; they seem also to be quite aware of plays by other dramatists on connected subjects. The scenes attributed to Fletcher tend to develop and stray away from Holinshed's accounts more than do the 'Shakespeare' scenes, in the sense both of dramatic extrapolation and of readier incorporation of other writers, including Stow and Speed. The 'Fletcher' scenes also seem for the most part to depend much more upon a tight mesh of biblical allusion, and the play's several echoes of the Prayer Book come in these sections (appropriate enough in a bishop's son, if biographical detail is considered relevant). On these premises, then, any collaborative model for *Henry VIII* which depends upon an idea of the master Shakespeare issuing instructions and the grateful Fletcher doing what he is told would seem wide of the mark.

But such models are highly suspect, at best, and the assumptions about the relationship of intentionality and textual production that are embodied in the distinctions I have drawn – as well as the convenient division of labour they suggest – have come under severe pressure in recent years. And while it could, for instance, be argued that the closeness of the collaboration can be seen in other ways – in, for instance, a comparison of the use of source material in 5.1 (a 'Shakespeare' scene) and 5.2 (a 'Fletcher' scene), in which the two playwrights work from the same section of Foxe, and even develop speeches from the same paragraph of narrative without overlapping, Shakespeare introducing the idea, and Fletcher extrapolating from it for the next scene – arguments of this kind cannot be conclusive because they can always be explained more easily – by the simple logic of Occam's razor – as evidence that the play was written by one person, not by two working closely together: as R.A. Foakes argued in 1957, 'If two authors wrote the play, they read the same parts of [Holinshed and Foxe] with a strangely similar attention to detail' (Ard², xxiii). Conversely, when the very first 'disintegrator' of the play, James Spedding, compared the first two scenes, he found that he could distinguish between styles the more easily because 'in both passages the true narrative of Cavendish is followed minutely and carefully, and both are therefore copies from the same original and in the same style of art' (Spedding, 119). Deployment of sources is therefore no determinant of authorship; on the contrary, the textual relationship embodied in the conjunction of a 'text' and its 'source' in fact compromises the notions of authority fundamental to attributive study.

Analogues

There are, over and above the chronicle sources, several texts which, if they are not actual sources, nonetheless serve as useful analogues for understanding *Henry VIII* in context. I have incorporated some examples into Appendix 5, notably two analogues for Cranmer's prophetic speech – one from John Bale's *King Johan* (1539, revised 1562) (which was probably originally performed for Cranmer himself and was reworked in Elizabeth's reign, but which is unlikely to have been available in that of James), the other from Christopher Ockland's *Valiant Acts and victorious Battles of the English Nation* (1585).[1] Both texts provide examples of the kinds of encomia produced for Elizabeth,

1 On *King Johan* and Cranmer, see Braunmuller, 16.

particularly in the form of extended prophecy, and demonstrate the tradition from which Cranmer's speech emerges. In the revised *King Johan*, Elizabeth is, as Gasper notes, 'the Angel who in Revelation marks out the servants of God, the elect or True Church' (Gasper, 'Reform', 68), 'whych maye be a lyghte to other princes all / For the godly wayes whome she doth dayly moue' because '[i]n Danyels sprete she hath subdued the Papistes'.[1] Ockland, in turn, describes Elizabeth's reign as a time in which:

> Peace shineth in those landes, and plenteous store of
>   fruite and grayne
> Throughout the fayre broad fieldes, with fragrant
>   hearbes adornisht growes,
> Such blessings from his heauenly throne almighty *Ioue*
>   bestowes,
> Both on those people, and their land which doe his
>   name adore
> And dread with suppliant hartes. . . .
> Gods worship true she hath restorde, suppresd, and
>   drownde before.
> And hath procurde that for the space of twentie yeares
>   and three
> Thy people wander may on land and surging salt
>   streames free
> From direfull harmes.
>
>   (*Valiant Acts*, D4^v)

These descriptions of Elizabeth's reign, prophetic and encomiastic, may not be direct sources for Cranmer's speech, but they make clear once again that *Henry VIII* offers a complex critical intervention in an already established field.

One particularly strong poetic analogue draws us back to the kinds of question about the interpretation of history raised in relation to Holinshed. Michael Drayton, to whom Henslowe's

---

1 *King Johan*, 133–4 (from the revised 'Hand B' section, 1562); see Appendix 5.

diary records payments in mid-1601 for his contributions to the collaborative *Life and Rising of Cardinal Wolsey* (itself very possibly a source for *Henry VIII* but, frustratingly, no longer extant), wrote a long poem in 1607 entitled *The Legend of Great Cromwell*, which draws on Foxe and on the anonymous play *Thomas, Lord Cromwell*, and which was included in the 1610 edition of *A Mirror for Magistrates*. For J. William Hebel, *The Legend of Great Cromwell* expresses 'perhaps for the first time, a detached critical attitude to events of Henry VIII's reign in a way that marks a definite break, not merely with Foxe (which would not be remarkable) but with Hall and his followers' (Hebel, 5.169). There are three stanzas towards the end of the poem which, while not source material *per se*, stand as analogues of certain aspects of *Henry VIII*, offering a view of the King which is markedly different from that in Holinshed.[1] The antipathy of Cromwell and Gardiner is central to Drayton's poem: Cromwell is characterized as a Protestant, though an equivocal one; Gardiner organizes Cromwell's downfall as he tries to arrange that of Cranmer in the play; and Henry appears unequivocally an intemperate tyrant (a marginal note to the 1619 text uses the precise word, 'Tyrannie'): 'For in his high distempra-ture of blood / Who was so great whose life he did regard?' (Drayton 1619, 392; Drayton 1610, 545; see Appendix 5).

In addition to such possible poetic influences as Drayton's *Cromwell*, the play can be located within (and is arguably pitched against) a tradition of dramatic history which included not only Shakespeare's own earlier epics of the Wars of the Roses but also other dramatic negotiations of more recent events. Some of these are lost (including another *Wolsey* play in addition to the one in which Drayton was involved), but others are extant and are worth examining, even if (or perhaps precisely because) they could not be described as having the same aesthetic qualities as *Henry*

---

1 Drayton was a friend of Francis Beaumont, Fletcher's erstwhile collaborator, and they shared a patronage milieu: he dedicated his *Cromwell* poem to Sir Walter Aston, the dedicatee of the published text of Fletcher's own *Faithful Shepherdess* a couple of years later (McMullan, *Unease*, 16, 56–8, 62–4).

VIII.[1] There is not space here to discuss this material in depth, but I wish briefly to mention three dramatic texts (in addition to Heywood's *If You Know Not Me, You Know Nobody*, discussed on pp. 134–5) that bear, or have been thought to bear, on *Henry VIII*: one which I have already noted, Samuel Rowley's *When You See Me, You Know Me*, and two which have led a twilight existence on the borders of the Shakespeare canon, *Thomas, Lord Cromwell* and *The Birth of Merlin*.

When You See Me, first performed probably in 1604, is important not only because it depicts the reign of Henry VIII or because it was reprinted topically in 1613, but because *Henry VIII*, as we have seen, quite specifically both utilizes and rejects it as a model for meditation on history: 'Only they / That come to hear a merry, bawdy play, / A noise of targets, or to see a fellow / In a long motley coat guarded with yellow, / Will be deceived' (Prologue 13–17). As we have seen, *When You See Me* is a Protestant play which alters chronology at will (Wolsey, for instance, is somehow still alive in 1546, when Gardiner charges Katherine Parr, the King's sixth wife, with heresy) and is clearly written for a very different audience from those of the Globe or the Blackfriars. Yet it provides a good sense of where the 'Bluff-King-Harry' tradition had reached by the beginning of James's reign – the King swears like a trooper, repeating 'Mother of God' numerous times (thus suggesting the range of oaths denied to the King of *Henry VIII* by the 1606 Act to Restrain Abuses), and shouts 'Ha!' when aroused – and it underlines the existence at this early stage of the Holbeinesque tradition: on the title-page, Henry is pictured in his familiar posture, legs straddled, fists on hips. When we see him, we know precisely who he is: we have a tradition, visual as well as verbal, with which to engage.

---

1 'Two plays on Cardinal Wolsey had been written for the Admiral's men, acting at the Fortune Theatre, in 1601. In a complicated series of payments Henslowe paid Chettle £6 in June and July 1601 for a play on the life of Cardinal Wolsey, and between August and December of the same year Chettle, Drayton, Munday, and Smith were paid £7 for a play called "the first Part of" or "the rising of" Cardinal Wolsey. The earlier play then became Part II' (Wilson, ix).

If Henry's oaths indelibly stamp him as Roman Catholic, Will Summers, his Fool, is the voice of Protestantism at court, mocking the Pope's material greed. He is also sharp on the King's repeated failures of continence, an integral part by this time of the tradition upon which *Henry VIII* draws. In the closing scene of the play, Summers – true to the linguistic levelling function of the stage fool – takes on King, Queen and Emperor in a flyting contest in which he makes overt reference to Henry's penchant for affairs:

> *King.* Answer this sir,
>   The bud is spread, the Rose is red, the leafe is greene,
> *Wil:* A wench t'is sed, was found in your bed, besides
>   the Queene. . . .
> *Empe:* . . . A ruddy lip, with a cherry tip, is fit for a King.
> *Wil:* I, so he may dip, about her hip, i'th tother thing.
>   (*When You See Me*, L1ᵛ)

The Prologue may overtly distance *Henry VIII* from Rowley's unsubtle entertainment, but the King's Company play nonetheless shares with it in negotiating an established popular tradition.

Two further plays mesh with *Henry VIII*. At one point in the King's Men's *Thomas, Lord Cromwell* (1602, reprinted 1613), Gardiner – Thomas Cromwell's chief antagonist – suborns two 'witnesses' in order to overthrow Cromwell in a move which resembles the Wolsey/Surveyor/Buckingham situation, especially when they appear and Norfolk warns them against perjury: 'My friends take heed of that which you haue said, / Your soules must answere what your tongues reports: / Therefore take heed, be wary what you doe' (F2ʳ). This is echoed in Katherine's intervention to warn the Surveyor, for which there is no basis in Holinshed: 'Take good heed / You charge not in your spleen a noble person / And spoil your nobler soul' (1.2.173–5). Moreover, the Second Witness (who is not, of course, a witness at all), when questioned, replies: 'My Lord we speake no more but truth' (F2ʳ), again looking forward to the Surveyor's response when faced with Katherine's questioning of his probity. Certain attitudes are also shared between the plays: Cromwell is made firmly Protestant, and the enmity between Gardiner and Cromwell is established quickly and is discussed at the beginning of 4.3 by two merchants, who appear forerunners of the Gentlemen in *Henry VIII* in their role as gossips and commentators on high events and rivalries.

A third play has been put forward as a possible influence upon *Henry VIII*. Joanna Udall, in her 1990 edition of *The Birth of Merlin, or The Child Hath Found His Father* – which was attributed to 'William Shakespear [*sic*], and William Rowley' on the title-page of the 1662 Quarto, but for which there is no evidence of Shakespearean involvement (*Birth of Merlin*, 23–31; Hope, *Authorship*, 131–3) – suggested that the latter part of the play has a great deal in common structurally with the last scene of *Henry VIII*, 'where action has given way to prophecy, and the future becomes the focus of attention' (*Birth of Merlin*, 101). As Merlin prophesies Britain's future, Uter responds by saying 'Thou speakst of wonders *Merlin*' (4.5.125), thus sharing Henry's awestruck response to Cranmer's speech at 5.4.55. 'In both cases', Udall notes, 'the comment is made by the current monarch . . . to the man who is telling him something about his country's future' (101), yet in the case of *The Birth of Merlin*, the prospects seem surprisingly bleak. Merlin appears determined to make the end of the play 'seem anti-climactic, and the succession precarious' (102), prophesying that Death will 'scarcely permit' Arthur 'to appoint one / In all his purchased Kingdoms to succeed him' (5.2.103–4). Udall, dating the play 'after 1607', suggests that there is a degree of awkward balancing between father and son; that, in his prophecy, Merlin:

> has to hold the balance between the praise of a father and a son, a common problem for those writing with enthusiasm about Prince Henry's prospects, who must nevertheless not seem to wish his father out of the way.
>
> (*Birth of Merlin*, 97–8)

She also argues 'that the final picture of the nation's hope, blasted by death, is a gesture towards the untimely death of Prince Henry in 1612' (103), though she acknowledges the speculative nature of these suggestions in the absence of authoritative dating evidence.

In 1996, however, Nigel Bawcutt published his account of the records of Sir Henry Herbert, Master of the Revels, which offers much newly discovered evidence for the dating of plays. One of his discoveries, from the Burn transcript of Herbert's office book (now held at the Beinecke Library at Yale), is an entry which notes Herbert's fee 'for perusing and allowing of a New Play' called 'The *Childe hath founde his Father* . . . acted by the Princes Servants at the Curtayne, 1622' (Bawcutt, 136). In this light, *Henry VIII* appears to be a source for *The Birth of Merlin* rather than vice versa, and the father/son balancing and general pessimism that Udall notes are likely therefore to reflect the relationship not between James and Henry but between James and Charles in the context of the tensions produced in England by the opening rounds of the Thirty Years' War.

Collaboration

> [T]he author does not precede the works, he is a certain functional principle by which, in our culture, one limits, excludes, and chooses.
>
> (Foucault, 'Author,' 159)

I have made it clear throughout this Introduction that I do not think Shakespeare wrote *Henry VIII* all by himself, but I have not explained myself, and it is now time to do so. I hope the Introduction and Commentary will have prompted a certain curiosity about this issue, which is, I believe, key to an adequate understanding of the production of early modern drama and which has, in the course of the twentieth century, been a major (arguably *the* major) determining factor in the critical neglect of the play. Critics who like the play have been happy to claim it for Shakespeare; those who do not have found it useful to be able to lay the blame on Fletcher. I do not share these sentiments – I like the play, I think it a fine play, and I think it a collaboration – and I wish to repeat that I have not placed the discussion of authorship at this point in the Introduction in order to reduce its significance. On the contrary, if there is no central, authoritative, 'principal' character in *Henry VIII* – a state of affairs which radically affects interpretation of the play – there is also no clear, authoritative, 'authorial' centre to the play, either, and this too has a radical effect upon interpretation.

The word 'collaboration' itself can mislead. For one thing, since 1940 or thereabouts, it has been loaded with connotations of betrayal, of a catastrophic failure of integrity, a connection which in fact predates the Second World War, originating in romantic aesthetic obsessions with unity and individuality in the field of artistic/literary production. It is used in two principal ways, to mean both the general collective agency involved in the production of a play-text and the specific process whereby two (or more) playwrights are responsible for producing the words of the script. The former is treated as too obvious to mention and, anyway, entirely after the event of, and subordinate to, authorship; the latter as a professional conjunction of two autonomous individuals always likely to produce inferior art (on the logic that a camel is a horse designed by a committee). Theatrical collaboration is thus treated as an unfortunate aberration by critics and editors and, at times, by theatre professionals. It can have its uses, though. An anonymous American reviewer, writing in *Variety* about the 1946 New York production of *Henry VIII*, noted that the director, Margaret Webster, 'states there was dual authorship, which permitted cuts and rearrangements from the original' (*Variety*) – the premise being, presumably, that since Shakespeare thought sufficiently little of the play that he was prepared to write it in collaboration with a lesser person, licence is thereby given to directors to alter what would otherwise be immutable.[1]

---

1   In a not-so-subtle variation on this theme, over and above the relaxed attitude directors have tended to show towards cutting the play, there has been 'a notable and curious correlation between the scenes . . . attributed to Fletcher and those usually most heavily cut in production' (Swayze, 304).

Collaboration, by definition, disperses the authority of the author, and while this might be deemed convenient by a director intent on reworking a text to her own taste, it is not something that was welcomed by the dominant modes of textual interpretation in the twentieth century, dependent as they were on ideas of unity, integrity and creative independence. This dispersal of authority is abundantly clear in the critical and publication history of *Henry VIII*, a play which has been the subject of a variety of authorship analyses (I provide a chart of the conclusions reached by several of these studies in Appendix 3) and which is currently in the anomalous position of being in print as part of two different early modern canons, not only as a 'Shakespeare' play but also as a play in the 'Beaumont and Fletcher' canon.[1] This dual location raises a series of interpretative questions which situate the issue of collaboration within larger debates not only about canonicity but also about authorship, the construction of the subject and the possibility of human agency. Editorial practice to date has responded haltingly, if at all, to these questions, and it is arguably only with the recent emphasis on writing as the product of reading (and consequently on the material conditions of both reading and writing in a given period) that the practical ramifications of collaboration can be fully acknowledged and appreciated.[2] *Henry VIII* is a fascinating test case for attitudes both to canonicity and to collaboration, hedged round as it is with the peculiar manifestations of proprietorship that are an inescapable part of Shakespeare studies; and an edition such as the current one, inclined to resist an editorial tradition largely dedicated to the maintenance of the play's status as 'minor Shakespeare', must address these issues, implicitly and explicitly, as a principal task.

1   The play belongs to the 'Shakespeare' canon because it appeared in the First Folio of 1623 (whereas a play such as *The London Prodigal*, say, which has been attributed both to Shakespeare and to Fletcher but which first appears only in a supplement to the Third Folio, is excluded). And, though it did not appear in the 1647 or the 1679 Beaumont and Fletcher Folios, it has most recently been included in an old-spelling form in Bowers.

2   For a fuller (and more speculative) account of some of the issues discussed here, see McMullan, 'Editing'. A key text in reconceptualizing the writing process is Chartier.

For twentieth-century editors, authors and their intentions held the key position as the source of meaning in a text, and the first task of any editor was to ensure that the writer's status in relation to the words on the page was demonstrably authoritative. James Thorpe, for instance, in his *Principles of Textual Criticism*, identified 'the central question . . . relating to the creation of the work of art: whose intentions are being fulfilled, who can properly be called the author?' (Thorpe, 14–15; see also Bowers, 'Multiple', 81). For the New Bibliographers (a term denoting a diverse group of scholars sharing a dedication to the injection of rigour into the process of the recovery of early texts in general and Shakespeare in particular), this entailed the deployment of a range of exacting techniques for the reconstruction – in the near-total absence of authorial manuscripts of early modern play-texts – of a stable 'original', channelled principally through research into the professional practice of early modern printing houses in the hope that input other than that of the author could be isolated and set aside. By the date of Thorpe's assertion, though, New Bibliographical scholarship had begun to demonstrate that Renaissance play-texts were generally either unstable or collaborative or both and that, as a result, the isolation of authorial input was highly problematic.

Ernst Honigmann had shown, for example, that the notion of a 'finalized' text was inadequate in view of the tendency of certain playwrights to alter the words they had written every time they transcribed them. He investigated instead the possibility of 'authorial "second thoughts" *before* [the play's] delivery to the actors', envisaging 'two copies of a play, each in the author's hand, disagreeing in both substantive and indifferent readings', and thus defining the Shakespearean text as always potentially unstable (Honigmann, *Stability*, 2). At the same time, G.E.Bentley had collated evidence showing that 'as many as half of the plays by professional dramatists in the period incorporated the writing at some date of more than one man' (probably, with hindsight, a very conservative estimate) and that '[i]n the case of the 282 plays mentioned in Henslowe's diary . . . nearly two-thirds are the work of more than one man' (Bentley, 199). As a result, he suggested, '[w]ell-known collaborations like those of . . . Shakespeare and Fletcher should not be looked upon as oddities, but as common occurrences in the careers of professional dramatists of the time' (234). Placing Honigmann's and Bentley's arguments together, there emerges the (for intentionalists) disturbing model of a play as an unstable series of texts written and sometimes rewritten by more than one writer. Thorpe's question – 'who can properly be called the author?' – had thus become even more difficult to answer than had at first been envisaged.

The New Bibliographers thus acknowledged that isolating authorial from other inputs into a given text was a problematic task, but insisted nonetheless that true authority could be invested only in a writer's intentions. Thorpe, for instance, acknowledges in his opening chapter that 'once works of art are performed, . . . complex questions begin in time to arise' (15) but does not see in this a threat to the pure analysis of 'what constitutes the integrity of the work of art' (15) which is his concern as a theorist of editorial principle. He accepts that 'in a complex way, the integrity of the work of art is . . . in some measure the effect of a juncture of intentions' (20) and that 'the literary work is often guided or directed or controlled by other people' (30), yet this acknowledgement serves only to increase his sense of duty to the author, leading him to assert carefully that, in view of the work's tendency to move towards collaborative status, 'the task of the textual critic is always to recover and preserve its integrity at that point where the authorial intentions seem to have been fulfilled' (48). Thus although Thorpe's textual aesthetic offers an ostensible admission of multiple agency, it is in fact only a modification of the intentionalist position. He acknowledges the inevitable acts of collaboration – between author and printing house, say – that operate in the production of the text, but his sense of the relative status of these operations remains dependent upon a hierarchy based in a fundamentally proprietorial notion of individual authorship.

The intentionalists' attitude to collaboration thus remained at best uncomfortable. What mattered above all was authorial intention, and in the case of jointly written texts, the key requirement was clarity about *which* author's intentions should be sought at any given moment. It was in this context that the New Bibliographers in the mid-twentieth century began to revisit and revise the long-dismissed 'disintegrative' practices of the mid- to late nineteenth century, by which plays could be attributed scene by scene to the collaborating writers.[1] Just as they aimed to replace editorial conjecture with a set of rigorous and coherent principles for the establishment of the text, so the New Bibliographers set out to formulate appropriate methods for distinguishing intentional input. They sought, in the words of Cyrus Hoy, efficient ways '[t]o distinguish any given dramatist's share in a play of dual or doubtful authorship' by way of 'some body of criteria which, derived from the unaided plays of the dramatist in question, will serve to identify his work in whatever context it may appear' (Hoy, 1, 130).[2]

There are three forms of evidence for authorship: external, intuitive and internal. The first of these signifies contemporary testimony – for instance, a title-page which names a particular writer. This evidence is sometimes supported elsewhere. Two good sources are the Stationers' Register, in which all plays to be printed were registered, generally with an authorship ascription of some sort, and the immensely valuable diary (i.e. account book) of the theatrical entrepreneur Philip Henslowe, who recorded payments to playwrights for their writing of, shares in or additions to particular plays. But often such external evidence is simply lacking, and scholars began in certain cases – often drawing on their sense of a writer's characteristic way with verse form, for instance – to suspect that plays attributed to one writer may in fact have been the products of another or that plays attributed to a single playwright may have been the result of

1   The term 'disintegration' to describe attempts to break down the authorship of collaborative texts by scenic attribution seems to have been coined by E.K.Chambers; see Chambers, *Gleanings*, 1–21.
2   I will take Hoy as my exemplary figure in attributional study because, through his work on the 'Beaumont and Fletcher' canon, he is most closely associated with the attribution of *Henry VIII*. Other significant studies of 'internal evidence' include Lake, and Jackson, *Attribution*. For a concise summary of attributional analyses of *Henry VIII*, see *TxC*, 133–4.

collaboration. Intuition, though, despite often producing results which have in due course been 'confirmed' by more quantifiable methods of inquiry, is, for obvious reasons, a wholly subjective and thus unsatisfactory analytical approach, and for the New Bibliographers it failed all the criteria for scholarly rigour. They sought instead techniques for authorship ascription that could be seen to be unaffected by personal prejudice, and it was with the work of Cyrus Hoy on internal authorship evidence in the 'Beaumont and Fletcher' canon that the determination to separate out the intentional inputs into collaborative texts first resulted in a systematic method.

For several reasons, *Henry VIII* presented itself as the most interesting case study. The play had begun to be considered as one of the most 'doubtful' in the Shakespeare canon (a term which is indicative of the prejudiced, bardolatrous environment out of which the study of authorship attribution grew), even though, at first sight, there appears to be no reason for it to be the subject of authorship debate at all. The only early text of the play is that in the Shakespeare First Folio, which offers no mention of the involvement of any other playwright. But *Henry VIII* was written in a brief period (1612–13) for which there is external evidence that Shakespeare worked with John Fletcher on at least two plays – *The Two Noble Kinsmen* (attributed on the title-page of the 1634 Quarto to 'Mr. John Fletcher, and Mr. William Shakspeare, Gent') and the lost *Cardenio* (attributed in the Stationers' Register in 1653 to 'Mr. Fletcher and Shakespeare') – and this evidence prompted scholars to wonder if Fletcher had also been involved in *Henry VIII*.[1] James Spedding's 'Who Wrote Shakespere's *Henry*

---

1   On 9 September 1653 the publisher Humphrey Moseley, who had published the 'Beaumont and Fletcher' Folio in 1647, entered in the Stationers' Register, along with a number of other plays, '*The History of Cardenio*, by Mr Fletcher and Shakespeare'. As *TxC* notes, 'Cardenio is a character in Part One of Cervantes' *Don Quixote*, published in English translation in 1612. Two earlier allusions suggest that the King's Men owned a play on this subject at the time that Shakespeare was collaborating with John Fletcher. . . . On 20 May 1613 the Privy Council authorized payment of £20 to John Heminges, as leader of the King's Men, for the presentation at court of six plays, one listed as "Cardenno". On 9 July of the same year Heminges received £6 13*s*. 4*d*. for his company's performance of a play "called Cardenna" before the ambassador of the Duke of Savoy' (*TxC*, 1191).

VIII?' – which is considered the foundational 'disintegrative' essay – offered an impressionistic division of the play into 'Shakespeare' scenes and 'Fletcher' scenes (the latter comprising over two-thirds of the play) which has since been broadly echoed by a variety of more rigorous analyses.[1] Spedding's curiosity was aroused in the first place by a suggestion from Tennyson and by what he perceived as a lack of structural and thematic coherence in the play. Drawing on Lamb's characterization of contrasting Shakespearean and Fletcherian styles in *Specimens of English Dramatic Poets* (Lamb, 419), Spedding noted a clear distinction between a style whose 'close-packed expression' and 'life, reality, and freshness' he associated with that 'master of harmony', William Shakespeare, and another style, 'full of mannerism', 'diffuse and languid' (Spedding, 118), which he associated with Fletcher. His method was initially wholly intuitive, but (for those 'less quick in perceiving the finer rhythmical effects', 121) he offered additional proof in the form of a metrical test, counting the occurrence of redundant syllables at the end of lines and, by selective quotation, demonstrating the similarity of this pattern in certain scenes with the style of Fletcher's 'middle period' plays. Behind this attempt at objectivity lay obvious prejudice: Fletcher's involvement meant that the play's 'want of moral

---

1   Spedding gives Shakespeare 1.1, 1.2, 2.3, 2.4, 3.2a and 5.1 and Fletcher the rest, including the Prologue and Epilogue; Hoy differs by claiming that 2.1, 2.2, 3.2b, 4.1 and 4.2 were all Shakespeare scenes only 'touched up' by Fletcher; Hope returns those scenes to Fletcher – in fact, with the exception of the Epilogue (which is simply too brief for effective statistical analysis), Hope reconfirms Spedding's division; see Hope, *Authorship*, 67–83, and Appendix 3. (For other attributional work, see, *inter alia*, Thorndike, 24–44; Farnham; Partridge; Oras; and Law.) Spedding's article appeared simultaneously with an essay by Samuel Hickson bearing the same title and attributional conclusions (see Ard[2], xvii). As I have noted already, Tennyson seems to have been the first to name Fletcher as the 'other hand' in the play; Spedding the first to outline a clear division between Shakespeare and Fletcher; but it was the pioneering Shakespearean editor Edmond Malone who first suggested the involvement of another hand, suspecting that the references to James in Cranmer's speech must have been 'added in 1613, after Shakspeare [*sic*] had quitted the stage, by that hand which tampered with the other parts of the play so much, as to have rendered the versification of it of a different colour from all the other plays of Shakspeare' (Malone, 139). Right from the beginning, then, reference to the 'other hand' in the play was negative and collaboration seen as a diminution of the great writer's work.

consistency and coherency needs no further explanation', since the lack of 'a just moral feeling is Fletcher's characteristic defect, and lies at the bottom of all that is most offensive in him' (123). To uncover collaborative authorship is thus also to redeem Shakespeare from charges of moral inadequacy. Bias notwithstanding, Spedding's metrical approach was the method championed by the best-known Victorian disintegrators, Fleay and Furnivall of the New Shakespere [*sic*] Society, who applied it to the entire Shakespeare canon and 'apocrypha' with what they felt was 'scientific' rigour.[1] Despite this claim to accuracy and objectivity, the results of their analyses varied widely, however, and accusations of miscounting and subjectivism led to acrimony and, finally, to the dissolution of the Society (see Grady). Nonetheless, the idea that *Henry VIII*'s 'difficulties' could be explained by collaborative authorship never died away, and several critics in the mid-twentieth century, all of whom held a high opinion of the play, provided eloquent resistance to those who continued to argue for collaborative ascription (Maxwell, 55–63; Alexander, 117; Knight, *Crown*, 256–72; Ard[2], xix–xxiv).

But by this time the New Bibliographical desire to pinpoint individual shares in a collaborative text had come to require refinements of the 'disintegrative' method, not dismissal. In returning to the fray in the late 1950s, Cyrus Hoy sought to rise above the various flaws of earlier disintegrative methods by seeking textual features which might be shown to be characteristic of a particular writer's style and by producing a careful statistical analysis in support of his claims. For Hoy, 'scholarly investigation of the authorial problems posed by collaborative drama' is no less than 'a necessary precondition to critical and aesthetic considerations of such drama' (Hoy, 'Collaboration', 4). The aim of his project, he announces, is:

---

1 'The great need for any critic who attempts to use these tests', Fleay observed, 'is to have a thorough training in the Naturall Sciences, especially in Mineralogy, classificatory Botany, and above all, in Chemical Analysis. The methods of all these sciences are applicable to this kind of criticism which, indeed, can scarcely be understood without them' (Fleay, 108); Fleay's book exemplifies the aims and methods of the New Shakespere Society.

to show (1) how the unaided plays of Fletcher can be sin-
gled out from the other plays of the canon, and (2) how
the pattern of linguistic preferences which emerges from
Fletcher's unaided plays contrasts sufficiently with the
language practices in the unaided plays of Massinger as
to afford a basis for distinguishing the work of the two
dramatists one from the other.

(Hoy, 1, 130)

To this end, he deploys 'linguistic' criteria, by which he means 'an
author's use of such a pronominal form as *ye* for *you*, of third person singular verb forms in *-th* (such as the auxiliaries *hath* and
doth), of contractions like *'em* for *them*', and so forth, suggesting
that the distinctive feature of his work in comparison with earlier
efforts is its scale and systematic nature. His analysis of the
authorship of *Henry VIII* is the culmination of his study partly
because it is a play which 'has its place . . . in a greater canon than
the Beaumont and Fletcher one' (Hoy, 7, 76) and partly because,
as a play for which no external evidence of collaborative authorship exists, it provides the toughest challenge for the analyst of
attribution.[1]

The simplest way to demonstrate the features on which Hoy's
analysis depends is to look back at the folios reproduced on
pp. 151–3 (Figs. 20–22) – and specifically at Katherine's speeches
at 2.4.72–82 (i.e. v2ᵛ, TLN 1431–41) and 3.1.102–11 (i.e. v3ᵛ–v4ʳ,
TLN 1733–42) – with a view this time to the question of authorship. I have chosen these particular brief passages both because
they are broadly comparable in content and context and because
they demonstrate on a small scale some of the features that have
led 'disintegrators' to distinguish between styles in *Henry VIII*,

---

1   These attitudes provide quiet testimony to the role both of Hoy's analyses of the
    Beaumont and Fletcher canon and of the Fredson Bowers edition of the plays in that
    canon (for which Hoy's articles were preliminary work) as secondary to, and a prac-
    tice ground for, a projected old-spelling edition of Shakespeare based on Bowers's
    editorial principles which was never, in the end, to see the light of day. The attribu-
    tional project thus takes place in the name of the canon's most definitive 'author'.

but I should point out that they are in no way statistically adequate for proper attributional study, and are offered here purely as a means of making visible in as compact a way as possible the kinds of feature Hoy was seeking. Both speeches are expressions of Katherine's frustration and anger with Rome's representatives, yet they exhibit noticeably different stylistic qualities: the second is, for example, heavily end-stopped, whereas in the first longer units of meaning extend across several lines of verse. Hoy, though, concentrated on features which he felt (on the basis of statistics drawn from 'solo' plays) could be said to be characteristic of the particular playwright for whose presence he was testing. For him, the contraction *'em* for *them* is one clear example of Fletcherian usage, as is a preference for *ye* over *you* (not that this is the only form used in Fletcher plays, but that it is the statistically dominant form). The speeches contain both an *'em* and a concentration of *ye* forms (eight in total, as well as several in adjacent speeches by Campeius) in the passage from 3.1, strongly suggesting (in Hoy's terms) the hand of Fletcher. The chosen speeches admittedly make a less than perfect comparison in the sense that there is no *them* in the passage from 2.4 to set against the *'em* of 3.1, but the presence of five *you* forms and no *ye* forms at all in the 2.4 passages marks a clear and measurable difference.

Hoy's method thus distinguishes between the two speeches, suggesting Shakespeare as the author of the one and Fletcher of the other. Measured across the play as a whole, the frequency of these features varies enough from scene to scene for Hoy to be able to demonstrate patterns which 'confirm' the collaborative nature of *Henry VIII*, and statistical comparison of these patterns with figures drawn from representative batches of 'solo' plays by each playwright enables him to offer attribution by scene, ascribing roughly half the play to each playwright. Even Foakes, in a 1962 postscript to his section on authorship, was obliged to admit that Hoy's evidence 'carries more weight' (Ard[2], xxvii) than that of his precursors and that he is probably right to conclude that Fletcher's hand is present (though less so than some analysts had claimed) and thus that, contrary to the view expressed in his first edition, 'the truth about Fletcher's share in *Henry VIII* is to be found where truth generally is: midway between the extreme views that have traditionally been held regarding it' (xxvii–xxviii).

This might seem to mark the end of debate, but truth, as we have seen repeatedly in the history of this play, is a matter of perspective. Ostensibly, features have been isolated which are characteristic of a particular writer's style, which can be applied generally, and which, when applied, allow for a clear division of authorship for *Henry VIII* (and, by implication, for any other collaborative play from the period). But Hoy makes a curious admission. 'In evaluating linguistic criteria as a test of authorship,' he notes, 'it is obvious that no linguistic form can be regarded as distinctive of a particular dramatist in any absolute sense' (Hoy, 1, 134). He thus acknowledges that '[t]he value to be attached to any piece of linguistic criteria is, in the end, completely relative: all depends upon the degree of divergence between the linguistic patterns that are to be distinguished' (134). Moreover, in discussing the linguistic characteristics that mark out one particular playwright – Francis Beaumont – from his coadjutors (principally, as it happens, Fletcher), Hoy is obliged to admit that 'Beaumont's linguistic practices are . . . so widely divergent as to make it all but impossible to predict what they will be from one play to another' (Hoy, 3, 86). 'Beaumont's presence will thus be ascertained', as Jeffrey Masten points out, 'as that which remains after Fletcher, Massinger, *et al.* have been subtracted' (Masten, *Intercourse*, 16–17). Identification is thus not a product of the absolute presence or absence of certain linguistic preferences in the 'unaided' work of a given writer, but rather of the frequency of usage of those preferences, and Hoy is obliged to acknowledge that 'no linguistic form can be regarded as the exclusive property of a single writer' (Hoy, 1, 137). This is a significant admission, since it suggests that the principal aim of the study – to find a way to determine which individual wrote which parts of a collaborative play – has still not been achieved.

Moreover, analyses such as Hoy's are faced with the problem of intervention by agents other than the collaborating writers, most notably the tendency of scribes and compositors to adjust the texts with which they work, evening out or erasing the very differences that are sought by the analyst. This is a particular problem in Hoy's analysis of *Henry VIII* because of the odd distribution ('clusters') of 'Fletcherian' features that he finds across the play, which may well be the result of the tendency of the First Folio's Compositor B to 'regularize' these forms during his stints.[1] The New Bibliographical response to problems of this sort is naturally to attempt to separate non-authorial intervention from authorial original, but the premises remain conjectural. In discussing 'clustering' in 3.2, for instance, Hoy is torn between the possibilities of intervention by, on the one hand, Compositor B (imagined as suppressing 'Fletcherian' forms most of the time, but not uniformly) and, on the other, Fletcher (imagined as intervening occasionally in a 'Shakespeare' scene) (Hoy, 7, 80–1). Yet there could be other explanations – from the possibility of active collaboration, in which both playwrights work simultaneously on a scene (a vision which is generally anathema to Shakespeareans) to the possibility of breaks in the compositor's work patterns tending to disrupt an otherwise pervasive process of regularization (it is noticeable, for instance, that the clusters of 'Fletcherian' forms in the First Folio text frequently come at column or page breaks).[2] We have, anyway, already noted the general inconsistency of early modern spelling and its dependence upon material factors rather than any kind of accepted orthography.

1   On the other hand, although the principal scenes in which such clustering occurs (3.2, 4.1 and 4.2) were set by Compositor B, there are also two Compositor I scenes (4.1 and 4.2) in which Hoy's 'Fletcherian' features appear fragmentarily.

2   This may of course not be at all significant, but it is typical of the kind of small-scale question that statistical analysis of the Hoy variety, by virtue of the need for an 'adequate sample of text', is unable to answer. Another source might be 'syntactic priming' on the part of the playwright(s), i.e. that a textual feature triggers a particular form which remains in use until a different feature triggers an alternative form. Again, this can never be proven.

As far as the notion of compositors' 'self-standardization' is concerned, Masten quotes A.W.Pollard's observation that, in the 1611 King James Bible, 'the only [spelling] consistency is that the form is always preferred which suits the spacing' – in other words, that a compositor will reduce or increase the length of a word (by deployment of final *e*, for example) to ensure largely uniform use of space across a given sheet, particularly if casting-off has been less than exact (Pollard, 6; see also Goldberg).[1] Some of the methods through which distinctions between textual agents are achieved can be shown, in other words, to be subject to the same criticisms as is authorial attribution itself.

The most recent attempt to solve the problem of the blurring of lines between compositorial and authorial 'responsibilities' for the text is Jonathan Hope's 'socio-historical linguistic' study of 'Shakespearean' authorship, which effectively supersedes Hoy and points successors in a much-needed 'worldly' direction. For Hope (whose study may be the last to involve 'manual' counting of variants in texts[2]), it is essential to recognize that language is process and that 'when a change [from one form to another] is in progress, the alternative forms will co-exist' (Hope, *Authorship*, 5). This provides a way to circumvent the problem of scribal or compositorial interference, since, in the case of *Henry VIII*, the linguistic features Hope chooses are not Hoy's easily altered *ye* and *'em*, but characteristics such as relative markers (*that* and *which*) and auxiliary *do*, on the principle that 'there are linguistic changes in progress in Early Modern English whose alternates (or more accurately variants) are not regarded as interchangeable by scribes and compositors, and which are therefore textually stable'

1 On the problems of determining compositorial identity by characteristic handling of spacing (another standard method), see McKenzie.
2 There is a burgeoning field of computational analysis of authorial characteristics that tends to concentrate on stylometry, an approach which has yet by and large (because of incompatible fields of understanding both about the nature of statistical study and about the significance of 'literary' concepts such as genre) to gain the approval of linguists and literary critics (Merriam; Hope, *Authorship*, 8–9). Once computer corpuses for all the relevant playwrights are available, linguistic analysis will no doubt benefit from becoming fully computational.

(5). Moreover, he notes that where '[c]hanges in progress in Early Modern English' did in fact offer:

> alternatives to writers and speakers where present-day Standard English offers none – for example, a choice between 'you' and 'ye' in the second person pronoun, and '-th' and '-s' as an ending for the third person singular present tense of verbs (e.g. 'hath' versus 'has'),
>
> (5)

the choices made are likely to map a particular language user's location in relation to those changes.

It is thus possible, he argues, to make certain assumptions about the likely preferences of writers in relation to their age, place of upbringing and other factors in the formation of a speaker's lect which offer the possibility of establishing a positive profile for a given playwright which is rooted not in 'individual choice' but in historical sociolinguistic development. In respect of the Shakespeare–Fletcher collaborations, he notes that 'John Fletcher was born in 1579 in the south-east and brought up in an upper-class, urban environment . . . and the evidence favours the view that [he] attended Cambridge University'; Shakespeare, on the other hand, was born 'fifteen years earlier in the rural south-west midlands', and this, combined with 'his lower-class status, and lack of higher education' would tend to suggest that Fletcher is much more likely to use incoming prestige variants than is Shakespeare. He is thus able to demonstrate a sociohistorical logic for the distinctions of style apparent in different scenes, and his analysis thus offers a way to move beyond the attribution of authorship on the basis of relative usage of revisable forms – not to the kind of fixed 'individual' style which has been the aim of such studies to date, but to the establishment of lects which can be associated with specific playwrights in relation to evidence about the linguistic contexts in which they operated. This approach – which produces a profile for the play more in line with Spedding's analysis than with Hoy's (see Appendix 3) – has the considerable advantage of looking to social rather than individual characteristics, projecting authors who are the products of their linguistic environment rather than autonomous agents freely choosing a particular, and unique, mode of expression.

There are problems, though, even with Hope's sophisticated version of 'disintegration'. For one thing, he is obliged to depend upon current knowledge of Early Modern English which is, as he acknowledges, decidedly less than complete. This effectively forces him both to make the uncomfortable assumption of equivalence between spoken and written forms and to depend upon sources which are subject to the same problems of scribal and other intervention as are dramatic texts (see Hope, 'Pronouns', 83–5). For another, the notion of a language user's distinct and unchanging relationship to that language is itself suspect. Since language is learned, any idiolect is the product of expressions and characteristics both consciously acquired and unconsciously absorbed from others and is by no means fixed at any point in the language user's life. There is, for instance, nothing to say that language users are consistent in their adoption or rejection of incoming forms.[1] Again, they may, consciously or unconsciously, change their 'style' over the course of a lifetime (Shakespeare and Fletcher both stepped into very different social situations when they became writers, the one upwardly mobile, the other downwardly, and their lects may well have altered to match), or they may adopt a different style as a result of working with another writer (linguistic 'accommodation theory' examines the effect of contact with other language users on a given user's lect) (Street & Giles).

Moreover, as Masten has suggested, the professional nature of the playwright's task undermines the notion of fixed style, since by definition, in creating dramatic personae, he or she 'im/personates another (many others) . . . and thus refracts the supposed singularity of the individual in language' (Masten, *Intercourse*, 17). As part of this creative process, changes in the status or

1 Hoy's emphasis on Fletcher's 'preference' for 'ye' over 'you' is a possible case in point: the younger, upper-class man retaining an idiosyncratic, outmoded linguistic form.

emotion of a particular character may be made by alterations in his or her style of speech. Looking back, for example, at Katherine's speeches from the reproduced pages, it may be possible to explain the differences in her turn of phrase and use of pronouns from one passage to the other by the increased emotional pressure she has come under between one scene and the other or by the subtle shifts of status embodied in the triad *thou/you/ye* as forms of address. Again, a playwright's style may be constrained by working within a particular genre (Hoy's and Hope's inability to incorporate the one-off pastoral tragicomedy *The Faithful Shepherdess*, with its oddly archaic style, into their statistics for Fletcher offers an overt example of the effect this can have). In other words, the quest for a stable 'fingerprint' which will be applicable to a given playwright, even one which takes into account the social and contextual construction of his 'style', conflicts with the basic instabilities and practicalities of the playwriting process in the early modern period.

It is, after all, obvious that Shakespeare did not create *Henry VIII* 'on his own'. No playwright does, not even the most fêted playwright in history. Playwrights pitch their writing into an environment – a theatre, a company of actors, set designers, carpenters, wig makers, an audience, as well as theatrical traditions, acting styles, professional protocols – which shapes what is written both before and after pen touches paper. Gary Taylor argues that 'dramatic texts are necessarily the most socialized of all literary forms' since the production of a play is 'a complex, layered process involving a substantial number of agents' (*TxC*, 15). And the particular conditions of early modern theatre placed severe limits on a playwright's opportunities for asserting ownership of 'his' texts. Extending Michel Foucault's groundbreaking work on the historical construction of the concept of authorship, Peter Stallybrass and Jeffrey Masten have shown that the proprietorship of individuals over 'their own' work (and, notably, of the playwright over a text which was owned not by him but by the company for which he wrote) in fact postdates the early modern period: Ben Jonson's highly conscious efforts to establish himself as an 'author' mark only the beginnings of a major shift in perceptions (see Foucault, 'Author'; Stallybrass; Masten, *Intercourse*; and Masten, 'Playwrighting'). Thus, when we look at the process of production:

> [i]nstead of a single author, we have a network of collaborative relations, normally between two or more writers, between writers and acting companies, between acting companies and printers, between compositors and proofreaders, between printers and censors.
>
> (Stallybrass, 601)

Moreover, this description still sells the extent of collaboration a little short, since at the exact physical moment of creation marked by the appearance of ink on paper, several further, and potentially conflicting, authorities come into play. Writers work, as I have suggested already, from sources which may be rewritten in new contexts but which may also substantially determine what is written. One 'author' of *Henry VIII*, in this sense, is Holinshed, whose words are regularly taken verbatim, only modified for purposes of metrification (an 'authority' which is itself called into question by the collaborative construction of the *Chronicles*). Another 'author' of *Henry VIII* is Shakespeare's younger self, in the sense that one of the things writers do is to collaborate with their former selves, to renegotiate repeatedly and insistently their previous textual expressions. Thus to treat the play as the product of collaboration by Shakespeare and Fletcher is, on one level, perfectly legitimate, and is, for several reasons, vastly preferable to the notion that it is 'Shakespeare's'. But to narrow down the event of collaboration to an imagined moment in which two playwrights work together in a single room is to limit the potential of collaboration for our own reimagining of the processes of dramatic creation.

The kind of collaborative endeavour that is exemplified in *Henry VIII* thus opens up our understanding of the complexities of, and the contradictions within, the idea of authorship that controls our approach to reading, and allows us to look beyond the restrictive paradigm of the 'solo' author to something more historically and theatrically appropriate. How, then, should we speak of *Henry VIII*? To describe it as 'Shakespeare's play' would be, for all sorts of reasons, to miss the point. Yet to call it 'Shakespeare's and Fletcher's play' would also be to depend on intentionalist premises which are powerfully challenged by the nature of the production of dramatic texts. It would arguably be better (as critics have been realizing in recent years) to group early modern plays, not by playwright at all, but within the repertoires for which they were originally written (so you would find on the bookshop shelf, for instance, not *Four Plays of John Webster*, but *Four Red Bull Plays*, which would include *The White Devil* because it belongs within a set of plays written for and performed by the company at the Red Bull Theatre). But this is not practically, commercially or emotionally viable in view of the romantic attitude to authorship that continues to dominate both academic courses and the publishing market across the English-speaking world. Nor does it take into account the weight of history that attends a text such as *Henry VIII*.

The play is *Shakespeare*'s in the sense that it has, at least since the publication of the First Folio, been read, performed and witnessed in a Shakespearean context, with all the professional, cultural and political implications of that context, and in the sense that it engages with, and has a particular place among, the other plays in the Shakespeare canon. It is *Shakespeare and Fletcher*'s, on the other hand (as the title-page of this edition claims), in the sense that a certain amount of evidence, mostly circumstantial, strongly suggests that, contrary to the impression given by its inclusion in the Shakespeare First Folio, the play was the product of two playwrights, William Shakespeare and John Fletcher, working together, and that to treat the play as a collaboration in this restricted sense is to complicate its canonic status in a potentially productive manner. Again, it is the *King's Company*'s in the sense that it was written for, and belonged to, a particular acting company at a particular historical moment, that it both advantaged them (in that it seems to have drawn audiences to at least one of the company's theatres) and disadvantaged them (in that its material realization caused the destruction of that theatre) and that, like any other play in the repertoire of that company, it is the product of all the various professional and cultural agencies called into being by the particular economic framework within which that company operated.

As such, *Henry VIII* is the product of a process which extends beyond the limited ramifications of these ascriptions, because the writing of any play is the result of a process of textual negotiation at a given historical moment which has a broader reach than can be encompassed by the comprehension of a writer or writers at any given moment (see, amongst others, Foucault, 'Author'; Nehemas, 'Author'; and Nehemas, 'Writer'). For our purposes, at the beginning of the twenty-first century, there are two key moves which can be made in relation to *Henry VIII*, each of which entails the recognition of the limitations of treating the play as wholly Shakespeare's. The first is to accept that the play is not just 'by Shakespeare' but 'by Shakespeare and Fletcher'. The second is to understand that the supplementarity embodied in this acknowledgement makes any attempt to limit responsibility for the play to two writers treated as autonomous 'authors' both an historically inappropriate gesture and a clear diminution of the processes of textual production. In other words, not only does *Henry VIII* offer us a much more subtle, complex and valuable textual experience than we might have been led to believe by Shakespearean tradition, it also requires us to reconsider the very basis of our understanding of the way in which texts – particularly early modern dramatic texts – come into being.

KING
HENRY VIII
(ALL IS TRUE)

LIST OF ROLES

Gardiner's PAGE		
Sir Anthony DENNY		
Thomas CRANMER	*Archbishop of Canterbury*	
Door KEEPER	*of the Council Chamber*	40
Doctor BUTTS	*the King's physician*	
PORTER		
Porter's MAN		

EPILOGUE

Musicians, Guards, Secretaries, Noblemen, Ladies, Gentlemen,   45
Masquers, Tipstaves, Halberdiers, Attendants, Common People,
Vergers, Scribes, Archbishop of Canterbury, Bishops of Ely, Rochester
and St Asaph, Priests, Gentleman Usher, Women attendant on Katherine,
Judges, Choristers, Lord Mayor of London, Marquess of Dorset,
four Barons of the Cinque Ports, Bishop of London, Duchess of Norfolk,   50
six Dancers (spirits) in Katherine's vision, Marchioness of Dorset,
Aldermen, Servants, Grooms

LIST OF ROLES not in F; first provided by Rowe

2 NORFOLK Thomas Howard became second Duke of Norfolk in 1514, restoring his family's status. Anne Bullen was his granddaughter through his eldest daughter Elizabeth; Henry's fifth wife, Katherine Howard, was his granddaughter through his third son Edmund. He was married twice: to Elizabeth Tilney (the 'old Duchess of Norfolk' of 4.1.36.20) and to Agnes Tilney. He died in 1524, but is conflated with his son Thomas Howard in the scenes in the play which postdate his historical death (e.g. at 4.1.18).

3 BUCKINGHAM Edward Stafford (not 'Bohun', as at 2.1.103), Duke of Buckingham, the eldest son of *R3*'s Buckingham, was executed for high treason in May 1521. On his possible claim to the throne, see 2.1.102n. His eldest daughter Elizabeth married Thomas Howard, the play's Earl of Surrey, later Duke of Norfolk; his second daughter Mary married George Neville, the play's Lord Abergavenny.

4 ABERGAVENNY George Neville, Lord Abergavenny, was Constable of Dover Castle and Warden of the Cinque Ports under Henry VIII. He married Mary Stafford, daughter of the Duke of Buckingham. Writing to Sir Edmund Bacon a year or so after his description of the burning of the Globe, Sir Henry Wotton makes mildly mocking reference to the son of the current Lord Abergavenny, Christopher Neville, MP, recently sent to the Tower for a speech 'against Kings' (Wotton/Bacon, B6ᵛ).

5 WOLSEY Thomas, Cardinal Wolsey, was born in 1471, the son of an Ipswich butcher. He became Archbishop of York in 1514, both Lord Chancellor and Cardinal in 1515, and effectively ran England for a decade. He was renowned for his overt displays of wealth and status. Henry began to lose confidence in him in 1527: he was deprived of both his property and the great seal (sign of his chancellorship) in 1529, and was

arrested and died in 1530. The play's emphasis on his lower-class origins (cf. 1.1.120) has been echoed by editors: Margeson, commenting on the BBC production, saw Timothy West as 'a stolid, calculating Wolsey with something of the butcher's plebeian beefiness about him' (Cam², 56).

7 BRANDON Buckingham was arrested, according to Holinshed, by Sir Henry Marney, but the arresting officer in the play is called 'Brandon', the family name of the Duke of Suffolk (see 1.1.197.1n). Marney became Lord Keeper of the Privy Seal in 1533.

9 KING Henry the Eighth was born in 1491, the second son of Henry VII and Elizabeth of York, daughter of Edward IV. He became King on 23 April 1509 and married Katherine of Aragon on 11 June. They had six children, only one of whom, a daughter, Mary, later Mary I (1553–8), lived longer than a few weeks. Cranmer declared their marriage unlawful on 23 May 1533; Henry had already married Anne Bullen in private on 25 January. In 1534, Parliament declared Henry head on earth of the Church of England. Anne was executed on 19 May 1536, and on 30 May Henry married Jane Seymour, who died in October 1537, twelve days after giving birth to a son, Edward, later Edward VI. Henry married three more times and died in 1547.

10 LOVELL Sir Thomas Lovell was Marshal of the House, Surveyor of the Court of Wards and Constable of the Tower under Henry VIII. He had fought at Bosworth and became Chancellor of the Exchequer under Henry VII. He retired from court in 1516. His funeral in 1524 was notable for its scale and the fullness of its Roman Catholic ritual.

11 KATHERINE Katherine of Aragon was born in 1485, the daughter of Ferdinand and Isabella of Spain (see 2.4.45n.). She married Arthur, eldest son of Henry VII, in 1501. When he died a year later, Katherine was immediately engaged to his brother, Henry.

Only one child, Mary, survived from her numerous pregnancies. After Henry had divorced her in favour of Anne Bullen in 1533, Katherine lived at Ampthill, then at Buckden, and finally at Kimbolton, where she died in January 1536.

12 SUFFOLK Charles Brandon became Duke of Suffolk in 1514: his elevation excluded the possibility of restoration for the de la Pole family (Gunn, 25–7). He was renowned as the epitome of chivalry. In 1515, to the King's initial fury, he married Henry's sister Mary, widow of Louis XII of France, but eventually he gained Henry's approval for the match and remained his close companion (the story features in *When You See Me*). He was an enemy of Wolsey and, later, of Gardiner; cf. also *Duchess of Suffolk* (1631).

13 SURVEYOR Charles Knevet, Buckingham's surveyor (see 1.1.115n., 1.2.171–3n.), was the Duke's distant relative but had been dismissed from his post. His nephew, Anthony Knevet, was one of Henry VIII's two gentleman ushers.

14 Lord CHAMBERLAIN officer of the royal household: his title derives from his duty to attend the King in his privy chamber, but he also had charge over the King's finances and diary. The post was in fact held by Lord Sandys at the time of the earlier events depicted in the play (see 15n; 1.4.31n.). His predecessor in the post, and presumably the play's Chamberlain throughout, was Charles Somerset, Earl of Worcester, who died in 1526.

15 SANDYS Sir William Sandys became Lord Sandys in 1523. He was Lord Chamberlain at the time of Wolsey's banquet, though in the play he is a separate character (see 14n., 1.3.0.1n.).

16 ANNE Anne Bullen was born in 1501 into a courtly family. By 1530 she was Henry's mistress; she became Marchioness of Pembroke in 1532. A keen Reformer, her ascendancy was opposed by Wolsey and she encouraged his arrest. She married Henry VIII in January 1533 and was crowned Queen in June. She was beheaded for (alleged) adultery in May 1536.

17 GUILDFORD Sir Henry Guildford was Henry VIII's Master of Horse and a prominent soldier. He was one of the fashionable young courtiers admonished by the Privy Council in 1519 for inappropriate behaviour after returning to the English court from France (see 1.3.1n.).

19, 20, 33 GENTLEMEN There are no specific historical counterparts for the three commentating gentlemen, who occupy a partially choric role.

21 VAUX Sir Nicholas Vaux was son and heir of the William Vaux who appears in *2H6* and who died at Tewkesbury. He was governor of Guînes under Henry VIII, who made him Lord Vaux of Harrowden shortly before he died.

22 CAMPEIUS Lorenzo Campeggio, who became a cardinal in 1517, was known for his staunch anti-Protestantism. He first came to England as papal legate in 1518, becoming absentee Bishop of Salisbury in 1524. He returned to England in 1528 to preside with Wolsey over the divorce case between Henry and Katherine. He was deprived of his see at the time of the Act of Supremacy in 1534, and died in Italy in 1539.

23 GARDINER Stephen Gardiner became the King's secretary in 1529 and Bishop of Winchester in 1531. He was a staunch enemy of Cranmer and of reform. He was imprisoned under Edward VI as an enemy of Protestantism, but was released by Mary, whom he crowned in 1553 (when he became Lord Chancellor); he also presided over her marriage to Philip of Spain. Foxe is the principal source for Gardiner's traditional malevolent image; he appears in *Thomas, Lord Cromwell* (1602, reprinted 1613), where his enmity with Cromwell is clearly established.

24 OLD LADY There is no apparent historical original for this character, who appears in 2.3 and again (presumably) in 5.1. She emerges from a tradition which includes Rojas's *Celestina* (see Round) and Juliet's Nurse in *RJ* (see 2.3n.).

25 LINCOLN John Longland became Bishop of Lincoln in 1528. He was Chancellor of Oxford University from 1532, assisting Wolsey with his plans for Cardinal College, now Christ Church (see 4.2.58n.).

26 GRIFFITH No-one of this name is mentioned in Holinshed's description of Katherine's death, but a Griffith is named in the account of the court proceedings at Blackfriars (see 2.4.119 SD–130 SDn., 124 SPn.). Holinshed draws on Cavendish's fuller description of the moment which notes that, leaving the courtroom, Katherine was 'leanyng (as she was wont allwayes to do /) vppon the arme of hir Generall receyvour called m^r Griffithe' (Cavendish, *EETS*, 82).

29 SURREY Thomas Howard, Earl of Surrey, eldest son of the second Duke of Norfolk, was Lord Admiral of England and then Lord Lieutenant of Ireland under Henry VIII. He became Duke of Norfolk at the death of his father in 1524, and would have been beheaded in 1547 had Henry not died the evening before the scheduled execution.

30 CROMWELL Thomas Cromwell was, like Wolsey, of low social origin, became a lawyer and an MP, and worked for the Cardinal. After Wolsey's fall, he became Henry's secretary. In 1535 he was appointed Vicar-General in Spirituals and oversaw the dissolution of the monasteries. He was an enemy of Anne Bullen. He became Lord Cromwell (1536) and Earl of Essex (1539), but he lost the King's favour for promoting the marriage with Anne of Cleves, was tried for high treason and beheaded in July 1540. His Protestantism and enmity with Gardiner are dramatized in *Thomas, Lord Cromwell*.

31 Lord CHANCELLOR the most important state administrator, who was entrusted with the great seal that authenticated royal documents. Wolsey held the post until 1529, when Sir Thomas More, humanist, writer and statesman, replaced him. More resigned in 1532, and was beheaded in 1535. Shakespeare wrote at least one scene of a play about him, *Sir Thomas More* (*c.* 1595). At More's resignation, Sir Thomas Audley became Chancellor (and walked in Anne Bullen's coronation procession in that capacity); he was succeeded at his death in 1544 by Sir Thomas Wriothesley (see 5.2.34.2n.), grandfather to Henry Wriothesley, third Earl of Southampton, Shakespeare's patron.

32 GARTER Garter King-of-Arms (or King-at-Arms, which is, according to *OED*, the less correct form) is the most important of the three chief heralds of the College of Arms (Garter, Clarenceux and Norroy), i.e. the main royal master of ceremonies (see 5.4.1–3, where Garter's role as continuity man is apparent). The post was occupied at the time of Anne's coronation by Thomas Wriothesley, who later became Lord Chancellor (see 31n., 4.1.36.6n.).

34 PATIENCE Of Katherine's four principal ladies-in-waiting, three were Spanish and one English. There is no historical record of anyone in her household with the name Patience, but it has obvious allegorical significance and is arguably an epithet transferred from Katherine herself (see, for instance, 2.4.71, 127, 3.1.137). Cavendish saw Katherine as 'a perfect Grysheld', a reference to the legend of 'Patient Griselda', best known from Chaucer's *Clerk's Tale*, which was highly popular in the sixteenth century; William Forrest's poem *The History of Grisild the Second* (1558) is a thinly veiled account of Katherine's sufferings (see Ives, 119; Cavendish, *EETS*, 35, 259–62).

36 CAPUTIUS Eustace Chapuys arrived in England in 1530 as ambassador from the Holy Roman Emperor, Charles V (Katherine of Aragon's nephew). He was a staunch supporter of Katherine and her daughter Mary and was 'delighted' to hear that Anne thought him responsible for her downfall (Ridley, *Henry*, 272). He was Katherine's last visitor at Kimbolton in the week of her death.

38 DENNY Sir Anthony Denny was Groom of the Stool and a member of the Privy Council under Henry VIII. A keen Reformer, he was one of the executors of Henry's will and a regent for Edward VI.

39 CRANMER Thomas Cranmer, who had written a treatise in favour of the King's divorce, was sent by Henry in 1530 to collect supportive clerical opinions on the Continent. He became Archbishop of Canterbury at the death of William Warham in 1532 and pronounced the decree of divorce. He survived two attempts by the Catholic faction at court to have him condemned for heresy, in 1543 and 1545, but was burnt at the stake at Oxford in March 1555 as a Protestant martyr.

41 BUTTS Sir William Butts was Henry VIII's personal physician, and is depicted in a painting by Holbein of the King presenting the Charter of the Barber–Surgeons' Company in 1541. Butts, who was an enthusiastic Reformer and friend of Cranmer, was sent by Henry to attend on Wolsey at Esher in his illness after his fall from favour.

47 *Archbishop of Canterbury* The Archbishop of Canterbury who appears at 2.4.0.3 and whom Henry addresses at 2.4.215 is not Cranmer, as the play makes clear, but William Warham, Cranmer's predecessor, who became Archbishop in 1504 and died in 1532. A mute role.

48 *Women attendant* See 34n.

49 *Lord Mayor* The Lord Mayor who appears at Anne's coronation (4.1) and Elizabeth's christening (5.4) was Sir Stephen Peacock, mayor from 1532 to 1533. A mute role.

KING
HENRY VIII
(ALL IS TRUE)

[*Enter*] PROLOGUE.

PROLOGUE

I come no more to make you laugh: things now
That bear a weighty and a serious brow,
Sad, high and working, full of state and woe,
Such noble scenes as draw the eye to flow,
We now present. Those that can pity here   5
May, if they think it well, let fall a tear:
The subject will deserve it. Such as give
Their money out of hope they may believe

PROLOGUE Generally ascribed to Fletcher (see Appendix 3), though there are not enough lines for an adequate linguistic or stylometric count. Presumably written for the first or an early performance, the Prologue sets out to prepare the audience for the kind of historical drama they are about to see: promising a particular (though barely delineated) kind of theatrical 'truth'; suggesting a structural return to early Shakespearean history (especially the *H6* plays); consciously distancing *H8* both from the second tetralogy and from *When You See Me*; and (arguably) hinting at a degree of topicality.

1–5 I . . . **present.** The Prologue sets out to assert the grandeur and seriousness of the play, insisting that this 'history play' will be tragic, not comic, in mode. Beerbohm Tree was the first director to restore the Prologue to his production (see Swayze, 309). In Tyrone Guthrie's 1949 production, the Prologue and Epilogue were spoken by the Old Lady; in Ian Judge's 1991 Chichester production, by one of the commentating Gentlemen; in the 1997 New York production, by the little girl who was also the angel of Katherine's vision. A clue to the original function of a Prologue within a particular repertoire was perhaps given by audience reaction to Greg Doran's RSC production in 1996/7: there was an immediate response to the opening line because many of the audience had seen Guy Henry, the actor playing the Lord Chamberlain/ Prologue, as a highly comic Dr Caius in the concurrent production of *MW*.

3 **Sad, high and working** serious, important and emotive

TITLE] KING HENRY VIII (ALL IS TRUE) *this edn;* The Famous History of the Life of King HENRY the Eight *F; All is True* Oxf **Prologue** 0.1] *Oxf;* THE PROLOGUE. *F* 1 SP] *Oxf; not in F* 3 high and] and high- *Staunton* full] fall *F2*

May here find truth, too. Those that come to see
Only a show or two and so agree   10
The play may pass, if they be still and willing
I'll undertake may see away their shilling
Richly in two short hours. Only they
That come to hear a merry, bawdy play,
A noise of targets, or to see a fellow   15
In a long motley coat guarded with yellow,
Will be deceived. For, gentle hearers, know
To rank our chosen truth with such a show

9 **truth** *Truth* is a key issue in *Henry VIII*: on its significance here, see Introduction, e.g. pp. 1–3, 67–70.

9–13 **Those . . . hours.** These lines appear to be directed humorously at a particular section of the audience, the affluent ('rich'), fashion-conscious and, by implication, vacuous theatre-goers who occupied the most expensive seats. It cost a penny to stand in the yard; a shilling (twelve pence) seems to have been the price for the most prominent seats, probably in the 'lord's room' to the side of the stage (Chambers, *ES*, 2.533–4; Gurr, 214–15).

13 **two short hours** Accounts of the duration of Jacobean plays vary, but 'two hours' is the standard figure; cf. *RJ*, Prologue 12: 'the two-hours' traffic of our stage'; Jonson, *The Alchemist*, Prologue 1: 'these two short houres'. There were no set changes and no lengthy intervals, but the pace of performance must still have been decidedly brisk. Wright believes that verse lines would have 'had to be spoken with some urgency, and without the metrically slack long pauses and preparations that distinguish most modern productions' (Wright, *Metrical*, 189). This line was altered in Tree's production (1910) to

'three short hours' in view of the time taken up by set changes and spectacle and despite the removal of all of Act 5.

14 **merry, bawdy play** The play referred to here is probably *When You See Me*, a comic history of Henry VIII's reign written in 1605 and revived in 1613; it is a loosely structured entertainment with a strong Protestant bias and an emphasis on the role of Henry's fool, Will Summers.

15 **targets** bucklers, shields; a probable reference to Henry's duel with Black Will the highwayman in *When You See Me*, sc. 4. The King, as he plans his nocturnal venture, maintains that 'Our swordes and bucklers shall conduct vs safe' (D1^r; Wilson, TLN 941). Sword and buckler, as the principal equipment for sporting swordplay, had given way to the rapier in the course of the 1590s, particularly for gentlemen, so the disparaging reference to *targets* is both a class and a fashion statement.

16 **long . . . yellow** the traditional costume of fools (as worn by Will Summers and Patch in *When You See Me*): this is presumably an indication that *H8* will not echo the king/fool juxtaposition of a play such as *KL*.

As fool and fight is, beside forfeiting
Our own brains and the opinion that we bring   20
To make that only true we now intend,
Will leave us never an understanding friend.
Therefore, for goodness' sake, and as you are known
The first and happiest hearers of the town,
Be sad, as we would make ye. Think ye see   25
The very persons of our noble story
As they were living; think you see them great,
And followed with the general throng and sweat
Of thousand friends; then, in a moment, see
How soon this mightiness meets misery;   30
And if you can be merry then, I'll say
A man may weep upon his wedding day.   [*Exit.*]

19 **fool and fight** Cf. Fletcher, *WPl* 5.1.156–7: 'To what end do I walk? for men to wonder at, / And fight, and foole?'
19–20 **forfeiting . . . brains** abandoning our claim to be intelligent
20–1 **opinion . . . intend** the reputation we have for making our planned performances truthful
22 **understanding** comprehending; standing under the stage, i.e. in the yard (a common joking reference to the 'groundlings'); presumably, the implication is that anyone in the audience who has been led to expect mere slapstick will be disappointed.
24 **first . . . hearers** a complimentary reference to the Globe (or Blackfriars) audience which reflects the dominant position of the King's Men in the London theatrical scene
25 **sad** serious
25–7 **Think . . . living** Cf. *H5* Prologue. 19–31. This could be either a simple exhortation to suspend disbelief or,

more likely, a hint that the representations on the stage have contemporary political resonance.
27–30 **think . . . misery** The audience is hereby notified to expect the kind of cyclical, episodic history reminiscent, for example, of the *H6* plays rather than of the second tetralogy.
29 **thousand** acceptable early modern usage without the article; cf. 4.2.89.
31 **And if** perhaps equals 'an if' (i.e. *if*); cf. 5.1.11.
31–2 **I'll . . . day** The hint of topicality at 25–7 is echoed here in a complexity of emotions familiar enough to an audience recently involved almost simultaneously in Prince Henry's funeral and Princess Elizabeth's wedding. The expression appears in Beaumont & Fletcher, *Maid's* 1.1.134–6: 'frowne not, I am for'st / In answere of such noble teares as those, / To weepe upon my wedding day'. It is also reminiscent, emotionally, if not verbally, of Claudius's remarks in *Ham*, 1.2.11-14.

19 beside] besides *Pope²*   21] *Rowe³;* To . . . true, . . . intend, *F;* That make . . . true, . . . intend, *Rowe;* Or make, – that only truth we now intend, – *Hudson² (Johnson);* (To . . true . . . intend,) *Malone*   32 SD] *Oxf; not in F*

1.1   *Enter the* Duke of NORFOLK *at one door. At the other,*
the Duke of BUCKINGHAM *and the* Lord ABERGAVENNY.

BUCKINGHAM
     Good morrow and well met. How have ye done
     Since last we saw in France?
NORFOLK   I thank your grace,
     Healthful, and ever since a fresh admirer
     Of what I saw there.
BUCKINGHAM   An untimely ague
     Stayed me a prisoner in my chamber when   5
     Those suns of glory, those two lights of men,
     Met in the vale of Andres.
NORFOLK   'Twixt Guînes and Ardres

1.1 Generally held to be a Shakespeare
scene (see Appendix 3), though Fleay,
Chronicle (251) believed it to be by
Massinger. The scene works closely
from Holinshed, though cutting his
lengthy description of the jousts at the
Field of the Cloth of Gold, and setting
up the hatred between Wolsey and
Buckingham broached a little later in
the *Chronicles*. The location is a room
at court.

2 **saw** i.e. each other; F3 treats *we* as the
aristocrat's (or pretender's) plural, and
adds 'y' (=ye) after *saw*.

3 **admirer** In the context that is gradually revealed to us, it is clear that this
word is by no means necessarily positive; cf. Goneril's contempt in *KL*:
'This admiration, sir, is much o'the
savour / Of other your new pranks'
(1.4.228–9). Norfolk is given a fairly
wry, arrogant, overtly aristocratic tone
throughout (see 3.2.1–3n.).

4 **saw** Norfolk picks up on Buckingham's verb from 2 and repeats it to
emphasize his own role as eyewitness.
untimely ague badly timed bout of
flu. The historical Buckingham did in

fact attend the Field of the Cloth of
Gold, but here Buckingham's absence
both prompts Norfolk's narrative and
suggests the Duke's disaffection (see
also 12–13). Several Jacobean aristocrats, including Fletcher's patron, the
fifth Earl of Huntingdon, found excus-
es to avoid attending royal ceremonies
they considered extravagant and tasteless (see McMullan, *Unease*, 22).

5 **Stayed me** forced me to stay
6 Henry VIII of England and François I
of France met at the Field of the Cloth
of Gold on 7 June 1520 in an expensive
and largely pointless display of
grandeur (see Holinshed, 853–61).
Knecht provides a concise description
of the occasion. Holinshed claims that
Wolsey was responsible for promoting
the meeting for his own ends.

7 **Andres . . . Ardres** I have modernized
the spelling of these northern French
place names: in Holinshed, they are
spelt 'Andren', 'Guisnes' and 'Ard'
(858). The Field of the Cloth of Gold,
still so called (*Le Camp du Drap d'Or*),
lies south of the village of Andres in
flat, damp, open ground between the

1.1] *(Actus Primus. Scœna Prima.)*   **2** saw in] saw y'in *F3*   **6** suns] *(Sunnes);* Sons *F3*   **7** Andres.
. . . Guînes . . . Ardres] *this edn;* Andren. . . . Guynes . . . Arde *F;* Arde . . . Guynes . . . Arde *F2;*
Ardres. . . . Guynes . . . Ardres *Rowe*

I was then present, saw them salute on horseback,
Beheld them when they lighted, how they clung
In their embracement as they grew together –   10
Which had they, what four throned ones could have
    weighed
Such a compounded one?
BUCKINGHAM   All the whole time
I was my chamber's prisoner.
NORFOLK   Then you lost

towns of Guines (where Henry initially camped, on soil he had acquired for
England at the beginning of his reign)
and Ardres (where François was based,
in French territory), an area a few
miles inland from the Channel port of
Calais. Following F2 (which gives
'Arde' for both of F's 'Andren' and
'Ard', editors have regularly failed to
distinguish correctly between Andres
and Ardres, presuming that the play
simply repeats Holinshed's supposed
error in spelling one place name in two
slightly different ways.
8–12 **I . . . one** Norfolk's apparently rap-
turous description, the implications of
which are rapidly soured by events,
injects pace and poetry into
Holinshed's account of the meeting:
'The two kings meeting in the field,
either saluted other in most loving
wise, first on horssebacke, and after
alighting on foote eftsoones embraced
with courteous words, to the great
rejoising of the beholders' (858).
9 **lighted** alternative form of 'alighted',
echoing *lights of men* (6); Staunton's
''lighted' (indicating elision) is unnecessary.
9–12 **clung . . . one** hermaphroditic
image for the 'compounding' of the
two kings. The excess of the image is
probably ironic, though there is an
apparently serious portrait of
'François I en travesti' (*c.* 1545) in the
Bibliothèque Nationale, Paris. And cf.

TNK 5.3.84–6: 'Were they metamor-
phosed / Both into one! – Oh, why?
There were no woman / Worth so
composed a man.' According to Lois
Potter, 'in a French version of the
Teseida, by Anne de Graville, written
about 1521, Boccaccio's descriptions of
Palamon and Arcite were adapted to
correspond to those of François I of
France and Henry VIII of England at
the time of their meeting at the Field
of the Cloth of Gold. Since this translation was not published until much
later, it is unlikely that the dramatists
knew it, but there are moments in
TNK reminiscent of their descriptions
of that event at the beginning of *H8*'
(LP).
10 **embracement** embrace
as as if
11–12 **four . . . one** a slightly convoluted
way of saying that the conflated
English and French kings would more
than equal (in honour, nobility, etc.)
four separate kings
12–13 **All . . . prisoner**. See 4n.;
Buckingham was in fact present,
Norfolk absent.
13–18 **Then . . . its**. Cf. *WT* 5.2.39–44:
'THIRD GENTLEMAN . . . Did you see
the meeting of the two kings? / SEC-
OND GENTLEMAN No. / THIRD
GENTLEMAN Then have you lost a
sight which was to be seen, cannot be
spoken of. There might you have
beheld one joy crown another.'

9 lighted] 'lighted *Staunton*   11] *Rowe³; F lines* they, / weigh'd /

213

The view of earthly glory. Men might say
Till this time pomp was single, but now married   15
To one above itself. Each following day
Became the next day's master, till the last
Made former wonders its. Today the French,
All clinquant, all in gold like heathen gods,
Shone down the English; and tomorrow they   20
Made Britain India. Every man that stood
Showed like a mine. Their dwarfish pages were
As cherubims, all gilt. The madams too,

14–16 **Men . . . itself.** a complex idea, by which each of the two kings, apparently unique in his individual grandeur, is made yet grander by their mutual *embracement*, thereby extending the image of the hermaphrodite (and the possible irony it brings with it) from 9–12

16–17 **Each . . . master** 'Every day learnt something from the preceding' (Johnson); *master* means 'schoolmaster' here. Capell, prompted by Theobald, inverted *next* and *last*, though the sense is much the same.

17–18 **till . . . its** until the last day subsumed the wonder caused by its predecessors (RP)

18 **its** This is *OED*'s first citation for 'its' as absolute possessive, i.e. 'used when no substantive follows' (*poss. pron.* B); *OED* also notes that 'its' 'does not appear in any of the works of Shakespere [*sic*] published during his lifetime, . . . but there are 9 examples of it's, and 1 of its, in the plays first printed in the Folio of 1623'.

19 **clinquant** glittering; originally a technical term for a thin plate lace of gold or silver (see Linthicum, 134)
heathen gods presumably with a negative implication

21 **Britain** As Kermode notes, *Britain* for 'England' is a usage only relatively recently validated in political terms by

the accession of James (VI of Scotland and I of England), and may therefore have had a more striking effect on the play's first audiences than it has on us (Kermode, 8).
India India was thought of as a source of untold wealth; cf. 4.1.45n.

22 **mine** natural Jacobean word-association after *India*; cf. *1H4* 3.1.164–5.

23 *****cherubims** angelic beings. The earliest English form of the word was 'cherubin', not 'cherub'; F's plural form, 'cherubins', is the typical Jacobean form (cf. *MV* 5.1.62; *Cym* 2.4.88) but was obsolete by the close of the seventeenth century (*OED Pl.* δ). I have therefore modernized to 'cherubims', following Steevens, despite *OED*'s assertion that this is, at best, a 'vulgar' plural form, the Hebrew plural being 'cherubim'. According to Shaheen, 'the word first appears at Genesis 3.24' [spelled, as it happens, 'Cherubims' in the Geneva Bible] and is associated with golden ornamentation (Shaheen, 196–7).
madams so F; Oxf corrects to 'mesdames', though curiously does not do so at *H5* 3.5.28, where the word is spoken by a Frenchman. If a mispronunciation is implied here, then, combined with *sweat* at 24, it arguably serves to undermine the grandeur of the scene.

23–6 **The . . . painting.** The women of

17 next . . . last] last . . . next *Capell (Theobald)* 23 cherubims] *Steevens;* Cherubins *F* madams] *mesdames Oxf*

Not used to toil, did almost sweat to bear
The pride upon them, that their very labour   25
Was to them as a painting. Now this masque
Was cried incomparable; and th'ensuing night
Made it a fool and beggar. The two kings,
Equal in lustre, were now best, now worst,
As presence did present them: him in eye,   30
Still him in praise, and being present both,
'Twas said they saw but one, and no discerner
Durst wag his tongue in censure. When these suns –
For so they phrase 'em – by their heralds challenged
The noble spirits to arms, they did perform   35
Beyond thought's compass – that former fabulous
   story
Being now seen possible enough, got credit

the court, unaccustomed to any kind of work, were on the verge of breaking into a sweat at the effort involved in wearing their costumes, which made them flush so that they looked heavily made-up.

26–8 Now . . . beggar. There is a possible, and not very positive, reference here to the masques performed on successive evenings (including one by Fletcher's erstwhile writing partner, Francis Beaumont) for the wedding of Princess Elizabeth and the Elector Palatine (see pp. 64, 69–70). Masques were proverbially ephemeral.

27 cried proclaimed

28 Made . . . beggar made it seem a cheap imposture

30–2 him . . . one Whichever king you were looking at seemed the grander; when you saw them simultaneously, they seemed identical in grandeur.

32–3 'Twas . . . censure one of a number of acknowledgements of surveillance. Those present *could* distinguish between the kings, but they would not

be advised to question the propaganda.

32 discerner Pooler (Ard[1]) and Foakes (Ard[2]) both suggest simply 'observer', but an ability specifically to distinguish is also implied.

33–6 When . . . compass Holinshed provides a long blow-by-blow description of the tournament, concluding (unsurprisingly) that 'the two kings surmounted all the rest in prowesse and valiantnesse' (859).

33 suns Cf. 6; a standard early modern metaphor for royal power; James I was often referred to as Phoebus or the Sun in court masques, e.g. Jonson, *Oberon*, 353.

34 phrase call, name

36 compass reach, range
former fabulous story old tales thought incredible until now

36–8 that . . . believed The kings' (staged) martial prowess was so great that the far-fetched old legend of Bevis seemed credible.

37 credit i.e. such credit

33 censure. When] *Rowe;* censure, when *F*

That Bevis was believed.

BUCKINGHAM   O, you go far.

NORFOLK

As I belong to worship and affect
In honour honesty, the tract of everything   40
Would by a good discourser lose some life
Which action's self was tongue to. All was royal;
To the disposing of it nought rebelled;
Order gave each thing view; the office did
Distinctly his full function.

BUCKINGHAM   Who did guide –   45
I mean, who set the body and the limbs
Of this great sport together, as you guess?

NORFOLK

One, certes, that promises no element

38 **Bevis** Bevis of Hampton (i.e. Southampton) was a legendary warrior whose prowess had recently been revived in Drayton's *Poly-Olbion* (1613; First Part 1612), 2.259–384.
O . . . **far**. You are going a bit too far, getting carried away.
39–42 **As** . . . **to**. a difficult passage, partly because it is hard to gauge the tone. 'As I am a nobleman and try to be truthful because that is the appropriately noble thing to do.' No matter how well told, any account of what took place would fall short of capturing the event as it was experienced by those present at the time. Cf. *TNK* 5.3.12–15.
40 **tract** the continued duration of an action (*OED sb.*[3] 2)
41 **discourser** raconteur
43 'There were no hitches in its execution' (RP); perhaps also hinting at a practical definition of a 'royal event' as one which ensures no criticism.
disposing of it way it was arranged
44 **Order** . . . **view** Everything was received in relation to its status; or the

sightlines were unimpeded (RP).
44–5 **office** . . . **function** All involved performed exactly as they should.
45–51 **Who** . . . **York**. Holinshed reports that 'both the kings committed the order and manner of their meeting . . . vnto the cardinall of Yorke' (853).
45–6 **Who** . . . **set** Buckingham fumbles for a way to ask who ran the show while not overtly questioning the royal authority that the tournament was designed to reinforce.
48–9 **One** . . . **business**. 'someone whose involvement in such activities looks inappropriate' (both because it contradicts the strict hierarchical order of the show and because a clergyman should not be involved in a military tournament)
48 **certes** certainly, surely; monosyllabic here (cf. *Oth* 1.1.15), though generally two syllables in Shakespeare
element the appropriate sphere of operation of any agency (*OED sb.* II 12); Norfolk is being ironic in his choice of word; cf. *TN* 3.1.58, 3.4.122; *Oth* 2.3.54.

40 everything] *(eu'ry thing)* 41 lose] *(loose)* 42 All] *Theobald; Buc.* All *F* 45 SP] *Theobald; not in F* 47 as you guess?] *F4; Nor.* As you guesse: *F* 48 SP] *Theobald; not in F* One] Once *F2*

In such a business.

BUCKINGHAM   I pray you who, my lord?

NORFOLK

All this was ordered by the good discretion   50
Of the right reverend Cardinal of York.

BUCKINGHAM

The devil speed him! No man's pie is freed
From his ambitious finger. What had he
To do in these fierce vanities? I wonder
That such a keech can with his very bulk   55
Take up the rays o'th' beneficial sun
And keep it from the earth.

NORFOLK   Surely, sir,
There's in him stuff that puts him to these ends;
For being not propped by ancestry, whose grace
Chalks successors their way, nor called upon   60

50–1 **good . . . reverend** ironic respect

52–7 **The . . . earth**. Buckingham's rage at hearing Wolsey's name stems from the antipathy between the two established by Holinshed, whose marginal note at this point is 'Great hatred betweene the cardinall, and the duke of Buckingham', and who reports that the Duke 'sticked not to saie, that it was an intollerable matter to obeie such a vile and importunate person' (855).

52–3 **No . . . finger**. proverbial: 'to have a finger in the pie' (Dent, F228)

54 **fierce vanities** warlike extravagances, i.e. the tournament

54–5 **I wonder / That** it is shocking how

55 **keech** a lump of congealed fat (*OED sb.* 1). This offensive description neatly encompasses both Wolsey's corpulence and his origins as the son of a butcher.

56–7 **Take . . . earth** On corruption in the sun, cf. *Ham* 2.2.182ff.; *MM* 2.2.170–3 (RP).

59–66 ***For . . . King** a difficult passage. Wolsey has neither the aristocratic background which, for Norfolk, would give him the right to power nor a history of major achievement nor close connections with people in high places; instead, he creates his own environment for power, and his sheer willpower and self-belief is such that his progress seems divinely ordained. Norfolk's haughtiness is clearly becoming emotional here, but F's punctuation fragments the sentence unhelpfully. Foakes's 'web, O, gives us note' (Ard²) improves F minimally and conforms to the rule of editorial conservatism, but Kellner's suggestion (based on Capell's 'he') adopted here ("a' for 'he' is Shakespearean usage elsewhere) is almost as restrained, and makes more sense of a complex passage.

59 **grace** prestige, renown

60 **successors** stress on first syllable; cf. *WT* 5.1.48; *TNK* 1.1.209, 5.3.69.

55 keech] Ketch *F4*

For high feats done to th' crown, neither allied
To eminent assistants, but spider-like,
Out of his self-drawing web, 'a gives us note
The force of his own merit makes his way
A gift that heaven gives for him, which buys   65
A place next to the King.

ABERGAVENNY   I cannot tell
What heaven hath given him – let some graver eye
Pierce into that – but I can see his pride
Peep through each part of him. Whence has he that?
If not from hell, the devil is a niggard   70
Or has given all before, and he begins
A new hell in himself.

BUCKINGHAM   Why the devil,
Upon this French going-out, took he upon him,
Without the privity o'th' King, t'appoint
Who should attend on him? He makes up the file   75

---

62 **assistants** those who aid in the execution of a purpose (*OED* B *sb.* 2);
seems to refer here and at *Ham*
2.2.167 to influence at a high level of
government
65 **gives . . . buys** Various editors have
come up with emendations which
make a more pleasing sentence without
altering the sense (see 65 t.n.).
66 **next to the King** i.e. next highest
status after the King
68 **pride** Lucifer's sin; cf. 3.2.371.
70 **niggard** a mean, stingy or parsimo-
nious person; a miser (*OED* A *sb.* 1)
71 **he** i.e. Wolsey
73 **going-out** journey
74 **privity** confidence; participation in

the knowledge of something private or
secret, usually implying concurrence
or consent (*OED* 5)
75–80 **He . . . papers**. 'He makes
arrangements such that any honour
conferred on an individual brings with
it a disproportionately high charge;
and, flouting the authority of the
Privy Council (*out* being an abbrevia-
tion for 'without', i.e. 'without asking
the Privy Council'), he issues sum-
monses on his own authority for
whomever he names'. Another problematic passage, textually speaking:
Capell's rearrangement of punctuation arguably makes the best sense. As
Malone suggested, the passage is

---

63 his self-drawing] his self-drawn *Rowe²;* himself drawing *(Theobald);* his self drawing *Staunton*
web, 'a gives us note] *Kittredge (Kellner) (*web, he gives us note, *Capell);* Web. O giues vs note, *F;* web;
this gives us note, *Pope;* web. O! it gives us note *Singer²;* web, – O! give us note! – *Knight;* web, – Oh,
give it note! – *Keightley;* web, O, gives us note, *Ard²;* web, O, gives us note *(Bowers)*
65 gives . . . buys] gives, which for him buys *Hanmer;* gives; which buys for him *Warburton;* gives to him,
which buys *Rann (Johnson);* gives him, and which buys *(Collier MS);* gives; for him which buys *(Jervis)*
69–70 that? . . . hell, the] *Theobald;* that, . . . Hell? The *F*   73 going-out] *Rann;* going out *F*

Of all the gentry, for the most part such
To whom as great a charge, as little honour
He meant to lay upon; and his own letter –
The honourable board of Council out –
Must fetch him in he papers.

ABERGAVENNY   I do know   80
Kinsmen of mine – three at the least – that have
By this so sickened their estates that never
They shall abound as formerly.

BUCKINGHAM   O, many
Have broke their backs with laying manors on 'em
For this great journey. What did this vanity   85
But minister communication of

drawn from Holinshed, 855: 'The peers . . . seemed to grudge, that such a costlie iournie should be taken in hand to their importunate charges and expenses, without consent of the whole boord of the councell.'

79 **Council** i.e. Privy Council, a body of advisers selected by the King, with *ex officio* members including the principal aristocrats, archbishops, and chief officers of state (*OED* 2)

80 **papers** sets down on paper (*OED v.* 1 *trans.*). Staunton's 'paupers' is ingenious but unnecessary; Campbell's 'the' for *he* is an understandable misreading of heavily condensed syntax.

82 **sickened** damaged, made ill; *OED*'s earliest recorded transitive use of 'sicken' (*v.* 5b)

83 **abound** be financially healthy

83–5 **O . . . journey.** conflation of two proverbial sayings: 'to break one's back' (Dent, B16; cf. *Tim* 2.1.24) and 'to wear a whole lordship on one's back' (Dent, L452 and W61); cf. 2.3.42–4, *2H6* 1.3.83, *KJ* 2.1.70. See

also Camden, in a passage attacking Wolsey's origins: 'a Nobleman . . . having lately sold a Mannor . . . came ruffling [*sic*] into the Court, in a new sute, saying: *Am not I a mightie man, that beare an hundred houses on my backe?* Which Cardinall *Wolsey* hearing, said: *You might have better employed it in paying your debts. Indeede my Lord (quoth he) you say well; for my Lord my father, owde my maister your father three half-pence for a Calf's head, hold, here is two pence for it'* (2F3ʳ) (see 120n.).

85 **this vanity** this pointless, self-aggrandizing event

86–7 **minister . . . issue** 'enable a deal of discussion to such little purpose'. The passage echoes Holinshed: 'he knew not for what cause so much monie should be spent about the sight of a vaine talke to be had, and communication to be ministred of things of no importance' (855). As Foakes points out (Ard²), 'issue' has procreative undertones, extending

76–7 such / To whom] such / On whom *Hanmer;* such / Too, whom *Capell;* such, too, / On whom *Keightley (Staunton)*   78–80 letter – / . . . Council out – / . . . him in he papers] *Pope;* Letter / . . . Councell, out / . . . him in, he Papers *F*   80 he papers] the papers *Campbell;* he paupers *(Staunton)*

A most poor issue?

NORFOLK   Grievingly, I think
The peace between the French and us not values
The cost that did conclude it.

BUCKINGHAM   Every man,
After the hideous storm that followed, was   90
A thing inspired and, not consulting, broke
Into a general prophecy, that this tempest,
Dashing the garment of this peace, aboded
The sudden breach on't.

NORFOLK   Which is budded out,
For France hath flawed the league, and hath attached   95
Our merchants' goods at Bordeaux.

ABERGAVENNY   Is it therefore
Th'ambassador is silenced?

NORFOLK   Marry, is't.

the preceding sentence about the sale of manors: the implication is that aristocratic children (possibly illegitimate children) are now born into impoverished families.

87 **Grievingly** sadly; first recorded adverbial usage in *OED*

88 **not values** is not worth (Ard[1])

89 **cost** Masques were known to be outrageously expensive: Fletcher, writing to his patron, the Countess of Huntington, claims not to be interested in 'whoe shall daunce i'th *maske*; nor whoe shall write / those braue things done: nor summe up the Expence; / nor whether ytt bee paid for ten yeere hence' (McMullan, *Unease*, 18).

90 **hideous storm** In the immediate wake of the meeting, there was 'an hideous storme of wind and weather, that manie coniectured it did prognosticate trouble and hatred shortlie after to follow betweene princes' (Holinshed, 861).

91–2 **inspired . . . prophecy** Holins-

hed's description of the weather here becomes a dark passage invoking a kind of inverse Pentecost, in which inspiration is equated with chaos; cf. Acts, 2.1–18 and 19.6; also 1.2.146–50n.

not . . . prophecy Without discussion, they all reached the same conclusion.

93 **aboded** presaged (*OED v.* 1)

94 **on't** of it
budded out turned out as expected; echoing *aboded* (93)

95 **flawed** broken
attached lawfully seized; from Holinshed: 'the French king commanded all Englishmens goods being in Burdeaux, to be attached, and put under arrest' (872)

97 **silenced** '[T]he [French] Ambassador was com[m]au[n]ded to kepe his house in silence, and not to come in presence, till he was sent for' (Hall, 3Q4[r]; fol. lxxxxiii).

87 issue?] *Pope;* issue. F   96 Bordeaux] *(Burdeux)*

ABERGAVENNY
A proper title of a peace, and purchased
At a superfluous rate.
BUCKINGHAM   Why, all this business
Our reverend Cardinal carried.
NORFOLK   Like it your grace,   100
The state takes notice of the private difference
Betwixt you and the Cardinal. I advise you –
And take it from a heart that wishes towards you
Honour and plenteous safety – that you read
The Cardinal's malice and his potency   105
Together; to consider further that
What his high hatred would effect wants not
A minister in his power. You know his nature,
That he's revengeful, and I know his sword
Hath a sharp edge: it's long, and't may be said   110
It reaches far, and where 'twill not extend,
Thither he darts it. Bosom up my counsel;
You'll find it wholesome. Lo, where comes that rock
That I advise your shunning.

98 **A . . . peace** ironic (underlined by allit-
eration): 'a fine thing to call a peace'
(Wright). A *proper title* is a 'true name',
but also relates to legal 'entitlement'
and thus to the notion of 'purchase'.

99 **a superfluous rate** too high a price
all this business Buckingham's
implication is that Wolsey was responsible not only for the Field of the
Cloth of Gold, but also for its failure,
and in suggesting this he provokes
Norfolk's warning (which turns out
already to be too late).

100 **Like . . . grace** an apology before
giving unsought advice (Ard[1]); on
modes of politeness, see Magnusson

101 **state** the government, ruling body,
grand council, or court (*OED sb.* III 26
collect. sing.); thus, the Privy Council;
or, perhaps, by implication, the King
private difference personal quarrel

104 **read** consider

106–8 **to . . . power** repeats 104–6;
Wolsey has the power practically to
demonstrate how much he detests you.

110–11 **long . . . far** Norfolk (with
implicit irony at the scale of Wolsey's
ambitions) echoes the proverbial saying 'kings have long arms' (Dent,
K87), and cf. Erasmus, 1.2.2 and 3:
'*multae regum aures atque oculi*' ('many
are the ears and eyes of kings') and
'*longae regum manus*' ('kings have long
hands'); cf. *2H6* 4.7.79, *R2* 4.1.10–12,
Per Sc. 2.8).

112 **Bosom up** take to heart, keep it
secret; first *OED* citation (*v.* 5 *fig.*) is
Isle of Gulls (1606): 'Ile bosome what I
thinke' (B4[v]).

113 **wholesome** valuable
where . . . rock Norfolk's comic
(though also arguably classical) image
of a moving rock foregrounds the awkwardness of tone of this encounter.

Enter Cardinal WOLSEY, *the purse borne before him, certain of the
Guard and two* Secretaries *with papers. The Cardinal, in his
passage, fixeth his eye on Buckingham, and Buckingham on him,
both full of disdain.*

WOLSEY

   The Duke of Buckingham's surveyor, ha?   115
   Where's his examination?

SECRETARY   Here, so please you.

WOLSEY

   Is he in person ready?

SECRETARY   Ay, please your grace.

WOLSEY

   Well, we shall then know more, and Buckingham
   Shall lessen this big look.   *Exeunt Cardinal and his train.*

BUCKINGHAM

   This butcher's cur is venom-mouthed, and I   120
   Have not the power to muzzle him: therefore best
   Not wake him in his slumber. A beggar's book

114.1–4 This is the first of F's substantial
   SDs, providing far more staging detail
   than is usual for plays in the
   Shakespeare canon.
114.1 *purse* a bag containing the great
   seal; see 3.2.229n.; see also 2.4.0.5–6,
   4.1.36.4.
115 **surveyor** an important subordinate to
   the steward of a large estate; the steward was sometimes himself a surveyor,
   a necessary professional skill at a time
   when estates were 'not definitively sur-
   veyed, discrete blocks of land', but
   were rather 'hopelessly intertwined,
   their boundaries still reliant more on
   the memories of "ancient men" than on
   surveyors' instruments' (Hainsworth,
   109).
116 **examination** deposition

119 **big** arrogant, haughty
120 **butcher's cur** butcher's dog, a
   proverbially vicious animal (Dent,
   B764.1); cf. Field, *Caveat*: 'You faune
   vpon her [i.e. Elizabeth] like gentle
   Spaniels, and yet most cruelly you bite
   her, . . . like butchers curres' (A5[r]); and
   R3 1.3.287–92. On Buckingham's class
   antagonism here, see List of Roles, 5n.
120–2 **cur . . . slumber** proverbial (Dent,
   W7: 'It is evil waking of a sleeping
   dog'); cf. *2H4* 1.2.154–5.
122–3 **A . . . blood.** 'A poor man's learning is more highly thought of than an
   aristocrat's breeding.' Foakes (Ard[2])
   suggests a possible pun on *book* and
   'bouk' (or 'bulk'), echoing the physi-
   cality of *keech* (55).

115+ SP] *Rowe (Wol.); Car.* F   119 this] his *F3*   120 venom-mouthed] *Pope;* venom'd-mouth'd
F; venom mouth'd *Rowe*   122 book] brood *Collier[2];* look *(Staunton)*

Outworths a noble's blood.

NORFOLK   What, are you chafed?

Ask God for temperance: that's th'appliance only

Which your disease requires.

BUCKINGHAM   I read in's looks   125

Matter against me, and his eye reviled

Me as his abject object. At this instant

He bores me with some trick. He's gone to th' King:

I'll follow and out-stare him.

NORFOLK   Stay, my lord,

And let your reason with your choler question   130

What 'tis you go about. To climb steep hills

Requires slow pace at first. Anger is like

A full hot horse, who being allowed his way

Self-mettle tires him. Not a man in England

Can advise me like you: be to yourself   135

As you would to your friend.

BUCKINGHAM   I'll to the King,

---

123 **chafed** hot, i.e. angry; cf. 3.2.206 and *Cor* 3.3.27.

124–5 **Ask . . . requires**. a conflation of proverbial sayings: 'God is a plaster for all sores' (Dent, P107) and 'God has provided a remedy for every disease' (Dent G189)

124 **temperance** two syllables (see t.n.); a key word in the construction of Renaissance masculinity (see pp. 81–93)

appliance only only treatment

126 **reviled** subjected to abuse (*OED v.* 2 *fig*)

127 **abject object** contemptible figure. *Abject* means 'despicable' or 'degraded' (*OED adj.* A 3), implying that the lower-class Wolsey is treating the aristocratic Buckingham as his social inferior. ' "Object" ', as Foakes observes (Ard²), 'is what is seen by the eyes and the emotion attached', and he compares *MND* 4.1.169–70: 'The object and the pleasure of mine eye / Is only Helena'; cf. also *TNK* 2.1.54–5.

128 **bores** cheats; cf. proverbial expression 'to bore one's nose' (Dent, N229), meaning to gull or cuckold someone; cf. Fletcher, *WP* 4.1.48: 'But when I have done all this, and think it duty, / Is't requisit an other bore my nostrils?'

130 **choler** supposedly a black liquid (bile, gall) secreted by the gall-bladder, which was the cause of, and came to mean, short temper or anger (*OED sb.* 2)

130–1 **let . . . about** moderate your anger by considering calmly what you intend (RP)

133–4 **horse . . . him** a proverbial expression (Dent, H642) equivalent to 'more haste less speed'; cf. *LLL* 2.1.119.

134 **Self-mettle** his own exertions

---

123 chafed] (chaff'd) 124 temperance] (Tempr'ance) 133 full hot] full-hot *F3*

And from a mouth of honour quite cry down
This Ipswich fellow's insolence, or proclaim
There's difference in no persons.

NORFOLK   Be advised:
Heat not a furnace for your foe so hot   140
That it do singe yourself. We may outrun
By violent swiftness that which we run at,
And lose by over-running. Know you not
The fire that mounts the liquor till't run o'er,
In seeming to augment it, wastes it? Be advised: 145
I say again there is no English soul
More stronger to direct you than yourself,
If with the sap of reason you would quench
Or but allay the fire of passion.

BUCKINGHAM   Sir,
I am thankful to you, and I'll go along   150
By your prescription; but this top-proud fellow –
Whom from the flow of gall I name not, but
From sincere motions – by intelligence

137–8 **mouth . . . insolence** Buckingham again emphasizes the class divide between himself and Wolsey. Ipswich, a provincial, politically unimportant town, was Wolsey's birthplace.

139 **difference** class distinction; cf. *KL* 1.4.88.

140–1 **Heat . . . yourself** proverbial expression (Dent, F251) presumably derived from the well-known OT story of King Nebuchadnezzar and the fiery furnace: 'Then was Nebuchadnezzar ful of rage . . . *therefore* he charged and commanded that they shulde heate the fornace at once seuen times more then it was wonte to be heat. . . . Therefore, because the Kings commandement was straite, that the fornace shulde be exceading hote, the flame of ye fyre slew those men y^t broght forthe Shadrach, Meshach, and Abednego' (Daniel, 3.19, 21).

144 **mounts . . . o'er** causes the liquid to boil over

147 **More stronger** acceptable early modern double comparative

149 **allay** restrain; but, as Foakes observes (Ard²), Shakespeare conflates *allay* and 'alloy' (to temper or mix); cf. *Tem* 1.2.393; *Cor* 5.3.85.

151 **top-proud** proud to the highest degree (*OED* top *sb.*¹ 34 *a.*); perhaps also, with emphasis on 'top', and by analogy with 'top-heavy' or 'top-gallant', possibly a reference to the Cardinal's hat (RP); cf. Suffolk's equation of *ambition* and *holy hat* at 3.2.324–5.

152–3 **Whom . . . motions** I have genuine motives for accusing him, not just rage. On the role of *gall* in inducing anger, see 130n. *Motions* conflates 'motives' (cf. *Cor* 2.1.50) and 'emotions' (cf. *Oth* 1.3.331).

153 **intelligence** secret reports; the Jacobean word for 'spy' was 'intelligencer'; cf. Beaumont & Fletcher, *WH* 1.3.169–79.

And proofs as clear as founts in July when
We see each grain of gravel, I do know   155
To be corrupt and treasonous.

NORFOLK   Say not 'treasonous'.

BUCKINGHAM

To th' King I'll say't, and make my vouch as strong
As shore of rock. Attend. This holy fox,
Or wolf, or both – for he is equal ravenous
As he is subtle, and as prone to mischief   160
As able to perform't – his mind and place
Infecting one another – yea, reciprocally –
Only to show his pomp as well in France
As here at home, suggests the King our master
To this last costly treaty, th'interview   165
That swallowed so much treasure and like a glass

157 **vouch** claim, allegation; cf. *MM*
2.4.156.
158 **shore of rock** Buckingham appropriates Norfolk's description of
Wolsey as a *rock* at 113.
Attend. listen (*OED v.* I 1); rather
peremptory, possibly because Norfolk
is disinclined to listen once he has
heard the word 'treason'
158–60 **fox . . . subtle** conflation of
proverbial sayings (Dent, F629: 'as
subtle as a fox', and W601.2: 'as ravenous as a wolf'), stemming in part from
biblical sources, e.g. Matthew, 7.15:
'Beware of false prophetes, which
come to you in shepes clothing, but
inwardely they are rauening wolues.'
For sectarian connotations, see
Spenser, *Shepherd's Calendar*, 'May'
Eclogue, especially 'E.K.'s' notes: 'By
the Foxe [is understood] the false and
faithlesse Papistes.' The implication is
that Wolsey will put Roman
Catholicism and the Pope's wishes
(and his own alleged Papal ambitions)
ahead of England and England's King.

159 **equal** equally
ravenous two syllables
161–2 **his . . . reciprocally** 'His desires and
his authority to put his desires into practice are mutually sustaining.' His *place* is
of course 'next to the King' (66). Capell
originated the emendation which moves
the closing parenthesis from after *perform't* to after *reciprocally*; but F's placing keeps the parenthetical lines as a
gloss on the fox/wolf metaphor.
164 **suggests** prompts, encourages, in a
negative sense; cf. *R2* 3.4.76, where, as
Foakes notes (Ard²), 'the word is used
of the devil's temptations'.
165, 180 **interview** meeting, but implying
the equality of the gaze of both kings.
The word is drawn (in a negative context) from Holinshed's description of
the build-up to the meeting: the
Emperor Charles V, meeting Henry
prior to the Field of the Cloth of Gold,
hoped to 'persuade . . . the king [that
he] should not meet with the French
king at anie interuiew' (856).

159 ravenous] *(*rau'nous*)*   161–2 perform't – . . . reciprocally –] perform't, . . . reciprocally) *Capell*

Did break i'th' rinsing.

NORFOLK   Faith, and so it did.

BUCKINGHAM

Pray give me favour, sir. This cunning Cardinal
The articles o'th' combination drew
As himself pleased; and they were ratified   170
As he cried, 'Thus let be', to as much end
As give a crutch to th' dead. But our Count–Cardinal
Has done this, and 'tis well: for worthy Wolsey,
Who cannot err, he did it. Now this follows –
Which, as I take it, is a kind of puppy   175
To th'old dam treason – Charles the Emperor,

---

167 **rinsing** F has 'wrenching'; *OED*
notes earlier forms of modern English
'rinse' including 'rynsche', 'rench' and
'wrench' (*OED v.* β), which make it an
appropriate modernization for F,
though Foakes (Ard²) is right to note
that the original spelling incorporates a
sense of the 'distortion of meaning' at
the Field of the Cloth of Gold, as well
as its more prosaic signification. Cf.
TNK 1.1.156 ('Wrinching', Q).

168 **Pray . . . favour** Allow me to continue.

169–70 **The . . . pleased** 'arranged the
terms of the treaty to his own liking';
drew signifies 'drew up'; see Holinshed, 858.

170–2 **as . . . dead** as much use as a crutch
would be to a dead person

171 **Thus let be** a pompous pronouncement; cf. the Schoolmaster at *TNK*
3.5.9.

172 **Count–Cardinal** I retain the reading in F as implying Wolsey's assumed
role as head of state, possibly with a
hint of the influence of foreign politics
over England (a 'count' is an un-
English kind of aristocrat). Cf. 2.2.18
for a similar composite term: *King–
Cardinal*. Pope's emendation to
'court–cardinal' is entirely possible,
though it seems to me slightly to lack

the contemptuous force of F. Capell's
suggestion, as reported by Foakes
(Ard²), 'that Wolsey was "Count-
Palatine" by virtue of holding the
bishopric of Durham *in commendam*",
is a little too tortured to be of help in
confirming F's reading; and, though
the title of the relevant English rank
was 'earl' not 'count', the equivalent
female rank was 'countess' and the Old
Lady uses the term happily enough (if
with a deliberate genital implication)
at 2.3.41.

176 **dam** a female parent (of animals)
(*OED sb.*² 2)

176–83 **Charles . . . him** Buckingham's
speech here echoes Holinshed's assessment of the logic behind the
Emperor's stay at Canterbury at
Whitsuntide, 1520: 'The chiefe cause
that mooued the emperour to come
thus on land at this time, was to persuade that by word of mouth, which he
had before done most earnestlie by letters; which was, that the king should
not meet with the French king at anie
interuiew: for he doubted least if the
king of England & the French king
should grow into some great friendship and faithfull bond of amitie, it
might turne him to displeasure' (856).

167 rinsing] *(wrenching)*   172 Count–Cardinal] Court–Cardinal *Pope*

Under pretence to see the Queen his aunt –
For 'twas indeed his colour, but he came
To whisper Wolsey – here makes visitation.
His fears were that the interview betwixt   180
England and France might through their amity
Breed him some prejudice, for from this league
Peeped harms that menaced him. He privily
Deals with our Cardinal, and as I trow –
Which I do well, for I am sure the Emperor   185
Paid ere he promised, whereby his suit was granted
Ere it was asked – but when the way was made
And paved with gold, the Emperor thus desired
That he would please to alter the King's course
And break the foresaid peace. Let the King know,   190
As soon he shall by me, that thus the Cardinal
Does buy and sell his honour as he pleases,
And for his own advantage.

NORFOLK   I am sorry

---

178 **colour** pretence, excuse
179 **visitation** early modern usage,
though by 1613 slightly archaic, signifying a 'visit' in the modern sense, but
shading into the ecclesiastical sense of
a formal occasion, a ceremony or
inspection; cf. *LLL* 5.2.179–81; *WT*
1.1.6. The word is still used in the
Church of England to denote the formal visit of a bishop.
181 **England and France** i.e. the Kings
of England and France
182 **prejudice** injury, detriment or damage (*OED sb.* I 1a)
183–90 **He . . . peace.** Buckingham's
words echo Holinshed's assessment of
Charles's intentions: 'forsomuch as he
knew the lord cardinall to be woone
with rewards, as a fish with bait: he
bestowed on him great gifts. . . . The
cardinall not able to susteine the least

assault by force of such rewards as he
presentlie received . . . promised to the
emperour, that he would so use the
matter, as his purpose should be sped'
(856).
183 ***privily** secretly; F2's addition of *He*
makes the line metrically complete,
though is not strictly necessary for
sense.
184–7 **and . . . asked** Various options
have been offered for punctuating
these lines. The sense is the same in
each case; the question is the extent to
which Buckingham's rage has got the
better of his grammar.
184 **trow** believe
186 **ere** before
187 **but** only
192 **buy . . . honour** 'To buy and sell' was
proverbial for deception (Dent, B787);
cf. *KJ* 5.4.10; *R3* 5.6.35.

183 him. He privily] *F2;* him. Priuily *F*   184–7 trow – / Which . . . asked –] *Steevens² (subst.);* troa /
Which . . . well; . . . ask'd. *F;* trow, – / Which . . . well, . . . sure, – . . . / . . . asked: *Staunton*

To hear this of him, and could wish he were
Something mistaken in't.
BUCKINGHAM   No, not a syllable.   195
I do pronounce him in that very shape
He shall appear in proof.

Enter BRANDON, *a* Sergeant-at-Arms *before him,*
and two or three of the Guard.

BRANDON
Your office, sergeant: execute it.
SERGEANT   Sir,
My lord the Duke of Buckingham, and Earl
Of Hereford, Stafford and Northampton, I   200
Arrest thee of high treason in the name
Of our most sovereign King.
BUCKINGHAM   Lo you, my lord,
The net has fallen upon me: I shall perish
Under device and practice.
BRANDON   I am sorry
To see you ta'en from liberty, to look on   205
The business present. 'Tis his highness' pleasure
You shall to th' Tower.
BUCKINGHAM   It will help me nothing
To plead mine innocence, for that dye is on me

194–5 **he . . . in't** 'he were in some way
misjudged (by other people) over this
issue'; F4's emendation to 'you' misses
the passive construction.
195 **Something** in some way; cf. 4.1.116.
196–7 The way I describe him is exactly
how his actions will reveal him.
197 **in proof** when put to the test; a possible printing metaphor, as if Norfolk
has hoped the evidence against Wolsey
has been inaccurately printed
197.1 *Enter* BRANDON 'The duke her-
upon was sent for up to London, & at
his comming thither, was streightwaies
attached, and brought to the Tower by

sir Henrie Marneie, capteine of the
gard' (Holinshed, 863). There is no
clear reason for the change of name
here: Foakes (Ard[2]) suggests that
'Shakespeare may have been thinking
here of Charles Brandon, who appears
as Suffolk in 2.2; if so, this would make
sense perhaps of "my lords", 226 (F)'.
202 **Lo** look
    my lord addressed to Norfolk
204 **device and practice** trickery and
plotting
205 **look on** observe, witness
207 **Tower** i.e. of London
    nothing not even slightly

194 he were] you were *F4*; ye were *(TxC)*   200 Hereford] *Capell*; Hertford *F*   203 fallen] *(falne)*
208 dye] die *Boswell*

Which makes my whitest part black. The will of
    heaven
Be done in this and all things: I obey. 210
O my lord Abergavenny, fare you well.

BRANDON

Nay, he must bear you company. [*to Abergavenny*]
                The King
Is pleased you shall to th' Tower, till you know
How he determines further.

ABERGAVENNY   As the Duke said,
The will of heaven be done, and the King's pleasure 215
By me obeyed.

BRANDON   Here is a warrant from
The King t'attach Lord Montague and the bodies
Of the Duke's confessor, John de la Court,
One Gilbert Park, his chancellor –

BUCKINGHAM   So, so;

209 **whitest part black** inversion of the proverbial 'to make black white' (Dent, B440); cf. *Mac* 4.3.53–4.

209–10, 215 **will . . . done** These remarks echo the Lord's Prayer: 'Thy wil be done euen in earth, as *it is* in heauen' (Matthew, 6.10); there are possible echoes, too, of Matthew, 26.39, 42, which might be taken as conscious overtones of martyrdom. 'The related expression "God's will be done" occurs twice in *When You See Me* (B2ᵛ, Wilson TLN 398; H2ʳ, Wilson TLN 2187–8), but it had no doubt become so embedded in popular speech that it had become more of a common expression than a conscious biblical reference' (Shaheen, 197–8).

211 ***Abergavenny** 'Though the place name is now pronounced with five syllables, the personal name continues to be pronounced with four. The unelided form is therefore a metrically acceptable modern spelling' (Montgomery, in Oxf). F's '*Aburgany*' indicates a four-

syllable pronunciation.

216–19 **Here . . . chancellor** 'There was also attached the foresaid Chartreux monke, maister John de la Car *alias* de la Court, the dukes confessor, and sir Gilbert Perke priest, the dukes chancellor. . . . And so likewise was the lord Montacute' (Holinshed, 863).

217 **Lord Montague** Henry Pole, whose sister had married Buckingham's son, was released shortly after his arrest in 1521, though he was eventually beheaded in 1539.

218 ***Court** I have preferred the emendation in Theobald², following Holinshed, 804, of F's '*Car*', which is presumably a phonetic rendering of the same word (as Holinshed's use of both versions suggests).

219 ***Park** F has '*Pecke*'. Holinshed and Hall both read 'Perke', probably in error for 'clerk' (Gilbert's occupation) but, since the playwrights could not have known this, it seems appropriate to follow Steevens in modernizing the

209 whitest] *(*whit'st*)* heaven] *(*Heau'n*)* 211 Abergavenny] *Rowe; Aburgany* F   212 SD] *Johnson (to Aberg.)*   217 Montague] *Rowe; Mountacute* F   218 Court] *Theobald² (after Holinshed); Car* F   219 Park] *Steevens; Pecke* F   chancellor] *Pope² (Theobald, after Holinshed); Councellour* F

These are the limbs o'th' plot. No more, I hope?   220

BRANDON

A monk o'th' Chartreux.

BUCKINGHAM   O, Nicholas Hopkins?

BRANDON   He.

BUCKINGHAM

My surveyor is false: the o'er-great Cardinal
Hath showed him gold. My life is spanned already.
I am the shadow of poor Buckingham,
Whose figure even this instant cloud puts on   225
By darkening my clear sun. My lord, farewell.   *Exeunt.*

---

proper name implied by F (the compositorial error 'Pecke' for 'Perke', i.e., secretary hand *c* for *r*, being an easy one to make).

220 **limbs** constituent parts; i.e. the individual plotters

221 **o'th' Chartreux** of the Carthusian order; probably named after Chatrousse village in Dauphiné, France, near which this austere, contemplative order was founded by St Bruno in 1086. The English word 'charterhouse' is a corruption of 'chartreuse'.

*Nicholas Theobald checked Holinshed in order to make his suggestion for correcting F's '*Michaell*', which is probably a compositor's error: as Foakes (Ard²) notes, '*Mic.* could be an easy misreading of *Nic.* in secretary hand'; see also 1.2.146–50n.

222 **surveyor** See 115n.

false deliberately ambiguous: it is unclear whether Buckingham means that the Surveyor is lying or that he has betrayed him.

223 **showed him gold** We know that Wolsey has paid the Surveyor to betray Buckingham; what is never entirely clear is whether Wolsey has bribed him to tell the truth or to lie.

spanned reached its conclusion; the idea of life as a short 'span' was proverbial (Dent, L251), stemming from Psalm 39.6–7 in Coverdale's

translation: 'Beholde, thou hast made my dayes as it were a spanne long.' See also Erasmus, 2.2.69.

224–6 **I . . . sun.** A complex passage, difficult to paraphrase but clear enough in intent: 'I am only poor Buckingham's shadow, as my appearance is clouded in this instant by the obstruction of my sun's light.' *Shadow* can mean either 'ghost' or 'image' but also implies a reduction in selfhood ('a shadow of my former self '); *figure* could simply mean 'shape' or 'silhouette' but might well also hint at 'prediction', as Foakes (Ard²) suggests; cf. Webster, *The Duchess of Malfi* (1614), 2.291–2: 'I'll presently / Goe set a figure for's Nativitie.' Margeson (Cam²) reads *instant* as adjectival and translates *this instant cloud* as 'this accusation', but it seems more likely that both *instant* and *cloud* are nouns, the latter lacking an article (being possibly the object rather than the subject of *puts*); *sun* may imply either Buckingham or the King, or both. Buckingham manages to compress a great deal of implication into the few words he has time to say before he is led away. The *cloud* may be Wolsey's bulky shadow falling between Buckingham and Henry; cf. 54–7.

226 **darkening** two syllables

*lord Rowe's correction of F's 'Lords'

---

221 Nicholas] *Pope²* (Theobald); *Michaell* F 226 By darkening] *(By Darkning)*; Be-darkening
(Steevens)   lord] *Rowe*; Lords F

1.2 *Cornetts. Enter* KING Henry, *leaning on the*
Cardinal*'s shoulder, the nobles, and* Sir Thomas LOVELL*;*
the Cardinal places himself under the King's feet on his right side.
[*A Secretary attends the Cardinal.*]

is convincing, since Abergavenny is
being led away with Buckingham, leaving Norfolk standing uncomfortably
and conspicuously alone as the scene
abruptly closes, and since it is hardly
likely that Buckingham is addressing
Brandon who is (i) not a noble (unless
this 'Brandon' is Charles Brandon,
Duke of Suffolk, who appears only as
'Suffolk' throughout, except when
Henry addresses him by his Christian
name; see 197.1n.; see also 5.1.59, 72,
78) and (ii) likely to go off with
Buckingham as the officer in charge of
his arrest.

1.2 Generally held to be a Shakespeare
scene (see Appendix 3). Henry is characterized in this scene as passive
(despite bluster): virtually everyone else
(Katherine, Wolsey, Norfolk, the
Surveyor) occupies an active political
role, while the King speaks in platitudes
and demonstrates his fear both that he
will *without issue die* (134) and that a
traitor will *sheathe his knife* (210) in him.
The scene follows Holinshed closely.
Katherine's interventions on the taxation question are dramatic interpola-
tions, not drawn from Holinshed, and
presumably serve to establish an active
political role for her at court: her phrasing on the subject does nonetheless
reflect that of the source. For one of
Katherine's interventions in the discussion, the play *Thomas, Lord Cromwell*,
in the course of which Gardiner suborns two 'witnesses' to accuse
Cromwell falsely, appears also to be a
source (see 173–5n.). The location is 'a
council-chamber' in the palace (Ard²).

0.1 *Cornetts* A cornett was a wooden, lip-
vibrated wind instrument with finger-
holes and a cup-shaped mouthpiece,

used mainly from the end of the fif-
teenth century to the end of the seventeenth. The English spelling was usually 'cornet', but the common variant
'cornett' has been widely adopted to
prevent confusion with the modern
valved cornet (*New Grove*, 4.788).

Enter KING Henry When Compton, in
When You See Me, searches for the
King in the City, he asks the watch if
they have seen 'a good lustie tall bigge
set man' (E1ʳ, Wilson TLN 1209).
Byrne, commenting on Anthony
Quayle in the 1949 Guthrie production,
noted that 'the producer . . . was presenting us not with the grossly corpu-
lent figure of the later years of the reign
but with the fine burly young man that
was Henry in his prime' (Byrne, 122).
Whatever casting decision is made,
Henry's late entry here, in a play named
(at least in its printed form) after him,
ought to make an impact.

0.1–2 *leaning . . . shoulder* Visually, this
gesture, along with Wolsey's position-
ing himself 'on [the King's] right side',
emphasizes Henry's dependence on
the Cardinal at this point of the play.

0.2 *the nobles* This SD, taken from F,
refers either to Norfolk and Suffolk,
the only specified noblemen to appear
in this scene (of whom only Norfolk
speaks), and is therefore redundant,
since they are given an entry SD at 8,
or else it refers to unspecified, non-
speaking 'nobles' who occupy the stage
for visual effect only (and who could
conceivably be any of the lords who
appear in 1.3 and 1.4).

0.3 *under . . . side* implies that the King
sits on his throne (or 'state'; see 8.4n.)
as soon as he enters

1.2] *(Scena Secunda.)*   **0.4**] *Cam² (Ard²)*

KING

    My life itself, and the best heart of it,

    Thanks you for this great care. I stood i'th' level

    Of a full-charged confederacy, and give thanks

    To you that choked it. Let be called before us

    That gentleman of Buckingham's: in person   5

    I'll hear him his confessions justify,

    And point by point the treasons of his master

    He shall again relate.

A noise within crying 'Room for the Queen!' *[who, as she enters, is]*
ushered by the Duke of NORFOLK. *Enter* Queen KATHERINE,
NORFOLK *and [the* Duke of] SUFFOLK. *[Katherine] kneels.* KING
riseth from his state, takes her up, [and] kisses [her.]

KATHERINE

    Nay, we must longer kneel. I am a suitor.

1–4 **My . . . it.** The first two sentences are addressed to Wolsey. The King begins the scene, for anyone in the audience who knew his or her Holinshed, as a dupe: as far as the chronicler was concerned, Wolsey was clearly responsible for framing Buckingham.

1 **best heart** very essence

2 **i'th' level** within the aim; cf. *AW* 2.1.156.

3 **full-charged** fully loaded, carrying on the military metaphor from 'level' **confederacy** plot, *coup*

4 **choked** crushed, put down

4–8 **Let . . . relate** presumably addressed to the courtiers in general

5 **gentleman** 'man of gentle birth attached to the household of a person of high rank' (Onions)

6 **justify** prove, confirm, verify; cf. *WT* 1.2.280.

8.1 *who . . . is* F's SD is a little compressed, lacking a proper subject for 'ushered'.

8.4 *state* A 'chair of state', perhaps with a canopy, is required for a number of scenes (1.2.0.3; 1.4.0.1; 1.4.34.1; 2.4.0.11; 3.2.135 SD; 5.2.147.1): it appears to have been envisaged, as Montgomery (Oxf) suggests at 1.1.0.1, as a fixture on the stage throughout the play, occupied either by Henry or by Wolsey, as a constant (and sometimes instructively empty) reminder of the hierarchy of power.

9 **Nay . . . kneel.** Presumably, Katherine kneels once more at this point, after the action of the SD; or, possibly, Katherine's and Henry's first lines should be spoken after '*kneels*' (8.3) and Katherine should kneel only once.

5 Buckingham's: in person] *Johnson (subst.); Buckinghams,* in person, F 8.1 *who . . . is] this edn (Ard² subst.); Enter the Queen, usher'd by the Dukes of Norfolk and Suffolk / Theobald* 8.2 Queen KATHERINE] *this edn; the Queene* F 8.3 *Katherine] this edn; she* F 8.4 *and . . . her] Oxf; kisses and placeth her by him* F 9+ SP] *Ard²; Queen.* F

KING

Arise, and take place by us.
[The King] placeth her by him.
　　　　　　　　　　Half your suit　　　　　10
Never name to us. You have half our power;
The other moiety ere you ask is given.
Repeat your will and take it.

KATHERINE　　　　　　　Thank your majesty.
That you would love yourself, and in that love
Not unconsidered leave your honour nor　　　15
The dignity of your office, is the point
Of my petition.

KING　　　　　　　Lady mine, proceed.

KATHERINE

I am solicited – not by a few,
And those of true condition – that your subjects
Are in great grievance. There have been commissions　　20

---

10 **take place** sit, in the rightful place for a queen, next to the King, not kneeling before him
11–12 **You . . . given** On the possible relationship of this remark to the story of Herod and Herodias's daughter in Mark, 6, see LN.
12 **moiety** portion, half; cf. *Ham* 1.1.89.
　ere . . . given phrasing redolent of several NT passages, especially Matthew, 6.8: 'your father knoweth whereof ye haue nede, before ye aske of him'; cf. Matthew, 7.7; Luke, 11.9; also 1.1.186–7.
14–17 **That . . . petition.** In 1525, Henry VIII asked his people, through aristocratic and clerical commissioners, to make an 'Amicable Grant' of a considerable proportion of their wealth to support his planned war with France. This demand was refused, led to a minor insurrection, and was eventually rescinded (see Bernard, *passim*). Holinshed reports the problem over tax-

ation but does not mention an intervention by Katherine, though her phrasing here reflects that of Holinshed: 'The king indeed was much offended that his commons were thus intreated, & thought it touched his honor, that his councell should attempt such a doubtful matter in his name' (892). The timeframe is compressed (Buckingham's betrayal by his surveyor took place in 1521; the resistance to the 'Amicable Grant' commissions in 1525), and the dispute serves to introduce Katherine, delineate a political role for her, and establish her opposition to Wolsey.
19 **true condition** genuinely loyal; *condition* is 'character' or 'temper', while *true* is, as generally in this play, a matter of perspective.
20 **commissions** government instructions (*OED sb.*[1] 1a), in this case for raising taxes. '[B]y the cardinall there was deuised strange commissions, and sent in the end of March into euerie shire,

---

10 SD *placeth her by him*] see 8.4 t.n.

Sent down among 'em which hath flawed the heart
Of all their loyalties; wherein although,
My good lord Cardinal, they vent reproaches
Most bitterly on you as putter-on
Of these exactions, yet the King our master –   25
Whose honour heaven shield from soil – even he
    escapes not
Language unmannerly, yea, such which breaks
The sides of loyalty and almost appears
In loud rebellion.

NORFOLK   Not almost appears,

and commissioners appointed, . . .
which was, that the sixt part of euerie
mans substance should be paid in
monie or plate to the king without
delaie, for the furniture of his war.
Hereof followed such cursing, weeping, and exclamation against both king
& cardinall, that pitie it was to heare'
(Holinshed, 891). Hamilton suggests
that this scene may also refer to topical
taxation demands in 1612–13 (168–73).

21–2 **flawed . . . loyalties** damaged their
    previously solid allegiance; for *flawed*,
    see 1.1.95n.
23 **vent** give voice to; cf. *Tem* 1.2.280.
24 **putter-on** instigator; cf. *WT* 2.1.143.
    Jane Lapotaire (RSC, 1996) treated
    this word as an instance (arguably the
    only instance) of the Spanish-born
    Katherine struggling to find the right
    English word. The choice of Gemma
    Jones and Lapotaire in successive RSC
    productions (1983, 1996) to speak with
    a marked accent, though unconvincing
    for some reviewers, served to distance
    the foreign Queen from the English
    courtiers from the outset. This effect
    seems to have been achieved less inten-
    tionally by the Polish actress Helena
    Modjeska, who played Katherine in
    1891 with a noticeable accent. It is nec-
    essary, though, to note Katherine's

own comments on her command of
English at 3.1.43–50.
26 **soil** blemish; here, moral blemish
28–9 **almost . . . rebellion** '[T]he bur-
    then was so greeuous, that it was gen-
    erallie denied, and the commons in
    euerie place so mooued, that it was like
    to grow to rebellion' (Holinshed, 891).
    The wording here is perhaps margin-
    ally closer to that of Speed: 'the
    paiment . . . was vtterly denied to the
    appointed Collectors, with weepings,
    Cursings, and great acclamations, yea
    and almost grew to an open rebellion'
    (Speed, 2.761). According to Bernard,
    '[n]ot a penny of the Amicable Grant
    was ever paid by anyone' (55). This is
    the only 'Shakespeare' scene in the
    play which offers the possibility that
    he consulted Speed; clearer echoes of
    Speed appear in the latter half of 3.2
    (generally considered Fletcher's).
29–37 **Not . . . them.** As Foakes notes
    (Ard²), this scene expands on the local
    revolt described by Holinshed to imply
    that there was a full-scale rebellion,
    though nonetheless following
    Holinshed's language closely: 'The
    duke of Suffolke . . . persuaded . . . the
    rich clothiers to assent therto: but
    when they came home, and went about
    to discharge and put from them their

21 hath] have *F4*   24 putter-on] *Capell;* (putter on)

It doth appear; for, upon these taxations, 30
The clothiers all, not able to maintain
The many to them longing, have put off
The spinsters, carders, fullers, weavers, who,
Unfit for other life, compelled by hunger
And lack of other means, in desperate manner, 35
Daring th'event to th' teeth, are all in uproar,
And danger serves among them.
KING   Taxation?
Wherein, and what taxation? My lord Cardinal,
You that are blamed for it alike with us,
Know you of this taxation?
WOLSEY   Please you, sir, 40
I know but of a single part in aught

spinners, carders, fullers, weauers, and
other artificers, which they kept in
worke afore time, the people began to
assemble in companies' (891). Though
not explicitly mentioned here (and not
entirely in character with the Norfolk
of the play), it was Norfolk's diplomatic skills and (according to Holinshed)
genuine sympathy for the rebels that
defused the revolt in Suffolk. The play
thus overplays this small-scale revolt,
possibly to underline the King's political impotence, since he doesn't even
know about it until Katherine intervenes.
32 **The . . . longing** the substantial number of people they employ; *longing* signifies 'belonging'; cf. *TS* 4.4.7.
put off laid off, made redundant; first
OED citation in this sense (*v.* 46f(*b*)).
Once the Duke of Suffolk had persuaded the clothiers of that county to
promise to pay the Amicable Grant in
full, they returned home and began to
lay off their workers (see Bernard,
141–2).
33 **spinsters, carders, fullers** different
roles within the clothing trade: *spinsters*

spun the cloth, a job generally done by
single women; *carders* combed out the
wool to prepare it for spinning; *fullers*
trod or beat the cloth in order to clean
and/or thicken it.
36 **Daring . . . teeth** pushing the situation to the very edge; proverbial (Dent,
TT4)
37 **serves** in the temporal sense of seeking
an opportunity, looking for an outlet
Taxation? The King's obvious ignorance in this scene exonerates him
from blame in the eyes of the audience
though, together with his immediately
turning to Wolsey, it again underlines
his political impotence at this stage of
the play. Historically, the King seems
to have been as responsible for the
commissions and their demands as was
Wolsey (Bernard, 53–72).
41–3 **I . . . me.** 'I only have the level of
knowledge available to an individual in
the process of government, and, while I
am indeed in charge, I do not presume
to make decisions by myself.' Wolsey
neatly ensures that, if there is to be
blame, it will not rest solely on him.
41 **aught** anything

32 longing] 'longing *F4*   36 to] *F2;* too *F*

Pertains to th' state, and front but in that file
Where others tell steps with me.

KATHERINE   No, my lord,
You know no more than others, but you frame
Things that are known alike, which are not wholesome   45
To those which would not know them and yet must
Perforce be their acquaintance. These exactions
Whereof my sovereign would have note, they are
Most pestilent to th' hearing, and to bear 'em
The back is sacrifice to th' load. They say   50
They are devised by you, or else you suffer
Too hard an exclamation.

KING   Still 'exaction'!
The nature of it? In what kind, let's know,
Is this exaction?

KATHERINE   I am much too venturous
In tempting of your patience, but am boldened   55
Under your promised pardon. The subjects' grief
Comes through commissions which compels from
            each

42 **front** march in the front rank
43 **tell . . . me** keep up with me (literally,
   count steps with me); share the same
   responsibilities
43–4 **No . . . others** Katherine's retort is
   both angry and sarcastic. F supplies a
   question-mark (which could anyway be
   the early modern equivalent of an exclamation mark), but following F4 makes
   more sense of the speech as a whole.
44–7 **but . . . acquaintance** 'Everyone
   knows the arrangements you make,
   with which people are stuck whether
   they agree with them or not.' So much
   for the power of the Privy Council.
47 **Perforce** forcibly, against their will; cf.
   KL 1.4.290.
48 **note** information, knowledge
52 **exclamation** complaint, accusation

53–60 **The . . . France.** See 20n. and
   Holinshed, 891: 'The king then came
   to Westminster to the cardinals palace,
   and . . . willed to know by whose
   meanes the commissions were so
   streictlie giuen foorth, to demand the
   sixt part of euerie mans goods.'
53–4 **The . . . exaction?** What form of
   tax is it?
54 **venturous** daring
55 **boldened** given confidence, made
   bold
56 **grief** grievance
57 **compels** third person plural -*s* ending;
   originally a northern form, but found in
   early modern texts by southerners by
   this date; see Abbott, 332–8; Barber,
   168–71 (JH). There is therefore no need
   to Pope's emendation to 'compel'.

43–4 lord, . . . others,] *F4;* Lord? . . . others? *F;* lord; . . . others! *Kittredge*   52 'exaction'] *(Exaction)*

The sixth part of his substance, to be levied
Without delay; and the pretence for this
Is named your wars in France. This makes bold mouths: 60
Tongues spit their duties out, and cold hearts freeze
Allegiance in them. Their curses now
Live where their prayers did, and it's come to pass
This tractable obedience is a slave
To each incensed will. I would your highness   65
Would give it quick consideration, for
There is no primer baseness.
KING   By my life,
This is against our pleasure.
WOLSEY   And for me,
I have no further gone in this than by
A single voice, and that not passed me but   70
By learned approbation of the judges. If I am

58 **The . . . substance** a sixth of his property and/or income. Bernard notes that '[t]he clergy were called upon to grant one-third of their yearly revenues. . . . No administrative document . . . survives to show the rates demanded of the laity[, though Hall] describes a sliding scale [and writes] of demands of a sixth of every man's substance' (Bernard, 56).
levied claimed and collected
59 **pretence** the assertion or alleging of a ground, cause, or reason for any action (*OED sb.* 6), probably shading into the modern sense of a groundless pretext
60 **bold mouths** inversion
62 **Allegiance** four syllables
64–5 **This . . . will.** What made the people loyal before now fuels their anger.
65 **incensed** incensèd
67 **no primer baseness** no more radical manifestation of evil. Hanmer's emendation to 'business' has had a deal of influence and is plausible, as Bowers

notes, if *primer* means 'urgent', but it lessens the force of Katherine's assertion and is unnecessary. Jane Lapotaire, experimenting with a Spanish accent (RSC, 1996), produced in effect a composite word for 'business'/'baseness' (Lapotaire, 139).
68–71 **And . . . judges.** 'The cardinall excused himselfe, and said, that when it was mooued in councell how to leuie monie to the kings vse; the kings councell, and namelie the iudges, said, that he might lawfullie demand anie summe by commission, and that by the consent of the whole councell it was doone' (Holinshed, 891).
70 **single voice** probably, 'unanimous support' (in the Privy Council), but Wolsey may mean that even his own vote was given in accord with the advice of the judges (RP)
71 **learned** learnèd
approbation approval, consent

58 sixth] *F4;* Sixt *F*   67 baseness] business *Hanmer (Warburton)*

Traduced by ignorant tongues, which neither know
My faculties nor person yet will be
The chronicles of my doing, let me say
'Tis but the fate of place and the rough brake   75
That virtue must go through. We must not stint
Our necessary actions in the fear
To cope malicious censurers, which ever,
As ravenous fishes, do a vessel follow
That is new-trimmed, but benefit no further   80
Than vainly longing. What we oft do best,
By sick interpreters, or weak ones, is
Not ours or not allowed; what worst, as oft,
Hitting a grosser quality, is cried up
For our best act. If we shall stand still   85
In fear our motion will be mocked or carped at,
We should take root here where we sit,

72 **Traduced** defamed, slandered
ignorant tongues Productions variously have Wolsey glance at either Katherine or Norfolk and Suffolk at these words, depending largely on the level of disrespect he is showing the Queen at this stage.
73 **faculties** qualities, disposition
75 **fate of place** occupational hazard of high office
rough brake wild woodland or thicket
76 **stint** limit, hold back; cf. *Tim* 5.5.88.
77–8 **in . . . censurers** out of fear that we might have to contend with people who are deliberately cruel about us
78 **cope** contend with
78–81 **which . . . longing** who are like sharks which persist in hopelessly pursuing a newly fitted-out ship even though there is no chance it will sink and thus provide them with food
81–5 **What . . . act**. Just as our best efforts are often rejected or maligned by the envious and disbelieving, so our

least impressive performance, catching on at a much more mundane level (or with coarser people), is made out to be our greatest achievement.
82 **sick . . . ones** *Sick* here means 'envious' (cf. *TC* 1.3.132); 'weak ones' probably has the biblical connotation of 'people of unsound faith', as Foakes suggests (Ard²), and thus perhaps a hint that anyone who doubts Wolsey is likely to be a heretic.
*or F's 'once', generally retained, makes limited sense, and Montgomery plausibly suggests a misreading of secretary hand 'ŏc(e)' for 'or(e)' (*TxC*).
83 **allowed** accepted, approved
84 **Hitting . . . quality** an ambivalent phrase, implying either that the unimpressive actions are popular with a particularly coarse group of people or that they operate on a very low level of achievement
86 **motion** both action and proposal

79 ravenous] *(*rau'nous*)* 80 new-trimmed] *(*new trim'd*)* 82 sick] such *(Keightley)* or] *Pope;* once F 83 oft,] *Capell;* oft F

Or sit state-statues only.

KING   Things done well,
And with a care, exempt themselves from fear;
Things done without example in their issue   90
Are to be feared. Have you a precedent
Of this commission? I believe not any.
We must not rend our subjects from our laws
And stick them in our will. Sixth part of each?
A trembling contribution! Why, we take   95
From every tree lop, bark and part o'th' timber,
And though we leave it with a root, thus hacked
The air will drink the sap. To every county
Where this is questioned send our letters with
Free pardon to each man that has denied   100
The force of this commission. Pray look to't:
I put it to your care.
WOLSEY [*apart to his Secretary*]   A word with you.
Let there be letters writ to every shire
Of the King's grace and pardon. The grieved
    commons
Hardly conceive of me: let it be noised   105

---

88 **state-statues** image of immobility to
contrast with *motion* in 86
90 **example** precedent
issue outcome
93–4 **We . . . will.** Henry points out
forcibly that he does not wish to be
seen as a tyrant, replacing the rule of
law with his own desires.
95 **trembling** frightening, disturbing
95–8 **Why . . . sap.** If we cut too much off
a tree, then even if we leave its roots
alone, our action will lead to the tree
drying up.
96 **lop** twigs and minor branches
98–101 **To . . . commission.** The King
'caused letters to be sent into all shires,
that the matter should no further be

talked of: & he pardoned all them that
had denied the demand openlie or
secretlie' (Holinshed, 892).
99 **questioned** resisted
101 **force** validity, effect
104 **grieved** aggrieved
104–7 **The . . . comes.** 'The cardinall, to
deliuer himselfe of the euill will of the
commons, purchased by procuring &
advancing of this demand, affirmed,
and caused it to be bruted abrode, that
through his intercession the king had
pardoned and released all things'
(Holinshed, 892).
105 **Hardly conceive** think harshly of
noised implied, rumoured

---

91 precedent] *(*President*)*   94 Sixth] *F4;* Sixt *F*   95 trembling] trebling *Collier²;* terrible
(Cartwright)   102 SD] *Rowe*

That through our intercession this revokement
And pardon comes. I shall anon advise you
Further in the proceeding.   *Exit Secretary.*

Enter Surveyor.

KATHERINE
I am sorry that the Duke of Buckingham
Is run in your displeasure.

KING   It grieves many.   110
The gentleman is learned and a most rare speaker,
To nature none more bound, his training such
That he may furnish and instruct great teachers
And never seek for aid out of himself. Yet see,
When these so noble benefits shall prove   115
Not well disposed, the mind growing once corrupt,
They turn to vicious forms, ten times more ugly
Than ever they were fair. This man so complete,
Who was enrolled 'mongst wonders – and when we,
Almost with ravished listening, could not find   120
His hour of speech a minute – he, my lady,
Hath into monstrous habits put the graces

---

106 **our** inappropriate plural for singular (the 'royal we'), which Wolsey uses with his secretary as he does not when speaking to the King (*I* at 69, 71) – a clear indication of his arrogance and presumption
revokement withdrawal, cancellation
110 **Is run in** has fallen into, incurred
111 **rare** fine
112 **To . . . bound** No-one has more natural talents for which to be grateful.
114 **out of** outside, beyond
115 **benefits** natural qualities, advantages
116 **disposed** arranged, directed; the effect being that the particular combination of abilities with which Buckingham was blessed in fact made him susceptible to corruption
117 **vicious** bad, evil
118 **complete** perfect, accomplished; stress on the first syllable
120 **ravished** engrossed, entranced
120–1 **could . . . minute** He was such a good speaker that an hour-long speech seemed to last no more than a minute.
122 **habits** guises, shapes, clothes, with a possible further sense of 'moral qualities'

108 SD *Secretary*] *(Secret.)*   111 learned] *(Learn'd)*   119–21 wonders – and . . . minute –] *Ard²*; wonders; and . . . minute: *F*   120 ravished listening] *(rauish'd listning);* list'ning ravish'd *Pope*

That once were his and is become as black
As if besmeared in hell. Sit by us. You shall hear –
This was his gentleman in trust – of him   125
Things to strike honour sad. Bid him recount
The fore-recited practices, whereof
We cannot feel too little, hear too much.

WOLSEY

Stand forth, and with bold spirit relate what you,
Most like a careful subject, have collected   130
Out of the Duke of Buckingham.

KING   Speak freely.

SURVEYOR

First, it was usual with him – every day
It would infect his speech – that if the King
Should without issue die, he'll carry it so
To make the sceptre his. These very words   135
I've heard him utter to his son-in-law,
Lord Abergavenny, to whom by oath he menaced
Revenge upon the Cardinal.

WOLSEY   Please your highness note

123–4 **black . . . hell** proverbial (Dent,
H397); cf. *inter alia KL* 3.7.59, *Ham*
3.3.94–5; see also *Birth of Merlin*,
2.2.71.
125 **gentleman in trust** trusted servant
127 **fore-recited practices** treacherous
activities outlined previously
130 **careful** caring, loving
130–1 **collected / Out of** gathered in
evidence against
132–8 **First . . . Cardinal.** 'And first he
vttered, that the duke was accustomed
by waie of talke, to saie, how he meant
so to vse the matter, that he would
atteine the crowne, if king Henrie
chanced to die without issue: & that he

had talke and conference of that matter on a time with George Neuill, lord
of Aburgauennie, . . . and also that he
threatned to punish the cardinall for
his manifold misdooings, being without cause his mortall enimie'
(Holinshed, 862).
132 **usual with him** his habit
134 **carry it so** arrange matters so as
135 **sceptre** symbol of royal authority
137 **Abergavenny** four syllables, not five;
see 1.1.211n.
138–40 **Please . . . person** In the context
of what he was hoping would happen
to you, please also note what he wanted
to do to your friends, i.e. me.

125 trust – of him] trust of him – *Oxf*   134 he'll] he'd *Pope*   137 Abergavenny] *Rowe; Aburgany
F;* Aberga'ny *Theobald*

His dangerous conception in this point,
Not friended by his wish to your high person; 140
His will is most malignant, and it stretches
Beyond you to your friends.

KATHERINE   My learned lord Cardinal,
Deliver all with charity.

KING   Speak on.
How grounded he his title to the crown
Upon our fail? To this point hast thou heard him 145
At any time speak aught?

SURVEYOR   He was brought to this
By a vain prophecy of Nicholas Hopkins.

KING
What was that Hopkins?

SURVEYOR   Sir, a Chartreux friar,

139 *His Pope's emendation undoes the
anticipation of *this* from later in the
line (see Bowers for detailed discussion
of these lines).
  His . . . point the dangerous way his
  thinking developed
143 Deliver . . . charity 'Don't be spiteful.' Katherine's sarcasm implies that
  Wolsey is being both selfish and
  unchristian in his eagerness to see
  Buckingham crushed and underlines
  his own sense of being (almost) as
  important as the King.
144–5 How . . . fail? On what basis did he
  intend to claim the throne when I die
  (or when I die childless)?
145 To this point on this topic
146–50 He . . . sovereignty. 'Then
  Kneuet . . . openlie confessed, that the
  duke had once fullie determined to
  deuise meanes how to make the king
  away, being brought into a full hope
  that he should be king, by a vaine
  prophecie which one Nicholas
  Hopkins, a monke of an house of the

Chartreux order beside Bristow, called
Henton, sometime his confessor had
opened vnto him' (Holinshed, 862–3).
Henton was one of ten Carthusian
institutions in Britain before the suppression of the monasteries (see also
1.1.221n.).
147, 148 *Hopkins F's '*Henton*' is an
apparently unintentional reverse
metonymy, monastery for monk (see
146–50n.). Doran (RSC, 1996) saw the
Surveyor's mistake here as evidence of
the nervous haste in which he is
'telling the tale he is supposed to tell'
(Doran, conversation with editor,
1996), though the source of the change
is more likely to be mechanical than
dramatic, since Buckingham also errs
in calling Hopkins/Henton 'Michael'
rather than 'Nicholas' at 1.1.221 in F.
This *vain prophecy*, along with the
popular prophesying at 1.1.92, provides an awkward context for
Cranmer's later prophetic speech over
the baby Elizabeth.

139 His] *Pope;* This *F*   139–40 point, . . . wish to . . . person;] point: . . . wish to . . . person, *Pope;*
point: . . . wish, to . . . person *Capell*   142 learned] *(learn'd)*   145 fail?] *Rowe³;* faile; *F*   147, 148
Hopkins] *Pope² (Theobald, after Holinshed); Henton F*

His confessor, who fed him every minute
With words of sovereignty.

KING   How know'st thou this?   150

SURVEYOR

Not long before your highness sped to France,
The Duke being at the Rose, within the parish
Saint Laurence Pountney, did of me demand
What was the speech among the Londoners
Concerning the French journey. I replied   155
Men feared the French would prove perfidious,
To the King's danger. Presently, the Duke

151–71 **Not . . . England.** Shakespeare
follows Holinshed very closely for the
Surveyor's testimony: '[T]he same
duke . . . at London in a place called
the Rose, within the parish of saint
Laurence Poultnie in Canwicke street
ward, demanded of the said Charles
Kneuet esquier, what was the talke
amongest the Londoners concerning
the kings iourneie beyond the seas:
And the said Charles told him, that
manie stood in doubt of that iourneie,
least the Frenchmen meant some
deceit towards the king. Whereto the
duke answered, that it was to be feared,
least it would come to passe, according
to the words of a certeine holie
moonke. For there is (saith he) a
Chartreux moonke, that diuerse times
hath sent to me, willing me to send
vnto him my chancellor: and I did send
vnto him John de la Court my chap-
leine, vnto whome he would not
declare anie thing, till de la Court had
sworne vnto him to keepe all things
secret, and to tell no creature liuing
what hee should heare of him, except
it were to me. And then the said
moonke told de la Court, that neither
the king nor his heires should prosper,
and that I should indeuour my selfe to
purchase the good wills of the com-

munaltie of England; for I the same
duke and my bloud should prosper,
and haue the rule of the realme of
England' (864).
152 **Rose** the name of a manor house
belonging to Buckingham which was
later converted for use as a school
153 **Saint Laurence Pountney** a church
on Candlewick Street, so called
because the original church of
St Laurence was developed into
Corpus Christi college by John de
Poulteney in 1344. It had one of the
tallest spires in the City, but was burnt
down in the Great Fire of 1666. All
that exists of it now is a commemora-
tive plaque and a few square yards of
churchyard on an alley called
Laurence Pountney Hill, surrounded
by Victorian and modern office blocks.
I have modernized to current spelling,
presumably a London phonetic rendering of 'Poulteney'.
154 what Londoners were saying
156 *feared F has 'feare', but it would be
the simplest of errors to read secretary
hand *d* as *e*.
156–7 **perfidious . . . danger** treacherous to the point of becoming a threat
to the King's life
157 **Presently** immediately, directly

---

153 Pountney] *(Poultney)*   156 feared] *Pope;* feare *F*

Said 'twas the fear indeed, and that he doubted
'Twould prove the verity of certain words
Spoke by a holy monk, 'that oft', says he,   160
'Hath sent to me, wishing me to permit
John de la Court, my chaplain, a choice hour
To hear from him a matter of some moment;
Whom after, under the confession's seal,
He solemnly had sworn that what he spoke   165
My chaplain to no creature living but
To me should utter, with demure confidence
This pausingly ensued: "Neither the King, nor's heirs –
Tell you the Duke – shall prosper. Bid him strive
To purchase the love o'th' commonalty. The Duke   170
Shall govern England." '

KATHERINE   If I know you well,
You were the Duke's surveyor, and lost your office

---

158 **doubted** suspected

162 **choice hour** convenient time

164–7 **Whom . . . utter** The slightly confused syntax here is made clearer when read alongside Holinshed (see 151–71n.): Hopkins the monk made Buckingham's chaplain swear while undergoing confession that he would tell no-one but the Duke what he had said.

164 ***confession's** F's 'Commissions' was first corrected by Theobald, presumably a slip echoing frequency of use of the word at the start of this scene (see 20n.). Theobald[2] also emends '*Car*' to '*Court*' (162) in line with Holinshed (also at 1.1.218 and 2.1.20; see 151–71n.).

165 **sworn** made to swear

167 **demure confidence** solemn assurance

168 **pausingly** with pauses, hesitantly; only adverbial citation in *OED* (*ppl. adv.*)

170 ***purchase** A word is missing in F between *To* and *the love*; F4's 'gain' has been generally accepted, though Sisson's 'win' has also been taken up. I prefer Bowers's 'purchase', after Holinshed (see 151–71n.).
commonalty the common people, from Holinshed's 'communaltie' (864), one of only two examples of this word in Shakespeare (cf. *Cor* 1.1.27)

171–3 **If . . . tenants**. Katherine's intervention breaks up the almost verbatim reporting of Knevet's speech from Holinshed and glances ahead to the analysis of blame in the *Chronicles*. Buckingham's dismissal of his Surveyor is seen to provide Wolsey with the opportunity he had been seeking to ruin the Duke: 'whilest he staid [at his estate in Kent,] greeuous complaints were exhibited to him by his farmers and tenants against Charles Kneuet his surueiour, for such

---

162 Court] *Theobald*[2] *(after Holinshed);* Car F   164 Whom] Who *Pope*   confession's] *Theobald (after Holinshed);* Commissions F   170 To . . . love] *Bowers (after Holinshed);* To the loue *F;* To gain the love *F4;* To win the love *Sisson*

On the complaint o'th' tenants. Take good heed
You charge not in your spleen a noble person
And spoil your nobler soul. I say, take heed –   175
Yes, heartily beseech you.

KING   Let him on:
[*to the Surveyor*] Go forward.

SURVEYOR   On my soul, I'll speak but truth.
I told my lord the Duke, by th' devil's illusions
The monk might be deceived, and that 'twas
      dangerous
For him to ruminate on this so far until   180

bribing as he had vsed there amongst them. Wherevpon the duke tooke such displeasure against him, that he depriued him of his office, not knowing how that in so dooing he procured his owne destruction, as after appeared' (Holinshed, 856).

173–5 Take . . . heed There is no basis in Holinshed for this warning. The likely source here is a moment in *Thomas, Lord Cromwell* in which Gardiner suborns two 'witnesses' to accuse Cromwell and Norfolk warns them: 'My friends take heed of that which you haue said, / Your soules must answer what your tongues reports: / Therefore take heed, be warie what you doe' (F2ʳ).

174 spleen the organ viewed as the seat of the passions (Onions), thus here spite, malice

174–5 noble . . . nobler Katherine is playing on the idea of nobility as a moral and as a hierarchical concept, suggesting that the individual's soul is much more precious than his or her status.

176 heartily with all my heart

177 On . . . truth. The Surveyor deliberately picks up Katherine's emphasis on the soul in order to reinforce his truth-

fulness. *Truth*, as throughout, is problematic here.

178 illusions deceptions

178–86 I . . . off. Shakespeare returns to the Surveyor's testimony as reported in Holinshed: 'Then said Charles Kneuet; The moonke maie be deceiued through the diuels illusion: and that it was euill to meddle with such matters. Well (said the duke) it cannot hurt me, and so (saith the indictment) the duke seemed to reioise in the moonkes woords. And further, at the same time, the duke told the said Charles, that if the king had miscaried now in his last sicknesse, he would haue chopped off the heads of the cardinall, of sir Thomas Louell knight, and of others' (864).

179–82 'twas . . . do It was dangerous for him to reflect on what the monk had said, particularly if he thought it credible, because doing so might encourage him to plot a *coup*.

180 *For him F's 'For this' anticipates the *this* later in the line; *For him* is metrically superfluous (producing, as it does, an atypical hexameter), may be the vestige of a deleted line, and could simply be dropped.

175 nobler] Noble *F2*   176–7 Let . . . forward] *Pope; one line F*   177 SD] *Capell (subst.)*
179–80 dangerous . . . to] *Rowe;* dangerous / For this to *F;* dangerous for him / To *Capell;*
dangerous / From this to *Collier²*   180 on . . . until] on this, until *Pope;* on it so far, until *Collier²*

It forged him some design – which, being believed,
It was much like to do. He answered, 'Tush,
It can do me no damage,' adding further
That had the King in his last sickness failed,
The Cardinal's and Sir Thomas Lovell's heads   185
Should have gone off.

KING   Ha? What, so rank? Ah, ha!
There's mischief in this man. Canst thou say further?

SURVEYOR
    I can, my liege.

KING   Proceed.

SURVEYOR   Being at Greenwich,
After your highness had reproved the Duke
About Sir William Bulmer –

KING   I remember   190

184 **failed** died; cf. 145.
186 **Ha?** This seems to have been Henry's characteristic exclamation. In *When You See Me*, it is underlined as a sign of the King's anger when he cries 'Am I not *Hary*, am I not Englands king, Ha', and the Fool, Will Sommers, whispers 'So la, now the watchwords giuen, nay and hee once cry ha, neare a man in the court dare for his head speake againe' (C1ᵛ, Wilson TLN 657–9).
  rank foul, corrupt
188–99 **Being . . . him**. The Surveyor vividly recounts the most damaging allegations (complete with reinforcement from Wolsey and Henry): '[T]he same duke . . . at east Greenwich in the countie of Kent, said vnto one Charles Kneuet esquier, after that the king had reprooued the duke for reteining William Bulmer knight into his seruice, that if he had perceiued that he should haue beene committed to the Tower (as he doubted hee should haue beene) hee would haue so wrought, that the principall doers therein should not haue had

cause of great reioising: for he would haue plaied the part which his father intended to haue put in practise against king Richard the third at Salisburie, who made earnest sute to haue come vnto the presence of the same king Richard: which sute if he might haue obteined, he hauing a knife secretlie about him, would haue thrust it into the bodie of king Richard, as he had made semblance to kneele downe before him' (Holinshed, 864); cf. *R3* 5.1.1.
190 *****Bulmer** corrected from F's '*Blumer*'; Holinshed had mentioned this event earlier in the context of the 'reformation' of the 'king's minions' on their return from France: 'the king specially rebuked sir William Bulmer knight, bicause he being his seruant sworne, refused the kings seruice, and became seruant to the duke of Buckingham' (852–3; on the behaviour of the courtiers after the French journey, see 1.3.1n.).
190–1 **remember / Of** recall; only example of this construction in the Shakespeare canon. Montgomery (Oxf)

190 Bulmer] *Cam (1892)*; *Blumer F*; Blomer *Pope*   190–1 I . . . servant] *Pope; one line F*   remember / Of such] remember / Such *Oxf*

Of such a time: being my sworn servant,
The Duke retained him his. But on: what hence?

SURVEYOR

'If', quoth he, 'I for this had been committed' –
As to the Tower, I thought – 'I would have played
The part my father meant to act upon   195
Th'usurper Richard who, being at Salisbury,
Made suit to come in's presence; which if granted,
As he made semblance of his duty would
Have put his knife into him.'

KING   A giant traitor.

WOLSEY

Now, madam, may his highness live in freedom   200
And this man out of prison?

KATHERINE   God mend all.

KING

There's something more would out of thee: what say'st?

SURVEYOR

After 'the Duke his father', with 'the knife',

---

notes this and the unmetrical quality of
the line and emends to 'remember'.

194 **As . . . thought** Editions typically
assume that this is part of
Buckingham's reported speech, but it
seems to me more likely to be an
explanatory aside from the Surveyor.

194–9 **I would . . . him** For the relationship of Richard III and Buckingham's
father, see *R3* 3.7, 4.2.86–125, 5.1.

198 **made . . . duty** made as if to kneel

199 **traitor** in context, a slightly awkward
remark, and certainly a fairly typical
failure of self-awareness on Henry's
part, since it was rebelling against and
killing Richard III (though mitigated by
the relative strength of his claim to the

throne) that brought Henry, Duke of
Richmond, Henry VIII's father, to the
throne as Henry VII (see *R3* 5.8.1–8)

201 **God mend all**. May God put everything right. Katherine's remark is conspicuously not an answer to Wolsey's
question, though it is not clear if *all*
refers to the state of government
under the Henry/Wolsey double act or
to Buckingham's alleged misdeeds.

203–9 **After . . . purpose**. The Surveyor
feigns reluctance to complete his testimony. Again his words closely follow
Holinshed: 'And in speaking these
words, he maliciouslie laid his hand
vpon his dagger, and said, that if he
were euill vsed, he would doo his best

---

191 time: being] *Collier;* time, being *F;* time, he being *Pope;* time. He being *Johnson;* time. Being
Steevens; time: – being *Steevens²*   193–4 committed' – / As . . . thought – 'I] *this edn;* committed,
/ As . . . thought; I *F*   196 Salisbury] *(Salsbury)*   203] *Capell (subst.);* After the Duke his Father,
with the knife *F*

He stretched him, and with one hand on his dagger,
Another spread on's breast, mounting his eyes,   205
He did discharge a horrible oath, whose tenor
Was, were he evil used, he would outgo
His father by as much as a performance
Does an irresolute purpose.

KING   There's his period:
To sheathe his knife in us. He is attached;   210
Call him to present trial. If he may
Find mercy in the law, 'tis his; if none,
Let him not seek't of us. By day and night,
He's traitor to th' height!   *Exeunt.*

1.3   *Enter* Lord CHAMBERLAIN *and* Lord SANDYS.

CHAMBERLAIN
Is't possible the spells of France should juggle

to accomplish his pretended purpose,
swearing to confirme his word by the
bloud of our Lord' (864).
204 **stretched him** stood upright
206 **whose tenor** the gist of which
207 **evil used** treated badly
208–9 **performance ... purpose** broadly
proverbial (Dent, P602); cf. 4.2.41–2;
also 3.2.154; in other words, he would
not hesitate to act.
209 **period** aim, conclusion of his plans
210 **sheathe his knife** Henry's expression of his fear here, in the context of
his horror of dying *without issue* and
his political passivity, takes on sexual
connotations, as his patriarchal dignity
as King has been compromised both
by the tax revolts and by Buckingham's
alleged plot and he is in a certain way
'feminized' by the details of the threatened stabbing; cf. the outrage the King
feels at 2.2.63–4 when Norfolk and
Suffolk interrupt his reading.
attached under arrest
211 **present** immediate, summary

214 **to th' height** in the highest possible
degree. On the back of a letter,
Henry's secretary Pace wrote '*credit
Rex quod a d[omini]s culpabilis in]veni-
etur et attaynte. D[ux] B[uckinghamiae]*'
('the King believes that the Duke of
Buckingham will be found guilty and
be condemned by the Lords') (*LP*, III
cxix, 453).
1.3 Generally held to be a Fletcher scene
(see Appendix 3). The scene satirically
updates Holinshed's account of the
'French' habits of young courtiers,
ensuring the audience's recognition of
contemporary relevance. The location
is a room at court.
0.1 SANDYS The 'y' is silent, and the
name has generally (and unnecessarily,
since the name still exists both as
'Sandys' and 'Sands') been modernized to the phonetic spelling 'Sands'.
1   **spells of France** A number of young
English aristocrats who had spent
time at the French court had, according to Holinshed, become 'all French,

1.3] *(Scæna Tertia.)*   0.1 SANDYS] Sands *Rowe*

Men into such strange mysteries?
SANDYS   New customs,
Though they be never so ridiculous –
Nay, let 'em be unmanly – yet are followed.
CHAMBERLAIN
As far as I see, all the good our English   5
Have got by the late voyage is but merely
A fit or two o'th' face – but they are shrewd ones,
For when they hold 'em you would swear directly
Their very noses had been counsellors
To Pepin or Clotharius, they keep state so.   10

in eating, drinking, and apparell, yea, and in French vices and brags, so that all the estates of England were by them laughed at' (850), and were purged at the insistence of the Privy Council (see 19n.). Foakes (Ard²) provides copious and very helpful annotation for the contemporary relevance of this affair for the court of 1613 (see notes below). Anne Bullen had gone to France to complete her education at the age of twelve in 1513 and had stayed there until 1521; her Protestantism was said (inaccurately) to have been inculcated into her while in the service of Marguerite of Angoulême (see 4.2.82.1 LN and pp. 132–5). It seems likely that this would still have been part of what was known of her a century later, and would doubtless have been equivocally viewed (the anti-Catholicism she picked up in France would have been approved but the cultural and sexual influence of the French suspected).

1–2 **spells . . . mysteries** terms associated with witchcraft: one meaning of *juggle* is 'to conjure'; *mysteries* imply either (mockingly) dark rites known only to the initiated or else (more simply but still contemptuously) daft behaviour. *Pace* Johnson, there is no allusion here

to the genre of the mystery play.
4 **let 'em be** even if they are
7 **fit . . . face** odd facial expression, grimace; from the rest of the passage, the Chamberlain is probably implying that these 'Frenchified' courtiers walk around haughtily, 'with their noses in the air', though Foakes (Ard²) quotes Dekker, *Work*, to show that there is also an association of French politics and facial expression: 'Deceipt . . . studies *Machiauell*, and hath a french face' (D4ʳ).
  shrewd early meanings included 'mischievous' and 'cunning, artful', but here the usage shades into the current sense of 'astute' (*OED a.* 1a and 13a)
8 **hold 'em** adopt the odd facial expressions
10 **Pepin or Clotharius** Kings of the Franks in the period 500–800. 'Clotharius' is either Clotaire I or Clotaire II, kings of France 511–61 and 584–628 respectively. 'Pepin' is presumably Pépin le Bref, who reigned 741–68 and whose consolidating achievements as king laid the ground for the conquests of his son Charlemagne. Each of these kings is representative of ancient French rule and perhaps also of barbarism (cf. *H5* 1.2.65–87).

2 mysteries] mimick'ries *Hanmer*; mockeries *Warburton*

SANDYS

   They have all new legs, and lame ones. One would
     take it,
   That never see 'em pace before, the spavin
   Or springhalt reigned among 'em.

CHAMBERLAIN　　　　　　　　　　　　Death, my lord,

   Their clothes are after such a pagan cut to't,
   That sure they've worn out Christendom.

Enter Sir Thomas LOVELL.

How now?　　　15

---

11 **legs** double meaning: new ways both of walking and of bowing ('making a leg')

11–13 **lame . . . 'em** This seems to have been criticism of courtiers not only in 1520 but also in 1613 (notably in sermons): Thomas Adams, in *The Gallant's Burden* (1612), for instance, demands to know 'Were these the sinnes of *Edom*, and are they not the sinnes of *England*? For the . . . Proude and gallant *Edomite* [adores] his gaye Cloathes, and studyed carriage' (H4^r) and Daniel Price, in his *Lamentations for the Death of Prince Henry* (1613), refers to 'the quaint *Crane-paced* Courtiers of this time' (C2^v) (Ard^2).

12 **see** Pope emended this to 'saw', since the sense seems to require a past tense, but recent editors have retained *see* as an acceptable if quirky early modern past tense (JH).
pace go through their paces. A possible misreading of secretary hand *d* as *e* would suggest 'pac(e)d', accentuating the equestrian image.
spavin a bony tumour produced by inflammation of the cartilage uniting the splint-bone and the shank in a horse's leg (*OED sb.* 1)

13 ***Or springhalt** a version (presumably to alliterate with *spavin*) of the word 'stringhalt', a disease affecting a horse's hind legs which causes certain muscles

to contract spasmodically (*OED*: an alteration of 'stringhalt'). F's 'A' makes an uncomfortable sentence, despite Foakes's defence (Ard^2); Dyce's 'Or' does not necessarily imply the interchangeability of *spavin* and *springhalt*, but rather a comic–grotesque escalation in Sandys's description.
Death a contraction of the oath 'by God's death'

14–15 Their clothes are of so foreign a design that you would think they had had to travel outside Christian countries to find such fashions.

14 **to't** conflation of idioms, i.e. 'of such a pagan cut'

14–43 **pagan . . . converting** As Slights (60) notes, this conversation about the influence of French fashion on the English court is couched in religious terms, especially at 14 (*pagan*), 15 (*Christendom*), 19 (*reformation*), 29 (*renouncing*), 30 (*faith*) and 43 (*converting*); of these terms, only the word *reformation* itself appears in the Holinshed passage from which this scene is drawn (see 19n.).

15 **worn out Christendom** used up every style available in the Christian world; but also implying the threat to Christianity posed by such rampant materialism

---

11] *Pope; F lines* legs, / it, /　12 see 'em] saw 'em *Pope;* saw them *Capell*　13 Or] *Collier;* A *F*
14 to't] *(*too't*); too' F3; too *Rowe*　15.1] *Capell (subst.); after* Lovell *16 F*

What news, Sir Thomas Lovell?
LOVELL   Faith, my lord,
I hear of none but the new proclamation
That's clapped upon the Court Gate.
CHAMBERLAIN   What is't for?
LOVELL
The reformation of our travelled gallants
That fill the court with quarrels, talk and tailors.   20
CHAMBERLAIN
I'm glad 'tis there. Now I would pray our monsieurs
To think an English courtier may be wise
And never see the Louvre.
LOVELL   They must either,

18 **Court Gate** The Court Gate was part
of the fifteenth-century section of York
Place, Wolsey's palace (see 4.1.94, 95n.),
which became Whitehall, and Henry
VIII's main residence, at Wolsey's fall.
Though overshadowed by the newer,
grander 'Holbein Gate' nearby and (in
James I's day) the Banqueting House
next door, it remained a principal
entrance to the palace, was a short distance from Charing Cross, and was a
conspicuous place to post a proclamation (see Thurley, 9–17). It was still in
use (at least notionally) in 1613, as
Chamberlain, in a letter to Dudley
Carleton, 25 March 1613, quotes 'a
flieng report . . . that there is a Bull
come from Rome against the King and
clapt upon the court gate'
(Chamberlain, 1.440).
19 **reformation** One of the courtiers
accused of francophilia by the Privy
Council in 1519 was Sir Henry
Guildford (see Scarisbrick, 161). The
King responded by saying that 'if they
saw anie about him misuse themselves,
he committed it vnto their reformation', and the Council summarily 'banished them the court for diverse considerations' (Holinshed, 852). The

word *reformation* appears to take on
larger significance here.
travelled gallants a current issue in
1613; Foakes (Ard²) quotes Walker,
Sermon, 'trauell did not infect him, nor
strange fashions marre his manners.
. . . O that our Gallants would imitate
the example of this noble Lord. . . .
Verely then they should not rush headlong, as now they doe, into all vice and
irreligion' (G2ʳ⁻ᵛ).
20 **quarrels . . . tailors** Duelling and high
fashion were the general targets of
Jacobean satire of the court. Duelling
seems to have been a particular problem
in 1613, since James I issued his *Edict
. . . against Private Combats* in October
of that year; George Wither complains
in the same year that 'braue gallant men
. . . / Quarrell, and fight with euery one
they meet' (Wither, P1ʳ).
21 **monsieurs** Oxf corrects to '*messieurs*',
but there are almost certainly (mis)pro-
nunciation implications in the inaccurate spelling; cf. 1.1.23.
23 **Louvre** the French court at Paris; pronounced in the English way as 'loover'
23–33 **They . . . playfellows**. On fashion, honour and the French court, cf.
AW 1.2.31–5, 58–63.

21] *Pope; F lines* there; / Monsieurs /   monsieurs] *F; 'messieurs' Oxf*

For so run the conditions, leave those remnants
Of fool and feather that they got in France,   25
With all their honourable points of ignorance
Pertaining thereunto – as fights and fireworks;
Abusing better men than they can be
Out of a foreign wisdom – renouncing clean
The faith they have in tennis and tall stockings,   30
Short blistered breeches, and those types of travel,
And understand again like honest men,

25 **fool and feather** proverbial association (Dent, F451.1); cf. Marston,
Malcontent (1604): 'no foole but haz
his feather' (G4ᵛ). Taylor 1612 (in a
work mentioned by Fletcher in his
verse-letter to the Countess of
Huntington) refers to a 'gallant Gull
. . . / With the great Feather, and the
Beauer Hat' (E4ʳ); Miramont mocks
the fashionable Eustace, whose 'understanding wav'd in a flaunting feather',
in Fletcher, *EB* 5.1.241; in [Beaumont
&?] Fletcher, *LP*, Mark Antonio sav-
ages those whose tastes do not last
'beyond the next fair feather' (2.3.93).
26–7 **their . . . thereunto** the trivia they
consider important; *points* are also laces.
27 **as** such as
fights and fireworks presumably
another reference to duelling, though,
as Foakes notes (Ard²), there is perhaps
satire at the expense of certain aspects
of Princess Elizabeth's wedding here –
the mock-battles staged on the Thames
– which Chamberlain, for instance,
refers to, in a letter of 4 February 1613,
as 'fireworks and fights upon the water'
(Chamberlain, 1.416). *Fireworks* seems
also to have been slang for 'prostitutes'
in their capacity as transmitters of
venereal disease.
29 **wisdom** ironic
30 **tennis** the game, French in origin, now
known as 'real tennis', the original form
of tennis, played on an enclosed court,
from which the modern game derives. It

was highly popular at both the Henrician
and Jacobean courts. An early real tennis
court survives at Hampton Court.
30–1 **tall . . . breeches** fashions associated both with the French (especially
the latter) and with the 1613 marriage
celebrations; Foakes (Ard²) notes that
James himself wore 'a longe stocking'
at the wedding, and Prince Henry had
been portrayed in long hose.
31 **blistered breeches** 'Hose', i.e. leg
garments, consisted of upper and
lower portions, the upper better
known as 'breeches'. *Blistered* breeches
were 'ornamented with puffs' (*OED
ppl. a.* 2), i.e. padded in a manner associated with French fashion; the reference is again anachronistic, since
padded breeches first became fashionable in the later sixteenth century (see
Linthicum, 204–5).
types of travel *Type* here is a distinguishing mark or sign (*OED sb.*¹ 3); thus,
fondness for tennis, tall stockings and
short breeches is a sure sign of the time
these courtiers have spent in France.
32 **understand** triple word-play: (i) use
their brains, (ii) be (proper English)
subjects, and (iii) walk or stand normally (cf. *TN* 3.1.78–9); with a possible additional nod at the audience in a
Jacobean theatre, where the fashionable would sit conspicuously at the
sides of the stage while the ordinary
spectators would either stand below
and around or sit in a gallery

31 blistered] *(*blistred*)*; bolstred *F4*

Or pack to their old playfellows. There, I take it,
They may, *cum privilegio, oui* away
The lag end of their lewdness and be laughed at.   35

SANDYS

'Tis time to give 'em physic, their diseases
Are grown so catching.

CHAMBERLAIN   What a loss our ladies
Will have of these trim vanities!

LOVELL   Ay, marry,
There will be woe indeed, lords. The sly whoresons
Have got a speeding trick to lay down ladies: 40
A French song and a fiddle has no fellow.

---

33 **pack** go away, depart, especially when
summarily dismissed (*OED v.*[1] II 10a)
There i.e. in France
34 *cum privilegio* abbreviated version of
cum privilegio ad imprimendum solum
('with the sole right to print'), a printer's
formula denoting a monopoly of publication; cf. *TS* 4.5.19–20. This tag is used
by Fletcher in ironic contexts. Cf.
Fletcher's manuscript verse-letter to the
Countess of Huntingdon: 'There I am
sure / I should have Brawne, and
Brakett, w[ch] indure / Longer then twentie Tryumphs; and good Swan, / Able to
choake Th'ambition of a churchman, /
And pyes *cum privilegio,* w[th]oute sinne /
forbydding all to Make 'um, but *Ralph
Goodwin*' (Hastings, 13333) (Goodwin
was the Huntingdons' cook); see also
Fletcher, *Capt* 4.4.3–10: 'Her looks are
nothing like her; would her faults / Were
all in Paris print upon her face, / *Cum
Privilegio,* to use 'em still. / I would
write an Epistle before it, on the inside of
her masque, and dedicate it to the whore
of *Babilon*, with a preface upon her nose
to the gentle Reader.'
oui Collier's suggestion, in his 1858 edition, seems the obvious modernization
of F's 'wee', though many editors have
followed F2's clumsy correction 'weare'.
'Wee', though, does sustain the image of

urinating courtiers, along with a possible
hint of venereal disease, picked up
immediately by Sandys. An alternative is
offered in Haughton, *Englishmen for My
Money*: 'I remember my great
Grandfathers Grandmothers sisters
coosen told mee, that Pigges and *Frenchmen*, speak one Language, *awee awee*'
(A4[r–v], TLN 177–9).
35 **lag end** last days
lewdness a range of possibilities: fool-
ishness, wickedness or lasciviousness
(*OED* 1, 2 and 3)
38 **trim vanities** either dapper courtiers
or empty fashions
marry abbreviated oath, 'by the
Virgin Mary'
40 **speeding** rapid, effective
41 **fiddle** a *double entendre*, both a musical
instrument for a serenade and sexual
contact; cf. Field, Fletcher &
Massinger, *HMF*: '*Lam.* You two will
make a pretty hansome Consort. /
Mont. Yes Madam, if my fiddle fail me
not. / *Lam.* Your fiddle? why your fiddle? I warrant thou meanest madly'
(5.1.63–6).
has no fellow cannot be equalled;
proverbial expression. Cf. *MND*
4.1.33; Fletcher, Field & Massinger,
KM 3.1.15 (a Fletcher scene, according
to Hoy, 4.97); Fletcher, *WPl* 3.2.93.

---

34 *oui*] *Collier*[4]; wee *F*; weare *F2*

SANDYS

> The devil fiddle 'em! I am glad they are going,
> For sure there's no converting of 'em. Now
> An honest country lord, as I am, beaten
> A long time out of play, may bring his plainsong   45
> And have an hour of hearing, and, by'r Lady,
> Held current music too.

CHAMBERLAIN   Well said, Lord Sandys.

> Your colt's tooth is not cast yet?

SANDYS   No, my lord,

> Nor shall not while I have a stump.

CHAMBERLAIN   Sir Thomas,

> Whither were you a-going?

LOVELL   To the Cardinal's.   50

> Your lordship is a guest too.

CHAMBERLAIN   O, 'tis true.

> This night he makes a supper, and a great one,
> To many lords and ladies. There will be
> The beauty of this kingdom, I'll assure you.

LOVELL

> That churchman bears a bounteous mind indeed,   55

43 **converting of 'em** changing their minds (with sectarian implication)

44–5 **honest . . . plainsong** Sandys emphasizes his 'simple' uncourtliness in contrast with *trim vanities*; 'court and country' was gradually becoming a recognizable distinction, though it never in James's reign attained the polarized, factional status often ascribed to it; *play*, like *fiddle* (41), is another *double entendre*, music/sex; 'plainsong' is a simple, unadorned melody, contrasted with the more ornamental *French song* (41); cf. *MND* 3.1.124, 'plainsong cuckoo', which suggests a possible further association with cuckoldry (RP).

46 **by'r Lady** by Our Lady; cf. *marry* (38).

47 **current** acceptable, up-to-date **Sandys** F spells the name '*Sands*' here (as elsewhere when it appears in a verse context) to emphasize monosyllabic pronunciation.

48 **colt's tooth** proverbial (Dent, C525) for the lustiness of youth appearing in older men

49 **stump** remains of a tooth; here also signifies 'penis'

52 **makes** provides, gives

55–63 **That . . . ones.** Lovell, Sandys and the Lord Chamberlain are distinctly wry about Wolsey and his magnanimity, implying that his generosity has ulterior motives.

42] *Pope; F lines* 'em, / going, /   47 SP] *(L. Cham.)* Sandys] *(Sands)*   50 a-going] *(a going)*
55] *Pope; F lines* Churchman / indeed /

A hand as fruitful as the land that feeds us:
His dews fall everywhere.
CHAMBERLAIN   No doubt he's noble –
He had a black mouth that said other of him.
SANDYS

He may, my lord; 'has wherewithal. In him
Sparing would show a worse sin than ill doctrine.   60
Men of his way should be most liberal:
They are set here for examples.
CHAMBERLAIN   True, they are so,
But few now give so great ones. My barge stays.
Your lordship shall along. Come, good Sir Thomas,
We shall be late else, which I would not be,   65
For I was spoke to, with Sir Henry Guildford,
This night to be comptrollers.
SANDYS   I am your lordship's. *Exeunt.*

56 **fruitful** generous
57 **His . . . everywhere** a common
enough image of beneficence (cf.
2.4.78, 4.2.133, *Cym* 5.6.352–3, and, as
OT source, Psalm 133.3), but deliberately ambivalent here, playing on
'dues', i.e. impositions, taxes (which
would also be spelt 'dewes', as in F)
58 **black mouth** calumnious, slanderous
mouth; proverbial also for someone on
the verge of death (Dent, M1246.11,
BB11), e.g. Middleton *et al.*, *Old Law*
(1656): 'Now by this hand hees almost
black ith mouth, indeed. / He should
die shortly then' (F3ᵛ), and thus possibly an image for the ruthlessness of
Wolsey's surveillance system (there are
no other examples of this usage in
either the Shakespeare or Fletcher
canons).
59 **'has wherewithal** He has the means.
61 **way** vocation
61–2 **Men . . . examples.** Shaheen suggests that these lines may be 'an indi-

rect reference to the qualifications for
bishops [and elders] as set out in the
NT' (199), e.g. 1 Timothy, 3.2: 'A
bishop therefore must be . . . harber-
ous' (i.e. hospitable); and 1 Peter, 5.3:
'that ye may be ensamples to the
flocke'. The tone is ironic, implying
that it is Wolsey's excessive wealth that
enables him to be so generous.
63 **stays** is waiting
64 **shall along** shall come along; a common early modern ellipsis (Abbott, 293)
65 **else** otherwise; cf. 2.2.21, 133.
66 **spoke to** invited, instructed
   Guildford modernized from F's phonetic *'Guilford'* (probably from
   Holinshed's 'Gilford')
67 **comptrollers** stewards, masters of
   ceremonies; the old spelling is current
   in the US and still used for state office
   in Britain and therefore does not
   require modernizing (see pp. 160–1).
   I . . . **lordship's** i.e. I am your servant;
   I will do as you suggest.

59] *Rowe³; F lines* Lord, / him; / 'has] *Dyce²;* Ha's *F* wherewithal. In] *Pope (*wherewithal; in*);*
wherewithall in *F* 61 way] sway *Collier²* 63] *Rowe³; F lines* ones: / stayes; / 66 Guildford]
Steevens; Guilford F

1.4 *Hautboys. A small table under a state for the Cardinal;*
a longer table for the guests. Then enter ANNE Bullen *and*
diverse other Ladies and Gentlemen, as guests, at one door.
At another door enter Sir Henry GUILDFORD.

GUILDFORD

Ladies, a general welcome from his grace
Salutes ye all. This night he dedicates
To fair content and you. None here, he hopes,
In all this noble bevy has brought with her
One care abroad: he would have all as merry   5
As, first, good company, good wine, good welcome
Can make good people.

1.4 Generally held to be a Fletcher scene (see Appendix 3). It originates in Holinshed's account of a 1527 banquet and masque at York Place, which appeared 'like a princes court for all kind of brauerie & sumptuousnesse' and 'was resorted to with noblemen and gentlemen, feasting and banketting ambassadors diuerse times, and all other right noblie' (921). The scene follows Holinshed quite closely, echoing his distaste for Wolsey's egotistic grandeur, but the occasion is principally engineered to create a first meeting between Henry and Anne, though in fact their relationship was already well established by 1527. They may have met as early as 1520 at the Field of the Cloth of Gold, or even earlier when, aged twelve, Anne was present at the Habsburg court during Henry's visit in 1513 (see Ives, 31, 40), though since Henry had had an affair with Anne's elder sister Mary in the early 1520s, their early acquaintance was not particularly auspicious. This in fact

added to the problems involved in divorcing Katherine and marrying Anne since, as a result of his affair with Mary Boleyn, Henry was technically related to Anne 'in the same degree of affinity as he was related to Catherine by virtue of her first marriage' (Scarisbrick, 215).

0.1 *Hautboys* An 'hautboy' or 'hautbois' was a shawm, a double-reed woodwind instrument (literally, a 'loud-wood'). In the late seventeenth century, the term transferred to the newly introduced 'oboe' or 'French hautbois' (*New Grove*, 17.237).
state Holinshed has 'the lord cardinal sitting vnder a cloth of estate, there hauing all his seruice alone' (922), as a sign of his self-regard. On the throne/state question, see 1.2.8.4n.

0.2 ANNE **Bullen** There is no suggestion in Holinshed that Anne was present at the 1527 banquet.

4 **bevy** a company of maidens or ladies, of quails or of larks (*OED* 1)

5 **abroad** away from home

1.4] *(Scena Quarta.)*   0.1 *Hautboys*] *(Hoboies)*   0.4 GUILDFORD] *Steevens; Guilford F*   1 SP] *Steevens; S. Hen. Guilf. F*   Ladies ... grace] *Pope; F lines* Ladyes, / Grace /   6 first, good] first-good *Theobald;* feast, good *(Staunton);* far as good *Dyce²* (*Halliwell*)

Enter Lord CHAMBERLAIN, Lord SANDYS
and [Sir Thomas] LOVELL.

O my lord, you're tardy.
The very thought of this fair company
Clapped wings to me.

CHAMBERLAIN   You are young, Sir Harry Guildford.

SANDYS

Sir Thomas Lovell, had the Cardinal   10
But half my lay thoughts in him, some of these
Should find a running banquet ere they rested
I think would better please 'em. By my life,
They are a sweet society of fair ones.

LOVELL

O, that your lordship were but now confessor   15
To one or two of these.

SANDYS   I would I were:
They should find easy penance.

LOVELL   Faith, how easy?

SANDYS

As easy as a down bed would afford it.

CHAMBERLAIN

Sweet ladies, will it please you sit? Sir Harry,
Place you that side; I'll take the charge of this.   20
His grace is entering. Nay, you must not freeze:

7.1 **Lord . . . SANDYS** In 1527, at the time of this banquet, Sandys was in fact Lord Chamberlain; but for the purposes of the play the event precedes Buckingham's trial in 1521, at which point the Lord Chamberlain was the Earl of Worcester (Humphreys).

9 **Clapped** attached

11 **lay thoughts** (i) thoughts of someone who is not a priest, (ii) sexual intentions; cf. 1.3.40.

12 **running banquet** buffet, the implica-

tion again being sexual; for an alternative signification, cf. 5.3.62–3.

14 **society** gathering

18 **down** feather

20 **Place** find places for (the guests)

21 **His . . . entering**. The Chamberlain anticipates Wolsey's entrance by thirteen lines: *entering* seems therefore to mean 'about to enter', unless either he is deliberately jumping the gun to get a reaction from the women or there is an implicit cue for entrance music (*haut-*

7.2 Sir Thomas] *Capell*   11 lay thoughts] *(*lay-thoughts*)*   12 banquet] *F4; (*Banket*)*   21 entering] *(*entring*)*

Two women placed together makes cold weather.
My lord Sandys, you are one will keep 'em waking:
Pray sit between these ladies.

SANDYS   By my faith,
And thank your lordship. By your leave, sweet ladies.   25
If I chance to talk a little wild, forgive me:
I had it from my father.

ANNE   Was he mad, sir?

SANDYS

O, very mad – exceeding mad in love, too –
But he would bite none. Just as I do now,
He would kiss you twenty with a breath.

CHAMBERLAIN   Well said, my lord.   30

---

boys, say, as at 34.1) to alert the party-goers to Wolsey's imminent arrival. Montgomery (Oxf) introduces a speculative SD ('*A noise within*').

entering two syllables

22 variant of the expression 'to make fair weather' (Dent, W221); cf., for example, *KJ* 5.1.21.

23 **waking** awake, lively; again, with sexual innuendo

25 **By . . . ladies**. In F, this appears to be preliminary to *If I chance*, but it is best seen (with Pope) as separate, representing Sandys's mock-courtly asking for permission to sit down. Oxf precedes this with a speculative SD: '*He sits between Anne and another*'.

28–9 **mad in . . . none** Sandys's laboured joke conflates proverbial expressions about mad dogs and their tendency to bite and about love as a kind of madness (Dent, L505.2, M2.1, M2.2); cf. Fletcher, *WPl* 4.3.1–2: 'She is mad with love, / As mad as ever unworm'd dogge was.'

29 **bite** Mad people were assumed to have a tendency to bite; madness in general was often particularized in images of

lycanthropy; cf. Fletcher, *Capt* 1.3.164.

30 **kiss you twenty** not the apparent 'kiss you twenty times', but 'kiss twenty women', an example of the 'ethic dative' (verb plus dative pronoun, not indicating that the action described is done to the addressee, but making the narration more immediate and personal), a conventional way to give dialogue a colloquial quality (or to produce comic misunderstanding; see *TS* 1.2.8ff.) (JH).

with a breath in the time it takes to draw a breath. In productions, Anne's response to Sandys's attempt to kiss her generally provides a key to the level of her sexual knowledge.

30–3 **Well . . . frowning**. F's punctuation does not make it clear whether the Chamberlain addresses his first two lines (to *seated*) to Sandys (i.e. 'Well said, sir: I'm pleased I've put you somewhere you're happy') and the rest of his lines (from *gentlemen*) to all the men in the room, as is generally assumed by editors, or whether, as I have assumed here, he addresses just 30 to Sandys and the rest to all the men

---

22 makes] make *Pope*   25 ladies.] *Pope (*ladies;*);* Ladies, *F*   28 mad in] *this edn;* mad, in *F*
29 none. Just] *Pope (*none; just*);* none, iust *F*

258

So, now you're fairly seated, gentlemen,
The penance lies on you if these fair ladies
Pass away frowning.

SANDYS   For my little cure
Let me alone.

Hautboys. Enter Cardinal WOLSEY *and takes his state.*

WOLSEY
You're welcome, my fair guests. That noble lady   35
Or gentleman that is not freely merry
Is not my friend. This, to confirm my welcome;
And to you all, good health!

SANDYS   Your grace is noble:
Let me have such a bowl may hold my thanks
And save me so much talking.

WOLSEY   My lord Sandys,   40
I am beholding to you. Cheer your neighbours.
Ladies, you are not merry. Gentlemen,
Whose fault is this?

SANDYS   The red wine first must rise
In their fair cheeks, my lord; then we shall have 'em

(i.e. 'Now that I have carefully arranged you all next to attractive women, it will be your fault if they go away displeased').

31 **fairly seated** The seating plan is described in some detail by Holinshed: 'then was there set a ladie with a noble man, or a gentleman and a gentlewoman throughout all the tables in the chamber on the one side, which were made and ioined as it were but one table, all which order and deuise was doone by the lord Sandes then lord chamberleine to the king and by sir Henrie Gilford comptroller of the kings maiesties house' (922).

33 **cure** (i) either 'spiritual office' (*OED*

sb.[1] I 4a; thus *confessor* at 15) or 'sphere of spiritual administration' (*OED sb.*[1] I 4b); (ii) remedy (for frowning)

34.1 *state* this time, the chair itself, not the canopy as at 0.1

37–8 **This . . . health!** Theobald first supplied the obvious but unnecessary SD '*Drinks*' after 38.

39 **such a bowl** i.e. full of good wine

41 **beholding** beholden, indebted
   Cheer entertain, amuse

43–4 **The . . . cheeks** Red wine was thought to produce blushing as it supplemented the bloodstream; cf. *TNK*: 'Drink a good hearty draught: it breeds good blood, man' (3.3.17); also Marlowe, *2 Tamburlaine*, 3.2.107–8.

33 cure] Cue *Rowe* 34.1 *Hautboys*] (*Hoboyes*) 35+ SP] (*Card.*) 41 neighbours] neighbour *F2*

Talk us to silence.

ANNE   You are a merry gamester,   45
My lord Sandys.

SANDYS   Yes, if I make my play.
Here's to your ladyship; and pledge it, madam,
For 'tis to such a thing –

ANNE   You cannot show me.

SANDYS

I told your grace they would talk anon.

Drum and trumpet. Chambers discharged.

WOLSEY   What's that?

CHAMBERLAIN

Look out there, some of ye.

WOLSEY   What warlike voice,   50

---

45 **gamester** a player of games, joker, or
rude person
46 **if . . . play** if I score (in the sense both
of winning the game and of sexual
success)
48 **thing** penis
49 **your grace** i.e. Wolsey
anon very soon, straight away
49 SD *Chambers* small cannon used for
ceremonial purposes, presumably fir-
ing blanks. It seems to have been these
blank charges that caused the burning
of the Globe during a performance of
the play (see pp. 9, 57–62). According
to Holinshed, the King came to
Wolsey's house via 'the water gate
without anie noise, where were laid
diuerse chambers and guns charged
with shot, and at his landing they were
shot off, which made such a rumble in
the aire, that it was like thunder' (921).
50–6 **Look . . . princes**. In the wake of
the cannonfire, 'the great chamberleine, and the said comptroller, sent to
looke what it should meane (as though
they knew nothing of the matter) who
looking out of the windowes into the

Thames, returned againe and shewed
him, that it seemed they were noblemen and strangers that arriued at his
bridge, comming as ambassadours
from some forren prince' (Holinshed,
922).
50 **Look . . . ye**. Editors since Capell have
frequently provided an exit line for a
servant here (which also requires an
entry line earlier, either with the guests
or with Wolsey), so that he can run out
to discover what is happening at this
point. This has then required emendation of 52.1 to '*Re-enter a servant*'.
However, Wolsey's order could just as
easily be addressed offstage to an
unseen servant, who then enters for
the first time at 52.1.
50–1 **What . . . this?** Holinshed recounts
how the sudden noise 'made all the
noblemen, gentlemen, ladies, and gentlewomen, to muse what it should
meane, comming so suddenlie, they
sitting quiet at a solemn banket, after
this sort' (921). The dramatized banquet is obviously not so solemn.

---

45 gamester] *F3;* Gamster *F*   49 SD] *Pope; after 48 F*

260

And to what end, is this? Nay, ladies, fear not:
By all the laws of war you're privileged.

Enter a Servant.

CHAMBERLAIN
How now, what is't?
SERVANT   A noble troop of strangers,
For so they seem. They've left their barge and landed,
And hither make, as great ambassadors   55
From foreign princes.
WOLSEY   Good Lord Chamberlain,
Go, give 'em welcome – you can speak the French
    tongue –
And pray receive 'em nobly, and conduct 'em
Into our presence, where this heaven of beauty
Shall shine at full upon them. Some attend him.   60
            [*Exit Lord Chamberlain, attended.*]
    All rise, and tables removed.
You have now a broken banquet, but we'll mend it.
A good digestion to you all, and once more

51–2 **ladies . . . privileged** If it is an attack, the enemy will, according to the rules of warfare, offer violence only to the men.

52.1 Editors since Capell have emended to 'Re-enter', which is logical in the context of the creation of the exit SD two lines previously; see 50n.

53 **strangers** foreigners, the assumption being that they are French; cf. 57 and 56–60n.

55 **make** make their way
    as like

56–60 **Good . . . them.** 'With that (quoth the cardinall) I desire you, bicause you can speake French, to take the paines to go into the hall,

there to receiue them according to their estates, and to conduct them into this chamber, where they shall see vs, and all these noble personages being merie at our banket, desiring them to sit downe with vs, and to take part of our fare' (Holinshed, 922). Wolsey's identification of the masquers as 'French' possibly reveals his complicity in the game; cf. 77–86 (RP).

61 **broken** interrupted
    banquet a sumptuous entertainment of food and drink (*OED sb.*[1] 1); cf. 98n.
    mend put right, rectify (*OED v.* I 3a. *trans.*)

52.1 *Enter*] *Re-enter / Capell*   60 SD] *Capell*   61 banquet] *(*Banket*)*

I shower a welcome on ye. Welcome all!

Hautboys. Enter KING *and others as Masquers, habited like*
shepherds, ushered by the Lord CHAMBERLAIN. *They pass directly*
before the Cardinal and gracefully salute him.

A noble company. What are their pleasures?

CHAMBERLAIN

Because they speak no English, thus they prayed   65
To tell your grace: that having heard by fame
Of this so noble and so fair assembly
This night to meet here, they could do no less,
Out of the great respect they bear to beauty,
But leave their flocks and, under your fair conduct,   70
Crave leave to view these ladies and entreat
An hour of revels with 'em.

WOLSEY   Say, Lord Chamberlain,
They have done my poor house grace; for which I pay
'em

63.1 *Enter . . . Masquers* On the masque
and its contexts, see LN.
   KING For Byrne, in her comments on
the 1949 Guthrie production, 'the
masquing costume gives us at precisely
the right moment the best possible
opportunity of realizing Henry as the
young man in the prime of life' (Byrne,
123).

63.1–2 *habited like shepherds* Pastoral
was the standard alternative realm for
early modern aristocratic fantasy, an
imaginative space in which courtly
structures could be escaped, reproduced and criticized. Shakespeare and
Fletcher had both been involved in the
Jacobean resurgence of popularity for
the pastoral mode, Shakespeare successfully (if circumspectly so) in *WT*
(1610–11) and *Tem* (1611), Fletcher
with less both of caution and of suc-

cess in *FSh*; on the latter, see
McMullan, *Unease*, 55–70.

65–74 **Because . . . pleasures.** '[T]he
lord chamberleine for them said: Sir,
for as much as they be strangers, and
can not speake English, they haue
desired me to declare vnto you, that
they hauing vnderstanding of this
your triumphant banket, where was
assembled such a number of excellent
dames, they could doo no lesse vnder
support of your grace, but to repaire
hither, to view as well their incomparable beautie, as for to . . . danse with
them. . . . To whom the cardinall said
he was verie well content they should
so doo' (Holinshed, 922).

66 **fame** rumour, report

70 **under . . . conduct** with your kind
permission

---

63 shower] (showre) 63.1 *Hautboys*] (Hoboyes) 73–4] *Pope; F lines* grace: / thankes, / pleasures. /

A thousand thanks and pray 'em take their pleasures.
[*The masquers*] *choose ladies. The King* [*chooses*] *Anne*
Bullen.

KING

The fairest hand I ever touched. O Beauty, 75
Till now I never knew thee. *Music. Dance.*

WOLSEY

My lord.

CHAMBERLAIN

Your grace?

WOLSEY Pray tell 'em thus much from me:
There should be one amongst 'em by his person
More worthy this place than myself, to whom,
If I but knew him, with my love and duty 80
I would surrender it.

CHAMBERLAIN I will, my lord.
[*Chamberlain talks in a*] *whisper* [*with the masquers*].

WOLSEY

What say they?

CHAMBERLAIN Such a one they all confess
There is indeed, which they would have your grace
Find out, and he will take it.

WOLSEY Let me see, then.

---

74 SD *choose ladies* The dance begins with
a symmetrical man/woman arrangement which echoes the seating plan.
75–6 **O . . . thee.** an effortless dismissal of
any thought of Katherine
75 **Beauty** abstract quality personified in
Anne
77–81 **Pray . . . it.** 'Then quoth the cardinall to the lord chamberleine, I praie
you (quoth he) that you would shew
them, that me seemeth there should be
a nobleman amongst them, who is more
meet to occupie this seat and place then

I am, to whome I would most gladlie
surrender the same according to my
dutie, if I knew him' (Holinshed, 922).
79 **this place** the chair of state (see
1.2.8.4n.)
82–4 **Such . . . it.** In Holinshed's account,
the Masquers 'confesse, that among
them there is such a noble personage,
whome, if your grace can appoint him
out from the rest, he is content to dis-
close himselfe, and to accept your
place' (922).
84 **take it** sit in the chair of state

74 SD] *Capell (subst.); Choose Ladies, King and An Bullen. F*   81 SD] *Capell (subst.); Whisper. /*
after surrender it *F*

By all your good leaves, gentlemen, here I'll make   85
My royal choice.

KING   Ye have found him, Cardinal.
    [*Unmasks.*]
You hold a fair assembly. You do well, lord:
You are a churchman, or I'll tell you, Cardinal,
I should judge now unhappily.

WOLSEY   I am glad
Your grace is grown so pleasant.

KING   My lord Chamberlain,   90
Prithee come hither. What fair lady's that?

CHAMBERLAIN
An't please your grace, Sir Thomas Bullen's daughter,
The Viscount Rochford, one of her highness' women.

KING
By heaven, she is a dainty one. [*to Anne*] Sweetheart,
I were unmannerly to take you out   95

---

86 **royal choice** In Holinshed's account, interestingly, Wolsey initially picks the wrong Masquer, choosing Sir Edward Neville, 'a comelie knight, that much more resembled the kings person in that maske than anie other' (922), so that the King is obliged to reveal himself. This error is erased here, presumably to demonstrate the (doomed) intimacy of King and Cardinal, and productions traditionally follow suit.

88–9 **You . . . unhappily** If you weren't a clergyman (and therefore above such things), I'd think you had gathered all these beautiful women for your own gratification; cf. 3.2.295–6.

89 **unhappily** unfavourably; critically

90 **so pleasant** so humorous, so inclined to jokes

92 **An't please** if it please (conditional third person singular)

93 **Viscount Rochford** Sir Thomas Bullen was made Viscount Rochford in 1525, i.e. between the date this scene occupies in the play (1521) and its historical date as recorded in the chronicles (1527).
   one . . . women i.e. one of Katherine's ladies-in-waiting; this is not the most tactful description the Chamberlain could offer in the context, but the King does not seem at this point to be suffering from his conscience.

94 **dainty** delicately pretty
   Sweetheart stressed on second syllable (F prints as two words)

95 **I were unmannerly** It would be rude of me. A correlation of manners and manliness is apparent in this remark; see pp. 83–4.
   take you out choose you for a dance

---

86 SD] *Capell (Unmasking)* 92–3] *Pope; F lines* Grace, / *Rochford*, / women. / 93 highness']
Rowe³; Highnesse *F* 94 SD] *Rowe (to Anne Bullen)*

And not to kiss you. A health, gentlemen!
Let it go round.

WOLSEY

Sir Thomas Lovell, is the banquet ready
I'th' privy chamber?

LOVELL   Yes, my lord.

WOLSEY   Your grace,
I fear, with dancing is a little heated.   100

KING

I fear too much.

WOLSEY   There's fresher air, my lord,
In the next chamber.

KING

Lead in your ladies, everyone. Sweet partner,
I must not yet forsake you. Let's be merry,
Good my lord Cardinal. I have half a dozen healths   105
To drink to these fair ladies, and a measure
To lead 'em once again, and then let's dream
Who's best in favour. Let the music knock it.

                              Exeunt with trumpets.

---

96 **kiss** It was customary at the conclusion of a dance for the man to kiss the woman and the woman to curtsy.

97 **Let . . . round.** Everyone is to drink in turn.

98 **banquet** here, a course of sweetmeats, fruit and wine, served as a continuation of the principal meal, usually in a different room (*OED sb.*[1] 3); cf. 61n.

99 **privy chamber** inner room in which one is not liable to disturbance (*OED* 1)

99–102 **Your . . . chamber.** a knowing, coded exchange between Wolsey and Henry; Wolsey hints that Henry might best move on from Anne, and Henry acknowledges that he has been a little

carried away. Henry follows Wolsey's advice up to a point by announcing the move to the banquet in the next room (*Lead in* then referring to the *next chamber*) but then ensures that he does not forfeit Anne's company.

103 **Lead in** i.e. to the *next chamber* for the banquet (see 99–102n.)

106 **measure** a stately dance

107 **once again** i.e. either before or after dinner (see 99–102n.)

108 **best in favour** either the best-looking woman or the person most highly regarded by either the King or the women: it is not clear which **knock it** strike up

---

98 banquet] *(*Banket*)*   105 I have] I've *(RP)*   half] *omitted in Rowe*[2]

2.1   *Enter two* Gentlemen *at several doors.*

1 GENTLEMAN
   Whither away so fast?
2 GENTLEMAN   O, God save ye.
   Even to the Hall to hear what shall become
   Of the great Duke of Buckingham.
1 GENTLEMAN   I'll save you
   That labour, sir. All's now done but the ceremony

2.1 A disputed scene: generally considered Fletcherian, though Hoy, 7 (79) considered it to be Shakespeare's writing reworked by Fletcher (see Appendix 3). The scene explores, and then abruptly finishes with, the fate of Buckingham (faction being subordinate to fashion in this play), and moves on to Katherine's decline and fall. In so doing, it echoes Holinshed's basic structure and often his turns of phrase but, by way of the comments of the gossipy Gentlemen and Buckingham's lengthy and detailed final speeches, expands on Holinshed's ambivalence about Buckingham's guilt and the role of Wolsey in his downfall. The location is a street in Westminster.

0.1 *two* **Gentlemen** The Gentlemen have a semi-choric role here and in 4.1; cf. the two Gentlemen who begin *Cym* by discussing the current state of the royal family and who set the troubled tone of the play (1.1.1–70); the three Gentlemen who describe the events following the rediscovery of Perdita in *WT* (5.2.1–111); and the two Citizens who lament Cromwell's arrest in *Thomas, Lord Cromwell* (F4^{r-v}). Productions, traditionally downplaying the subversive role of the Gentlemen, tend to economize on actors: Byrne notes that Guthrie, for instance, for his 1949 production, gave the second Gentleman's part to Sandys; Doran

(RSC, 1996) conflated the first Gentleman and Sir Thomas Lovell; the 1997 New York production turned the Gentlemen into bitchy Ladies, thereby also (presumably unintentionally) creating gender stereotypes. The Gentlemen's social status is often reduced, as in Davies (RSC, 1983), in which the second Gentleman had a Cockney accent and both put out barriers as if they were functionaries; this pattern – one upstairs, one downstairs, vocally speaking – was repeated in Doran (RSC, 1996), but reversed.
several i.e. separate

1   **Whither . . . fast?** a slightly old-fashioned expression by 1613, which seems often to be used with a touch of irony (Dent, W316.1); cf. Wager, *Enough* (1570), 353: 'What, brother Covetous? whither away so fast?'; *King Leir* (1605), D3^r: 'My honest friend, whither away so fast?' It is difficult to be certain of the dynamic of the dialogic relationship between the Gentlemen, but the First Gentleman is generally subordinate in conversation and is clearly an even fiercer gossip than his friend; in this case, the Second Gentleman is perhaps hoping to avoid him.

2   **Even** monosyllabic
    Hall Westminster Hall, also scene of the trials of Sir Thomas More, of Anne Bullen, and (decades later) of Charles I

2.1] *(Actus Secundus. Scena Prima.)* 1 SP+ 1 GENTLEMAN] *Rowe (1 Gen.);* 1. *F* SP2+ 2 GENTLEMAN] *Rowe (2 Gen.);* 2. *F* 2 Even] *(Eu'n)*

Of bringing back the prisoner.

2 GENTLEMAN   Were you there?   5

1 GENTLEMAN

Yes, indeed was I.

2 GENTLEMAN   Pray speak what has happened.

1 GENTLEMAN

You may guess quickly what.

2 GENTLEMAN   Is he found guilty?

1 GENTLEMAN

Yes, truly is he, and condemned upon't.

2 GENTLEMAN

I am sorry for't.

1 GENTLEMAN   So are a number more.

2 GENTLEMAN   But pray, how passed it?   10

1 GENTLEMAN

I'll tell you in a little. The great Duke
Came to the bar, where to his accusations
He pleaded still not guilty and alleged
Many sharp reasons to defeat the law.
The King's attorney, on the contrary,   15
Urged on the examinations, proofs, confessions,
Of diverse witnesses, which the Duke desired
To have brought *viva voce* to his face;
At which appeared against him his surveyor,

10 **how . . . it** What happened at the trial?
11 **in a little** briefly
11–25 **Duke . . . not** The First Gentleman's account of the trial and of Buckingham's behaviour follows Holinshed closely: there are many direct verbal echoes (see Holinshed, 865).
12 **his accusations** i.e. the accusations brought against him
13 **still** always, consistently
13–14 **alleged . . . reasons** produced a number of good arguments

14 **defeat the law** exonerate himself, resist the charges; though the expression perhaps suggests that the First Gentleman thinks Buckingham guilty
15 **King's attorney** John Fitzjames, later Chief Justice of the King's Bench (Cam[1])
16 **Urged on** emphatically called in evidence
18 *viva voce* Latin expression meaning to speak 'in person' (pleonastic in the context of *to his face*)

8] *Pope; F lines* he, / vpon't. /   18 have] *F4;* him *F*

Sir Gilbert Park his chancellor, and John Court,   20
Confessor to him, with that devil monk,
Hopkins, that made this mischief.

2 GENTLEMAN   That was he
That fed him with his prophecies.

1 GENTLEMAN   The same.
All these accused him strongly, which he fain
Would have flung from him, but indeed he could not.   25
And so his peers, upon this evidence,
Have found him guilty of high treason. Much
He spoke, and learnedly, for life, but all
Was either pitied in him or forgotten.

2 GENTLEMAN
After all this, how did he bear himself?   30

1 GENTLEMAN
When he was brought again to th' bar to hear
His knell rung out, his judgement, he was stirred
With such an agony he sweat extremely

---

20 **Sir** a courtesy title for a priest, not a knight of the realm
*Park I have followed Steevens in modernizing the proper name implied by F, but cf. 1.1.219n.
chancellor a nobleman's secretary (*OED* I 1d, quoting this line)
*John Court See 1.1.216–19n. and 218n.

22 **mischief** harm or evil considered as the work of an agent (*OED sb.* 2a); cf. 66

24 **which** i.e. the accusations made by the witnesses

24–5 **fain / Would** would gladly

26 **his peers** i.e. the other lords. According to Holinshed, Buckingham was 'found giltie of high treason, by a duke, a marques, seuen earles, & twelue barons' (865); the Duke in question, and principal judge, was Norfolk (as Wolsey obliquely reminds him at 3.2.269).

28 **learnedly** three syllables (learnèdly)

28–9 **all . . . forgotten** Nothing he could say could induce anything other than pity in his audience, and for the most part his words had no effect at all.

32 **His . . . judgement** the pronouncement of the death sentence

32–3 **stirred . . . extremely** This detail originates in Holinshed: 'The duke was brought to the barre sore chafing, and swet marvellouslie' (865). But by juxtaposing *agony* and *sweat*, the First Gentleman arguably echoes the language of the Litany, which refers to Christ's 'agonie and bloody Sweate' (*Common Prayer*, B2ᵛ), echoing Luke, 22.44: 'But being in an agonie, he prayed more earnestly: and his sweate was like droppes of blood, trickling downe to the grounde' (see Shaheen, 199); cf. 2.4.205.

33 **such an agony** such inner conflict

20 Park] *Steevens; Pecke* F   Court] *Theobald² (after Holinshed); Car* F   23 prophecies.] prophecies? *Capell*

And something spoke in choler, ill and hasty;
But he fell to himself again, and sweetly   35
In all the rest showed a most noble patience.

2 GENTLEMAN
I do not think he fears death.

1 GENTLEMAN   Sure he does not;
He never was so womanish. The cause
He may a little grieve at.

2 GENTLEMAN   Certainly
The Cardinal is the end of this.

1 GENTLEMAN   'Tis likely,   40
By all conjectures: first, Kildare's attainder,
Then Deputy of Ireland, who removed,
Earl Surrey was sent thither, and in haste too,

---

34 **ill** sour, ill judged
37–9 **I . . . at.** typical of the construction
of exchanges between the Gentlemen:
platitudes from both modulate into
irony from one.
37–8 **fears . . . womanish** Fear was
proverbially a female trait (Dent,
W724.1); cf. *TC* 1.1.103, *RJ* 4.1.119,
and Fletcher & Massinger, *FO* 4.3.157.
40 **end** root cause
41–4 **first . . . father** The Gentlemen
here echo Holinshed's analysis of
Wolsey's tactics: 'bicause he doubted
his freends . . . and cheeflie the earle of
Surrie lord admerall, which had married the dukes daughter, he thought
good first to send him some whither
out of the waie. . . . At length there was
occasion offered him to compasse his
purpose, by occasion of the earle of
Kildare his comming out of Ireland. . . .
[H]e was committed to prison, and
then by the cardinals good preferment
the earle of Surrie was sent into
Ireland as the kings deputie . . . there
to remaine rather as an exile, than as
lieutenant to the king, euen at the cardinals pleasure, as he himselfe well

perceiued' (855); cf. 3.2.260–5. Ireland
was often used as a destination for
unwanted politicians, though in this
case Surrey took up his post there
twelve months before Buckingham's
arrest and trial.
41–3 **Kildare . . . thither** Gerald
Fitzgerald, ninth Earl of Kildare, was
head of the most powerful family in
Ireland, with its strength concentrated
around the English Pale: he held the
post of Lord Deputy, the Crown's
chief representative there, from 1513.
He was summoned to England in 1519
to answer various charges, and Surrey
went out as Lord Lieutenant in May
1520. Kildare was reappointed Lord
Deputy several times, though he eventually died in the Tower in 1534
(Gwyn, 241–50).
41 **attainder** disgrace (not here in the
technical sense of the practical dishonour, loss of property rights, etc., that
follows upon a death sentence); F's
'attendure' is a rare spelling used also
by Holinshed (928), though not in the
immediate source passages for this
scene.

41 attainder] *Rowe;* Attendure *F;* Attaindure *F3*

269

Lest he should help his father.

2 GENTLEMAN   That trick of state
Was a deep envious one.

1 GENTLEMAN   At his return   45
No doubt he will requite it. This is noted,
And generally: whoever the King favours,
The Cardinal instantly will find employment –
And far enough from court, too.

2 GENTLEMAN   All the commons
Hate him perniciously and, o'my conscience,   50
Wish him ten fathom deep. This Duke as much
They love and dote on, call him 'bounteous
     Buckingham,
The mirror of all courtesy' –

Enter BUCKINGHAM *from his arraignment, Tipstaves before
him, the axe with the edge towards him, Halberds on each side,
accompanied with* Sir Thomas LOVELL, Sir Nicholas VAUX,
Lord SANDYS, [*Attendants*] *and Common People.*

---

44 **father** often used, as here, to mean 'father-in-law'
45 **envious** malicious, spiteful
47 **generally** universally, by everyone
     whoever i.e. for whomsoever
47–9 **whoever . . . too** Holinshed mentions, in this regard, Richard Pace (872; cf. 2.2.120–8) and Sir William Compton (878) (Vaughan).
48 **Cardinal** two syllables
49–52 **All . . . on** This passage echoes Holinshed's claims about the relative popularity of Wolsey and Buckingham: 'the cardinall chieflie procured the death of this noble man, no lesse fauoured and beloued of the people of this realme in that season, than the cardinall himselfe was hated and enuied' (864).
50 **perniciously** enough to want him dead (derived from Latin *pernecare*, 'to kill

outright')
53 **mirror . . . courtesy** *Mirror* here means 'model' or 'exemplar'. The phrase comes from Holinshed: 'the floure & mirrour of all courtesie' (870).
53.1 *Tipstaves* court officers appointed to take the accused into custody, named after the staff tipped with metal that was their badge of office
53.2 *the axe . . . him* sign that the accused has been condemned to death
     Halberds i.e. halberdiers; a halberd was a long-handled weapon with both a spear-point and an axe-head.
53.4 ***Lord** SANDYS F has '*Sir Walter Sands*'; I have emended to 'Lord Sandys' for continuity and because of two problems with F: Sandys was ennobled prior to the events depicted in 1.3 and 1.4, but this scene turns back to his-

---

47 And generally:] *Capell;* (And generally) *F*   48 Cardinal] *(Cardnall)*   employment –] imployment, *F*   51 fathom] *(faddom)*   53 courtesy' –] *Steevens;* courtesie. *F*   53.4 Lord] *Bowers; Sir Walter F*   *Attendants . . . People] this edn (see 97 SD); and common people, &c. F; and Others, common people / Capell*

1 GENTLEMAN   Stay there, sir,
And see the noble ruined man you speak of.
2 GENTLEMAN
Let's stand close and behold him.
BUCKINGHAM   All good people,   55
You that thus far have come to pity me,
Hear what I say, and then go home and lose me.
I have this day received a traitor's judgement,
And by that name must die; yet heaven bear witness,
And if I have a conscience, let it sink me,   60
Even as the axe falls, if I be not faithful.
The law I bear no malice for my death –
'T has done upon the premises but justice –
But those that sought it I could wish more Christians.
Be what they will, I heartily forgive 'em.   65
Yet let 'em look they glory not in mischief

torically earlier events; since Holinshed gives Sandys's forename as 'William', F's *'Walter'* may be due to a compositor's erroneous expansion of a 'W' in the manuscript. He does not speak in this scene.

54 **noble ruined man** inversion for 'ruined nobleman'; putting *noble* first emphasizes subjective quality rather than objective rank; cf. 114–15.

55 **close** as near as possible, but also with undertones of silence, secrecy and sympathy

57 **lose me** forget me

58 **traitor's judgement** the death sentence for treason; usually, the graphic violence of hanging, drawing and quartering, but for Buckingham, high in the aristocratic hierarchy, beheading

60 **conscience** the first deployment of many of this word at moments of personal crisis in the play; conscience and judgement seem rarely to coincide
    sink me ruin me

62 **The law** i.e. to the law

63 **upon the premises** carefully phrased

to imply that the judgement was not based on the full facts

64–6 Buckingham is trying his best to voice the Christian platitudes expected of a man facing execution (see Ives, 392, on the conventions within which the condemned person worked), but his resentment is at best barely contained. His words here struggle to invoke the basic Christian principle of forgiveness for enemies (cf. Matthew, 5.44, Colossians, 3.13). Buckingham's speeches as reported by Holinshed (865) are expanded considerably from here to 135, forcing the audience to confront the contradictions of the verdict.

65 **Be . . . will** a proverbial construction ('Whatever they're like') (Dent, B112.1); cf. *R2* 2.1.147, *2H4* 1.2.116.
    heartily with all my heart. Buckingham's next line suggests this is not strictly accurate.

66 **mischief** either 'harm done by an agent' (*OED sb.* 2a) (cf. 22), or 'misfortune' (*OED sb.* 1a), with 'my' understood

56 thus far have] thus have *F2*   62 The law] To th'law *F3*

Nor build their evils on the graves of great men,
For then my guiltless blood must cry against 'em.
For further life in this world I ne'er hope,
Nor will I sue, although the King have mercies   70
More than I dare make faults. You few that loved me
And dare be bold to weep for Buckingham,
His noble friends and fellows, whom to leave
Is only bitter to him, only dying,
Go with me like good angels to my end,   75
And as the long divorce of steel falls on me,
Make of your prayers one sweet sacrifice,
And lift my soul to heaven. Lead on, i'God's name.

LOVELL

I do beseech your grace, for charity,
If ever any malice in your heart   80
Were hid against me, now to forgive me frankly.

BUCKINGHAM

Sir Thomas Lovell, I as free forgive you

---

67 **build . . . men** The primary sense is clear enough – develop their immoral or criminal activities by way of the deaths of prominent men – but *evil* could have a number of obscure meanings at this time, ranging from 'hovel' to 'privy' (*OED sb.*[2], quoting this line as one of two cases); the image of dishonour and shame is, in each case, pervasive.

70–1 **the . . . faults** No matter how awful a crime I were to commit, the King has power to be merciful if he were so to choose.

72 **dare be bold** pleonastic, but reminding us that, once someone has been condemned, sympathy is not permitted

73 **noble** Since Buckingham is addressing a crowd, he is presumably both flattering the *Common People* who make up the bulk of that crowd by referring to them as *noble* and implying the lack of true nobility in his peers who, Norfolk included, have colluded in his death.

74 **only dying** dying alone

76 **long . . . steel** Execution as the divorce of soul and body is a common image (cf. *TN* 3.4.231); here the word *divorce* is, for the audience, replete with foreshadowings, both for Katherine and, most specifically in the context of a beheading, for Anne.

77–8 **Make . . . heaven** a possible echo of Psalm 141.2: 'Let my praier be directed in thy sight *as* incense, & the lifting vp of mine hands *as* an euening sacrifice.'

78 **i'God's name** I have followed Oxf in modernizing F's 'a Gods name' in view of *OED* ''a' *prep.*[1] 10.

79–81 Cf. 1.2.185–6, where the Surveyor reports Buckingham's alleged wish to have Lovell beheaded.

82–3 **I . . . all** Lovell's interruption seems to produce a calmer tone from

---

71] *Rowe*[3]; F lines faults. / me, /   78] *Pope; F lines* Heauen. / name. /   i'] *Oxf*; a F; o' *Theobald*

As I would be forgiven. I forgive all.
There cannot be those numberless offences
'Gainst me that I cannot take peace with. No black envy   85
Shall make my grave. Commend me to his grace,
And if he speak of Buckingham, pray tell him
You met him half in heaven. My vows and prayers
Yet are the King's and, till my soul forsake,
Shall cry for blessings on him. May he live   90
Longer than I have time to tell his years;
Ever beloved and loving may his rule be;
And when old Time shall lead him to his end,
Goodness and he fill up one monument.

LOVELL

To th' waterside I must conduct your grace,   95
Then give my charge up to Sir Nicholas Vaux,
Who undertakes you to your end.

VAUX [*to Attendants*]   Prepare there:

Buckingham, who sticks more closely to
NT sentiment, presumably with an eye
to the afterlife; cf. Matthew, 6.14–15:
'For if ye do forgiue men their trespaces,
your heauenlie father will also forgiue
you. / But, if ye do not forgiue men
their trespaces, no more wil your father,
forgiue *you* your trespaces.'

85 **take** make
86 **make** Hanmer's emendation (from
Warburton's conjecture) to 'mark' is
plausible, certainly more so than
Johnson's suggestion that *take* (85) and
make should be inverted, but there is
no need for emendation: 'I do not wish
to die bearing grudges.'
his grace i.e. the King
89 **forsake** leave me (my body); F4's
addition of 'me' is unnecessary.
93 **Time** a personification
94 **monument** tomb and memorial

97 **undertakes** takes charge of, responsibility for
97–103 **Prepare . . . Bohun.** This scene
returns to Holinshed for the exchanges
between Lovell, Vaux and
Buckingham: 'Then was . . . he led into
a barge. Sir Thomas Louell desired
him to sit on the cushins and carpet
ordeined for him. He said nay; for
when I went to Westminster I was duke
of Buckingham, now I am but Edward
Bohune the most caitife of the world'
(865). Buckingham's surname was
Stafford, which Holinshed gives correctly in a later passage (870). As
Wright noted, he was descended from
the family of Bohun, Earls of
Hereford, through the female line, 'but
Bohun was never the family name of
the Dukes of Buckingham' (127). But
for the relationship between the

85–6] *Pope; F lines* with: / Graue. / Grace: /   take . . . make] take . . . mark *Hanmer (Warburton);* make
. . . take *(Johnson);* take . . . wake *(Vaughan)*   89 forsake] forsake me *F4*   92 beloved] *(*belou'd*)*
97 SD] *Oxf (to an attendant)*

273

The Duke is coming. See the barge be ready,
And fit it with such furniture as suits
The greatness of his person.

BUCKINGHAM   Nay, Sir Nicholas,   100
Let it alone. My state now will but mock me.
When I came hither, I was Lord High Constable
And Duke of Buckingham; now, poor Edward Bohun.
Yet I am richer than my base accusers,
That never knew what truth meant. I now seal it, 105
And with that blood will make 'em one day groan for't.
My noble father, Henry of Buckingham,
Who first raised head against usurping Richard,

Bohuns and the Staffords, and the claim implied in Buckingham's use of the name, see 102n.

99 **furniture** fittings, embellishments

100–35 **Nay . . . me.** The decision of the 1997 New York production to have a young girl in angel's wings, who later reappears as Katherine's angelic vision in 4.2, appear to Buckingham during this speech ignored the deliberate refusal of the play to tell us for certain whether Buckingham is guilty as charged; see 1.1.223n.

102 **Lord High Constable** originally, one of the principal officers of the royal household, whose powers included being commander-in-chief of the army in the absence of the monarch and supreme arbiter of issues of chivalry (*OED* 2b). The post had become a purely ceremonial one by the early sixteenth century, but Buckingham viewed it as his hereditary right, 'being vested in three estates that had been in the Staffords' possession for almost a hundred years, [all three of which] formed part of the Bohun inheritance [which, e]ver since Henry IV's marriage to one of the Bohun heiresses, . . . had caused difficulties between the Stafford family and successive kings of England'

(Gwyn, 166). In this context, 'Buckingham's claim to the throne was no worse than Henry VIII's, . . . [and] the fact that Buckingham's claim to the great constableship also emphasized his royal connection probably did not greatly please the king' (Gwyn, 166); see 107–23n. It is noticeable that the names and titles by which Buckingham refers to himself here are rather different from those accorded him by the Sergeant-at-Arms at 1.1.199–200.

105 **truth** *Truth* here means 'allegiance', but is part of the sequence of references to and invocations of truth that runs throughout the play (see pp. 2–3, 93–106)

106 **will** i.e. which will

107–23 **My . . . service.** The history recounted by Buckingham here is drawn directly from Holinshed's account of the Duke's father (the Buckingham of *R3*), on his downfall, and on the restitution of the dukedom to his son by Henry VII, all of which appears in Holinshed's list of High Constables of England '*which office* ceassed and tooke end at the duke of *Buckingham*' (869–70); the comment on the parallel circumstances of their downfalls does not come from the source.

108 **raised head** began a rebellion

Flying for succour to his servant Banister,
Being distressed, was by that wretch betrayed, 110
And, without trial, fell. God's peace be with him.
Henry the Seventh succeeding, truly pitying
My father's loss, like a most royal prince,
Restored me to my honours and out of ruins
Made my name once more noble. Now his son, 115
Henry the Eighth, life, honour, name, and all
That made me happy at one stroke has taken
For ever from the world. I had my trial,
And must needs say a noble one, which makes me
A little happier than my wretched father. 120
Yet thus far we are one in fortunes: both
Fell by our servants, by those men we loved most –
A most unnatural and faithless service.
Heaven has an end in all. Yet, you that hear me,
This from a dying man receive as certain: 125
Where you are liberal of your loves and counsels,
Be sure you be not loose; for those you make friends
And give your hearts to, when they once perceive
The least rub in your fortunes, fall away
Like water from ye, never found again 130

113 **prince** used in the general sense of
'sovereign ruler' (*OED sb.* I 1a)
114–15 **ruins . . . noble** For this conjunction, see 54.
117 **stroke** i.e. the fall of the execution-
er's axe
119 **must needs say** splendidly ambivalent phrasing: must Buckingham say
this out of justice or obligation?
121–3 **both . . . service** Cf. *When You
See Me*: 'Thus kings & Lords I see, /
Are oft abusde by seruants treacherie'
(E1ᵛ; Wilson TLN 1271–2), a sentiment based on Psalm 41.9.
124 **end** logic, purpose
125 alluding to the belief that people on

the point of death are most likely to
tell the truth
127 **loose** careless
127–30 **friends . . . ye** The basis of the
phrasing here is of Psalm 58.6 in the
Psalter (i.e. Coverdale's) translation
('let them fall away lyke water that
runneth apace'; cf. Job, 6.15), though
the general idea is proverbial (Dent,
R103; Proverbs, 14.20, 19.4).
129 **rub** downturn, snag; a metaphor
drawn from the game of bowls, i.e. an
obstacle by which a bowl is hindered
in, or diverted from, its proper course
(*OED sb.*¹ 2a); cf. *R2* 3.4.4, *Ham* 3.1.67.

116 Eighth] *F4*; Eight *F*

But where they mean to sink ye. All good people,
Pray for me. I must now forsake ye. The last hour
Of my long weary life is come upon me.
Farewell, and when you would say something that is
    sad,
Speak how I fell. I have done, and God forgive me.   135

Exeunt Duke and train.

1 GENTLEMAN

O, this is full of pity. Sir, it calls,
I fear, too many curses on their heads
That were the authors.

2 GENTLEMAN   If the Duke be guiltless,
'Tis full of woe. Yet I can give you inkling
Of an ensuing evil, if it fall,   140
Greater than this.

1 GENTLEMAN   Good angels keep it from us.
What may it be? You do not doubt my faith, sir?

2 GENTLEMAN

This secret is so weighty 'twill require
A strong faith to conceal it.

1 GENTLEMAN   Let me have it;
I do not talk much.

2 GENTLEMAN   I am confident;   145

---

131 **sink** ruin (cf. 60); [Beaumont &?] Fletcher, *LP* 3.2.22; Fletcher, *WPl* 2.3.35
133 **long weary life** melodramatic; Buckingham was in fact forty-three in 1521.
136–9 **it . . . woe** The First Gentleman's immediate response is to assume Buckingham's innocence. The notion that curses can be reflexive was proverbial (Dent, C924), stemming from a range of OT passages (e.g. Joshua, 2.19, Esther, 9.25, Psalm 7.17); cf. *Ham* 5.2.338–9, *R3* 3.4.92–3. The Second Gentleman qualifies this reaction with an *If*, and the Gentlemen's concentration span is shown to be remarkably (and humorously) limited as they move off straightaway into gossip and Buckingham is forgotten: as audience response to the Duke's speech, their attitude is crushing.
139 **inkling** a hint
140 **fall** happen
142, 144 **faith** trustworthiness
145 The First Gentleman's wide-eyed denial of his fondness for political gossip usually gets a laugh in performance: the Second Gentleman's response is presumably ironic, if willing.

134] *Capell lines* Farewel: / sad, /   135] *Pope; F lines* fell. / me. /

You shall, sir. Did you not of late days hear
A buzzing of a separation
Between the King and Katherine?
1 GENTLEMAN   Yes, but it held not,
For when the King once heard it, out of anger
He sent command to the Lord Mayor straight   150
To stop the rumour and allay those tongues
That durst disperse it.
2 GENTLEMAN   But that slander, sir,
Is found a truth now, for it grows again
Fresher then e'er it was, and held for certain
The King will venture at it. Either the Cardinal   155
Or some about him near have, out of malice
To the good Queen, possessed him with a scruple

---

147 **buzzing** rumour, report
    separation Buckingham was convict-
ed and executed in 1521; it was not
until 1527 that rumours began to
appear about a possible divorce. The
two events are juxtaposed as evidence
of Wolsey's constant machinations.
148–52 **Yes . . . it**. Holinshed reports the
beginnings and the suppression of the
divorce rumour: 'There rose a secret
brute in London that the kings confessor doctor Longland, and diuerse other
great clerks had told the king that the
marriage betweene him and the ladie
Katharine, late wife to his brother
prince Arthur was not lawfull:
wherevpon the king should sue a
diuorse, and marrie the duchesse of
Alanson. . . . The king was offended
with those tales, and sent for sir Thomas
Seimor maior of the citie of London,
secretlie charging him to see that the
people ceassed from such talke' (897).
Later, Holinshed seems more inclined
to blame Wolsey than Longland for sow-
ing the seed of divorce.
148 **held not** did not last long
150 **straight** immediately
151 **allay** quell, i.e. quieten, censor (*OED*

$v.^1$ I 9)
152 **disperse** spread about, disseminate
(*OED v.* 6a)
152–5 **slander . . . at it** development of a
proverbial ambivalence over the status
of slander; *RJ* 4.1.33 offers the standard opposition – 'That is no slander,
sir, which is a truth' – but Dent (S520)
quotes Melbanke, *Philotimus* (1583): 'I
had better slaunder them trulye, which
is no Slaunder indeede, then flatter
them falsely as thou doest' (N3^r). The
Second Gentleman's comment underlines the relativity of truth, particularly
in the reporting of royal business, in *H8*
(see pp. 98–103); cf., in a Reformation
context, Drayton 1610: 'What late was
truth conuerted heresie' (201).
154 **held for certain** it is believed true
that
156 **some . . . near** some of the King's
confidants; the Second Gentleman's
vagueness echoes Holinshed's ambivalence (see 148–52n.).
157 **possessed . . . scruple** put a doubt
in his mind. *OED* defines *scruple* (*sb.*^{2}
1) as 'a thought or circumstance that
troubles the mind or conscience'; see
also 2.2.86, 2.4.147, 168.

153 Is found a] Is a sound *F3*

That will undo her. To confirm this, too,
Cardinal Campeius is arrived, and lately,
As all think, for this business.

1 GENTLEMAN   'Tis the Cardinal;   160
And merely to revenge him on the Emperor
For not bestowing on him at his asking
The archbishopric of Toledo this is purposed.

2 GENTLEMAN
I think you have hit the mark. But is't not cruel
That she should feel the smart of this? The Cardinal   165
Will have his will, and she must fall.

1 GENTLEMAN   'Tis woeful.
We are too open here to argue this.
Let's think in private more.   *Exeunt.*

---

158 **undo** destroy, ruin
159 **Campeius** The King 'desired the court of Rome to send into his realme a legat. . . . At whose request the whole consistorie of the college of Rome sent thither Laurence Campeius, a preest cardinall, a man of great wit and experience' (Holinshed, 906). Again, the time compression is severe: Lorenzo Campeggio (latinized to Campeius) reached England in September 1528, seven years after Buckingham's trial. He had previously visited England as legate, again jointly with Wolsey, in 1518 to seek support for a crusade (Ridley, *Henry*, 110).
160 **'Tis the Cardinal** i.e. Wolsey is responsible for this
161–3 Holinshed reports that '[t]he cardinall verelie was put in most blame for this scruple now cast into the kings conscience, for the hate he bare to the emperor, bicause he would not grant to him the archbishoprike of Toledo, for the which he was a suter' (906).

161 **revenge** presumably because anything done to Katherine would be bound to affect and annoy her nephew, Charles V, the Holy Roman Emperor (the ruler, broadly, of what we would think of as Germany)
Emperor Charles V was also King of Spain, and had in 1523 secured from the Pope the right to bestow Spanish bishoprics. He had recently defeated and captured the French king, and had promised to marry Mary, Henry and Katherine's daughter, though he was in fact disinclined to do so. (He would, of course, have been marrying his cousin, but that was not considered a bar to dynastic exchange.)
164 **hit the mark** a proverbial expression for accuracy (Tilley, M667)
165 **smart** pain (*OED sb.*[1] 1b)
167 **too open** indicative of the atmosphere of surveillance and censorship that pervades the play; for *open* as meaning 'public' or 'on display', see 3.2.404.

164] *Pope; F lines* thinke / cruell, /

2.2 *Enter* Lord CHAMBERLAIN, *reading this letter.*

CHAMBERLAIN *My lord, the horses your lordship sent for,*
with all the care I had I saw well chosen, ridden and
furnished. They were young and handsome and of the best
breed in the north. When they were ready to set out for
London, a man of my lord Cardinal's, by commission and 5
main power, took 'em from me with this reason: his master
would be served before a subject, if not before the King,
which stopped our mouths, sir.
I fear he will indeed. Well, let him have them;
He will have all, I think. 10

Enter to the Lord Chamberlain the Dukes of
NORFOLK *and* SUFFOLK.

NORFOLK Well met, my lord Chamberlain.
CHAMBERLAIN Good day to both your graces.
SUFFOLK
How is the King employed?
CHAMBERLAIN I left him private,
Full of sad thoughts and troubles.
NORFOLK What's the cause?
CHAMBERLAIN
It seems the marriage with his brother's wife 15

2.2 Generally considered a Fletcher
scene, though Hoy thought it Shakespeare's writing reworked by Fletcher
(see Appendix 3). The location is a
room at court.

1–8 *My . . . sir.* There is no source for
this letter in Holinshed, but Nichol
Smith suggested one possible point of
origin in *When You See Me*: 'Another
Cittizen there is, complaines / Of one
belonging to the *Cardinall,* / That one
his Maisters name hath taken vp /
Commodities, valued at a thousand

pound' (E1ᵛ; Wilson TLN 1266–8).
Most of this letter (especially the latter
part) can be relined as blank verse,
though no editor has done so to date.
2–3 *ridden and furnished* broken in and
properly equipped
5–6 *by . . . power* by a combination of a warrant and sheer strength. Hamilton suggests contemporary reference here (171).
8 *stopped our mouths* proverbial (Dent,
M1264); cf. *H5* 5.2.270; *Oth* 5.2.71;
KL 5.3.152–3; Fletcher, *WWM* 5.3.47.
14 **sad** serious

2.2] *(Scena Secunda.)* 1 SP] *Capell; not in F* 9–10] *Theobald; prose F*

Has crept too near his conscience.

SUFFOLK   No, his conscience

Has crept too near another lady.

NORFOLK   'Tis so;

This is the Cardinal's doing. The King–Cardinal,

That blind priest, like the eldest son of Fortune,

Turns what he list. The King will know him one day.   20

SUFFOLK

Pray God he do. He'll never know himself else.

NORFOLK

How holily he works in all his business,

And with what zeal! For now he has cracked the league

Between us and the Emperor, the Queen's great
     nephew,

He dives into the King's soul and there scatters   25

Dangers, doubts, wringing of the conscience,

Fears and despairs – and all these for his marriage.

And out of all these, to restore the King,

He counsels a divorce, a loss of her

That like a jewel has hung twenty years   30

16–17 **No . . . lady** *Conscience* begins here
to acquire the sexual connotations that
it bears in the rest of the play. It is
unclear if Suffolk's ironic observation
is, as Vaughan conjectured, an aside,
since Norfolk's *'Tis so* could (both in
sense and metrically) be a response
either to Suffolk or to the Lord
Chamberlain. It is also unclear if
Suffolk has Anne Bullen specifically in
mind as he makes this remark or is simply thinking of Henry's general suscep-
tibility, especially since Norfolk goes on
to talk about Wolsey's plans for Henry
to marry the Duchess of Alençon (40).

18 **King–Cardinal** It is effectively no
longer clear who is the *de facto* head of
state. The compound is akin to
Count–Cardinal at 1.1.172.

19–20 **That . . . list** *blind* presumably in

the sense of being careless of the
state's well being as well as inheriting,
in his capacity as *eldest son*, the attributes of Fortune, including her blind-
ness and her wheel

20 **Turns** i.e. Fortune's wheel; with the
implication that Wolsey determines
others' futures
list desires, wishes (*OED v.*[1] 2)

21 **He'll . . . else.** Cf. 133 and 1.3.65n.
know himself ancient proverbial
expression (Dent, K175): 'Ovid gives
Pythagoras as the author of this rule;
Socrates in Plato thinks it started with
Apollo', Erasmus, 1.6.95: 'Nosce teip-
sum' ('Know thyself'); cf. 3.2.378;
AYLI 3.5.57; *AC* 2.1.5; *Cor* 2.1.66.

24 **nephew** See 2.1.161n.

26 **wringing . . . conscience** guilt, remorse

28 **the King** i.e. the King's peace of mind

16 SP] SUFFOLK *aside (Vaughan)*   21] *Pope; F lines* doe, / else. /   22 his] this *Capell*

About his neck yet never lost her lustre;
Of her that loves him with that excellence
That angels love good men with; even of her
That, when the greatest stroke of Fortune falls,
Will bless the King – and is not this course pious?   35
CHAMBERLAIN
Heaven keep me from such counsel! 'Tis most true:
These news are everywhere – every tongue speaks 'em,
And every true heart weeps for't. All that dare
Look into these affairs see this main end:
The French king's sister. Heaven will one day open   40
The King's eyes, that so long have slept upon
This bold bad man.
SUFFOLK   And free us from his slavery.

---

34 **stroke** Cf. Buckingham's use of the word to denote execution at 2.1.117.
35 **course** i.e. of action
36 **counsel** This may refer, 'following the sarcastic mention of piety at 35, to the theological concept of the counsels or precepts of Christ in the gospels which the churchman, Wolsey, seems to be denying in offering such advice' (Cam²).
37 **news** new occurrences as a subject of report or talk (*OED sb. (pl.)* 2a); tends to be treated as singular in modern English, but could be construed as either singular or plural in the seventeenth century
38 **true** again, a pointed invocation of 'truth', meaning 'loyal'
39 **main end** principal goal
40 **French King's sister** According to Holinshed, Wolsey 'sought a divorce betwixt the king and the queene, that the king might haue had in marriage the duchesse of Alanson, sister vnto the French king' (906); cf. 3.2.85–6, 4.2.82.1 LN.
41 **slept upon** failed to notice the crimes of
42–3 **This . . . pray** It is not clear from F, which provides three part-lines ranged left (as it generally does both with lines which are metrically incomplete and

with the component parts of divided verse lines), whether these lines should be retained as separate part-lines or, as here, a part-line and a divided line, or, if the latter, which of the Chamberlain's or Norfolk's part-lines should form the complete line with Suffolk's part-line. Pope chose to make 43–4 into one line, omitting *our* for metrical reasons. I have opted to form a complete verse line without altering F's half-line structure, and since each of the two alternatives works equally well metrically speaking, I have preferred the combination of the Chamberlain's and Suffolk's part-lines since it seems to me both that Suffolk's *And* conjoins his desire for liberty with the Chamberlain's frustration at royal inactivity and that the resultant pause after *pray* places emphasis on prayer as the only apparent option in face of Wolsey's political dominance.
42 **bold bad man** cf. its opposite, *bold brave gentleman*, at 4.1.40; a common-place phrase, perhaps originally coined by Spenser, *Faerie Queene* (1.1.37), not found elsewhere in Shakespeare, but later used by Fletcher in the plural: see *LS* (1618), 4.5.90.

39 this] his *F4*

NORFOLK   We had need pray,
And heartily, for our deliverance,
Or this imperious man will work us all   45
From princes into pages. All men's honours
Lie like one lump before him, to be fashioned
Into what pitch he please.
SUFFOLK   For me, my lords,
I love him not nor fear him: there's my creed.
As I am made without him, so I'll stand,   50
If the King please. His curses and his blessings
Touch me alike: they're breath I not believe in.
I knew him and I know him; so I leave him
To him that made him proud, the Pope.
NORFOLK   Let's in,
And with some other business put the King   55
From these sad thoughts that work too much upon him.
My lord, you'll bear us company?
CHAMBERLAIN   Excuse me;
The King has sent me otherwhere. Besides,

46 **princes into pages** Holinshed provides various (not always credible) examples of Wolsey's arrogance, e.g. 'Before masse, two barons gave him water, and after the gospell two earles; and at the last lavatorie, two dukes' (873).

46–8 **All . . . please**. Wolsey has total control over the maintenance, elevation or degradation of the aristocracy; the phrase echoes Romans, 9.21 ('Hath not the potter power over the clay, euen of the same lumpe to make one vessel vnto honour, and another vnto dishonour'); see also Wisdom, 15.7.

48 **pitch** appears, in context, to mean 'shape, manner', though the nearest definition in *OED* (*sb.*[2] *v.* 22a) is only approximate ('comparative height or intensity of any quality or attribute') *OED* (*sb.*[1] 1) 'tar' is also relevant; cf. *Oth* 2.3.355

49 **there's my creed** The word *creed*

does not appear in Shakespeare's solo plays, but cf. Fletcher, verse-letter to countess of Huntingdon: 'as I knowe that creede / I take from' (ll. 12–13; see McMullan, *Unease*, 17–18).

50–1 **As . . . please**. Extending Norfolk's pottery metaphor from 46–8, Suffolk makes it clear that his own nobility is not subject to Wolsey's will, and that the only person who can alter that state of affairs is the King.

50 **stand** stand firm; stay as I am; retain my rank

54 **Pope** instead of the expected word, 'Devil' (Cam[1])

58 **otherwhere** elsewhere. The obvious question is where. The answer presumably comes in the next scene when the Lord Chamberlain arrives to tell Anne Bullen of her new status. Henry's conscience is not so troubled with 'sad thoughts and troubles' (14)

43–4] *one line in Pope, omitting* our   47 Lie like] Lie in *Steevens–Reed*[2]

You'll find a most unfit time to disturb him.

Health to your lordships.

NORFOLK   Thanks, my good lord Chamberlain.   60

Exit Lord Chamberlain, and the King draws the curtain
and sits reading pensively.

SUFFOLK

How sad he looks. Sure he is much afflicted.

KING

Who's there? Ha?

NORFOLK   Pray God he be not angry.

KING

Who's there, I say? How dare you thrust yourselves

Into my private meditations?

Who am I? Ha?   65

NORFOLK

A gracious king that pardons all offences

Malice ne'er meant. Our breach of duty this way

that he stops making plans for Anne. The Doran production (RSC, 1996) made this explicit by having Henry give the Lord Chamberlain a purse at the beginning of this scene, which he then hands to Anne in 2.3. The mission also enables the Lord Chamberlain to avoid going back to face the King, whom he knows to be in a foul mood.

59 Cf. the Chamberlain's earlier comment on the King's mood at 13–14.
   find with ellipsis of 'it'
60 **Thanks** presumably said ironically, since the Chamberlain is demonstrating his skill at avoiding being in the wrong place at the wrong time (which eventually deserts him at 5.2.143)
60.1 KING . . . *curtain* The King is revealed to be sitting inside the 'discovery space', concealed by a curtain which is drawn to reveal him. Since he

is furious that his privacy has been disturbed, it seems incongruous that he should himself draw the curtain (as stated in F SD), and editors since Rowe have offered a range of other possibilities derived from the theatrical practice of their time. Presumably, as the King rages at the Dukes, he comes forward onto the platform stage.

62, 65 **Ha?** See 1.2.186n.
63–4 **How . . . meditations?** Cf. 1.2.210 and n. Again, the language of intrusion into royal space and passivity is implicitly sexual.
65 **Who am I?** rhetorical question demanding acknowledgement of authority (Dent, W318.1); cf. *KL* 1.4.76 and Wager, *Longer* (1580): 'No cappe of, no knee bowed, no homage, / Who am I:' (D3ᵛ).
67 **this way** in this regard

60.1 SD] *F; The Scene draws, and discovers the King sitting and reading pensively. / Rowe; They go towards the Door: Door opens; and the King is discover'd, sitting at a Table, pensively, and reading. / Capell*

Is business of estate, in which we come
To know your royal pleasure.
KING   Ye are too bold.
Go to. I'll make ye know your times of business.   70
Is this an hour for temporal affairs? Ha?

Enter WOLSEY *and* CAMPEIUS *with a commission.*

Who's there? My good lord Cardinal? O my Wolsey,
The quiet of my wounded conscience,
Thou art a cure fit for a king. [*to Campeius*] You're
    welcome,
Most learned reverend sir, into our kingdom;   75
Use us and it. [*to Wolsey*] My good lord, have great
    care
I be not found a talker.
WOLSEY   Sir, you cannot.
I would your grace would give us but an hour
Of private conference.
KING [*to Norfolk and Suffolk*]   We are busy. Go.
NORFOLK [*aside to Suffolk*]
This priest has no pride in him!
SUFFOLK [*aside to Norfolk*]   Not to speak of.   80

---

68 **estate** i.e. state
71 **temporal** worldly (as opposed to
'spiritual') (*OED a.*[1] 2); see also 2.3.13.
71.1 *commission* See 102–5n.
73 **quiet of** salve for
74 **cure** remedy, with an undertone of
spiritual concern (*OED sb.*[1] II and I);
cf. different usage but similar undertone at 1.4.33.
76 **Use . . . it** 'Take full advantage of my
authority and of the resources of the
kingdom.' *Use* had multiple significa-
tions in this period, some of them neg-

ative, but Henry is here simply exer-
cising royal magnanimity.
77 **talker** proverbial: 'The greatest talk-
ers are the least doers' (Dent, T64); cf.
R3 1.3.349. Henry is ordering Wolsey
to ensure that all necessary resources
are made available to Campeius.
79 **private conference** conversation
only for the ears of Henry and the
Cardinals. Wolsey finds yet another
way to be offensive to the nobles.
80 furious irony from Norfolk and Suffolk
This priest i.e. Wolsey

---

74 a king] the King *F2* SD] *Theobald* 76 SD] *Johnson* 79 SD] *Theobald* 80 SD *aside to*
Suffolk] *Capell (subst.)* SD2 *aside to Norfolk*] *Capell (subst.)*

I would not be so sick, though, for his place.
But this cannot continue.
NORFOLK [*aside to Suffolk*]   If it do,
    I'll venture one have-at-him.
SUFFOLK [*aside to Norfolk*]   I another.
                         Exeunt Norfolk and Suffolk.
WOLSEY
    Your grace has given a precedent of wisdom
    Above all princes in committing freely   85
    Your scruple to the voice of Christendom.
    Who can be angry now? What envy reach you?
    The Spaniard, tied by blood and favour to her,
    Must now confess, if they have any goodness,
    The trial just and noble. All the clerks –   90
    I mean the learned ones in Christian kingdoms –
    Have their free voices. Rome, the nurse of judgement,
    Invited by your noble self, hath sent
    One general tongue unto us: this good man,

---

81 I would not be so appallingly proud
even to have all of his power.

83 *have-at-him F's 'one; haue at him'
gives 'have at him' its customary role
as an exclamation but leaves an incomplete sentence in *I'll venture one*;
Dyce's suggestion, after Boswell, that
have-at-him is a noun coined from the
exclamation makes much more sense
of the whole line.

84–96 Your . . . highness. If the authorial attribution is accurate, Fletcher has
kept his Holinshed open at the same
place as at 2.1.159: 'the king . . . called
togither the best learned of the realme,
which were of severall opinions.
Wherfore he thought to know the
truth by indifferent iudges, least
peraduenture the Spaniards, and other

also in fauour of the queene would
saie, that his owne subiects were not
indifferent iudges in this behalfe. And
therefore he wrote his cause to Rome,
and also sent to all the vniuersities in
Italie and France, and to the great
clearkes of all christendome, to know
their opinions' (906); cf. 2.1.159n.

86 scruple worry that marrying Katherine
was against God's will; see 2.1.157n.
voice judgement or vote; cf. 92, where
voices clearly means votes.

87 envy malice, ill will
88 Spaniard singular for plural
90 clerks clerics and/or scholars
91, 95, learned learnèd
92 Have . . . voices may vote freely
94 One general tongue a representative
voice

81 sick, though,] *Rowe²* *(subst.)*; sick though *F*; sick, though *F4*   82 SD] *Capell (subst.)*   82–3 If . . .
have-at-him] *Pope; one line F*   83 one have-at-him] *Dyce (Boswell subst.)*; one; haue at him *F*; one heaue
at him *F2*   SD *aside to Norfolk*] *Capell (subst.)*   84 precedent] *(*President*)*   92 Have] Gave *White*

This just and learned priest, Cardinal Campeius,   95
Whom once more I present unto your highness.
KING
And once more in mine arms I bid him welcome,
And thank the holy conclave for their loves:
They have sent me such a man I would have wished
      for.
CAMPEIUS
Your grace must needs deserve all strangers' loves,   100
You are so noble. To your highness' hand
I tender my commission, by whose virtue,
The court of Rome commanding, you, my lord
Cardinal of York, are joined with me their servant
In the unpartial judging of this business.   105
KING
Two equal men. The Queen shall be acquainted
Forthwith for what you come. Where's Gardiner?
WOLSEY
I know your majesty has always loved her
So dear in heart not to deny her that
A woman of less place might ask by law –   110
Scholars allowed freely to argue for her.

95 **Cardinal** two syllables
98 **conclave** collective noun for cardinals; this is the first example cited in _OED_ loosely to describe 'the body of cardinals' rather than specifically to mean the assembly of cardinals for the election of a new pope.
100 **strangers'** foreigners'; cf. 1.4.53, 2.3.17.
102–5 **commission . . . business** 'The college of Rome sent thither Laurence Campeius, a preest cardinall . . . and with him was joined in commission the cardinall of Yorke' (Holinshed, 906).
105 **unpartial** a version of 'impartial', very common from _c._ 1590 to _c._ 1660

(_OED a._ 1a), but not found in any other play in either the Shakespeare or the Fletcher canon
106 **equal** equally impartial; Henry may also be quietly reminding Campeius that coming from Rome to join with Wolsey for the divorce business did not necessarily give him precedence over the English Cardinal.
107 **Gardiner** Further time-compression: Stephen Gardiner, later Bishop of Winchester (see 5.2.92), replaced Richard Pace as the King's secretary on 28 July 1529; see 120n.
109 **that** i.e. that which
110 **less place** lower status

95 Cardinal] _(Card'nall)_   103 commanding, you] _F4;_ commanding. You _F_   105 unpartial] impartiall _F3_

KING

    Ay, and the best she shall have – and my favour

    To him that does best: God forbid else. Cardinal,

    Prithee call Gardiner to me, my new secretary:

    I find him a fit fellow.   115

Enter GARDINER.

WOLSEY [*aside to Gardiner*]

    Give me your hand. Much joy and favour to you;

    You are the King's now.

GARDINER [*aside to Wolsey*]   But to be commanded

    For ever by your grace, whose hand has raised me.

KING   Come hither, Gardiner.

    [*The King*] *walks and whispers* [*with Gardiner.*]

CAMPEIUS

    My lord of York, was not one Doctor Pace   120

    In this man's place before him?

WOLSEY   Yes, he was.

CAMPEIUS

    Was he not held a learned man?

WOLSEY   Yes, surely.

---

115 **fit** suitable, useful

120 **Pace** Holinshed reports that '[a]bout this time the king receiued into fauour doctor Stephan Gardiner, whose seruice he vsed in matters of great secrecie and weight, admitting him in the roome of doctor Pace, the which being continuallie abroad in ambassages, and the same oftentimes not much necessarie, by the cardinals appointment, at length he tooke such greefe therewith, that he fell out of his right wits' (907). Wolsey had two principal secretaries, Richard Pace and William Burbank. Pace, who became Dean of St Paul's in 1519, was deployed by Henry VIII as an ambas-

sador to Rome in 1524 to try to secure Wolsey's accession to the papacy, but by 1524–5, suffering from accelerating mental illness, he had begun to criticize Wolsey in public (Gwyn, 553). The implication that Wolsey was responsible for his death is absent from Holinshed – anyway, Pace did not die until 1536 – but by 1528 he was in custody at Beaulieu and considered quite mad (Gwyn, 554). Pooler (Ard[1]) notes that Pace was imprisoned several times while on embassies on the Continent, which may well have contributed to the deterioration of his health.

122 **learned** learnèd

116 SD] *Capell (subst.)*   117 SD] *Capell (subst.)*   119 SD] *(Walks and whispers.)*

CAMPEIUS

Believe me, there's an ill opinion spread, then,

Even of yourself, lord Cardinal.

WOLSEY   How? Of me?

CAMPEIUS

They will not stick to say you envied him,   125

And fearing he would rise – he was so virtuous –

Kept him a foreign man still, which so grieved him

That he ran mad and died.

WOLSEY   Heaven's peace be with him:

That's Christian care enough. For living murmurers

There's places of rebuke. He was a fool,   130

For he would needs be virtuous.

[*Gestures towards Gardiner.*]   That good fellow,

If I command him, follows my appointment.

I will have none so near else. Learn this, brother:

We live not to be griped by meaner persons.   134

KING

Deliver this with modesty to th' Queen.   *Exit Gardiner.*

---

125 **stick to say** refrain from saying

127 **foreign man** i.e. kept him away from court; cf. 120n.

127–8 **grieved . . . died** Fletcher's own father, Richard Fletcher, Bishop of London, was reported to have died from grief at being out of favour at court: 'he lost the *Queens favour*, . . . and died suddainly, more of grief then any other disease' (Fuller, 9.233; McMullan, *Unease*, 9–11).

128–34 **Heaven's . . . persons**. This passage makes Wolsey's Machiavellianism overt, and he clearly assumes his interlocutor will not demur, a thoroughly Protestant assumption about cardinals.

128 **Heaven's** monosyllabic

129–30 **For . . . rebuke**. Wolsey is effectively acknowledging the public opinion that he kept Pace away from the King: *murmurers* embraces anyone

who disagrees with his policies. It was common Renaissance practice for rulers to send their political opponents on long foreign embassies (as we have already seen in the case of Surrey at 2.1.40–6): James I, for instance, kept Sir Thomas Roe, friend to Fletcher's patron the Earl of Huntingdon, away from England for much of his career.

129 **murmurers** grumblers, complainers

132 **appointment** instructions, directions

133 **near** familiar, intimate, i.e. with the King

134 **griped** clutched at (and thus pulled down) (*OED v.*[1] 1a); cf. 5.2.134.

meaner socially inferior

135 **Deliver . . . modesty** Henry is keen that the message he sends by Gardiner should not in any way be provocative or triumphant.

128 Heaven's] (Heau'ns)   131 SD] *Capell (subst.)*

The most convenient place that I can think of
For such receipt of learning is Blackfriars:
There ye shall meet about this weighty business.
My Wolsey, see it furnished. O my lord,
Would it not grieve an able man to leave   140
So sweet a bedfellow? But conscience, conscience –
O, 'tis a tender place, and I must leave her.   *Exeunt.*

2.3   *Enter* ANNE Bullen *and an* Old Lady.

ANNE
Not for that neither. Here's the pang that pinches:

136–7 **convenient** . . . **Blackfriars**
Blackfriars, as its name suggests
(Dominican monks wear black robes),
was a Dominican friary prior to the dissolution of the monasteries. It was
convenient in two senses: its hall was
large enough to accommodate the necessary personnel for a legatine court
and it was connected via a gallery (pas-
sageway) to the royal palace at
Bridewell (see 3.1 headnote). To the
Jacobean audience, Blackfriars was not
only the venue for the divorce hearing,
but also the 'private' (i.e. indoor) theatre recently occupied by the King's
company: the first performances of the
play may well have taken place there
(see pp. 9–10). The effect of the word
on the audience would presumably be
similar to that on the Globe audience at
H5 Prologue 13, and *Tem* 4.1.153.
137 **For** . . . **learning** in which to hear
the scholars' arguments
139 **furnished** prepared, equipped (*OED
ppl. a.* c); possibly also with the more
general sense of 'accomplished' or
'brought about' (*OED v.* 1)
140 **able** sexually potent
141 **bedfellow** i.e. Katherine. This is the
only time in the play when Henry
speaks of his wife in terms of compan-
ionship and sexual pleasure rather

than conscience and reproduction.
141–2 **conscience** . . . **tender** proverbial
(Dent, C598); cf. 2.4.167.
142 **tender place** one of the moments in
the play in which conscience and vagina become curiously synonymous (see
pp. 80–1; also 2.3.32, 66–7); Henry
unintentionally expresses the dominance of the sexual over the spiritual
in his internal motivations.
2.3 Generally considered a Shakespeare
scene (see Appendix 3). The relationship – especially the bawdy talk – of
Anne and the Old Lady draws on
Terentian tradition via that of Juliet
and the Nurse in *RJ*, but is also
indebted to Rojas's *Celestina* (see
Round), first dramatized for the
English stage in John Rastell's *Calisto
and Melibea* (1516–33). The location is
'a room in the Queen's apartments'
(Theobald subst.).
1 **Not** . . . **neither**. Anne's opening
words are her response to an unheard
remark by the Old Lady about
Katherine's plight; but if Anne and the
Old Lady are already entering as Henry
is leaving the stage, Anne's negative
can sound like a direct rejection of
Henry's hypocrisy about his conscience
at 2.2.142 (i.e. 'no, you're not leaving
her because of your conscience').

2.3] *(Scena Tertia.)*

His highness having lived so long with her and she
So good a lady that no tongue could ever
Pronounce dishonour of her – by my life,
She never knew harm-doing – O, now, after   5
So many courses of the sun enthroned,
Still growing in a majesty and pomp the which
To leave a thousandfold more bitter than
'Tis sweet at first t'acquire – after this process,
To give her the avaunt, it is a pity   10
Would move a monster.

OLD LADY   Hearts of most hard temper
Melt and lament for her.

ANNE   O, God's will! Much better
She ne'er had known pomp: though't be temporal,
Yet if that quarrel and Fortune do divorce

---

pang a shooting pain; hence, figuratively, a sudden sharp mental pain or feeling of intense mental anguish (*OED sb.* 1 and 2); see also 15 and 3.2.370.
pinches i.e. tortures; much harsher than it sounds (see Breight, 24–7)
4   **Pronounce** declare, make public
6   **courses . . . sun** years; the sun was thought to revolve around the earth.
7   This line appears to be an alexandrine (twelve syllables), unless either *growing in a* or *majesty and* is elided to two syllables.
7–9 **the . . . t'acquire** which is vastly more painful to lose than it is enjoyable to get in the first place
9   **process** history (of the royal relationship)
10 **avaunt** order to be off, to depart (*OED sb.*[2])
11 **monster** Cf. *WT* 4.4.770.
13 **temporal** wordly, as opposed to spiritual, and therefore (supposedly) not as important; see 2.2.71n.
14 ***quarrel . . . do** Foakes's suggestion

(Ard[2]) that F's full stop is a compositor's misreading of a vague ampersand makes acceptable sense of an otherwise unresolvable crux, and his worry that *quarrel* would then indicate a direct reference to Katherine and Henry which is dissipated into the generalized *bearer* (15) seems unfounded; this would not, after all, be the only point in this play of surveillance and unease at which fear of offence can be seen to modify a speech in progress. 'Cruel' in Collier[2] makes good sense, but is difficult to derive plausibly from 'quarrel'; Staunton's 'squirrel' (meaning 'prostitute') is entertainingly far-fetched; only Johnson's argument that 'quarrel' is the abstract noun substituted for the agent 'quarreller' carries conviction, though it still leaves an uncomfortable line. Bowers provides an alternative defence of 'quarreller', suggesting that '[a]n outside chance may exist that Compositor *I*, who had a high tolerance for intrusive strong stops, mistook

---

7–8] *Pope lines* pomp, / bitter /   14 quarrel . . . do] *this edn (Ard[2]);* quarrell. Fortune, do *F;* quarrel, Fortune, do *F2;* quarr'lous fortune do *(Warburton);* quarr'ler fortune do *Hanmer;* quarrel fortune to *(Steevens);* cruel fortune do *Collier[2]*

It from the bearer, 'tis a sufferance panging 15
As soul and body's severing.

OLD LADY   Alas, poor lady,
She's a stranger now again.

ANNE   So much the more
Must pity drop upon her. Verily,
I swear, 'tis better to be lowly born
And range with humble livers in content 20
Than to be perked up in a glistering grief
And wear a golden sorrow.

OLD LADY   Our content
Is our best having.

ANNE   By my troth and maidenhead,
I would not be a queen.

OLD LADY   Beshrew me, I would,
And venture maidenhead for't; and so would you, 25
For all this spice of your hypocrisy.

a scribbled "er" for some punctuation, which he translated as a full stop'; in which case perhaps the missing word is 'or' (RP).

14–16 divorce . . . severing In the heavy irony (for the audience) of these remarks, divorce and execution are again seen as effectively interchangeable; see 2.1.76n.

15 sufferance suffering, pain
panging (as) painful (see 1n.)

17 stranger foreigner; cf. 1.4.53, 2.2.100.

18 verily another questionable assertion of truth

20 range . . . livers be aligned with those of low status

21 perked spruced, trimmed ('as a bird does its plumage') (*OED v.*[1] II *trans.* 2a)
glistering sparkling, glittering (*OED ppl. a*); two syllables

22–3 Our . . . having. a splendidly pious (and, as we discover, utterly hypocritical) platitude from the Old Lady.

23 By . . . maidenhead At 23 and then at 33, Anne uses *troth* as a 'form of asseveration' (*OED sb.* I 1b); at 34, the Old Lady twists it slightly to mean 'truth' (*sb.* II 4); it also holds a residual sense of 'troth' as a promise to marry (*sb.* 2); and cf. *Verily* at 18. We have already seen the equation of conscience and vagina at 2.2.141–2; here *troth* is awkwardly equated with virginity even as it brings thoughts of marriage to mind. Does this mean 'experience' moves a person beyond a simple, clear form of 'truth'? In this context, 'by my maidenhead' would appear a rash oath from Anne, bearing in mind the fondness for the extended sexual pun that the Old Lady shows as the scene progresses.

24 Beshrew me May evil strike me (if I'm lying).

25 venture maidenhead risk my virginity

26 despite the flavour of hypocrisy in what you say

16 body's] *(bodies)*   21 glistering] *(glistring)*

You, that have so fair parts of woman on you,
Have, too, a woman's heart which ever yet
Affected eminence, wealth, sovereignty;
Which, to say sooth, are blessings; and which gifts –　　30
Saving your mincing – the capacity
Of your soft cheverel conscience would receive,
If you might please to stretch it.

ANNE　　　　　　　　　　　　　　　Nay, good troth.

OLD LADY

Yes, troth and troth. You would not be a queen?

ANNE

No, not for all the riches under heaven.　　35

OLD LADY

'Tis strange: a threepence bowed would hire me,
Old as I am, to queen it. But I pray you,
What think you of a duchess? Have you limbs
To bear that load of title?

ANNE　　　　　　　　　　　　　　No, in truth.

---

27 **fair parts** beauty
28–9 **woman's . . . sovereignty**
Women's proverbial (Dent, W707.2)
desire for sovereignty over men is the
basis of Chaucer's *Wife of Bath's Tale*
and of Fletcher's *WPl*, a free adaptation of Chaucer's tale: 'The riddle that
Silvio is set . . . is the same as in the
Wife of Bath's Tale – to find what
women most desire; and the answer is
the same, too, to have their will. But
this promotion of female sovereignty
is . . . rendered safe by Fletcher, both
by the phrasing of the riddle and by
the twists of the plot' (Cooper, 191–2).
29 **Affected** aspired to, desired
30 **sooth** truth
31 **Saving your mincing** despite your
pretend delicacy; *OED* defines *mincing*
as 'the action or habit of speaking or
acting in an affectedly nice or elegant
manner' (*vbl. sb.* 3).
32 **cheverel conscience** Cheverel leather
(used to make gloves) was 'noted for its

pliancy and capability of being
stretched', was figuratively used to
mean 'flexible, yielding, elastic' (*OED
sb.* 1 and 2b) (cf. *TN* 3.1.12; *RJ*
2.3.77–8) and was proverbial particularly for a pliable conscience (Dent,
C608). As Judith Anderson notes,
there is a strong sexual implication
here (conscience/vagina; see pp. 80–1;
cf. also 2.2.142, 2.3.66–7) which offers
a cynical commentary on Anne's route
to power.
34 **queen** punning here, as throughout
this scene, on the early modern word
'quean' (i.e. whore)
36 **threepence bowed** a bent coin of
negligible value; the pun on 'bawd'
matches that of queen/quean.
37 **queen it** presumably also 'quean it',
i.e. play the whore
38–9 **limbs / To bear** a range of punning
implications: the Old Lady's image is
sexual and procreative, a duke on top of
Anne, and Anne bearing the duke's child

---

32 cheverel] *(Chiuerell)*　36 bowed would] bow'd now would *F2*

OLD LADY

Then you are weakly made. Pluck off a little: 40
I would not be a young count in your way
For more than blushing comes to. If your back
Cannot vouchsafe this burden, 'tis too weak
Ever to get a boy.

ANNE   How you do talk!
I swear again, I would not be a queen   45
For all the world.

OLD LADY   In faith, for little England
You'd venture an emballing. I myself

(the latter sense made explicit at 43–4).

40 Pluck . . . little literally, undress a little, but here meaning drop a notch or two in rank, to the level of *count* (the Continental equivalent of the English earl, whose wife is a countess, and who is below a duke in rank)

41–2 I . . . to This assertion works on (at least) two levels. *Count* (deliberately used despite its inappropriateness in the English context; see 40n.) would, in early modern pronunciation, probably have sounded much like 'cunt' (and can be made to do so in performance, particularly if the Old Lady is played as Welsh, as the text seems to imply at 48); *in your way* means 'in your condition', i.e. still a virgin. Anne is presumably blushing at the sexual puns; thus the sense is 'I wouldn't delay losing my virginity for modesty's sake'; at the same time, *in your way* can mean 'in your path', so the sense is 'I don't believe you'd be so coy if you met a handsome young earl'. Cf. Fletcher, *Wife* 1.1.85–6: 'I would not be a hansome wench in your way Sir, / For a new gowne.'

42–4 If . . . boy. Cf. 1.1.83–5.

43 vouchsafe lower itself to accept

44 get conceive, become pregnant with

45–9 I . . . that. This dialogue recalls Desdemona's defence of fidelity against Emilia's arguments in *Oth*

4.3.60–104.

45 queen Once more, the dividing line between queen and whore is blurred; it would seem the techniques required to become the King's wife are much the same as those required to become a prostitute.

46 little England James I assumed the title of 'King of Great Britain' as his accession brought about the union of the kingdoms (practically, if not constitutionally); *little England* was a way gently to mock James's grandeur. At the same time, it was a fond way of referring to England, and, as Humphreys notes, here it anticipates Anne's future status as Queen. The Old Lady may be referring not to England at all, however, but to Pembrokeshire, a coastal county of South Wales known as 'little *England* beyond *Wales*' (Taylor 1653, B2ʳ) because the majority of people there spoke English and not Welsh; this would make sense of *Caernarfonshire* in 48, since land in Pembrokeshire was the more valuable of the two, and looks forward to the Lord Chamberlain's announcement at 63.

47 emballing investiture with the orb as a sign of royalty, but again with a sexual implication

43 burden] *(*burthen*)*   47 emballing] empalling *(Malone); emballing *(Whalley); empaling *(Jackson)*

Would for Caernarfonshire, although there longed
No more to th' crown but that. Lo, who comes here?

Enter Lord CHAMBERLAIN.

CHAMBERLAIN
Good morrow, ladies. What were't worth to know   50
The secret of your conference?
ANNE   My good lord,
Not your demand: it values not your asking.
Our mistress' sorrows we were pitying.
CHAMBERLAIN
It was a gentle business, and becoming
The action of good women. There is hope   55
All will be well.
ANNE   Now I pray God, amen.
CHAMBERLAIN
You bear a gentle mind, and heavenly blessings
Follow such creatures. That you may, fair lady,
Perceive I speak sincerely, and high note's
Ta'en of your many virtues, the King's majesty   60
Commends his good opinion of you, and

48 **Caernarfonshire** a coastal county of North Wales (historically anglicized to 'Carnarvonshire'), still a rural, substantially Welsh-speaking area **longed** belonged
51 **conference** conversation
52 **Not . . . asking** It is not worth your while asking, i.e. it is not a deeply secret (or, perhaps, comfortable?) topic.
54–5 **becoming . . . of** appropriate activity for
55–6 **There . . . amen**. magnificently ironic; ostensibly, they are both hoping that the rift between Henry and Katherine will be healed, but Anne's potential as future Queen is in fact the issue.

57 **heavenly** two syllables
   blessings Cf. 76–9; see also 3.2.50–2.
59–60 **and . . . Ta'en** and [that] high note [is] taken; i.e. close attention is being paid. The passive construction is coy.
61 ***Commends . . . you** wants you to know how high an opinion he has of you; F1–4's 'of you, to you' is not entirely unlikely, but is awkward metrically and 'may be a literal copying by a scribe or the compositor of an insufficiently deleted revision, although a memorial error in transmission cannot be overlooked whereby "to you" was anticipated from the next line' (Bowers).

48 longed] 'long'd *Capell*; belong'd *Pope*   57 heavenly] *(*heau'nly*)*   59 note's] *Theobald*; notes *F*
61 of you, and] *Capell*; of you, to you; and *F*; to you, and *Pope*

Does purpose honour to you no less flowing
Than Marchioness of Pembroke, to which title
A thousand pound a year annual support
Out of his grace he adds.

ANNE   I do not know   65
What kind of my obedience I should tender.
More than my all is nothing; nor my prayers
Are not words duly hallowed, nor my wishes
More worth than empty vanities; yet prayers and wishes
Are all I can return. Beseech your lordship,   70
Vouchsafe to speak my thanks and my obedience,
As from a blushing handmaid, to his highness,
Whose health and royalty I pray for.

CHAMBERLAIN   Lady,
I shall not fail t'approve the fair conceit

63–4 **Marchioness . . . support** 'on the first of September [1532] being sundaie, the K. being come to Windsor, created the ladie Anne Bullongne marchionesse of Penbroke, and gaue to hir one thousand pounds land by the yeare' (Holinshed, 928)

63 **Pembroke** See 46n.

65–6 **I . . . tender**. The audience, however, knows exactly what kind of *obedience* is required, especially since the word *tender* recalls the sexualizing of the conscience at 2.2.142.

65–8 **not . . . nothing; nor . . . not . . . nor** All the negatives create the impression of a (suitably modest) affirmative.

66–7 **tender . . . nothing** echoes *tender place* at 2.2.142, if *nothing* has its early modern signification of 'vagina' (cf. also 2.3.32); 'More than my all is nothing' thus acknowledges that Anne's importance lies solely in her sexuality/procreativity.

67 **More . . . nothing** ostensibly complete self-effacement

70 **Beseech** i.e. I beseech

71 **Vouchsafe** be so good as; recalling the word in its sexual context at 43

72 **handmaid** literally, a female personal attendant (*OED sb.* 1), but with biblical overtones – most resonantly, in a context of fertility, Luke, 1.38, 48, in the passage prescribed for 25 March (Lady-day or Annunciation) in *Common Prayer* (though not in Geneva, where Mary simply describes herself as a 'servant': I am grateful to George Walton Williams for pointing me to the *Common Prayer* translation, which is based on the 'Great' Bible (1539)). This, in conjunction with the Chamberlain's invocation of *heavenly blessings* at 57 (c.f. Luke, 1.28, 48), suggests that we are witnessing a secular Annunciation, with the Chamberlain in the role of the angel Gabriel. I am grateful to Thomas Merriam for this suggestion. The scene both apotheosizes Elizabeth I and undercuts that apotheosis through the Old Lady's attitude to Anne (c.f. 5.1.158).

74 **approve . . . conceit** confirm the high opinion

The King hath of you. [*aside*] I have perused her well.   75
Beauty and honour in her are so mingled
That they have caught the King, and who knows yet
But from this lady may proceed a gem
To lighten all this isle. [*to Anne*] I'll to the King
And say I spoke with you.

ANNE   My honoured lord.   80
                       Exit Lord Chamberlain.

OLD LADY   Why, this it is: see, see!
I have been begging sixteen years in court –
Am yet a courtier beggarly, nor could
Come pat betwixt too early and too late
For any suit of pounds – and you (O, fate!),   85
A very fresh fish here – fie, fie, fie upon
This compelled fortune! – have your mouth filled up

---

75 SD Guthrie, in his 1949 production, had the Chamberlain address these observations to the Old Lady, which seems a little clumsy.
  perused considered, examined
78 **gem** Anne's daughter, the future Elizabeth I; cf. 5.4.17–38. Jewels were thought to produce light in dark places.
79 **lighten** another word with biblical resonance: the phrase 'a light to lighten the Gentiles' appears in the *Nunc dimittis* ('Now lettest thou thy servant departe in peace'), said daily at Evening Prayer (as prescribed in *Common Prayer*), the words spoken by Simeon (Luke 2.32) when he saw the infant Jesus in the temple (GWW).
83 **courtier beggarly** a very poor courtier, still begging
84–5 **Come . . . pounds** get the timing right with regard to a request for money; but since *pannus* was Latin for cloth or rag and 'pane' is, as Foakes notes (Ard²), an obsolete English word for a piece or strip of cloth (*OED sb.*[1]

2a), there is also a play on *suit of pounds* as a suit of clothes made of rags. There is a possible play on 'pawn', too, the Scottish form of which is 'pand' (*OED sb.*[2]), which would also underline the practical conditions of the Old Lady's poverty. 'Pond' and 'pound' can be interchangeable (see *OED* 'pond' *sb.* and *v.*), and one meaning of 'pound' is 'an enclosure for fish' (*OED sb.*[2] II 5), which thus produces *fresh fish* (which also, inevitably, has sexual undertones) in 86.
87 **compelled fortune** luck forced upon her
87–8 **mouth . . . it** contrast with *begging* (82); Anne is never going to go short of food. There is a range of other possibilities: Anne is a fish who has been waiting no time at all to be hooked (i.e. in the mouth); since this is the Old Lady speaking, possibly an image of oral sex; perhaps, ominously, a reference to the classical custom of putting a coin in the mouth of the dead to pay the ferryman on the way to the underworld.

---

75 SD] *Pope*   78 gem] (*Iemme*)   79 SD] *Malone (subst.); * To them *Humphreys*   80 SD] *Capell; after* you *F*   86–7 here – fie . . . fortune! –] *Hanmer (subst.); * heere; fye . . . fortune: *F*

Before you open it.

ANNE   This is strange to me.

OLD LADY

How tastes it? Is it bitter? Forty pence, no.

There was a lady once – 'tis an old story –   90

That would not be a queen, that would she not,

For all the mud in Egypt. Have you heard it?

ANNE

Come, you are pleasant.

OLD LADY   With your theme I could

O'ermount the lark. The Marchioness of Pembroke?

A thousand pounds a year, for pure respect?   95

No other obligation? By my life,

That promises more thousands: honour's train

Is longer than his foreskirt. By this time,

I know your back will bear a duchess. Say,

Are you not stronger than you were?

ANNE   Good lady,   100

Make yourself mirth with your particular fancy

And leave me out on't. Would I had no being

---

89 **tastes . . . bitter** further play on the image of oral sex at 87–8, perhaps
Forty pence the amount of a standard bet or fee; a slightly derogatory expression

91 **queen** The reference to *Forty pence* ensures that the queen/quean pun is still quietly in operation here.

92 **mud in Egypt** an earthy image for wealth, the rising Nile being the source, as Steevens noted, of Egypt's fertility and therefore its wealth. Cespedes suggests that this might recall *AC* and similarly anticipate the 'audience's knowledge of the famous story and traditional interpretations of it [in order] to move its audience into a novel and ambiguous perspective on

the heroic lovers' (Cespedes, 418).

93 **pleasant** humorous, comical

94 **O'ermount** fly higher, and sing louder, than

97 **more** F's 'mo' is a valid, but archaic, form of 'more' (*OED adv.* C2); I have therefore modernized to *more*.

97–8 **honour's . . . foreskirt** These first signs of the King's appreciation will be eclipsed by those to come; *foreskirt* is the first example cited in *OED* (*prefix.* 3a).

99 **duchess** The Old Lady refers sarcastically to their exchange at 37–9.

101 **particular fancy** individual imaginings, capricious or arbitrary fantasy (*OED sb.* 8a)

102 **on't** of it

97 more] (mo)

If this salute my blood a jot. It faints me
To think what follows.
The Queen is comfortless, and we forgetful   105
In our long absence. Pray do not deliver
What here you've heard to her.
OLD LADY   What do you think me?

Exeunt.

2.4   *Trumpets, sennet and cornetts. Enter two Vergers with
short silver wands; next them two* Scribes *in the habit of doctors;
after them, the Archbishop of Canterbury alone; after him, the*

103 **salute . . . jot** excites the slightest
physical response from me
It faints me I feel faint.
104 The short line presumably indicates
the strength of emotion holding Anne
at this point.
106 **deliver** recount; for all her apparent
concern for Katherine, Anne has no
intention of risking the King's favour
merely to be loyal to the Queen.
107 **What . . . me?** a marvellously open-
ended way to close the scene (underlined by the long dash that follows 'me'
in F). The unspoken answer, presumably, is 'a bawd'.
2.4 Generally considered Shakespeare's
(see Appendix 3), this scene is key in
the establishment both of Katherine's
personality and of the King's vacillat-
ing conscience, providing both characters with lengthy set-piece speeches
in a formal context. The scene's formality is underlined by the second
longest of the play's extensive stage
directions, drawn closely from
Holinshed's description. The Queen's
speech is almost entirely versified
Holinshed, but with some important
changes and additions, notably in the
vehemence   of   the   dramatic
Katherine, whose departure from the
court has much more impact in the

play than it does in Holinshed's
account. The King's speeches also
follow Holinshed closely, but again
with a number of crucial differences,
including the nervous way in which
Henry begins his narrative. The location, as we know from 2.2.137, is
Blackfriars, which had recently been
opened as a theatre by the King's
company and was probably the venue
for early, if not the first, performances
of *H8* (see pp.9–10).
0.1 **sennet** a particular kind of fanfare,
of either trumpets or cornetts; its exact
significance is unclear (see Appendix 6).
0.2 **Scribes** one speaking role (6, 9), one
mute
habit of doctors i.e. the academic
robes of Doctors of Law: 'the cheefe
scribe   was   doctor   Steevens'
(Holinshed, 907).
0.3–4 *Archbishop . . . Asaph* Shakespeare
takes the names of the defence team
from Holinshed's somewhat wry
account: 'And bicause the king meant
nothing but uprightly therein, and
knew well that the queene was somewhat wedded to hir owne opinion, and
wished that she should do nothing
without counsell, he had hir choose the
best clearks of his realme to be of hir
counsell. . . . Then she elected William

103 salute] elate *Collier² (Collier MS);* shall heat *(Bailey)*   **2.4**] *(Scena Quarta.)*   0.2 *habit*]
(habite); habits F3   0.3 *Archbishop*] *Johnson; Bishop* F

298

Bishops of LINCOLN, *Ely, Rochester and St Asaph; next them,*
with some small distance, follows a Gentleman, bearing the purse
with the great seal and a cardinal's hat; then two Priests, bearing
each a silver cross; then a Gentleman Usher, bare-headed,
accompanied with a Sergeant-at-arms, bearing a silver mace;
then two Gentlemen, bearing two great silver pillars; after them, side
by side, the two Cardinals; *two Noblemen with the sword and mace.*
The KING *takes place under the cloth of state. The two Cardinals sit*

Warham archbishop of Canturburie, and Nicholas Weast bishop of Elie, doctors of the laws; and John Fisher bishop of Rochester, and Henrie Standish bishop of saint Asaph, doctors of diuinitie' (907). For Warham, see List of Roles, 47n. Knowledge of Fisher's eventual Catholic martyrdom in 1535 would presumably limit the sympathy of some members of the audience for Katherine's cause if they recognized him in the procession.

0.4 *St Asaph* There has been a Bishop in the small town of Llanelwy (St Asaph) in North Wales, roughly halfway between Conwy and Chester, since 1143. The Jacobean bishop, William Morgan, had translated the Bible into Welsh in 1588.

0.6–9 *great . . . pillars* In his summing-up of Wolsey's pomp, Holinshed describes the details of his daily procession to Westminster Hall: 'Before him was borne first the broad seale of England, and his cardinals hat, by a lord, or some gentleman of worship, right solemnlie: & as soone as he was once entered into his chamber of presence, his two great crosses were there attending to be borne before him: . . . Thus went he downe through the hall with a sergeant of armes before him, bearing a great mace of siluer, and two gentlemen carieng two great pillers of siluer' (921). Holinshed has already mentioned the silver crosses (in a passage repeated verbatim in Stow 1592, 838): 'Then had he his two great crosses of siluer, the one of his archbish-

oprike, the other of his legacie, borne before him whither soeuer he went or rode, by two of the tallest priests that he could get within the realme' (Holinshed, 920). Foakes (Ard²) notes that Wolsey's substitution of a pair of silver pillars for the usual cardinal's mace was already seen at the time as a particularly arrogant gesture; Holinshed, though, mentions both mace and pillars. On Wolsey's fondness for such displays of wealth and status, see Glanville.

0.7 *Gentleman Usher* This is unlikely to be Griffith, Katherine's gentleman usher (see 4.2.0.2), since it would be highly inappropriate for one of Katherine's servants to be involved in the middle of the Cardinals' section of the procession (though editors have generally assumed that must be the case). If any historical individual is meant, it is in fact more likely to be George Cavendish, Wolsey's gentleman usher who later became his biographer (and a source for the play via Stow 1592); see pp. 169–71.

0.11–15 *The* KING *. . . Scribes* Holinshed describes the scene: 'The court was platted in tables and benches in manner of a consistorie, one seat raised higher for the iudges to sit in. Then as it were in the midst of the said iudges aloft aboue them three degrees high, was a cloth of estate hanged, with a chaire roiall vnder the same, wherein sat the king; and besides him, some distance from him sat the queene, and vnder the iudges feet sat the scribes' (907).

under him as judges. Queen KATHERINE[, *attended by* GRIFFITH,]
  *takes place some distance from the King. The Bishops place
  themselves on each side the court in manner of a consistory; below
  them the Scribes* [*and a* Crier]. *The Lords sit next the Bishops. The
  rest of the attendants stand in convenient order about the stage.*

WOLSEY
  Whilst our commission from Rome is read,
  Let silence be commanded.
KING   What's the need?
  It hath already publicly been read,
  And on all sides th'authority allowed;
  You may then spare that time.
WOLSEY   Be't so. Proceed.   5
SCRIBE
  Say, 'Henry, King of England, come into the court.'
CRIER
  Henry, King of England, come into the court.
KING   Here.
SCRIBE
  Say, 'Katherine, Queen of England, come into the
    court.'

0.12 GRIFFITH In the spirit of 0.7n., an
  entry SD is required here; see also 124
  SPn.
0.13 *takes place* sits, here meaning
  specifically 'in state'; see 1.2.8.4n
0.14 *consistory* a court of judgement, a
  tribunal; a bishop's court for ecclesiastical causes (*OED* I 3 and II 7)
0.15 **Crier** An entry SD is required
  because the Crier speaks at 7 and 10.
1–5 **Whilst . . . time.** According to
  Holinshed, '[t]he iudges commanded
  silence whilest their commission was
  read, both to the court and to the people
  assembled. That doone the scribes commanded the crier to call the king' (907).

Henry's intervention is not in Holinshed,
  and is possibly added simply to avoid a
  tedious recital of the commission, but
  also to demonstrate the King's unease.
1 **commission** See 2.2.102–5n.; four
  syllables.
2–3 **What's . . . read** Henry shows clear
  signs of impatience here, in the 'Bluff-
  King-Harry' tradition; see pp.74–5,
  177–8.
4 **th'authority allowed** its authority
  acknowledged
6–10 **Say . . . court.** direct from
  Holinshed, down to the etceteras in F
  which I have expanded in the process
  of modernizing

0.12 Queen KATHERINE] *this edn; The Queene F   attended by* GRIFFITH] *Oxf; and her Train /
Capell*   0.15 *and a* Crier] *Capell*   7, 10 come into the court] *Humphreys;* &c. F   9] *Capell; F lines*
England, / Court /

CRIER

Katherine, Queen of England, come into the court.　　10
The Queen makes no answer, rises out of her chair, goes
about the court, comes to the King, and kneels at his
feet; then speaks.

KATHERINE

Sir, I desire you do me right and justice,
And to bestow your pity on me, for
I am a most poor woman and a stranger,
Born out of your dominions, having here
No judge indifferent nor no more assurance　　15
Of equal friendship and proceeding. Alas, sir,
In what have I offended you? What cause
Hath my behaviour given to your displeasure
That thus you should proceed to put me off
And take your good grace from me? Heaven witness　　20
I have been to you a true and humble wife,
At all times to your will conformable,
Ever in fear to kindle your dislike,
Yea, subject to your countenance, glad or sorry
As I saw it inclined. When was the hour　　25

10.1–3 Again, this comes direct from Holinshed: 'And bicause shee could not come to the king directlie, for the distance seuered betweene them, shee went about by the court, and came to the king, kneeling downe at his feet' (907). The SD subtly alters Katherine's movement, suggesting that she is making a virtue out of necessity and deliberately slowing the pace of the proceedings in the wake of Henry's peremptory beginning, preparing the court (and the audience) for her speech.

11–55 Sir . . . fulfilled. Katherine's speech is effectively versified

Holinshed, but with some important changes and additions as noted below (for the entire speech, see Holinshed, 907). Katherine's speech here (and her situation in general) bears close comparison with that of Hermione at *WT* 3.2, especially 21–53; and cf. 68n.

13 stranger foreigner
15 indifferent impartial
16 equal fair, impartial
19 put me off put me aside
20 your good grace your favour, yourself
24 countenance the look or expression of a person's face; show of feeling towards another (*OED sb.* I 4 and II 7)

11 SP] *Malone (Q. Cath.); not in F; Queen. / Warburton* **25 inclined.]** *Rowe³ (subst.); inclin'd? F*

I ever contradicted your desire,
Or made it not mine too? Or which of your friends
Have I not strove to love, although I knew
He were mine enemy? What friend of mine
That had to him derived your anger did I   30
Continue in my liking? Nay, gave notice
He was from thence discharged? Sir, call to mind
That I have been your wife in this obedience
Upward of twenty years, and have been blessed
With many children by you. If, in the course   35
And process of this time, you can report,
And prove it too, against mine honour aught,
My bond to wedlock, or my love and duty
Against your sacred person, in God's name
Turn me away and let the foulest contempt   40
Shut door upon me, and so give me up
To the sharpest kind of justice. Please you, sir,
The King your father was reputed for
A prince most prudent, of an excellent

27–9 **Or which . . . enemy?** Cf.
Holinshed's phrasing: 'I loued for your
sake all them whome you loued,
whether they were my freends or
enimies' (907). Shakespeare's modification here implies Katherine's particular rage with Wolsey.
28 **strove** past tense for past participle, a
common substitution
29–32 **What . . . discharged?** These
lines are not in Holinshed.
30 **derived** drawn
33–5 **wife . . . children** Henry and
Katherine's marriage, which lasted
twenty years, 'yielded several miscarriages, three infants who were either
still-born or died immediately after

birth (two of them males), two infants
who had died within a few weeks of
birth (one of them a boy) and one girl,
Princess Mary' (Scarisbrick, 201); see
186.
37 **aught** anything
39 **Against** towards
39–42 **in . . . justice** In Holinshed,
Katherine simply says that if anything
can justly be alleged against her, she
will be 'content to depart to [her]
shame and rebuke' (907); the dramatic
Katherine expresses herself much
more vehemently.
40 **foulest** monosyllabic
42 **sharpest** monosyllabic

31 Nay, gave notice] nay, gave not notice *Hanmer;* nor gave notice *(Steevens)*   40 foulest] *(*fowl'st*)*
42 sharpest] *(*sharp'st*)*

And unmatched wit and judgement. Ferdinand, 45
My father, King of Spain, was reckoned one
The wisest prince that there had reigned by many
A year before. It is not to be questioned
That they had gathered a wise council to them
Of every realm, that did debate this business, 50
Who deemed our marriage lawful. Wherefore I humbly
Beseech you, sir, to spare me till I may
Be by my friends in Spain advised, whose counsel
I will implore. If not, i'th' name of God,
Your pleasure be fulfilled.

WOLSEY   You have here, lady, 55
And of your choice, these reverend fathers, men
Of singular integrity and learning,
Yea, the elect o'th' land, who are assembled
To plead your cause. It shall be therefore bootless
That longer you desire the court, as well 60
For your own quiet as to rectify
What is unsettled in the King.

CAMPEIUS   His grace

---

45 **wit** intelligence
  Ferdinand Ferdinand of Aragon married Isabella of Castile in 1469; the
  marriage led, on their respective acces-
  sions in 1474 and 1479, to the union of
  the two most powerful kingdoms of
  Spain. Their daughter Katherine was
  born in 1485. The 'Catholic
  Monarchs' (a title given them by the
  Pope in 1496) oversaw the removal of
  the last elements of Muslim rule in the
  peninsula, introduced a rigorous and
  intolerant Inquisition, and established
  Spain as a major power in Europe.
  Isabella died in 1504 and Ferdinand in
  1516.
46–7 **one / The wisest** the very wisest
48 **questioned** doubted
55–119 **You . . . him.** Holinshed men-

tions no argument between Katherine
and the Cardinals at this point, and
Katherine's language at 76–82 is
drawn from slightly later in the chronicle (see 76–82n.).
56 **of your choice** chosen by you; see
  0.3–4n.
58 **the elect o'** the very best in; literally
  'the chosen of'
59 **bootless** useless, pointless
60 **desire** Malone saw *desire* as a contraction, expanding it as 'That you desire
  to protract the business of the court';
  F4's emendation to 'defer' is appealing,
  but Foakes's (Ard²) gloss of *desire* as
  'entreat' or 'plead with' (cf. *TC* 4.5.158)
  makes change unnecessary.
61 **quiet** peace of mind
  rectify remedy

60 desire] defer *F4;* defy *(Vaughan)*

Hath spoken well and justly. Therefore, madam,
It's fit this royal session do proceed
And that without delay their arguments   65
Be now produced and heard.
KATHERINE   Lord Cardinal,
To you I speak.
WOLSEY   Your pleasure, madam.
KATHERINE   Sir,
I am about to weep; but, thinking that
We are a queen, or long have dreamed so, certain
The daughter of a king, my drops of tears   70
I'll turn to sparks of fire.
WOLSEY   Be patient yet.
KATHERINE

I will, when you are humble – nay, before,
Or God will punish me. I do believe,
Induced by potent circumstances, that
You are mine enemy, and make my challenge   75
You shall not be my judge. For it is you
Have blown this coal betwixt my lord and me,

---

65 **their** i.e. those of the *reverend fathers* (56)
67 **Your pleasure** i.e. I await your pleasure, what you wish to say
68 **weep** Cf. 11–55n., *WT* 2.1.107–12.
68–71 **I . . . me . . . my . . . I'll** modulation from first person singular to evoke sympathy to royal plural used to full haughty effect and back to singular for intensity of personal anger
72–3 **when . . . me** Pride, which is (as far as his enemies are concerned; see 107–8; 2.2.54, 79) Wolsey's chief characteristic, is the first of the seven deadly sins (see also 105–7n., 3.1.103–4n.).
74 **Induced . . . circumstances** persuaded by powerful evidence
75 **challenge** an objection made to one or more of the jurymen in a trial (*OED sb.*

3a), so by extension a formal objection to Wolsey as judge
76 **shall** must
76–82 **For . . . truth.** Katherine's words here are extrapolated from Holinshed's account of her rejection of Wolsey as judge: '[T]he queene in presence of the whole court most greeuouslie accused the cardinall of vntruth, deceit, wickednesse, & malice, which had sowne dissention betwixt hir and the king hir husband; and therefore openlie protested, that she did vtterlie abhorre, refuse, and forsake such a iudge, as was not onelie a most malicious enimie to hir, but also a manifest aduersarie to all right and iustice' (908).
77, 92 **blown this coal** encouraged this dispute; proverbial (Dent, C465,

66+ SP KATHERINE] *Malone (Q. Cath.); Qu.; Que., Queen F*   66–7 Lord . . . speak] *Pope; one line F*   67–8 Sir . . . that] *Pope; one line F*

Which God's dew quench. Therefore, I say again,
I utterly abhor, yea, from my soul
Refuse you for my judge, whom yet once more   80
I hold my most malicious foe and think not
At all a friend to truth.
WOLSEY   I do profess
You speak not like yourself, who ever yet
Have stood to charity and displayed th'effects
Of disposition gentle and of wisdom   85
O'er-topping woman's power. Madam, you do me
    wrong.
I have no spleen against you, nor injustice
For you or any. How far I have proceeded,
Or how far further shall, is warranted
By a commission from the Consistory,   90
Yea, the whole Consistory of Rome. You charge me
That I have 'blown this coal': I do deny it.
The King is present. If it be known to him
That I gainsay my deed, how may he wound,
And worthily, my falsehood – yea, as much   95
As you have done my truth. If he know
That I am free of your report, he knows
I am not of your wrong. Therefore in him

though *H8* provides his only citations); cf., in a slightly different context, 5.2.147; also Isaiah, 54.16.
78 **dew** metaphorical for blessings pour-
ing down from heaven; cf. *Cym*
5.6.352–3.
79 **abhor** detest and reject; cf. 76–82n.
82 **friend to truth** Cf. Beaumont &
Fletcher, *LC*, 1.149.
84 **stood to** demonstrated
86 **power** one syllable
87 **spleen** See 1.2.174n.
89 **shall** F's '(Shall)' is an example of
Honigmann's 'swib' (single word in
brackets); see p. 155n.

90 **Consistory** the ecclesiastical senate in
which the Pope, presiding over the
whole body of Cardinals, deliberates
upon the affairs of the (Roman
Catholic) Church (*OED* II 6); cf.
0.14n., where the term is used slightly
differently.
94 **gainsay my deed** refuse to acknowledge my own action
95 **falsehood** deceitfulness, faithlessness
(*OED* 1)
96–8 **If . . . wrong.** If he knows that I am
innocent of the wrongdoing you claim I
have done, then he also knows that you
have done me wrong in so claiming.

86 power] *(powre)*   89 shall] *(Shall) F*   96 If he] But if he *Pope;* If he then *Keightley*

It lies to cure me, and the cure is to
Remove these thoughts from you, the which before   100
His highness shall speak in, I do beseech
You, gracious madam, to unthink your speaking,
And to say so no more.
KATHERINE   My lord, my lord,
I am a simple woman, much too weak
T'oppose your cunning. You're meek and humble-
        mouthed;   105
You sign your place and calling, in full seeming,
With meekness and humility; but your heart
Is crammed with arrogancy, spleen and pride.
You have, by fortune and his highness' favours,
Gone slightly o'er low steps, and now are mounted   110
Where powers are your retainers, and your words,
Domestics to you, serve your will as't please
Yourself pronounce their office. I must tell you,

100–1 **the . . . in** 'but before the King addresses these issues'; *in* is 'in reference to', 'on the subject of'.

105–7 **You're . . . humility** Katherine names the characteristics associated with Christians, particularly those called to the ministry, in order to demonstrate Wolsey's need for reformation. See especially Colossians, 3.12: 'Now therefore as the elect of God holie & beloued, put on tender mercie, kindnes, humblenes of minde, mekenes, long suffring.' Holinshed observes that Wolsey was more interested in his honour than his 'spirituall profession, wherin should be shewed all meekenes, humilitie, and charitie' (917).

106 **sign** advertise, label
   in full seeming in an entirely convincing manner

108 **arrogancy** the only use of this form of 'arrogance' in the Shakespeare

canon, presumably acquired from Holinshed, 917 ('pride and arrogancie'; cf. Proverbs, 8.13), where it is repeated as a marginal note

110 **slightly** effortlessly

111 **powers . . . retainers** There are several possible connected meanings of *powers* (one syllable here): (i) 'the power you have by virtue of your position'; (ii) 'powerful people'; (iii) the kind of power over the elements wielded by Prospero in *Tem*; (iv) evil forces (cf. Ephesians, 6.12: 'For we wrestle not against flesh and blood, but against principalities, against powers') (RP). The overall implication is that everything and everyone representing or wielding power is at Wolsey's beck and call.

111–13 **your . . . office** Your words are slaves to carry out your wishes in any way you like.

112 **Domestics** servants, slaves

103 SP] *Malone (Q. Cath.); Queen. F*   110 slightly] lightly *(Walker)*   111 powers] *(Powres)* your words] your wards *Singer (Tyrwhitt);* our lords *(Mason)*

You tender more your person's honour than
Your high profession spiritual; that again   115
I do refuse you for my judge; and here
Before you all, appeal unto the Pope,
To bring my whole cause 'fore His Holiness,
And to be judged by him.
She curtsies to the King and offers to depart.

CAMPEIUS   The Queen is obstinate,
Stubborn to justice, apt to accuse it, and   120
Disdainful to be tried by't. 'Tis not well.
She's going away.

KING   Call her again.

CRIER   Katherine, Queen of England, come into the court!

GRIFFITH   Madam, you are called back.

KATHERINE
What need you note it? Pray you keep your way.   125
When you are called, return. Now the Lord help:
They vex me past my patience. Pray you, pass on.

---

114 **tender** cherish, respect
115–19 **again . . . him** According to
Holinshed, Katherine 'did appeale
vnto the pope, committing hir whole
cause to be iudged of him' (908). Here
her departure has considerable impact,
but in Holinshed's account, the trial
simply carries on: 'notwithstanding
this appeale, the legats sat weekelie,
and euerie daie were arguments
brought in on both parts' (908).
116–19 **and . . . him** Cf. Hermione's
appeal to the oracle in *WT* 3.2.113–15.
119 SD–130 SD *She . . . Attendants*.
These exchanges come directly from
Holinshed: 'she arose vp, making a
lowe curtesie to the king, and departed
from thence. The king being aduertised that shee was readie to go out of
the house, commanded the crier to call
hir againe, who called hir by these

words; Katharine queene of England,
come into the court. With that (quoth
maister Griffith) Madame, you be
called againe. On on (quoth she) it
maketh no matter, I will not tarrie, go
on your waies. And thus she departed,
without anie further answer at that
time, or anie other, and neuer would
appeare after in anie court' (907).
119 SD *offers to* makes to, begins to
120 **Stubborn** resistant
     apt to accuse quick to impugn
124 SP *It seems appropriate to emend
F's 'Gent. Vsh' for continuity, since
Holinshed names Griffith specifically
(see 119 SD–130 SDn.) and since he is
described as Katherine's gentleman
usher at 4.2.0.2; see also 0.7n.
125 **keep your way** carry on walking in
the same direction
127 **pass on** keep going

124 SP] *Steevens–Reed²* (GRIF.); *Gent. Vsh.* F

> I will not tarry: no, nor ever more
> Upon this business my appearance make
> In any of their courts.   *Exeunt Queen and her Attendants.*
> KING   Go thy ways, Kate.   130
> That man i'th' world who shall report he has
> A better wife, let him in naught be trusted
> For speaking false in that. Thou art alone –
> If thy rare qualities, sweet gentleness,
> Thy meekness saint-like, wife-like government,   135
> Obeying in commanding, and thy parts
> Sovereign and pious else, could speak thee out –
> The queen of earthly queens. She's noble born,
> And like her true nobility she has

130 **Kate** the only time in the play when Henry refers to his wife by the diminutive *Kate*. The name has obvious Shakespearean resonances, which would have been both positive and less positive for a Jacobean audience: Kate (Katharina) in *TS*, of whom the audience had recently been reminded in Fletcher's *WP*; Kate (Katherine) in *LLL*; Hotspur's Kate (historically named Elizabeth) in *1H4*; Kate (Princess Katharine) in *H5*, another foreign woman married to an English Harry (see p. 124). It also has an affectionate, domestic quality to it which contrasts markedly with the harsh formality of the legatine court.

131–40 **That . . . me.** Henry's praise of Katherine here (wistful or hypocritical, according to taste) is loosely based on Holinshed – 'For as much (quoth he) as the queene is gone, I will in hir absence declare to you all, that shee hath beene to me as true, as obedient, and as conformable a wife, as I would wish or desire. She hath all the vertuous qualities that ought to be in a woman of hir dignitie, or in anie other of a baser estate' (907) – but perhaps

most reminiscent, in the list of Katherine's *rare qualities*, of Hall's account: 'I dare saie that for her womanhode, wisedom, nobilitie, and gentlenes, neuer Prince had suche another, and therfore if I would willyngly chaunge I wer not wise' (Hall, 3H2ʳ; fol. clxxxii).

134 **rare** excellent, splendid

134–7 a standard list of wifely virtues, domestic and religious. See, *inter alia*, Dod & Cleaver, Gouge, and Brathwait (also Aughterson, 67–101, and Keeble, 96–111, for helpful extracts) for the paradox of the aristocratic woman's domestic and social role neatly summed up in *Obeying in commanding*.

135 **government** restraint, control, extending to others as well as self (Humphreys), with an additional sense of her ability to control the household, a management skill associated with excellent huswifery

138 **noble born** a remark presumably designed to hurt Wolsey's feelings, as he was incapable, according to the theory of genetically inherited aristocratic qualities, of such behaviour himself

130 SD *Exeunt*] Rowe; *Exit* F

Carried herself towards me.

WOLSEY   Most gracious sir,   140
In humblest manner I require your highness
That it shall please you to declare in hearing
Of all these ears – for where I am robbed and bound,
There must I be unloosed, although not there
At once and fully satisfied – whether ever I   145
Did broach this business to your highness, or
Laid any scruple in your way which might
Induce you to the question on't, or ever
Have to you, but with thanks to God for such
A royal lady, spake one the least word that might   150
Be to the prejudice of her present state
Or touch of her good person?

KING   My lord Cardinal,
I do excuse you – yea, upon mine honour,
I free you from't. You are not to be taught

---

140 **Carried herself** behaved

140–52 **Most . . . person?** This speech of Wolsey's expands Holinshed's account: 'With that quoth Wolseie the cardinall: Sir, I most humblie require your highnesse, to declare before all this audience, whether I haue beene the cheefe and first moouer of this matter vnto your maiestie or no, for I am greatlie suspected herein' (907). Wolsey is quietly insisting that Henry fulfil the function the Cardinal had outlined for him at 93–101.

141 **require** not as abrupt a demand as it sounds to us, meaning simply 'ask' or 'request' (*OED v.* I 3); Holinshed is being quoted almost word for word here.

145 **satisfied** compensated, reinstated

147 **scruple** See 2.1.157n.

148 **on't** of it

152 **touch of** stain on, doubt about
person name, character

152–206 **My . . . you?** This important speech has often been savagely cut in performance, yet the audience's opinion of the King is consolidated here as either honestly vulnerable or unforgivably hypocritical.

152–64 **My . . . him.** Holinshed's wording, expanded for dramatic purposes: 'My lord cardinall (quoth the king) I can well excuse you in this matter, marrie (quoth he) you haue beene rather against me in the tempting heereof, than a setter forward or moouer of the same' (907). Henry seems inclined to dismiss Wolsey's request quickly (*You're excused*), but the actor playing Wolsey is presumably, at 159, required to find a non-verbal way to express his wish for more justification.

154 **You . . . taught** You don't need to be told.

145 At once] Atton'd *Hanmer (Warburton)*

309

That you have many enemies that know not   155
Why they are so but, like to village curs,
Bark when their fellows do. By some of these
The Queen is put in anger. You're excused.
But will you be more justified? You ever
Have wished the sleeping of this business, never desired   160
It to be stirred, but oft have hindered, oft,
The passages made toward it. On my honour,
I speak my good lord Cardinal to this point
And thus far clear him. Now, what moved me to't,
I will be bold with time and your attention: 165
Then mark th'inducement. Thus it came: give heed
    to't.
My conscience first received a tenderness,

156–7 **curs . . . do** proverbial (Dent, D539, who cites Webster, *The White Devil* (1612): 'one dog / Still sets another a-barking' (5.3.95–6))
162 **The . . . it** the development of the debate
162–4 **On . . . him**. As various editors have noted, there are two possible ways of reading these lines. My own preference, following Theobald, is to assume that Henry turns at this point to address the court as a whole, making known his support for Wolsey's assertion. But 'my good lord Cardinal' might possibly be parenthetical, in which case the lines are still addressed to Wolsey, though *him* would then refer to *point*, which seems unlikely. Foakes (Ard^2) suggests that Henry addresses the entire court but makes a parenthetical gesture toward Wolsey in mid-sentence: 'I treat (my lord, bowing to Wolsey) of this point, this accusation, and clear him of it.' *OED* gives an (unlikely) earliest date of 1610 for 'speaking to' as dealing with or discussing items on an agenda (*v.* B II 14e); cf. 5.2.35.
163 I support the Cardinal in this matter.

Cardinal two syllables
164–6 **Now . . . to't** Henry draws attention to the beginning of his narrative with a peremptory nervousness absent from Holinshed.
166 **th'inducement** what persuaded me; see 74n.
167–72 **My . . . Mary**. follows Holinshed closely: 'The speciall cause that mooued me vnto this matter, was a certeine scrupulositie that pricked my conscience, vpon certeine words spoken at a time when it was, by the bishop of Baion the French ambassador, who had beene hither sent, vpon the debating of a marriage to be concluded betweene our daughter the ladie Marie, and the duke of Orleance, second son to the king of France' (907).
167 See 2.2.141–2n. and 142n. Conscience is again tender, and in the context of the previous ambivalent signified for *tender* – Anne's (or Katherine's) vagina – the echo of Holinshed's word *prick* (168) seems deliberately phallic. Henry again seems metaphorically feminized by the workings of his conscience (see pp. 81–3).

163 Cardinal] *(Cardnall)*   164] *Rowe^3*; F lines him. / too't, /

Scruple and prick on certain speeches uttered
By th' Bishop of Bayonne, then French ambassador,
Who had been hither sent on the debating 170
A marriage 'twixt the Duke of Orléans and
Our daughter Mary. I'th' progress of this business,
Ere a determinate resolution, he –
I mean the Bishop – did require a respite,
Wherein he might the King his lord advertise 175
Whether our daughter were legitimate
Respecting this our marriage with the dowager,
Sometimes our brother's wife. This respite shook

168 **on** from, caused by
171 **Duke of Orléans** The Duke was
second son to the king of France,
François I, and later became Henri II
of France. Orléans is a city not far
from Paris on the river Loire.
172–8 **I'th'** . . . **wife.** Again, this follows
Holinshed closely – 'Upon the resolu-
tion and determination whereof, he
desired respit to aduertise the king his
maister thereof, whether our daughter
Marie should be legitimate in respect of
this my marriage with this woman, being
sometimes my brothers wife' (907) –
though the use of the word *dowager*
looks forward to 4.1.23 and the title
(*Princess Dowager*) that Katherine is
obliged to assume after the divorce as she
returns to her earlier temporary status as
'widow to Prince Arthur' (3.2.70–1). A
dowager is a woman whose husband is
dead and who is in the enjoyment of
some title or some property that has
come to her from him (*OED* a).
173 **Ere** prior to
determinate resolution clear conclusion
174 **require** See 141n.
175 **advertise** inform (accent on the second syllable)
178 **Sometimes** previously
wife 'To sustain the mounting climax
initiated by the Queen's abrupt and

contemptuous exit, the confusion in
the Court, and the noisy departure of
the citizenesses', Tree (1910) cut from
here to 222 (Booth, 148).
178–81 **This** . . . **breast** Henry's language of conscience, as at 167, seems
metaphorically to feminize him. Here,
conscience is again perceived as physical and perhaps sexual ('the bosom of
my conscience'); as a result the
Bishop's inquiry into the legitimacy of
Princess Mary 'enters' the King 'with
a spitting (see 180n.) power' (cf.
1.2.210), making him *tremble*, and
'forcing [its] way' into him. It is as if
the *prick* is raping him. Cf. 3.2.100, for
a parallel use of *bosom*.
178–93 **This . . . me.** considerable amplification of the Holinshed passage:
'Which words once conceiued within
the secret bottome of my conscience,
ingendered such a scrupulous doubt,
that my conscience was incontinentlie
accombred, vexed, and disquieted;
whereby I thought my selfe to be
greatlie in danger of Gods indignation. Which appeared to be (as me
seemed) the rather, for that he sent vs
no issue male: and all such issues male
as my said wife had by me, died incon-
tinent after they came into the world,
so that I doubted the great displeasure
of God in that behalfe' (907).

171 A] *Rowe³;* And *F*

The bosom of my conscience, entered me,
Yea, with a spitting power, and made to tremble   180
The region of my breast; which forced such way
That many mazed considerings did throng
And pressed in with this caution. First, methought
I stood not in the smile of heaven, who had
Commanded nature that my lady's womb,   185
If it conceived a male child by me, should
Do no more offices of life to't than
The grave does to th' dead: for her male issue
Or died where they were made, or shortly after
This world had aired them. Hence I took a thought   190
This was a judgement on me, that my kingdom –
Well worthy the best heir o'th' world – should not

179 **bosom . . . conscience** On the
nature and location of the conscience,
see LN.
180 **spitting** impaling, as on a spit. F2
emends to 'splitting', a reading which
has been adopted by many editors, but
there is no need to emend: the idea is
one of insertion, not division; cf. *H5*
3.3.38; *RJ* 4.3.55.
182 **mazed** puzzled, confused
182–3 **throng . . . in** This passage has
metaphorical connections with later
crowd scenes (4.1.57–81; 5.3) which
can perhaps be seen to embody the
mazed considerings that led to the
divorce/remarriage process, implying
that Henry's private conscience is both
unpredictable and anything but private: rather, it is a public matter, and
the King's internal doubts appear akin
to the material anarchy of the crowds;
cf. *Luc* 1301–2: 'Much like a press of
people at a door / Throng her inven-
tions'. Moments of privacy are constantly interrupted in this play:
Katherine's domestic activities at
3.1.15; her vision at 4.2.100; Henry's

meditations at 2.2.64; Wolsey's
masque at 1.4.49; and the conversation
of Anne and the Old Lady at 2.3.50.
183 **pressed** pushed or strained forward,
as through a crowd (*OED v.*[1] III 14a,
15a); rather than 'press', as might be
expected if the word were coordinated
under the auxiliary 'do' (i.e. 'did
throng and press'), but the point is that
two different actions are performed:
gathering ('thronging') and then
forced entry ('pressed in') (JH)
184 **smile of heaven** favour of God;
Foakes (Ard[2]) notes that *heaven* may be
one of the erratic substitutions in F for
'God' that resulted from the Act of
Abuses of 1606 which restrained pro-
fanity in stage plays (cf. 5.1.153n.).
186 **male child** See 33–5n.
187 **offices** services, playing also on the
funeral service
189 **Or . . . or** either . . . or
189–90 **after . . . them** i.e. after they
were born. *Aired* means 'given them air
to breathe' and puns a little uncomfortably with *heir* in 192: 'made them
my heir by giving them life'.

179 bosom] bottom *Theobald*[2] *(after Holinshed) (Thirlby)*   180 spitting] splitting *F2*

Be gladded in't by me. Then follows that
I weighed the danger which my realms stood in
By this my issue's fail, and that gave to me   195
Many a groaning throe. Thus hulling in
The wild sea of my conscience, I did steer
Toward this remedy whereupon we are
Now present here together: that's to say,
I meant to rectify my conscience – which   200
I then did feel full sick, and yet not well –
By all the reverend fathers of the land
And doctors learned. First, I began in private
With you, my lord of Lincoln. You remember
How under my oppression I did reek   205
When I first moved you?

LINCOLN   Very well, my liege.

---

193 **gladded** made glad
193–203 **Then . . . learned.** Holinshed's
account is condensed and reordered:
'Thus my conscience being tossed in the
waues of a scrupulous mind, and partlie
in despaire to haue anie other issue than
I had alredie by this ladie now my wife,
it behooued me further to consider the
state of this realme, and the danger it
stood in for lacke of a prince to succeed
me, I thought it good in release of the
weightie burthen of my weake conscience, & also the quiet estate of this
worthie relme, to attempt the law therin,
whether I may lawfullie take another
wife more lawfullie, by whome God may
send me more issue' (907–8).
194 **weighed** considered
195 **fail** death; cf. 1.2.144–5n.
196 **groaning throe** pain bad enough to
make him cry out: the language of
childbirth. Cf. Prospero in the boat
with Miranda at *Tem* 1.2.156: 'Under
my burden groaned'.
hulling to drift to the wind with sails
furled (*OED v.*² 1); i.e. being at sea
without control over direction, though

steer (197) suggests the ability to reclaim
control instantly; cf. *TN* 1.5.195.
197 **wild sea** 'technical for "open sea"'
(Cam¹)
201 **full** completely, entirely (*OED adv.*
2a)
yet still
202 **By** i.e. with the assistance of
203 **doctors** legal scholars, but also continuing the metaphors of illness and
childbirth
203, 235 **learned** one syllable
203–14 **First . . . here.** Lincoln has a rather
more decisive role here than he does in
Holinshed: 'Wherein, after that I perceiued my conscience so doubtfull, I
mooued it in confession to you my lord
of Lincolne then ghostlie father. And
for so much as then you your selfe were
in some doubt, you mooued me to aske
the counsell of all these my lords' (908).
204 **Lincoln** See List of Roles, 25n.
205 **reek** sweat, perspire; cf. Buckingham's
agony (2.1.33) and the people *broiling*
during Anne's coronation (4.1.56).
206 **moved you** broached the subject
with you

---

193 gladded in't] glad in't *F2;* glad in one *Pope*   196 throe] *Pope;* throw *F*   203, 235 learned]
(learn'd)   205 reek] reel *Rowe*

KING

    I have spoke long. Be pleased yourself to say
    How far you satisfied me.

LINCOLN   So please your highness,

    The question did at first so stagger me,
    Bearing a state of mighty moment in't   210
    And consequence of dread, that I committed
    The daringest counsel which I had to doubt
    And did entreat your highness to this course
    Which you are running here.

KING   I then moved you,

    My lord of Canterbury, and got your leave   215
    To make this present summons. Unsolicited
    I left no reverend person in this court,
    But by particular consent proceeded
    Under your hands and seals. Therefore go on,
    For no dislike i'th' world against the person   220
    Of the good Queen, but the sharp thorny points
    Of my alleged reasons, drives this forward.
    Prove but our marriage lawful, by my life

---

209 **stagger** bewilder, nonplus (*OED v.* II 7 *fig.* a)

210–11 **Bearing . . . dread** involving, as it did, important state matters and fearful consequences

211–12 **I . . . doubt** 'I began to be unsure about my most radical suggestion', i.e. he would have counselled a divorce right away but could see the King was in two minds.

212 **daringest** two syllables

214–19 **I . . . seals.** Holinshed's account is again condensed: 'wherevpon I mooued you my lord of Canturburie, first to haue your licence, in as much as you were metropolitane, to put this matter in question, and so I did of all you my lords: to which you granted vnder your seals, heere to be shewed' (908).

215 **Canterbury** See 0.3–4n. and List of Roles, 47n.

216 **summons** i.e. to the hearing

216–17 **Unsolicited . . . court** I asked the advice of every cleric present here.

219 **Under . . . seals** with your written acquiescence, signed and sealed

219–27 **Therefore . . . world.** In Holinshed's account, Henry claims he is thinking of another marriage purely for the good of the realm, 'without anie carnall concupiscence, and not for anie displeasure or misliking of the queenes person and age, with whome I would be as well contented to continue, if our marriage may stand with the laws of God, as with anie woman aliue' (908).

222 **alleged reasons** the reasons I have outlined (allegèd)

223 **Prove but** only prove

212 daringest] *(*daringst*)*   216 summons. Unsolicited] *Theobald (subst.);* Summons vnsolicited. *F*

And kingly dignity, we are contented
To wear our mortal state to come with her,   225
Katherine, our Queen, before the primest creature
That's paragoned o'th' world.
CAMPEIUS   So please your highness,
The Queen being absent, 'tis a needful fitness
That we adjourn this court till further day.
Meanwhile must be an earnest motion   230
Made to the Queen to call back her appeal
She intends unto His Holiness.
KING [*aside*]   I may perceive
These cardinals trifle with me. I abhor
This dilatory sloth and tricks of Rome.
My learned and well-beloved servant, Cranmer,   235

---

225 **state** royal status; being, existence
226 **primest** most excellent; possibly hinting at 'youngest' (RP)
227 **paragoned** 'set forth as a perfect model' (Onions); it is hard not to hear a reference to Anne in this description.
228 **a needful fitness** necessary and appropriate
229 **adjourn** According to Holinshed, Campeius adjourns the trial because he feels it is 'verie doubtfull', not because the Queen is absent. Moreover, he specifically announces that he wishes to inform the Pope of the current state of play: 'I will not giue iudgement till I haue made relation to the pope of all our proceedings. . . . Wherfore I will adiourne this court for this time, according to the order of the court of Rome. And with that the court was dissolued, and no more doone' (908).
further another
230 **motion** See 206, 214–19n.
232–4 **I . . . Rome.** Holinshed describes Henry's fury at Campeius for delaying judgement: 'This protracting of the

conclusion of the matter, king Henrie tooke verie displeasantlie' (908). Henry's aside echoes Holinshed's description of his growing suspicions of the legates' motives: 'The king would gladlie haue had an end in the matter, but when the legats draue time, and determined vpon no certeine point, he conceiued a suspicion, that this was doone of purpose, that their dooings might draw to none effect or conclusion' (908).
235–6 **My . . . return.** Some productions have brought Cranmer on stage at this point, an interpretation for which there is no authority in the text but which establishes his face with the audience, especially if, as is often the case, the interval takes place at this point. The Archbishop mentioned at 0.3 is William Warham (see 0.3–4n.).
235 **beloved** belovèd
235–7 **Cranmer . . . along** looking forward to Cranmer's exemplary status later in the play, especially in 5.4. Cf. 4.1.105; 3.2.71–3, 400–1.

---

227 paragoned o'th'] paragon'd i'th' *Pope;* paragon o'th' *Hanmer*   232 SD] *Capell*

Prithee return. With thy approach I know
My comfort comes along. – Break up the court!
I say, set on.   *Exeunt in manner as they entered.*

3.1 *Enter* Queen [KATHERINE] *and her* Women, *as at work.*

KATHERINE
Take thy lute, wench. My soul grows sad with troubles.
Sing, and disperse 'em if thou canst. Leave working.
WOMAN (*Sings.*)
          Orpheus, with his lute, made trees

237 **Break up** dissolve, put an end to (*OED v.* VIII 57d)
238 **set on** proceed, get going (*OED v*[1]. XI 148d *a*)
3.1 Generally considered a Fletcher scene (see Appendix 3). Cut entirely by Kemble. Holinshed's account of the Cardinals' visit to Katherine places it before Campeius' adjournment of the trial. Here the playwright expands the moment into a powerfully emotive scene which marks Katherine's reluctant capitulation to Wolsey's (and the King's) will. The scene is the Queen's rooms at Bridewell Palace, which adjoined Blackfriars.
0.1 *as at work* See 74n.
1, 3 **lute** a guitar-like instrument popular in the Renaissance (though not in ancient Greece)
1 **wench** unspecified, though Doran (RSC, 1996) had Claire Marchionne as Anne Bullen play the lute and begin the song, her presence during the discussion thereby ensuring an element of tension (though *wench* would hardly have been an appropriate way for anyone, the Queen included, to address a woman of Anne's social position, who would anyway not perform such menial tasks). Productions have in fact often had Anne on stage for this scene

as one of Katherine's ladies-in-waiting, and find different moments for Katherine to express her fury at her subordinate and for Anne to depart once she knows her 'secret' is out.
2 **Leave** stop
3–14 This song appears to be a recycled version of a speech by the character Julio in Fletcher's *Capt*, written a year or two prior to *H8* and performed in 1612 (see Appendix 6). It is also possible that this song echoes one of the performances for the wedding of Elizabeth and Frederick, since Campion's *Lord's Masque*, commissioned as a replacement for the controversial, Prince Henry-sponsored *Masque of Truth* (see pp. 68–70), focuses on Orpheus. In the Doran production (RSC, 1996), the song began as a melancholy piece, but modulated into a Spanish dance, in which Katherine eventually joined, as her Spanish attendants set out to cheer her up. The positive mood thus created was broken suddenly by announcement of the Cardinals' arrival.
3 **Orpheus** Despite, or perhaps in ironic counterpoint to, the song's relationship with the royal wedding, it is fitting that, as Anderson notes in the context of the play's obsession with forms of divorce, this scene should begin 'with a

236 return … approach] *F2 (subst.);* returne, with thy approch: *F*   **3.1]** *(Actus Tertius. Scena Prima.)* 1–101 SP KATHERINE] *Malone (Q. Cath.);* Queen. *F*   1] *Pope; F lines* wench, / troubles /   3 SP] *Humphreys (subst.);* SONG. *F*   3–14] *indented for rhyme Pope; stanzas Warburton; not indented F*

And the mountain tops that freeze
Bow themselves, when he did sing.   5
To his music, plants and flowers
Ever sprung, as sun and showers
There had made a lasting spring.

Everything that heard him play,
Even the billows of the sea,   10
Hung their heads and then lay by.
In sweet music is such art,
Killing care and grief of heart
Fall asleep or, hearing, die.

Enter GRIFFITH.

KATHERINE   How now?   15
GRIFFITH
An't please your grace, the two great Cardinals

---

song about Orpheus, that Renaissance
favorite for the evocation of ideas of
harmony, inspiration, and perfection'
(127), who was separated from
Eurydice and who suffered 'soul and
body's severing' (2.3.16) at the hands
of the frenzied Bacchantes (see also
Cutts, 'Song', 187–8). The two stanzas
of the song do in fact evoke rather different moods. In 3–8, Orpheus's music
seems productive and renewing; in
9–14, it is soporific and enervating (see
Anderson, 127). In fact, the mood of
the second stanza would more appropriately evoke Morpheus (god of
sleep) than Orpheus. Perhaps the playwright is already examining the
sources for Katherine's dream; see
4.2.82.1 LN (see Appendix 6 and p.
134).
7   as as if
11   lay by reclined, rested

12–14 'There is such art in sweet music
that life-threatening stress and grief
fade or disappear when it is heard.'
Hearing is displaced, but the implication is that listening to music either
puts care and grief to sleep or destroys
them altogether.
13 **Killing** used as an adjective, i.e. care
which kills; cf. Fletcher, *Bon* 1.2.133:
'must my killing griefs make others
May-games?'
14.1 *GRIFFITH I have followed Oxf in
emending this from F's *a Gentleman* in
line with Holinshed – 'The cardinals
being in the queenes chamber of presence, the gentleman vsher aduertised
the queene that the cardinals were
come to speake with hir' (908) – and for
continuity with 2.4.0.7, 0.12, 124 and
4.2.0.2. There seems little point in a
production bringing on a separate
character at this point.

7 sprung] spring *F2;* rose *Pope*   14.1 GRIFFITH] *Oxf; a Gentleman.* F   16, 18 SP GRIFFITH]
Oxf; Gent. F   16 An't] *(*and't*)*

Wait in the presence.
KATHERINE   Would they speak with me?
GRIFFITH
They willed me say so, madam.
KATHERINE   Pray their graces
To come near.   *[Exit Griffith.]*
        What can be their business
With me, a poor weak woman, fallen from favour?   20
I do not like their coming. Now I think on't,
They should be good men, their affairs as righteous –
But all hoods make not monks.

Enter the two Cardinals, WOLSEY *and* CAMPEIUS.

WOLSEY   Peace to your highness.

---

17 **presence** i.e. presence-chamber, a
room in which meetings with royalty
took place, reception room. As *private
chamber* (28) makes clear, the typical
early modern three-room pattern for
great houses applies here: the reception room for formal meetings, the
main room in which the lady would
live and work with her ladies-in-waiting, and the closet into which the lady
would retire for privacy, meals with
intimates, etc.
18 **willed me** desired me to
19–23 **What . . . monks.** Katherine's
reflection on the meaning of the visit is
dramatic invention; there is no equivalent moment in Holinshed. Either this
question is ironic (i.e. she has a pretty
good idea of what they want from her,
as 37–9 suggests) or now that her fate
has been effectively settled, Katherine
seems to have lost much of her
strength of character. If the latter,
then she regains much of her presence
of mind in the course of this scene

(notably at 102ff.), only to lose it again
towards the end.
21 **coming . . . on't** Capell's transposi-
tion is, as Bowers notes, 'extremely
tempting', since the F reading (punctuated most bluntly in Knight³)
requires her to express 'puzzlement,
then dislike, but then, after reflecting
on her dislike, she charitably alters her
feeling since the Cardinals by their
office ought to be good men, and their
business with her . . . as well-intended
as their goodness' (Bowers). But these
emotional shifts do perhaps underline
Katherine's decline and prepare us for
her succumbing to the Cardinals' pressure in the end.
22 **as righteous** i.e. as they are good
23 **hoods . . . monks** Not everyone who
seems good is good; proverbial (Dent,
H586), usually in its Latin form, *cucul-
lus non facit monachum*, as in *TN*
1.5.51–2, *MM* 5.1.260, and Jonson,
Chapman & Marston, *Eastward Ho!*,
3.3.176.

---

19 SD] *Capell (Exit Gentleman)*   20 fallen] *(falne)*   21 coming. . . . on't,] *(comming; . . . on't,)*;
coming, . . . on't. *Capell*   23.1 CAMPEIUS] *F4; Campian F*

KATHERINE

Your graces find me here part of a housewife:
I would be all, against the worst may happen.   25
What are your pleasures with me, reverend lords?

WOLSEY

May it please you, noble madam, to withdraw
Into your private chamber? We shall give you
The full cause of our coming.

KATHERINE   Speak it here.

There's nothing I have done yet, o'my conscience,   30
Deserves a corner. Would all other women
Could speak this with as free a soul as I do.
My lords, I care not – so much I am happy
Above a number – if my actions
Were tried by every tongue, every eye saw 'em,   35
Envy and base opinion set against 'em,
I know my life so even. If your business

---

24 **part of** partly
25 'I would like to be a proper housewife, in case I have no other role left'; also a sense of the wish to be restored to the status of wife.
 against the worst broadly proverbial (Dent, W912); cf. *TC* 3.2.69–70: 'To fear the worst oft cures the worse.'
26 drawn directly from Holinshed: 'quoth she, What is your plesure with me?' (908)
27–9 **May . . . coming**. Again, this is almost verbatim Holinshed: 'If it please your grace (quoth cardinall Wolseie) to go into your priuie chamber, we will shew you the cause of our comming' (908).
28 **private chamber** closet (see 17n.); Wolsey would like to get rid of any who might hear the conversation; Katherine clearly has no wish to let enemies into the inner room, her most personal space.
29–39 **Speak . . . dealing**. expansion of

Holinshed's version: 'My lord (quoth she) if yee haue anie thing to saie, speake it openlie before all these folke, for I feare nothing that yee can saie against me, but that I would all the world should heare and see it, and therefore speake your mind' (908).
30–1 **nothing . . . corner** proverbial assertion (Dent, T587: 'Truth seeks no corners'), which firmly associates Katherine with the truth
31–2 **Would . . . do**. sometimes taken by directors as a cue for Katherine to glance at Anne, if present (though see 1.1n.)
32 **free** untroubled
34 **a number** i.e. many people
36 **Envy . . . opinion** i.e. every form of envy and base opinion
37 **even** true, straightforward
37–9 **If . . . boldly**. If you are here because of me, and because of my position as the King's wife, say so boldly.

26 reverend] *F2;* reuerent *F*   35 every . . . every] *(eu'ry . . . eu'ry)*

Seek me out, and that way I am wife in,
Out with it boldly. Truth loves open dealing.

WOLSEY   *Tanta est erga te mentis integritas, Regina*   40
          serenissima –

KATHERINE

O, good my lord, no Latin.
I am not such a truant since my coming
As not to know the language I have lived in.
A strange tongue makes my cause more strange,
    suspicious.   45
Pray speak in English. Here are some will thank you,
If you speak truth, for their poor mistress' sake.
Believe me, she has had much wrong. Lord Cardinal,
The willingest sin I ever yet committed
May be absolved in English.

WOLSEY   Noble lady,   50

39 **Truth . . . dealing**. See 30–1n.; this expression, for which there is no equivalent in Holinshed, conflates two proverbial sayings – Dent, T587 ('Truth seeks no corners') (cf. 30–1n.) and P383 ('Plain dealing is best'). Dekker, *Whore*, includes characters named 'Truth' and 'Plaine-dealing'.

40–1 Wolsey's Latin can be translated as 'So honourable are my intentions towards you, most serene queen'; Holinshed simply mentions that Wolsey began 'to speake to hir in Latine' (908), but does not provide a sample.

42–50 **O . . . English**. Katherine's admonition makes explicit much that is implicit in Holinshed's understated report: 'Naie good my lord (quoth she) speake to me in English' (908). To address the Queen in Latin was to distance her emotionally from both the situation and the nation, and to make her seem a foreigner to those listening; her response emphasizes her status as

Queen of England, despite her Spanish birth (but compare 82–91, 149–51, and 2.4.13, 53). She also makes clear at 46–7 that she intends to have witnesses, in the form of her women, to the Cardinals' proposals.

43 **truant** Katherine pictures herself as a good pupil, not one who misses school; cf., as Foakes (Ard²) suggests, *1H4* 3.1.202–3: 'I will never be a truant, love, / Till I have learnt thy language'.

45 **strange, suspicious** There is no need, with Dyce², to hyphenate this into a compound word. Katherine is afraid that using a foreign language will make her cause seem foreign and therefore suspect.

49 **willingest** two syllables

50–61 **Noble . . . cause**. Again, the bare bones of Holinshed's account are fleshed out: 'Forsooth (quoth the cardinall) good madame, if it please you, we come both to know your mind how you are disposed to doo in this matter betweene the king and you, and also to

38 wife] Wise *Rowe*   40, 50 SP] *Rowe; Card.* F   45 strange, suspicious] strange-suspicious *Dyce²* (*Walker*); strange suspicious (*Vaughan*)   49 willingest] (willing'st)

320

I am sorry my integrity should breed –
And service to his majesty and you –
So deep suspicion where all faith was meant.
We come not by the way of accusation,
To taint that honour every good tongue blesses,   55
Nor to betray you any way to sorrow –
You have too much, good lady – but to know
How you stand minded in the weighty difference
Between the King and you, and to deliver,
Like free and honest men, our just opinions   60
And comforts to your cause.

CAMPEIUS   Most honoured madam,
My lord of York, out of his noble nature,
Zeal, and obedience he still bore your grace,
Forgetting, like a good man, your late censure
Both of his truth and him – which was too far –   65
Offers, as I do, in a sign of peace,
His service and his counsel.

KATHERINE [*aside*]   To betray me.
    [*to them*] My lords, I thank you both for your good
        wills.

---

declare secretlie our opinions and
counsell vnto you: which we doo onelie
for verie zeale and obedience we beare
vnto your grace' (908). The expansion,
as Foakes (Ard²) notes, ensures that we
see Wolsey's personal priorities,
especially at 51–2: his own honour
first, then others' as an afterthought.
51 **breed** Jane Lapotaire notes that
    'Wolsey, in his attempt to placate her,
    uses the most inflammatory word pos-
    sible to Katherine' (Lapotaire, 145),
    which might explain the awkward
    structure of his sentence as he realizes
    the inappropriateness of the word and
    attempts to recoup.
53 **faith** honour, loyalty
54 **by . . . accusation** in order to accuse

60 **free** unbiased
61 **comforts** here, 'encouragement, aid,
    support' (*OED sb.* + 1a), though cf. 104
63 **still** always
65 **which . . . far** in which you went too far
66 **in** as
68–80 After her aside, Katherine's speech
    echoes and develops Holinshed's
    report: 'I thanke you for your good
    will, but to make you answer in your
    request I cannot so suddenlie, for I was
    set among my maids at worke, thinking
    full little of anie such matter, wherein
    there needeth a longer deliberation,
    and a better head than mine to make
    answer: for I need counsell in this case
    which toucheth me so neere' (908).

61 your] *F2;* our *F*   67 SD] *Capell (subst.)*   68 SD] *Capell (subst.)*

Ye speak like honest men – pray God ye prove so.
But how to make ye suddenly an answer   70
In such a point of weight, so near mine honour –
More near my life, I fear – with my weak wit,
And to such men of gravity and learning,
In truth I know not. I was set at work
Among my maids, full little, God knows, looking   75
Either for such men or such business.
For her sake that I have been – for I feel
The last fit of my greatness – good your graces,
Let me have time and counsel for my cause.
Alas, I am a woman friendless, hopeless.   80

WOLSEY

Madam, you wrong the King's love with these fears:
Your hopes and friends are infinite.

KATHERINE   In England

But little for my profit. Can you think, lords,
That any Englishman dare give me counsel?

---

69 **pray ... so** This parenthetical remark, along with *More . . . fear* at 72, could reasonably be marked (and certainly directed) as an aside (following Capell at 67), since it would appear to negate the rhetorical strategy of Katherine's speech for her to let the Cardinals hear her doubts about them. I have nonetheless chosen not to interpolate an SD, since it seems to me that an actress could make sense of the speech either way and since *suddenly* at 70 seems to me to be the key term: she simply has not had time to prepare what she will say, and the speech lacks coherence as a result.

70 **suddenly** off the cuff

71 **point of weight** serious matter
   near closely concerning

72 **wit** intellect

74 **set** seated; cf. current Northern English 'I was sat'.

75–6 **looking / Either for** expecting either

77–8 **for ... greatness** It is particularly difficult to know if this should be marked as an aside, looking forward as it seems to do to Katherine's capitulation.

78 **fit** period, hour

82–91 **In . . . lords.** Despite her assertions of Englishness earlier in the scene (see 41–9), Katherine acknowledges her foreign, beleaguered status. The speech parallels Holinshed's version closely: 'for anie counsell or freendship that I can find in England, they are not for my profit. What thinke you my lords, will anie Englishman counsell me, or be freend to me against the K. pleasure that is his subiect? Naie forsooth. And as for my counsell in whom I will put my trust, they be not here, they be in Spaine in my owne countrie' (908).

81] *Pope; F lines* Madam / . . . feares, /   83 profit. Can] *F2 (subst.);* profit can *F*

Or be a known friend 'gainst his highness' pleasure –   85
Though he be grown so desperate to be honest –
And live a subject? Nay, forsooth, my friends,
They that must weigh out my afflictions,
They that my trust must grow to, live not here:
They are, as all my other comforts, far hence   90
In mine own country, lords.

CAMPEIUS   I would your grace
Would leave your griefs and take my counsel.

KATHERINE   How, sir?

CAMPEIUS

Put your main cause into the King's protection.
He's loving and most gracious. 'Twill be much
Both for your honour better and your cause,   95
For if the trial of the law o'ertake ye,
You'll part away disgraced.

WOLSEY   He tells you rightly.

KATHERINE

Ye tell me what ye wish for both – my ruin.
Is this your Christian counsel? Out upon ye!
Heaven is above all yet: there sits a judge   100

---

86 **so ... honest** reckless enough to try to
be honest
87 **And ... subject** i.e. think he could
carry on behaving as if he were one of
Henry's loyal subjects without being
punished for his defence of a cause
contrary to the King's wishes
forsooth in truth, truly
88 **weigh out** balance, compensate for
90 **as** like
93–7 **Put ... disgraced**. reworked from
Holinshed's opening sentence about the
Cardinals' visit: 'the king sent the two
cardinals to the queene (who was then in
Bridewell) to persuade with her by their
wisdoms, and to aduise her to surrender
the whole matter into the kings hands by

hir owne consent & will, which should
be much better to hir honour, than to
stand to the triall of law, and thereby be
condemned, which should seeme much
to hir dishonour' (908).
93 **main** principal
97 **part away** depart
97–176 **He ... unmannerly**. There is no
parallel in Holinshed for this section,
which amplifies the antipathetic relations between Katherine and the
Cardinals, especially Wolsey, and characterizes the Queen as passionate in
the face of injustice.
100 **Heaven ... all** proverbial (Dent,
H348); cf. *R2* 3.3.17.
100–1 **Heaven ... corrupt**. Katherine's

98 both –] *Collier (subst.);* both, *F*

That no king can corrupt.

CAMPEIUS   Your rage mistakes us.

KATHERINE

The more shame for ye. Holy men I thought ye,

Upon my soul, two reverend cardinal virtues –

But cardinal sins and hollow hearts I fear ye.

Mend 'em for shame, my lords. Is this your comfort?   105

The cordial that ye bring a wretched lady,

A woman lost among ye, laughed at, scorned?

I will not wish ye half my miseries:

I have more charity. But say I warned ye.

Take heed, for heaven's sake take heed, lest at once   110

The burden of my sorrows fall upon ye.

WOLSEY

Madam, this is a mere distraction.

You turn the good we offer into envy.

KATHERINE

Ye turn me into nothing. Woe upon ye,

rage expresses itself unguardedly here, as she implies that, in the divorce proceedings, the King is trying to corrupt God. For God as judge, see Psalms, 7.8, 9.8, 50.6, and (doubtless best known of all) the Creed: 'he shall come to iudge the quicke and the dead' (*Common Prayer*, 'Morning Prayer'). For God as impartial, see for example 2 Chronicles, 19.7 and Romans, 2.11.

103–4 **cardinal virtues . . . cardinal sins** punning on 'carnal' *(cardinal* being disyllabic*)*: the Seven Deadly Sins, or *cardinal sins* – pride, covetousness, envy, wrath, gluttony, sloth, lechery – and their counterparts, the *cardinal virtues* – justice, prudence, temperance, fortitude – to which were added the 'theological' virtues – faith, hope, charity – to equal the sins

105 **comfort** picks up on Wolsey's use of the word *comforts* at 61, though here Katherine uses the word in a slightly different sense, as 'relief or aid in want, pain, sickness, etc.' (*OED sb.* + 4)

106 **cordial** a medicine which invigorates the heart; a comforting drink (*OED* B *sb.* 1)

107 **woman . . . scorned** 'Laughed to scorn' is familiar biblical phrasing; see especially 2 Kings, 19.21: 'O virgine, daughter of Zion, he hathe despised thee, *and* laughed thee to scorne.'

110 **at once** at some time in the future

112 **mere** downright, sheer
    distraction frenzy; evasion of the facts

113 **envy** ill will, malice, enmity (*OED sb.* + 1)

114–15 **Woe . . . professors!** Cf. Matthew, 23.15: 'Wo *be* vnto you, Scribes and Pharises, hypocrites: for ye

111 burden] *(*burthen*)*   112+ SP WOLSEY] *Rowe; Car.* F   114 SP] *Malone (Q. Cath.); Quee.* F

And all such false professors! Would you have me –   115
If you have any justice, any pity,
If ye be anything but churchmen's habits –
Put my sick cause into his hands that hates me?
Alas, 'has banished me his bed already;
His love, too, long ago. I am old, my lords,   120
And all the fellowship I hold now with him
Is only my obedience. What can happen
To me above this wretchedness? All your studies
Make me a curse, like this.

CAMPEIUS   Your fears are worse.

KATHERINE

Have I lived thus long – let me speak myself,   125
Since virtue finds no friends – a wife, a true one –
A woman, I dare say without vainglory,

compasse sea and land to make one of your profession'; *professors* are those who profess to believe (in this case, in the Gospel); cf. 157, 167.

117 **habits** See 23n.

120 **His . . . ago** F4's (and Rowe's) relocation of the comma clarifies the balance between *bed* and *love*, and implies 'that Katherine lost Henry's love before she was banished from his bed, a correct order of events after he had fallen in love with Anne Boleyn' (Bowers).

old Katherine was in fact forty-three in 1529 when the interview with the Cardinals took place: assuming the playwright(s) were reflecting this, the implication is that she is *old* only in the sense that, in the wake of a number of miscarriages and still births, she is highly unlikely now to produce an heir. Obviously, Henry has also demonstrated a sexual preference for younger women. Productions often tend to por-

tray Katherine as being in her fifties, thereby emphasizing Henry's patriarchal equation of female maturity and redundancy.

121 **fellowship** The word refers to intimacy in general, but clearly implies principally the cessation of sexual relations between Henry and Katherine.

123 **above** that is worse than

124 **a curse** awkwardly compressed phrasing; Hoeniger emends to 'accursed' in line with Foakes's plausible suggestion (Ard²) that secretary hand *d* or *t* has been misread as *e*. The more likely, though admittedly more elliptical, meanings of 123–4, however (either 'everything you do results in the misery you see when you look at me' or 'you have put a great deal of research into putting me under a curse in this way'), do not require emendation.

125 **speak** defend

127 **vainglory** boasting

119 'has] *Dyce²*; ha's *F*; he has *Capell*   120 love, too,] *F4 (subst.)*; Loue, too *F*   122 my obedience] by obedience *F2*   124 a curse] accursed *Hoeniger (Ard²)*   125+ SP KATHERINE] *Malone (Q. Cath.)*; Qu. *F*

Never yet branded with suspicion –
Have I with all my full affections
Still met the King, loved him next heaven, obeyed
  him,   130
Been, out of fondness, superstitious to him,
Almost forgot my prayers to content him,
And am I thus rewarded? 'Tis not well, lords.
Bring me a constant woman to her husband,
One that ne'er dreamed a joy beyond his pleasure,   135
And to that woman, when she has done most,
Yet will I add an honour: a great patience.

WOLSEY

Madam, you wander from the good we aim at.

KATHERINE

My lord, I dare not make myself so guilty
To give up willingly that noble title   140
Your master wed me to. Nothing but death
Shall e'er divorce my dignities.

WOLSEY   Pray hear me.

128 **suspicion** i.e. of adulterous behaviour or any other activity that might merit divorce
129 **full affections** genuine love, powerful emotions
130 **Still** always
131 **fondness** a word neatly balanced at this stage in its development between love and stupidity (*OED* 1, 2, 3)
superstitious to fond to the point of idolatry of
137 **great patience** This particular expression invokes the figure of 'patient Griselda', a much put-upon royal wife from Boccaccio's *Decameron*, who was the subject of a poem presented to Mary Tudor in 1558 by William Forrest, her chaplain, which focused upon '[y]oure Mothers meeke life', and

sustained a specific analogy between the charmless king of the story and Henry and between Katherine and Griselda: 'Her I heere lyken to *Grysilde* the goode, / As well I so maye, for her great patience' (Forrest, 5). This appropriation of the Griselda story both empowers Katherine by way of her exemplary humility and severely criticizes Henry for his immoderate behaviour towards his wife. Ironically perhaps, the image of Griselda was one which Elizabeth I later adopted for her own relationship with her male advisers. See also Jones & Stallybrass, 'Griselda'.
142 **dignities** a combination of quality and rank (*OED* 1 and 2); cf. 184, 3.2.328–9, 379; see also *1H4* 1.3.205, *TC* 2.2.193.

129 Have I] *Alexander;* Haue I, F   130 King, loved] *Alexander;* King? Lou'd F   heaven] *(*Heau'n*)*
heaven, obeyed him,] *Alexander;* Heau'n? / Obey'd him? F   131, 132 him,] *Alexander;* him? F
138–9] *Rowe³; F lines* good / at. / Lord, / guiltie, /

KATHERINE

Would I had never trod this English earth
Or felt the flatteries that grow upon it.
Ye have angels' faces, but heaven knows your hearts.   145
What will become of me now, wretched lady?
I am the most unhappy woman living.
[*to her women*] Alas, poor wenches, where are now
    your fortunes?
Shipwrecked upon a kingdom where no pity,
No friends, no hope, no kindred weep for me,   150
Almost no grave allowed me, like the lily
That once was mistress of the field and flourished,
I'll hang my head and perish.

WOLSEY   If your grace
Could but be brought to know our ends are honest,
You'd feel more comfort. Why should we, good lady,   155
Upon what cause, wrong you? Alas, our places,
The way of our profession, is against it.

145 **angels'** . . . **hearts** a conflation of the proverbial saying 'fair face foul heart' (Dent, F3) (cf. *RJ* 3.2.73, *Mac* 1.7.82) with a reference to St Gregory's famous, if somewhat unlikely, description of the English as '*non Angli sed angeli*' ('not Angles, but angels') because of their (alleged) good looks; see also 1 Samuel, 16.7: 'man loketh on the outward appearance, but the Lord beholdeth the heart'.

146 **me** . . . **lady** characteristic rhetoric from Katherine, moving from self (first person) to objectification of self (third person) (JH)

147–52 **I** . . . **perish** This is syntactically odd. I have punctuated, contrary to editorial tradition, in the belief that *Alas* . . . *Fortunes?* is a single line of concern for the others, the rest Katherine's reflection on her predicament. Thus '*Shipwrecked*' refers to Katherine, though it is hard not to assume a primary connection between the wormen's

fortunes and the shipwreck.

148–9 **wenches** . . . **kingdom** Three of Katherine's principal ladies-in-waiting were Spanish; see List of Roles, 34n.

151–3 **lily** . . . **perish** biblical phrasing, familiar from the Sermon on the Mount (Matthew, 6.28: 'Learne, how the lilies of the field do growe'), but the allusion in this negative context is most probably to Psalm 103.15–16: 'The daies of man are as grasse: as a flower of the field, so florisheth he. / For the winde goeth ouer it, and it is gone, and the place therof shal knowe it no more'; cf. also Spenser, *Faerie Queene*, 2.6.16: 'The lilly, Lady of the flowring field'.

154 **ends** intentions

156 **places** positions, vocations

157 **The** . . . **profession** the manner of life chosen by a person entering a religious order (*OED profession* I 1a) or, more generally, the lifestyle required by the faith one professes (II 5 *spec.* a); cf. 115, 167.

148 SD] *Rowe*   150–1 me, . . . me,] *Capell;* me? . . . me? *F*

We are to cure such sorrows, not to sow 'em.
For goodness' sake, consider what you do,
How you may hurt yourself, ay, utterly   160
Grow from the King's acquaintance, by this carriage.
The hearts of princes kiss obedience,
So much they love it, but to stubborn spirits
They swell and grow as terrible as storms.
I know you have a gentle, noble temper,   165
A soul as even as a calm. Pray think us
Those we profess: peacemakers, friends, and servants.

CAMPEIUS

Madam, you'll find it so. You wrong your virtues
With these weak women's fears. A noble spirit,
As yours was put into you, ever casts   170
Such doubts as false coin from it. The King loves you:
Beware you lose it not. For us, if you please
To trust us in your business, we are ready
To use our utmost studies in your service.

KATHERINE

Do what ye will, my lords, and pray forgive me   175
If I have used myself unmannerly.

159 **For goodness' sake** Cf. Prologue 23; Humphreys glosses this as 'out of your own good nature (not the modern colloquial sense)'.
161 **carriage** behaviour
166 **as even . . . calm** a simile not found elsewhere in the Shakespeare canon, but cf. Fletcher, *Pilg*: 'as easy as a calme' (1.1.39)
167 **profess** avow, affirm oneself to be something (sometimes, as here, with omission of both reflexive pronoun and infinitive) (*OED v.* II 2 *trans.* a); cf. 115, 157.
  peacemakers Wolsey locates the Cardinals' mission in relation to the seventh beatitude ('Blessed are the peace makers'), which, in its Latin form (*beati pacifici*), was James I's personal motto.

169 **weak women's fears** Campeius means either that Katherine's 'natural' weakness as a woman is overshadowing her inherited and acquired strength as 'a queen and daughter to a king' (4.2.172), or that, as a strong woman, she should not behave like weaker members of her sex.
174 **studies** efforts
175–6 Ard² returned to F's reading, making *If . . . unmannerly* a preliminary clause to 'You know I am a woman'; but F4 more accurately reflects the play's use of the source. In Holinshed, Katherine begins her sentence simply 'I am a poore woman' (908), with no preliminary apologetic clause (see 177–84n.).
176 **used myself** behaved

168] *Pope; F lines* so: / Vertues / 170 was] *Pope;* was, F 172 lose] *(loose)* 175] *Rowe³; F lines* Lords: / me; / 175–6 me . . . unmannerly.] *F4 (*me, . . . unmannerly;*) ;* me; . . . vnmannerly, F

You know I am a woman, lacking wit
To make a seemly answer to such persons.
Pray do my service to his majesty:
He has my heart yet, and shall have my prayers   180
While I shall have my life. Come, reverend fathers,
Bestow your counsels on me. She now begs
That little thought when she set footing here
She should have bought her dignities so dear.   *Exeunt.*

3.2   *Enter the* Duke of NORFOLK, Duke of SUFFOLK,
          Lord SURREY *and* Lord CHAMBERLAIN.

NORFOLK
    If you will now unite in your complaints
    And force them with a constancy, the Cardinal
    Cannot stand under them. If you omit
    The offer of this time, I cannot promise

177–84 Katherine's speech of surrender is drawn loosely from Holinshed: 'I am a poore woman, lacking wit, to answer to anie such noble persons of wisedom as you be, in so weightie a matter, therefore I praie you be good to me poore woman, destitute of freends here in a forren region, and your counsell also I will be glad to heare. And therewith she tooke the cardinall by the hand, and led him into hir priuie chamber with the other cardinall' (908).

177 **wit** intellect, understanding

183 **set footing** arrived, entered (the country) (*OED vbl. sb.* 1a)

184 **bought . . . dear** had to negotiate over her status as Queen, paid so high a price for eminence; for *dignities*, see 142n.

3.2 The only scene in the play generally held to contain the work of more than one hand (see Appendix 3). Spedding's analysis suggested that the scene was Shakespeare's until line 203 and Fletcher's from there on (Spedding, 382; see also Hickson, 198). Fleay

(*Chronicle*, 251) thought the first half was by Massinger. Hoy, 7(80) suggested that the second half of the scene was also Shakespeare's, but was reworked by Fletcher. Hope (*Authorship*, 67–83) agrees (on different grounds) with Spedding. Again, the scene is primarily dependent upon Holinshed, but in a complex relationship with a range of other sources (see pp. 168–73). The location is a room at court.

1–3 **If . . . them.** Norfolk's opening lines reveal the change in Wolsey's fortunes. Compare Holinshed: 'When the nobles of the realme perceiued the cardinall to be in displeasure, they began to accuse him of such offenses as they knew might be proued against him, and thereof they made a booke conteining certeine articles, to which diuerse of the kings councell set their hands' (909).

2 **force . . . constancy** persevere steadily with them

3–4 **omit . . . time** neglect the current opportunity

But that you shall sustain more new disgraces   5
With these you bear already.
SURREY   I am joyful
    To meet the least occasion that may give me
    Remembrance of my father-in-law the Duke,
    To be revenged on him.
SUFFOLK   Which of the peers
    Have uncontemned gone by him, or at least   10
    Strangely neglected? When did he regard
    The stamp of nobleness in any person
    Out of himself?
CHAMBERLAIN   My lords, you speak your pleasures.
    What he deserves of you and me, I know;
    What we can do to him – though now the time   15
    Gives way to us – I much fear. If you cannot
    Bar his access to th' King, never attempt
    Anything on him, for he hath a witchcraft
    Over the King in's tongue.
NORFOLK   O, fear him not:
    His spell in that is out. The King hath found   20
    Matter against him that for ever mars
    The honey of his language. No, he's settled,

8 **Duke** i.e. Buckingham; cf. 2.1.41–4.
9 **on him** i.e. on Wolsey
10 **uncontemned** without being treated
   with contempt (*OED ppl. a.* from *v.* 1)
11 **Strangely neglected** ignored as a
   stranger or foreigner
13 **Out of** beside, other than
   speak your pleasures tell us your
   wishes; effectively a meaningless phrase
   here. As Maxwell notes, the typically
   careful Lord Chamberlain finds 'a
   polite way of expressing [his] refusal to
   commit himself to agreement' (186).
16 **way** opportunity
   I much fear I have my doubts.
17–18 **never . . . him** Don't try to attack
   (or trick) him.

20 **His . . . out** His influence has come to
   an end.
22–8 **No . . . enemy.** Holinshed recounts
   Wolsey's desire to slow down the
   divorce process because his plans were
   threatened by the King's liaison with
   Anne Bullen. He wrote to the Pope
   that he should 'defer the iudgement of
   the diuorce, till he might frame the
   kings mind to his purpose'; the King
   found out (see 30–7n.), and 'tooke so
   high displeasure with such his cloked
   dissimulation, that he determined to
   abase his degree' (909).
22 **he** Wolsey, though not inconceivably
   Henry

5 more] *(moe)*

330

Not to come off, in his displeasure.
SURREY   Sir,
   I should be glad to hear such news as this
   Once every hour.
NORFOLK   Believe it, this is true.   25
   In the divorce his contrary proceedings
   Are all unfolded, wherein he appears
   As I would wish mine enemy.
SURREY   How came
   His practices to light?
SUFFOLK   Most strangely.
SURREY   O, how, how?
SUFFOLK
   The Cardinal's letters to the Pope miscarried   30
   And came to th'eye o'th' King, wherein was read
   How that the Cardinal did entreat his holiness
   To stay the judgement o'th' divorce; for if
   It did take place, 'I do', quoth he, 'perceive
   My King is tangled in affection to   35
   A creature of the Queen's, Lady Anne Bullen.'

23 **Not . . . off** He has no way to get out of this.
   his Henry's
26–8 **In . . . enemy**. Anderson notes the ambiguous syntax: Norfolk means that the King has now recognized that Wolsey's proceedings in respect of the divorce have not reflected his wishes, but his words could just as easily be read to imply that 'the very concept of the divorce . . . is the distillation of [Wolsey's] contradictory career' (Anderson, 127).
26 **contrary proceedings** either contradictory actions or opposition to the King's preferences (see 32–6); possibly both
29 **practices** schemes, plots

30–7 **The . . . this?** Holinshed implies that Wolsey's covert activity was under royal surveillance: 'the cardinall required the pope by letters and secret messengers, that in anie wise he should defer the iudgement. . . . Howbeit he went about nothing so secretlie, but that the same came to the kings knowledge' (909); see also 124n.
30 **miscarried** a usefully ambivalent way to say that the letters never reached their destination, though whether accidentally or by intervention is not clear
33 **stay** delay, defer
36 **creature** servant, one who owes her position to a patron (*OED* 5); cf. 49.

30 letters] letter *Steevens²*

331

SURREY

Has the King this?

SUFFOLK   Believe it.

SURREY   Will this work?

CHAMBERLAIN

The King in this perceives him how he coasts

And hedges his own way. But in this point

All his tricks founder, and he brings his physic   40

After his patient's death. The King already

Hath married the fair lady.

SURREY   Would he had!

SUFFOLK

May you be happy in your wish, my lord,

For I profess you have it.

SURREY   Now all my joy

Trace the conjunction.

SUFFOLK   My amen to't.

NORFOLK   All men's.   45

SUFFOLK

There's order given for her coronation.

Marry, this is yet but young, and may be left

To some ears unrecounted. But, my lords,

39–40 in . . . founder All his tricks are wrecked with this revelation.

40–1 he . . . death proverbial (Dent, D133); cf. Dekker, *Match Me*: 'You giue me physicke after I'm dead' (G1ʳ).

40 physic cure, medicine

42 married Holinshed recounts that on 14 November, 1532, on his return from a trip to Calais to enlist the French king's support for the divorce, Henry 'married priuily the ladie Anne Bullongne, . . . which marriage was kept so secret, that verie few knew it till Easter next insuing, when it was perceiued that she was with child' (929). This demonstrates, once again, the play's creative attitude to time:

Wolsey's fall in fact came three years earlier, and he was dead by 1530.

45 Trace the conjunction literally, follow the process of the marriage, but also with an astrological sense, suggesting the hand of fate in the event

46 There's order given Orders have been issued.

47, 54 Marry a standard interjection, derived from the name of Mary, mother of Jesus, though in this case, as occasionally, perhaps reflecting 'marriage', too

47 yet but young very recent news

47–8 may . . . unrecounted (i) may not yet be known to everyone; (ii) is not suitable for all ears. This is *OED*'s only citation for *unrecounted* (*ppl. a.*).

She is a gallant creature, and complete
In mind and feature. I persuade me from her   50
Will fall some blessing to this land which shall
In it be memorized.

SURREY   But will the King
Digest this letter of the Cardinal's?
The Lord forbid.

NORFOLK   Marry, amen.

SUFFOLK   No, no:
There be more wasps that buzz about his nose   55
Will make this sting the sooner. Cardinal Campeius
Is stolen away to Rome; hath ta'en no leave;
Has left the cause o'th' King unhandled; and
Is posted as the agent of our Cardinal
To second all his plot. I do assure you   60
The King cried 'Ha!' at this.

CHAMBERLAIN   Now God incense him,
And let him cry 'Ha!' louder.

NORFOLK   But, my lord,
When returns Cranmer?

---

49 **creature** created being (*OED* 1a);
there is a possible echo of *creature* as
'servant' at 36, though there is no obvious irony in Suffolk's words.
complete perfect

51 **fall** befall; playing on the idea of giving birth
blessing one of the foretastes the play
offers of Cranmer's concluding
prophecy of Elizabeth's future; cf.
2.3.57.

52 **memorized** remembered as of great
importance

53 **Digest** absorb and forget

56–60 **Cardinal . . . plot**. This contradicts Holinshed, who reports that 'cardinall *Campeius* tooke his leaue of the
king' (908), but echoes Hall – 'Thus

departed out of England in high displeasure, the crafty Cardinall
Campeius, leauyng behynd him hys
subtle felowe, whiche after their
departinge from the kyng at Grafton,
neuer sawe the kynge, nor came in his
presence' (B3ᵛ; fol. clxxxiii) – or (less
likely) Foxe, who notes that Campeius
'craftily shifted himselfe out of the
Realme' (Foxe 1596, 906).

57 **stolen** one syllable

58 **left . . . unhandled** abandoned his
role of overseeing the divorce

59 **Is posted** has been publicly
denounced; possibly also, has hastened
away

60 **second** support, encourage

61, 62 **Ha!** See 1.2.186n.

---

55 more] *(moe)*   57 stolen] *(stolne)*   Rome; . . . leave;] *Capell;* Rome, . . . leave, *F*

SUFFOLK

He is returned in his opinions, which
Have satisfied the King for his divorce,   65
Together with all famous colleges,
Almost, in Christendom. Shortly, I believe,
His second marriage shall be published, and
Her coronation. Katherine no more
Shall be called 'Queen', but 'Princess Dowager',   70
And 'widow to Prince Arthur'.

NORFOLK   This same Cranmer's

A worthy fellow, and hath ta'en much pain
In the King's business.

SUFFOLK   He has, and we shall see him

For it an archbishop.

NORFOLK   So I hear.

SUFFOLK   'Tis so.

Enter WOLSEY *and* CROMWELL.

The Cardinal.

NORFOLK   Observe, observe: he's moody.   75

[*They stand apart.*]

WOLSEY

The packet, Cromwell: gave't you the King?

64–7 **He . . . Christendom**. For versions
  of Cranmer's return, see LN.
68 **published** announced
69–71 **Katherine . . . Arthur**. It was
  decreed by Act of Parliament early in
  1533 'that queene Katharine should no
  more be called queene, but princesse
  Dowager, as the widow of prince Arthur'
  (Holinshed, 929); see also 2.4.172–8n.
72 **worthy fellow** characteristic haughtiness from Norfolk
72–3 **ta'en . . . In** put a great deal of

effort into
74 **archbishop** Holinshed follows his
  account of Katherine's loss of the title
  of 'Queen' with a report of Cranmer's
  installation as Archbishop of
  Canterbury early in 1533 in the wake
  of the death of Warham the previous
  summer (see Holinshed, 929).
75 **Observe** yet more surveillance
76 **packet** bundle of letters; specifically,
  the early modern equivalent of the
  'diplomatic bag'

64 in his] with his *Rowe;* in wise *(Vaughan)*   66 colleges] colleges' *Neilson-Hill (Vaughan)*   74.1]
after Cardinal. *Steevens*   76–252 SP WOLSEY] *(Car(d).)*   75 SD] *Collier 2 (Collier MS) (They
stand back.)*   76] *Steevens-Reed²; F lines* Cromwell, / King? /

CROMWELL

To his own hand, in's bedchamber.

WOLSEY   Looked he

O'th' inside of the paper?

CROMWELL   Presently

He did unseal them, and the first he viewed,

He did it with a serious mind; a heed   80

Was in his countenance. You he bade

Attend him here this morning.

WOLSEY   Is he ready

To come abroad?

CROMWELL   I think by this he is.

WOLSEY   Leave me a while.   *Exit Cromwell.*

It shall be to the Duchess of Alençon,   85

The French King's sister: he shall marry her.

---

78 **Presently** immediately
80 **heed** careful attention (*OED sb.* 1); *OED* offers no usage with the indefinite article.
83 **abroad** out of his private rooms
85–6 Wolsey had not, of course, supported the divorce proceedings only to have the King marry the wrong woman; see 2.2.40n.
85 **It shall be** Rowe marked asides for Wolsey here and at 94 which have been generally echoed by editors, but defining the 'aside' is difficult in this passage. Wolsey must be unaware that he has company at this point; he is thus soliloquizing (or, very possibly, addressing the audience and therefore in a position well removed from the doors) rather than speaking aside. An alternative might be to mark asides at 75, 91, 92, 104, 105 and 106, since once they see Wolsey on stage, it is the courtiers who speak surreptitiously, but strictly speaking this would

require asides to be marked also between the King's opening line at 107 and the moment at 135 when Lovell alerts Wolsey to the King's presence, since the King's brief initial speech and subsequent conversation with the courtiers is premised on Wolsey's being out of earshot. It could perhaps best be argued that the scene offers conversation in counterpoint, none of which is truly 'aside', but all of which requires directorial decisions.

Duchess of Alençon Marguerite of Angoulême, Duchess of Alençon, was sister to François I of France and widow of Charles, Duke of Alençon, grandson of the Duke of Alençon in *1H6*. Marguerite married Henri II, King of Navarre, in January 1527. For a curious tacit conflation of Katherine and Marguerite, see pp. 132–5; 4.2.82.1 LN.
86 **her** stressed metrically

77–8] *Ard²*; F *lines* Bed-chamber. / Paper? / Presently / 78 paper] papers *Keightley*
82–3] *Hanmer*; F *lines* Morning. / abroad? / is. / 85] SD *aside* / *Rowe* Alençon] *(Alanson)*

Anne Bullen? No, I'll no Anne Bullens for him:
There's more in't than fair visage. Bullen?
No, we'll no Bullens. Speedily I wish
To hear from Rome. The Marchioness of Pembroke?   90
NORFOLK
He's discontented.
SUFFOLK   Maybe he hears the King
Does whet his anger to him.
SURREY   Sharp enough,
Lord, for thy justice.
WOLSEY
The late Queen's gentlewoman? A knight's daughter
To be her mistress' mistress? The Queen's Queen?   95
This candle burns not clear. 'Tis I must snuff it;
Then out it goes. What though I know her virtuous
And well-deserving? Yet I know her for

87, 88, 89 **Bullen** Wolsey's repetition of Anne's surname is evidence of his snobbery: he is furious that his efforts have been turned to the advantage of a mere Bullen rather than a princess (compare 90n. and 94–5n.). The Bullens were in fact a major courtly family (though this is not apparent in the play), but Wolsey would expect a royal marriage to serve a dynastic and diplomatic function on the European, not domestic, stage.

87–9 **I'll no . . . we'll no** The understood verbs are not clear, but the meaning is: 'I won't be arranging any marriage for the King with this politically and socially inappropriate woman'.

88 **fair visage** Wolsey's speech makes clear both his opinion of the King's sexual motivations and the generally perceived irrelevance of love and desire in marriage arrangements for Renaissance heads of state. Henry's later rejection of Anne of Cleves because he found her sexually un-

attractive was the ultimate diplomatic *faux pas* and a strong indication of his capriciousness.

90 **The . . . Pembroke?** a combination of incredulous rhetorical question and exclamation, probably more of the former – either way, said with rage and contempt. Wolsey again reveals his snobbishness: Anne was, as we have seen (cf. 2.3.63), only recently ennobled and solely as a result of Henry's desire for her.

94–5 Since Wolsey's anger can hardly stem from sympathy for Katherine, it can only be further evidence of his snobbery, a deeply-felt sense of status portrayed as the product of his struggle against the contempt of the nobility for his own lower-class roots.

96–7 **candle . . . goes** proverbial (Dent, C49); 'possibly, as Staunton thought, there is a play on "bullen" meaning "hemp-stalks peeled", . . . and hence the wick of a candle' (Ard²).

90 Pembroke] (Penbroke)   94] SD *aside* / Rowe   94] *Pope; F lines* Gentlewoman? / Daughter /

A spleeny Lutheran, and not wholesome to
Our cause, that she should lie i'th' bosom of   100
Our hard-ruled King. Again, there is sprung up
An heretic, an arch-one, Cranmer, one
Hath crawled into the favour of the King
And is his oracle.

NORFOLK   He is vexed at something.

Enter KING, *reading of a schedule*[*, and* LOVELL.]

SURREY
I would 'twere something that would fret the string,   105

99 **spleeny** impulsive, emotional; possibly alluding to dependence upon the
motions of the Spirit, suggesting over-
emotionalism (RP)
Lutheran The branch of the
Protestant Church (the other main one
being Calvinism) that followed the religious principles of Martin Luther,
most famously expressed in the Ninety-
five Theses of 1517 which attacked
indulgences (a way of 'paying off' sins)
and other aspects of Roman Catholic
theology and ritual. For Wolsey, the
term *Lutheran* would be an expression
of contempt for sectarianism and
heresy. Cf. Gardiner's chronologically
inappropriate remark to Wolsey after
the death of Queen Jane in *When You
See Me*: 'I feare false *Luthers* doctrins
spread so farre, / Least that his highnesse now vnmaried, / Should match
amongst that sect of *Lutherans*, / You
saw how soone his maiestie was wonne,
/ To scorne the Pope, and Romes religion, / When Queene *Anne Bullen* wore
the diadem' (B4ᵛ; Wilson TLN 523–8).
99–104 **Lutheran . . . oracle** In *When You
See Me*, Wolsey worries about Henry's
sudden desire to marry Catherine Parr:
'Holy Saint *Peter* sheeld his Maiestie, /
She is the hope of *Luthers* heresie: / If

she be Queene, the Protestants will swell,
/ And *Cranmer*, Tutor to the Prince of
Wales, / Will boldly speake gainst *Romes*
Religion' (E4ᵛ; Wilson TLN 1489–93).
100–1 **lie . . . King** have sex with the King,
and thus share his secrets. There is a
quiet but pointed reference to 1 Kings,
1.2 ('3 Kings' in Bishops' Bible): 'Let
there be soght for my lord the King a
yong virgin, . . . & let her lye in thy
bosome, that my lord the King may get
heate'. David is old, and despite the
beauty of the girl, Abisag, 'the King
knewe her not' (1.4). Wolsey seems to be
implicitly condemning the age difference
between Henry and Anne, and perhaps
also hinting at Henry's possible impotence. His expression here associates sex,
intimacy and religious influence in a
manner that perhaps sheds further light
on Henry's expression 'the bosom of my
conscience' at 2.4.179; see 2.4.178–81n.
102 **arch-one** punning on 'archbishop';
cf. 5.1.45.
102–3 **one / Hath** one who has
104 **his oracle** 'regarded by him as infal-
lible'; cf. *R3* 2.2.122; *TC* 1.3.74; *Mac*
3.1.9.
105–6 **fret . . . heart** fray his heart-
strings, defined in *OED* as, 'in old
notions of Anatomy, the tendons or

100–1 cause, that . . . King.] Cause!–that . . . king! *Rowe*   101 hard-ruled] (*hard ruled*)   102 arch-
one] arch one *Rowe*   104.1 *and* LOVELL] *Theobald*; *SD after line 106* / *Cam (1892)*

The master-cord on's heart.

SUFFOLK   The King, the King.

KING

What piles of wealth hath he accumulated
To his own portion! And what expense by th'hour
Seems to flow from him! How i'th' name of thrift
Does he rake this together? – Now, my lords,   110
Saw you the Cardinal?

NORFOLK   My lord, we have
Stood here observing him. Some strange commotion
Is in his brain. He bites his lip, and starts,
Stops on a sudden, looks upon the ground,
Then lays his finger on his temple; straight   115
Springs out into fast gait; then stops again,
Strikes his breast hard, and anon he casts
His eye against the moon. In most strange postures
We have seen him set himself.

KING   It may well be
There is a mutiny in's mind. This morning,   120
Papers of state he sent me to peruse
As I required; and wot you what I found
There – on my conscience, put unwittingly?

nerves supposed to brace and sustain the heart' (*sb. pl.* 1); also in the musical sense of holding the strings down on the frets of the instrument
106 on's of his
107–10 What . . . together? Holinshed expands at length on Wolsey's acquisitiveness, devoting two full pages (920–1) to descriptions of his possessions; see also 126n.
108 To . . . portion for his own use
112 commotion rebellion of the senses; cf. 'mutiny' in 120.
113–19 He . . . himself. a conventional

description (cf. *R3* 3.5.1–11; *Oth* 5.2.37–44), but also a challenging passage for director and actor – pinpointing, as it does, a very particular (and, to modern actors, uncomfortable) acting style – which is sometimes cut
116 gait walking; pace
118 against towards
122 required requested
wot you do you know
123 on . . . unwittingly the conscience to the fore at a moment of ambivalence; the question is whether we think the incriminating papers were planted or

108–9 portion! . . . him!] *Rowe;* portion? . . . him? *F*   110 together? – Now,] *this edn;* together? Now *F;* SD [*to them*] *after* together / *Collier MS*   116 gait] *(gate)*   119 be] *Hudson² (Walker);* be, *F;* be; *Capell*   123 There – . . . conscience, . . . unwittingly?] *F (subst.) (*There (. . . Conscience . . . vnwittingly*));* There, . . . conscience . . . unwittingly? *Rowe;* There, . . . conscience, . . . unwittingly? *Capell*

Forsooth, an inventory, thus importing
The several parcels of his plate, his treasure,   125
Rich stuffs and ornaments of household, which
I find at such proud rate that it outspeaks
Possession of a subject.

NORFOLK   It's heaven's will;
Some spirit put this paper in the packet
To bless your eye withal.

KING   If we did think   130
His contemplation were above the earth
And fixed on spiritual object, he should still
Dwell in his musings. But I am afraid

simply included in error; certainly, to judge by 30–1, Suffolk is unaware of this inventory.

124 **inventory** This fatal error appears in Holinshed's account of the reign of Henry VII, where it is told of Thomas Ruthall, Bishop of Durham. Here it is transferred to Wolsey, a change presumably influenced by Holinshed's description of the King's discovery of Wolsey's letters to the Pope (see Holinshed, 796). Holinshed does mention an inventory, but as an effect, not a cause, of Wolsey's fall: once he had lost the great seal, he 'called all his officers before him, and tooke accompt of them for all such stuffe, whereof they had charge . . . and so was there inuentaries of all things in order against the kings comming' (909). Foxe also describes an occasion on which Henry is shown letters written by Wolsey which contradict what the Cardinal has told him, after which 'the King neuer put any more confidence or trust in the Cardinall' (Foxe 1596, 901).
importing signifying, listing

125 **several parcels** various items
plate Household plate provided a convenient way both to store and to display wealth. On Wolsey's plate, see Glanville: 'Because plate was the essen-

tial indicator of status, it was crucial in the ritual of gift-exchange which was the visible cement holding the hierarchy together; it also played an essential role in every ceremonial occasion' (134).

126 **Rich . . . household** Henry's description here echoes Holinshed's preliminary account of Wolsey's acquisitions: 'And in his gallerie were set diuerse tables, wherevpon laie a great number of goodlie rich stuffe, as whole peeces of silke of all colours, veluet, sattin, damaske, taffata, grograine, and other things' (909).
stuffs material, cloth

127 **at . . . rate** in such grandiose quantities

127–8 **outspeaks . . . subject** lists far too much wealth for someone who is not himself King

128–30 **It's . . . withal**. It is difficult for an actor playing Norfolk to speak these lines without implying that he had been involved in making the substitution, although there is nothing to suggest Norfolk could have had access to the inventory.

130 **To . . . withal** with which to bless your eye

132–3 **he . . . musings** I would let him continue in his introspection or, possibly, in his doubts.

131 contemplation] contemplations *F2*   132 object] objects *F4*

His thinkings are below the moon, not worth
His serious considering.

*King takes his seat; [and] whispers Lovell, who goes to
the Cardinal.*

WOLSEY   Heaven forgive me.   135
[*to the King*] Ever God bless your highness.

KING   Good my lord,
You are full of heavenly stuff, and bear the inventory
Of your best graces in your mind, the which
You were now running o'er. You have scarce time
To steal from spiritual leisure a brief span   140
To keep your earthly audit. Sure, in that
I deem you an ill husband, and am glad
To have you therein my companion.

WOLSEY   Sir,
For holy offices I have a time; a time

---

134 **below the moon** worldly, unspiritual
135 SD *whispers* transitive for 'whispers to'
137 **stuff . . . inventory** *Stuff* means 'qualities', 'characteristics', but Henry is repeating his own words at 124–6 with heavy irony. This brief speech is full of the language of accountancy, from *span* to *audit* to *husband* (see 140n., 141n., 141–3n.).
140 **steal** metaphoric usage, but with literal implication
leisure possibly in *OED*'s obsolete sense 4, 'deliberation', though the suggested emendation in *Collier³* to 'labour' makes more sense to post-seventeenth-century ears. Henry's subsequent metaphors for the way Wolsey spends his time are of material acquisition, not spiritual devotion.
span See 1.1.223n.
141 **earthly audit** material reckoning, in contrast with the day of judgement (one of *OED*'s definitions of 'audit', *sb*. 3)

141–3 **Sure . . . companion.** *Ill husband* primarily means 'poor manager', with the abstract 'husbandry' (household economy) in mind rather than marriage; Henry is implying that he has been profligate by giving Wolsey so much financial responsibility. Humphreys denies that Henry could possibly have his own marital relations in mind; certainly, if he is acknowledging his own inadequacy in the marital (or, for that matter, economic) sphere, this is a moment of remarkable frankness; Foakes (Ard²) offers a helpful compromise by suggesting that he is quoting what he knows to be Wolsey's opinion of him.
143–9 **Sir . . . to.** Wolsey's speech is careful, formal, religious and tense (all of which are conveyed by the convoluted syntax), as he provides an appropriate audit for the religious life. The repetition of *time* echoes Ecclesiastes, 3.1: 'To al things *there is* an appointed time, and a time to euerie purpose vnder the heauen.'

---

136 SD] *Rowe (subst.)*   140 leisure] labour *(Collier³)*   142 glad] *F2;* gald *F*

To think upon the part of business which   145
I bear i'th' state; and nature does require
Her times of preservation which, perforce,
I, her frail son, amongst my brethren mortal,
Must give my tendance to.

KING   You have said well.

WOLSEY

And ever may your highness yoke together,   150
As I will lend you cause, my doing well
With my well saying.

KING   'Tis well said again,
And 'tis a kind of good deed to say well –
And yet words are no deeds. My father loved you:
He said he did, and with his deed did crown   155
His word upon you. Since I had my office,
I have kept you next my heart, have not alone
Employed you where high profits might come home,
But pared my present havings to bestow
My bounties upon you.

WOLSEY [*aside*]   What should this mean?   160

SURREY [*aside*]

The Lord increase this business!

KING   Have I not made you
The prime man of the state? I pray you tell me

---

147 **perforce** necessarily

149 **tendance** attention, heed

149–54 **You . . . deeds**. The tension of this exchange between King and Cardinal is established by Henry's turning Wolsey's bland proverbial expression back against him (Dent, S119/D402 and Dent, *Exclusive*, S123); cf. *Ham* 1.3.24–8; *TC* 3.2.54; Fletcher & Beaumont, *Cox* 4.3.21–2: 'You can say well: / If you be mine, Wench, you must doe well too.'

155–6 **with . . . you** Wolsey was Henry

VII's chaplain, and was promoted initially to the deanship of Lincoln.

157–60 **have not. . . you** have not only put you in a position from which you could make a great deal of money, but have also reduced my own wealth by giving you gifts.

157 **alone** only

159 **pared** reduced, brought down in amount (*OED v.*[1] I 5)

162 **prime . . . state** executive head of government, prime minister

If what I now pronounce you have found true,
And, if you may confess it, say withal
If you are bound to us or no. What say you?   165
WOLSEY
My sovereign, I confess your royal graces,
Showered on me daily, have been more than could
My studied purposes requite, which went
Beyond all man's endeavours. My endeavours
Have ever come too short of my desires,   170
Yet filed with my abilities. Mine own ends
Have been mine so that evermore they pointed
To th' good of your most sacred person and
The profit of the state. For your great graces
Heaped upon me – poor undeserver – I   175
Can nothing render but allegiant thanks;
My prayers to heaven for you; my loyalty,
Which ever has and ever shall be growing,
Till death, that winter, kill it.
KING   Fairly answered:
A loyal and obedient subject is   180
Therein illustrated. The honour of it
Does pay the act of it, as i'th' contrary
The foulness is the punishment. I presume
That as my hand has opened bounty to you,

163 **pronounce** have claimed
164 **withal** in addition
167–8 **more . . . requite** 'more than I
    could repay, despite my best efforts';
    this is repeated, in effect, at 169–70.
171 ***filed** kept pace with, cf. 1.2.42; F
    has 'fill'd', but Hanmer's emendation
    has been generally accepted as making
    sense of an otherwise opaque line.
    ends goals, aims
171–2 **Mine . . . so** my goals can be said
    to be 'mine' only in the sense that

175 **undeserver** unworthy person
176 **allegiant** loyal; first citation in *OED*
    (*a.*)
181 **illustrated** main stress on second
    syllable (RP)
    it i.e. loyalty; which is rewarded by
    respect, just as disloyalty brings
    opprobrium
183 **foulness** bad reputation
184–5 **opened . . . dropped . . . rained**
    Henry's language consistently situates
    him in the same relationship to his

171 filed] *Hanmer;* fill'd *F*   172 so that] *Cam;* so, that *F*

My heart dropped love, my power rained honour, more   185
On you than any, so your hand and heart,
Your brain, and every function of your power,
Should, notwithstanding that your bond of duty,
As 'twere in love's particular, be more
To me, your friend, than any.

WOLSEY   I do profess   190
That for your highness' good I ever laboured
More than mine own that am, have and will be.
Though all the world should crack their duty to you
And throw it from their soul – though perils did
Abound as thick as thought could make 'em, and   195
Appear in forms more horrid – yet my duty,
As doth a rock against the chiding flood,
Should the approach of this wild river break
And stand unshaken yours.

KING   'Tis nobly spoken.

subjects as God to his creation, vertical movement metaphors emphasizing the (theoretical) fixity of hierarchy; we have, however, already seen Wolsey as the centrepiece of such metaphors; cf. 1.3.57, despite the irony.

188 **notwithstanding . . . duty** ambiguous; Henry could mean either 'despite your duty to the Pope and the Church' or 'not just because of a general sense of loyalty'.
   that your bond that bond of yours
189 **love's particular** the special loyalty which comes from close friendship
190–9 ***I . . . yours.** All sorts of emendations have been suggested for F's grammatically awkward parentheses, generally on the assumption that Wolsey's emotions are getting the better of his sentence structure. Berdan and Brooke's modernization (Yale),

ending the first sentence at *be*, makes the resulting sentence beginning *Though* logical, and simply requires acknowledgement of the compression embodied in 192.
192 more than for anything of my own in the past, right now, and at any future point
197 a possible echo of the man who 'hath buylded his house on a rocke: / And the raine fell, and the floods came, and the windes blewe, and beat vpon that house, and it fell not' (Matthew, 7.24–5).
   chiding angry noise, figuratively of wind, waters, etc. (*OED vbl. sb.* 3)
198 **break** stand as an obstacle in the way of (*OED v.* II 10)
199 **spoken** again, the menacing emphasis only on the saying, not the doing

192 own . . . be] *Yale;* own: that am, haue, and will be *F;* own: that am I, have been, will be: *Pope;* own: that aim I have, and will. *Collier³ (Knight);* own: that I am true, and will be, *Singer²*

Take notice, lords: he has a loyal breast,   200
For you have seen him open't.
[*Gives him papers.*]   Read o'er this,
And after, this, and then to breakfast with
What appetite you have.
                              Exit King, frowning upon the Cardinal; the nobles
                              throng after him, smiling and whispering.
WOLSEY   What should this mean?
What sudden anger's this? How have I reaped it?
He parted frowning from me, as if ruin   205
Leaped from his eyes. So looks the chafed lion
Upon the daring huntsman that has galled him,
Then makes him nothing. I must read this paper –
I fear, the story of his anger. 'Tis so:
This paper has undone me. 'Tis th'account   210
Of all that world of wealth I have drawn together
For mine own ends – indeed to gain the popedom
And fee my friends in Rome. O, negligence,

200–1 **breast . . . open't** *breast* signifies
'heart'; 'to open the breast' is to display emotions.
203–459 **What should . . . dwell.** The
consensus of the authorship analysts is
that the rest of this scene was written
by Fletcher (see Appendix 3).
206 **chafed** furious (chafèd)
207 **galled** injured, angered
208 **makes him nothing** destroys him
209 **I . . . anger** which, I am afraid,
explains why he is angry (or, is the
cause of his anger)
210 **account** a statement of moneys
received and expended (*OED sb.* II 2a)
211 **world** i.e. vast amount
212 **mine own ends** Cf. Wolsey's assertion at 171–4.
212–13 **gain . . . Rome** Wolsey was well
known for his papal ambitions. His last
fully fledged attempt to win a papal

election came a few months before the
divorce hearings when he received a
(false) report of the death of Clement
VII (see Ridley, *Statesman*, 209).
213 **negligence** See 124n. If the authorship analysts are correct, then this passage shows that Fletcher has read
Holinshed on Henry VII too. Here he
echoes the phraseology of the story of
Ruthall's error: 'But see the mishap!
that a man in all other things so provident, should now be so negligent: and
at that time so forget himselfe, when (as
it after fell out) he had most need to
haue remembred himselfe' (796). That
a 'Fletcher' section and a 'Shakespeare'
section demonstrate knowledge of the
same page in Holinshed's 'Henrie the
seuenth' underlines the closeness of
the collaboration (or the irrelevance of
authorial attribution).

201 SD] *Pope (Giving)*   202 after, this] *Theobald;* after this *F*   209 fear, the] *Rowe;* fear the *F*
210 account] *(Accompt)*

Fit for a fool to fall by! What cross devil
Made me put this main secret in the packet   215
I sent the King? Is there no way to cure this?
No new device to beat this from his brains?
I know 'twill stir him strongly. Yet I know
A way, if it take right, in spite of fortune
Will bring me off again. What's this? 'To th' Pope'?   220
The letter, as I live, with all the business
I writ to's Holiness. Nay then, farewell.
I have touched the highest point of all my greatness,
And from that full meridian of my glory
I haste now to my setting. I shall fall   225
Like a bright exhalation in the evening,
And no man see me more.

Enter to Wolsey the Dukes *of* NORFOLK *and* SUFFOLK, *the*
Earl *of* SURREY *and the* Lord CHAMBERLAIN.

NORFOLK

Hear the King's pleasure, Cardinal, who commands
    you

214 **cross** perverse, contrary
215 **main** key, crucial
217 **device** trick, scheme
219 **take right** works properly
220 **bring me off** allow me to escape
    What's this? Wolsey realizes there is a
    second incriminating letter, and looks at
    the address written on it ('To th' Pope').
224–5 **meridian . . . setting** The *meridian*
    is 'the point at which the sun attains its
    highest altitude' at midday; this line is
    OED's first figurative example (*sb.* 2b),
    though the transition from astronomi-
    cal to metaphorical can be seen in the
    source, Speed, 2.769: 'but now his
    Sunne hauing passed the Meridian of
    his greatnesse, began by degrees againe
    to decline, till lastly it set vnder the

cloud of his fatall eclipse'. This is one
of two apparent echoes of Speed (see
also 359n.), both in the section of this
scene attributed to Fletcher.
226 **exhalation** shooting star, meteor; cf.
    Fletcher, Beaumont & Massinger, *T&T*
    4.1.105–6: 'kings from height of all their
    painted glories / Fall, like spent exhala-
    tions, to this center'. Meteors, lightning,
    etc., were thought to be uprushes of
    vapour falling back to earth.
227.2 SURREY, CHAMBERLAIN Holin-
    shed describes an encounter between
    Wolsey and the two Dukes only.
228–32 **Hear . . . highness**. The scene
    now returns to Holinshed, extrapolat-
    ing from the chronicle account of the
    confrontation of Wolsey and the

227.1 *Enter*] *Re-enter* / *Capell*   228] *Pope; F lines* Cardinall, / you /

To render up the great seal presently
Into our hands, and to confine yourself   230
To Esher House, my lord of Winchester's,
Till you hear further from his highness.
WOLSEY   Stay.
Where's your commission, lords? Words cannot carry
Authority so weighty.
SUFFOLK   Who dare cross 'em,
Bearing the King's will from his mouth expressly?   235
WOLSEY
Till I find more than will or words to do it –

Dukes, and incorporating from slightly later in Holinshed the list of charges brought against the Cardinal. Norfolk's opening speech is almost verbatim Holinshed: 'the seuenteenth of Nouember the king sent the two dukes of Norfolke and Suffolke to the cardinals place at Westminster, who went as they were commanded and finding the cardinall there, they declared that the kings pleasure was that he should surrender vp the great seale into their hands, and to depart simplie vnto Asher, which was an house situat nigh vnto Hampton court, belonging to the bishoprike of Winchester' (909).

229 **great seal** the engraved stamp of metal used to make an impression in wax for authentication of documents issued in the name of the sovereign. Prior to the union of England and Scotland under James I (James VI of Scotland), the custodian was normally the Lord Chancellor; see 245–51 for details of Wolsey's custody of the seal. **presently** at once

231 **Esher** I have modernized the spelling from F's (and Holinshed's; see 228–32n.) 'Asher'. Esher House, in Surrey, was in fact Wolsey's own, since he was himself Bishop of Winchester, though soon to be deprived of the see.

As Foakes (Ard[2]) suggests, the subtle alteration of Holinshed's wording may be designed to bring to mind Stephen Gardiner, erstwhile secretary to Wolsey and the next Bishop of Winchester (see Boswell-Stone, 474, n. 2), and therefore to create continuity with 4.1.101–2.

232–5 **Stay . . . expressly?** This exchange closely parallels Holinshed: 'The cardinall demanded of them their commission that gaue them such authoritie, who answered againe, that they were sufficient commissioners, and had authoritie to doo no lesse by the kings mouth' (909).

233 **commission** warrant in writing; cf. 2.2.71.1.
     Words i.e. spoken words, as opposed to written (signed and sealed) authority

234 **cross** disagree with, resist

236–50 Holinshed's account is the basis for Wolsey's defiance here: 'Nothwithstanding, he would in no wise agree in that behalfe, without further knowledge of their authoritie, saieng; that the great seale was deliuered him by the kings person, to inioy the minstration thereof, with the roome of the chancellor for the terme of his life, whereof for his suertie he had the kings letters patents' (909).

231 Esher House] *(Asher-House)*   233 commission, lords?] *Rowe;* Commission? Lords, *F*

I mean your malice – know, officious lords,
I dare, and must, deny it. Now I feel
Of what coarse metal ye are moulded – envy!
How eagerly ye follow my disgraces 240
As if it fed ye, and how sleek and wanton
Ye appear in everything may bring my ruin!
Follow your envious courses, men of malice:
You have Christian warrant for 'em, and no doubt
In time will find their fit rewards. That seal 245
You ask with such a violence, the King –
Mine and your master – with his own hand gave me;
Bade me enjoy it, with the place and honours,
During my life; and to confirm his goodness,
Tied it by letters patents. Now, who'll take it? 250

SURREY

    The King that gave it.

WOLSEY   It must be himself, then.

SURREY

    Thou art a proud traitor, priest.

WOLSEY   Proud lord, thou liest.

237 **officious** here in the familiar sense of 'meddlesome', though early modern usage could still also be positive ('dutiful')

239 **envy** ill will, malice (cf. 3.1.113)

241 **it** envy
sleek oily, plausible, specious (*OED a.* 3)
wanton lawless, merciless

242 **ruin** echoes Katherine's attack on the Cardinals at 3.1.98

243–4 **Follow . . . 'em** a possible allusion to Pontius Pilate's recognition of the reasons for the condemnation of Jesus: 'For he knewe wel, that for enuie they had deliuered him' (Matthew, 27.18)

245 **rewards** punishments

246 **with . . . violence** so precipitately, with such force

248 **place and honours** i.e. the status and honour of the post of Lord Chancellor, which is associated with the holding of the great seal

249 **During my life** until death; the implication being that if the King really has demanded it back, he has reneged on his earlier promise that Wolsey would hold the office for life

250 **letters patents** open letters or documents from the sovereign issued to confer a privilege (*OED patent a.* I 1)

252–349 This entire disagreement stems from one line in Holinshed: 'This matter was greatlie debated betweene them with manie great words' (909).

239 coarse metal] *Pope;* course Mettle *F;* course metal *Rowe;* base metal *Capell* moulded – envy!] *Rowe (subst.);* molded, Enuy, *F*

Within these forty hours Surrey durst better
Have burnt that tongue than said so.
SURREY   Thy ambition,
    Thou scarlet sin, robbed this bewailing land   255
    Of noble Buckingham, my father-in-law.
    The heads of all thy brother cardinals,
    With thee and all thy best parts bound together,
    Weighed not a hair of his. Plague of your policy!
    You sent me Deputy for Ireland,   260
    Far from his succour, from the King, from all
    That might have mercy on the fault thou gavest him,
    Whilst your great goodness, out of holy pity,
    Absolved him with an axe.
WOLSEY   This, and all else
    This talking lord can lay upon my credit,   265
    I answer, is most false. The Duke by law
    Found his deserts. How innocent I was
    From any private malice in his end,
    His noble jury and foul cause can witness.
    If I loved many words, lord, I should tell you   270
    You have as little honesty as honour,

253 **forty hours** a round number, not an exact period; cf. 2.3.89.
255 **scarlet sin** a double reference to a cardinal's red robes and to Isaiah, 1.18: 'thogh your sinnes were as crimsin, they shalbe made white as snowe: thogh they were red like skarlet, they shal be as woll'. As Foakes (Ard²) notes, 'scarlet' is a kind of cloth; cf. 280.
258 **parts** abilities, characteristics
259 **Weighed . . . hair** proverbial (Dent, H19); cf. *1H4* 3.1.135–6, Beaumont & Fletcher, *Maid's* 5.3.220.
    Weighed not were not equal in value to
    Plague of a plague on
260 **Deputy for Ireland** See 2.1.41–4n.
    Ireland three syllables

262 **fault . . . him** crime you claimed he had committed; cf. 2.1.71.
    gavest monosyllabic
265 **credit** reputation
268 **From** of
    in his end in the process that led to his execution
269 **His noble jury** Wolsey no doubt means this to be uncomfortable for Norfolk, who was the highest-ranking member of the group of peers who found Buckingham guilty; cf. 2.1.26 and n.
270 **If . . . words** proverbial (Dent, W813.1), if a little ironic; cf. *AW* 3.6.84.

257 brother cardinals] *(*Brother-Cardinals*)*   262 gavest] *(*gau'st*)*

That in the way of loyalty and truth
Toward the King, my ever royal master,
Dare mate a sounder man than Surrey can be,
And all that love his follies.

SURREY   By my soul,   275
Your long coat, priest, protects you; thou shouldst feel
My sword i'th' lifeblood of thee else. My lords,
Can ye endure to hear this arrogance?
And from this fellow? If we live thus tamely,
To be thus jaded by a piece of scarlet,   280
Farewell, nobility: let his grace go forward
And dare us with his cap, like larks.

WOLSEY   All goodness
Is poison to thy stomach.

SURREY   Yes, that 'goodness'
Of gleaning all the land's wealth into one,
Into your own hands, Cardinal, by extortion;   285
The 'goodness' of your intercepted packets
You writ to th' Pope against the King – your
   'goodness',
Since you provoke me, shall be most notorious.

---

272 **That** qualifies *I* at 270
   in . . . truth as far as loyalty and truth
   go; once again, *truth* is in dispute.
274 **mate** vie or cope with (*OED v.*²
   1a); not used in this sense elsewhere in
   the Shakespeare canon, but cf.
   Fletcher, *Rule* 3.1.109: 'he stood up to
   me / And mated my commands'
276 **coat** i.e. the visible evidence of your
   privileged status as a priest. In productions, Surrey tends to draw his sword
   at this point and require restraint by
   the other lords.
279 **fellow** In line with the aristocrats'
   attitude to Wolsey throughout, this is a
   deeply offensive way to refer to someone of the Cardinal's status; cf.

4.2.100.
280 **jaded** made fools of
   piece of scarlet metonymy: robe for
   cardinal; cf. 255n.
281 **Farewell, nobility** Cf. Fletcher &
   Massinger, *EB* 4.1.58 (a Fletcher
   scene, according to Hoy, 2.148).
282 **dare . . . larks** mesmerize, immobi-
   lize. On the connotations of *larks*, see
   LN.
284 **gleaning** gathering, collecting
285 **Cardinal** two syllables; this is an
   example of a 'swib' (single word in
   brackets); see p. 155
   extortion wresting something from a
   person by undue exercise of authority
   (*OED sb.* 1)

272 That in the] That I, i'th' *Theobald*   276] *Rowe³; F lines* you, / feele /   282, 297 SP WOLSEY]
(Car(d).)   285 Cardinal] *((Card'nall))*

349

My lord of Norfolk, as you are truly noble,
As you respect the common good, the state   290
Of our despised nobility, our issues –
Who, if he live, will scarce be gentlemen –
Produce the grand sum of his sins, the articles
Collected from his life. I'll startle you
Worse than the sacring-bell when the brown wench   295
Lay kissing in your arms, lord Cardinal.

WOLSEY

How much, methinks, I could despise this man,
But that I am bound in charity against it.

NORFOLK

Those articles, my lord, are in the King's hand;
But thus much: they are foul ones.

WOLSEY   So much fairer,   300

289 **truly noble** as opposed, presumably, to an upstart like Wolsey

290 **common good** common, presumably, to the peers, rather than to every member of the 'commonwealth', since so much of Surrey's rage continues to focus on the threat Wolsey has posed to the power of the nobility

291 **issues** children, but here, specifically, 'sons'

292 ***Who** This is the grammatically correct F2 form, but Montgomery (Oxf) makes a case for retaining F's 'Whom', noting that *OED (whom, pron.* II) 'records confusion of these two forms in the 17th c.', and adding that '*Whom* was apparently acceptable to [the editors] of F1, and may well not have been recognized by the author as an error'. It could equally well, however, have been a slip, and it seems appropriate, for a modernized edition, to adopt the F2 form.
will . . . gentlemen will hardly (if Wolsey has his way) be allowed on even the first rung of respectability (as claimed for himself by Shakespeare's father), never mind the properly elevated status due to sons of the nobility

293 **sum** total

295 **sacring-bell** Before the Reformation, this would mean the bell rung during the mass when the priest lifts up and consecrates the bread; after the Reformation (as it is anachronistically used here), it came to signify the church bell rung to announce morning prayers.
brown wench implying a suntanned and therefore lower-class woman (Surrey continues to harp on Wolsey's social inferiority), since aristocratic women went out of their way to avoid getting a tan. On Wolsey's failure of celibacy, see 282 LN.

297–8 Wolsey clearly maintains his sense of irony even at times like this.

299 **in . . . hand** a quibble: in the handwriting of the King, i.e. drawn up by the King himself; in the King's possession right now. Productions vary over whether or not the nobles have copies of the articles with them, though Surrey's dependence on his memory at 303–4 makes it clear that they do not.

300 **foul . . . fairer** Despite being in the King's handwriting, and therefore 'fair', the sins outlined are nonetheless *foul*. Wolsey picks up on the implied fair/foul opposition immediately in the next line.

292 Who] *F2;* Whom *F*   295 sacring-bell] *(Sacring Bell)*

And spotless, shall mine innocence arise
When the King knows my truth.

SURREY   This cannot save you.
I thank my memory I yet remember
Some of these articles, and out they shall.
Now, if you can blush and cry 'Guilty', Cardinal,   305
You'll show a little honesty.

WOLSEY   Speak on, sir;
I dare your worst objections. If I blush,
It is to see a nobleman want manners.

SURREY

I had rather want those than my head. Have at you!
First, that without the King's assent or knowledge,   310
You wrought to be a legate, by which power
You maimed the jurisdiction of all bishops.

NORFOLK

Then, that in all you writ to Rome, or else
To foreign princes, '*ego et rex meus*'

---

304 **articles** Holinshed lists nine of the
   articles used to indict Wolsey in 1529;
   here six of them (1, 2, 4, 5, 7 and 9) are
   quoted almost verbatim. For one of
   the omitted articles, see 330–2n. In
   When You See Me, the King rages at
   Wolsey himself, echoing (in a rather
   garbled way) two of the articles listed
   by Holinshed: 'How durst ye sirra, in
   your ambassage, / Vnknowne to vs,
   stampe in our royall coyne / The base
   impression of your Cardinall hat, / As
   if you were copartner in the Crowne? /
   Ego & Rex meus: you and your king
   must be / In equal state, and pompe,
   and Maiestie' (K4ᵛ; Wilson TLN
   2987–92).
307 **dare** meet defiantly (*OED v.*¹ B 4); cf.
   282.
   objections charges, accusations
308 **want** lack; direct retaliation, this, for

Surrey's snobbery
309 **Have at you!** here goes (implying the
   beginning of a personal assault); cf.
   2.2.83 and n.
311 **wrought** arranged, negotiated
   legate papal representative
312 **maimed the jurisdiction** undermined the authority
314 *ego et rex meus* This Latin fragment
   is quoted directly from Holinshed
   (912), which appears, as various editors have observed, to misunderstand
   the import of the phrase, since it is the
   normal form equivalent to 'my King
   and I', implying equality, and need not
   be read as 'I and my King', implying
   superiority. The simple assertion of
   equality of King and Cardinal would,
   after all, be enough to bring the weight
   of the law upon Wolsey. See 304n.

305 can blush] can, blush *Pope*   309] *Rowe*³; F lines head; / you. /   314 *et*] *Steevens–Reed*²; *& F*

Was still inscribed, in which you brought the King 315
To be your servant.

SUFFOLK   Then, that without the knowledge
Either of King or Council, when you went
Ambassador to the Emperor, you made bold
To carry into Flanders the great seal.

SURREY

Item, you sent a large commission 320
To Gregory de Cassado, to conclude,
Without the King's will or the state's allowance,
A league between his highness and Ferrara.

SUFFOLK

That out of mere ambition you have caused
Your holy hat to be stamped on the King's coin. 325

SURREY

Then, that you have sent innumerable substance –

---

315 **still** always
318 **Emperor** the Holy Roman Emperor, Charles V; cf. 1.1.176.
   made bold had the audacity
319 **Flanders** What is now the Flemish-speaking part of Belgium was, in Henry VIII's day, a general term for the Low Countries. Taking the seal out of the King's territories, where it could be used against him, was strictly forbidden.
320 **commission** not here, as at 1.2.20, 'instructions', but rather the body of persons charged to carry out the instructions (*OED sb.*[1] 6)
321–3 **Gregory . . . Ferrara** 'Item, he without the kings assent, sent a commission to sir Gregorie de Cassado, knight, to conclude a league betweene the king & the duke of Ferrar, without the kings knowledge' (Holinshed, 912). Gregory de Cassado (also spelled Casale or Cassalis) was English ambassador to the Papal court in Rome, 'a member of an Italian family which rendered continual service to Henry and

was well versed in the ways of Rome' (Scarisbrick, 268); he worked for both Henry and Wolsey to try to secure Papal permission for the divorce from Katherine. Ferrara was one of the city-states that made up early modern Italy; Alphonso d'Este, the Duke of Ferrara, was a longstanding enemy of the Papacy, though he had joined the League of Cognac to fight the Emperor in November 1527 (Gwyn, 540).
322 **allowance** permission
324 **mere** absolute, sheer, downright (*OED a.*[2] A 4); cf. 329.
325 **hat . . . coin** 'Archbishop Warham of Canterbury struck half-groats, pence and halfpence bearing his initials. At York the privilege of the archbishop was . . . limited to the half-groat and halfpenny.' By issuing the 'York Groat . . . bearing his initials and cardinal's hat', Wolsey 'usurped the king's prerogative' (Brooke, 175, 177).
326 **innumerable substance** incalculable wealth

---

325 holy hat] *(holy-Hat)*

By what means got, I leave to your own conscience –
To furnish Rome and to prepare the ways
You have for dignities, to the mere undoing
Of all the kingdom. Many more there are,   330
Which since they are of you, and odious,
I will not taint my mouth with.

CHAMBERLAIN   O my lord,
Press not a falling man too far. 'Tis virtue.
His faults lie open to the laws: let them,
Not you, correct him. My heart weeps to see him   335
So little of his great self.

SURREY   I forgive him.

SUFFOLK

Lord Cardinal, the King's further pleasure is,
Because all those things you have done of late
By your power legative within this kingdom
Fall into th' compass of a *praemunire*,   340
That therefore such a writ be sued against you
To forfeit all your goods, lands, tenements,

328–9 To . . . **dignities** 'to send bribes to Rome as part of your plan to become Pope'; for *dignities*, see 379, 3.1.142, 184.

330–2 **Many . . . with.** presumably a veiled reference to the sixth item in Holinshed's list: 'that he hauing the French pockes presumed to come and breath on the king' (912)

333 **Press . . . far** a slightly trite sentiment, coming as late in the day as it does; the Lord Chamberlain, cautious politician that he is, is making a show of moderation.

'Tis virtue. i.e. to leave him alone

334 **lie . . . laws** have been exposed and are now susceptible to the process of justice

336 **I forgive him.** probably, but not necessarily, ironic

339 **legative** as a papal deputy; the emen-

dation in Rowe[2] to 'legatine' was presumably suggested by F4's (and Holinshed's) 'Legantine', but is unnecessary, as *legative* is a perfectly acceptable word (i.e. 'as a papal representative').

340 'come within the scope of a charge of asserting papal jurisdiction in England (and therefore of denying the ecclesiastical supremacy of the sovereign)' (*OED praemunire sb.* 1). The term stems from the medieval Latin phrase *praemunire facias* ('give warning'), which appears in the writ that summons the defendant to answer the charge. If found guilty, the defendant could be outlawed and have his possessions confiscated.

341 **sued** legally initiated

339 legative] Legantine *F2;* Legantive *F4;* legatine *Rowe[2]*   340 *praemunire*] *(*Premunire*)*

Chattels and whatsoever, and to be
Out of the King's protection. This is my charge.

NORFOLK

And so we'll leave you to your meditations   345
How to live better. For your stubborn answer
About the giving back the great seal to us,
The King shall know it and, no doubt, shall thank
    you.
So fare you well, my little good lord Cardinal.

Exeunt all but Wolsey.

WOLSEY

So, farewell to the little good you bear me.   350
Farewell? A long farewell to all my greatness.
This is the state of man. Today he puts forth
The tender leaves of hopes; tomorrow blossoms,

---

343 *Chattels F has 'Castles', but Theobald's suggestion, derived from the form of the word given at the relevant moment in Holinshed ('cattels', 909), has been generally accepted. Foakes (Ard²) is right, though, to point out that 'Castles' would make a logical climax to the list and that Wolsey was notorious for building vast homes (notably, Hampton Court and York Place).

344 **Out . . . protection** i.e. outlawed, in line with the charge of *praemunire* (see 340n)

346–8 **For . . . you.** Holinshed recounts that 'the dukes were faine to depart againe without their purpose, and rode to Windsore to the king, and made report accordinglie' (909).

349 **my . . . lord** a sarcastic version of the usual 'my good lord'

350–459 Wolsey's language from here to the end of the scene, both in soliloquy and in dialogue with Cromwell, is crammed with biblical allusion, imply- ing Wolsey's renewal as a Christian in

the immediate wake of his downfall, though the image of Lucifer falling '[n]ever to hope again' (372) darkens this personal reformation.

351 **Farewell?** a rhetorical question implying that it is time to say goodbye not only to the lords' malice but also to every other aspect of his life in the cor- ridors of power

A long farewell This particular phrase appears only once elsewhere in the Shakespeare canon (*AC* 5.2.291), but is frequent in Fletcher; e.g. *WP* 5.1.155; *Bon* 4.4.113.

352–8 **This . . . do.** Wolsey's swansong is modelled on Isaiah, 40.6–8: 'All flesh *is* grasse, and all the grace thereof *is* as yᵉ floure of the field. / The grasse with- ereth, the floure fadeth, because the Spirit of the Lord bloweth vpon it'; cf. 1 Peter, 1.24. Cf. also *Son* 73, *Tim* 4.3.260–7, *Cym* 3.3.44–64, *Mac* 5.3.24–30.

353 **blossoms** has a capital in F, and has therefore been treated as a noun by the

---

343 Chattels] *Theobald;* Castles *F*   351 Farewell? A] Farewell, a *Rowe;* Farewell! A *Staunton*
353 hopes] hope *Steevens*

And bears his blushing honours thick upon him;
The third day comes a frost, a killing frost,   355
And when he thinks, good easy man, full surely
His greatness is a-ripening, nips his root,
And then he falls, as I do. I have ventured,
Like little wanton boys that swim on bladders,
This many summers in a sea of glory,   360
But far beyond my depth. My high-blown pride
At length broke under me and now has left me,
Weary and old with service, to the mercy
Of a rude stream that must for ever hide me.
Vain pomp and glory of this world, I hate ye!   365
I feel my heart new opened. O, how wretched
Is that poor man that hangs on princes' favours!
There is betwixt that smile we would aspire to,
That sweet aspect of princes, and their ruin
More pangs and fears than wars or women have;   370

compositor, but could equally be (and
is perhaps better as) a verb
356 **easy** credulous, accepting
359 **wanton** playful
  bladders This image was apparently
  prompted by reading Speed's description of Wolsey's downfall (see pp.
  171–3). Children generally learnt to
  swim with the help of inflated bladders: cf. Rowley's additions to *Fair
  Quarrel*: 'Did'st thou bargain for the
  bladders with the butcher? / . . . Ay, sir
  . . . I'll practise to swim too, sir' (47,
  50).
360 **This** i.e. in the course of; for
361–2 **high-blown . . . broke** continues
  the simile from 359
363 **old** Wolsey was approaching sixty at
  the time of his fall.
364 **rude stream** rough torrent
365 Wolsey echoes a question put to the

child's sponsors in the Anglican bap-
tismal service – 'Doest thou forsake
. . . the vaine pompe, and glory of the
world . . . ?' (*Common Prayer*, B4ᵛ) –
presumably implying his own reformation and rededication.
366 **I . . . opened.** further evidence of
  Wolsey's conscious regeneration as a
  Christian; cf. Acts, 16.14: 'whose heart
  the Lord opened'; cf. 200–1.
366–7 **O . . . favours!** Cf. Psalms, 118.9
  ('It is better to trust in the Lord, then
  to haue confidence in princes') and
  146.2 ('Put not your trust in princes:
  nor in the sonne of man, for there is
  none helpe in him').
369 **aspect** stressed on second syllable
  their ruin i.e. the ruin they can
  cause
370 **pangs** pains; see 2.3.1n.
  have a) cause; b) experience

360 This] These *Pope*   369 their] our *Pope;* his *Hanmer*

> And when he falls, he falls like Lucifer,
> Never to hope again.

Enter CROMWELL, *standing amazed.*

Why, how now, Cromwell?

CROMWELL
I have no power to speak, sir.

WOLSEY   What, amazed
At my misfortunes? Can thy spirit wonder
A great man should decline? Nay, an you weep   375
I am fallen indeed.

CROMWELL   How does your grace?

WOLSEY   Why, well.

371 **falls like Lucifer** As described in the Homily 'against disobedience and wilfull rebellion', *Homilies*, 2Y6ᵛ (and of course graphically later in the century in Milton's *Paradise Lost*), the result of the angel Lucifer's rebellion against God was his fall from heaven; cf. Isaiah, 14.12: 'How art thou fallen from heauen, ô Lucifer, sonne of the morning?', and Luke, 10.18: 'I sawe Satan, like lightening, falle downe from heauen'. Holinshed characterizes Wolsey as 'a diuelish and luciferian vice' (837). Malone noted a parallel with two lines – 'Your fault not halfe, so great as was my pride, / For which offence, fell *Lucifer* from skies' – from Churchyard's *Life of Wolsey* in *Mirror* 1610, 2M2ᵛ, though Pooler considered this 'very doubtful' (Ard¹, xxx); see also Kiefer; Anderson, 227n.

372 **Never . . . again** proverbial (Dent, H604.1); cf. *R3* 1.2.187–8.

372–459 Cavendish, EETS, is the ultimate, though indirect, source for this exchange, channelled via Stow 1592. Holinshed, drawing its Cavendish material from Stow 1580, mentions Cromwell simply as one of Wolsey's 'chiefe coun-

sell, and chiefe dooer for him in the suppression of abbeies', who along with a number of Wolsey's servants, 'departed from him to the kings seruice' (913). Stow 1592, however, incorporates more from Cavendish, including the assertion that Cromwell's 'honest estimation' (cf. *honest* at 430) and 'earnest behauour in his masters cause, grew so in euerie mans opinion, how that he was the most faithfull seruant to his master of all other, wherein hee was greatly of all men commended' (Stow 1592, 927; cf. 931, also Cavendish, EETS, 113). Cavendish's *Life* was not published until 1641 (and then in a partial version as *The Negotiations of Thomas Wolsey*), and there is no reason to presume that the playwrights had access to a manuscript; Fletcher must have consulted Stow 1592 as well as Holinshed and Speed (see 169–71; Anderson, 136–42).

376 **fallen** monosyllabic
How . . . grace? Cf. Stow 1592: 'My lord returned into his chamber lamenting the departure from his seruants, making his mone to master *Cromwell*, who comforted him the best he could' (925).

373+ SP WOLSEY] *(Car(d).)*   375 an] *(and)*   376 fallen] *(falne)*

Never so truly happy, my good Cromwell.
I know myself now, and I feel within me
A peace above all earthly dignities,
A still and quiet conscience. The King has cured me,   380
I humbly thank his grace, and from these shoulders,
These ruined pillars, out of pity, taken
A load would sink a navy – too much honour.
O, 'tis a burden, Cromwell, 'tis a burden
Too heavy for a man that hopes for heaven.   385
CROMWELL
I am glad your grace has made that right use of it.
WOLSEY
I hope I have. I am able now, methinks,
Out of a fortitude of soul I feel,
To endure more miseries and greater far
Than my weak-hearted enemies dare offer.   390
What news abroad?
CROMWELL   The heaviest and the worst

378 **know myself** understand my limitations and can see them in a larger, spiritual context; see 2.2.21n.
379 **above . . . dignities** beyond that produced by high status during life; on
dignities, see 328–9, 3.1.142, 184.
380 **conscience. The King** Other con-
junctions of *King* and *conscience* in the
play (e.g. at 4.1.45–7) may either suggest the fragility of Wolsey's 'reformation' here or contrast with its sincerity.
382 **pillars** possibly a reference to
Holinshed's description of Wolsey in
his pomp; see 2.4.0.6–9n.
386 **right** positive
388 **fortitude of soul** a spiritual courage
supposed to come over true Christians
at times of crisis: a recurrent idea in
this play, affecting Katherine and
Cranmer, as well as Wolsey

391 **What news abroad?** This sudden
shift of interest to the external world
echoes Stow's version of the comfort
given by Cromwell to Wolsey in
Cavendish and perhaps suggests that
Wolsey has not yet learnt to focus
solely on spiritual matters. Cavendish
reports an uncomplimentary dream
about Anne Bullen which Stow omits,
filling the gap with a general survey of
current affairs, including More's promotion to chancellor and other religious events parallel to those mentioned here (see Anderson, 139–40;
Stow 1592, 932–3; Cavendish, EETS,
127–8). This section of Stow would
also have had a certain significance for
Fletcher because it contains a reference to George Hastings, Earl of
Huntingdon, great-great-grandfather
of his patron, the fifth Earl.

386–7] *Pope; F lines* Grace, / it. / haue: / (me thinkes) /

Is your displeasure with the King.
WOLSEY   God bless him.
CROMWELL
The next is that Sir Thomas More is chosen
Lord Chancellor in your place.
WOLSEY   That's somewhat sudden.
But he's a learned man. May he continue   395
Long in his highness' favour, and do justice
For truth's sake and his conscience, that his bones,
When he has run his course and sleeps in blessings,
May have a tomb of orphans' tears wept on him.
What more?
CROMWELL   That Cranmer is returned with welcome,   400
Installed lord Archbishop of Canterbury.
WOLSEY
That's news indeed.
CROMWELL   Last, that the Lady Anne,
Whom the King hath in secrecy long married,

392 **your displeasure** the disgrace you are in
393–406 **Sir . . . coronation** Cromwell's report of 'current' events compresses events spread over five years. More became chancellor on 25 November 1529, Wolsey died in 1530, Cranmer became archbishop on 30 March 1533 (see 74n.), and Henry secretly married Anne on 25 January 1533.
395 **learned** learnèd
395–6 **May . . . favour** The audience would, of course, hear heavy irony in these lines, knowing as they did of More's martyrdom in 1535.
398 'when he has died and gone to heaven'
399 **tomb . . . tears** a curious image; the relevant sense of *tomb* is perhaps a mound or pile, as well as a memorial, and is possibly informed by 'hecatomb', originally a group of animals offered for sacrifice, hence a large number or quantity (*OED sb.* 2 *fig.*)

especially in a context of death
orphans' tears The Lord Chancellor had ultimate official responsibility for minors, i.e. for those under twenty-one. Steevens notes a parallel with one of the elegies for Prince Henry in Drummond: 'The Muses . . . have raised of their teares / A Crystal Tomb to Him' (B2ʳ).
402–6 **Last . . . coronation.** Holinshed reports that Henry 'married priuilie the ladie Anne Bullongne . . . which marriage was kept so secret, that verie few knew it till Easter next insuing, when it was perceiued that she was with child. . . . After that the king perceiued his new wife to be with child, he caused all officers necessarie to be appointed to hir, and so on Easter even as she went to hir closet openlie as queene' (929). There is no mention of Anne's pregnancy in the play, unless 4.1.76–9 is a displacement (see note).

399 orphans'] *Theobald²;* Orphants *F;* Orphan's *F3*

This day was viewed in open as his Queen,
Going to chapel, and the voice is now   405
Only about her coronation.

WOLSEY

There was the weight that pulled me down. O
    Cromwell,
The King has gone beyond me. All my glories
In that one woman I have lost for ever.
No sun shall ever usher forth mine honours,   410
Or gild again the noble troops that waited
Upon my smiles. Go get thee from me, Cromwell:
I am a poor fallen man, unworthy now
To be thy lord and master. Seek the King –
That sun I pray may never set. I have told him   415
What, and how true, thou art. He will advance thee:
Some little memory of me will stir him –
I know his noble nature – not to let
Thy hopeful service perish too. Good Cromwell,
Neglect him not. Make use now, and provide   420
For thine own future safety.

CROMWELL   O my lord,

---

404 **in open** in public; see 2.1.167n.
405 **voice** public discussion
406 **coronation** five syllables
408 **gone beyond me** overreached me, acted outside my influence; implies also the inevitability of the King's continuing in his place as his advisers rise and fall
410–12 **No . . . smiles.** For the wistful tone, cf. *TNK* 2.2.8–25.
410 **sun** metonymic for a new day; also metaphoric for king; cf. 415, and 1.1.6 and n.
411 **noble troops** According to Holinshed, Wolsey had 'a great number dailie attending upon him, both of noblemen & worthie gentlemen, with no small

number of the tallest yeomen' (920).
412 **Go . . . Cromwell** As Anderson puts it, '[i]n Stow, Cromwell leaves Wolsey more willingly than in Shakespeare [*sic*], where he has virtually to be ordered away' (138). Stow 1592 recounts Cromwell's request that Wolsey 'giue him leaue, to go to London, wheras he would either make or marre' (925).
413 **poor fallen man** See 371n. and 2.1.127–30n.; *fallen* is monosyllabic.
419 **hopeful** promising, of great potential
420 **Make use** make the most of the opportunity; *use* is the legal term for profit or benefit derived from property (*OED sb.* 18).

407] *Pope; F lines* downe. / *Cromwell,* /   413 fallen] *(*falne*)*

Must I then leave you? Must I needs forgo
So good, so noble and so true a master?
Bear witness, all that have not hearts of iron,
With what a sorrow Cromwell leaves his lord.   425
The King shall have my service, but my prayers
For ever and for ever shall be yours.

WOLSEY

Cromwell, I did not think to shed a tear
In all my miseries, but thou hast forced me,
Out of thy honest truth, to play the woman.   430
Let's dry our eyes, and thus far hear me, Cromwell,
And when I am forgotten, as I shall be,
And sleep in dull cold marble, where no mention
Of me more must be heard of, say I taught thee.
Say Wolsey, that once trod the ways of glory   435
And sounded all the depths and shoals of honour,
Found thee a way, out of his wreck, to rise in,
A sure and safe one, though thy master missed it.
Mark but my fall and that that ruined me.

424–5 a curiously direct address to the audience as contemporaries
424 **hearts of iron** a proverbial expression (Dent, H310.1); cf. *Tim* 3.4.84.
425 Cf. 412n.
428 **tear** Again, as at 372.1, this is dependent not upon Holinshed but upon Stow's fuller appropriation of Cavendish: 'the teares ran downe his cheekes, which fewe teares perceiued by his seruants, caused the fountaines of water to gush out of their faithfull eies' (Stow 1592, 924; cf. Cavendish, EETS, 107).
430 **honest truth** The word *truth* here looks forward to Cromwell's Protestantism; cf. *martyr* (449).
play the woman Weeping was proverbially a female trait (Dent, W637.2).

433 **dull** both 'inanimate' and 'dismal'
436 **sounded** tested the depth of
437 **way . . . in** Cavendish and Stow both make fairly explicit Cromwell's ability to improvise success from Wolsey's downfall, noting that 'Wolsey coaches Cromwell on how to answer . . . in Parliament' and that it is these answers which identify Cromwell as 'a paragon of fidelity' and that Wolsey and Cromwell cooperate on a scheme to advance the latter so that he will be 'in a better position to help his old master' (Anderson, 138–9; cf. Stow 1592, 927; Cavendish, EETS, 113). Downplaying this practical side to Cromwell's pragmatism arguably enhances the play's representation of him as a good Protestant.

---

435 trod the ways] rode the waves *(Warburton)*

Cromwell, I charge thee, fling away ambition. 440
By that sin fell the angels. How can man then,
The image of his maker, hope to win by it?
Love thyself last; cherish those hearts that hate thee.
Corruption wins not more than honesty.
Still in thy right hand carry gentle peace 445
To silence envious tongues. Be just, and fear not.
Let all the ends thou aimest at be thy country's,
Thy God's, and truth's. Then if thou fallest, O
    Cromwell,
Thou fallest a blessed martyr.
Serve the King. And prithee lead me in: 450
There take an inventory of all I have.
To the last penny, 'tis the King's. My robe
And my integrity to heaven is all
I dare now call mine own. O Cromwell, Cromwell,

440 As Anderson observes (138), Wolsey
here 'turns surprisingly moral' in the
presence of his servant, reflecting
Stow's (and thus Cavendish's)
Cardinal, who claims that he 'wil neuer
during [his] life, esteeme the goods of
[*sic*] riches of this world any otherwise,
then which shal be sufficient to main-
taine' him in an appropriate manner
(Stow 1592, 924; cf. Cavendish, EETS,
108). This again implies recourse to
Stow 1592 and perhaps implies that
Wolsey realizes Cromwell will make
the most he can of the 'way . . . to rise
in' (437) with which the Cardinal provides him.
440–1 **fling . . . angels** See 371n. As is
made clear in Isaiah, 14.13–14 ('Yet
thou saidest in thine heart, I wil ascend
into heauen, and exalt my throne
aboue beside the starres of God'),
pride was the chief cause of the fall of
Lucifer and the angels who had
rebelled with him; cf. 2 Peter, 2.4;
Revelation, 12.9.
441–2 **man . . . maker** Cf. Genesis, 1.26:

'God said, Let vs make man in our
image.'
443 **Love thyself last** Cf. Philippians, 2.3
('in mekenes of minde euerie man
esteme other better then him self'); see
also 1 Corinthians, 10.24 and 13.5.
cherish . . . thee Cf. Luke, 6.27 ('Loue
your enemie: do wel to them w^c hate
you'); see also Matthew, 5.44.
445 probable echoes of various biblical
passages, including Romans, 12.18 and
Hebrews, 12.14. *Still*, as at 315, means
'always'.
447 **ends** goals, results
aimest monosyllabic
448, 449 **fallest** monosyllabic
449–50 **Thou . . . King** Rowe^3 plausibly
moved *Serve the King* back to 449, but
it is perhaps better left as in F, as both
a formulaic dismissal of Cromwell and
a shift of focus to Wolsey's (now the
King's) possessions (Ard^2).
449 **blessed martyr** See List of Roles,
30n.; Cromwell's career is dramatized
in the play *Thomas, Lord Cromwell*; see
pp. 178–9.

447 aimest] *(*aym'st*)*   448, 449 fallest] *(*fall'st*)*   449–50] *Rowe^3 lines* king: / in. /

Had I but served my God with half the zeal   455
I served my King, he would not in mine age
Have left me naked to mine enemies.

CROMWELL

Good sir, have patience.

WOLSEY   So I have. Farewell,
The hopes of court: my hopes in heaven do dwell.   *Exeunt.*

4.1   *Enter two* Gentlemen, *meeting one another.*

1 GENTLEMAN

You're well met once again.

2 GENTLEMAN   So are you.

1 GENTLEMAN

You come to take your stand here and behold
The Lady Anne pass from her coronation?

2 GENTLEMAN

'Tis all my business. At our last encounter,

455–7 These famous deathbed words of Wolsey (spoken not to Cromwell but to Sir William Kingston) stem from Cavendish: 'If I had serued god as dyligently as I haue don the kyng he wold not haue gevyn me ouer in my gray heares' (Cavendish, *Negotiations*, P1ʳ; Cavendish, EETS, 178–9). They include a double reference to Psalm 71.9–10 ('Cast me not off in the time of age: forsake me not when my strength faileth. / For mine enemies speake of me') and 18 ('Yea, euen vnto *mine* olde age and graie head, ô God: forsake me not'). Holinshed (917) quotes Cavendish directly: 'if I had serued God as diligentlie as I haue doone the king, he would not haue giuen me ouer in my greie haires' (Bullough, 476) – but, as Anderson notes, Stow 1592 is the basis of the play's version. On the same page as the description of 'faithful' Cromwell, Stow's Wolsey says 'I . . . was alwaies contented, and glade to please him before God, whom I ought most chiefely to haue obeyed' (Stow 1592, 927).

457 **naked** defenceless, unarmed

4.1 Generally considered a Fletcher scene (see Appendix 3), though Hoy, 7 (80–1) thought it Shakespeare's, with Fletcherian reworking. Kemble cut the scene completely; Tree retained the procession and inserted it after 4.2 as the conclusion of his production. The coronation took place on 1 June 1533. The location is a street outside Westminster Abbey.

4 **'Tis . . . business**. It is the only reason I'm here.

4–7 **At . . . joy**. The conscious juxtaposition of sadness and joy here would

---

4.1] *(Actus Quartus. Scena Prima.)*   1+ SP 1 GENTLEMAN . . . 2 GENTLEMAN] *Rowe (1 Gen . . . 2 Gen); 1 . . . 2 F*

The Duke of Buckingham came from his trial.   5

1 GENTLEMAN

'Tis very true. But that time offered sorrow,
This, general joy.

2 GENTLEMAN   'Tis well. The citizens,
I am sure, have shown at full their royal minds –
As, let 'em have their rights, they are ever forward –
In celebration of this day with shows,   10
Pageants, and sights of honour.

1 GENTLEMAN   Never greater,
Nor, I'll assure you, better taken, sir.

2 GENTLEMAN

May I be bold to ask what that contains,
That paper in your hand?

1 GENTLEMAN   Yes, 'tis the list
Of those that claim their offices this day   15
By custom of the coronation.
The Duke of Suffolk is the first, and claims

have struck a strong chord with the audience in 1613 in the immediate wake of the death of Prince Henry and the marriage of Princess Elizabeth (see pp. 63–5).

8 **royal** generous, munificent (*OED* 9ᵃ), though with a certain irony at the citizens' lack of restraint

9 **let . . . rights** give them their due

11 **Pageants** Holinshed describes the process of the coronation in great detail over three pages, with a section devoted to 'sundrie pageants' (932). As Foakes suggests (Ard²), it is likely that one effect of the playwrights' dramatization of the coronation procession would be to recall recent, rather more sophisticated, Jacobean pageants and masques.

12 **taken** received

15–16 **claim . . . coronation** Holinshed notes that 'the king caused open

proclamations to be made, that all men that claimed to doo anie service, or execute anie office at the . . . coronation . . . should put their grant . . . in the Starrechamber before Charles duke of Suffolke' (930).

17–19 **The . . . Marshal**. These details are taken directly from Holinshed, though with alterations for dramatic reasons (see 36.1–25n.): 'After all these rode the lord William Howard with the marshalles rod, deputie to his brother the duke of Norffolke marshall of England, which was ambassador then in France. . . . Then went . . . the duke of Suffolke in his robe of estate also for that daie being high steward of England' (933). The play ignores William Howard's deputizing for his brother, as reported in Holinshed.

8 royal] loyal *Pope*   8–9 minds – / As . . . forward –] *Keightley;* minds, / As . . . forward *F*

To be High Steward; next, the Duke of Norfolk,
He to be Earl Marshal. You may read the rest.

2 GENTLEMAN

I thank you, sir. Had I not known those customs,   20
I should have been beholding to your paper.
But I beseech you, what's become of Katherine,
The Princess Dowager? How goes her business?

1 GENTLEMAN

That I can tell you too. The Archbishop
Of Canterbury, accompanied with other   25
Learned and reverend fathers of his order,
Held a late court at Dunstable, six miles off

18 **High Steward** Since the accession of
Henry IV, this officer has been appointed only for the trial of a peer or on the
occasion of a coronation, at which he
presides (*OED* steward *sb.* 3a).

19 **Earl Marshal** a high officer of state,
formerly the deputy of the High
Constable (see 2.1.102n.) as judge of
the court of chivalry. Originally just
'marshal', but since the twelfth century the post has never been held by a
person of lower rank than an earl. It is
a ceremonial post, including as one of
its duties the presidency of the
Heralds' College (*OED*).

20–1 **Had . . . paper.** part of the Gentlemen's habitual game of one-upmanship;
possibly also an invocation of the knowledge the audience had recently gained
from the wedding of Princess Elizabeth
and the Elector Palatine

21 **beholding** beholden, indebted

23 **Princess Dowager** 'As soon as
Cranmer had delivered his judgement
[that the marriage of Henry and
Catherine was, and had always been,
unlawful,] Henry ordered that Catherine
should no longer have the title of Queen,
but should be known as the Princess
Dowager of Wales, to which she was
entitled as the widow of Arthur, her only

lawful husband' (Ridley, *Henry*, 221,
223); see 2.4.172–8n.

24–33 **Archbishop . . . effect** The First
Gentleman's account of the divorce is
almost verbatim Holinshed: '[T]he
archbishop of Canturburie accompanied with the bishops of London,
Winchester, Bath, Lincolne, and
diuers other learned men in great
number, rode to Dunstable, which is
six miles from Ampthill, where the
princesse Dowager laie, and there by
one doctor Lee she was cited to
appeare before the said archbishop in
cause of matrimonie in the said towne
of Dunstable, and at the daie of
appearance she appeared not, but
made default, and so she was called
peremptorie ['peremptorilie' in mar-
gin] euerie daie fifteene daies togither,
and at the last, for lacke of appearance,
by the assent of all the learned men
there present, she was divorced from
the king, and the marriage declared to
be void and of none effect' (929–30).

26, 32 **Learned** learnèd

26 **order** rank, status (i.e. other bishops)

27 **late** recent
    Dunstable a town in Bedfordshire,
    approximately thirty-five miles north-
    west of London

20 SP] *F4;* I *F*

From Ampthill, where the Princess lay; to which
She was often cited by them, but appeared not;
And, to be short, for not appearance and   30
The King's late scruple, by the main assent
Of all these learned men, she was divorced,
And the late marriage made of none effect;
Since which she was removed to Kimbolton,
Where she remains now sick.

2 GENTLEMAN   Alas, good lady.   [*Trumpets.*]
The trumpets sound. Stand close. The Queen is coming.   36

The order of the coronation
1   A lively flourish of trumpets.

28 **Ampthill** a small town, in fact about
nine miles north of Dunstable
lay was staying
29 **cited** summoned to appear before the
bishops
30 **not appearance** Holinshed does not
provide this slightly odd combination:
his version is 'for lacke of appearance'
(930; see 24–33n.). There is no need
either to hyphenate or to emend. Cf.
LFL 3.2.82.
31 **main assent** general agreement
32 **learned** learnèd
33 **late** former, erstwhile
of none effect null and void
34 ***Kimbolton** Katherine's last home is
first mentioned by name in Holinshed
not in the passage from which the bulk
of this speech is drawn but in a later
section (which is the basis for
4.2.108–19): 'The princesse Dowager
lieng at Kimbalton, fell into hir last
sicknesse' (939). I have accepted F3's
modern spelling of the place name; F
has 'Kymmalton', which may well, as
Foakes notes (Ard²), represent Jacobean
pronunciation.
36 **Stand close.** Be still and silent.
Queen an example either of the brevity

of the Gentlemen's political memories
or of the efficiency with which the
royal will is enforced: Anne is now
firmly established in their discussions
as the Queen, and Katherine as the
Princess Dowager.
36.1–25 another vast stage direction given
in unprecedented detail in F, carefully
compiled from Holinshed but managed
so as not to require an impractically
large cast (though the number of actors
required is still substantial). Presumably
for reasons of dramatic economy, various figures not called for elsewhere in
the play are omitted, including the Earl
of Oxford, and others replaced, with the
Earl of Surrey substituted for Arundel
and the Duke of Norfolk for William
Howard. I note below some of the
details at the relevant points; for the full
procession, see Holinshed, 933. The
Gentlemen's dialogue at 37ff must
begin at the latest when Dorset passes
near them, i.e. by 36.8.
36.2 *flourish* a fanfare of wind instruments (trumpets or cornetts), usually
denoting entrance or exit; not in
Holinshed at this point; see 36.25n.
and Appendix 6.

30 not appearance] non-appearance *(Steevens)*; not-appearance *Hudson²*   34 Kimbolton] *F3;*
Kymmalton *F*   35 SD] *Capell, replacing 36 SD Ho-boyes F*   36] *Pope; F lines* close, / comming. /
36.1] *F prints line as a heading between rules*

2   *Then, two Judges.*

3   *Lord* CHANCELLOR, *with purse and mace before him.*

4   *Choristers singing. Music.*   36.5

5   *Mayor of London, bearing the mace. Then* GARTER, *in his coat of arms, and on his head he wears a gilt copper crown.*

6   *Marquess Dorset, bearing a sceptre of gold, on his head a demi-coronal of gold. With him the* Earl *of* SURREY, *bearing the rod of silver with the dove, crowned with an* 36.10 *earl's coronet. Collars of esses.*

7   Duke *of* SUFFOLK, *in his robe of estate, his coronet on his head, bearing a long white wand, as High Steward. With him, the* Duke *of* NORFOLK, *with the rod of marshalship, a coronet on his head. Collars of esses.*   36.15

36.3 *judges* 'the iudges in their mantels of scarlet and coiffes' (Holinshed, 933)

36.4 **Lord** CHANCELLOR 'the lord chancellor in a robe of scarlet open before' (Holinshed, 933)

purse See 1.1.114.1n.; 2.4.0.5–6.

36.5 *Choristers* abbreviated from Holinshed's unwieldy 'the kings chapell and the moonks solemnelie singing with procession' (933)

Music 'While the F direction may simply be a call for off-stage music, the third gentleman's comment that "the Quire / With all the choysest Musicke of the Kingdome, / Together sung *Te Deum*" [4.1.90–2] suggests that we here, also, should interpret "Musicke" to mean "musicians playing"' (*TxC*, 621). At the same time, F's 'Musicke' is roman, not italic as is the rest of the SD, raising the possibility that it was not written in the principal hand of the MS (RP).

36.6 *Mayor . . .* GARTER 'after them went the maior of London with his mace and garter in his cote of armes' (Holinshed, 933). On Garter King-of-Arms, see List of Roles, 32n.

36.7 *wears F reads '*wore*': 'The past tense is curious; the likeliest explanation is that the writer was so engrossed in closely following Holinshed's retrospective account as to slip into the past tense for his one finite verb' (Humphreys), i.e. he accidentally imported Holinshed's past into his present-tense narrative. On this basis, emendation to present tense is justified. Alternatively *wore*, the only finite verb in the SD, might be the product of memory rather than reading, and as such evidence of a post-production addition (RP).

36.8 *Dorset* 'then went the marquesse Dorset in a robe of estate which bare the scepter of gold, and the earle of Arundell which bare the rod of iuorie with the doue both togither' (Holinshed, 933). For the substitution of Surrey for Arundel, see 36.1–25n.

36.9 *demi-coronal* a small coronet

36.11, 15 *Collars of esses* i.e. they are wearing chains made up of linked 'S' shapes, 'originally a Lancastrian badge in the Wars of the Roses, and still worn by some officials' (Ard[2])

36.12–14 SUFFOLK . . . NORFOLK See 17–19n.

36.12 *estate* state

36.5 *Choristers*] (Quirristers) 36.7 *wears*] Cam; *wore* F; omitted in Rowe

8   *A canopy, borne by four of the Cinque Ports; under it, the*
    Queen [ANNE] *in her robe, in her hair, richly adorned with*
    pearl; crowned. On each side her, the Bishops of London
    and Winchester.

9   *The old Duchess of Norfolk, in a coronal of gold wrought*   36.20
    with flowers, bearing the Queen's train.

10 *Certain Ladies or Countesses, with plain circlets of gold*
    without flowers.

            Exeunt, first passing over the stage in order and state,
                    and then a great flourish of trumpets.

2 GENTLEMAN

A royal train, believe me. These I know.

36.16–19 'Then proceeded foorth the
queene . . . in hir here coiffe and circlet
. . . and ouer hir was borne the canopie
by foure of the fiue ports, . . . and the
bishops of London and Winchester
bare vp the laps of the queenes robe'
(Holinshed, 933).

36.16 *four of* i.e. four barons of
Cinque Ports a group of sea ports
(originally five, whence the name) situated on the south-east coast of
England; the original ports were
Hastings, Sandwich, Dover, Romney
and Hythe, to which were added Rye
and Winchelsea; other coastal towns
have associate membership of the
group. One of the ancient rights of the
barons of the Cinque Ports was to
carry the canopy over the King during
processions (*OED*).

36.17 *in her hair* with her hair hanging
loose, as was customary for brides; cf.
TNK: '*Enter* EMILIA *in white, her hair
about her shoulders*' (5.1.136.1–2). This
may well again be a reference to the
wedding of Princess Elizabeth, who is
described on that occasion as being 'in
her haire that hung downe long, with
an exceding rich coronet on her head'
(Chamberlain, 1.424). Also, as Foakes
notes (Ard²), there is no mention of

'pearls' in Holinshed's description of
Anne.

36.18 *side her* i.e. side of her
36.19 **Winchester** i.e. Stephen Gardiner;
see List of Roles 23n.
36.20 *Duchess* 'The queenes traine which
was verie long was borne by the old
duches of Norffolke' (Holinshed, 933).
The Duchess was the second wife and
widow of the second Duke of Norfolk,
who had died in 1524 (though the play
conflates the second and third Dukes).
36.21 *train* The 'train' is the excess material trailing behind the wedding dress
(*OED sb.*¹ 5a); cf. 37.
36.25 *great flourish* Holinshed notes that
'the trumpets plaied maruellous fresh-
lie' (933).
37–55 The two Gentlemen provide a
commentary on the procession which
is much more interesting when it
diverges from Holinshed's account
than when it echoes it. Clearly, their
comments should run at the same time
as the procession, not after it (as the
layout on the F page might suggest);
see 36.1–25n.
37 **royal** finely arrayed, grand or impos-
ing (*OED a.* II 8b)
train here refers to the coronation
procession (*OED sb.*¹ 9a)

36.17 *in her hair,*] her hair *Dyce²* *(Walker)*

Who's that that bears the sceptre?

1 GENTLEMAN   Marquess Dorset,
And that the Earl of Surrey with the rod.

2 GENTLEMAN
A bold brave gentleman. That should be   40
The Duke of Suffolk.

1 GENTLEMAN   'Tis the same: High Steward.

2 GENTLEMAN
And that my lord of Norfolk?

1 GENTLEMAN   Yes.

2 GENTLEMAN [*Sees Anne.*]   Heaven bless thee!
Thou hast the sweetest face I ever looked on.
Sir, as I have a soul, she is an angel.
Our King has all the Indies in his arms,   45
And more, and richer, when he strains that lady.
I cannot blame his conscience.

1 GENTLEMAN   They that bear
The cloth of honour over her are four barons
Of the Cinque Ports.

2 GENTLEMAN
Those men are happy, and so are all are near her.   50
I take it she that carries up the train
Is that old noble lady, Duchess of Norfolk?

---

40 bold brave gentleman Cf. its opposite *bold bad man* at 2.2.42.

44 as . . . soul i.e. upon my life

45 Indies either or both of the East and West Indies, especially India and America, thought of as realms of vast wealth: a colonial image for a sexual relation; cf. Donne, 'The Sun Rising', 16–18: 'Looke, . . . / Whether both the'India's of spice and Myne / Be where thou leftst them, or lie here with mee'.

46 strains holds, hugs, with a clear sexual implication

47 conscience After some lines of simple description, this sudden plunge into ironic interpretation is, to say the least, startling, particularly since the Second Gentleman here makes explicit the play's equation of the King's conscience with his sexual desires. The First Gentleman seems to ignore his friend's remark and continues with straight commentary, but it is he who adopts the role of cynic a few lines later (55).

50 and . . . her stress on the final two syllables (both *near* and *her*)

41 Suffolk.] Suffolk? *Dyce*   42 SD] *Johnson (subst.) (Looking on)*   50] *Pope; F lines* happy, / her. /

1 GENTLEMAN

It is, and the rest are countesses.

2 GENTLEMAN

Their coronets say so. These are stars indeed –

1 GENTLEMAN

And sometimes falling ones.

2 GENTLEMAN   No more of that.   55

Enter a Third Gentleman.

1 GENTLEMAN

God save you, sir. Where have you been broiling?

3 GENTLEMAN

Among the crowd i'th' Abbey, where a finger
Could not be wedged in more. I am stifled

---

53 **countesses** All the women in the procession are of equivalent rank to earls.
54–6 ***Their . . . sir**. F assigns 54–5,
'Their . . . ones', to the Second
Gentleman, and then 55, 'No . . . that',
also to the Second Gentleman, with no
intervening speech (see t.n.): I have
followed Hudson's emendations in
reallocating the lines.
55 **falling ones** The First Gentleman
is implying, fairly gracelessly, that
courtly ladies are sexually available,
and his friend hastily controls him. We
have already seen that Wolsey's downfall was in part the result of courtly
surveillance systems (see 3.2.30–7n.),
and we have noted the Gentlemen's
wariness before (see 2.1.167n.). The
idea of a falling star offers a distant
echo of the characterization of Wolsey
as Lucifer (see 3.2.371), and seems to
offer little redemption to individuals of
high social status.
56 **broiling** a combination of two *OED*
definitions of 'broil': to become heated
with excitement ($v.^1$ 3b); to contend in
a confused struggle ($v.^2$ 3). Sweating,
as a sign of uncontrolled or barely controlled emotion, is a persistent motif of
the play; cf. Buckingham at 2.1.33 and
Henry at 2.4.205.
57–81 **finger . . . piece** This entire section (for which, with the exception of
62–7, there is no precedent in
Holinshed) is remarkable for its sensu-
ousness and the intensity of its
description of popular energy channelled into royal occasion. Its emphasis
on sexuality and procreation, from the
implications of *a finger / Could not be
wedged in more* to the *great-bellied
women* who *shake the press* and the
inability of men to distinguish their
own wives in the crowd, centres on the
figure of Anne, who becomes both the
sexual sublime and at the same time
unintentionally responsible for a kind
of sexual anarchy.

---

54 indeed –] *Hudson (Walker);* indeed, *F*   54–6 2 GENTLEMAN Their . . . / 1 GENTLEMAN And . . .
2 GENTLEMAN No . . . / 1 GENTLEMAN God] *Hudson (Walker);* 2 Their . . . And . . . 2 No . . . / 1 God
F; 2 Their . . . / And . . . 1 No . . . / God *F3*

With the mere rankness of their joy.

2 GENTLEMAN　　　　　　　　　　　You saw
　　The ceremony?

3 GENTLEMAN　　　That I did.

1 GENTLEMAN　　　　　　　　How was it?　　　　　　　　　60

3 GENTLEMAN
　　Well worth the seeing.

2 GENTLEMAN　　　　　　　Good sir, speak it to us.

3 GENTLEMAN
　　As well as I am able. The rich stream
　　Of lords and ladies, having brought the Queen
　　To a prepared place in the choir, fell off
　　A distance from her, while her grace sat down　　　　65
　　To rest a while – some half an hour or so –
　　In a rich chair of state, opposing freely
　　The beauty of her person to the people –
　　Believe me, sir, she is the goodliest woman
　　That ever lay by man – which when the people　　　70
　　Had the full view of, such a noise arose
　　As the shrouds make at sea in a stiff tempest,

59 **mere rankness** sheer excess, both of excitement and of body odour; for *mere*, cf. 3.2.324n.
61 **Well . . . seeing.** The Third Gentleman seems well equipped to join in the usual game of one-upmanship played by the other two.
　　speak it describe it
62–7 **The . . . state** This part of the Third Gentleman's description is drawn from Holinshed: 'When she was thus brought to the high place made in the middest of the church, betweene the queere and the high altar, she was set in a rich chaire. And after that she had rested a while, she descended downe to the high altar' (933).
64 **fell off** stood back
67 **opposing freely** making entirely visible; Holinshed makes no mention of

Anne displaying the beauty of her person to the people in the course of the coronation, noting only that she rested a while 'in a rich chaire'. The play creates the impression of a ritual of public display and approval almost akin to the consular ritual Coriolanus cannot abide (*Cor* 2.2, 2.3), except that *freely* suggests that Anne has no objection to presenting herself to the public gaze; on the contrary, she is represented as effectively inviting the kind of comment made by the Second Gentleman at 42–6.
69 **goodliest** most attractive
72 **shrouds** a set of ropes, usually in pairs, leading from the deck to the head of a mast and serving to relieve the mast of lateral strain; they form part of the standing rigging of a ship (*OED sb.*[1] 1).

59–60 You . . . ceremony] *Hanmer; one line F*　　64, 90 choir] *(Quire)*

As loud and to as many tunes. Hats, cloaks –
Doublets, I think – flew up, and had their faces
Been loose, this day they had been lost. Such joy   75
I never saw before. Great-bellied women
That had not half a week to go, like rams
In the old time of war, would shake the press
And make 'em reel before 'em. No man living
Could say 'This is my wife' there, all were woven   80
So strangely in one piece.

2 GENTLEMAN   But what followed?

3 GENTLEMAN

At length her grace rose, and with modest paces
Came to the altar, where she kneeled and, saint-like,
Cast her fair eyes to heaven and prayed devoutly;
Then rose again and bowed her to the people,   85
When by the Archbishop of Canterbury
She had all the royal makings of a queen,

73–5 Hats ... lost. classic carnivalesque personification and grotesque exaggeration: here, items of clothing spontaneously fly, and *faces* can be imagined as detachable components of a loosely structured human body.

74 Doublets closely fitting jackets, with or without sleeves (or with detachable sleeves), straight-bodied in Henry VIII's reign, fitted in James's, and generally heavily buttoned (see Linthicum, 197–9)

76 Great-bellied women further carnivalesque imagery; cf. 5.3.

77 rams battering rams

78 press crowd

81 strangely The metre seems to require this word to be trisyllabic.

82–92 At ... Deum. After Anne had rested, Holinshed reports, 'she descended downe to the high altar and there prostrate hir selfe while the archbishop of Canturburie said certeine collects: then she rose, and the bishop annointed hir on the head and on the brest, and then she was led vp againe, where after

diuerse orisons said, the archbishop set the crowne of saint Edward on hir head, and then deliuered hir the scepter of gold in hir right hand, and the rod of iuorie with the doue in the left hand, and then all the queere soong *Te Deum, &c.*' (933). There are a number of changes in phrasing, though the description retains Holinshed's order.

82 modest It would be inappropriate for Anne to rush gleefully towards the crown.

84 fair eyes Again, Anne's physical grace is emphasized.

85 bowed ... people Holinshed makes no mention of this gesture: Anne is repeatedly portrayed in this scene in terms of her relationship with her new subjects. *Bowed*, now an intransitive verb, could at this time still be (a slightly emphatic) reflexive.

87 She had received the material trappings of royalty; this is the first citation in *OED* for *makings (vbl. sb.[1] 8a).*

78 press] *(prease)*

As holy oil, Edward Confessor's crown,
The rod, and bird of peace, and all such emblems
Laid nobly on her; which performed, the choir,   90
With all the choicest music of the kingdom,
Together sung *Te Deum*. So she parted,
And with the same full state paced back again
To York Place, where the feast is held.

1 GENTLEMAN   Sir,
You must no more call it 'York Place' – that's past;   95
For since the Cardinal fell, that title's lost.
'Tis now the King's, and called 'Whitehall'.

3 GENTLEMAN   I know it,
But 'tis so lately altered that the old name
Is fresh about me.

2 GENTLEMAN   What two reverend bishops
Were those that went on each side of the Queen?   100

3 GENTLEMAN
Stokesley and Gardiner, the one of Winchester,

88–9 **holy oil . . . bird** See 82–92n.
91 **choicest music** best band of musicians
92 *Te Deum* Latin shorthand for the rousing
  prayer of praise – '*Te Deum laudamus*'
  ('We praise thee, O Lord') – prescribed
  for 'Morning Prayer' by *Common
  Prayer*
  parted departed
93 **with . . . state** accompanied by the
  same procession
94, 95 **York Place** a house originally
  belonging to the Archbishops of York,
  occupied briefly by Edward I in the
  1290s, and reconstructed in the fif-
  teenth century. The last Archbishop to
  live there was Wolsey; he extended it in
  the 1520s, making it bigger than anything owned by Henry VIII, who
  acquired it in 1530 at the Cardinal's fall
  and enlarged it to be his own Whitehall
  Palace. It had acquired new significance
  for the Jacobean audience since James
  had a new Banqueting House built in

1606. This burnt down in 1619 and was
replaced by Inigo Jones's Banqueting
House, which still stands (see Thurley,
9–21). Henry and Anne's wedding feast
was in fact held not at Whitehall but at
Westminster Hall (Holinshed, 933): the
change here serves to reintroduce the
topic of Wolsey's fall from power.
96 **lost** gone, erased
98 **so lately altered** another example of
  time compression, since York Place/
  Whitehall had changed hands and
  names a year earlier
99 **fresh about me** still the one that
  comes instantly to mind; cf. 5.2.65.
100–3 **those . . . London** Holinshed
  reports that 'the bishops of London
  and Winchester bare vp the laps of the
  queenes robe' during the ceremony
  (933); see 36.16–19.
101–3 **Stokesley . . . London** The structure of the Third Gentleman's reply is
  chiasmic: John Stokesley became Bishop

94, 95 York Place] *(York-Place, Yorke-place)*   101 Stokesley] *F4; Stokeley F*

Newly preferred from the King's secretary;
The other, London.

2 GENTLEMAN He of Winchester
Is held no great good lover of the Archbishop's,
The virtuous Cranmer.

3 GENTLEMAN All the land knows that. 105
However, yet there is no great breach. When it comes,
Cranmer will find a friend will not shrink from him.

2 GENTLEMAN
Who may that be, I pray you?

3 GENTLEMAN Thomas Cromwell,
A man in much esteem wi'th' King, and truly
A worthy friend. The King has made him 110
Master o'th' Jewel House,
And one already of the Privy Council.

2 GENTLEMAN
He will deserve more.

3 GENTLEMAN Yes, without all doubt.
Come, gentlemen, ye shall go my way,
Which is to th' court, and there ye shall be my guests: 115
Something I can command. As I walk thither
I'll tell ye more.

1 & 2 GENTLEMEN You may command us, sir. *Exeunt.*

of London on 27 November 1530; for Gardiner, see List of Roles, 23n.

102 **preferred from** promoted from the office of

103–5 **He . . . Cranmer**. The Second Gentleman's comment prepares us for the clash between Gardiner and Cranmer dramatized in 5.1 and 5.2.

105 **virtuous Cranmer** one of a number of references which prepare the audience for the Archbishop's prophetic role in 5.4; cf. 3.2.71–3, 400–1.

108–12 **Thomas . . . Council**. In his account of the previous year,

Holinshed mentions 'Thomas Cromwell, maister of the kings iewell house, & councellor to the king, a man newlie receiued into high fauour' (929).

111 **Master o'th' Jewel House** officer with responsibility for the Crown Jewels in the Tower of London (*OED* master *sb*.[1] II 19a).

116 **Something . . . command** I have a certain amount of influence; cf. 1.1.195; *Something* is picked up humorously by the First and Second Gentlemen in their stress on *us* (117) (RP).

106 However] Howe'er *(RP)* there is] there's *Pope* When it] when't *Pope* 109 wi'th'] (with th') 110–11] *Collier*[3] *lines* master / House. / 114–15] *Capell lines* which / guests: / 117 SP] *F (Both)*

4.2   *Enter* KATHERINE Dowager, *sick, led between*
GRIFFITH, *her gentleman usher, and* PATIENCE, *her woman.*

GRIFFITH
How does your grace?

KATHERINE   O Griffith, sick to death.
My legs like loaden branches bow to th'earth,
Willing to leave their burden. Reach a chair. [*She sits.*]
So. Now, methinks, I feel a little ease.
Didst thou not tell me, Griffith, as thou leddest me,   5
That the great child of honour, Cardinal Wolsey,
Was dead?

GRIFFITH   Yes, madam, but I think your grace,
Out of the pain you suffered, gave no ear to't.

KATHERINE
Prithee, good Griffith, tell me how he died.
If well, he stepped before me happily   10
For my example.

4.2 Generally considered a Fletcher scene, though Hoy, 7 (80–1) thought it Shakespeare's, with Fletcherian reworking (see Appendix 3). The scene expands substantially on Holinshed's description of Katherine's death, providing her with a slightly unsettling near-apotheosis (see pp. 132–5). Again, there is substantial time-compression: Wolsey died in 1530, Katherine in 1536. The location is Kimbolton.

0.2 GRIFFITH See List of Roles, 26n.
PATIENCE See List of Roles, 34n.
1   **sick to death** standard biblical phrase for terminal illness; cf. 2 Kings, 20.1; 2 Chronicles, 32.24. This scene was considered one of Siddons's very finest, demonstrating her exemplary attention to detail: she 'displayed through her feeble and falling frame, and death-stricken expression of features, that morbid fretfulness of look, that restless desire of changing place and position, which frequently attends our last decay – . . . playing, during discourse, among her drapery with restless and uneasy fingers, . . . [creating] a most affecting portraiture of nature fast approaching its exit' (Genest, 8.304).

2   **loaden** weighed down with leaves, blossom, or (most likely, in context) snow; cf. Fletcher, *Cha* 1.3.25; *FSh* 5.3.37; *Pilg* 5.3.15.
3   **leave** get rid of
5   **leddest** monosyllabic
6   **child of honour** person born for great (generally chivalric) achievement; cf. *1H4* 3.2.139 (though see p. 108).
10   **happily** fittingly
11   **the voice goes** rumour has it

4.2] *(Scena Secunda.)*   2 loaden] loaded *F2*   3 SD] *Rowe (Sitting down)*   4 So. Now] *Rowe (So-now);* So now *F*   5 leddest] *(*lead'st*)*   7 think] *F2;* thanke *F*

GRIFFITH   Well, the voice goes, madam.
For after the stout Earl Northumberland
Arrested him at York and brought him forward,
As a man sorely tainted, to his answer,
He fell sick suddenly and grew so ill   15
He could not sit his mule.

KATHERINE   Alas, poor man.

GRIFFITH

At last, with easy roads, he came to Leicester;
Lodged in the abbey, where the reverend abbot,
With all his convent, honourably received him;

12–13 **For . . . York** The Earl arrested
Wolsey at Cawood, ten miles south of
York: '[T]he earle of Northumberland
. . . came to the hall at Cawood. . . .
[T]he earl said vnto the cardinall with
a soft voice, laieng his hand vpon his
arme: My lord I arrest you of high
treason' (Holinshed, 915).
14 **sorely** in such a manner as to press
hardly or severely upon a person (*OED
adv.* 3)
    tainted infected, corrupted; touched
with putrefaction (*OED ppl. a.* 1)
    answer his plea in respect of the
charges
15–16 **sick . . . mule** Wolsey fell ill on his
journey south while staying at the Earl
of Shrewsbury's house at Sheffield
Park. 'When night came, the cardinall
waxed verie sicke with the laske [diar-
rhoea], the which caused him continuallie to go to the stoole all that night, in
so much that he had that night fiftie
stooles' (Holinshed, 916–17). He continued south, but by the time he
reached Leicester, he 'waxed so sicke
that he was almost fallen from his
mule' (916).
17–25 Wolsey reached 'the abbeie of
Leicester, where at his comming in at
the gates, the abbat with all his conu-
ent met him with diuerse torches light,
whom they honorablie receiued and

welcomed. To whom the cardinall
said: Father abbat, I am come hither to
lay my bones among you, riding so still
vntill he came to the staires of the
chamber, where he alighted from his
mule, and master Kingston led him vp
the staires, and as soone as he was in
his chamber, he went to bed. This was
on the saturday at night, and then
increased he sicker and sicker, vntill
mondaie, that all men thought he
would haue died' (Holinshed, 917).
17 **with easy roads** in short stages. Like
Holinshed, Foxe worked (indirectly)
from Cavendish for his description of
Wolsey's death, and he picks up
Cavendish's phrase 'by easie iournies'
where Holinshed does not (Foxe 1596,
909; Cavendish, EETS, 171). The
importation of *easy* here perhaps suggests that Fletcher consulted Foxe's
account of the Cardinal's death as well
as that of Holinshed.
19 **convent** I have followed Rowe – modernizing, not emending, F's word
'Covent', which is a form of 'convent'
(as in 'Covent Garden') that was common up to the seventeenth century.
The word originally referred to any
group of people, not just women,
adopting a monastic life (*OED sb.* 3a,
citing this line). 'Covent' is the form in
Stow 1592 but not in Holinshed.

19 convent] *Rowe;* Couent *F*

To whom he gave these words: 'O father abbot,   20
An old man, broken with the storms of state,
Is come to lay his weary bones among ye.
Give him a little earth, for charity.'
So went to bed, where eagerly his sickness
Pursued him still, and three nights after this,   25
About the hour of eight, which he himself
Foretold should be his last, full of repentance,
Continual meditations, tears and sorrows,
He gave his honours to the world again,
His blessed part to heaven, and slept in peace.   30

KATHERINE

So may he rest: his faults lie gently on him.
Yet thus far, Griffith, give me leave to speak him,
And yet with charity. He was a man
Of an unbounded stomach, ever ranking

21 **old** See 3.2.363n.

26–30 On the Tuesday, 'the clocke stroke eight, and then he gaue vp the ghost, and departed this present life: which caused some to call to remembrance how he said the daie before, that at eight of the clocke they should loose their master' (Holinshed, 917).

27 **repentance** Holinshed does not explicitly state that Wolsey repents: he implies the Cardinal's 'pensiuenes', not his penitence (917), though compare 3.2.454–7 (words which are drawn from Holinshed's description of his death) and 48–68n. below.

28 **sorrows** laments

30 **blessed** blessèd

31–3 **So ... charity**. Katherine's ostensible forgiveness and *charity* soon fade away in her frank appraisal of the Cardinal's failings.

32 **thus . . . him** Let me comment on particular aspects of his life.

33–44 **He . . . example**. There are two views of Wolsey in Holinshed, formally presented to the audience here by Katherine and Griffith, the one rather more unyielding than the other (see pp. 103–5). Katherine's speech closely follows the second, less generous description, which was not in fact the work of Raphael Holinshed, but drawn from Hall by Holinshed's collaborator Abraham Fleming (see Patterson, *Holinshed*, 7): 'This cardinall ... was of a great stomach, for he compted himselfe equall with princes, & by craftie suggestion gat into his hands innumerable treasure: he forced little on simonie, and was not pittifull, and stood affectionate in his owne opinion: in open presence he would lie and saie vntruth, and was double both in speach and meaning: he would promise much & performe little: he was vicious of his bodie, & gaue the clergie euill example' (Holinshed, 922).

34 **unbounded stomach** boundless pride or ambition; *stomach* in general signifies emotional strength, here either 'pride, haughtiness, obstinacy' (*OED* 8b) or possibly 'malice, ill-will, spite' (*OED* 8c).

31] *Pope; F lines* rest, / him: /

Himself with princes; one that by suggestion   35
Tied all the kingdom. Simony was fair play.
His own opinion was his law. I'th' presence
He would say untruths, and be ever double
Both in his words and meaning. He was never,
But where he meant to ruin, pitiful.   40
His promises were as he then was, mighty;
But his performance, as he is now, nothing.
Of his own body he was ill, and gave
The clergy ill example.
GRIFFITH   Noble madam,
Men's evil manners live in brass, their virtues   45
We write in water. May it please your highness
To hear me speak his good now?
KATHERINE   Yes, good Griffith;

35–6 by . . . kingdom controlled the state by intrigues
35 suggestion incitement to evil (*OED* 1a); manipulation (*OED* 2a; 3)
36 Tied Hanmer's 'Tyth'd' (i.e. took ten per cent of everyone's wealth) is possible because of a passage in Holinshed describing Wolsey's plan to oblige 'euerie man' to admit 'the true valuation of that they were woorth' and then demand 'a tenth part thereof to bee granted towards the kings charges now in his warres' (874). But the passage quoted at 33–44n. connects the word *suggestion* to Wolsey's extortions for his own benefit; and F is therefore best left unemended.
Simony . . . play. Simony was the word used to describe the taking or giving of money for ecclesiastical preferments, so called after Simon of Samaria, who offered the Apostles money in exchange for the power of the Holy Spirit (see Acts, 8.9–24).
37 presence the room in which the King enacted state business
38 double two-faced, ambiguous

39 words and meaning a basic Renaissance sense of the duality of language: words as the superficial 'ornaments' of hidden meaning
40 But except
41–2 promises . . . nothing proverbial (Dent, P602); cf. *Oth* 4.2.184–5 and *Tim* 5.1.23–9, where the saying becomes a vehicle for commentary on the courtly perversion of manners; and cf. 1.2.208–9.
43 Of . . . body in his practical or sexual morality
ill ill-disciplined, unchaste
45–6 Men's . . . water a conflation of two proverbial expressions, 'to live in brass' (Dent, B607.1; cf. *H5* 4.3.97) and 'to write in water' (Dent, W114; cf. Jonson, *Poetaster* (1601), 'To the Reader', 169–70: 'what they write 'gainst me, / Shall like a figure, drawne in water, fleete'; Beaumont & Fletcher, *Phil* 5.3.83–4: 'all your better deeds / Shall be in water writ, but this in Marble'; and Erasmus, 1.4.56: '*In aqua scribis*' ('You write in water')
47 speak his good outline his good points

36 Tied] *Knight;* Ty'de *F;* Tyth'd *Hanmer*

I were malicious else.

GRIFFITH   This Cardinal,

Though from an humble stock, undoubtedly

Was fashioned to much honour. From his cradle   50

He was a scholar, and a ripe and good one,

Exceeding wise, fair-spoken and persuading;

Lofty and sour to them that loved him not,

But to those men that sought him, sweet as summer.

And though he were unsatisfied in getting –   55

Which was a sin – yet in bestowing, madam,

He was most princely: ever witness for him

Those twins of learning that he raised in you,

---

48 **I . . . else**. Cf. 1.3.65n.

48–68 **This . . . God**. Holinshed's first description of Wolsey is taken word for word from Campion: '[t]his cardinall . . . was a man vndoubtedly borne to honor: I thinke (saith he) some princes bastard, no butchers sonne, exceeding wise, faire spoken, high minded, full of reuenge, vitious of his bodie, loftie to his enimies, were they neuer so big, to those that accepted and sought his friendship woonderfull courteous, a ripe schooleman, thrall to affections, brought a bed with flatterie, insatiable to get, and more princelie in bestowing, as appeareth by his two colleges at Ipswich and Oxenford, the one ouerthrowne with his fall, the other vnfinished, and yet as it lieth for an house of students, considering all the appurtenances incomparable thorough Christendome, whereof Henrie the eight is now called founder, bicause he let it stand. . . . [He was] neuer happie till this his ouerthrow. Wherein he showed such moderation, and ended so perfectlie, that the houre of his death did him more honor, than all the pompe of his life passed' (Campion, 115, K4ʳ; Holinshed, 917). Griffith's version emphasizes the positive

aspects of Campion's account, thereby providing clearer contrast with Katherine's critical view.

50 **From his cradle** proverbial expression meaning 'from his earliest years' (Erasmus, 1.7.53: *Ab incunabulis* ('From the cradle'); not in Dent). That the expression was proverbial supports F's punctuation over Theobald's emendation, which was designed to remove the hyperbolic suggestion that Wolsey had been a scholar when still a baby; cf. Holinshed: 'a man vndoubtedly borne to honor', and, further down the same column, 'being but a child, verie apt to be learned' (917).

53 **Lofty** condescending, haughty

54 **sought him** i.e. as a patron or friend

55 **unsatisfied** insatiable
   getting acquiring material possessions

56 **bestowing** giving, philanthropy

58 **twins of learning** Wolsey created two new colleges, at Oxford and at his birthplace, Ipswich. Only the former – planned as Cardinal College and renamed Christ Church, one of the grandest of the constituent colleges of Oxford University – survived its founder, though its main quadrangle was left architecturally incomplete at his downfall and has never been finished

---

50 honour . . . cradle] honour, from his cradle; *Theobald;* honour from his cradle: *Hanmer*

Ipswich and Oxford – one of which fell with him,
Unwilling to outlive the good that did it;   60
The other, though unfinished, yet so famous,
So excellent in art, and still so rising,
That Christendom shall ever speak his virtue.
His overthrow heaped happiness upon him,
For then, and not till then, he felt himself,   65
And found the blessedness of being little.
And, to add greater honours to his age
Than man could give him, he died fearing God.

KATHERINE

After my death I wish no other herald,
No other speaker of my living actions,   70
To keep mine honour from corruption
But such an honest chronicler as Griffith.
Whom I most hated living, thou hast made me,
With thy religious truth and modesty,
Now in his ashes honour. Peace be with him.   75
Patience, be near me still, and set me lower.
I have not long to trouble thee. Good Griffith,
Cause the musicians play me that sad note

(see Holinshed, 891, 913, 917; see also
Newman, 103–15).
raised built
60 **the . . . it** the goodwill that made it
possible. I have retained F's reading,
accepting *did* as itself a main verb
rather than an auxiliary to a missing
main verb, despite various editors'
suggestions, each of which seems
unnecessary for both meaning and
metre.
61 **unfinished** See 58n.
62 **art** scholarship
   still so rising continuing to gain
fame; with a play on the fact that it has
yet to be fully 'raised'

65 **felt himself** understood what he was
worth; cf. 3.2.378n.
66 **blessedness** blessèdness
   little i.e. a subject and not a ruler
68 **fearing** revering
69 **herald** someone to proclaim her qualities
70 **living** while alive
72 **chronicler** a possible acknowledg-
ment of Holinshed, *et al.*
74 **modesty** restraint
76 **be . . . still** Stay close to me.
   set me lower This suggests that the
chair she called for at 3 is substantial
enough to lie back in.
78 **sad note** melancholy tune

60 good . . . it] good he did it *Pope;* good man did it *(Collier³);* good that did it nourish *Keightley;*
good one built it *(Cartwright)*

I named my knell, whilst I sit meditating
On that celestial harmony I go to.   *Sad and solemn music.*

GRIFFITH

She is asleep. Good wench, let's sit down quiet,   81
For fear we wake her. Softly, gentle Patience.

The vision
Enter, solemnly tripping one after another, six
Personages, clad in white robes, wearing on their heads
garlands of bays, and golden vizards on their faces,
branches of bays or palm in their hands. They first   82.5
congé unto her, then dance; and at certain changes, the
first two hold a spare garland over her head, at which
the other four make reverent curtsies. Then the two
that held the garland deliver the same to the other next

79 **knell** i.e. the music to be played at her death
80 **celestial harmony** See 94–5n.
82.1 *The vision* For the sources and implications of Katherine's vision, see LN; see also pp. 132–6.
82.2–17 There are two traditions for dealing with Katherine's vision. The nineteenth century made a great deal of fuss out of it, with complex special effects and regiments of angels on carefully concealed ladders (see p. 11). Twentieth-century directors often went to the other extreme, doing away with a visible vision altogether. In the 1949 Guthrie production, for instance, Katherine 'saw the vision in the vacant air above our heads, playing the whole thing straight at us' (Byrne, 128), i.e. as visible only to her imagination; this was also the case in the Doran production (RSC, 1996).
82.3–5 *clad . . . hands* The lengthy SD describes Katherine's vision in terms redolent of Revelation, especially 7.9: 'a great multitude . . . stode before the throne, and before the Lambe, clothed

with long white robes, and palmes in their hands'; *bays* indicate celebration.
82.4 *golden vizards* These appear to have been standard stage properties signifying spirits; the dance is a kind of masque, but diametrically opposed in focus to the thoroughly sensual festivity we have already seen in 1.4. That earlier masque proved the beginning of Katherine's downfall; this is her (circumscribed) apotheosis. Davies's 1983 RSC production quite specifically choreographed this vision as a redemptive version of the dance at Wolsey's party (see p. 11; and cf. 87–90n.).
82.6 *congé* make a formal bow or curtsey *changes* stages of or figures in the dance
82.9 *other next* I have retained F's reading, though it is tautologous. RP conjectures that *other* may have been deleted when the scribe realized that there were still two more couples to come and substituted *next*, but that the compositor retained both words.

80 celestial] *(Cœlestiall)*   82.6 *congé*] *(Conge)*; *congee* F3

> *two, who observe the same order in their changes and* 82.10
> *holding the garland over her head. Which done, they*
> *deliver the same garland to the last two, who likewise*
> *observe the same order. At which (as it were by*
> *inspiration) she makes in her sleep signs of rejoicing and*
> *holdeth up her hands to heaven. And so, in their* 82.15
> *dancing, vanish, carrying the garland with them.*
> *The music continues.*

KATHERINE

  Spirits of peace, where are ye? Are ye all gone,

  And leave me here in wretchedness behind ye?

GRIFFITH

  Madam, we are here.

KATHERINE   It is not you I call for. 85

  Saw ye none enter since I slept?

GRIFFITH   None, madam.

KATHERINE

  No? Saw you not even now a blessed troop

  Invite me to a banquet, whose bright faces

  Cast thousand beams upon me, like the sun?

  They promised me eternal happiness 90

  And brought me garlands, Griffith, which I feel

  I am not worthy yet to wear. I shall, assuredly.

82.15–16 *in their dancing* still dancing

83–4 **Are . . . ye?** Cf. *Cym* 5.5.221–3: 'Poor wretches . . . / . . . dream as I have done, / Wake and find nothing'. Unlike Posthumus, Katherine is given no token of the truth of the vision except her own assurance of faith (see 92).

87–90 **Saw . . . happiness** Katherine interprets her vision in appropriately biblical terms, though the invitation to a *banquet* she mentions is not in the SD; cf. Revelation, 19.9 ('Blessed *are* they which are called vnto the Lambes supper').

87 **blessed** blessèd

89 **thousand** acceptable usage without the article; cf. Prologue 29.

92 perhaps best regarded as an alexandrine with a feminine ending; Foakes (Ard²) notes the odd metrical structure of this line and its 'slurring' effect, possibly suggestive of Katherine's increasing illness or tiredness.

92 I am] F; I'm *Keightley*   92–3] *Capell lines* shall, / dreams /

GRIFFITH

I am most joyful, madam, such good dreams
Possess your fancy.

KATHERINE   Bid the music leave.
They are harsh and heavy to me.   *Music ceases.*

PATIENCE   Do you note   95
How much her grace is altered on the sudden?
How long her face is drawn? How pale she looks,
And of an earthy cold? Mark her eyes.

GRIFFITH

She is going, wench. Pray, pray.

PATIENCE   Heaven comfort her.

Enter a Messenger.

MESSENGER

An't like your grace –

KATHERINE   You are a saucy fellow.   100

94 **fancy** imagination
   Bid . . . leave. Tell the musicians to
   stop playing.
94–5 **Bid . . . me.** At 78, Katherine had
   requested melancholy music to help
   her reflect upon the afterlife,
   metaphored as the 'music of the
   spheres', the perfect sound believed to
   be made by the spheres – 'concentric,
   transparent, hollow globes imagined as
   revolving round the earth' (*OED sb.* 2)
   – as they revolve, to which only a soul
   released from the body could listen;
   now that she has heard that celestial
   music, mere earthly music has become
   harsh and heavy.
95 **heavy** tedious, depressing
98 **earthy cold** Earth was thought of as
   the cold, dry element, and associated
   with death (cf. *KL* 5.3.259: 'She's dead
   as earth'); emendations of *cold* – 'coldness', 'colour' – have been suggested to

complete the line metrically; Capell
suggested 'Mark you her eyes' as an
alternative way to improve the metre.
100 **An't . . . grace** a brisk, offhand, formulaic way of beginning a message;
   clearly not an appropriate way to
   address a queen (even one reduced in
   status to *Princess Dowager*). The
   bureaucracy sustains Henry's insensitive treatment of Katherine to the end.
100–8 **You . . . again.** Katherine may be
   dying, but she has lost none of her dignity. As Foakes suggests (Ard²), this
   brief sequence is probably drawn from
   Holinshed's report of changes effected
   in Katherine's household after the
   Pope, at her request, had published a
   curse on King and kingdom for the
   divorce: 'the duke of Suffolke being
   sent to her . . . discharged a a great sort
   of hir houshold seruants, and yet left a
   conuenient number . . . which were

95 They are] They're *Hudson²*   98 cold] coldness *Collier²;* colour *Dyce² (Walker)*   Mark her eyes]
Mark you her eyes *Capell*   100 An't] *(And't)*

Deserve we no more reverence?

GRIFFITH [*to the Messenger*]   You are to blame,
Knowing she will not lose her wonted greatness,
To use so rude behaviour. Go to, kneel.

MESSENGER

I humbly do entreat your highness' pardon.
My haste made me unmannerly. There is staying   105
A gentleman sent from the King to see you.

KATHERINE

Admit him entrance, Griffith. But this fellow
Let me ne'er see again.   *Exit Messenger.*

Enter Lord CAPUTIUS.

If my sight fail not,
You should be lord ambassador from the Emperor,
My royal nephew, and your name Caputius.   110

CAPUTIUS

Madam, the same. Your servant.

KATHERINE   O my lord,

sworne to serue hir not as queene, but
as princesse Dowager. Such as tooke
that oth she vtterlie refused' (936).

102 **lose** forget; F's spelling, 'loose', may
also suggest 'let go of'.
wonted habitual
greatness eminence of rank or station
(*OED* 4)

103 **Go to** Behave yourself.

108 SD–108.1 *Exit* . . . CAPUTIUS.
Because of Katherine's exhortation at
107, editors have tended to supply an
additional SD here to send Griffith out
and have him return with Caputius; as
Foakes (Ard²) notes, though, there is
no absolute need for this additional
action. The movement to the door,
however, leaves Katherine isolated
centre-stage.

108.1 CAPUTIUS 'F represents a quasi-
phonetic spelling of the Latinized
form of *Chapuys*, the historical character's name' (Montgomery in Oxf);
Holinshed gives the standard
Latinization. Holinshed reports
Caputius's visit to the dying
Katherine: 'The princesse Dowager
lieng at Kimbalton, fell into hir last
sicknesse, whereof the king being
aduertised, appointed the emperors
ambassador that was legier here with
him named Eustachius Caputius, to go
to visit hir, and to doo his commendations to hir, and will hir to be of good
comfort. The ambassador with all dili-
gence did his duetie therein, comforting hir the best he might' (939).

101, 103 to] *F3;* too *F*   102 lose] *(loose)*   108.1 CAPUTIUS] *(Capuchius) (after Holinshed)*

The times and titles now are altered strangely
With me since first you knew me. But I pray you,
What is your pleasure with me?

CAPUTIUS   Noble lady,
First, mine own service to your grace; the next,   115
The King's request that I would visit you,
Who grieves much for your weakness and by me
Sends you his princely commendations
And heartily entreats you take good comfort.

KATHERINE
O my good lord, that comfort comes too late;   120
'Tis like a pardon after execution.
That gentle physic given in time had cured me,
But now I am past all comforts here but prayers.
How does his highness?

CAPUTIUS   Madam, in good health.

KATHERINE
So may he ever do, and ever flourish   125
When I shall dwell with worms and my poor name
Banished the kingdom. Patience, is that letter
I caused you write yet sent away?

PATIENCE   No, madam.

---

112 **strangely** both 'oddly' and 'considerably', with a hint of her status as a
  foreigner in England
118 **commendations** regards, compliments
122 **physic** medicine
  had i.e. would have
123 **here** i.e. in this world
126–7 **When . . . kingdom** biblical
  phrasing; cf. Job, 24.20 ('the worm *shal*
  fele his swetenes: he shalbe no more
  reme*m*bred'), Job, 21.26, Isaiah, 51.8.
127–58 **letter . . . right** Holinshed's brief
  report becomes a deathbed speech of
  some pathos. According to Holinshed,

'feel[ing] death approching at hand',
Katherine 'caused one of hir gentlewomen to write a letter to the king,
commending to him hir daughter and
his, beseeching him to stand good
father vnto hir: and further desired
him to haue some consideration of hir
gentlewomen that had serued hir, and
to see them bestowed in marriage.
Further, that it would please him to
appoint that hir seruants might haue
their due wages, and a yeeres wage
beside. This in effect was all that she
requested, and so immediatlie here-
upon she departed this life' (939).

113] *Rowe³; F lines* me. / you, /

KATHERINE

Sir, I most humbly pray you to deliver
This to my lord the King.

CAPUTIUS   Most willing, madam.   130

KATHERINE

In which I have commended to his goodness
The model of our chaste loves, his young daughter –
The dews of heaven fall thick in blessings on her! –
Beseeching him to give her virtuous breeding –
She is young and of a noble, modest nature;   135
I hope she will deserve well – and a little
To love her for her mother's sake that loved him,
Heaven knows how dearly. My next poor petition
Is that his noble grace would have some pity
Upon my wretched women, that so long   140
Have followed both my fortunes faithfully;
Of which there is not one, I dare avow –
And now I should not lie – but will deserve,

---

130 **willing** willingly (*OED ppl. a.* 2f)

131–58 **In . . . right**. This speech is modified from Holinshed, and is generally played with heavy pathos. In a specifically legal context, however, Katherine's deathbed requests constitute a deliberate, continued rejection both of the divorce and of Henry's legal moves to enforce his control of her property. As Jones and Stallybrass note, she is here asserting 'her right to give away the money . . . that she is simultaneously asking Henry to give to her' (Jones & Stallybrass, 'Griselda', 19).

132 **model** image; both evidence and representation
chaste loves Katherine continues to remind her listeners that she did not deserve to be discarded.
daughter Mary, the mention of whose name is likely to have tempered the sympathy Katherine may have evoked in at least some of the audience

133 **dews . . . her** biblical image for the prospect of prosperity (cf. Deuteronomy, 33.28: 'The*n* Israel . . . shal dwel alone in safety in a land of wheat & wine: also his heaue*n*s shal drop the dewe'), without the negative overtones of 1.3.57.

134 **virtuous breeding** a good upbringing

136 **I . . . well** This would provide a particularly strong sense of irony for the audience, who would be well acquainted with the details of the reign of 'Bloody Mary'.

141 **both my fortunes** i.e. when she was Queen and now she has been superseded

143 **And . . . lie** alluding to the belief that the dying have no interest in telling anything other than the truth; cf. Buckingham at 2.1.125.

---

129 most] must *Rowe*   130 willing] willingly *F2*   138] *Rowe³; F lines* deerely. / Petition, / 143 will] well *F3*

For virtue and true beauty of the soul,
For honesty and decent carriage,   145
A right good husband – let him be a noble –
And sure those men are happy that shall have 'em.
The last is for my men – they are the poorest,
But poverty could never draw 'em from me –
That they may have their wages duly paid 'em,   150
And something over to remember me by.
If heaven had pleased to have given me longer life
And able means, we had not parted thus.
These are the whole contents, and, good my lord,
By that you love the dearest in this world,   155
As you wish Christian peace to souls departed,
Stand these poor people's friend, and urge the King
To do me this last right.
CAPUTIUS   By heaven, I will,
Or let me lose the fashion of a man.
KATHERINE

I thank you, honest lord. Remember me   160
In all humility unto his highness.
Say his long trouble now is passing

---

145 **honesty . . . carriage** chastity and
appropriate behaviour
decent in accordance with proper
standards of conduct (*OED a.* 3a); not
found in any other play in the
Shakespeare canon
146 **noble** perhaps a little optimistic, but
a reminder nonetheless that these are
gentlewomen, not servants; there is
nonetheless a complex irony here in
that Anne Bullen was, as we know, *one
of her highness' women* (1.4.93)
147 **happy** fortunate
153 **able means** adequate funds

158 **right** I have retained F's 'right' here,
though Oxf's 'rite' has force because of
the conjunction with *last*, since the
scene, in effect, arguably constitutes
Katherine's last rites. The two
spellings were interchangeable in the
seventeenth century.
159 **fashion** title, character
162 This nine-syllable line may recommend slow delivery.
long trouble a bitter self-appellation:
the person who has caused Henry
trouble for so long a time

148–9 men – they . . . poorest, / But . . . me –] *Pope (subst.);* men, they . . . poorest, / (But . . . me)
F; men – they . . . poorest / (But . . . me) – *Kittredge*   153 able] abler *Hudson² (Walker)*   158 right]
rite *Oxf*   159 lose] *(loose)*

Out of this world. Tell him in death I blessed him,
For so I will. Mine eyes grow dim. Farewell,
My lord. Griffith, farewell. Nay, Patience,   165
You must not leave me yet: I must to bed.
Call in more women. When I am dead, good wench,
Let me be used with honour. Strew me over
With maiden flowers, that all the world may know
I was a chaste wife to my grave. Embalm me,   170
Then lay me forth. Although unqueened, yet like
A queen and daughter to a king inter me.
I can no more.   *Exeunt leading Katherine.*

167 **Call . . . women** This may be an
implicit SD to call in more women to
assist Patience in helping the dying
Queen from the stage.

168 **Let . . . honour** Treat my body with
appropriate ritual for a person of my
status (*OED v.* I 1b, in light of *sb.* II
12b and 13a)

168–70 **Strew . . . grave.** Katherine's
wish here echoes Desdemona's pre-
scient request at *Oth* 4.2.107–8.
Flowers appropriate to the dead person's status were traditionally strewn
on the body (see *WT* 4.4.113–29, *Cym*
4.2.219–25).

171 **lay me forth** Lay me out for burial.

171–2 **Although . . . me.** a bitter echo
of 2 Kings (4 Kings in Bishops'
Bible), 9.32–37, which describes the
destruction of Jezebel by Jehu who,
after he had had her thrown from a
high window, relented a little –

'Visite now yonder cursed woman,
and bury her: for she is a Kings
daughter' (9.34) – only to find that
there was little left to bury after the
dogs had finished with her. These last
words clearly indicate Katherine's
continued resentment of the King's
callousness.

172 **inter** bury

173 **can no more** have no strength left
SD *Exeunt* This implies that Patience,
Caputius and Griffith all help
Katherine off-stage, although there
might be a case for providing exit SDs
for Caputius and Griffith at 165, on
the grounds that the farewells suggest
Katherine is left in female company for
her death (GWW); see 167n. Oxf suggests that Caputius and Griffith leave
'at one door' and Katherine and
Patience 'at another'.

171 forth. Although] *Pope;* forth (although *F*

5.1 *Enter* GARDINER, Bishop of Winchester, *a* Page
with a torch before him, met by Sir Thomas LOVELL.

GARDINER
It's one o'clock, boy, is't not?
PAGE   It hath struck.
GARDINER
These should be hours for necessities,
Not for delights; times to repair our nature
With comforting repose, and not for us
To waste these times. Good hour of the night, Sir
    Thomas.   5
Whither so late?
LOVELL   Came you from the King, my lord?
GARDINER
I did, Sir Thomas, and left him at primero
With the Duke of Suffolk.
LOVELL   I must to him, too,

5.1 Generally considered a Shakespeare scene, though Fleay (*Chronicle*, 251) believed it to be by Massinger (see Appendix 3). Cut entirely by both Irving and Tree. Both this scene and 5.2 (attributed to Fletcher) draw primarily upon Foxe 1596 and alter this source in parallel ways, especially in the characterization of Cranmer. The location is a gallery at court near the King's private rooms.

0.1 GARDINER Gardiner is principal villain and the protagonist's chief enemy in another King's Men play, *Thomas, Lord Cromwell* (1602; reprinted 1613); cf. 31n. Byrne notes, and criticizes, the theatrical tradition of giving the part of Gardiner 'to the first comic actor' (Byrne, 128).

2–3 These ... delights This immediately establishes Gardiner's Lenten, killjoy character. He is referring to the King's playing a game of cards with Suffolk

(see 7–8).

2 necessities i.e. rest, sleep

3–5 times . . . times Cf. Ecclesiastes, 3.1; see 3.2.143–9n. and pp. 84–5.

6 Whither i.e. where are you going?
Came . . . lord? Lovell, preoccupied with his task and answering a question with a question, initially evades telling Gardiner the nature of his mission, though he acknowledges, implicitly at 6 and explicitly at 8, that he is going to talk to the King.

7 primero a card game similar to modern poker. 'The game is called primero because it holds a primary place among the games of chance, either because of its beauty or because it consists of four primary associations . . . which is the number of primary elements [i.e. earth, air, fire, water] from which we . . . are composed' (Cardano, 185). See LN for a description of the game.

8 must to him must go to him

5.1] *(Actus Quintus. Scena Prima.)*   1 o'clock] *(*a clocke*)*   SP PAGE] *(Boy)*

Before he go to bed. I'll take my leave.

GARDINER

Not yet, Sir Thomas Lovell. What's the matter?   10
It seems you are in haste. And if there be
No great offence belongs to't, give your friend
Some touch of your late business. Affairs that walk,
As they say spirits do, at midnight have
In them a wilder nature than the business   15
That seeks dispatch by day.

LOVELL   My lord, I love you,
And durst commend a secret to your ear
Much weightier than this work. The Queen's in
    labour –
They say in great extremity, and feared
She'll with the labour end.

GARDINER   The fruit she goes with   20
I pray for heartily, that it may find

---

9   **go** subjunctive
10 Gardiner is quite bluntly disinclined to
    let Lovell go without finding out the
    nature of his haste, though he modu-
    lates his forcefulness a little at 11ff.
11 **And if** perhaps equals 'an if' (i.e. *if*);
    cf. Prologue 31.
11–12 **if . . . offence** 'if I am not intrud-
    ing too much' or, possibly, 'if it would
    not be breaching a trust'
13 **touch** sense, hint
    late here both 'recent' and 'late at
    night'
    walk the customary term for the
    movement of a ghost
14 **midnight** in the middle of the night;
    not, in this instance, a specific time (we
    know from 1 that it is, in fact, 1 a.m.);
    cf. 72.
17–20 **And . . . end** Lovell flatters
    Gardiner and offsets his initial reluc-
    tance to stop and talk by telling him

that he would be more than happy to
divulge a genuine state secret to him if
he knew one, but that his business is
simply to inform the King of the dangerous state of Anne's labour, thereby
implying that pregnancy and childbirth are women's matters and thus of
minimal significance – an unconvincing stance, even given the misogynistic
premises of their conversation, considering that the child is potentially
Henry's son and heir.
17 **durst commend** would dare to
    entrust
18 **weightier** more important
    this work the business I have been
    engaged in
19 **in great extremity** exhausted; near
    to death
    feared i.e. it is feared that
20 **The . . . with** i.e. the child she carries
21 **heartily** genuinely, with all my heart

---

18 work] Word *Rowe²*

389

Good time, and live. But, for the stock, Sir Thomas,
I wish it grubbed up now.

LOVELL   Methinks I could
Cry the amen, and yet my conscience says
She's a good creature and, sweet lady, does   25
Deserve our better wishes.

GARDINER   But sir, sir –
Hear me, Sir Thomas. You're a gentleman
Of mine own way. I know you wise, religious,
And let me tell you, it will ne'er be well –
'Twill not, Sir Thomas Lovell, take't of me –   30
Till Cranmer, Cromwell (her two hands) and she
Sleep in their graves.

---

22 **Good time** i.e. a good time to be born; cf. *WT* 2.1.21: 'good time encounter her'.

22–3 **stock . . . now** Gardiner is here living up to his name with an image from horticulture: he wants the fruit to survive but the tree on which it has grown to be uprooted and destroyed. There are few starker images than this of the instrumental function accorded to women of childbearing age within patriarchal culture: once she has produced a viable heir, Anne becomes instantly expendable (see Noling, 291). This perhaps echoes a moment in *When You See Me*, when Gardiner and Bonner congratulate themselves on the success of their coup against the Queen: 'Twas excellent,' says Bonner, 'that Ceder once orethrowne, / To crop the lower shrubs let vs alone' (I3^r, Wilson TLN 2554–5).

24 **Cry the amen** agree with you. Some editors have suggested emendation to 'thee' or 'ye'. While there are examples of the construction 'cry amen' in Fletcher (*Capt* 2.1.66), in Shakespeare (*H5* 5.2.21) and in another Shakespeare/Fletcher collaboration (*TNK* 1.4.3), there is only one example of the construction with the second person singular in either canon (*KJ*

3.1.107: 'cry thou "Amen"'), and this means '[I ask] you [to] cry "Amen"', not, as here, 'I could cry "Amen" to you'. Moreover, emending in this way, while feasible, would necessitate ignoring the speakers' use of 'you' as their preferred second person form throughout their exchange (JH).

amen biblical, and hence liturgical, response by clerk or congregation, indicating concurrence

28 **way** i.e. of thinking, specifically theological/ecclesiological thinking; both are Catholic and fiercely anti-Lutheran.

31 **Cranmer, Cromwell** Foxe 1596 repeatedly cites Cranmer and Cromwell as a pair as the chief motivators of the Henrician schism (see Fig. 14) and sets up Gardiner as principal papist villain, naming him as the person responsible for the charges against Cranmer that are enacted in this scene and the next (cf. 37–8 and see 40–52n.). *Thomas, Lord Cromwell* casts Gardiner as Cromwell's chief antagonist: 'Shall *Cromwell* liue a greater man then I? / My enuie with his honour now is bred, / I hope to shorten *Cromwell* by the head' (E1^r).

her two hands her two principal supporters

LOVELL   Now, sir, you speak of two
The most remarked i'th' kingdom. As for Cromwell,
Beside that of the Jewel House, is made Master
O'th' Rolls and the King's secretary; further, sir,   35
Stands in the gap and trade of more preferments,
With which the time will load him. Th'Archbishop
Is the King's hand and tongue, and who dare speak
One syllable against him?
GARDINER   Yes, yes, Sir Thomas,
There are that dare, and I myself have ventured   40
To speak my mind of him; and indeed this day,
Sir – I may tell it you, I think – I have
Incensed the lords o'th' Council that he is –
For so I know he is, they know he is –

---

33 **remarked** celebrated, notable
33–5 **As . . . secretary** Cromwell was
 appointed Master of the King's Jewel
 House on 14 April 1532, King's secretary in April 1534 and Master of the
 Rolls on 19 October 1534. Norfolk
 and Bedford provide a similar list of
 promotions in *Thomas, Lord
 Cromwell*: 'Norf. Cromwell the
 maiestie of England, / . . . Makes thee
 maister of the iewell house, / Chiefe
 Secretarie to himselfe, and with all, /
 Creates thee one of his highnesse
 priuie Councell. / . . . Bed. The King
 creates him Lord keeper of his priuie
 Seale: / And maister of the Roules'
 (D4ᵛ).
34 **Beside** as well as
 is he is
34–5 **Master / O'th' Rolls** high legal
 office; 'The Master of the Rolls was
 keeper of the rolls, patents, and grants
 made under the great seal, and records of
 the Court of Chancery' (Humphreys).
36 **Stands** i.e. he stands
 gap and trade opportunity and well-

trodden path; *trade* is any road used by
 traders.
37 **time** course of events, with a sense
 perhaps of *OED* 3, 'the age now present' or 5a, 'the general state of affairs'
40 **There are that** i.e. there are men
 who, some men
40–52 **I . . . convented** Gardiner here ini-
 tiates the sequence taken from Foxe
 1596: '[C]ertaine of the Counsaile,
 whose names neede not to be repeated,
 by the intisement & prouocation of his
 ancient enemie the Bishop of
 Winchester, . . . attempted the king
 against him' (1693–4). The next scene
 returns to this passage from Foxe for
 speeches by the Lord Chancellor and
 Gardiner (see 5.2.49–53n., 61–5n.).
43 **Incensed** aroused the anger of; Rann's
 emendation ('Insens'd') means 'informed' and was current usage, but is
 weaker in effect and unnecessary.
44 Gardiner is suggesting that he has told
 the Council everything he knows, but
 there is also an implication that he has
 them in his pocket.

---

34 is] he's *Theobald;* he is *Capell*   36 trade of] trade for *F4;* tread for *Warburton*   more] *(moe)*
37 time] *F4;* Lime *F*   42 – I . . . you, I think –] *Staunton;* (I . . . you), I think *F;* I . . . you, I think
Johnson   43 Incensed] *(Incenst);* Insens'd *Rann*

A most arch heretic, a pestilence   45
That does infect the land; with which they, moved,
Have broken with the King, who hath so far
Given ear to our complaint, of his great grace
And princely care foreseeing those fell mischiefs
Our reasons laid before him, hath commanded   50
Tomorrow morning to the Council board
He be convented. He's a rank weed, Sir Thomas,
And we must root him out. From your affairs
I hinder you too long. Good night, Sir Thomas.

LOVELL

Many good nights, my lord. I rest your servant.   55

Exeunt Gardiner and Page.

Enter KING *and* SUFFOLK.

KING

Charles, I will play no more tonight:
My mind's not on't. You are too hard for me.

SUFFOLK

Sir, I did never win of you before.

KING   But little, Charles,
Nor shall not, when my fancy's on my play.   60
Now, Lovell, from the Queen what is the news?

LOVELL

I could not personally deliver to her

---

45 **most arch** a double superlative, with
   arch punning again on 'archbishop' (cf.
   3.2.102 and n.)
46 **moved** angered
47 **broken** broached the subject
49 **fell** dreadful, cruel
50 **reasons** arguments, warnings
   hath Malone's subtle emendation to
   ''hath' assumes an absent 'he'; the
   word is in fact better seen as a compressed version of 'that he hath'.
52 **convented** summoned, required to

attend; cf. *TNK* 1.5.9–10
52–3 **rank . . . out** Gardiner returns to
   the kind of horticultural metaphor he
   used of Anne at 20–3.
55 **rest** remain
56–60 Cf. *TNK* 1.3.27–33.
57 **too . . . me** playing too well for me to
   defeat
60 **when . . . play** when I can concentrate
   properly on the game; when I am in
   the mood to play
62 **deliver** tell, recount

---

45 arch heretic] *(Arch-Heretique)*   46 which they,] which, they *F*   49 foreseeing] *(fore-seeing)*
50 hath] he hath *Pope;* 'hath *Malone*   55 SD] *Capell; after* Thomas, *line 54 F (Exit)*

What you commanded me, but by her woman
I sent your message, who returned her thanks
In the greatest humbleness and desired your highness   65
Most heartily to pray for her.

KING   What sayest thou? Ha?
To pray for her? What, is she crying out?

LOVELL
So said her woman, and that her sufferance made
Almost each pang a death.

KING   Alas, good lady.

SUFFOLK
God safely quit her of her burden, and   70
With gentle travail, to the gladding of
Your highness with an heir.

KING   'Tis midnight, Charles.
Prithee to bed, and in thy prayers remember
Th'estate of my poor Queen. Leave me alone,
For I must think of that which company   75
Would not be friendly to.

SUFFOLK   I wish your highness
A quiet night, and my good mistress will
Remember in my prayers.

KING   Charles, good night. *Exit Suffolk.*

---

65 **greatest** monosyllabic
66 **Most heartily** with all your heart
  sayest monosyllabic
68 **sufferance** two syllables
69 **pang** There is no reference to a difficult labour in Holinshed, though there
  may be some displacement from one of
  Henry's future wives: in *When You See
  Me*, Jane Seymour dies while giving
  birth to the future Edward VI.
70 **quit her of** release her from
71 **gentle travail** relatively painless contractions
71–2 **to . . . heir** making your highness
  happy by presenting you with a son

72 **midnight** Cf. 14n.
74 **estate** condition, well being
75–6 **I . . . to** It is not entirely clear
  whether Henry has genuinely forgotten that he has summoned Cranmer or
  does not want Suffolk to be part of the
  conversation (and he is certainly irritated with Lovell's eavesdropping at
  84–7). His response to Denny at 81–2
  perhaps suggests that Cranmer's
  appointment has slipped his mind in
  the context of Anne's labour, but the
  subsequent scene would be shaped
  very differently if Suffolk knew about
  Henry's discussion with Cranmer.

65 greatest] *(great'st)* 66 sayest] *(say'st)* 68 sufferance] *(suffrance)* 70 burden] *(Burthen)*
76 to] *(too)*

Enter Sir Anthony DENNY.

Well, sir, what follows?

DENNY

Sir, I have brought my lord the Archbishop,   80
As you commanded me.

KING   Ha? Canterbury?

DENNY

Ay, my good lord.

KING   'Tis true. Where is he, Denny?

DENNY

He attends your highness' pleasure.

KING   Bring him to us. [*Exit Denny.*]

LOVELL [*aside*]

This is about that which the Bishop spake.
I am happily come hither.   85

Enter CRANMER *and* DENNY.

KING

Avoid the gallery!   (*Lovell seems to stay.*)
                  Ha? I have said. Be gone.

78.1 Foxe 1596 recounts the King's decision to commit Cranmer to the Tower
at the request of the Council, and continues: 'When night came, the king
sent Sir Anthonie Denie about midnight, to Lambeth to the Archbishop,
willing him forthwith to resort vnto
him at the Court. The message done,
the Archbishop speedily addressed
himselfe to the Court' (1694).
84–86 SD1 **This . . .** *stay.* The King may
have his subjects under surveillance,
but he is not to be spied on himself. An
oddly abortive sequence, nonetheless,
in an enigmatic scene.
84 **which** of which
85 **happily** fortunately
86 **Avoid** get out of

gallery According to Foxe 1596,
Cranmer went 'into the Galerie where the
king walked, and taried for him' (1694). A
gallery was a long room in large houses
used for taking exercise. As the *gallery* is
the setting for the scene, this must be represented on the main stage and not on the
upper level, although some critics assume
that it was staged above. In staging terms,
the 'gallery' is sometimes taken to mean
the upper level, but it does not have that
significance here.
seems to stay does not appear to be in a
hurry to leave
I have said I have already told you;
proverbial assertion (Dent, S118.1); cf.
Oth 4.2.203; *Mac* 4.3.214; *AC* 1.2.59;
Fletcher & Beaumont, *Cox* 1.1.72.

78.1] *Johnson; after* followes *F*   80 Archbishop] *(*Arch-byshop*)*   83 us] *(*Vs*)*   SD] *Rowe*   84 SD]
Rowe   86] *Capell; F lines* gallery. / gone. /

What?   *Exeunt Lovell and Denny.*
CRANMER [*aside*]   I am fearful. Wherefore frowns he
    thus?
'Tis his aspect of terror. All's not well.
KING
    How now, my lord? You do desire to know
    Wherefore I sent for you.
CRANMER [*Kneels.*]   It is my duty   90
    T'attend your highness' pleasure.
KING   Pray you, arise,
    My good and gracious lord of Canterbury.
    Come, you and I must walk a turn together:
    I have news to tell you. Come, come: give me your
        hand.
    Ah, my good lord, I grieve at what I speak,   95
    And am right sorry to repeat what follows.
    I have, and most unwillingly, of late
    Heard many grievous – I do say, my lord,
    Grievous – complaints of you, which, being
        considered,
    Have moved us and our Council that you shall   100
    This morning come before us, where I know

---

87 **fearful** Foxe 1596 does not explicitly
say that Cranmer was afraid, but his
narrative of summons, delay and test
implies it.
88 **'Tis . . . terror**. This is what he looks
like when he is angry; an internal SD
to guide the actor.
93–108 **Come . . . you**. Henry's speech is
loosely based on Foxe 1596, though the
King in Foxe's narrative does not at
this stage imply his sympathy for
Cranmer's cause: 'his highnesse saide:
Ah my Lorde of Canturbury, I can tell

you newes. . . . [T]he Counsell haue
requested me, for the triall of the matter, to suffer the[m] to commit you to
the tower, or else no man dare come
forth, as witnesse in these matters, you
being a Counsellor' (1694).
93 **walk a turn** take a short walk (presumably, along the gallery)
98, 99 **grievous** serious, grave
99 **of** about
100 **moved us** made us decide
    shall must, are to

87 SD] *Capell*   89–90] *Rowe³*; F *lines* Lord? / wherefore / you. / dutie /   90 SD] *Johnson (Kneeling)*   94] *Pope (omits second* come); F *lines* you. / hand. /   98–9 grievous – I . . . Grievous –] *this edn;* greeuous. I . . . Greeuous F   100 us] (Vs)

You cannot with such freedom purge yourself
But that, till further trial in those charges
Which will require your answer, you must take
Your patience to you and be well contented   105
To make your house our Tower. You a brother of us,
It fits we thus proceed, or else no witness
Would come against you.

CRANMER [*Kneels.*]   I humbly thank your highness,
And am right glad to catch this good occasion
Most throughly to be winnowed, where my chaff   110
And corn shall fly asunder. For I know
There's none stands under more calumnious tongues
Than I myself, poor man.

KING   Stand up, good Canterbury.
Thy truth and thy integrity is rooted
In us, thy friend. Give me thy hand. Stand up.   115

---

102 You will not be able to free yourself
so totally from the charges made
against you.

104–5 **take . . . you** similar construction
to the proverbial expression 'to take a
man's heart to thee'; see Dent, H328.1;
cf. *AYL* 4.3.174 and Fletcher, *WGC*
2.3.44. Here and at *WT* 3.2.230,
patience replaces 'heart'.

106 **You . . . us** 'since you are one of my
immediate advisers'

108 SD Cf. 113: *Stand up*. Foxe 1596 indicates that 'the Archb. kneeled downe'
(1694) at this point.

108–13 **I . . . man**. Cranmer's reply is
based (for sense, though not for phrasing) on Foxe 1596: 'I am content if it
please your grace, with al my hart, to go
thither at your highnes commandement,
and I most humbly thank your maiesty
that I may come to my triall, for there be
that haue many waies slandered me, and
nowe this way I hope to trie my selfe not
worthy of such report' (1694). Foxe
provides little precedent for the pathos

of Cranmer's speech in the play.

110–11 **Most . . . asunder** Cranmer uses
appropriately apocalyptic language as
he looks forward formally to the judgement process. The principal echo is of
Matthew, 3.12 ('Which hathe his fanne
in his hand, & wil make cleane his
floore, and gather his wheat into his
garner, but wil burne vp the chaffe
with vnquencheable fyre'); the word
'winnow' may come from Luke, 22.31
('Satan hathe desired you, to wynnow
you, as wheat'), though the context is
different.

110 **throughly** a standard spelling of
'thoroughly'. Modernizing to 'thoroughly' would sacrifice the metre by
introducing an extra syllable.

112 **stands under** is the object of
calumnious lying, deceitful

113 **I . . . man** Compare Katherine's
rhetorical strategy at 3.1.146.

114 **is** Two singular nouns as subjects are
often followed by a singular verb in
Early Modern English.

---

106 You . . . us,] *F2;* you, a Brother of us *F;* you, a Brother of us, *F4*   108 SD] *Johnson (Kneeling)*

Prithee, let's walk. Now, by my halidom,
What manner of man are you? My lord, I looked
You would have given me your petition that
I should have ta'en some pains to bring together
Yourself and your accusers and to have heard you   120
Without endurance further.

CRANMER   Most dread liege,
The good I stand on is my truth and honesty.
If they shall fail, I with mine enemies
Will triumph o'er my person, which I weigh not
Being of those virtues vacant. I fear nothing   125
What can be said against me.

KING   Know you not
How your state stands i'th' world, with the whole
     world?

116 **halidom** F's 'Holydame' is a corruption of 'haligdom' (holiness), sometimes confused with 'Our Lady' (*OED* 1), e.g. by Rowe ('holy Dame'). A problem for a modernizing editor, since there is no truly modern form: I have adopted the *OED* (and Hudson[2]) form.

117–21 **What . . . further** Foxe 1596 reports that Henry, 'perceiuing the mans uprightnesse, ioyned with such simplicitie, saide: Oh Lorde, what maner a man be you? . . . I had thought that you would rather haue sued to vs to haue taken the paines to haue heard you, and your accusers together for your triall, without any such indura[n]ce' (1694).

117 **looked** expected, predicted

121 **endurance** imprisonment (*OED* 1b); though *OED* cites this passage as its only instance of a connected meaning 'protraction of an existing condition' (*OED* 2b),which amounts to the same thing (cf. Foxe 1596 quotation at 5.2.183–7n.); modernized from F's 'indurance,' the form in use in the six-

teenth to eighteenth centuries

121–6 **Most . . . me**. In Foxe 1596, Cranmer makes no such intervention in Henry's speech.

122 **The . . . on** the basis of my confidence

123–5 **If . . . vacant**. If I am not genuinely truthful and honest, my spirit will join my enemies in condemning my earthly self, which would be worthless in such circumstances.

124 **weigh not** consider valueless

125 **nothing** not at all

126 **What** whatever

126–40 **Know . . . destruction**. In Foxe 1596, Henry's words are: 'Do not you know, what state you be in with the whole world, and how many great enemies you haue? Do you not consider what an easie thing it is, to procure three or foure false knaues to witnesse against you? Think you to haue better lucke that waie, then your maister Christ had? I see by it, you will run headlong to your vndoing, if I would suffer you' (1694). The parallels with Buckingham's trial are clear, especially at 131–3.

116 halidom] *Hudson[2]*; Holydame *F;* holidame *Cam;* holy Dame *Rowe*   121 endurance] *(*indurance*)*

Your enemies are many and not small: their practices
Must bear the same proportion, and not ever
The justice and the truth o'th' question carries   130
The due o'th' verdict with it. At what ease
Might corrupt minds procure knaves as corrupt
To swear against you? Such things have been done.
You are potently opposed, and with a malice
Of as great size. Ween you of better luck –   135
I mean in perjured witness – than your master,
Whose minister you are, whiles here he lived
Upon this naughty earth? Go to, go to:
You take a precipice for no leap of danger,
And woo your own destruction.
CRANMER   God and your majesty   140
Protect mine innocence, or I fall into

128 F's fourteen-syllable line arguably
contains redundancy. RP conjectures
that 134–5, which stress the power of
Cranmer's enemies, might be invoked
in favour of emending to produce
either 'are many: their practices' or
'are not small: their practices' (the
choice depending on whether *and not
small* is read as redundant or as reinforcement of 134–5).
    not small i.e. powerful
128–9 **their . . . proportion** Their plots
will be as effective as they are plentiful
and powerful.
129–31 **not . . . it** It is not always the side
telling the truth that wins the case.
131–3 **At . . . you?** Cf. 1.2.173–5 and
Gardiner's subversion of two witnesses
in *Thomas, Lord Cromwell*, E4ᵛ–F2ʳ.
131 **At what ease** how effortlessly
134 **potently** powerfully
135–8 **Ween . . . earth?** biblical reference
to the perjury used to condemn Jesus
to death in Matthew, 26.59–60: 'Now
the chief Priests & the Elders, and all
the whole council soght false witnes
against Iesus, to put him to death. /

But they founde none, and thogh many
false witnesses came, yet founde they
none: but at the last came two false
witnesses'; cf. 131–3n.
135 **Ween you of** do you expect to have
(*OED v.* 2)
136 **in perjured witness** in the matter of
false evidence
137 **whiles** while (*OED conj.* II 4)
138 **naughty** sinful
139 You are behaving as if jumping off a
cliff is not dangerous.
    *precipice F's 'Precepit' may well be
the playwright's precise spelling (*OED*
lists it as a variant form, not an error,
though this is the only instance cited),
though the easy confusion of *c* and *t* in
secretary hand makes the modern
spelling quite possible. The lack of a
final *e* suggests the *t* may well be correct,
though final *c* is taken by some (partly
on the basis of the Hand D evidence in
STM) as a characteristic Shakespearean
spelling (RP). Either way, *precipice* is the
appropriate modernized form.
140 **woo** invite, bring on
141 **or** might possibly signify 'ere' (RP)

131 due] *(dew)*   139 precipice] *(Precepit)*   140 woo] *(woe)*

The trap is laid for me.

KING   Be of good cheer.

They shall no more prevail than we give way to.

Keep comfort to you, and this morning see

You do appear before them. If they shall chance,   145

In charging you with matters, to commit you,

The best persuasions to the contrary

Fail not to use, and with what vehemency

Th'occasion shall instruct you. If entreaties

Will render you no remedy, this ring   150

Deliver them, and your appeal to us

There make before them. – Look, the good man weeps.

He's honest, on mine honour. God's blest mother,

---

142 **trap is** The relative marker ('that' or 'which') is understood.

143–52 **They . . . them.** Again, this passage follows Foxe 1596 quite closely: 'Your enemies shall not so preuaile against you, for I haue otherwise deuised with my selfe to keepe you out of their handes. Yet notwithstanding to morrow when the Counsaile shall sit, and send for you, resort vnto them, and if in charging you with this matter, they do commit you to the tower, . . . vse for yourselfe as good perswasions that way as you may deuise, and if no intreatie or reasonable request will serue, then deliuer vnto them this my ring, . . . and saie vnto them, if there be no remedie my Lords, . . . then I . . . appeale to the kinges owne person by this his token vnto you all' (1694).

143 They will succeed only to the extent I permit.

146 **commit** i.e. (as in Holinshed) have you confined to the Tower of London

148 **vehemency** energy, persistence; *vehemency* was an alternative form of 'vehemence'.

152–5 **Look . . . kingdom.** Henry's switch of mode from direct address to public utterance either acts as an

engaging aside or, if played to include Cranmer, serves to distance and objectify the Archbishop; cf. Polonius in *Ham* 2.2.521–2: 'Look whe'er he has not turned his colour, and has tears in 's eyes', where the first Player, though not directly addressed, is not excluded either (RP). Either way, the change of mode allows for a brief commentary, including the epithet *true-hearted* for Cranmer the Protestant, though the Archbishop seems a little less in control of his emotions than he does in Foxe 1596: 'The Archbishop perceiuing the kinges benignity so much to him wards, had much ado to forbeare teares. Well, said the K. go your waies my Lord, and do as I haue bidden you' (1694).

152 **good man** F's 'goodman' underlines that the stress is on the first word/syllable.

153 **God's blest mother** one of the few examples of swearing to remain in the play despite the strictures of the 1606 Act to Restrain Abuses (see 2.4.185n.). Apart from the exclamation 'Ha!', Henry's most characteristic phrase in Rowley's *When You See Me* is 'Mother of God' and variants including 'God's holy mother', neither of which (unsur-

143 to] *(too)*   152 good man] *F3;* goodman *F*

I swear he is true-hearted, and a soul
None better in my kingdom. – Get you gone,   155
And do as I have bid you.   *Exit Cranmer.*
                    He has strangled
His language in his tears.

Enter Old Lady[*; * LOVELL *follows.*]

LOVELL (*within*)   Come back! What mean you?
OLD LADY
I'll not come back. The tidings that I bring
Will make my boldness manners. [*to the King*] Now
        good angels
Fly o'er thy royal head and shade thy person   160
Under their blessed wings.
KING   Now by thy looks
I guess thy message. Is the Queen delivered?

prisingly) appears in Foxe 1596 and
which mark the absence of a reformation in Henry's vocabulary at least. It is
hard to know whether the oath here
stems specifically from Rowley or
more broadly from the 'Bluff-King-
Harry' tradition; the last few lines of
this scene, however, bear a strong
resemblance to lines in *When You See
Me* (see 162–76n.).
157.1 **Old Lady** presumably, the same
Old Lady with whom Anne was in dialogue in 2.3; her sudden unmannerly
intrusion is reminiscent of 4.2.99.1.
157 SP *F has '*Gent. within*' but it seems
in accordance with the logic of dramatic economy to accept Humphreys's
emendation.
158–61 **tidings . . . wings** Where at
2.3.72 we are offered an ambivalent
Annunciation, here we see an equally
ambivalent Nativity scene, though this
time with the Old Lady in the unlikely

role of angel; cf. Luke, 2.10. As at
2.3.72, I am grateful to Thomas
Merriam for this suggestion.
159 **manners** Again, at a moment crucial for the well being of Henry's
sense of manliness, the issue of manners arises; cf. e.g. 1.2.27; 1.4.95.
162–76 **Is . . . issue.** When Queen Jane is
in labour in *When You See Me*, Henry
says that 'Who first brings word that
Harrie hath a Son / Shall be rewarded
well' (B1[r]; Wilson TLN 286–7), and the
Fool, Will Sommers, adds 'I, Ile bee his
suertie: but doe you heare wenches, shee
that brings the first tydings howsoeuer it
fall out, let her be sure to say the Childs
like the father, or els she shall haue nothing' (B1[r-v]; Wilson TLN 288–90).
162 **delivered** 'The seuenth of September
[1533] being sundaie, betweene three &
foure of the clocke in the afternoone,
the queene was deliuered of a faire
yoong ladie' (Holinshed, 934).

156–7 He . . . tears] *Hanmer (subst.); one line in F*   157 His language] all his language *F2;* All language *Hanmer*   157.1 LOVELL *follows*] *Capell (subst.)*   157 SP LOVELL] *Humphreys;* Gent. *F*
158+ SP OLD LADY] *Lady. F*   159 SD] *Capell (subst.)*

Say 'Ay, and of a boy'.

OLD LADY   Ay, ay, my liege,

And of a lovely boy. The God of heaven

Both now and ever bless her: 'tis a girl   165

Promises boys hereafter. Sir, your Queen

Desires your visitation and to be

Acquainted with this stranger. 'Tis as like you

As cherry is to cherry.

KING   Lovell.

LOVELL   Sir?   169

KING

Give her an hundred marks. I'll to the Queen.

                        Exeunt King [and Lovell].

163–4 **Say . . . boy**. This puts the Old Lady in an impossible (and comical) position, since she is obliged to obey the King's order, even though doing so is only going to make matters worse.

165 **her** ambiguous, referring either to Anne or Elizabeth. The Doran production (RSC, 1996) had Henry – ecstatic that at last he has a son and heir – perform a quick impromptu dance of joy with Lovell, only to come to an abrupt halt at the word *girl*.

165–6 **'tis . . . hereafter** The Old Lady's phrasing makes the instrumental role of women in the royal family apparent, though it is not entirely clear whether she means that, having had a healthy daughter, Anne may in time produce a son or that the baby girl will grow up to be the mother of a son (in either case, the audience would no doubt note the irony).

167 **your visitation** you to visit her
to be i.e. for you to be

168–9 **like . . . to cherry** proverbial for identical (Dent, C276.1), probably derived from the ancient Greek expression ὁμοιότερος σύκου ('as like as two figs'), which Erasmus lists as specifical-

ly humorous (2.8.7). The Old Lady is naïvely hoping to head off the King's impending rage by making a little joke.

170 **an hundred marks** not an ungenerous sum, since the mark originally represented the sum of money equivalent to eight ounces (approximately 250g) of silver, but clearly the Old Lady was expecting considerably more. As Foakes notes (Ard[2]), the courtier who defied the Privy Council and rode to Scotland to tell James of Elizabeth's death was given high office; perhaps the Old Lady is hoping now for the preferment that, to judge by her remarks in 2.3, had always eluded her. Either way, her reaction serves as an oblique way to demonstrate Henry's (to the post-Elizabethan audience, ironically misplaced) disappointment at the birth of yet another daughter.

Exeunt . . . Lovell No exit is marked in F for Lovell, and editions assume he departs with the Old Lady at 176, but F SD for 176 is clear (*Exit Ladie.*) and it makes good stage sense to have Henry and Lovell exit (perhaps by different doors), leaving the Old Lady on her own.

170] *Pope; F lines* Markes. / Queene. /   170 SD *Exeunt*] *this edn (GWW); Exit. F   and Lovell*] *this edn (GWW)*

OLD LADY

An hundred marks? By this light, I'll ha' more.
An ordinary groom is for such payment.
I will have more or scold it out of him.
Said I for this the girl was like to him? I'll
Have more, or else unsay't; and now, while 'tis hot,   175
I'll put it to the issue.   *Exit [Old] Lady.*

5.2   *Enter* CRANMER, Archbishop of Canterbury.

171 **By this light** a standard expression, originally 'by God's light'
172 **groom** servant of 'low birth'
174 **Said . . . him?** Cf. 162–76n.; this mocking of Henry's claims to paternity serves two purposes: as another undermining of his manliness (see pp. 81–7), and as a comment on the difference in character between Henry and Elizabeth.
174–6 **him . . . issue** Though F's lineation is metrically awkward, I agree with Maxwell (Cam¹) that the attempts of Steevens² and many subsequent editors to rearrange these lines – expanding the contractions 'Ile' and ''tis' as 'I will' and 'it is' in order to establish a new, and more regular, metrical pattern – are arbitrary.
175 **while 'tis hot** a shorthand version of the proverbial 'to strike while the iron is hot' (Dent, I94); cf. *KL* 1.1.309: 'and i'the heat'.
176 **put . . . issue** bring the matter to a close
5.2 Generally considered a Fletcher scene (see Appendix 3). If so, then it is Fletcher who returns to the section of Foxe 1596 that Shakespeare had begun to mine in the previous scene, and who develops the contrast and enmity set up between Cranmer and Gardiner. Chronology is again heavily compressed for dramatic immediacy: the near-imprisonment of Cranmer in fact took place twelve or so years after the

birth of Elizabeth. Productions (including Kemble, Kean, Irving and Tree) have often cut this scene and the next in order to move directly from the announcement of the birth of Elizabeth to the christening. For discussion of staging possibilities, see pp. 13–15. The location is the council chamber and its ante-room.
0.1 CRANMER The portrayal of Cranmer here is extrapolated from that in 5.1. The Archbishop seems much weaker and more emotional here than he does in Foxe 1596, and is at times portrayed almost comically. His weakness here sets up a somewhat equivocal background for the final prophecy in 5.4. Editors often insert a stage direction here (e.g. '*pursuivants, pages &c. are in attendance at the door*' (Ard²)) in anticipation of Cranmer's and Butts's references at 17 and 23–4 to the company the Archbishop is forced to keep while the door is barred to him. As became clear in the course of a workshop on this scene at the new Globe in March 1999, however, the repeated references to *pursuivants et al.* install them in the audience's imagination without necessitating their actual presence on stage, though productions have tended to include them. Davies (RSC, 1983), for instance, had Cranmer

174–6 him . . . issue/] him? / I will have . . . now, / While it is hot, I'll . . . issue / *Steevens²;* him? / I'll . . . hot, / . . . issue *Ard²*   176 SD] *F; Exeunt. Capell*   **5.2]** *(Scena Secunda.)*

CRANMER

    I hope I am not too late, and yet the gentleman

    That was sent to me from the Council prayed me

    To make great haste. All fast? What means this? Ho!

    Who waits there?

Enter [Door] Keeper.

                  Sure you know me?

KEEPER   Yes, my lord,

    But yet I cannot help you.

CRANMER   Why?

KEEPER   Your grace   5

    Must wait till you be called for.

Enter Doctor BUTTS.

CRANMER   So.

BUTTS [*aside*]

    This is a piece of malice. I am glad

    I came this way so happily. The King

---

play football (i.e. soccer) with the footboys to pass the time. There is a similar moment in Fletcher & Massinger, *JVOB* (1619), 1.3.49ff., when the Prince of Orange finds that the States have barred the door against him.

1–6 I hope . . . for. Again, the bare facts provided by Foxe 1596 are given dramatic treatment: 'On the morrow about 9. of the clocke before noone, the counsaile sent a gentleman Usher for the Archbishop, who when hee came to the Counsaile chamber dore, could not be let in, but of purpose (as it seemed) was compelled there to waite among the Pages, Lackies, and seruing men all alone' (1694).

3 **All fast?** all locked up

4 **Sure** surely

6.1 BUTTS F spells the doctor's name as 'Buts', (modernized here to *Butts*) after Foxe 1596: 'D. Buts the kings phisition resorting that way, and espying how my lord of Cant. was handled, went to the kings highnesse' (1694).

7 **piece of malice** malicious thing to do

8 **happily** fortunately, by accident (though, arguably, surveillance is too widespread in this play ever to be entirely accidental)

4.1] *Oxf; after* me? *F*   5–6] Your . . . for] *Ard²; one line F*   7 SD *Dyce*   piece] *F2;* Peere *F*

Shall understand it presently.   *Exit Butts.*

CRANMER [*aside*]   'Tis Butts,

The King's physician. As he passed along,   10

How earnestly he cast his eyes upon me.

Pray heaven he sound not my disgrace. For certain,

This is of purpose laid by some that hate me –

God turn their hearts: I never sought their malice –

To quench mine honour. They would shame to make me   15

Wait else at door, a fellow Councillor

'Mong boys, grooms and lackeys. But their pleasures

Must be fulfilled, and I attend with patience.

Enter the KING *and* BUTTS *at a window above.*

BUTTS

I'll show your grace the strangest sight –

KING   What's that, Butts?

BUTTS

– I think your highness saw this many a day.   20

KING

Body o'me, where is it?

BUTTS   There, my lord:

9   **Shall understand** i.e. must hear about
     presently immediately
12   **sound** proclaim, make known (*OED*
     v.[1] II 10); Cam[1] sees the term as figu-
     rative ('sound' signifying 'fathom');
     there is a possible secondary reference
     to medical 'probing'.
13   **laid** set up, organized
14   **turn their hearts** change their atti-
     tudes
17   **boys . . . lackeys** This is a version of
     Foxe 1596: 'Pages, Lackies, and seru-
     ing men'; cf. 1–6; also 22–4. *Lackeys* is
     derogatory. Metrical considerations

perhaps support emendation of *boys* to
'footboys' (as at 24) (RP).
17–18   **their . . . fulfilled** I am obliged to
     obey their wishes.
18   **attend** wait
18.1 As Foakes observes (Ard[2]), this is
     'the only certain indication of the use
     of the upper stage in this play' (see
     p. 13).
21   **Body o'me** another of Henry's char-
     acteristic phrases; cf. 5.1.153n. and
     When You See Me, I3[v], Wilson TLN
     2601; and I4[v], Wilson TLN 2678
     ('Body a me').

9 SD *aside*] *Johnson*   12 sound] found *Rowe*   17] *Rowe*[3]; *F* lines Lackeyes. / pleasures /   19 sight –]
Rowe; sight. *F*   21 o'me] *Pope;* a me *F*

The high promotion of his grace of Canterbury,
Who holds his state at door 'mongst pursuivants,
Pages and footboys.
KING   Ha? 'Tis he indeed.
Is this the honour they do one another?   25
'Tis well there's one above 'em yet. I had thought
They had parted so much honesty among 'em –
At least good manners – as not thus to suffer
A man of his place, and so near our favour,
To dance attendance on their lordships' pleasures –   30
And at the door, too, like a post with packets.
By holy Mary, Butts, there's knavery!
Let 'em alone, and draw the curtain close:
We shall hear more anon.

22–4 **high . . . footboys** drawn closely from Foxe 1596: 'My Lorde of Cant. if it please your grace is well promoted: for nowe he is become a Lackey or a seruing man, for yonder he standeth this halfe hower at the Counsaile Chamber doore amongst them' (1694); cf. 1–6, 17.

23 **holds his state** stands in a place appropriate to his status (ironic, obviously); also suggests 'contains himself with dignity'
pursuivants servants, official messengers

24 **footboys** servants, errand-boys

26 **there's . . . yet** neatly ambiguous, associating Henry with God

26–34 **I . . . anon**. The King's speech is loosely based on Foxe 1596: 'It is not so (quoth the king) I trowe, nor the Counsaile hath not so little discretion as to vse the Metropolitane of the Realme in that sort, specially being one of their own number. But let them alone (saide the king) and wee shall heare more soone' (1694).

27 **parted . . . honesty** shared sufficient respect

29 **place** rank, status

30 **To dance attendance** proverbial (Dent, A392); cf. *2H6* 1.3.174, *R3* 3.7.56.

31 **like . . . packets** like a courier with letters

32 **holy Mary** Again, Henry's choice of exclamation would suggest to Protestants in the audience that he needs a reformation of the vocabulary; cf. 5.1.153n.

33 **curtain** 'From the upper stage window the King and Butts survey the street outside the council chamber where Cranmer is waiting. . . . The drawing of the curtain chiefly helps the transition from street to chamber and incidentally removes what would have been a distraction from the audience if it had observed the King's reactions above to the events and dialogue below, on which attention must be concentrated' (Bowers). It also serves as an exit for Butts and allows the King to make his way quietly down to stage level, ready to enter suddenly at 147.1, thereby surprising not only the Privy Council but also the audience, who expect him still to be listening unseen above.

A council table brought in with chairs and stools and placed under the
   state. Enter Lord CHANCELLOR, *places himself at the upper end of*
   the table, on the left hand; a seat being left void above him, as for
      Canterbury's seat. Duke of SUFFOLK, Duke of NORFOLK,
   SURREY, Lord CHAMBERLAIN, GARDINER *seat themselves in*
      order on each side; CROMWELL *at lower end, as secretary.*

CHANCELLOR
   Speak to the business, master secretary.   35
   Why are we met in Council?
CROMWELL   Please your honours,
   The chief cause concerns his grace of Canterbury.
GARDINER
   Has he had knowledge of it?
CROMWELL   Yes.
NORFOLK   Who waits there?

34.1–6 There is no such description of the scene in Foxe 1596, who names only the Earl of Bedford (and, by implication, Gardiner, Bishop of Winchester) of those present at the hearing. The occasion serves here to reintroduce some of the nobility who have appeared earlier in the play. Editors have regularly begun a new scene at this point, principally to enable Cranmer, Henry and Butts to leave the stage, but it seems clear that F envisages Cranmer's remaining on stage, to one side (probably near one of the stage doors), for the whole scene, and the King's eavesdropping on the debate is entirely in keeping both with the culture of surveillance throughout the play and the physical possibilities of the Globe and the Blackfriars. Despite the drawing of the curtain, 'by the physical necessity of the stage the King's observation post remains constant since he is to be a hearer (and presumably a hidden spectator) of the action below. The necessity for the King's continued presence, as well as the awkwardness of an exit for Cranmer, seem to have dic-

tated a continuous scene here, a fluidity with which the Elizabethan stage could readily cope' (Bowers).

34.2 *state* another suggestion that there might be a throne or *state* on stage throughout the play; see 1.2.8.4n.
   Lord CHANCELLOR This, as we know from 3.2.393, is Sir Thomas More, though in fact the post was held by Sir Thomas Wriothesley at the time of the council meeting depicted in this scene. It is not clear why More is not named unless it is for this reason or else simply, as Foakes suggests (Ard²), to 'avoid the intrusion of a personality'.
   upper end in terms of a non-theatrical building, the end of the table furthest from the door, and therefore the position of highest status; on stage, however, the end nearest to the tiring-house wall. The Lord Chancellor sits *on the left hand*, that is, one seat down from the top of the long stage right side of the table, leaving the seat to his left *as for* Cranmer.

35 **Speak . . . business** Introduce the topic of the meeting.

38 **had knowledge of** been told about

34.1] scene 5 *Pope;* scene 3 *Cam (and many other eds)*   35 master] *Steevens²;* M. F; Mr. *F3*

KEEPER

Without, my noble lords?

GARDINER   Yes.

KEEPER   My lord Archbishop,

And has done half an hour to know your pleasures.   40

CHANCELLOR

Let him come in.

KEEPER   Your grace may enter now.

Cranmer approaches the council table.

CHANCELLOR

My good lord Archbishop, I'm very sorry

To sit here at this present and behold

That chair stand empty. But we all are men,

In our own natures frail, and capable   45

Of our flesh – few are angels – out of which frailty

And want of wisdom, you that best should teach us

Have misdemeaned yourself, and not a little,

---

39 **Without** outside
41 The Keeper is given no exit line, so presumably stays on stage until the general *Exeunt* at 215.
43 **present** time
44 **chair** i.e. Cranmer's place at the council table
44–9 **But . . . laws** Stokesley, the then Bishop of London, addresses his clergy in the wake of Wolsey's downfall: 'My friendes all, you knowe well that we be men fraile of condition and no Aungels, and by frailtie and lacke of wisdome, we haue misdemeaned our selfe towarde the king our soueraigne Lord and his lawes . . .' (Foxe 1596, 959).This address is drawn from a 1531 speech by Stokesley reported in Hall (L3^v, fol. 201^v) and reprinted in Foxe 1596 (959–60) in a passage which appears 700–odd pages before the Cranmer material, just after his narrative of the

divorce proceedings, Katherine's diatribe against Wolsey, and the issue of the *praemunire*. Fletcher (assuming the attribution is accurate) may have been checking Holinshed on those subjects against Foxe; the one or two possible hints of material drawn from Hall earlier in the play come in scenes attributed to Shakespeare.
44–6 **men . . . frailty** a conflation of two proverbial expressions (confused by textual problems): 'flesh is frail' (Dent, F363; cf. *1H4* 3.3.167–9, *MM* 2.4.122) and 'men are not angels' (Dent, M544)
45–6 **capable . . . flesh** subject to bodily urges. *Capable* can mean 'susceptible', 'open to' (*OED a.* 3); Malone's 'incapable' and 'culpable' in Collier^2 are therefore unnecessary emendations.
47 **want** lack
48 **misdemeaned yourself** behaved inappropriately

45–6 frail . . . angels] *(*fraile, and capable / Of our flesh, few are Angels;*)*; frail, and capable / Of frailty *Pope;* frail, incapable; / Of our flesh, . . . angels *Malone;* frail, and culpable / Of our flesh; . . . angels *Collier^2*

Toward the King first, then his laws, in filling
The whole realm, by your teaching and your
    chaplains' –   50
For so we are informed – with new opinions,
Diverse and dangerous, which are heresies
And, not reformed, may prove pernicious.

GARDINER
Which reformation must be sudden too,
My noble lords, for those that tame wild horses   55
Pace 'em not in their hands to make 'em gentle,
But stop their mouths with stubborn bits and spur 'em
Till they obey the manage. If we suffer,
Out of our easiness and childish pity
To one man's honour, this contagious sickness,   60
Farewell, all physic. And what follows then?
Commotions, uproars, with a general taint
Of the whole state, as of late days our neighbours,
The upper Germany, can dearly witness,

49–53 **filling . . . pernicious** This is drawn from the beginning of a Foxe 1596 narrative which provided material for the previous scene (see 5.1.40–52n.): 'the Realme was so infected with heresies . . . that it was daungerous for his highnesse, farther to permit it vnreformed' (1694). For the rest of this passage, see 61–5n.

53, 54 **reformed, reformation** To the audience, the choice of words here would have the effect of turning this criticism of Protestants by Roman Catholics back on the speakers.

53 **pernicious** immensely dangerous

56 Do not lead them by hand in order to tame them.

57 **stop their mouths** See 2.2.8n.
    stubborn hard, unyielding

58 **manage** anglicized form of *manège*, i.e. horsemanship (*OED sb.* 1a); cf. *TNK* 5.4.69.

59 **easiness** indulgence

61–5 **And . . . memories.** Gardiner's

speech returns to the passage from Foxe 1596 begun at 5.1.40–52 and continued in this scene at 49–53: 'least peraduenture by long suffering, such contention should arise, and ensue in the Realme among his subiects, that thereby might spring horrible commotions, and vprores, like as in some partes of Germanie, it did not long ago' (1694). The reference may be either to the Peasants' Rising in Saxony and Thuringia in 1524 or to the Anabaptist Rising at Münster in 1535. In *When You See Me*, Gardiner provides details of the horrors to come if England succumbs to Protestantism: 'Much bloodshed there is now in Germanie, / About this difference in religion, / With Lutherans, Arians, and Anabaptists, / As halfe the Prouince of *Heluetia*, / Is with their tumults almost quite destroyde' (H2^r, Wilson TLN 2201–5).

62 **taint** corruption, infection

64 **upper** i.e. inland

Yet freshly pitied in our memories.　　　　　　　　65

CRANMER

My good lords, hitherto, in all the progress
Both of my life and office, I have laboured,
And with no little study, that my teaching
And the strong course of my authority
Might go one way, and safely; and the end　　　　　　70
Was ever to do well. Nor is there living –
I speak it with a single heart, my lords –
A man that more detests, more stirs against,
Both in his private conscience and his place,
Defacers of a public peace than I do.　　　　　　75
Pray heaven the King may never find a heart
With less allegiance in it. Men that make
Envy and crooked malice nourishment
Dare bite the best. I do beseech your lordships
That in this case, of justice, my accusers,　　　　　　80
Be what they will, may stand forth face to face
And freely urge against me.

SUFFOLK　　　　　　　　　　　　Nay, my lord,
That cannot be. You are a Councillor,
And by that virtue no man dare accuse you.

66–132 **My . . . say**. This entire section is
dramatic invention or, rather, extrapolation from the narrative in Foxe 1596,
forcefully echoing the antithesis set up
in Foxe between Gardiner and
Cranmer (in alliance with Cromwell).
Cranmer's speeches at 66–82 and
92–103 make him seem a stronger
character than we have so far been led
to believe, though we need to bear in
mind that he knows what the Council
do not yet know, that he has the talis-
manic ring and thus the King's vicarious power.
72 **single heart** i.e. not duplicitous; a
proverbial expression (Dent, H330.1),

derived from various biblical passages,
most exactly Genesis, 20.5 in the
Bishops' translation ('with a single
heart, and innocent handes'); cf. *MA*
2.1.261.
73 **more stirs** is more active
74 **place** the context of his office
80 ***case, of justice** F's punctuation creates the phrase 'case of justice', which
is meaningless; it makes much more
sense to see *of justice* as a version of the
modern 'in all fairness'.
81 **Be . . . will** no matter who they are
82 **urge** put forward their charges
84 **by that virtue** as a result

73 stirs] strives *Collier²*　75 of a] of the *Rowe*　80 case, of] *Ard²;* case of F

GARDINER

My lord, because we have business of more moment,　　85
We will be short with you. 'Tis his highness' pleasure
And our consent, for better trial of you,
From hence you be committed to the Tower,
Where, being but a private man again,
You shall know many dare accuse you boldly –　　90
More than, I fear, you are provided for.

CRANMER

Ah, my good lord of Winchester, I thank you;
You are always my good friend. If your will pass,
I shall both find your lordship judge and juror,
You are so merciful. I see your end:　　95
'Tis my undoing. Love and meekness, lord,
Become a churchman better than ambition.
Win straying souls with modesty again;
Cast none away. That I shall clear myself,
Lay all the weight ye can upon my patience,　　100
I make as little doubt as you do conscience
In doing daily wrongs. I could say more,
But reverence to your calling makes me modest.

GARDINER

My lord, my lord, you are a sectary.

85–6 **because . . . you** magnificent condescension from Gardiner. We know from 37 that the examination of Cranmer is in fact the chief cause of the Council's session.
85 **moment** importance
87 **consent** Gardiner makes it sound as if Cranmer's examination is Henry's idea, with which he and the other Councillors have gone along, rather than something he had himself initiated (which we know about from 5.1.42–6).
89 **private man** i.e. not a Privy Councillor, and therefore protected

93 **friend** Gardiner's arrogance is matched by Cranmer's ironic gentleness.
　　pass gains the upper hand
95 **end** aim
98 **Win . . . again** win back
　　modesty restraint, moderation (also at 103)
100 however much you may try my powers of endurance
101 I have no more doubt than you have conscience.
104 **sectary** someone who belongs to a sect, or heretical offshoot from the 'true Church'

90 know many] know, many *Theobald*

That's the plain truth. Your painted gloss discovers,   105
To men that understand you, words and weakness.
CROMWELL
My lord of Winchester, you're a little,
By your good favour, too sharp. Men so noble,
However faulty, yet should find respect
For what they have been. 'Tis a cruelty   110
To load a falling man.
GARDINER   Good master secretary,
I cry your honour mercy: you may worst
Of all this table say so.
CROMWELL   Why, my lord?
GARDINER
Do not I know you for a favourer
Of this new sect? Ye are not sound.
CROMWELL   Not sound?   115
GARDINER
Not sound, I say.
CROMWELL   Would you were half so honest!
Men's prayers then would seek you, not their fears.
GARDINER
I shall remember this bold language.
CROMWELL   Do.

---

105 **painted gloss** both 'false exterior'
and 'baseless charges'
discovers reveals
106 **words** See 4.2.39n.
107–19 **My . . . life, too** This bitter,
sarcastic exchange between Cromwell
and Gardiner forcefully confirms
Cromwell's Protestant zeal, in line
with Foxe's account; cf. *Thomas, Lord
Cromwell*, E2^{r-v}.
108 metrical stress in this line falls on *too*
sharp quick to pass judgement
110–11 **'Tis . . . man.** Cf. 3.2.333 and n.
This is a more genuine expression of

the sentiment, underlining the 'manly'
moderation of Cranmer and the
reforming tendency (see pp. 84–5).
112 **cry . . . mercy** beg your pardon
worst with least justification
113 **table** metonymic for 'council'
115 **sect** i.e. Lutheranism
sound theologically correct, loyal;
Nichol Smith suggests that this word
may owe something to two lines in *When
You See Me*: 'I doe suspect that *Latimer*
and *Ridly* / . . . Are not sound Catho-
lickes' (F1^r, Wilson TLN 1499, 1501).
118, 119 **bold** shameless, unrestrained

109 faulty] *F2;* faultly *F*   111 master] *Steevens^2;* M. *F;* Mr. *F3*

Remember your bold life, too.

CHANCELLOR   This is too much.

Forbear, for shame, my lords.

GARDINER   I have done.

CROMWELL   And I.   120

CHANCELLOR [*to Cranmer*]

Then thus for you, my lord. It stands agreed,

I take it, by all voices, that forthwith

You be conveyed to th' Tower a prisoner,

There to remain till the King's further pleasure

Be known unto us. Are you all agreed, lords?   125

ALL

We are.

CRANMER   Is there no other way of mercy

But I must needs to th' Tower, my lords?

GARDINER   What other

Would you expect? You are strangely troublesome.

Let some o'th' guard be ready there.

Enter the Guard.

CRANMER   For me?

Must I go like a traitor thither?

GARDINER   Receive him,   130

And see him safe i'th' Tower.

CRANMER   Stay, good my lords,

119, 121 CHANCELLOR *F's SP '*Cham.*'
   for 'Lord Chamberlain' at these lines
   (and at 136) appears to be a compositor's error or misreading (understandable in a scene which includes the SPs
   '*Chan.*', '*Cham.*' and '*Cran.*'), since the
   character speaks with more authority
   than the Chamberlain could claim. RP,
   noting that Compositor I set x3^{r-v} seri-
   atim as he was setting the second half
   of the final two-sheet gathering of the

play, suggests that if in that time he got
'*Chan.*' right three times, then wrong
three times, and then right again once,
it might be reasonable to suppose that
the error originated in the copy from
which he was working.
120 **Forbear** restrain yourselves
123 **conveyed** taken, escorted; cf. *R2*
   4.1.306–7.
128 **strangely** unusually
130 **Receive** take into custody

119, 121 SP CHANCELLOR] *Capell; Cham. F*   121 SD] *Capell (subst.) (after* lord)

I have a little yet to say. Look there, my lords.
By virtue of that ring, I take my cause
Out of the gripes of cruel men and give it
To a most noble judge, the King my master.   135
CHANCELLOR
This is the King's ring.
SURREY   'Tis no counterfeit.
SUFFOLK
'Tis the right ring, by heaven. I told ye all,
When we first put this dangerous stone a-rolling,
'Twould fall upon ourselves.
NORFOLK   Do you think, my lords,

132 **Look there** Cranmer displays the ring, often in productions placing it on the council table for inspection.

133 **ring** This marks a return to Foxe's (1596) account: '[I]n the end, when he perceiued that no maner of perswasion or intreatie could serue, he deliuered them the kings ring, reuoking his cause into the kings hands' (1694); see also *When You See Me*: 'here, take my ring, / Bid Doctor *Cranmer* haste to Court againe, / Give him that token of king *Henries* love' (K1ʳ, Wilson TLN 2703–5).

134 **gripes** clutches (*OED sb.*[1] 1b); cf. 2.2.134.

136 CHANCELLOR *Most editors have accepted F's '*Cham.*' at this point, but I think Bowers is probably right that '[t]he recognition of the king's ring is most suitably made by the person in authority' (though his second argument, that 'it is obvious' that the speaker of this line cannot also speak 141–3, seems less convincing).

136–41 **This . . . vexed?** In this dramatization of Foxe's (1596) description, the 'whole Counsaile' is represented by nobles and courtiers who have already appeared in the play and the words spoken by the Earl of Bedford in Foxe's account are divided between Suffolk

and Norfolk: 'The whole Counsaile being thereat somewhat amazed, the Earle of Bedford with a loud voice confirming his words with a solemne othe, said: when you first began the matter my Lordes, I told you what would come of it. Do you thinke that the king will suffer this mans finger to ake?' (1694). Bedford features prominently, as Cromwell's chief patron, in *Thomas, Lord Cromwell*, but is conspicuous by his absence here. The Jacobean Bedford had never received a pardon for his involvement with the Essex Rebellion in 1601, was near bankruptcy, and thus had no involvement in Jacobean politics. The presence of an Earl of Bedford on stage as a significant political figure would thus contradict the play's conscious equation of Henrician and Jacobean England. I am grateful to Conrad Russell for discussion of Bedford.

137 **heaven** monosyllabic

138–9 **stone . . . ourselves** proverbial reflexivity (Dent, S889). Proverbs, 26.27 provides the most direct source for these lines: 'He that diggeth a pit, shal fall therein, and he that rolleth a stone, it shal returne vnto him.' This proverb is inserted into the midst of material drawn from Foxe 1596.

136 SP CHANCELLOR] *Boswell; Cham. F*   137 heaven] *(*Heau'n*)*

The King will suffer but the little finger   140
Of this man to be vexed?
CHAMBERLAIN   'Tis now too certain.
How much more is his life in value with him?
Would I were fairly out on't.
CROMWELL   My mind gave me,
In seeking tales and informations
Against this man, whose honesty the devil   145
And his disciples only envy at,
Ye blew the fire that burns ye. Now have at ye!

Enter KING, *frowning on them. [He] takes his seat.*

GARDINER
Dread sovereign, how much are we bound to heaven
In daily thanks, that gave us such a prince,
Not only good and wise but most religious;   150
One that, in all obedience, makes the Church
The chief aim of his honour and, to strengthen
That holy duty out of dear respect,
His royal self in judgement comes to hear

142 **in value with** valued by
143 **gave me** i.e. misgave, made me suspicious
144 **tales and informations** rumour and gossip
146 **only envy at** can only begrudge (because they cannot dent it)
147 **Ye . . . ye** See 1.1.140–1n., 2.4.77, 92n.; and cf. Ecclesiasticus, 28.12: 'If thou blowe the sparke, it shal burne'.
have at ye See 2.2.83 and n.
147.1 *Enter* KING In the account of Foxe 1596, the Council 'all rose, and caried to the K. his ring' (1694); here, Henry makes a dramatic entrance into the Council chamber.
frowning Foxe 1596 describes the King's 'seuere countenance' (1694)

when the Council come to him with the ring.
takes his seat Presumably this is the *state*, still on stage (see 1.2.8.4n.).
148–63 **Dread . . . bloody.** The prominence of Gardiner in this scene stems entirely from Foxe's assertion that it was his 'prouocation' that initiated the attempt to unseat Cranmer. In the account of Foxe 1596, the Bishop has no active, speaking role. Here, though, he is the principal Catholic protagonist throughout the scene (and the act).
151–2 **makes . . . honour** treats the welfare of the church as his principal object
153 **dear respect** genuine regard

148] *Pope; F lines* Soueraigne, / Heauen, /

The cause betwixt her and this great offender.   155

KING

You were ever good at sudden commendations,
Bishop of Winchester, but know I come not
To hear such flattery now, and in my presence
They are too thin and bare to hide offences.
To me you cannot reach, you play the spaniel   160
And think with wagging of your tongue to win me.
But whatsoe'er thou takest me for, I'm sure
Thou hast a cruel nature and a bloody.
[*to Cranmer*] Good man, sit down. Now let me see the
     proudest –
He that dares most – but wag his finger at thee.   165
By all that's holy, he had better starve,
Than but once think his place becomes thee not.

SURREY

May it please your grace –

KING   No, sir, it does not please me.
I had thought I had had men of some understanding
And wisdom of my Council, but I find none.   170

---

156 **sudden commendations** impro-
vised compliments
159 **They** i.e. the *sudden commendations*
*bare Malone's suggested emendation
of F's 'base' makes sense in context,
since *thin* and *hide* both imply some
kind of cloth or cover, for which 'base'
would be irrelevant and *bare* (i.e.
threadbare) appropriate; cf. *Oth*
1.3.109.
160 **me you** me whom you
spaniel Spaniels were proverbially
fawning in their behaviour (Dent,
S704); cf. *AC* 4.12.21.
162 **takest** monosyllabic
165 **He** the man

166 **starve** die a lingering death, as from
hunger, cold, grief or slow disease
(*OED v.* I 1); suffer extreme poverty or
want (*v.* I 4a)
167 **his place** i.e. the status of the proudest Privy Councillor. F4's 'this' would
make equal sense in reference either to
the chair Cranmer occupies as a
Councillor or to the chamber as a
whole.
169–81 **I had thought . . . live.** This
speech is patterned on, and frequently
echoes, the King's speech to the
Council in Foxe 1596: 'Ah my Lordes,
I thought I had had wiser men of my
counsaile then now I find you. What

158 flattery] flatteries *Rowe³*   159 bare] *Singer (Malone);* base *F*   159–60 offences. . . . reach, you]
Johnson; offences, . . . reach. You *F*   162 takest] *(*tak'st*)*   164 SD] *Rowe*   164–5 proudest – / He]
*Collier (*proudest, / He*);* proudest / He, *F*   167 his] this *F4*   169 I . . . had had] I had thought I
had *Rowe²;* I thought I had *Pope;* I thought, I had had *Theobald*

Was it discretion, lords, to let this man,
This good man – few of you deserve that title –
This honest man, wait like a lousy footboy
At chamber door? And one as great as you are?
Why, what a shame was this! Did my commission   175
Bid ye so far forget yourselves? I gave ye
Power as he was a Councillor to try him,
Not as a groom. There's some of ye, I see,
More out of malice than integrity,
Would try him to the utmost, had ye mean,   180
Which ye shall never have while I live.

CHANCELLOR   Thus far,
My most dread sovereign, may it like your grace
To let my tongue excuse all. What was purposed
Concerning his imprisonment was rather –
If there be faith in men – meant for his trial   185

discretion was this in you, thus to make the Primate of the realme, & one of you in office, to waite at the counsaile chamber doore amongst seruing men? You might haue considered that he was a counsellor as wel as you, and you had no such commission of me so to handle him. I was content that you should trie him as a Counseller, and not as a meane subiect. But now I well perceiue that things be done against him maliciouslie, and if some of you might haue your mindes, you woulde haue tried him to the vttermost' (1694).

173 **lousy** Both senses were available at this time: infected by lice (*OED a.* A 1a) and vile, contemptible, inferior (*a.* A 2 *fig.*).

174 **And ... are?** someone just as important as you too

175 **shame** i.e. shameful way to treat someone

180–1 **try ... live** *Try* means both to 'put

on trial' and to 'make life difficult for'; the audience would understand these lines as prophetic, looking forward to Cranmer's martyrdom in Mary's reign.

180 **mean** opportunity; power; Pope's 'means' is entirely feasible, especially in view of the ease with which a compositor can drop a final *s*.

182 **like** please

183–7 **What ... me.** The Chancellor's excuse is drawn from the middle of Foxe's (1596) account of the discussion: 'one or two of the chiefest of the Counsaile, making their excuse, declared, that in requesting his indurance, it was rather ment for his triall, and his purgation against the common fame, and slander of the worlde, then for any malice conceiued against him' (1694).

185 **If ... men** if ever anyone spoke truth

180 mean] means *Pope*   181 SP] *(Chan.); Cham. F3*

And fair purgation to the world than malice,
I'm sure, in me.

KING   Well, well, my lords, respect him.
Take him, and use him well: he's worthy of it.
I will say thus much for him: if a prince
May be beholding to a subject, I   190
Am, for his love and service, so to him.
Make me no more ado, but all embrace him.
Be friends, for shame, my lords! My lord of
    Canterbury,
I have a suit which you must not deny me:
That is, a fair young maid that yet wants baptism.   195
You must be godfather and answer for her.

CRANMER
The greatest monarch now alive may glory
In such an honour. How may I deserve it,
That am a poor and humble subject to you?

KING Come, come, my lord, you'd spare your spoons! You   200

---

186 **purgation** the clearing of his name
188–93 **Take . . . lords!** This speech condenses and rearranges the rest of the speech from Foxe 1596 broached at 183–7: 'But I doe you all to wit, and protest, that if a Prince may bee beholding vnto his subiect (and so solemnelie, laying his hand vpon his brest) said: by the faith I owe to God, I take this man here my Lord of Canturburie, to bee of all other a most faithfull subiect vnto vs, and one to whome wee are much beholding. . . . Well, well my Lordes (quoth the king) take him and well vse him, as hee is worthy to be, and make no more adoe. And with that euery man caught him by the hand' (1694).
190 **beholding** indebted to, dependent upon

192 **Make . . . ado** Waste no more time.
195 **baptism** Connecting the council chamber scene with the baptism of Elizabeth is dramatic invention to create a clear impression of Cranmer prior to the prophecy; the details of the christening come from Holinshed, 934; see 5.4.0.1–0.9n.
196 **answer for her** 'make the responses on her behalf at the christening'; and, by implication, 'take responsibility for her spiritual upbringing'
200 **spoons** The allusion is to the traditional godparent's gift of a set of twelve 'apostle spoons', with the figure of an apostle on each handle. Henry is humorously suggesting that Cranmer is trying to save money. Royal christening gifts were not inexpensive, though; cf. 5.4.0.4.

190 beholding] beholden *Rowe²*   192 him] *omitted in Johnson*   200–2 Come . . . Dorset] *Pope lines as verse* have / Dutchess / Dorset – /

shall have two noble partners with you: the old Duchess
of Norfolk and Lady Marquess Dorset. Will these
please you?
Once more, my lord of Winchester, I charge you
Embrace and love this man.

GARDINER   With a true heart   205
And brother's love I do it.

CRANMER   And let heaven
Witness how dear I hold this confirmation.

KING

Good man, those joyful tears show thy true heart.
The common voice, I see, is verified
Of thee, which says thus: 'Do my lord of Canterbury   210
A shrewd turn, and he's your friend forever.'
Come, lords, we trifle time away. I long
To have this young one made a Christian.
As I have made ye one, lords, one remain: 214

---

201 **partners** co-sponsors, godparents; a
child generally had two godparents of
its own sex and one of the other
204–5 **Once ... Embrace** This is generally taken to imply that Gardiner had
failed so far to obey Henry's injunction
at 192, though in the 1997 New York
production Henry obliged him to
embrace Cranmer a second time.
206 ***brother's love** F reads 'Brother; loue
I doe it'; F2 provides the most plausible
emendation, since 'Brother;' is an easy
misreading of MS 'Brothers'. Other
versions have been offered, notably
'brother-love' in Steevens–Reed².
Foakes (Ard²), on the other hand, notes
that F's 'Brother; loue I doe it', may be
the result of a slight misreading of
'brother, lo(w)e, I do it', in which case
hyphenating the words compounds the
error. Productions vary over the tone
in which Gardiner speaks these words:
for some, Gardiner is won over by

Cranmer's goodness; for others, the
words have to make their way past grit-
ted teeth.
208 **joyful tears** Cf. Prologue 32.
209 **common voice** popular rumour
210–11 **Do ... forever.** Foxe 1596 reports
that 'it was known that [Cranmer] had
many cruel enemies . . . and yet whatsoeuer hee was that . . . sought his hin-
derance . . . hee woulde both forget the
offence . . . and also euermore afterwards
friendly intertaine him: . . . Insomuch
that it came into a common prouerbe:
Doe vnto my lord of Canturbury displeasure or a shrewd turne, and then you
may bee sure to haue him your friend
whiles he liueth' (1691).
211 **shrewd turn** injury, harm an expression in Foxe 1596; see 210–11.
213 **made a Christian** a rather blunt,
but theologically accurate, way to
describe the function of baptism
214 **one** united

202–3 Will . . . you] *omitted in Pope*   206 brother's love] *F2;* Brother; loue *F;* brother-love *Steevens-
Reed²*   208 heart] *F2;* hearts *F*

So I grow stronger, you more honour gain. *Exeunt.*

5.3 *Noise and tumult within. Enter* Porter *and his* Man.

PORTER   You'll leave your noise anon, ye rascals. Do you
take the court for Parish Garden? Ye rude slaves, leave
your gaping.

[ONE] *(within)*   Good master porter, I belong to th' larder.

PORTER   Belong to th' gallows, and be hanged, ye rogue! Is   5
this a place to roar in? Fetch me a dozen crab-tree staves,
and strong ones: these are but switches to 'em. I'll
scratch your heads. You must be seeing christenings?
Do you look for ale and cakes here, you rude rascals?

---

215 a politically questionable (and clichéd) assertion to round out the scene: '[i]f Henry grows in stature, we do not see it happen' (Anderson, 135).

5.3 Generally considered the work of Fletcher (see Appendix 3), and often cut (by, for example, Kemble, Kean, Irving and Tree), though always to the detriment of productions. There is nothing in Holinshed *et al.* to suggest an original for this carnivalesque scene; there is, however, an apparent blueprint in *Maid's* 1.2.1–106 (see specific references below), which was Beaumont & Fletcher's fourth collaboration for the King's company (see Appendix 4). The location is the main entrance to the court, through which the procession will be passing on its return from the christening.

1   **leave** cease, stop

2   **Parish Garden** alternatively spelt 'Paris Garden', this was an arena for the barbaric activities of bull- and bear-baiting (setting dogs onto a chained animal for the entertainment of spectators). It was situated on the Bankside, near the Globe, and was notorious for noise: the din made by the animals and the spectators could presumably be all too easily heard by the Globe audience.

rude primitive, uneducated

3   **gaping** shouting, yelling

4   SP-5 ONE . . . **rogue** Cf. Beaumont & Fletcher, *Maid's* 1.2.47–8: '[*A Voice*] *within.* I pray you, can you help me to the speech of the master-cook? / *Diagoras.* If I open the door I'll cook some of your calves' heads. Peace, rogues!'

4   **belong to** i.e. work in (and should therefore be allowed past)

6   **roar** riot, rampage; the term 'roaring boy' was used to describe young bullies and troublemakers.

crab-tree staves Crab-apple wood was considered proverbially hard (Tilley, C787).

7   **these . . . 'em** These heavy cudgels seem like little twigs to them.

switches slender shoots cut from a tree

7–8 **I'll . . . heads.** Cf. Beaumont & Fletcher, *Maid's* 1.2.39–40: 'Ay, do your heads itch? I'll scratch them for you!'

9   **ale and cakes** traditional holiday or church-festival fare, unpopular with strict Protestants; cf. *TN* 2.3.111.

5.3] *(Scena Tertia.)*   1–9] *Capell lines as verse* noise / court / gaping. / larder. / rogue: / in? – / ones; / 'em. – / christnings? / rascals? /   2 Parish Garden] Paris-Garden *F4*   4, 26 SP] *White*
4 master] *Steevens;* M. *F*

419

MAN

Pray, sir, be patient. 'Tis as much impossible,   10
Unless we sweep 'em from the door with cannons,
To scatter 'em as 'tis to make 'em sleep
On May-day morning – which will never be.
We may as well push against Paul's as stir 'em.

PORTER   How got they in, and be hanged?   15

MAN

Alas, I know not. How gets the tide in?
As much as one sound cudgel of four foot –
You see the poor remainder – could distribute,
I made no spare, sir.

PORTER   You did nothing, sir.

MAN

I am not Samson, nor Sir Guy, nor Colbrand,   20
To mow 'em down before me; but if I spared any
That had a head to hit, either young or old,
He or she, cuckold or cuckold-maker,
Let me ne'er hope to see a chine again –

---

13 **May-day morning** Early morning on 1 May was another festive occasion frowned on by 'puritans', during which people would go out into the fields while it was still dark, in order, in Stow's probably euphemistic words, to 'reioyce their spirites with the beuty and sauour of sweete flowers' (Stow, *Survey*, F4ᵛ).

14 **Paul's** St Paul's Cathedral, by far the largest structure in London at this date

18 **remainder** The Porter's Man presumably holds up a short piece of broken-off cudgel.

19 **made no spare** spared nobody

20 **Samson . . . Colbrand** legendary strong men: according to Judges, 15.15, Samson killed a thousand of his enemies, the Philistines, with the 'newe iawe bone of an Asse'; Sir Guy was the hero of the fourteenth-century romance *Guy of Warwick* (see Zupitza, especially

576–607): his battle against Danish invaders, and notably the giant Colbrand, is also mentioned in Stow and Holinshed, as well as featuring in Drayton, *Poly-Olbion*, Song 12, 129–334; on the romance's popularity, see Crane; cf. *KJ* 1.1.225. As Braunmuller notes, 'during the sixteenth century, Guy's sword was preserved at Warwick Castle (not far from Shakespeare's home town of Stratford)'.

23 **cuckold or cuckold-maker** a husband whose wife has committed adultery and either a woman who has done so or the man with whom she has done so (presumably the former, in keeping with *He or she*)

24 **chine** a piece of meat consisting of the whole or part of the backbone of an animal, with the adjoining flesh; in beef, any part of the back (ribs or sirloin) (*OED sb.*² 3)

---

14 Paul's] *(Powles)*   20–5] *prose Pope*   24 chine] queen *Collier*²

And that I would not for a cow, God save her!   25
[ONE] (*within*)   Do you hear, master porter?
PORTER
  I shall be with you presently, good master puppy.
  [*to his Man*]   Keep the door close, sirrah.
MAN   What would you have me do?
PORTER   What should you do, but knock 'em down by th'   30
dozens? Is this Moorfields to muster in? Or have we
some strange Indian with the great tool come to court,

25 **not . . . her** This appears to have been
a common and fairly meaningless
phrase, unless there is a connection
with the *chine* in the previous line (the
joke being partly that the Porter's Man
would give up a whole cow for a joint of
beef). Editors have come up with a
range of ingenious explications, none
of which is convincing; Foakes (Ard²),
for example, speculates about a possible
bawdy implication. RP suggests, more
straightforwardly, that a cow was the
most valuable possession of many poor
farming families; the predicament of
such a family when conned out of their
cow by a Usurer is graphically dramatized by Lodge & Greene.
26 SP presumably the same person who
earlier claimed to work in the kitchens
Do . . . hear Are you listening? Can
you hear me? (probably angrily)
28 **close** shut
30 **What . . . do** F's lining arguably rejects
Capell's wish to treat the speech as
verse, since the separate line might signify the last verse line before prose.
31 **Moorfields** an area of reclaimed
marshland just outside Moorgate (on
the northern side of the city), which was
at one point, according to Stow, used as
a field for archery practice (see Stow,
Survey, Z8ʳ) and probably under James
a site for training the citizens' militia;

this perhaps explains the military over-
tone of *muster*
32 **strange** foreign
Indian *Indian* could signify a person
from the East or West Indies, the Far
East or America, but in this case almost
certainly refers to a native American
brought back from the New World.
The first North American in England
was brought over in 1502. While there
is no record of any native American in
England during the reign of Henry
VIII, several are recorded during James
I's reign, willing and unwilling. In 1611,
a man called Epenew was captured at
Capawick (Martha's Vineyard) and
brought to London: he was described as
'of so great stature, he was shewed up
and downe *London* for money as a wonder', and he had 'learned so much
English as to bid those that wondred at
him, welcome, welcome'; perhaps surprisingly, he was taken back in 1614
(Salmon, 160–2). The 'chiefe Maskers'
of Chapman's *Masque of the Middle
Temple* (1613), performed for the wedding of Princess Elizabeth, were
dressed 'in Indian habits . . . like the
Virginian Princes they presented'
(A1ᵛ–A2ʳ), and the other masquers
'were likewise of the *Indian* garb' (A3ʳ).
great tool large penis. The Porter provides a carnivalesque gloss on the native

25 a cow] a crow *Blair;* a crown *Collier²;* my cow *(Staunton)*   26–7 master . . . master] *Steevens;* M. .
. . M. *F*   28 SD] *Capell (subst.)*   30–63] *Capell lines as verse* do, / *Morefields,* / *Indian,* / us? / me,
/ door! / christening will / godfather, / together. / sir. / door, / face, / dog-days / are / penance: /
head, / me; / us. / wit / me, / head, / state: / woman, / far / succour, / quarter'd: / length / still; /
'em, / pebbles, / in, / work: / surely. / playhouse, / audience, / *Tower-hill,* / are / *Limbo* / days; /
beadles, / come. /   30 What . . . do,] *Rowe; separate line in F*

421

the women so besiege us? Bless me, what a fry of fornication is at door! On my Christian conscience, this one christening will beget a thousand: here will be father, godfather, and all together.

MAN The spoons will be the bigger, sir. There is a fellow somewhat near the door – he should be a brazier by his face, for, o'my conscience, twenty of the dog-days now reign in's nose. All that stand about him are under the line: they need no other penance. That fire-drake did I hit three times on the head, and three times was his nose discharged against me. He stands there like a mortar-piece, to blow us. There was a haberdasher's

American's physical wondrousness. Unusually large genitalia were a predictable Jacobean talking-point: cf. *Birth of Merlin*: 'if you grow in all things as your Beard does, you will be talkt on' (3.4.85–6); and Beaumont, *Knight*, in which the Grocer's Wife speaks enthusiastically of 'the little child that was so faire growne about the members' (3.[1.]275–6).

33 **fry** swarm. *Fry* are both fish-eggs and the mass of recently hatched baby fish.

34–6 **On . . . together**. a powerful image converting the scene to one of general (and uncontrolled) fertility, carnivalizing the christening we are about to watch, and once again juxtaposing *conscience* with sexual activity

37 **spoons** apostle spoons; see 5.2.200n.; cf. Whorehound's phallic 'godfather's' gift to his new-born illegitimate daughter of 'a fair high standing cup, and two great postle spoons, one of them gilt' in Middleton, *Chaste Maid*, 3.2.50–1.

38 **brazier** a brass-worker, who would work all day in high temperatures

39 **dog-days** the period of high summer (approximately forty days in all) preceding the rise of the dog-star, Sirius, on or about 11 August, considered the hottest and therefore least healthy time of year

40–1 **under the line** at the equator; cf. *Tem* 4.1.237.

41 **penance** another residually Catholic expression, referring to the temperature in Purgatory (humorously considered similar to that at the equator)
fire-drake a dragon, but metaphorically a meteor or firework (cf. 47)

43 **discharged** combined meaning of 'fired' (like a gun) and 'emitted, poured forth' (*OED sb.* 2 and 3a)

44 **mortar-piece** a small large-bore cannon with a high elevation; metaphorically, gaping upwards, ready to discharge shot
blow us blow us down or up; F3 has 'blow us up'

44–5 **haberdasher's wife** A haberdasher was originally a seller of hats and caps, but by the Jacobean period the term could be used of anyone who sold small items relating to clothing, such as ribbons and thread (*OED* a and b). Foakes notes (Ard[2]) that, while there is no known source for this scene, Holinshed does mention that, of the London trades which organized pageants for Anne's coronation, 'commandement was giuen to the haberdashers (of which craft the maior sir Stephan Pecocke then was)' (930).

44 blow us] blow us up *F3*

wife of small wit near him that railed upon me till her   45
pinked porringer fell off her head for kindling such a
combustion in the state. I missed the meteor once and
hit that woman, who cried out 'Clubs!', when I might
see from far some forty truncheoners draw to her
succour, which were the hope o'th' Strand, where she   50
was quartered. They fell on; I made good my place; at
length they came to th' broomstaff to me; I defied 'em
still, when suddenly a file of boys behind 'em, loose
shot, delivered such a shower of pebbles that I was fain
to draw mine honour in and let 'em win the work. The   55

45 **small wit** Haberdashers seem not to have been noted for their intellectual qualities; cf. Jonson, *The Magnetic Lady*: 'all Haberdashers of small wit' (Induction 12).
railed upon shouted abuse at
46 **pinked** 'Pinking' was 'a term applied to the cutting of small holes or slits . . . either in the materials or in the finished garment' (Linthicum, 153–4), i.e. a kind of perforation often serving to display a brightly coloured lining.
porringer originally, a small soup-bowl and thus a hat shaped like a dish (*OED* b: first citation). The use of the term is anachronistic: Linthicum (218–9) notes that it was an Elizabethan/Jacobean fashion, both useless and trendy enough for the reference to amuse the audience of 1613. It is entirely appropriate for a haberdasher's wife to be wearing fashionable headgear. This kind of contemporary reference also has the effect of diminishing the distance between the events on stage and the England of 1613 (cf. Prologue 25–7; and see pp. 144–7), underscoring the role of the audience as active interpreters of political events.
46–7 **kindling . . . combustion** causing such a riot
47 **meteor** i.e. the *brazier* (see 41n.)
48 **Clubs!** the rallying cry summoning

apprentices to leave work and intervene in a fight; cf. Dekker, *The Shoemaker's Holiday* (1599) 5.2.28: 'Villaines? downe with them, cry "clubs for prentises"'. See also *RJ* 1.1.70–2; cf. *STM*, Add.II.D, 29–31.
49 **truncheoners** apprentices with clubs; this is the first citation in *OED* (after *sb.* truncheon 8).
50 **hope o'th' Strand** apprentices belonging to the workshops on the Strand, a wide street running parallel to the Thames which at that time was the site of a number of fashionable merchants' houses with workshops at ground level (though cf. 51)
51 **was quartered** lived. This perhaps casts doubt on her morals. At the end of Middleton, *Chaste Maid* (1613), for example, the Allwits plan to 'take a house in the Strand' (5.2.170) and open a brothel.
They . . . place They attacked; I defended my position successfully.
52 **came . . . broomstaff** began fighting at close quarters, near enough to use sticks; earliest citation for *broomstaff* in *OED*
53–4 **loose shot** marksmen not attached to a company (*OED a.* 1k)
54–5 **was fain to** had no choice but to
55 **work** short for 'earthwork', i.e. fort or barricade

50 Strand] (Strond) 52 to me] with me *Pope* 54 pebbles] (Pibbles)

devil was amongst 'em, I think, surely.

PORTER   These are the youths that thunder at a playhouse
and fight for bitten apples, that no audience but the
'Tribulation' of Tower Hill or the 'Limbs' of
Limehouse, their dear brothers, are able to endure. I   60
have some of 'em in *Limbo Patrum* – and there they are
like to dance these three days – besides the running
banquet of two beadles that is to come.

Enter Lord CHAMBERLAIN.

CHAMBERLAIN
Mercy o'me, what a multitude are here!

57 **youths** apprentices. This reference, together with Bluett's account of the rescue of 'a child which otherwise had been burnt' in the Globe fire (see pp. 57–8), suggests the wide age range in attendance at the theatres.

58–60 **the . . . Limehouse** two gangs of troublemakers from Tower Hill, where people would gather to watch executions, and from Limehouse, a robust dockyard town a couple of miles east of London on the Thames; I have followed Theobald's conjecture that *Tribulation* is a proper name and extended it to *Limbs*.

59 **Tribulation** condition of great affliction, oppression, or misery (*OED* 1); here, a cant name for a gang of disturbers (*OED* 1 and 1c)

61 *Limbo Patrum* Limbo was the traditional afterlife destination of just souls who had either died before the coming of Christ or else had not been baptized, an extra-biblical concept associated with Roman Catholicism: it was different from Purgatory, where souls were tormented, as the ghost of Hamlet's father says, 'Till the foul crimes done in my days of nature / Are burnt and purged away' (*Ham* 1.5.12–13). In *When You See Me*, Cranmer makes sure that the young Edward VI rejects the

idea of Purgatory which he has heard from his 'Sister *Marie* and her Tutors' (G3^v, Wilson TLN 1998). The persistence of such pre-Protestant notions is a good indication of the rapidity of ecclesiastical and political change in the English Reformation upon which the play meditates. If '*Limbs*' *of Limehouse* is the name of a street gang, then the Porter deliberately and mockingly puns on the word 'limb' as he relishes having caught a few of them; he is perhaps also offering a comical sense of London's boroughs as the circles of hell. On prison as *Limbo Patrum*, see Nashe, *The four Letters Confuted* (1.299–300): 'Wert thou put in the Fleete for pamphleting? . . . Wast paper made thee betake thy selfe to *Limbo Patrum*.'

62 **three days** perhaps an allusion to Christ's descent to Hell before resurrection (RP)

62–3 **running banquet** a buffet meal (cf. 1.4.12); here, a humorous term for a public flogging, especially since convicted criminals were often whipped along the street

63 **beadles** minor city officials, who would make arrests and administer whippings

64 **Mercy o'me** abbreviated version of 'God have mercy on me'

59 'Tribulation'] *(tribulation)* 'Limbs'] *(Limbes); lambs (Steevens)*

They grow still, too. From all parts they are coming,   65
As if we kept a fair here! Where are these porters,
These lazy knaves? You've made a fine hand, fellows!
There's a trim rabble let in! Are all these
Your faithful friends o'th' suburbs? We shall have
Great store of room, no doubt, left for the ladies,   70
When they pass back from the christening.
PORTER   An't please your honour,
We are but men, and what so many may do,
Not being torn a-pieces, we have done:
An army cannot rule 'em.
CHAMBERLAIN   As I live,
If the King blame me for't, I'll lay ye all   75
By th' heels, and suddenly, and on your heads
Clap round fines for neglect. You're lazy knaves,
And here ye lie, baiting of bombards, when
Ye should do service. Hark, the trumpets sound:

67 **You've . . . hand** You've done a great job (sarcastic); a variation on the proverb 'to make a fair hand' of something (Dent, H99); cf. *Cor* 4.6.123; Beaumont & Fletcher, *KNK* 1.1.1.
68 **trim** neatly dressed, elegant (sarcastic)
69 **suburbs** a rather different connotation from today: the *suburbs* were the areas outside City jurisdiction and therefore thought of as lawless.
70 **Great . . . room** vast amounts of space (again, sarcastic)
72 **We . . . men** shorthand variation on the proverbs 'Men are but men' (Dent, M541; cf. *Oth* 2.3.237) and 'We are but men, not gods' (Dent, M593; cf. *Mac* 3.1.92; Fletcher, *Val* 2.3.42).
75 **If . . . for't** Cf. Beaumont & Fletcher, *Maid's* 1.2.1–2: 'look to the doors better, for shame: you let in all the world, and anon the King will rail at me'.

75–6 **lay . . . heels** put you all in shackles or in the stocks
76 **suddenly** without warning
77 **Clap round fines** impose substantial fines
78 **baiting of bombards** three possible meanings: 'drinking from bottles', 'giving drink to drunkards' or 'harassing drunkards'. *Baiting* can mean 'taking refreshment' (*OED v.*[1] II 8), 'giving drink to someone' (*v.*[1] II 5), or 'harassing someone' (*v.*[1] I 2b), while *bombards* were leather bottles shaped like small cannon (*sb.* 3a), and the term was extended to refer to people drinking from such bottles and/or shaped like them (notably, Falstaff at *1H4* 2.5.456). The first meaning is the most likely, in context, because of the inaction implied in the verb 'lie'.
79 **do service** get on with your job

They're come already from the christening.   80
Go break among the press and find a way out
To let the troop pass fairly, or I'll find
A Marshalsea shall hold ye play these two months.
PORTER
Make way there for the Princess!
MAN   You, great fellow,
Stand close up, or I'll make your head ache!   85
PORTER
You i'th' chamblet, get up o'th' rail –
I'll peck you o'er the pales else.   *Exeunt.*

---

81 **press** crowd
82 **troop** procession
   fairly without hindrance
83 **Marshalsea** a prison in Southwark
   amongst whose inmates were members
   of the King's household who had committed crimes
   hold ye play keep you from enjoying
   yourselves; *hold* implies keeping in a
   specific place (*OED v.* B I 7b), in this
   case, jail.
84 **Make . . . Princess!** Cf. Beaumont &
   Fletcher, *Maid's* 1.2.104: 'Make room
   there!'
86 **chamblet** otherwise spelt 'camlet' or
   'chamlet'; an expensive material made
   from silk and hair (see Linthicum,
   73–4). Foakes (Ard²) quotes Wither,
   Abuses Stript (1613), to suggest that the
   cloth was in fashion at this particular
   time; there are mentions of it in
   Beaumont & Fletcher, *Phil* 5.4.10, and
   in Fletcher, *WP* 5.1.87, where it
   appears in the context of a christening.

rail a low railing round the stage that
appears in illustrations on some title-
pages. The implication, for Saunders,
is that the *press* is the audience itself
and not an unseen crowd behind the
stage doors (see Saunders, especially
70–1).
87 **peck . . . pales** chuck you over the
   fence. *Peck* is an alternative for 'pitch'
   (*OED v.²* 1), to fling or throw. *Pale* for
   'fence' (*OED sb.¹* 2a) is best known to
   us from the term 'beyond the pale',
   which stems from the colonization of
   Ireland and refers to the land outside
   the secure area established around
   Dublin.
   Exeunt The Chamberlain, the Porter
   and his Man may leave the stage but
   there is no interruption of the action.
   Either way, their role must be to ensure
   a clear space for the entry of the procession. The *trumpets* at 79 and at
   5.4.0.1 are almost certainly the same.

84–7 You . . . else] *prose Pope*   86–7] *Keightley lines* camblet / else. /   86 chamblet] camblet *Pope*;
camlet *Steevens–Reed²*

5.4 *Enter Trumpets sounding; then two Aldermen,*
Lord Mayor, GARTER, CRANMER, Duke of NORFOLK
with his marshal's staff, Duke of SUFFOLK, *two Noblemen bearing*
great standing bowls for the christening gifts; then four Noblemen
bearing a canopy, under which the Duchess of Norfolk, godmother,
bearing the child richly habited in a mantle, etc., train borne by a
Lady; then follows the Marchioness Dorset, the other godmother, and
Ladies. The troop pass once about the stage, and Garter speaks.

GARTER   Heaven, from thy endless goodness, send
prosperous life, long and ever happy, to the high and

5.4 Critics invariably treat (or want to treat) this scene, with its climactic status, as Shakespeare's; attributional methods suggest, however, that it is a Fletcher scene (see Appendix 3). Tree omitted it, along with all of Act 5. Henry was in fact almost certainly absent when Elizabeth was christened (Scarisbrick, 421). The christening took place at Grey Friar Church, Greenwich, on 10 September 1533, though editors since Theobald have generally stated that the location is the court, since the action follows directly from 5.3.

0.1–0.8 This opening SD echoes Holinshed's report of the christening, with one or two modifications: '[T]he duke of Norffolke came home to the christening, which was . . . accomplished . . . with all such solemne ceremonies as were thought conuenient. The godfather at the font, was the lord archbishop of Canturburie, the godmothers, the old dutches of Norffolke & the old marchionesse Dorset widow; . . . the child was named Elizabeth. . . . [T]he archbishop of Canturburie gaue to the princesse a standing cup of gold' (934).

0.1 *Trumpets* trumpeters

0.3 *marshal's staff* the insignia of the office of Earl Marshal, which Norfolk had 'claimed' at the coronation; see 4.1.36.14–15.

0.4 *standing bowls* bowls with a base or legs
for as

0.6 *richly habited* sumptuously dressed
mantle The specificity of this description may have reminded some in the audience of Henry's offensive demand (which was refused) that Katherine provide for the baby Elizabeth the 'triumphal cloth', i.e. christening robe, which had been part of her dowry and which Mary had worn at her christening (see Paul, 136; Ridley, *Henry*, 227; Jones & Stallybrass, *Clothing*).

1–3 Holinshed records that '[w]hen the ceremonies and christening were ended, Garter cheefe king of armes cried alowd, God of his infinite goodnesse send prosperous life & long to the high and mightie princesse of England Elizabeth: & then the trumpets blew' (934). As Foakes notes (Ard[2]), this speech, though formulaic, is likely to have evoked for the audience the recent wedding of Princess

---

5.4] *(Scena Quarta.)*   0.2 *Lord Mayor*] *(L. Maior)*   1–3] *prose Capell; F lines as verse* Heauen / life, / Mighty / *Elizabeth. /; Pope lines as verse* life, / mighty / *Elizabeth. /*   2 *prosperous*] long *Pope* long] *om. Pope*

mighty Princess of England, Elizabeth.

Flourish. Enter KING *and Guard.*

CRANMER [*Kneels.*]
   And to your royal grace and the good Queen,
   My noble partners and myself thus pray   5
   All comfort, joy, in this most gracious lady
   Heaven ever laid up to make parents happy
   May hourly fall upon ye.
KING   Thank you, good lord Archbishop.
   What is her name?
CRANMER   Elizabeth.
KING   Stand up, lord.
   [*to the child*] With this kiss, take my blessing. God
      protect thee,   10
   Into whose hand I give thy life.
CRANMER   Amen.
KING
   My noble gossips, you've been too prodigal.
   I thank ye heartily: so shall this lady,
   When she has so much English.
CRANMER   Let me speak, sir,

Elizabeth and the Elector Palatine; cf.
Peacham: 'Mr. *Garter* Principall *King
of Armes*, published the stile of the
Prince and Princesse to this effect. *All
Health, Happinesse and Honour be to the
High and Mightie Princes*, Frederick . . .
and Elizabeth' (H2ᵛ).
3.1 *Flourish* See 4.1.36.2n.
5 My . . . partners the godmothers
9 What . . . name For the benefit, presumably, of the crowd, Henry echoes
   the celebrant's words as prescribed in
   Common Prayer: 'Then shall the Priest
   demaunde the name of the chylde,
   whych beyng by the Godfathers and

Godmothers pronounced . . . ' (N8ʳ).
Cranmer answers as godfather; on the
slippage of function from Henry to
Cranmer, see pp. 70, 87–8.
12 gossips godparents; used in its original signification from 'God-sibs',
   implying that the godparents have a
   new spiritual kinship with Henry as
   the child's father
   prodigal excessively generous in gift-
   giving (i.e. the *great standing bowls* of
   0.4 rather than the *spoons* joked about
   earlier)
14–62 Let . . . her On political prophecy, see LN. Cranmer's speech has no

4 SD] *Johnson (Kneeling.)*   10 SD] *Capell (subst.)*   11 hand] hands *Boswell*

For heaven now bids me; and the words I utter   15
Let none think flattery, for they'll find 'em truth.
This royal infant – heaven still move about her –
Though in her cradle, yet now promises
Upon this land a thousand thousand blessings,
Which time shall bring to ripeness. She shall be –   20
But few now living can behold that goodness –
A pattern to all princes living with her
And all that shall succeed. Saba was never
More covetous of wisdom and fair virtue

chronicle source. Bale's *King Johan* had culminated in a prophecy of Elizabeth, seeing her as 'a quene . . . / Whych maye be a lyghte to other princes all / For the godly wayes whome she doth dayly moue / To hir liege people, through Gods wurde specyall', and characterizing her as 'that Angell, as saynt Iohan doth him call, / That with the lordes seale doth marke out hys true seruauntes' (*King Johan*, 147, 2671–6). But as Foakes shows (Ard²), the speech has distinct topical significance, relating as much, if not more, to James I's reign than to that of Elizabeth I, and in particular depending upon the audience's awareness of the direct parallels drawn between Elizabeth and her namesake, James's daughter. See Leigh: 'Shee a kings daughter, so are you: shee a maiden *Queene*, you a Virgin *Prince*: her name is yours, her blood is yours, her carriage is yours, her countenance yours, like pietie towards God, like pittie towards men: onely the difference stands in this; that the faire flower of her youth is fallen; yours flourisheth like a Rose of *Saram*, and a Lilly of the *Valley*' (A6ᵛ); see also pp. 70–3.

17 **heaven . . . her** May God always be with her.

19 **thousand thousand** i.e. a million

20 **time . . . ripeness** In the context of the explicit invocation of *truth* at 16,

this evokes the iconography of *veritas filia temporis* ('Truth, the daughter of Time'); see pp. 67–70.

22 **pattern** The prophecy repeatedly implies that James should be modelling himself on Elizabeth. Certainly in James's reign, poets criticized him obliquely by singing the praises of his predecessor.

23 **Saba** 1 Kings, 10, describes the arrival of the Queen of Sheba ('Saba' in pre-1611 translations, except in the text of the Geneva Bible, though 'Saba' still in the headings) to test Solomon's wisdom by asking 'hard questions. . . . / Then the quene of Sheba sawe all Salomons wisdome, . . . / And she said vnto the King, It was a true worde that I heard in mine owne land of thy sayings, and of thy wisdome' (1, 4, 6). The Sheba/Solomon reference arguably invokes, too, the politically sensitive story of David, Bathsheba and Nathan the prophet at 2 Samuel, 11–12, possibly prompted by Speed, who hints at the relevance of the David and Bathsheba story to Henry's treatment of Anne, e.g. 2.772: 'And albeit *Queene Anne* in her lifetime had sinned as *David*; or by frailety fell, as who sinneth not; . . . the quiet of her conscience at her death, did well witnes the contrary' (see pp. 88–93).

24 **covetous of** greedy for

23 Saba] Sheba *Rowe³*

429

Than this pure soul shall be. All princely graces   25
That mould up such a mighty piece as this is,
With all the virtues that attend the good,
Shall still be doubled on her. Truth shall nurse her;
Holy and heavenly thoughts still counsel her.
She shall be loved and feared. Her own shall bless her;   30
Her foes shake like a field of beaten corn,
And hang their heads with sorrow. Good grows with
    her.
In her days, every man shall eat in safety
Under his own vine what he plants, and sing
The merry songs of peace to all his neighbours.   35
God shall be truly known, and those about her
From her shall read the perfect ways of honour

26 **mould . . . is** go to create such a powerful person; *piece* ('masterpiece', presumably) possibly refers specifically to women; cf. *Tem* 1.2.56.
28 **still** always
   Truth again, a distinctly Protestant personification (see 20n.)
30 **Her own** her own people
31 **beaten** presumably, wind-beaten
33–5 These images stem from a range of OT passages, especially 1 Kings, 4.20, 25 ('Iudah and Israel *were* manie, as the sand of the sea in nomber, eating, drinking, and making meary. . . . / And Iudah and Israel dwelt without feare, euerie man vnder his vine, and vnder his fig tre, from Dan to Beersheba, all the dayes of Salomon'); Micah, 4.4 ('But thei shall sit euery ma*n* vnder his vine, and vnder his fig tre, and none shal make them afraied'); and Isaiah, 65.21–2 ('and thei shall plant vineyardes, and eat the frute of them. / Thei . . . shall not plant, and another eat'). These texts were repeatedly associated with James I. Thomas Adams, in *The Gallant's Burden*, for example, suggests that '[o]ur feare of

warre is lesse then theirs [because] *Wee sitte vnder our owne Figge-trees, and eate the fruites of our owne Vineyards'* (D2ʳ). Daniel Price, in *Lamentations*, addresses Prince Henry's courtiers, who 'liued vnder the *Branches* of our *Princely Cedar* . . . : *you* onely returne to your owne *Families* to drinke of your owne *Vines*, and to eate vnder your owne *Figge-trees'* (E3ʳ). Fletcher seems not to have held these lines in much reverence, since they are parodied in *BB* 2.1.113–15: 'under him / Each man shall eate his own stolne eggs, and butter, / In his owne shade, or sun-shine'.
36–8 **those . . . blood** a curiously egalitarian (and utopian) rejection of the attitude of the nobility throughout the play, most notably in their struggle with Wolsey (see, e.g., 1.1.59–66n., 122–3n., 127n.; 3.2.96–7n., 279n., 295n.); possibly a residual element of the subversive function of the Henrician prophecies (see 14–62 LN)
37 ***ways** I have followed F4 in emending F's 'way' to *ways* to agree with *those* at 38. It is easy enough for a compositor to drop a final *s*.

32] *Rowe³; F lines* sorrow / her /   37 read] tread *(Collier³)*   37–8 ways . . . by those] *F4;* way . . . by those *F;* way . . . by that *Capell*

And by those claim their greatness, not by blood.
Nor shall this peace sleep with her, but as when
The bird of wonder dies, the maiden phoenix,   40
Her ashes new create another heir
As great in admiration as herself,
So shall she leave her blessedness to one,
When heaven shall call her from this cloud of
     darkness,
Who from the sacred ashes of her honour   45
Shall star-like rise as great in fame as she was
And so stand fixed. Peace, plenty, love, truth, terror,
That were the servants to this chosen infant,
Shall then be his, and like a vine grow to him.
Wherever the bright sun of heaven shall shine,   50
His honour and the greatness of his name

39–55 Guthrie's 1949 production cut this entire passage. Byrne, reviewing the production, asserts that '[t]o concentrate on Elizabeth gives immediate theatrical effect, but to delete James destroys dramatic intention' (Byrne, 129).

40 **phoenix** On this mythical bird and its significance, see LN.

42 **admiration** i.e. her tendency to instil in people the emotion of wonder, arguably the characteristic emotion of the 'late plays' (cf. Miranda in *Tem*)

43 **one** i.e. James I

44 **cloud of darkness** an expression with biblical echoes: e.g. Psalm 97.2 ('Cloudes and darkenes *are* round about him'); Zephaniah, 1.15 ('a day of obscuritie and darkenes, a day of cloudes & blacknes')

46 **star-like rise** as opposed, presumably, to falling *Like a bright exhalation* (3.2.226)

47 **fixed** i.e. not subject to the earthly rises and falls that have provided the structure for the play; fixed stars were contrasted with mobile planets, comets and meteors.

49 **vine** Dekker's pageant *The Mag-* *nificent Entertainment*, produced for James on his arrival in London in 1603, suggests the hope placed in James and his sons after the death of the childless Elizabeth: 'I am the places *Genius*, whence now springs / A *Vine*, whose yongest Braunch shall produce Kings' (B1ᵛ).

50–2 **Wherever . . . nations**. This passage is drawn from Genesis, 17.4, 6: 'thou shalt be a father of manie nacions. . . . / I wil make thee exceading fruteful, and wil make nacions of thee: yea, Kings shal procede of thee'. The language of Genesis, 17, was prominent in sermons preached at the time of the wedding of Princess Elizabeth and Frederick, Elector Palatine. John King, Bishop of London, in his *Vitis Palatina*, applies the passage to Elizabeth: 'that she may be *the mother of nations, and kings of the people may come of her*' (F2ʳ); George Webbe, in his 'Epistle Dedicatorie' to *The Bride Royal*, applies it to Frederick: '*That your Highnesse (right worthie Prince) may be as* Abraham, *a Father of many Nations*' (A5ʳ).

Shall be, and make new nations. He shall flourish,
And, like a mountain cedar, reach his branches
To all the plains about him. Our children's children
Shall see this and bless heaven.

KING   Thou speakest wonders.   55

CRANMER

She shall be to the happiness of England
An aged princess. Many days shall see her,
And yet no day without a deed to crown it.
Would I had known no more. But she must die:
She must, the saints must have her. Yet a virgin,   60
A most unspotted lily, shall she pass to th' ground,
And all the world shall mourn her.

KING   O lord Archbishop,
Thou hast made me now a man. Never before
This happy child did I get anything.
This oracle of comfort has so pleased me   65
That when I am in heaven I shall desire
To see what this child does and praise my maker.
I thank ye all. To you, my good Lord Mayor,

---

52 **new nations** presumably a reference, as Malone first suggested, to the colonization of America, most notably at this point being carried out by the Virginia Company, with which James had a fairly antagonistic relationship. For a range of reasons, notably James's failure to achieve a formal union of England and Scotland, the idea of the 'nation' was seen to be practically and conceptually complex (see e.g. Howard & Rackin, 14).

52–4 **He . . . him.** On the significance of the cedar, see LN.

55 **Thou speakest wonders.** instant fulfilment of 42; cf. *Birth of Merlin*, in which, as Merlin prophesies Britain's

future, Uter exclaims: 'Thou speakst of wonders *Merlin*' (4.5.125); see pp. 179–80. Cf. also *WT* 5.2.23–5: 'The King's daughter is found. Such a deal of wonder is broken out within this hour, that ballad-makers cannot be able to express it.'

57 **aged** agèd

58 **deed** i.e. positive achievement

63 **Thou . . . man** On Henry's position in relation to early modern definitions of manliness, see pp. 81–8. Cf. Maria in *WP* 1.2.102–4: 'there's a fellow / Must yet . . . / Be made a man, for yet he is a monster'.

64 **get** i.e. both 'gain' and 'beget'

---

60 her . . . virgin,] her yet a Virgin; *Theobald*   61] *this edn (RP); F lines* passe / her   62] *this edn (Walker); F lines* her / Archbishop

And your good brethren, I am much beholding:
I have received much honour by your presence,   70
And ye shall find me thankful. Lead the way, lords:
Ye must all see the Queen, and she must thank ye –
She will be sick else. This day, no man think
'Has business at his house, for all shall stay: 74
This little one shall make it holiday.   *Exeunt.*

[*Enter*] EPILOGUE.

EPILOGUE

'Tis ten to one this play can never please
All that are here. Some come to take their ease,
And sleep an act or two (but those, we fear,
We've frighted with our trumpets, so 'tis clear
They'll say 'tis naught), others to hear the city   5
Abused extremely and to cry 'That's witty!'
(Which we have not done neither), that I fear

---

69 ***your** Theobald's emendation of F's
'you' both recognizes that the King
would not address aldermen as 'brothers' and echoes Holinshed's 'maior . . .
with his brethren' (934). As Foakes
(Ard²) notes, 'final *r* in secretary hand
is often so attenuated as almost to disappear'.
  beholding indebted, obliged
73 **She . . . else** Cf. 1.3.65n.
  sick hurt, frustrated
75 **holiday** The word derives from 'Holy-
day' (as it is spelled in F), a reminder
that this implies a spiritual as well as
festive occasion. Some late twentieth-
century productions have attempted to
undermine the apparent optimism of
these final lines. 'Trevor Nunn's production ended as it began, with Henry
in the Holbein stance – but at the end
he was left holding the infant

Elizabeth, with an expression of deep
perplexity on his face' (RP). Greg
Doran (RSC, 1996) strove for a similarly unsettling (if slightly melodramatic)
effect, bringing Anne Bullen back on
behind Henry in the last few moments:
in the split second before the lights
went down, she raised her hand slowly
to her throat in apprehension.
EPILOGUE Generally held to be
Fletcher's (see Appendix 3), though
there are too few lines for effective
stylistic analysis.
5 **naught** useless, worthless
5-6 **others . . . extremely** a reference to
the popularity amongst some members
of the audience (e.g. law students from
the Inns of Court) for plays which
mock London citizens; cf. Field,
Woman, D4ᵛ: 'Such a Cittizen / as the
Playes flout still'.

---

70 your] *Theobald (Thirlby);* you *F*   beholding] beholden *Pope*   76 holiday] *Steevens²;* Holy-day
F; holy day *Johnson*   **Epilogue**   0.1] *Oxf;* THE EPILOGUE *F*   1 SP] *Oxf; not in F*

All the expected good we're like to hear
For this play at this time is only in
The merciful construction of good women,   10
For such a one we showed 'em. If they smile
And say 'twill do, I know within a while
All the best men are ours – for 'tis ill hap
If they hold when their ladies bid 'em clap.   *[Exit.]*

FINIS

10 **construction** interpretation, report
11 **such a one** probably a deliberately
   ambivalent reference to one or all of
   Katherine, Anne and Elizabeth,
   though generally taken to refer only to
   Katherine

14 **clap** applaud (*OED v.*[1] II. 5b); with a
   possible archery (and therefore sexual)
   pun, if *clap* is taken also in the sense of
   OED's *v.*[1] IV 10c: 'to shoot an arrow
   with promptness and effect'; cf. *2H4*
   3.2.45.

14 SD] *Oxf; not in F*

LONGER NOTES

1.2.11–12 You . . . given Shaheen suggests a tentative relationship between this ostensibly magnanimous remark of Henry's and Mark, 6.22–3: 'And the daughter of the same Herodias came in and danced, and pleased Herode and them that sate at table together, the King said vnto yᵉ maide, Aske of me what thou wilt, and I wil giue it thee. / And he sware vnto her, Whatsoeuer thou shalt aske of me, I wil giue it thee, *euen* vnto the halfe of my kingdome.' Shaheen observes that '[a]lthough the spirit of Henry's words and those of Herod are the same, the comparison of Henry and Katherine to Herod and Herodias's daughter is strange, and at first glance appears to be farfetched' (Shaheen, 8); he notes that there are no known parallels for this passage in any of the other sources, and concludes that Mark is drawn on without heed to context. Yet the reference may be deliberately grotesque: if Henry were invoking Herodias's daughter, then this might both imply that he wishes Katherine were young and beautiful and suggest that he is on the lookout for such a dancing girl. This might then provide a mythic underpinning for the encounter of Henry and Anne during a dance (see 1.4).

1.4.63.1 Enter . . . Masquers The term 'masque' had a range of meanings in the Renaissance, from a brief dance by masked performers to a full-blown royal entertainment complete with special effects. Henry VIII seems to have been particularly fond of appearing, disguised, in such events (see Scarisbrick, 36–7). By 1613, masques had become considerably more sophisticated than in Henry's day, and were an integral part of courtly display. The wedding of Elizabeth and Frederick was marked by a significant amount of masquing activity (see pp. 63–70). On the occasion dramatized here, according to Holinshed, 'the king came . . . in a maske with a dozen maskers all in garments like sheepheards, made of fine cloth of gold. . . . [T]hey went directlie before the cardinall, where he sate and saluted him reuerentlie' (921–2). Cf. *LLL* 5.2.120–4: 'apparelled thus / Like Muscovites, or Russians, as I guess. / Their purpose is to parley, court, and dance, / And every one his love-suit will advance / Unto his several mistress'. The entrance of the courtiers and the subsequent dance has tended to be directed as a formal, elegant, Holbeinesque scene, though both Davies (RSC, 1983) and Doran (RSC, 1996) echoed Tree (1910) in turning the moment into something much more full-blooded: Tree's courtiers 'execute[d] a Bacchanalian dance . . . a triumph of flesh and the devil' (*Times*); Doran's, sporting huge papier-mâché phalluses, stamped their way through a comically atavistic sequence.

2.4.179 bosom ... conscience There were arguments in the Renaissance over the physical location of the conscience (i.e. head or heart), though in this case *bosom* appears to imply a different part of the anatomy (see 178–81n.). Henry here is caught up in the emotion of his failure to produce a son: there is little in his words that truly suggests the operation of reason. Christopher St German, writing of the conscience after the Henrician schism, and formulating an attitude to equity which would delegitimate the church courts, sees 'conscyence' as a faculty of the reason: 'a law of man is always to be sette as a rewle in conscyence so that it is not lawfull for no man to go fro it on the one syde ne on the other / for suche a lawe of man hath not only the strength of mannes law / but also of the lawe of reason / or of the law of god / wherof it is dyryuyed / for lawes made by man whiche haue receyued of god power to make lawes be made by god' (St German, 111; see also Guy, 181). Theobald, following Thirlby's suggestion, emended *bosom* to 'bottom' with an eye to Holinshed (see 178–93n.), assuming a compositorial error of *s* for *tt* (or for *t*).

3.2.64–7 He ... Christendom. 'Cranmer has come back to England with the same views he held all along, views that have convinced both the King and the colleges.' Foakes (Ard²) notes that it might also be possible to read this as 'he has come back with the views of the colleges, which, together with his own opinion, have convinced the King', a reading which was preferred by Rowe and Vaughan. Cam (1892), however, citing Tyrwhitt, reads this differently: 'that is, not in person, but having sent in advance the opinions he had gathered'. According to Holinshed, it was Edmund Bonner, Bishop of London, not Cranmer, whom the King sent 'to the chiefe vniuersities of all christendome, to know their opinion and iudgement' of the marriage question (923). Foxe, however, in the 1563 edition, reports (mistakenly) that Cranmer 'was straight way sent into France, and with him . . . Stokisley Byshop of London, [to] debate this matter in Paris & other Uniuersities. . . . Cranmer takynge his iourney through Germany, drewe manye into his opinion' (1471); this may well be the source for this passage, though by the 1596 edition the account was altered, the French journey omitted, and the description of Cranmer's success in Germany rephrased (1689–90).

3.2.282 dare ... larks Continuing the clothing metonymy from 280, this alludes, according to *OED* (*v.*² 5), to a slightly bizarre method of catching larks by dazing or confusing them using a piece of brightly coloured material (possibly scarlet? cf. 255), in this case a cap; or else by deploying a trained bird of prey (a hobby, say) to make the lark sit tight before throwing a net over it. More to the point, this is almost certainly an oblique reference to Wolsey's mistress Joan Lark, the mother of his son Thomas Winter and the sister of his confessor, Thomas Lark. Wolsey eventually arranged a marriage for Joan, but he was widely known to have overlooked his clerical obligation to celibacy – as Surrey makes plain at 295–6 – and this allusion would doubtless have been caught by at least some in the audience. The pun had already been made in a dramatic context in about 1520 by John Skelton in his *Magnificence*, in which Abusion offers Magnificence a 'lusty lass', and he responds by crying 'I would hawk whilst my head did wark, / So I might hobby for such a lusty lark' (1564–5). Neuss notes the same pun in Skelton's 'Colin Cloute': 'For some say ye hunte in parkes, / And hauke on hobby larkes, / And other wanton warkes, / Whan the nyght darkes' (193–6; *Magnificence*, 35). I am grateful to Mark Lawhorn for alerting me to these references.

4.2.82.1 *The vision* There is no evidence for this vision in Holinshed; but two other possible sources have been mooted. (1) E.E.Duncan-Jones notes that 'Katherine's biographers do not relate that she had this assurance of heavenly happiness' (142), but points out that Marguerite of Angoulême, Duchess of Alençon and Queen of Navarre (mentioned at 2.2.40 and 3.2.85–6), a pious Catholic with reforming tendencies, had such a dream prior to her death; interestingly, Anne Bullen was at one time one of Marguerite's ladies-in-waiting. (2) Margeson (Cam²) suggests that the description of the vision may have been influenced by Holinshed's report of a dream dreamt by Anne Bullen shortly before her death: 'this good queene was forwarned of hir death in a dreame, wherein *Morpheus* the god of sleepe (in the likenesse of hir grandfather) appeered vnto hir' (Holinshed, 940). This seems a likely source, yet to give Katherine one of Anne's dreams – and one, above all, that looks forward to Elizabeth's reign after the death of Katherine's daughter Mary – seems to offer a curious interchangeability between Katherine and Anne (cf. 'No man living / Could say "This is my wife" there', 4.1.79–80), rather than the expected contrast. Even more remarkably, the vision may be indebted to Heywood's *If You Know Not Me, You Know Nobody* (first published 1605), in which the young Princess Elizabeth, persecuted by her sister Mary, dreams of angels fending off friars 'offering to kill her', one of whom then 'opens the Bible and puts it in her hands'. When she wakes, she asks her maid Clarentia if she saw or heard anything and, when the maid says no, decides the vision must have been the 'inspiration' of 'heaven' (D4ʳ).

5.1.7 **primero** the most fashionable Tudor card game. There is a painting of an Elizabethan card party, attributed to Zuccaro, which shows Lord Burleigh playing primero. Skill at primero seems to have remained a courtly characteristic in James's reign (see Middleton, *NVal* 1.1.42). The game appears to be Italian, not (as might be assumed from the name) Spanish, in origin: Katherine of Aragon, according to Parlett, preferred Gleek. It is known as 'primiera' in Italian and remains 'the major native vying game of Italy' (Parlett, 91). Francesco Berni describes it as '*vno gioco tanto bello: / Et tanto trauagliato: tanto vario*' (Berni, B1ʳ). Gerolamo Cardano treats it as 'the noblest of all' card games (Cardano, 206), and an English translation of his description of primero can be found in Ore. However, for general interest, I provide Parlett's modern reconstruction of the sixteenth-century form of the game from *A History of Card Games (Parlett, 91–2)*:

Four or more players, 40–card pack lacking Eights, Nines, and Tens. Players ante to a pot, are dealt two cards face down, stake again, and receive two more. The winning combinations are, from lowest to highest:

1. Point (*numerus*): two or three cards of the same suit. A point of higher card-value beats one of lower value, for which purpose courts count 10 each, Two 12, Three 13, Four 14, Five 15, Ace 16, Six 18, and Seven 21.
2. Prime (*primiera*): four cards, one of each suit.
3. Fifty-five (*supremus*): the highest possible three-flush, i.e. Ace + Six + Seven (= 16 + 18 + 21 = 55) plus an unrelated fourth card.
4. Flush (*fluxus*): four of a suit.
5. Quartet (*chorus*): four of the same rank.

Anyone holding a prime or flush may call 'Vada!' ('Go!'), which brings an immediate showdown won by the best hand. Failing that, there is a draw and another betting round. If no one bets, the stakes are carried forward to the next deal; but if one stays in, at least one other must contest the pot, this obligation ultimately falling upon the player immediately ahead of the last bettor if everyone else has folded. In a showdown the better of equal combinations is that with the higher point. Thus a quartet of Aces ($4 \times 16 = 64$) beats a quartet of Fives (60) but is beaten by four Sixes (72). Four Kings will not beat four Queens or Jacks, as these hands all count 40. Such ties are broken in favour of the eldest hand competing. Players 'vie' by stating how high a hand they are claiming to have, and may 'bluff' by overstating it. What they apparently must not do is to underbid their hand; for, as Cardano puts it, 'If anyone wins with the greater point, he is obliged to show another card; otherwise he loses his deposit because he could have a flush. . . . Similarly, if he vies on the basis of point, he is obliged to show two different cards and one of a matching suit, so that no one may suspect him of having a flush or prime'.

5.4.14–62 **Let . . . her.** The political prophecy was an important Tudor (and thus, here, Jacobean) genre. As Fox notes, under Henry VIII, prophecies became 'an instrument whereby ordinary Englishmen could objectify their feelings about the course history was taking' (Fox, 89–90). Such prophecies circulated most widely at the lower end of the social scale; the authorities reacted both by suppressing them and by manipulating them 'to create a myth of destiny which foreshadowed, and perhaps even promoted, the later idea of England as the elect nation. . . . To see past and future political disturbances as part of an apocalyptic pattern with a happy out-come was to make them bearable' (78, 91). Here the political prophecy is carefully updated, and is both legitimized and problematized by its incorporation into a history play, enabling the audience to verify the events which have already taken place and thus presume the accuracy of those which have not (see pp. 71–2). Updating the function of the prophecy has been part and parcel of the play's afterlife. For instance, lines 14–38 and 50–5 of this speech (spoken by 'Saint George' rather than Cranmer, with 'Lady' substituted for *infant* and 'girlhood' for *cradle* and omitting line 21) were incorporated at the climax of a performance, *The Masque of Hope. Presented for the Entertainment of HRH Princess Elizabeth on the occasion of her visit to University College, 25 May 1948, by Oxford University Dramatic Society* (London, 1948). This was 'written by Nevill Coghill on a theme devised by Glynne Wickham', with the part of Fear proleptically played – as Michael Dobson notes ('Costume drama', 33) – by Kenneth Tynan, then a student, but later London's leading theatre critic; cf. the revival of Guthrie's production for the coronation of Elizabeth II in 1953.

5.4.40 **phoenix** A mythical bird, of gorgeous plumage, fabled to be the only one of its kind and to live five or six hundred years in the Arabian desert, after which it would burn itself to ashes on a funeral pile of aromatic twigs ignited by the sun and fanned by its own wings, only to emerge from its ashes with renewed youth to live through another cycle of years (*OED*); thus proverbial for rarity (Dent, P256) and longevity; cf. *AYL* 4.3.18, *Cym* 1.6.1. See Erasmus, 2.1.57, *Phoenice vivacior* ('Living longer than the phoenix') and 2.7.10, *Phoenice rarior* ('Rarer than the phoenix'), who refers to Pliny, *Naturalis historia*, 10.3, Ovid, *Metamorphoses*, 15.392–407, and Lactantius, *Carmen de ave phoenice* (*Clavis patrum latinorum*, 90). Dekker, *Four Birds*, makes a direct correlation between the phoenix and Christ: 'Christ is the true Phoenix' (I11^r). The analogy for the relationship of Elizabeth and James was standard: Joshua Sylvester, dedicating his translation of Du Bartas's *Divine Weeks* to King James, claims that '[f]rom Spicie Ashes of the sacred Vrne / Of Our dead Phœnix (dear ELIZABETH) / *A new true* PHOENIX *lively flourisheth,* / *Whom greater glories than the First adorne*' (A2^r).The image of the phoenix also appears in Rowley's *When You See Me* at the birth not of Elizabeth but of Edward VI (and the death in childbirth of Jane Seymour): 'One Phenix dying, giues another life, / Thus must we flatter our extreamest griefe' (B3^v, Wilson TLN 491–2). Cf. also *TNK* 1.3.70. Again, the image of the phoenix fits with the parallels drawn between the two Princesses Elizabeth, past and present. But see also pp. 72–3.

5.4.52–4 **He . . . him.** See 33–5n, and cf. *Cym* 5.6.440. The image of the cedar was also popular with preachers in 1612–13: for example, in the sermon referred to in 50–2n.: '*that she may . . . be set vp as a Cedar in Libanus*' (F2^r). It was drawn most probably from Psalm 92.12–13: ('The righteous shal florish like a palme tre, & shal growe like a cedre in Lebanon. / Suche as be planted in the House of the Lord, shal florish in ye courts of our God'; but cf. Ezekiel, 17.22–3, and 31.3, 6–7. The metaphor of the cedar perhaps connects (a little uneasily) with other organic/tree images in the play, notably Gardiner's desire to 'grub up the stock'; there is an uncomfortable reference to a cedar in this context in *When You See Me* (I3ʳ, Wilson TLN, 2554–5), but this does not appear to relate to the way in which the cedar is deployed here, and the interchangeability of such metaphors is apparent in Dekker, *Wonderful Year* (1603), in which the cedar is an image of infertility and the olive is the tree which promises generativity: 'The losse of a Queene, was paid with the double interest of a King and Queene. The Cedar of her gouernment which stood alone and bare no fruit, is changed now to an Oliue, vpon whose spreading branches grow both Kings and Queenes' (C1ᵛ); see also 5.1.22–3n. and pp. 130–2. Curiously, there are no references here to Revelation, an odd omission in the context of the Tudor poet–prophets' apocalyptic reworkings of vernacular prophetic traditions (especially those of Merlin) (see Fox, 79 and 5.4.14–62n.); this may, however, be a quite deliberate omission.

APPENDIX 1

CONTEXTUAL CHRONOLOGY FOR THE EVENTS OF *HENRY VIII*

1491	28 June	Birth of Henry, second son of Henry VII and Elizabeth of York
1501	14/15 November	Arthur, Prince of Wales, marries Katherine of Aragon
1502	2 April	Death of Arthur
1503	18 February	Henry is invested as Prince of Wales
	23 June	Initial contract for marriage of Henry and Katherine
	26 December	Pope Julius II grants a dispensation for this marriage plan
1509	22 April	Death of Henry VII
	23 April	Accession of Henry VIII
	11 June	Marriage of Henry and Katherine
	24 June	Coronation of Henry and Katherine
1511	1 January	Birth of a son, Henry, to Henry VIII and Katherine
	22 February	Death of baby Henry
	13 November	Alliance between England, Spain, and the Holy Roman Empire against France
1512	20 March	Pope Julius II conditionally invests Henry with the kingdom of France
1513	July	Henry invades France

1514	9 July	Peace treaty between England and France
	13 August	Henry's sister Mary marries Louis XII of France by proxy
	5 November	Mary becomes Queen of France
1515	1 January	Death of Louis XII; accession of François I
	February	Charles Brandon, Duke of Suffolk, secretly marries Mary, widowed Queen of France
1516	23 January	Death of Ferdinand of Aragon, Katherine's father
	18 February	Birth of Mary, future Mary I (ruled 1553–8)
1518	2 October	'Treaty of Universal Peace' between England, France, Spain, and the Holy Roman Empire
1519	January	Death of Emperor Maximilian; Charles of Castile and Austria becomes Charles V, Holy Roman Emperor, after defeating Henry VIII and François I in election (28 June)
	May	Purge of 'French' courtiers (1.3)
	Autumn	Kildare summoned to London to answer charges
1520	May	Surrey goes to Ireland as Lord Lieutenant
	27–9 May	Meeting of Henry and Charles V at Dover and Canterbury
	7–23 June	Meeting of Henry and François I at Field of the Cloth of Gold (1.1)
1521	April/May	Arrest and trial of Duke of Buckingham (1.1, 1.2, 2.1)
	17 May	Execution of Buckingham
	25 August	Secret treaty between Henry and Charles V against François I
	October	Henry's book against Luther presented to the Pope, who grants Henry title of 'Defender of the Faith'
1522		Surrey returns from Ireland
	June/July	Charles V visits England; Henry declares war on France

1523		England invades France
1524		Peace negotiations between England and France
1525	24 February	François I captured by Charles V's army at Pavia
		'Amicable Grant' and its failure (**1.2**)
1526	14 January	Treaty of Madrid between Charles V and François I, who is released
1527		Wolsey's banquet (**1.3, 1.4**)
	April	Treaty of Westminster between Henry and François I
	6 May	Sack of Rome by Charles V's army
	17 May	Henry initiates divorce proceedings against Katherine
1528	January	England and France declare war on Charles V
	September	Campeggio arrives in England for divorce proceedings (**2.1, 2.2**)
1529	18 June	Legatine court begins at Blackfriars (**2.4**)
	late July	Wolsey and Campeggio visit Katherine (**3.1**)
	31 July	Campeggio announces adjournment of court (**2.4**)
	9 October	Wolsey is removed from office (**3.2**)
	25 November	More becomes Lord Chancellor (**3.2**)
	1 December	44 articles against Wolsey (**3.2**)
1530	4 November	Wolsey is arrested
	29 November	Death of Wolsey (**4.2**)
1532	16 May	More resigns as Chancellor
	24 May	Death of William Warham, Archbishop of Canterbury
	September	Anne created Marchioness of Pembroke (**2.3**)
1533	25 January	Marriage in secret of Henry and Anne Boleyn
	30 March	Cranmer is ordained Archbishop of Canterbury (**3.2**)
	23 May	Cranmer invalidates marriage of Henry and Katherine

	28 May	Cranmer validates marriage of Henry and Anne (**3.2**)
	1 June	Coronation of Anne (**4.1**)
	7 September	Birth of Elizabeth, future Elizabeth I (ruled 1558–1603) (**5.1**)
	10 September	Christening of Elizabeth (**5.3, 5.4**)
1534	25 January	Henry declared Head on earth of the Church of England
	13 April	Oath of Succession; More and Fisher refuse to take Oath
1535	20 May	Fisher appointed Cardinal
	23 June	Execution of Fisher
	6 July	Execution of More
	August	Inspection of monasteries by agents of Cromwell
1536	8 January	Death of Katherine (**4.2**)
	February	Dissolution of smaller monasteries
	19 May	Execution of Anne
	30 May	Marriage of Henry and Jane Seymour
	October	'Pilgrimage of Grace' rebellions
1537	January–July	Suppression of Pilgrimage of Grace
	12 October	Birth of Edward, future Edward VI (ruled 1547–53)
	24 October	Death of Jane Seymour
1540	28 July	Execution of Cromwell
1545		Probable date of attempt by Catholic faction to have Cranmer arrested for heresy (**5.2**)
1547	28 January	Death of Henry; accession of Edward VI

APPENDIX 2

COMPARATIVE CHRONOLOGY (1603–13) FOR PLAYS IN THE FLETCHER AND SHAKESPEARE CANONS

All dates given are approximate. Authorial attribution is subject to the caveats offered in the Introduction (pp. 180–99).

Date	Title of play	Attribution	Company
1603	*Measure for Measure*	Shakespeare (with Middleton?)	King's
1603–4	*Sir Thomas More* (revised)	Munday, Chettle, Dekker, Heywood, Shakespeare	King's (?)
1604–5	*All's Well That Ends Well*	Shakespeare	King's
1605	*Timon of Athens*	Shakespeare and Middleton	King's
1605–6	*King Lear*	Shakespeare	King's
1606	*Macbeth*	Shakespeare	King's
	Antony and Cleopatra	Shakespeare	King's
	The Woman Hater	Beaumont, with Fletcher	Paul's
1607	*Pericles*	Shakespeare (and Wilkins?)	King's
	The Knight of the Burning Pestle	Beaumont	Queen's Revels

445

Date	Title of play	Attribution	Company
1607–8	*Cupid's Revenge*	Beaumont and Fletcher	Queen's Revels
	The Faithful Shepherdess	Fletcher	Queen's Revels
1608	*Coriolanus*	Shakespeare	King's
1608–10	*The Coxcomb*	Beaumont and Fletcher	Queen's Revels
	Philaster	Beaumont and Fletcher	King's
1609	*The Winter's Tale*	Shakespeare	King's
1610	*The Scornful Lady*	Fletcher, with Beaumont	Queen's Revels
	Cymbeline	Shakespeare	King's
1610–11	*The Maid's Tragedy*	Beaumont and Fletcher	King's
	Bonduca	Fletcher	King's
	Valentinian	Fletcher	King's
1611	*A King and No King*	Beaumont and Fletcher	King's
	The Woman's Prize	Fletcher	King's
	The Night Walker	Fletcher	Lady Elizabeth's (?)
	The Tempest	Shakespeare	King's
1612	*The Captain*	Fletcher, with Beaumont	King's
	Cardenio	Shakespeare and Fletcher (lost)	King's
1613	*Henry VIII*	Shakespeare and Fletcher	King's
	The Two Noble Kinsmen	Shakespeare and Fletcher	King's

Date	Title of play	Attribution	Company
	The Honest Man's Fortune	Field, with Fletcher and Massinger	Lady Elizabeth's (?)
	Monsieur Thomas	Fletcher	Lady Elizabeth's (?)
1613 (?)	*Four Plays*	Fletcher and Field	unknown

APPENDIX 3

ATTRIBUTION AND COMPOSITION

Attribution is subject to the caveats offered in the Introduction (pp. 180–99). F = Fletcher; S = Shakespeare; M = Massinger; S(F) = scenes considered by Hoy to be mainly by Shakespeare with 'Fletcherian interpolation' (Hoy, 7.82). There is evidence for Folio typesetting by two compositors, currently known as 'B' and 'I'.

	Pro.	Act 1 1.1	1.2	1.3	1.4	Act 2 2.1	2.2	2.3	2.4
Spedding 1850	F	S	S	F	F	F	F	S	S
Fleay 1886	F	M	S	F	F	F	F	S	S
Farnham 1916	F	S	S	F	F	F	F	S	S
Hoy 1962	–	S	S	F	F	S(F)	S(F)	S	S
Hope 1994	F	S	S	F	F	F	F	S	S
Compositor attribution	B	B>137 I 138<	I	I	I	I	I	I	B>119 SD I 119<

	Act 3			Act 4		Act 5				Epi.
	3.1	3.2a 1–203	3.2b 203–end	4.1	4.2	5.1	5.2	5.3	5.4	
	F	S	F	F	F	S	F	F	F	F
	F	M	F	F	F	M	F	F	F	F
	F	S	F	F	F	S	F	F	F	F
	F	S	S(F)	S(F)	S(F)	S	F	F	F	–
	F	S	F	F	F	S	F	F	F	F
	I>108 B109<	B	B	B	B	B	B>20 I 21<	I	I	I

APPENDIX 4

THE MAID'S TRAGEDY

Elements of *Henry VIII*, 5.3, derive from Beaumont and Fletcher's *The Maid's Tragedy*, 1.2, the relevant sections of which are provided here (Bowers 2, 35–8).

The scene begins with the efforts of Calianax, an old courtier, and Diagoras, a servant, to restrain a crowd eager to see the masque the King has sponsored to celebrate the marriage of Evadne, sister to the general Melantius (and also, secretly, the King's mistress).

Enter Calianax, *with* Diagoras.

Calianax. *Diagoras* looke to the dores better for shame, you let in all the world, and anon the King will raile at me: why very well said, by *Jove* the King will have the show i'th Court.

Diagoras. Why doe you sweare so my Lord? you know heele have it here.

Calianax. By this light if he be wise, he will not.

Diagoras. And if he will not be wise, you are forsworne.

Calianax. One may swear his heart out, and get thankes on no side, ile be gone, looke too't who will.

Diagoras. My Lord I shall never keepe them out. Pray stay, your lookes will terrifie them.

Calianax. My lookes terrifie them? you coxcomely asse you, ile be judgd by all the company, whether thou hast not a worse face then I.

Diagoras. I meane because they know you, and your office.

Calianax. Office, I would I could put it off, I am sure I sweat quite through my office, I might have made room at my daughters wedding, they ha neere kild her amongst them. And now I must doe service for him that hath forsaken her, serve that will. *Exit* Calianax.

Diagoras. Hee's so humerous since his daughter was forsaken? hark, hark, there, there, so, so codes, codes, (*knock within*) – what now?

Melantius (*within*). Open the dore.

Diagoras. Whose there?

Melantius [*within*]. *Melantius.*

Diagoras. I hope your Lord-ship brings no troope with you, for if you doe, I must returne them.

Enter Melantius *and a* Lady.

Melantius. None but this Lady sir.

Diagoras. The Ladies are all plac'd above, save those that come in the Kings troope, the best of *Rhodes* sit there, and theres roome.

Melantius. I thanke you sir, – when I have seene you placed madam, I must attend the King, but the maske done, ile waite on you againe.

Exeunt Melantius, Lady *other dore.*

Diagoras. Stand backe there, roome for my Lord *Melantius*, pray beare back, this is no place for such youthes and their truls, let the dores shut agen: I, do your heads itch? ile scratch them for you, so now thrust and hang: [*knock within*] againe, – who i'st now? I cannot blame my Lord *Calianax* for going away, would he were here, he would run raging amongst them, and breake a dozen wiser heads than his own in the twinckling of an eye: what's the newes now?

Within. I pray you can you helpe mee to the speech of the maister Cooke?

Diagoras.　If I open the dore Ile cooke some of your
　　calves heads. Peace rogues? – [*knock within*] againe, –
　　who i'st?
Melantius (*within*).　*Melantius?*

Enter Calianax.

Calianax.　Let him not in.
Diagoras.　O my Lord a must, – make roome there for
　　my Lord. . . .

Calianax.　Make roome there.　　　*Hoboyes play within.*

Enter King, Evadne, Aspatia, *Lords and Ladies.*

King.　*Melantius* thou art welcome, and my love
　　Is with thee still; but this is not a place
　　To brable in, – *Calianax*, joyne hands.
Calianax.　He shall not have mine hand.
King.　　　　　　　　　　　This is no time
　　To force you too't, I doe love you both,
　　Calianax you looke well to your office,
　　And you *Melantius* are welcome home, –
　　Begin the maske.

　　　　　　　　　　　　　　　(1.2.1–48, 98–106)

APPENDIX 5

UNCOLLECTED SOURCES/ANALOGUES

1. From Michael Drayton's *The Life and Death of the Lord Cromwell*, on the subject of Henry VIII:

> For in his high distemprature of blood
> Who was so great whose life he did regard?
> Or what was it that his desires withstood
> He not inuested were it nere so hard?
> Nor held he me so absolutely good,
> That though I crost him yet I should be spar'd,
>   But with those things I lastly was to go,
>   Which he to ground did violently throw.
>
> When *Winchester* with all those enemies
> Whom my much power from audience had debarr'd,
> The longer time there mischiefes to deuise,
> Feeling with me how lastly now it far'd,
> When I had done the King that did suffice,
> Lastly thrust in against me to be heard,
>   When all was ill contrarily turn'd good,
>   Making amaine to th'shedding of my blood.
>
> And that the King his action doth deny,
> And on my guilt doth altogether lay,
> Having his riot satisfied thereby,
> Seemes not to know how I therein did sway,
> What late was truth conuerted heresie:
> When he in me had purchased his pray,

Himselfe to cleere and satisfie the sin,
Leaues me but late his instrument therein.
(Drayton 1610, 545)

2. From John Bale's *King Johan* (1539; revised 1562), in which Nobility, Clergy and Civil Order discuss Elizabeth's reign:

Nobylyte   Englande hath a quene, Thankes to the lorde aboue
whych maye be a lyghte, to other princes all
for the godly wayes, whome she doth dayly moue
To hir liege people, through Gods wurde specyall
She is that Angell, as saynt Iohan doth hym call
That with the lordes seale, doth marke out hys true seruauntes
Pryntynge in their hartes, hys holy wourdes and Covenauntes.

Clergye   In Danyels sprete, she hath subdued the Papistes
with all the ofsprynge, of Antichristes generacyon. . . .

Ciuyle ordre   Praye vnto the lorde, that hir grace maye contynewe
The dayes of Nestor, to our sowles consolacyon;
And that hir ofsprynge, maye lyue also to subdewe
The great Antichriste, with hys whole generacyon
In Helias sprete, to the confort of thys nacyon
Also to preserue, [the qu] hir most honourable counsell
To the prayse of God, and glorye of the Gospell.
(*King Johan*, 133–4, ll. 2625–33, 2639–45)

3. From Christopher Ockland's *Valiant Acts* (1585), vol. 2, '*Elizabeth Queen*', in which Elizabeth's reign is praised:

Peace shineth in those landes, and plenteous store of fruite and grayne

Throughout the fayre broad fieldes, with fragrant hearbes
    adornisht growes,
Such blessings from his heauenly throne almighty *Ioue* bestowes,
Both on those people, and their land which doe his name adore
And dread with suppliant hartes, and of hye *Ioue* obey the lore,
And wise are in the Lord: for this true wisedome is in deede,
To know *Iehoue*, and *Christ* his sonne, which from him did
    proceede.
Descending downe into the earth from filthy sinnes to cleanse,
Those which beleu'd, and to preserue from hells infernall
    dennes.
O natiue land, God graunt O *England* that thy wisedome bright,
Herein appeare, that *Gods* good giftes thou doe acknowledge right,
And meekely thankes condign bestow, on him with gratefull
    hart.
What better or what greater gift may *Ioue* with thee impart:
A guider of thine *Imperie* adornd with heauenly minde
He gentlie hath bestowde, both learned, wise, seuere and kinde.
Of maiestie to be honoured, chast bold, and to be fear'd
Who since she bore the regall mace, such profitt hath vp reard
Vnto thy coastes, as neuer haue thine auncient kings of yore.
Gods worship true she hath restorde, suppresd, and drownde
    before.
And hath procurde that for the space of twentie yeares and three
Thy people wander may on land and surging salt streames free
From direfull harmes, which gastly broyles of *Mars* procure, and
    heape,
Nor onely in tranquillitie she doth her subiectes keepe,
At home, but would with all her hart, and her indeuour eke,
The externe peoples furious rage compresse, who dayle seeke
Their owne destruction fell and reare vp dreadfull skirmage still,
Wherein with mutuall wound the brother doth his brother kill
And neighbour doth with goary knife his neighbours hart bloud
    spill.

                    (*Valiant Acts*, D4ᵛ)

4. From John Speed's *Theatre of the Empire of Great Britain* (1611), in which Wolsey's death is described:

But whatsoeuer the cause was, that *Campeius* denied his sentence for the Diuorce, certaine it is, that Cardinall *Wolsey*, fell likewise in great displeasure of the King, though he sought to excuse himselfe with want of sufficient authority: but now his Sunne hauing passed the Meridian of his greatnesse, began by degrees againe to decline, till lastly it set vnder the cloud of his fatall eclipse.

Formerly wee haue spoken of the rising of this man, who now being swolne so bigge by the blasts of promotion, as the bladder not able to conteine more greatnesse, suddenly burst, and vented foorth the winde of all former fauours. Vaine glorious he was, in state, in diet, and in rich furniture for house, and in prodigall intertainements, more like to a Prince then a Prelate, attended with so many officers, and seruants as is almost incredible, were not his Check-roll yet to be seene. At his masse he was serued by Dukes, and Earles, who tooke the assaie of his wine on their knees, and held him his Basen at the Lauatorie. And being Ambassador vnto the Emperour at *Bruxels*, was there waited vpon by manie noble men of *England*, and serued at Table by his seruitors vpon their knees, to the great admiration of the *Germaines* which behelde it: and indeed so much ouertopped the Pompe of a spirituall function, as he seemed to the more humble, to be mad for ioy; and him doth *Campian* judge, rather to be a Bastard of some Prince, then the sonne of a Butcher, so moulded for the one, and so farre mounting from the other: exceedingly wise he was and very wel spoken, but full of reuenge and vicious of body, thrall to affection, and lulled asleepe with flattery, insatiable to get, but princely in bestowing, lofty to his enemies, and not easily reconciled, which hastened his fall, when he first began

for to slippe. *Queene Katherine* in her cause, did grieu-
ously accuse him, the Counsell for their parts, did article
against him, the Law found him in a premunire vnto the
King, and Sir *Thomas Moore* in the high Court of
Parliament inueighed bitterly against him.

The first steppe of his discent was his dislike of the
Kings affection vnto *Anne Bullen*, a Gentlewoman nothing fauourable to his Pontificall Pompe, nor no great
follower of the Rites of those times, which moued the
Cardinall (the *Pope* hauing assumed the sentence of
Queene Katherines cause vnto himselfe) to write vnto his
holinesse to deferre the iudgement of Diuorce, till he had
wrought the Kings minde in another mould. This was
not done so secretly, but that it came to the Kings eare,
and lastly cost the proud Cardinall his life. For the broad
Seale first taken from him, and his other Bishopricks elsewhere bestowed, his House and furniture seazed vpon,
and himselfe remoued into the North, at *Cawood* Castle
seuen miles from Yorke, was suddenly arrested (for arrogant words importing a desire of reuengement, saith
Sleidan) by the Earle of *Northumberland*, whence he was
conueied toward *London* by the Lieutenant of the Tower,
in which iourney at *Leicester Abbey* he ended his life,
whose death himselfe had hastened bytaking an ouer-
much quantity of a confection to breake winde from off
his stomacke, and in that Church was there enterred.

(Speed, 2.769)

APPENDIX 6

MUSIC

Despite its reputation as a play of ceremony (and Henry VIII's own reputation as a composer), *Henry VIII* is not thought of as one of the more musical plays in the Shakespeare canon, yet the Folio text calls for numerous fanfares of various sorts (1.2.0.1; 1.4.0.1; 1.4.34.1; 1.4.49 SD; 1.4.63.1; 1.4.108 SD; 2.4.0.1; 4.1.35 SD; 4.1.36.2; 4.1.36.25; 5.4.0.1; 5.4.3.1), as well as music for dancing (1.4.76 SD), music for choristers (4.1.36.5), '*Sad and solemn music*' just prior to Katherine's vision (4.2.80 SD), and a two-stanza song, 'Orpheus, with his lute' (3.1.3–14). Certainly, the musical forces required are, by the standards of Jacobean drama, considerable: according to Long 'a cry of trumpets (probably nine or more), a consort of hautboys, a consort of cornets, a "broken" consort of mixed strings and woodwinds, and . . . a lutenist', as well as 'a solo singer – perhaps a choirboy – and a choir possibly composed of men and choirboys' (261). We have a reasonable idea both of the kind of music that accompanied productions of Shakespearean plays and of the instruments used, but very little of the actual original music is extant and none for *Henry VIII*.

'Orpheus, with his lute', appears to be a recycled version of a speech by the character Julio in Fletcher's *The Captain*, which was first performed in 1612:

<blockquote>

musick

(Such as old *Orpheus* made, that gave a soule

To aged mountaines, and made rugged beasts

Lay by their rages; and tall trees that knew

No sound but tempests, to bow downe their branches
</blockquote>

> And heare, and wonder; and the Sea, whose surges
> Shooke their white heads in heaven, to be as midnight
> Still, and attentive) steales into our soules
> So suddenly, and strangely, that we are
> From that time no more ours, but what she pleases.
>
> (3.1.31–40)

Cutts attempts to argue that this is Fletcher's reworking (inferior, of course) of the 'Shakespearean' original in *Henry VIII*, but he has to fudge the chronology in order to do so (Cutts, 'Song', 190); for a comparable, but more complete, instance of a song appearing in both a 'Shakespeare' and a 'Fletcher' play (*MM* and *Rollo*), see Taylor & Jowett, 123–40; Williams in Bowers, 10.2.363–7. It is possible that the development of the speech into the song was connected to one of the performances for the Palatine wedding, since Campion's *Lords' Masque*, commissioned as a replacement for the controversial, Prince Henry-sponsored *Masque of Truth* (see pp. 68–70, 70n.), revolves around Orpheus's benign influence. It is likely that the King's Company musician Robert Johnson set 'Orpheus, with his lute', since he was working for both playwrights at the time: he wrote settings of songs for Shakespeare's *Macbeth, Cymbeline, The Winter's Tale* and *The Tempest* and for Fletcher's *Valentinian, The Chances, The Mad Lover* and, most notably, *The Captain* (Cutts, 'Johnson', 110–21). Matthew Locke, composer to Charles II, may have had access to Johnson's original for his *c*. 1663 setting of the song (Gooch & Thatcher, 1.521), though Long is sceptical of this claim (Long, 253).

The earliest extant music for the play after Locke was written by William Shield for a Covent Garden production in 1780 (Gooch & Thatcher, 1.523). A substantial number of nineteenth- and twentieth-century composers (including Zoltán Kodály, amongst the better known) produced incidental music (Gooch & Thatcher, 1.517–43), and in one case did so for more than one significant production – for Beerbohm Tree's production, Edward German reworked and added to the music he had written for

Irving's *Henry VIII*. There is, as Gooch & Thatcher note, 'no substantive evidence' for the claim 'that Beethoven's *Sonate pour le Piano Forte*, Opus 111, was inspired by *Henry VIII*' (1.542). 'Orpheus, with his lute' has received a substantial number of later (mostly non-theatrical) settings by, amongst others, Arthur Sullivan (1877), Gerard Manley Hopkins (unfinished, 1887), Eric Coates (1907–8), Ivor Gurney (1912–13), Wilhelm Stenhammar (1917–24), Mario Castelnuovo-Tedesco (1921), Ralph Vaughan Williams (1925) and William Schuman (1945). Few of these have been recorded, but the following are notable exceptions:

> Arthur Sullivan's 1877 'Orpheus with His Lute', on an LP of Dame Janet Baker's 'Favourite Encores', with Gerald Moore, piano, on HMV Greensleeve (EMI ESD 1024391).

> Vaughan Williams's 1925 'Orpheus with His Lute' (BM MS 50480), song for voice and pianoforte, first performed in 1904 by a soprano, Beatrice Spencer; sung by Robert Tear, tenor, with Philip Ledger, piano, on London CD 430 368-2 (originally on Argo records, 1972).

> William Schuman's 1945 'Orpheus with His Lute', on an LP, *Twentieth Century Music for Voice and Guitar* (Turnabout TV34727, 1978), with Rosalind Rees (soprano) and David Starobin (guitar and piano).

The Folio stage directions raise questions about distinctions between types of fanfare, notably 'sennets' and 'flourishes'. The exact significance of a 'sennet' is unclear, especially at 2.4.0.1, which reads '*Trumpets, sennet and cornets*'. *TxC* argues that a 'sennet' was customarily played on trumpets alone and that the form of F's stage direction implies that '*Trumpets*' may be 'a playhouse marginal annotation which either the scribe or the compositor incorporated in the main direction' (620), but the evidence for a trumpets-only sennet seems to me unclear. Early in Act 1 of Part 1 of Marston's *Antonio and Mellida*, first a flourish and then a

'*Synnet*' are played on cornetts (B2ᵛ): evidently, both a 'flourish' and a 'sennet' can be played on cornetts – which were wooden instruments with finger holes, quite unlike the modern brass cornet with valves (Sider, 401; see 1.2.0.1n.) – as well as on trumpets. In this context, I prefer to assume that the opening stage direction calls for trumpets first, then either trumpets or cornetts playing a sennet (or perhaps trumpets and cornetts together, though Long argues that '[t]he two kinds of instrument were seldom played in consort'; see Long, 251), then cornetts alone. Experiments with trumpets at the reconstructed Globe suggest that they are too loud to be played in the tiring-house, which might suggest cornetts as an indoor theatre alternative. Trumpets seem often to have signified the arrival of royalty, cornetts that of minor dignitaries: Manifold notes a 'correlation' between cornetts and Wolsey's entrances (Manifold, 49; Sider, 404). If so, *Henry VIII* contradicts the norm at one point, since the King enters to the sound of cornetts at 1.2.0.1, which might, at least in the context of one critical reading of Henry's development (see pp. 87–8; Manifold, 49), imply aurally that he has yet to assert his authority over that of the Cardinal. At 1.4.49, on the other hand, it is possible that the sound of a trumpet announcing the arrival of the 'noble troop of strangers' suggests to the audience that one of the masquers will turn out to be the King – though the King's actual entrance is marked by '*hautboys*' alone. As Manifold observes, '[t]rumpets sound alone for the first time in 5.5 [*sic*], at the christening of Princess Elizabeth' (Manifold, 49), one implication being that this is the first entry of a genuinely royal character onto the stage.

APPENDIX 7

DOUBLING CHART

Roles marked with an asterisk (*) are mute; with a plus (+) are played by boys; in brackets are optional. See King, *Casting*, 93, 246–8, for an alternative arrangement.

Actor	Pro.	1.1	1.2	1.3	1.4	2.1	2.2	2.3	2.4	3.1	3.2	4.1	4.2	5.1	5.2	5.3	5.4	Epi.
1			King		King		King		King		King			King	King		King	
2		Wol	Wol		Wol		Wol		Wol	Wol	Wol							
3+			Kath						Kath	Kath			Kath					
4		Nor	Nor				Nor				Nor	Nor			Nor		Nor	
5		Buck				Buck					Crom				Crom			
6	Pro			Cham	Cham			Cham			Cham				Cham	Cham		Epi
7						1 Gent	1 Gent					1 Gent		Cran	Cran		Cran	
8			Suff				Suff				Suff	Suff		Suff	Suff		Suff	
9			Surv				Gard					Gard		Gard	Gard			

462

Actor	Pro.	1.1	1.2	1.3	1.4	2.1	2.2	2.3	2.4	3.1	3.2	4.1	4.2	5.1	5.2	5.3	5.4	Epi.
10		Aber				Vaux					Surr	Surr			Surr			
11				Sand	Sand	Sand						L. Chan			L. Chan			
12+					Anne			Anne				Anne					Lady	
13+								OL						OL				
14					Guil				Linc			3 Gent	Cap					
15			Lov	Lov	Lov	Lov					Lov			Lov		Port		
16		Serg			Serv		Camp		Camp	Camp		Garter			Keep		Garter	
17									Griff	Griff			Griff		Butts			
18		Brand				2 Gent			Crier			2 Gent		Den		P. Man		
19		Guard	Secr						Verg			Judge	Mess		Guard		Ald	
20+					Lady	Tip			Scribe				Pat				March	
21+					Lady	Tip			Gent			Lady					Lady	
22*		Guard			Masq	Hal			Verg			Judge		Page	Guard		Ald	
23*		(Guard)			Masq	Hal			Arch			Mayor					Mayor	
24*					Masq	Att			Scribe			Dorset					Noble	
25*					Masq	Att			Roch			London					Noble	
26*						Com			Ely			Cinque					Noble	
27*			(Noble)		Gent				St A			Cinque					Noble	
28*			(Noble)		Gent				Gent			Cinque					Noble	
29*					Gent				Priest			Cinque					Noble	

Actor	Pro.	1.1	1.2	1.3	1.4	2.1	2.2	2.3	2.4	3.1	3.2	4.1	4.2	5.1	5.2	5.3	5.4	Epi.
30*						Com			G. Ush				Spirit				Guard	
31*						Com			Serg				Spirit				Guard	
32*									Noble				Spirit					
33*									Noble									
34*+					Lady				Priest			Lady	Spirit				Lady	
35*+						Com			Gent			Duch	Spirit				Duch	
36*+						(Com)			K. Att	Wom			Spirit					
37*+						(Com)			K. Att	Wom								

ABBREVIATIONS AND REFERENCES

In all references, unless otherwise stated, the place of publication is London. Where I have been able to consult the earliest printed texts, I have done so; otherwise, I quote from editions generally held to be standard. Biblical references are taken from the Geneva Bible (1560) unless otherwise specified. Abbreviations of parts of speech are those used in the *OED*, 2nd edition.

ABBREVIATIONS

ABBREVIATIONS USED IN NOTES

F	the Shakespeare First Folio (see Editions Collated)
LN	Longer Note
n.	(in cross-references) commentary note
n.s.	new series
NT	New Testament
om.	omitted by
OT	Old Testament
Q	a quarto text
SD	stage direction
SP	speech prefix
subst.	substantively
this edn	a reading adopted for the first time in this edition
TLN	Through Line Number (lines in a document numbered consecutively as in copytext)
t.n.	the textual notes at the foot of the page
*	precedes commentary notes involving substantive readings altered from the text on which this edition is based (i.e. F)
( )	surrounding a F reading in textual notes indicates original spelling; surrounding an editor's or scholar's name indicates conjectural reading not actually included in an edited text

WORKS IN THE SHAKESPEARE CANON

References to works in the Shakespeare canon other than *Henry VIII* are to the Arden 3 editions published to date, namely *AC*, *H5*, *JC*, *KL*, *LLL*, *Oth*, *Son*, *TC*, *Tem*, *Tit* and *TNK*; otherwise, to William Shakespeare, *The Complete Works*, gen. eds Stanley Wells and Gary Taylor (Oxford, 1986). The following abbreviations are used for works in the Shakespeare canon and some attributed plays:

AC	*Antony and Cleopatra*
AW	*All's Well that Ends Well*
AYL	*As You Like It*
Car	*The History of Cardenio*
CE	*The Comedy of Errors*
Cor	*Coriolanus*
Cym	*Cymbeline*
DF	Lewis Theobald, *Double Falsehood*
E3	*King Edward III*
Ham	*Hamlet*
1H4	*King Henry IV, Part 1*
2H4	*King Henry IV, Part 2*
H5	*King Henry V*
1H6	*King Henry VI, Part 1*
2H6	*King Henry VI, Part 2*
3H6	*King Henry VI, Part 3*
H8	*King Henry VIII*
JC	*Julius Caesar*
KJ	*King John*
KL	*King Lear*
LC	*A Lover's Complaint*
LLL	*Love's Labour's Lost*
Luc	*The Rape of Lucrece*
MA	*Much Ado About Nothing*
Mac	*Macbeth*
MM	*Measure for Measure*
MND	*A Midsummer Night's Dream*
MV	*The Merchant of Venice*
MW	*The Merry Wives of Windsor*
Oth	*Othello*
Per	*Pericles*
PP	*The Passionate Pilgrim*
PT	*The Phoenix and the Turtle*
R2	*King Richard II*
R3	*King Richard III*
RJ	*Romeo and Juliet*
Son	*Sonnets*

STM	*The Book of Sir Thomas More*
TC	*Troilus and Cressida*
Tem	*The Tempest*
TGV	*The Two Gentlemen of Verona*
Tim	*Timon of Athens*
Tit	*Titus Andronicus*
TN	*Twelfth Night*
TNK	*The Two Noble Kinsmen*
TS	*The Taming of the Shrew*
VA	*Venus and Adonis*
WT	*The Winter's Tale*

WORKS IN THE FLETCHER CANON

References to works in the Fletcher canon other than *Henry VIII* are to Fredson Bowers (gen. ed.), *The Dramatic Works in the Beaumont and Fletcher Canon* (Cambridge, 1966–96), except where otherwise specified. For a comparative chronology of plays in the Shakespeare and Fletcher canons between 1603 and 1613, see Appendix 2; for a fuller, though tentative, chronology and attribution chart for plays in the Fletcher canon, see McMullan, *Unease*, 267–9. The following abbreviations are used for plays in the Fletcher canon:

BB	Fletcher, *Beggars' Bush*
Bon	Fletcher, *Bonduca*
Capt	Fletcher, with Beaumont, *The Captain*
Cha	Fletcher, *The Chances*
Cox	Fletcher & Beaumont, *The Coxcomb*
EB	Fletcher & Massinger, *The Elder Brother*
FO	Fletcher & Massinger, *The False One*
FP	Field & Fletcher, *Four Plays in One*
FSh	Fletcher, *The Faithful Shepherdess*
HMF	Field, Fletcher & Massinger, *The Honest Man's Fortune*
JVOB	Fletcher & Massinger, *Sir John Van Olden Barnavelt*
KM	Fletcher, Field & Massinger, *The Knight of Malta*
Knight	Beaumont, *The Knight of the Burning Pestle*
KNK	Beaumont & Fletcher, *A King and No King*
LC	Beaumont & Fletcher, rev. Massinger (?), *Love's Cure*
LFL	Fletcher & Massinger, *The Little French Lawyer*
LP	[Beaumont &?] Fletcher, *Love's Pilgrimage*
LS	Fletcher, *The Loyal Subject*
Maid's	Beaumont & Fletcher, *The Maid's Tragedy*
NVal	Middleton, *The Nice Valour* (re-ascribed)
Phil	Beaumont & Fletcher, *Philaster*
Pilg	Fletcher, *The Pilgrim*
Rollo	Fletcher, Massinger (& Field?), *Rollo, Duke of Normandy*
Rule	Fletcher, *Rule a Wife and Have a Wife*

T&T	Fletcher, Beaumont & Massinger, *Thierry and Theodoret*
Val	Fletcher, *Valentinian*
WGC	Fletcher, *The Wild Goose Chase*
WH	Beaumont with Fletcher, *The Woman Hater*
Wife	Fletcher, *A Wife for a Month*
WP	Fletcher, *The Woman's Prize*
WPl	Fletcher, *Women Pleased*
WWM	Fletcher, *Wit Without Money*

REFERENCES

EDITIONS OF SHAKESPEARE COLLATED

Alexander	*William Shakespeare: The Complete Works*, ed. Peter Alexander (1951)
Ard[1]	*The Famous History of the Life of King Henry VIII*, ed. C. Knox Pooler, Arden Shakespeare (1915)
Ard[2]	*King Henry VIII*, ed. R.A.Foakes, Arden Shakespeare (1957)
Bantam	*King John and Henry VIII*, ed. David Bevington with David Scott Kastan, James Hammersmith, and Robert Kean Turner (New York, 1988)
BBC	*Henry VIII*, BBC TV Shakespeare (1979) (includes text by Alexander)
Blair	*The Works of Shakespear*, ed. Hugh Blair, 8 vols (Edinburgh, 1753), vol. 5
Boswell	*The Plays and Poems of William Shakespeare*, ed. James Boswell, 21 vols (1821), vol. 19
Bowers	*Henry VIII*, ed. Fredson Bowers, in Bowers (gen. ed.), *The Dramatic Works in the Beaumont and Fletcher Canon* (Cambridge, 1989) vol. 7
Bullen	*The Works of William Shakespeare*, ed. A.H.Bullen, 10 vols (Stratford-upon-Avon, 1906), vol. 6
Cam	*The Works of William Shakespeare*, ed. W.G.Clark and W.A.Wright, 9 vols (Cambridge, 1863–6), vol. 6 (1865); reprinted in one vol. as Globe edn (1864)
Cam (1892)	*The Works of William Shakespeare*, ed. W.A.Wright, 9 vols (Cambridge, 1891–3), vol. 5 (1892)
Cam[1]	*King Henry the Eighth*, ed. J.C.Maxwell, New Shakespeare (Cambridge, 1962)
Cam[2]	*King Henry VIII*, ed. John Margeson, New Cambridge Shakespeare (Cambridge, 1990)
Campbell	Thomas Campbell, *The Dramatic Works of William Shakspeare, with Remarks on His Life and Writings*, 2 vols (1838)

Capell	*Mr. William Shakespeare His Comedies, Histories and Tragedies*, ed. Edward Capell, 10 vols (1767–8), vol. 7
Collier	*The Works of William Shakespeare*, ed. John Payne Collier, 9 vols (1842), vol. 5
Collier[2]	*The Plays of Shakespeare*, ed. John Payne Collier (1853)
Collier[3]	*Shakespeare's Comedies, Histories and Tragedies*, ed. John Payne Collier, '2nd edn', 6 vols (1858), vol. 4
Collier[4]	*The Plays and Poems of William Shakespeare*, ed. John Payne Collier, 8 vols (1878), vol. 5
Collier MS	Manuscript annotations (the subject of a forgery debate, but probably by Collier, not the alleged 'Old Corrector') in the Perkins–Collier–Devonshire copy of F2 in the Huntington Library; partially listed in Samuel Taylor Coleridge, *Seven Lectures on Shakespeare and Milton*, ed. John Payne Collier (1856), 231–3
Craig	*The Complete Works of Shakespeare*, ed. W.J.Craig (Oxford, 1892)
Craig-Bevington	*The Complete Works of Shakespeare*, ed. Hardin Craig (Chicago, Ill., 1951), revised by David Bevington (1973)
Deighton	*King Henry the Eighth*, ed. Kenneth Deighton, Macmillan English Classics (1895)
Dyce	*The Works of Shakespeare*, ed. Alexander Dyce, 6 vols (1857), vol. 4
Dyce[2]	*The Works of Shakespeare*, ed. Alexander Dyce, 9 vols (1864–7), vol. 5
F	*Comedies, Histories, and Tragedies*, The First Folio (1623)
F2	*Comedies, Histories, and Tragedies*, The Second Folio (1632)
F3	*Comedies, Histories, and Tragedies*, The Third Folio (1663)
F4	*Comedies, Histories, and Tragedies*, The Fourth Folio (1685)
Halliwell	*The Works of William Shakespeare*, ed. James O. Halliwell, 16 vols (1853–65), vol. 12
Hanmer	*The Works of Shakespear*, ed. Thomas Hanmer, 6 vols (Oxford, 1743–4), vol. 4
Harness	*The Dramatic Works of Shakespeare*, ed. Rev. W. Harness, 8 vols (1825), vol. 6
Henley	*The Works of William Shakespeare*, ed. W.E.Henley, 10 vols (1901–4), vol. 6
Hoeniger	*King Henry the Eighth*, ed. F. David Hoeniger, in Alfred Harbage (gen. ed.), *William Shakespeare: The Complete Works*, Pelican Shakespeare (Harmondsworth, England, 1966)
Hudson	*The Works of William Shakespeare*, ed. Henry N. Hudson, 11 vols (Boston, Mass., 1851–9), vol. 7

469

Hudson[2]	*The Works of William Shakespeare*, ed. Henry N. Hudson, 20 vols (Boston, Mass., 1881), vol. 12
Humphreys	*King Henry the Eighth*, ed. A.R.Humphreys, New Penguin Shakespeare (Harmondsworth, England, 1971)
Johnson	*The Plays of William Shakespeare*, ed. Samuel Johnson, 8 vols (1765), vol. 5
Keightley	*The Plays of William Shakespeare*, ed. Thomas Keightley, 6 vols (1864), vol. 4
Kittredge	*The Complete Works of Shakespeare*, ed. George L. Kittredge (Boston, Mass., 1936)
Knight	*The Pictorial Edition of the Works of William Shakespeare*, ed. Charles Knight, 8 vols (1838–43), vol. 2
Knight[3]	*The Pictorial Edition of the Works of William Shakespeare*, ed. Charles Knight, 'The Second Edition, Revised', 6 vols (1864–7), 'Histories', vol. 2
Malone	*The Plays and Poems of William Shakespeare*, ed. Edmond Malone, 10 vols (1790), vol. 7
Marshall	*The Works of William Shakespeare*, Henry Irving Marshall, 8 vols (1887–90), vol. 8
Munro	*The London Shakespeare*, ed. John Munro, 6 vols (1958), vol. 4
Neilson	*The Complete Dramatic and Poetic Works of William Shakespeare*, ed. William A. Neilson (Cambridge, 1906)
Neilson & Hill	*The Complete Plays and Poems of William Shakespeare*, ed. William A. Neilson and Charles J. Hill (Boston, Mass., 1942)
New Temple	*The Life of King Henry the Eighth*, ed. M.R.Ridley, New Temple Shakespeare (New Haven, Conn., 1925)
Nichol Smith	*King Henry the Eighth*, ed. D. Nichol Smith (1899), in the Warwick Shakespeare, ed. C.H.Herford *et al.* (1893–9)
Oxf	*William Shakespeare: The Complete Works*, ed. Stanley Wells, Gary Taylor *et al.* (Oxford, 1986)
Oxf (Orig)	*William Shakespeare: The Complete Works*, ed. Stanley Wells, Gary Taylor *et al.*, Original-Spelling Edition (Oxford, 1986)
Pope	*The Works of Shakespear*, ed. Alexander Pope, 6 vols (1723–5), vol. 4
Pope[2]	*The Works of Shakespear*, ed. Alexander Pope, 9 vols (1728), vol. 6
Rann	*The Dramatic Works of William Shakespeare*, ed. Joseph Rann, 6 vols (Oxford, 1786), vol. 4
Reed	*The Plays of William Shakespeare*, ed. Samuel Johnson, George Steevens and Isaac Reed, 5th edn, 21 vols (1803), vol. 15
Reed[2]	*The Plays of William Shakespeare*, ed. Samuel Johnson, George Steevens and Isaac Reed, 6th edn, 21 vols (1813), vol. 15

Riv	*The Riverside Shakespeare*, ed. G. Blakemore Evans (Boston, Mass., 1974)
Rowe	*The Works of Mr. William Shakespear*, ed. Nicholas Rowe, 6 vols (1709), vol. 4
Rowe²	*The Works of Mr. William Shakespeare*, ed. Nicholas Rowe, 2nd edn, 6 vols (1709), vol. 4
Rowe³	*The Works of Mr. William Shakespear*, ed. Nicholas Rowe, 8 vols (1714), vol. 5
Schoenbaum	*The Signet Shakespeare*, ed. S. Schoenbaum (New York, 1967)
Singer	*The Dramatic Works of Shakespeare*, ed. Samuel W. Singer, 10 vols (1826), vol. 7
Singer²	*The Dramatic Works of William Shakespeare*, ed. Samuel W. Singer, 10 vols (1856), vol. 7
Sisson	*William Shakespeare: The Complete Works*, ed. Charles J. Sisson (1954)
Staunton	*The Plays of Shakespeare*, ed. Howard Staunton, 3 vols (1858–60), vol. 2
Steevens	*The Plays of William Shakespeare*, ed. Samuel Johnson and George Steevens, 10 vols (1773), vol. 7 (otherwise known as *Var. 1773*)
Steevens²	*The Plays of William Shakespeare*, ed. Samuel Johnson and George Steevens, 2nd edn, 10 vols (1778), vol. 7 (otherwise known as *Var. 1778*)
Steevens–Reed	*The Plays of William Shakespeare*, ed. Samuel Johnson, George Steevens and Isaac Reed, 3rd edn, 10 vols (1785), vol. 7
Steevens–Reed²	*The Plays of William Shakespeare*, ed. Samuel Johnson, George Steevens and Isaac Reed, 4th edn, 15 vols (1793), vol. 11
Theobald	*The Works of Shakespeare*, ed. Lewis Theobald, 7 vols (1733), vol. 5
Theobald²	*The Works of Shakespeare*, ed. Lewis Theobald, 2nd edn, 8 vols (1740), vol. 5
Theobald³	*The Works of Shakespeare*, ed. Lewis Theobald, 3rd edn, 8 vols (1752), vol. 5
Warburton	*The Works of Shakespear*, ed. William Warburton, 8 vols (1747), vol. 5
Wright	*The Works of William Shakespeare*, ed. William Aldis Wright, Clarendon Shakespeare (Oxford, 1891)
White	*The Works of William Shakespeare*, ed. Richard Grant White, 12 vols (Boston, Mass., 1865), vol. 8
White²	*Mr. William Shakespeare's Comedies, Histories, Tragedies and Poems*, ed. Richard Grant White, 3 vols, Riverside Shakespeare (1883), vol. 2

471

Wordsworth	*Shakespeare's Historical Plays: Roman and English*, ed. Charles Wordsworth, 3 vols (Edinburgh, 1883), vol. 3
Yale	*The Life of King Henry the Eighth*, ed. John M. Berdan and C.F.Tucker Brooke, Yale Shakespeare (New Haven, Conn., 1925)

OTHER WORKS

Abbott	E.A.Abbott, *A Shakespearian Grammar*, 3rd edn (1870)
Adams	Thomas Adams, *The Gallant's Burden: A sermon preached at Paul's Cross, the twenty nine of March, being the fifth Sunday in Lent. 1612* (1612)
Alter	Iska Alter, ' "To reform and make fitt": *Henry VIII* and the making of "bad" Shakespeare', in Maurice Charney (ed.), *'Bad' Shakespeare: Revaluations of the Shakespeare Canon* (Rutherford, N.J., 1988), 176–86
Anderson	Judith H. Anderson, *Biographical Truth: The Representation of Historical Persons in Tudor–Stuart Writing* (New Haven, Conn., 1984)
Archer	Ian W. Archer, *The Pursuit of Stability: Social Relations in Elizabethan London* (Cambridge, 1991)
Armstrong	Isobel Armstrong, *Jane Austen: Mansfield Park*, Penguin Critical Studies (Harmondsworth, 1988)
Atkinson	Brooks Atkinson, review of Webster production, *New York Times*, 7 November 1946
Auberlen	Eckhard Auberlen, 'Shakespeare's break with the "Bluff-King-Harry" tradition', *Anglia*, 98 (1980), 319–47
Aughterson	Kate Aughterson (ed.), *Renaissance Woman: Constructions of Femininity in England* (1995)
Austen	Jane Austen, *Mansfield Park*, ed. Kathryn Sutherland (1996)
Bailey	Samuel Bailey, *On the Received Text of Shakespeare's Dramatic Writing and its Improvement* (1862)
Baillie	William Baillie, '*Henry VIII*: a Jacobean history', *SSt*, 2 (1979), 247–66
Baldwin	Thomas W. Baldwin, *Shakspere's Five-Act Structure* (Urbana, Ill., 1947)
Ball	Robert Hamilton Ball, *Shakespeare on Silent Film* (New York, 1968)
Barber	Charles Barber, *Early Modern English* (Edinburgh, 1996)
Barrett	Debbie L. Barrett, '*Pericles*, social redemption, and the iconography of "veritas filia temporis"', *Shakespeare Yearbook*, 2 (1991), 77–94
Barton	Anne Barton, *Essays, Mainly Shakespearean* (Cambridge, 1994)

Bate   Jonathan Bate, chapter 5, 'The Romantic Stage', in Bate &
                        Jackson, 92–111
Bate & Jackson   Jonathan Bate and Russell Jackson (eds), *Shakespeare: An
                        Illustrated Stage History* (Oxford, 1996)
Bawcutt   N.W.Bawcutt, *The Control and Censorship of Caroline
                        Drama: The Records of Sir Henry Herbert, Master of the
                        Revels 1623–73* (Oxford, 1996)
Bentley   G.E. Bentley, *The Profession of Dramatist in Shakespeare's
                        Time, 1590–1642* (Princeton, N.J., 1971)
Bernard   G.W.Bernard, *War, Taxation and Rebellion in Early Tudor
                        England: Henry VIII, Wolsey and the Amicable Grant of
                        1525* (Brighton, England, 1986)
Berni   Gelasino de Fiesoli [i.e. Francesco Berni], *Capitolo del
                        Gioco della Primiera* (Rome, 1534)
Bible   See *Geneva Bible*
Billington,   Michael Billington, *Peggy Ashcroft* (1988)
    Ashcroft
Billington,   Michael Billington, review of Doran production,
    Guardian   *The Guardian*, 29 November 1996
Birmingham Post   R.C.R., '"King Henry VIII" at Cambridge: a Festival
                        Theatre production: amusing methods of Mr. Terence
                        Gray', *Birmingham Post*, 11 February 1931
Birth of Merlin   Joanna Udall (ed.), *A Critical, Old-Spelling Edition of The
                        Birth of Merlin (Q 1662)*, Modern Humanities Research
                        Association Texts and Dissertations, no. 31 (1990)
Bishop   Thomas Bishop, *Shakespeare and the Theatre of Wonder*
                        (Cambridge, 1996)
Bliss   Lee Bliss, 'The wheel of fortune and the maiden phoenix
                        in Shakespeare's *King Henry the Eighth*', *ELH*, 42 (1975),
                        1–25
Booth   Michael Booth, *Victorian Spectacular Theatre 1850–1910*
                        (1981)
Booth, Stokes,   Michael R. Booth, John Stokes, Susan Bassnett, *Three
    Bassnett   Tragic Actresses: Siddons, Rachel, Ristori* (Cambridge, 1996)
Boswell-Stone   W.G.Boswell-Stone, *Shakespeare's Holinshed* (1896)
Bowers   Fredson Bowers (gen. ed.) *The Dramatic Works in the
                        Beaumont and Fletcher Canon*, 10 vols (Cambridge 1966–96)
Bowers, 'Multiple'   Fredson Bowers, 'Multiple authority: new problems and
                        concepts of copy-text', *Library*, 5th Series, 27 (1972), 81–115
Bowers, *Principles*   Fredson Bowers, *Principles of Bibliographical Description*
                        (Princeton, N.J., 1949)
Brathwait   Richard Brathwait, *The English Gentlewoman, drawn out to
                        the full body: expressing what habiliments do best attire her,
                        what ornaments do best adorn her, what complements do best
                        accomplish her* (1631)

473

Braunmuller	William Shakespeare, *King John*, ed. A.R.Braunmuller (Oxford, 1994)
Breight	Curt Breight, ' "Treason doth never prosper": *The Tempest* and the discourse of treason', *SQ*, 41 (1990), 1–28
Brightman	Thomas Brightman, *Revelation of the Revelation* (Leyden, Holland, 1615; first published in Latin, 1609)
Brooke	George C. Brooke, *English Coins: From the Seventh Century to the Present Day*, 3rd edn (1976)
Browne	Thomas Browne, *Religio Medici*, in C.A.Patrides (ed.), *Sir Thomas Browne: The Major Works* (Harmondsworth, England, 1977), 57–161
Bullough	Geoffrey Bullough (ed.), *Narrative and Dramatic Sources of Shakespeare*, vol. 4 (1962), *Later English History Plays*
Butler	Martin Butler, *Theatre and Crisis, 1632–1642* (Cambridge, 1984)
Byrne	Muriel St Clare Byrne, 'A Stratford Production: *Henry VIII*', *SS 3* (1950), 120–9
Camden	William Camden, *Remains of a Greater Work, Concerning Britain* (1605)
Campion	Edmund Campion, *History of Ireland* (1571), in James Ware (ed.), *The History of Ireland* (Dublin, 1633)
Candido	Joseph Candido, 'Fashioning Henry VIII: what Shakespeare saw in *When You See Me You Know Me*', *Cahiers Élisabéthains*, 23 (1983), 47–59
Cardano	Gerolamo Cardano, *The Book on Games of Chance (Liber de Ludo Aleae)* (1564), trans. Sydney Henry Gould, in Ore, 181–241
Cartwright	Robert Cartwright, *New Readings in Shakespeare; or, Proposed Emendations of the Text* (1866)
Cascardi	Anthony J. Cascardi (ed.) *Literature and the Question of Philosophy* (Baltimore, Ma., 1987)
Cave	Richard Cave, *Terence Gray and the Cambridge Festival Theatre*, 'Theatre in Focus' series (Cambridge and Teaneck, N.J., 1980)
Cavendish, EETS	George Cavendish, *The Life and Death of Cardinal Wolsey*, ed. Richard S. Sylvester, Early English Texts Society, no. 243 (Oxford, 1959)
Cavendish, *Negotiations*	George Cavendish, *The Negotiations of Thomas Wolsey, The Great Cardinal of England* (1641)
Cespedes	Frank V. Cespedes, ' "We are one in fortunes": the sense of history in *Henry VIII*', *ELR*, 10 (1980), 413–38
Chamberlain	*The Letters of John Chamberlain*, ed. Norman Egbert McClure, Memoirs of the American Philosophical Society, 2 vols (Philadelphia, Penn., 1939), vol. 12
Chambers, *ES*	E.K.Chambers, *The Elizabethan Stage*, 4 vols (Oxford, 1923)

Chambers, *Gleanings*	E.K.Chambers, *Shakespearean Gleanings* (Oxford, 1944)
Chapman	George Chapman, *The Memorable Mask of the two Honourable Houses or Inns of Court, the Middle Temple and Lincoln's Inn* (1613)
Chartier	Roger Chartier, *The Order of Books: Readers, Authors, and Libraries in Europe Between the Fourteenth and Eighteenth Centuries*, trans. Lydia G. Cochrane (Stanford, Calif., 1994)
Chew	Samuel C. Chew, *The Virtues Reconciled: An Iconographic Study* (Toronto, 1947)
Clapp	Henry Austin Clapp, review of Irving production of *Henry VIII*, *Advertiser*, 9 Jan. 1894
Clapp, *Reminiscences*	Henry Austin Clapp, *Reminiscences of a Dramatic Critic* (Boston, Mass., and New York, 1902)
Clare	Janet Clare, *'Art made tongue-tied by authority': Elizabethan and Jacobean Dramatic Censorship* (Manchester, 1990)
Clark	Cumberland Clark, *A Study of Shakespeare's Henry VIII* (1931, revised 1938)
Cole	Letter of Henry Bluett to Richard Weeks, 4 July 1613, in Maija Jansson Cole, 'A New Account of the Burning of the Globe', *SQ*, 32 (1981), 352
Collier, *Harlequinade*	Constance Collier, *Harlequinade: The Story of My Life* (1929)
Collinson	Patrick Collinson, *The Birthpangs of Protestant England: Religious and Cultural Change in the Sixteenth and Seventeenth Centuries* (1988)
Common Prayer	*The Book of Common Prayer* (1559)
Concordance	*Henry VIII: A Concordance to the Text of the First Folio*, Oxford Shakespeare Concordances (Oxford, 1971)
Cooper	Helen Cooper, 'Jacobean Chaucer: *The Two Noble Kinsmen* and Other Chaucerian Plays', in Theresa M. Krier (ed.), *Refiguring Chaucer in the Renaissance* (Gainesville, Fla., 1998), 189–209
Cope	Anthony Cope, *The History of two the most noble Captains in the World* (1544)
Coras	Jean de Coras, *Arrest Memorable du Parlement de Tholose contenant une Histoire prodigieuse* (Paris, 1572)
Coveney	Michael Coveney, review of Doran production, *Observer*, 1 December 1996
Cox	John D. Cox, '*Henry VIII* and the masque', *ELH*, 45 (1978), 390–409
Cox & Kastan	John D. Cox and David Scott Kastan (eds), *A New History of Early English Drama* (New York, 1997)

Crane	R.S.Crane, 'The vogue of *Guy of Warwick* from the close of the middle ages to the Romantic revival', *PMLA*, 30 (1915), 125–94
Cutts, 'Johnson'	John P. Cutts, 'Robert Johnson: King's musician in His Majesty's public entertainment', *Music and Letters*, 36 (1955), 110–25
Cutts, 'Song'	John P. Cutts, 'Shakespeare's song and masque hand in *Henry VIII*', *Shakespeare Jahrbuch*, 99 (1963), 184–95
Daily Mail	'E.B.', review of Tree production, *Daily Mail*, 2 September 1910
Daniel	Samuel Daniel, *The Complete Works*, ed. Alexander B. Grosart, 5 vols (1896)
Davenant	William Davenant, *The Prologue to His Majesty at the First Play Presented at the Cock-pit in Whitehall; Being Part of That Noble Entertainment Which Their Majesties Received Novemb. 19. from His Grace the Duke of Albermarle* (1660)
Davies	Thomas Davies, *Memoirs of the Life of David Garrick, Esq.*, 2 vols (1753)
Davis	Natalie Zemon Davis, *The Return of Martin Guerre* (Cambridge, Mass., 1983)
Dean	Paul Dean, 'Dramatic mode and historical vision in *Henry VIII*', *SQ*, 37 (1986), 175–89.
Dekker, *Dramatic Works*	Fredson Bowers (ed.), *The Dramatic Works of Thomas Dekker*, 3 vols (Cambridge, 1953–8)
Dekker, *Four Birds*	Thomas Dekker, *Four Birds of Noah's Ark* (1609)
Dekker, *Magnificent Entertainment*	Thomas Dekker, *The Magnificent Entertainment: Given to King* James, *Queen* Anne *his wife, and* Henry Frederick *the Prince, upon the day of his Majesty's Triumphant Passage . . . through his Honourable City . . . of* London (1603)
Dekker, *Match Me*	Thomas Dekker, *A Tragi-comedy Called, Match Me in London* (1631)
Dekker, *Whore*	Thomas Dekker, *The Whore of Babylon* (1607)
Dekker, *Wonderful Year*	Thomas Dekker, *The Wonderful year* (1603)
Dekker, *Work*	Thomas Dekker, *Work for Armourers: or, The Peace is Broken* (1609)
Dening	Greg Dening, *Mr. Bligh's Bad Language: Passion, Power, and Theatre on the Bounty* (Cambridge, 1992)
Dent	R.W.Dent, *Shakespeare's Proverbial Language: An Index* (Berkeley and Los Angeles, Calif., 1981)
Dent, *Exclusive*	R.W.Dent, *Proverbial Language in English Drama Exclusive of Shakespeare, 1495–1616: An Index* (Berkeley and Los Angeles, Calif., 1984)
Dobson, 'Costume drama'	Michael Dobson, 'Costume drama', draft chapter in Dobson and Nicola Watson, *England's Elizabeth: National Fictions of Elizabeth I, 1603–1990* (forthcoming)

Dobson, *National*	Michael Dobson, *The Making of the National Poet: Shakespeare, Adaptation and Authorship, 1600–1769* (Oxford, 1992)
Dod & Cleaver	R.C. (i.e. Robert Dod and John Cleaver), *A Godly Form of Household Government* (1598)
Donne	John Donne, *'The Elegies' and 'The Songs and Sonnets'*, ed. Helen Gardner (Oxford, 1965)
Downes	John Downes, *Roscius Anglicanus, or An Historical Review of the Stage* (1708)
Drayton 1610	Michael Drayton, *The Life and Death of the Lord Cromwell*, in *Mirror* (1610), 520–47
Drayton 1619	Michael Drayton, *The Legend of Great Cromwell*, in Drayton, *The Legends* (1619), 370–94
Drayton, *Poly-Olbion*	Michael Drayton, *Poly-Olbion* (1613), in Hebel, vol. 4
Drummond	William Drummond, *Tears on the Death of Moeliades* (third edition 1614)
Du Bartas	[Guillaume de Saluste du Bartas,] *Bartas his Device Weeks and Works translated by J. Sylvester* (1605)
Duchess of Suffolk	[Thomas Drue,] *The Life of the Duchess of Suffolk* (1631)
Duncan-Jones	E.E.Duncan-Jones, 'Queen Katherine's vision and Queen Margaret's dream', *N&Q*, 8 (1961), 142–3
Dutton	Richard Dutton, *Mastering the Revels: The Regulation and Censorship of English Renaissance Drama* (1991)
East Anglian Daily Times	'F.B.', review of Tree production, *East Anglian Daily Times*, 3 September 1910
Edmond	Mary Edmond, *Rare Sir William Davenant* (Manchester, 1987)
ELH	*A Journal of English Literary History*
ELR	*English Literary Renaissance*
Era	'Sir Herbert Tree's table talk', *Era*, 22 October 1910
Erasmus	*Collected Works of Erasmus*, vols 31–4: *Adages*, vol. 31, trans. Margaret Mann Philips, annotated R.A.B.Mynors; vols 32–4, trans. and annotated R.A.B.Mynors (Toronto, 1982–92)
Ewbank, 'David'	Inga-Stina Ewbank, 'The House of David in Renaissance drama: a comparative study', *RenD*, 8 (1965), 3–40
Ewbank, 'Triumph'	Inga-Stina Ewbank, 'The triumph of time in *The Winter's Tale*', in Maurice Hunt (ed.), *'The Winter's Tale': Critical Essays* (New York, 1995), 139–55
Fair Quarrel	Thomas Middleton and William Rowley, *A Fair Quarrel*, ed. George R. Price (Lincoln, Nebr., 1976); includes appendix of Rowley's additions to issue 2 of Q1
Farnham	W. Farnham, 'Colloquial contractions in Beaumont, Fletcher, Massinger and Shakespeare as a test of authorship', *PMLA*, 31 (1916), 326–58

Felman & Laub	Shoshana Felman and Dori Laub, *Testimony: Crises of Witnessing in Literature, Psychoanalysis, and History* (New York, 1992)
Felperin	Howard Felperin, *Shakespearean Romance* (Princeton, N.J., 1972)
Fenton	James Fenton, review of Davies production, *Sunday Times*, 19 June 1983
Field, *Caveat*	John Field, *A Caveat for Parson's Howlet* (1581)
Field, *Woman*	Nathan Field, *A Woman is a Weathercock* (1612)
Firth	Katharine R. Firth, *The Apocalyptic Tradition in Reformation Britain, 1530–1645* (Oxford, 1979)
Fisher	John Fisher, *Treatise concerning the fruitful sayings of David the king and prophet in the seven penitential psalms* (1509)
FitzGerald	Ann FitzGerald, review of Doran production, *Stage*, 5 December 1996
Fleay	F.G.Fleay, *Shakespeare Manual* (1878)
Fleay, *Chronicle*	F.G.Fleay, *A Chronicle History of the Life and Work of William Shakespeare* (1886)
Foakes, 'Folio'	R.A.Foakes, 'On the First Folio text of *Henry VIII*', *SB* 11 (1958), 55–60
Forrest	William Forrest, *The History of Grisild the Second*, ed. W.D.Macray, Roxburghe Club (1875)
Foucault, 'Author'	Michel Foucault, 'What is an author?' in Josué V. Harari, *Textual Strategies: Perspectives in Post-Structuralist Criticism* (Ithaca, N.Y., 1979), 141–60
Foucault, *Sexuality*	Michel Foucault, *The History of Sexuality*, vol. 2, *The Use of Pleasure*, trans. Robert Hurley (Harmondsworth, England, 1987)
Foulkes	Richard Foulkes, 'Tree's *Henry VIII*: expenditure, spectacle, and experiment', *Theatre Research International*, 3.1 (1977), 23–32
Fox	Alistair Fox, 'Prophecies and politics in the reign of Henry VIII', in Fox & Guy, 77–94
Fox & Guy	Alistair Fox and John Guy, *Reassessing the Henrician Age: Humanism, Politics and Reform, 1500–1550* (Oxford, 1986)
Foxe 1563	John Foxe, *Acts and Monuments (The Book of Martyrs)* (1563)
Foxe 1583	John Foxe, *Acts and Monuments*, 2 vols (1583)
Foxe 1596	John Foxe, *Acts and Monuments*, 2 vols (1596)
Foxe, *Christus*	John Foxe, *Christus Triumphans. Comœdia Apocalyptica*, ed. T.C. (1672)
Fuller	Thomas Fuller, *The Church-History of Britain: from the Birth of Jesus Christ Until the Year M. DC. XLVIII* (1655)
Gardiner	Samuel Rawson Gardiner, *History of England from the Accession of James I*, 2 vols (1863)

Gasper, *Dragon*   Julia Gasper, *The Dragon and the Dove: The Plays of Thomas Dekker* (Oxford, 1990)

Gasper, 'Reform'   'The Reformation plays on the public stage', in J.R.Mulryne and Margaret Shewring (eds), *Theatre and Government under the Early Stuarts* (Cambridge, 1993), 190–216

GD   Greg Doran, conversation with editor, 1996

Gell   Robert Gell, letter to Sir Martyn Stuteville, 9 August 1628, BL Harleian MS 383, fol. 65

Genest   John Genest, *Some Account of the English Stage, from the Restoration in 1660 to 1830*, 10 vols (Bath, 1832)

Geneva Bible   *The Bible and Holy Scriptures contained in the Old and New Testaments* (1560)

Glanville   Philippa Glanville, 'Cardinal Wolsey and the goldsmiths', in Gunn & Lindley, 131–48

Glover & Waller   *The Works of Francis Beaumont and John Fletcher*, ed. Arnold Glover and A.R.Waller, 10 vols (Cambridge, 1906–12)

Goldberg   Jonathan Goldberg, *Writing Matter: From the Hands of the English Renaissance* (Stanford, Calif., 1989)

Gooch & Thatcher   Bryan N. S. Gooch and David Thatcher, with Odean Long, *A Shakespeare Music Catalogue*, 5 vols (Oxford, 1991)

Gouge   William Gouge, *Of Domestical Duties: Eight Treatises* (1622)

Grady   Hugh Grady, 'Disintegration and its reverberations', in Jean I. Marsden (ed.), *The Appropriation of Shakespeare: Post-Renaissance Reconstructions of the Works and the Myth* (Hemel Hempstead, England, 1991), 111–27

Gray   Terence Gray, 'Historical Drama', *Festival Theatre Review*, vol. 2, no. 4 (1928), 6–8

Greenblatt   Stephen J. Greenblatt, *Renaissance Self-Fashioning: From More to Shakespeare* (Chicago, Ill., 1980)

Greg   W.W.Greg, *The Shakespeare First Folio: Its Bibliographical and Textual History* (Oxford, 1955)

Griffin   William J. Griffin, 'An omission in the folio text of *Richard III*', *Review of English Studies*, 13 (1937), 329–32

Gunn   S.J.Gunn, *Charles Brandon, Duke of Suffolk, c. 1484–1545* (Oxford, 1988)

Gunn & Lindley   S.J.Gunn and P.G.Lindley (eds), *Cardinal Wolsey: Church, State and Art* (Cambridge, 1991)

Gurr   Andrew Gurr, *The Shakespearean Stage, 1574–1642*, 3rd edn (Cambridge, 1992)

Gurr & Orrell   Andrew Gurr, with John Orrell, *Rebuilding Shakespeare's Globe* (1989)

Guthrie   Tyrone Guthrie, *A Life in the Theatre* (1960)

Guy   John Guy, 'Law, equity and conscience in Henrician juris-
                   tic thought', in Fox & Guy, 179–98
GWW   George Walton Williams, private communication
Gwyn   Peter Gwyn, *The King's Cardinal: The Rise and Fall of
                   Thomas Wolsey* (1990)
Hackett   Helen Hackett, *Virgin Mother, Maiden Queen: Elizabeth I
                   and the Cult of the Virgin Mary* (1995)
Haigh   Christopher Haigh, *English Reformation: Religion, Politics,
                   and Society under the Tudors* (Oxford, 1993)
Hainsworth   D.R.Hainsworth, *Stewards, Lords and People: The Estate
                   Steward and His World in Later Stuart England*
                   (Cambridge, 1992)
Hall   Edward Hall, *The Union of the two noble and illustre fami-
                   lies of Lancaster and York . . . to the reign of the high and
                   prudent prince king Henry the eighth* (1548)
Hamilton   Donna Hamilton, *Shakespeare and the Politics of Protestant
                   England* (Hemel Hempstead, 1992)
Hastings   *The Aristocracy, the State and the Local Community: The
                   Hastings Collection of Manuscripts from the Huntington
                   Library in California.* Part 1: The Hastings Correspondence
                   1477–1701 (Brighton, 1986)
Haughton   William Haughton, *Englishmen for My Money* (*c.* 1598/9;
                   printed 1616), ed. W.W.Greg, Malone Society Reprint
                   (Oxford, 1912)
Healy   Thomas Healy, 'History and judgement in *Henry VIII*',
                   in Richards & Knowles, 158–75
Hebel   J. William Hebel *et al.* (eds), *The Works of Michael
                   Drayton*, 5 vols (Oxford, 1933–56)
Herman   Peter C. Herman (ed.), *Rethinking the Henrician Era:
                   Essays on Early Tudor Texts and Contexts* (Urbana and
                   Chicago, Ill., 1994)
Herrick   Marvin T. Herrick, *Tragicomedy: Its Origins and Development
                   in Italy, France, and England*, Illinois Studies in Language
                   and Literature, vol. 39 (Urbana, Ill., 1955; reprinted 1962)
Hickson   Samuel Hickson, 'Who wrote Shakespeare's *Henry VIII*?'
                   N&Q, 43 (1850), 198
Hinman   Charlton Hinman, *The Printing and Proof-Reading of the
                   First Folio of Shakespeare*, 2 vols (Oxford, 1963)
Hobson 1949   Harold Hobson, review of Guthrie production, *Sunday
                   Times*, 24 July 1949
Hobson 1969   Harold Hobson, review of Nunn production, *Sunday
                   Times*, 12 October 1969
Holinshed   Raphael Holinshed, *The Third volume of Chronicles, begin-
                   ning at duke William the Norman . . . First compiled by
                   Raphael Holinshed, . . . Now newly . . . augmented* (1587)

Homilies	*Certaine Sermons appointed by the Queenes Maiestie, to be declared and read, by all Parsons, Vicars and Curates . . .* (1582)
Honigmann, *Lost*	E.A.J.Honigmann, *Shakespeare: The Lost Years* (Manchester, 1985)
Honigmann, *Stability*	E.A.J.Honigmann, *The Stability of Shakespeare's Text* (1965)
Honigmann, *Texts*	E.A.J.Honigmann, *The Texts of 'Othello' and Shakespearian Revision* (1996)
Hope, *Authorship*	Jonathan Hope, *The Authorship of Shakespeare's Plays: A Socio-linguistic study* (Cambridge, 1994)
Hope, 'English'	Jonathan Hope, 'Shakespeare's "Natiue English"', in Kastan, *Companion*, 239–55
Hope, 'Pronouns'	Jonathan Hope, 'Second person singular pronouns in records of Early Modern 'spoken' English', *Neophilologische Mitteilungen*, 94 (1993), 83–100
Howard & Rackin	Jean E. Howard and Phyllis Rackin, *Engendering a Nation: A Feminist Account of Shakespeare's English Histories* (1997)
Hoy, 1	Cyrus Hoy, 'The shares of Fletcher and his collaborators in the Beaumont and Fletcher canon (I)', *SB*, 8 (1956), 129–46
Hoy, 2	Cyrus Hoy, 'The shares of Fletcher and his collaborators in the Beaumont and Fletcher canon (II)', *SB*, 9 (1957), 143–62
Hoy, 3	Cyrus Hoy, 'The shares of Fletcher and his collaborators in the Beaumont and Fletcher canon (III)', *SB*, 11 (1958), 85–106
Hoy, 4	Cyrus Hoy, 'The shares of Fletcher and his collaborators in the Beaumont and Fletcher canon (IV)', *SB*, 12 (1959), 91–116
Hoy, 7	Cyrus Hoy, 'The shares of Fletcher and his collaborators in the Beaumont and Fletcher canon (VII)', *SB*, 15 (1962), 71–90
Hoy, 'Collaboration'	Cyrus Hoy, 'Critical and aesthetic problems of collaboration in Renaissance drama', *Research Opportunities in Renaissance Drama*, 19 (1976), 3–6
Hutson, 'Chivalry'	Lorna Hutson, 'Chivalry for merchants; or, Knights of Temperance in the Realms of Gold', *Journal of Medieval and Early Modern Studies*, 29 (1996), 29–59
Hutson, *Usurer's*	Lorna Hutson, *The Usurer's Daughter: Male Friendship and Fictions of Women in Sixteenth-Century England* (1994)
If You Know Not Me	[Thomas Heywood,] *If you know not me, you know no body: Or the troubles of Queen Elizabeth* (1606)
Isle of Gulls	[John Day,] *The Isle of Gulls* (1606)
Ives	E.W.Ives, *Anne Boleyn* (Oxford, 1986)

Jackson	Z. Jackson, *Shakespeare's Genius Justified: Being Restorations and Illustrations of Seven Hundred Passages in Shakespeare's Plays* (1819)
Jackson, *Attribution*	Macdonald P. Jackson, *Studies in Attribution: Middleton and Shakespeare* (Salzburg, 1979)
Jameson	Anna Jameson, *Characteristics of Women, Moral, Poetical and Historical*, 2 vols (1832)
Jervis	Swynfen Jervis, *Proposed Emendations of the Text of Shakespeare's Plays* (1860)
Jesson	Paul Jesson, 'Henry VIII', in Smallwood, 114–31
JH	Jonathan Hope, private communication
Jones & Stallybrass, 'Griselda'	Ann Rosalind Jones and Peter Stallybrass, '(In)alienable possessions: Griselda, clothing and the exchange of women', draft of chapter forthcoming in Jones & Stallybrass, *Clothing*
Jones & Stallybrass, *Clothing*	Ann Rosalind Jones and Peter Stallybrass, *Renaissance Clothing and the Materials of Memory* (forthcoming)
Jonson, *Poems*	*Ben Jonson*, ed. Ian Donaldson, 'The Oxford Authors' series (Oxford, 1985)
Jonson, *Works*	C.H.Herford, Percy Simpson and Evelyn Simpson, *Ben Jonson*, 11 vols (Oxford, 1925–52)
Jourda	Pierre Jourda, *Marguerite d'Angoulême*, 2 vols (Paris, 1930)
Kamps	Ivo Kamps, *Historiography and Ideology in Stuart Drama* (Cambridge, 1996)
Kastan, *Companion*	David Scott Kastan (ed.), *A Companion to Shakespeare* (Oxford, 1999)
Kastan, *Shapes*	David Scott Kastan, *Shakespeare and the Shapes of Time* (1982)
Kay	Dennis Kay, *Melodious Tears: The English Funeral Elegy from Spenser to Milton* (Oxford, 1990)
Keeble	N.H.Keeble (ed.), *The Cultural Identity of Seventeenth-Century Woman: A Reader* (1994)
Kellner	L. Kellner, *Restoring Shakespeare* (1925)
Kermode	Frank Kermode, 'Writing about Shakespeare', *London Review of Books*, 9 December 1999, 3–8
Kiefer	Frederick Kiefer, 'Churchyard's "Cardinal Wolsey" and its influence on Shakespeare's *Henry VIII*', *Essays in Literature (Western Illinois University)*, 6 (1979), 3–10
King, 'Henry'	John N. King, 'Henry VIII as David: The King's image and Reformation politics', in Herman, 78–92
King Johan	John Bale, *King Johan*, ed. John Pafford, Malone Society Reprints (Oxford, 1931)
King Leir	Anon., *The True Chronicle History of King Leir, and his three daughters, Gonorill, Ragan, and Cordella* (1605)
King, *Casting*	T.J.King, *Casting Shakespeare's Plays: London Actors and their Roles, 1590–1642* (Cambridge, 1992)

King, *Tudor*	John N. King, *Tudor Royal Iconography: Literature and Art in an Age of Religious Crisis* (Princeton, N.J., 1989)
King, *Vitis Palatina*	John King, *Vitis Palatina: A Sermon Appointed to Be preached at Whitehall* (1614)
Knecht	Robert Knecht, 'The Field of the Cloth of Gold', in Charles Giry-Deloison (ed.), *François Ier et Henry VIII: deux princes de la Renaissance (1515–1547)* (Villeneuve d'Ascq and London, 1995)
Knight, *Crown*	G. Wilson Knight, *The Crown of Life: Essays in Interpretation of Shakespeare's Final Plays* (Oxford, 1947)
Knight, *Principles*	G. Wilson Knight, *Principles of Shakespearian Production* (1936)
Knight, 'Propaganda'	G. Wilson Knight, 'A Royal Propaganda', unpublished typescript (1956)
Knowles	Ronald Knowles (ed.), *Shakespeare and Carnival: After Bakhtin* (1998)
Knutson, *Company*	Roslyn L. Knutson, *The Repertory of Shakespeare's Company, 1594–1613* (Fayetteville, Ark., 1991)
Knutson, 'Repertory'	Roslyn L. Knutson, 'The Repertory', in Cox & Kastan, 461–80
Lake	David J. Lake, *The Canon of Thomas Middleton's Plays: Internal Evidence for the Major Problems of Authorship* (Cambridge, 1975)
Lamb	Charles Lamb, *Specimens of English Dramatic Poets, Who Lived About the Time of Shakespeare* (1808)
Langbaine	Gerard Langbaine, *An Account of the English Dramatic Poets* (Oxford, 1691)
Lapotaire	Jane Lapotaire, 'Queen Katherine in *Henry VIII*', in Smallwood, 132–51
Laqueur	Thomas Laqueur, *Making Sex: Body and Gender from the Greeks to Freud* (Cambridge, Mass., 1990)
Law	R.A.Law, 'The Double Authorship of *Henry VIII*', *Studies in Philology*, 56 (1959), 471–88
Leech	Clifford Leech, 'The structure of the last plays', *SS* 11 (1958), 19–30
Leigh	William Leigh, *Queen Elizabeth, Paralleled in her Princely virtues, with David, Joshua, and Hezekia* (1612)
Lindley, *Howard*	David Lindley, *The Trials of Frances Howard: Fact and Fiction at the Court of King James* (1993)
Lindley, *Masque*	David Lindley (ed.), *The Court Masque* (Manchester, 1984)
Linthicum	Marie Channing Linthicum, *Costume in the Drama of Shakespeare and His Contemporaries* (Oxford, 1936)
Liverpool Post	'Shakespearean effects', *Liverpool Post*, 4 February 1931
Lodge & Greene	Thomas Lodge and Robert Greene, *A Looking-Glass for London and England* (1594)

London Stage	Emmett L. Avery, Charles Beecher Hogan, A.H.Scouten, George Winchester Stone and William Van Lennep (eds), *The London Stage 1660–1800: A Calendar of Plays, Entertainments, and Afterpieces*, 5 parts in 11 vols (Carbondale, Ill., 1960–8)
Long	John H. Long, *Shakespeare's Use of Music: The Histories and Tragedies* (Gainesville, Fla., 1971)
Lords' Masque	Thomas Campion, *The Lords' Masque*, ed. I.A.Shapiro, in *A Book of Masques in Honour of Allardyce Nicoll* (Cambridge, 1967), 95–123
Lorkins	Thomas Lorkins, letter to Sir Thomas Puckering, 30 June 1613, BL Harleian MS 7002, fol. 268
LP	Lois Potter, private communication
LP	*Letters and Papers, Foreign and Domestic, of the Reign of Henry VIII*, ed. J.S.Brewer and J. Gairdner (1862–1932)
Lucky Chance	Aphra Behn, *The Lucky Chance, or An Alderman's Bargain* (1687)
Luttrell	Narcissus Luttrell, *A Brief Historical Relation of State Affairs*, 6 vols (Oxford, 1857)
McClure	Norman E. McClure (ed.), *The Letters and Epigrams of Sir John Harington* (Philadelphia, Penn., 1930)
McIlwain	Charles H. McIlwain, *The Political Works of James I* (Cambridge, Mass., 1918)
McKenzie	D.F.McKenzie, 'Stretching a point: or, the case of the spaced-out comps', *SB*, 37 (1984), 106–21
McMullan, 'Editing'	Gordon McMullan, '"Our whole life is like a play": collaboration and the problem of editing', *Textus*, 9 (1996), 437–60
McMullan, 'History'	Gordon McMullan, 'Shakespeare and the end of history', *Essays and Studies*, 48 (1995), 16–37
McMullan, 'Reforming'	Gordon McMullan, '"Thou hast made me now a man": reforming man(ner)liness in *Henry VIII*', in Richards & Knowles, 40–56
McMullan, 'Swimming'	Gordon McMullan, 'Swimming on bladders: the dialogics of Reformation in Shakespeare & Fletcher's *Henry VIII*', in Knowles, 211–27
McMullan *Unease*	Gordon McMullan, *The Politics of Unease in the Plays of John Fletcher* (Amherst, Mass., 1994)
McMullan & Hope	Gordon McMullan and Jonathan Hope (eds), *The Politics of Tragicomedy: Shakespeare and After* (1992)
Magnificence	John Skelton, *Magnificence*, ed. Paula Neuss (Manchester, 1980)
Magnusson	A.Lynne Magnusson, 'The rhetoric of politeness and *Henry VIII*', *SQ*, 43 (1992), 391–409

Manifold	John S. Manifold, *Music in English Drama from Shakespeare to Purcell* (1956)
Marguerite, *Godly*	Marguerite of Angoulême, *A Godly Meditation of the Christian Soul*, trans. Elizabeth I, ed. John Bale (Marburg, Germany, 1548)
Marguerite, *Miroir*	Marguerite of Angoulême, *Miroir de l'âme pécheresse* (Paris, 1531)
Marlowe	*The Complete Works of Christopher Marlowe*, ed. Fredson Bowers, 2 vols (Cambridge, 1973, 1981)
Marshall, *Theatre*	Norman Marshall, *The Other Theatre* (1947)
Marston, *Antonio I*	John Marston, *The History of Antonio and Mellida, The first part* (1602)
Marston, *Malcontent*	John Marston, *The Malcontent* (1604)
Mason	John Monck Mason, *Comments on the Last Edition of Shakespeare's Plays* (1785)
Masten, *Intercourse*	Jeffrey Masten, *Textual Intercourse: Collaboration, Authorship, and Sexualities in Renaissance Drama* (Cambridge, 1997)
Masten, 'Playwrighting'	Jeffrey Masten, 'Playwrighting: authorship and collaboration', in Cox & Kastan, 357–82
Maxwell	Baldwin Maxwell, *Studies in Beaumont, Fletcher, and Massinger* (Chapel Hill, N.C., 1939)
Melbanke	Brian Melbanke, *Philotimus: The War betwixt Nature and Fortune* (1583)
Merriam	Thomas Merriam, 'The Authorship of *Sir Thomas More*', *Association for Literary and Linguistic Computing Bulletin*, 10 (1982), 1–8
Middleton, *Chaste Maid*	Thomas Middleton, *A Chaste Maid in Cheapside*, ed. Alan Brissenden, 'The New Mermaids' series (1968)
Middleton, *Triumphs*	Thomas Middleton, *The Triumphs of Truth* (1613)
Milhous & Hume	John Downes, *Roscius Anglicanus*, ed. Judith Milhous and Robert D. Hume (1987)
Millgate	Michael Millgate, *Testamentary Acts: Browning, Tennyson, James, Hardy* (Oxford, 1992)
Mirror 1587	John Higgins *et al.*, *The Mirror for Magistrates, wherein may be seen, by examples passed in this Realm, with how grievous plagues vices are punished in great Princes and Magistrates* (1587)
Mirror 1610	John Higgins *et al.*, *A Mirror for Magistrates: being a True Chronicle History of the Untimely Falls of . . . Princes and men of note* (includes Thomas Churchyard's *Life of Wolsey* and Michael Drayton's *Legend of Great Cromwell*) (1610)
Moore	J.K.Moore, *Primary Materials Relating to Copy and Print in English Books of the 16th and 17th Centuries*, Oxford Bibliographical Society: Occasional Papers, no. 24 (Oxford, 1992)

Muir   Kenneth Muir, *Last Periods of Shakespeare, Racine, and Ibsen* (Liverpool, 1961)

N&Q   *Notes and Queries*

Nashe   *The Works of Thomas Nashe*, ed. Ronald B. McKerrow, 5 vols (Oxford, 1904–10; reprinted 1958)

Nehemas, 'Author'   Alexander Nehemas, 'The postulated author: critical monism as a regulative ideal', *Critical Inquiry*, 8 (1981), 133–49

Nehemas, 'Writer'   Alexander Nehemas, 'Writer, text, work, author', in Cascardi, 267–91

Nevo   Ruth Nevo, 'Shakespeare's comic remedies', in Maurice Charney (ed.), *Shakespearean Comedy* (New York, 1980), 3–15

Newman   John Newman, 'Cardinal Wolsey's collegiate foundations', in Gunn & Lindley, 103–15

New Grove   Stanley Sadie (ed.), *The New Grove Dictionary of Music and Musicians*, 20 vols (1980)

New York Evening Mail   Review of Tree production, *New York Evening Mail*, 15 March 1916

Noling   Kim Noling, ' "Grubbing up the stock": dramatizing queens in *Henry VIII*', *SQ*, 39 (1988), 291–306

Norbrook, 'Reformation'   David Norbrook, 'The reformation of the masque', in Lindley, *Masque*, 94–110

Norbrook, 'Truth'   David Norbrook, ' "The Masque of Truth": court entertainments and international Protestant politics in the early Stuart period', *Seventeenth Century*, 1 (1986), 81–110

Odell   George C. D. Odell, *Shakespeare from Betterton to Irving*, 2 vols (1921)

OED   *Oxford English Dictionary*, 2nd edn, prepared by J.A.Simpson and E.S.C.Weiner (Oxford, 1989)

Old Law   Philip Massinger, Thomas Middleton and William Rowley, *The Old Law: or, A New Way to Please You* (1656)

Old Maid   'Mary Singleton, Spinster' [i.e. Frances Brooke], *The Old Maid* (1764)

Onions   C.T.Onions, *A Shakespeare Glossary*, revised Robert D. Eagleson (Oxford, 1986)

Oras   Ants Oras, 'Extra monosyllables in *Henry VIII* and the problem of authorship', *Journal of English and Germanic Philology*, 52 (1953), 198–213

Ore   Oystein Ore, *Cardano, The Gambling Scholar* (Princeton, N.J., 1953)

Orgel   William Shakespeare, *The Winter's Tale*, ed. Stephen Orgel (Oxford, 1996)

Orrell, *Human*   John Orrell, *The Human Stage: English Theatre Design, 1567–1640* (Cambridge, 1988)

Orrell, *Quest*	John Orrell, *The Quest for Shakespeare's Globe* (Cambridge, 1983)
Palfrey	Simon Palfrey, *Late Shakespeare: A New World Of Words* (Oxford, 1997)
Parkes	M.B.Parkes, *The Medieval Manuscripts of Keble College, Oxford* (1979)
Parlett	David Parlett, *A History of Card Games* (Oxford, 1991)
Partridge	A.C.Partridge, *The Problem of Henry VIII Reopened* (Cambridge, 1949)
Patterson, 'All Is True'	Annabel Patterson, ' "All is True": negotiating the past in *Henry VIII*', in R.B.Parker and S.P.Zitner (eds), *Elizabethan Theater: Essays in Honour of S. Schoenbaum* (Newark, Del., 1996), 147–66
Patterson, *Censorship*	Annabel Patterson, *Censorship and Interpretation: The Conditions of Writing and Reading in Early Modern England* (Madison, Wis., 1984)
Patterson, *Holinshed*	Annabel Patterson, *Reading Holinshed's 'Chronicles'* (Chicago, Ill., 1994)
Paul	John E. Paul, *Katherine of Aragon and Her Friends* (1966)
Peacham	Henry Peacham, *The Period of Mourning . . . In Memory of the Late Prince* (1613)
Pepys	*The Diary of Samuel Pepys*, ed. Robert Latham and William Matthews, 11 vols (1970–83)
Platt	Peter Platt, *Reason Diminished: Shakespeare and the Marvelous* (Lincoln, Nebr., 1997)
PMLA	*Publications of the Modern Language Association of America*
Pollard	Alfred W. Pollard, 'Elizabethan spelling as a literary and bibliographical clue', *Library*, 4th series, 4 (1923), 1–8
Prayer Book	*The Book of Common Prayer, and Administration of the Sacraments, And Other Rites and Ceremonies of the Church of England* (1605 edn)
Price, *Lamentations*	Daniel Price, *Lamentations for the death of the late Illustrious Prince Henry* (1613)
Price, *London's*	Sampson Price, *London's Warning by Laodicea's Luke-warmness* (1613)
Psalter	*The Psalter or Psalms of David, after the translation of the great Bible* (1566 edn)
Queen's	*The Queen's Majesty's Passage through the City of London to Westminster the Day before her Coronation* (1559)
Readings	Bill Readings, 'When did the Renaissance begin? the Henrician court and the Shakespearean stage', in Herman, 283–302
Réau	Louis Réau, *Iconographie de l'art chrétien*, vol. 2 (Paris, 1956)
Rehearsal	[George Villiers, 2nd Duke of Buckingham,] *The Rehearsal* (1672)

RenD   *Renaissance Drama*
Review   [Christopher Christian?] 'Bringing Shakespeare back into the
                theatre', *Festival Theatre Review*, vol. 4, no. 67 (1931), 1–6
Richards &   Jennifer Richards and James Knowles (eds), *Shakespeare's
  Knowles   Late Plays: New Readings* (Edinburgh, 1999)
Richmond   Hugh M. Richmond, *Henry VIII*, 'Shakespeare in
                Performance' series (Manchester, 1994)
Ridley, *Henry*   Jasper Ridley, *Henry VIII* (1984)
Ridley, *Statesman*   Jasper Ridley, *The Statesman and the Fanatic: Thomas
                Wolsey and Thomas More* (1982)
Rigby, *Eastern*   Charles Rigby, review of Gray production, *Eastern Daily
  Daily Press*   Press*, 11 February 1931; reprinted in Rigby, *Maddermarket*,
                103–8
Rigby,   Charles Rigby, *Maddermarket Mondays* (Norwich, 1933)
  Maddermarket
Rosenblatt   Jason P. Rosenblatt, 'Aspects of the Incest Problem in
                Hamlet', *SQ*, 29 (1978), 349–64
Round   Nicholas G. Round, 'Rojas' Old Bawd and Shakespeare's
                Old Lady: Celestina and the Anglican Reformation',
                Celestinesca, 21 (1997), 93–110
RP   Richard Proudfoot, private communication
Rudnytsky   Peter L. Rudnytsky, '*Henry VIII* and the deconstruction
                of history', *SS 43* (1991), 43–58
Sahel   Pierre Sahel, 'The strangeness of a dramatic style: rumour
                in *Henry VIII*', *SS 38* (1985), 145–51
St German   Christopher St German, *Doctor and Student* (1531), in
                T.F.T.Plucknett and J.L.Barton (eds), *St. German's Doctor
                and Student* (1974)
Sainte Marthe   Charles de Sainte Marthe, *Oraison funèbre de la mort de
                l'incomparable Marguerite Reine de Navarre et duchesse
                d'Alençon* (Paris, 1550), quoted in Jourda, 1.337
Salmon   Vivian Salmon, 'Thomas Harriot (1560–1621) and the
                English origins of Algonkian linguistics', in Salmon,
                *Language and Society in Early Modern England: Selected
                Essays 1981–1994*, ed. Konrad Koerner (Amsterdam,
                1996), 143–72
Saunders   J.W.Saunders, 'Vaulting the rails', *SS 7* (1954), 69–81
Saxl   Fritz Saxl, '*Veritas filia temporis*', in R. Klibansky and
                H.J.Paton (eds), *Philosophy and History: Essays Presented
                to Ernst Cassirer* (Oxford, 1936)
SB   *Studies in Bibliography*
Scarisbrick   J.J.Scarisbrick, *Henry VIII* (1968)
Schäfer   Jürgen Schäfer, *Documentation in the OED: Shakespeare
                and Nashe as Test Cases* (Oxford, 1980)
Schlueter   June Schlueter, 'Rereading the Peacham drawing', *SQ*, 50
                (1999), 171–84

Schoch   Richard W. Schoch, *Shakespeare's Victorian Stage: Performing
                        History in the Theatre of Charles Kean* (Cambridge, 1998)
Scott   Clement Scott, review of Irving production, *Daily
                        Telegraph*, 6 January 1892
Seed   *The Seed*, trans. I.M.Lonie, in G.E.R.Lloyd (ed.), *Hippocratic
                        Writings*, trans. J. Chadwick, W.N.Mann, I.M.Lonie and
                        E.T.Withington (Harmondsworth, England, 1978)
Shaheen   Naseeb Shaheen, *Biblical References in Shakespeare's
                        History Plays* (Newark, Del., 1989)
Shaughnessy   Robert Shaughnessy, ' "Ragging the Bard": Terence Gray,
                        Shakespeare, and *Henry VIII*', *Theatre Notebook*, 51
                        (1997), 92–111
Sider   John W. Sider, 'Shakespeare's cornets', *SQ*, 22 (1971),
                        401–4
Sinden   Donald Sinden, *Laughter in the Second Act* (1986)
Sisson, *Readings*   C.J.Sisson, *New Readings in Shakespeare*, 2 vols (Cambridge,
                        1956), vol. 2
Slights   Camille Wells Slights, 'The politics of conscience in *All Is
                        True* (or *Henry VIII*)', *SS 43* (1991), 59–68
Smallwood   Robert Smallwood (ed.), *Players of Shakespeare 4: Further
                        Essays in Shakespearian Performance by Players with the
                        Royal Shakespeare Company* (Cambridge, 1998)
Smith   John Hazel Smith (ed.), *Two Latin Comedies by John Foxe
                        the Martyrologist: Titus et Gesippus; Christus Triumphans*
                        (Ithaca, N.Y., 1973)
Spedding   James Spedding, 'Who Wrote Shakespere's *Henry VIII*?'
                        Gentleman's Magazine, n.s. 34 (1850), 115–24, 381–2
Speed   John Speed, *The Theatre of the Empire of Great Britain*, 2
                        vols (1611)
Spenser,   Edmund Spenser, *The Faerie Queene* (1590)
  Faerie Queene
Spenser,   Edmund Spenser, *The Shepherd's Calendar*, in *Poetical
  Shepherd's   Works*, ed. J.C.Smith and E. de Sélincourt (Oxford, 1912)
Spikes   Judith Doolin Spikes, 'The Jacobean history play and the
                        myth of the Elect Nation', *RenD*, 8 (1977), 117–49.
Sprague, *Actors*   Arthur Colby Sprague, *Shakespeare and the Actors: The Stage
                        Business in His Plays (1660–1905)* (Boston, Mass., 1945)
Sprague, *Histories*   Arthur Colby Sprague, *Shakespeare's Histories: Plays for
                        the Stage* (1964)
SB   *Studies in Bibliography*
SQ   *Shakespeare Quarterly*
SS   *Shakespeare Survey*
SSt   *Shakespeare Studies*
Stallybrass   Peter Stallybrass, 'Shakespeare, the individual, and the
                        text', in Lawrence Grossberg, Cary Nelson and Paula
                        Treichler (eds), *Cultural Studies* (New York, 1992), 593–610

Stern	Virginia F. Stern, *Gabriel Harvey: His Life, Marginalia and Library* (Oxford, 1979)
Stow 1580	[John Stow,] *The Chronicles of England, from Brute unto this present year of Christ* (1580)
Stow 1592	[John Stow,] *The Annals of England, faithfully collected out of the most authentical Authors . . .* (1592)
Stow 1615	*The Annals, or General Chronicle of England, begun first by master John Stow, and after him continued . . . by* Edmond Howes, gentleman (1615)
Stow, *Survey*	John Stow, *A Survey of London* (1598)
Street & Giles	Richard L. Street, Jr, and Howard Giles, 'Speech accommodation theory: a social and cognitive approach to language and speech behaviour', in Michael E. Roloff and Charles R. Berger (eds), *Social Cognition and Communication* (Beverly Hills, Calif., 1982), 193–226
Strong	Roy Strong, *Henry, Prince of Wales, and England's Lost Renaissance* (1986)
Stuart	Arabella Stuart, letter to James I, BL Harleian MS 7003, fol. 82
Swayze	Margaret Swayze, 'A history of the literary criticism and stage production of *Henry VIII*', University of Birmingham Ph.D thesis, 1973
Tate	William Tate, 'James I and the Queen of Sheba', *ELR*, 26 (1996), 561–85
Taylor 1612	John Taylor, 'the Water Poet', *The Sculler* (1612)
Taylor 1653	John Taylor, 'the Water Poet', *A Short Relation of a Long Journey* (1653)
Taylor, *Prophecy*	Rupert Taylor, *The Political Prophecy in England* (New York, 1911; reprinted 1967)
Taylor, 'Shrinking'	Gary Taylor, 'The shrinking Compositor A of the Shakespeare First Folio', *SB*, 34 (1981), 96–117
Taylor & Jowett	Gary Taylor and John Jowett, *Shakespeare Reshaped, 1606–23* (Oxford, 1993)
Thirlby	Styan Thirlby, unpublished conjectures in correspondence with Theobald and Warburton, transcribed in John Nichols, *Illustrations of the Literary History of the Eighteenth Century*, 8 vols (1817–58), vol. 2, 189–647
Thomas, Lord Cromwell	*The True Chronicle History of the whole life and death of Thomas Lord Cromwell . . . Written by* W.S. (1602; reprinted 1613)
Thorndike	Ashley Thorndike, *The Influence of Beaumont and Fletcher on Shakspere* (Worcester, Mass., 1901)
Thorpe	James Thorpe, *Principles of Textual Criticism* (San Marino, Calif., 1972)
Thurley	Simon Thurley, *The Lost Palace of Whitehall* (1998)

Tilley	Morris Palmer Tilley, *A Dictionary of the Proverbs in England in the Sixteenth and Seventeenth Centuries* (Ann Arbor, Mich., 1950)
Times	Review of Tree production, *Times*, 2 September 1910
Tree, *Henry*	Herbert Beerbohm Tree, *Henry VIII and His Court* (1910)
Tree, *Thoughts*	Herbert Beerbohm Tree, *Thoughts and After-Thoughts*, 3rd edn (1915)
Trewin, *Birmingham Post*	J.C.Trewin, review of Davies production, *Birmingham Post*, 15 June 1983
Trewin, *Lady*	J.C.Trewin, review of Guthrie production, *Lady*, 4 August 1949
TxC	Stanley Wells and Gary Taylor, with John Jowett and William Montgomery, *William Shakespeare: A Textual Companion* (Oxford, 1987)
Tyndale	William Tyndale, *The obedience of a Christian man and how Christian rulers ought to govern* (Antwerp, 1528)
Tyrwhitt	Thomas Tyrwhitt, *Observations and Conjectures upon Some Passages of Shakespeare* (Oxford, 1766)
Underdown	David Underdown, *Fire from Heaven: Life in an English Town in the Seventeenth Century* (1992)
Usher	Shaun Usher, review of Doran production, *Daily Mail*, 29 November 1996
Valiant Acts	Christopher Ockland, *The Valiant Acts and victorious Battles of the English Nation*, 2 vols (1585)
Variety	Review of Webster production, *Variety*, 13 November 1946
Vaughan	H.H.Vaughan, *New Readings in Shakespeare* (1886)
Virtue Betrayed	John Banks, *Virtue Betrayed, or Anna Bullen* (1682)
Wager, *Enough*	William Wager, *Enough is As Good As a Feast*, ed. R. Mark Benbow (1968)
Wager, *Longer*	William Wager, *A Very Merry and Pithy Comedy, called The Longer thou livest, the more fool thou art* (1580)
Walker	W.S.Walker, *A Critical Examination of the Text of Shakespeare*, 3 vols (1860)
Walker, *Sermon*	William Walker, *A Sermon Preached at the Funerals of . . . William, Lord Russell* (1614)
Warner	William Warner, *Albion's England* (1612)
Webbe	George Webbe, *The Bride Royal, or The Spiritual Marriage between Christ and his Church* (1613)
Webster	Margaret Webster, *The Same Only Different: Five Generations of a Great Theatre Family* (1969)
Webster, *Works*	F.L.Lucas (ed.), *The Complete Works of John Webster*, 4 vols (1927)
Whalley	Peter Whalley, *An Enquiry into the Learning of Shakespeare* (1748)

491

When You See Me	Samuel Rowley, *When You See Me, You Know Me, Or the famous Chronicle History of king Henry the eighth, with the birth and virtuous life of Edward Prince of Wales, As it was played by the high and mighty Prince of Wales his servants* (1605)
Wickham	Glynne Wickham, 'The dramatic structure of Shakespeare's *King Henry the Eighth*: an essay in rehabilitation', in *British Academy Shakespeare Lectures, 1980–89*, introduced by E.A.J.Honigmann (Oxford, 1993)
Wiggins	Martin Wiggins, chapter 2, 'The King's Men and after', in Bate & Jackson, 23–44
Willet, *Fruitful*	Andrew Willet, *Certain Fruitful Meditations upon the 122. Psalm*, appended to his *Ecclesia Triumphans: that is, The Joy of the English Church, for the Happy Coronation of . . . James* (1604; 2nd edn 1614)
Willet, *Salomon's*	Andrew Willet, *A Treatise of Salomon's Marriage* (1612)
Wilson	*When You See Me, You Know Me*, by Samuel Rowley (1605), ed. F.P.Wilson, Malone Society Reprints (Oxford, 1952)
Wiseman	Susan Wiseman, *Drama and Politics in the English Civil War* (Cambridge, 1998)
Wither	George Wither, *Abuses Stripped, and Whipped, or Satirical Essays* (1613)
Worden	Blair Worden, 'Shakespeare and politics', *SS* 44 (1992), 1–15
Wotton	*The Life and Letters of Sir Henry Wotton*, ed. Logan Pearsall Smith, 2 vols (Oxford, 1907)
Wotton/Bacon	*Letters of Sir Henry Wotton to Sir Edmund Bacon* (1661)
Woudhuysen	Henry Woudhuysen, '*King Henry VIII* and "All Is True"', *N&Q*, 31 (1984), 217–18
Wright, *Metrical*	George T. Wright, *Shakespeare's Metrical Art* (Berkeley, Calif., 1988)
Wyatt	Sir Thomas Wyatt, *Collected Poems*, ed. R.A.Rebholz (Harmondsworth, England, 1978)
Yates	Frances Yates, *Shakespeare's Last Plays: A New Approach* (1975)
Young	C.B.Young, 'Stage-history' (1960), in Cam[1], xxxviii–l
Zim	Rivkah Zim, *English Metrical Psalms: Poetry as Praise and Prayer, 1535–1601* (Cambridge, 1987)
Zupitza	Julius Zupitza (ed.), *The Romance of Guy of Warwick*, Early English Texts Society, extra series, 42, 49, 59 (1883, 1887, 1891)

MODERN PRODUCTIONS CITED

Atkins	Old Vic Theatre, London, directed by Robert Atkins, 1924
Chichester	Chichester Festival Theatre, directed by Ian Judge, 1991
Davies	Royal Shakespeare Company (RSC), Royal Shakespeare Theatre, Stratford-upon-Avon, directed by Howard Davies, 1983
Doran	Royal Shakespeare Company, Swan Theatre, Stratford-upon-Avon and Young Vic Theatre, London, directed by Greg Doran, 1996
Gray	Festival Theatre, Cambridge, directed by Terence Gray, 1931
Greet	Old Vic Theatre, London, directed by Ben Greet, 1916
Guthrie	Memorial Theatre, Stratford-upon-Avon, directed by Tyrone Guthrie, 1949 (revived 1950 and 1953, Old Vic Theatre, London)
New York	Joseph Papp Public Theatre/New York Shakespeare Festival, Delacorte Theatre, Central Park, New York, directed by Mary Zimmerman, 1997
Nunn	Royal Shakespeare Company, Royal Shakespeare Theatre, Stratford-upon-Avon and Aldwych Theatre, London, directed by Trevor Nunn, 1969
Tree	His Majesty's Theatre, London, directed by Herbert Beerbohm Tree, 1910
Webster	American Repertory Company, International Theatre, New York, directed by Margaret Webster, 1946

FILM/TELEVISION PRODUCTIONS CITED

Henry VIII (GB, 1911): film; b/w; silent; production company: Barker Motion Photography; directed by William G. B. Barker; with Arthur Bourchier as Henry, Herbert Beerbohm Tree as Wolsey, Violet Vanbrugh as Katherine, and Henry Ainley as Buckingham

Henry VIII (GB, 1979): TV; colour; production company: Cedric Messina (BBC); directed by Kevin Billington; designed by Alun Hughes; with Claire Bloom as Katherine, John Stride as Henry and Timothy West as Wolsey

INDEX

This Index covers Preface (except the acknowledgements), Introduction, Commentary and Appendix 6. It omits *Henry VIII* and all *OED* entries except those listed as first or only citations. It also provides separate entries for historical personalities and for their dramatic counterparts. Entries for the *dramatis personae* cover the Introduction only.